Government Finance
Economics of the Public Sector

Government Finance
Economics of the Public Sector

JOHN F. DUE

Professor of Economics
University of Illinois, Urbana

ANN F. FRIEDLAENDER

Professor of Economics
Massachusetts Institute of Technology

1977

Sixth Edition

RICHARD D. IRWIN, INC.   Homewood, Illinois   60430
Irwin-Dorsey Limited   Georgetown, Ontario   L7G 4B3

Sixth Edition

First Printing, February 1977

ISBN 0-256-01911-8
Library of Congress Catalog Card No. 76–47771
Printed in the United States of America

To Jean, Allan, and Kevin
Stephen, Lucas, and Nathaniel

Preface

The previous edition of this text involved substantial reorganization and rewriting. This Sixth Edition, retaining that basic organization, involves less drastic change. The major modifications have sought to simplify the exposition in Chapters 2 and 3, and to bring the remaining material up to date, both in terms of institutional changes and contributions to the theory of public finance. The income and death tax chapters reflect the 1976 tax reform legislation. With Chapter 3, the more advanced material removed from the text has been retained as an appendix to the chapter, so that the material is still available for those instructors wishing to use it. Other changes involve reorganization of the material on consumption taxation and some simplification of the fiscal policy chapters.

The writing of this edition has been greatly facilitated, as were previous editions, by the various publications of the Brookings Institution, and appreciation is expressed to Brookings, and particularly to Joseph Pechman, for the contributions of the Brookings volumes. The various editions, over the years, have been greatly influenced by the work of Richard Musgrave, James M. Buchanan, Paul Samuelson, George Break, Wallace Oates, Carl Shoup, and many others.

We would like to express our personal appreciation to several persons who have provided assistance over the years: Professor Emeritus Malcolm M. Davisson of the University of California, Berkeley, for his encouragement for the original and subsequent editions; Jane Leuthold of the University of Illinois for her comments; Edward J. Kane of Ohio State University, Richard Tresch, David Belsley, and Alice Bourneuf of Boston College, and Peter Diamond of the Massachusetts Institute of Technology for their suggestions on various portions of the manuscript.

Appreciation is expressed to the Brookings Institution for permission to reproduce material from Joseph A. Pechman, *Federal Tax Policy* (Washington, D.C.: Brookings Institution, 1971c.); from Joseph A. Kershaw, *Government Against Poverty* (Washington, D.C.: Brookings Institution, 1970c.); Henry J. Aaron, *Who Pays the Property Tax?* (Washington, D.C.: Brookings Institution, 1975c.); George F. Break and Joseph A. Pechman, *Federal Tax Reform* (Washington, D.C.: Brookings Institution, 1975c.); Joseph A. Pechman and Benjamin A. Okner, *Who Bears the Tax Burden?* (Washington, D.C.: Brookings Institution, 1974c.); C. Schultze et al., *Setting National Priorities: The 1973·Budget* (Washington, D.C.: Brookings Institution, 1972c.); to the Tax Foundation, for permission to reproduce material from *Tax Burdens and Benefits of Government Expenditures* (New York: Tax Foundation, 1967c.); to the Canadian Tax Foundation to reproduce material from the *Canadian Tax Journal;* to Praeger Publishers, Inc., for permission to reproduce material from L. C. Thurow, *The Impact of Taxes on the American Economy* (New York: Praeger Publishers, 1971c.); to Johns Hopkins Press to reproduce material from John F. Due, *Indirect Taxation in Developing Economies* (Baltimore, Md.: Johns Hopkins Press, 1970c.).

January 1977   JOHN F. DUE
                                  ANN F. FRIEDLAENDER

Contents

Technological Externalities. Negative Externalities and Spill-over Effects. The Reciprocal Nature of the Problem. Income Effects and Compensation. Corrective Actions. The Level of Charges. Conclusion.

PART II
Allocation and Distribution: Taxation

Future Generations and the Preference for Borrowing. Other Influences on the Choice of Borrowing. Government versus Individuals. Charges for Governmental Services. Taxation: Attitudes toward Use of Taxes: *Levels of Taxation. Attitudes toward Structures.* Tax Incidence—The Distributional Effects of a Tax: *Sources versus Uses of Income. Changes in the Level of Employment. Relative Price Changes. The Problem of Analysis of Distributional Effects. Excess Burden.* Criteria of Tax Structures: Pareto Optimality: *Resource Allocation. Factor Supplies. Production Efficiency. Collection. Stabilization.* Criteria: Equity: *Benefit Received or Generalized User Charges. Ability.* Conflict of Standards. Attitudes of Governments. Appendix I—The Process of Enactment of Tax Legislation: *Preparation of Recommendations. Congressional Consideration. State Tax Measures.* Appendix II—Constitutional Restrictions: United States. The Federal Government: *Specific Limitations. Implied Restrictions.* The Taxing Powers of the States: *Specific Federal Restrictions. Implied Restrictions. Restrictions Imposed by State Constitutions.* The Taxing Powers of the Local Governments. Appendix III—Constitutional Taxing Powers: Canada. Appendix IV—Tax Legislation in Canada and Other Commonwealth Countries.

10. The Structure of Income Taxation I: The Concept of Income   221

General Requirements. Definition of Income: *Nonmonetary Transfers. Self-Produced Goods. Owner-Occupied Housing. Gifts and Bequests Received. Life Insurance Proceeds and Annuities.* The Definition of Income: Capital Gains: *Are Capital Gains Income? Peculiarities of Capital Gains. Special Treatment. Objectionable Features. Reforms within the Present Structure. Basic Reforms–The Accrual Approach. Basic Reform: Proration or Averaging. Defense of Preferential Treatment.* Items Excluded from Income by Specific Provisions of the Law: *Welfare, Social Security, and Various Veterans' Benefits. Interest on State and Local Bonds.* Gross versus Net Income: The Expenses of Gaining Income: *Minimum Living Expenditures. Education. Expenses for Child Care and Housework, Particularly for Working Wives. Commuting and Moving Expenses. Travel, Entertainment, Hobby, and Related Expenditures.*

11. The Structure of Income Taxation II: Adjustments in Income, Reform   246

Problems of Timing of Income: *Irregular Incomes and Averaging. Acceleration of Expenses for Tax Purposes. Retirement Income.* The Taxpaying Unit: *Individual Persons. Pooling of Income: Husband and Wife. Income of Children.* Exemptions for the Taxpayer and Dependents: *Height of Exemption. Exemption versus Credit. Uniformity of Exemption or Credit. Definition of Dependents.* Other Adjustments: Personal Deductions: *Medical Expenses. Casualty Losses. Interest Paid. Taxes Paid. Contributions. The Optional or Standard Deduction. The Tax-Rate*

Structure. Adjustments for Inflation. Tax Shelters. Comprehensive Income Tax Proposals: *The Canadian Royal Commission Proposals. United States–The Defects. The Defects as of 1977.* The Pechman Study. Conclusion. Appendix—Canadian Income Tax Rates, 1976.

The Basis of Analysis. Income Taxes and Capital Formation: *Income Taxes and Savings: The Maximum Rate of Capital Formation. The Investment Schedule and Capital Formation. Risk-Taking. Nonfull Employment: Effects of the Tax.* The Income Tax and the Supply of Labor: *The Indifference-Curve Analysis. Reactions to Taxes. Progression. Empirical Studies. Long-Run Supply. Relative Supply of Labor in Various Occupations.* Distributional Effects: *The Differential Approach. A Proportional Income Tax. A Progressive Income Tax.* Economic Efficiency: *Effects of the Income Tax.* Overall Evaluation of Income Taxation: *Equity. Economic Efficiency. Administration and Compliance.* Conclusion. Appendix—Payroll Taxes: *Distributional Effects. Other Economic Effects. Equity. Alternative Reforms.*

The Significance of the Corporation. The Present Tax. The Distributional Pattern of the Tax: *The Traditional Approach. Application of the Harberger Model. Nonperfectly Competitive Conditions. Backward Shifting. Restricted Capital Mobility. Econometric Studies–Behavior of the Rate of Return. The Factor-Shares Approach. The Gordon Study.* Other Economic Effects: *Effects upon Factor Supplies. Economic Efficiency. The Corporate Income Tax as a Built-in Stabilizer.* The Role of Depreciation: *The Formal Analysis. The Investment Credit. Empirical Studies of the Effectiveness of Changes in Depreciation Policy.* Evaluation of the Present Corporate Income Tax: *Defense. The Primary Criticisms.* Reform Proposals—Integration of the Corporate and Personal Income Taxes: *The Partnership Approach. Dividend Received Credits. Dividend-Paid Credit. General Evaluation of Reform Proposals.* Appendix—Business Taxes: *General Business Levies. Special Levies.*

The Rationale of Consumption Taxation: *Equity. Economic Efficiency. Administrative Considerations.* The Spendings (Expenditure) Tax: *The Nature of the Tax. The Advantages. The Problems. Economic Effects and Equity. Experience.* The Indirect or Commodity Tax Alternative. Sales Taxation: Shifting: *Complete Shifting Models. Modifications from the Uniform Pattern. Separate Quotation of Tax. Nonretail Taxes. Longer Period Adjustments. Empirical Studies.* Excise Taxes: Shifting: *Perfect Competition. Complete Monopoly. Nonperfectly Competitive Models. Empirical Studies of Price Responses to Excise Taxes.* Conclusion. Excise Taxation—Structure and Evaluation: *Excises Designed to Improve Efficiency in the Use of Resources (Sumptuary Excises). Excise Taxes in Lieu of Charges. Excises for General Revenue. Miscellaneous Excises. Summary.* Appendix—Canadian Federal Excise Taxes, 1976.

PART III
Fiscal Federalism

PART IV
The Overall Impact of the Fiscal Structure on the Economy

PART V
Development

1

Introduction

As governments have played a growing role in all economies, they have used increasing amounts of resources for their activities, and taxes have constituted increasing percentages of national income. In recent years all levels of government have absorbed some 30 percent of total income in the United States. Either directly or indirectly, the various levels of government provide most education and pay a major proportion of medical bills. They provide national defense, police and fire protection, and provide or support a substantial amount of housing, recreation facilities, and parklands. They set health standards and ensure adequate water supplies, transportation, and other public facilities. They seek to attain a distribution of income regarded as equitable, to stabilize the economy from periods of excessive inflation or unemployment, and to ensure an adequate rate of growth. Not incidentally, they affect innumerable decisions of individuals by the large amount of national income they collect in taxes to finance these various activities.

The scope and role of government obviously varies from country to country. Governments in Western Europe undertake more activities than governments in the United States. In socialist countries, government carries on most production activities. In less-developed countries, the role of government is large, at least with respect to the non-subsistence portion of the economy.

The various roles of government in different economies are subjects in themselves.[1] This book will concentrate upon the role of government in the United States economy, with some reference to Canada, although it will at times branch out to discuss government activities in

[1] For a good discussion see R. A. Musgrave, *Fiscal Systems* (New Haven, Conn.: Yale University Press, 1969).

other economies and other countries. Basically, it is concerned with four questions:

First: Why is government necessary in a market economy?

Second: What determines the optimal scope and level of government activity?

Third: What criteria should be used in determining how this activity should be financed?

Fourth: What are the consequences of government activity and its financing on the economy?

The role of government in present-day economies is largely a consequence of the growing complexities and interdependencies of modern society. In a primitive society, governmental activity in the contemporary sense was unknown. There was typically a hierarchical organization, it is true, with a chief or other ruler, but the ruler in practice exercised little influence over the conduct of the almost wholly subsistence economy. For a time in the late Middle Ages, governments did exercise substantial control over the economies and used substantial resources in the conduct of war. The controls and the role of government declined in the laissez-faire reaction to excessive governmental intervention, and the United States gained its independence in large part in a reaction against British economic restrictions. Thus our early history was characterized by extreme laissez-faire doctrines, as was 19th-century England: "The best government is the government that does the least."

In defense of minimizing the role of government, Adam Smith and others stressed the "invisible hand" doctrine: If persons are left to pursue their own endeavors, the best interest of society as a whole is served. If there are large numbers of small producers, as was typical of the era, each firm in seeking to maximize profits will produce the goods offering the most profitable market and hence satisfying consumer wants, and the firm will operate at the point of lowest average cost. The flow of firms into and out of industries will bring price to equal average cost. When price equals lowest average cost it also equals marginal cost—the real cost to society of producing additional units of the commodity. Not only will consumers obtain goods at the lowest possible price, but the inequities of monopoly profits will be avoided and production will be directed to the optimal satisfaction of consumer wants, given the pattern of income distribution.

Thus, laissez-faire was expected by its defenders to bring about the attainment of what came to be called *Pareto optimality*, named for Vilfredo Pareto.[2] He was the first to develop systematically the theory

---

[2] Pareto was born in 1848, educated primarily in Italy in engineering, and served in railway and industrial management positions until 1892. Meanwhile he studied economics extensively and in 1893 succeeded Leon Walras, the distinguished economist at the University of Lausanne, when Walras retired. Until his death in 1923, Pareto lived in Switzerland, writing extensively in the fields of economics and sociology.

of economic efficiency. Pareto optimality is reached when resource allocation is most efficient: When no further changes in resource allocation (the relative allocation of factors among the production of various commodities) or in methods of production can be made that will increase the welfare of one person without decreasing that of others. This adjustment will be explained in detail in Chapter 2.

While laissez-faire brought rapid economic development, it also brought the evils so well portrayed in England by Charles Dickens and in the United States by Upton Sinclair—the exploitation of unskilled labor, appalling housing conditions, and great fortunes built out of monopolistic exploitation and land speculation.

As time passed, the evils of laissez-faire became increasingly apparent, and the role of government has steadily increased throughout the world. Why has this change occurred? First is the question of equity. Polanyi and others[3] have argued that the market-determined efficient pattern of economic activity is not necessarily (and in fact will not usually be) the pattern regarded by society as equitable. In a world of competition, owners of scarce factors of production will have high incomes while owners of plentiful factors of production will have low incomes. Thus, in the 19th century, capitalists who owned substantial amounts of the scarce means of production, capital, were rich, while most of the workers existed in unbelievable squalor and poverty. It was precisely this pattern of distribution of income that led Marx to his dire predictions of class war and the eventual demise of capitalist society.

How an equitable distribution can be defined and achieved will be the subject of several chapters of this book. But in general, democracies have found extreme inequality to be politically intolerable. Thus, one of the earliest functions of government was to set standards to limit the exploitation of the poor (and implicitly limit the supply of labor) by passing laws against child labor and to undertake taxation and expenditure measures to redistribute income to achieve a less unequal distribution of income.

Second, there are some goods—called public goods—that the private market economy cannot provide. They have the basic quality that if they are made available at all, they must be made available equally to all individuals. Since no one can be excluded from their benefits, they cannot be produced and sold on a profit-making basis. National defense is the most obvious example.

Third, production activities of firms and consumption activities of individuals are often not independent. The upstream paper firm, polluting the water supply of a downstream city, is an obvious example. By educating my children, I am increasing the overall productivity of the work force. Thus where private and social valuations diverge be-

---

[3] See Karl Polanyi, *The Great Transformation* (New York: Farrar and Rinehart, 1944).

cause of these interdependencies—called externalities—some form of governmental intervention is needed.

Fourth, some activities cannot be produced under competitive conditions. The efficient scale is so large that the activity can be provided efficiently by only one enterprise. Government regulation and/or subsidy is needed to ensure an economically efficient output and check income inequality.

Fifth, the market economy may not be capable of functioning in a sufficiently stable fashion. Unexpected shifts in aggregate demand (or its various components) may occur that cause the economy to experience periods of inflation or recession. Accordingly, governmental action may be needed to stabilize the economy through appropriate fiscal and/or monetary policies.

Sixth, the rate of capital formation may be too high or too low to achieve what is thought to be an acceptable rate of growth. Thus government may be needed to change the parameters that affect the rate of growth—saving, investment, productivity, the rate of growth of the labor force, and so forth.

Clearly, the scope of government activity is substantial. To perform all of these functions, government must have extensive sources of revenue.

The study of governmental activity is essentially the study of tax and expenditure policy to obtain the answers to the four questions noted above: (1) Why is government activity necessary? (2) What determines its proper scope and level? (3) How should this activity be financed? (4) What are the consequences of this activity?

For purposes of analysis, it is useful, following the precedent of Richard Musgrave, to divide governmental activity into three parts or branches:[4]

1.   Allocation: the activities involving the provision of various governmental services to society and thus involving the allocation of resources to the production of these services rather than private-sector output. Some of the services are strict public goods (e.g., national defense); some are ones involving externalities (e.g., education); some are provided by government to avoid private monopoly and costs of collection of charges (e.g., highways).

2.   Distribution: the activities involved in the redistribution of income: welfare programs, progressive tax structures, etc.

3.   Stabilization and growth: the activities designed to increase economic stability by lessening unemployment and inflation and influencing, if thought desirable, the rate of economic growth.

While this conceptual approach is useful and is followed to some

---

[4] This classification was developed by Musgrave in his classic work, *The Theory of Public Finance* (New York: McGraw-Hill, 1959). Since its publication, this book has been the standard work in public finance at an advanced level.

extent in this book, the interdependency of the functions must be recognized. The government does not have three separate branches that deal exclusively with each of the three activities. Provision of various governmental services (e.g., education) and the levying of taxes to finance them affect real-income distribution patterns, while distributional activities inevitably affect relative prices and consumer demands and thus, allocation of resources to the production of various goods.

Stabilization policies also affect both income distribution and resource allocation.

Briefly, this book takes the following form. Part I discusses government expenditures: Why are they undertaken and how are they allocated in the United States? What are their distributional consequences? Part II then discusses how these activities are financed and analyzes the allocational and distributional impact of the tax structure, both in theory and in practice. Part III relates to intergovernmental fiscal relationships. Part IV is concerned with problems of stabilization and growth; it discusses the theories of economic stabilization and growth and applies these theories to the experience of the United States. Finally, Part V considers the role which government plays in economic development and discusses how government expenditure and taxation policies can help the less-developed countries increase their levels of income.

The general approach is to provide an analytical framework for consideration of various aspects of the subject and then to consider actual policies in light of the analysis. Alternative policies can be evaluated only on the basis of an analytical framework and a statement of objectives.

Many of the most significant political questions of the contemporary period are essentially questions of public finance. The list below notes a few major ones, which will be discussed in subsequent chapters:

1. The appropriate levels of defense spending, which have a major impact on the economy and virtually every individual in society.
2. The best approaches to budgeting, to ensure that governmental activities coincide with preferences in society.
3. The evaluation of long-range governmental investment projects: highways, river valley projects, transit facilities, etc.
4. The negative income tax, as an alternative or supplement to the existing welfare programs, which are generally regarded as unsatisfactory and inadequate to meet the problems of poverty.
5. Optimal levels and programs of education, particularly in low-income areas of large cities.
6. Continued use of the revenue-sharing system and possible changes in its structure.

7. The financing of education. The traditional system has been under attack politically and in the courts for more than a decade.
8. Criticisms of the property tax and debate over where the burden actually rests.
9. Proposals for a federal value added tax, which have been recurring for a decade or more.
10. The issue of loopholes in the federal income tax, which allow many wealthy persons to escape tax and greatly reduce progression below the intended levels.
11. The effects of the tax structure upon economic incentives and economic growth and the desirability of investment credits and other devices to stimulate investment.
12. The complexity of the income tax structure.
13. The serious financial plight of New York City and other large metropolitan areas.
14. The bitter dilemma of simultaneous inflation and unemployment.

PART I

Allocation and Distribution: Activities and Expenditures

2

Economic Optimality

As noted in the first chapter, political support for governmental participation in economic activity arises in situations in which the private sector fails to maximize economic welfare. Analysis of governmental activities, therefore, requires a preliminary statement of the concept of economic welfare and of the requirements that must be fulfilled if economic welfare is to be maximized.

THE CONCEPT OF OPTIMAL ECONOMIC WELFARE

Maximum economic welfare may be defined as a situation in which overall levels of satisfaction are maximized—that is, everyone in society is as well off, in terms of attainment of individual preferences, as is possible, given the constraints: resources (natural, human, capital); the production functions, which are determined by available technology and express the outputs possible with given input combinations; and tastes as described in individuals' utility or preference functions.

The Elements in Welfare Optimization

Maximum economic welfare involves three elements:

1. Economic efficiency, or Pareto optimality; in nontechnical terms, the allocation of resources such that no change is possible that would increase the output of one commodity or the welfare of one individual without reducing the output of another commodity or the welfare of another individual.

2. Optimal income distribution, in the sense of the distribution pattern that the consensus in society regards as most equitable, as expressed through its social welfare function, which weights the

well-being of different members of society. The social welfare function may be defined as the consensus reached by the political process about the relative importance of the well-being of various members of society.

3. Attainment of the rate of growth and degree of price level stability regarded as most desirable in the particular society.

Each of these requires more detailed analysis.

PARETO OPTIMALITY

Pareto optimality, or economic efficiency in the broad sense of that term, is defined as a situation in which no output changes can be made that will make any one person better off without making someone else worse off. If Pareto optimality has not been attained, movement toward it involves either (1) production of more of some goods without the need to reduce the output of others; or (2) change in the composition of total output in such a way that the satisfaction of some persons will be increased without a reduction in the satisfaction of others. Thus, if so many paperclips are being produced that the utility of the marginal unit is zero, shifting steel from paperclips to frying pans will allow greater satisfaction on the part of persons who want more frying pans without reducing the satisfaction of the paperclip users.

Accordingly, Pareto optimality requires the attainment of (1) technical efficiency—the allocation of resources such that no change in production is possible that would increase the output of one commodity without reducing the output of another; (2) consumption efficiency—the allocation of commodities among consumers such that no change in consumption is possible that would increase the welfare of one individual without reducing the welfare of another; and (3) allocative efficiency—the allocation of factors and commodities among producers and consumers such that no change is possible that would not lead to the reduction in output of one commodity *and* the reduction in welfare of one consumer.

Technical Efficiency of the Firm

Technical efficiency not only requires that resources are allocated within a firm to minimize resource costs for a given output, but also that they are allocated among firms to minimize total resource costs for specified outputs. Thus, we will first consider the concept of technical efficiency within a firm and then extend it to the industry and finally extend it to the allocation of resources among industries.

The analysis of technical efficiency assumes: (1) given schedules of factors of production available at various levels of real incomes of their owners, (2) given quality of factor units, and (3) given technology. In less-technical terms—for example, there are certain numbers of workers available, given the wage levels; workers have certain given skills and aptitudes; and the methods of production are given. These are not unrealistic assumptions at any particular point in time.

Technical efficiency for each firm requires:

1. The selection of the optimal techniques available, including methods of organization of production, that will lead to a maximum output for a given resource input.

2. The attainment of the efficient factor combination, that is, the use of the amounts of various types of capital, labor, and other resource inputs that permit the production of a given output at the lowest possible cost. This adjustment, in turn, requires:

a. That the marginal rate of technical substitution between any factors (MRTS), which measures the number of units of one factor that must be substituted for one unit of another to maintain a given output level, is equal to the ratio of the prices of the two factors. Since the marginal rate of technical substitution is also equal to the ratio of the marginal products of each factor, cost minimization requires that the ratio of the marginal products of any two factors is equal to the ratio of their prices.[1]

b. That the amount of each factor acquired is such that the marginal revenue product (MRP) of the factor is equal to the price paid for the factor unit. Marginal revenue product is the contribution of the factor unit to the revenue of the firm, and thus, is equal to the marginal product of the factor multiplied by the marginal revenue of the additional unit of output. Because of the law of diminishing returns, MRP falls as factor units are added beyond a certain point. If MRP is greater than the price of the factor, the firm will add factor units; if MRP is less, it will hire fewer units. Because the marginal rate of technical substitution between any two factors (MRTS) is defined to equal the ratio of the marginal products of those factors, the equality of MRP and factor price will ensure that the MRTS equals the ratio of factor prices.[2]

3. While not precisely an aspect of technical efficiency, profit maximization will lead the firm to produce at the point where marginal

---

[1] In terms of formal definitions, for any two factors K and L, we define

$$MRTS = -\left(\frac{dK}{dL}\right) = \frac{MPL}{MPK}$$

where MPK and MPL respectively represent the marginal product of factors K and L. Then technical efficiency requires that $MRTS = MPL/MPK = P_L/P_K$, where P_L and P_K respectively reflect the costs of factors L and K.

[2] Stated more formally, the marginal revenue product for any factor i is defined as $MRP_i = (MR)(MP_i)$, where MR equals the marginal revenue from the firm's output. Since efficiency requires that $MRP_i = P_i$, it should be clear that for any two factors K and L, $MP_L/MP_K = P_L/P_K$. As indicated in the footnote above, however, $MRTS$ for K and L is defined as $MRTS = MPL/MPK$. Thus, as long as $MRP_i = P_i$ for all factors ($i = K$, L, . . .), the equality between $MRTS$ and the ratio of factor prices will be fulfilled.

cost equals marginal revenue. If we assume that the firm is a price taker, it cannot influence the price it receives for its products. Thus, price equals marginal revenue and a firm will be in equilibrium where price equals marginal cost.

This statement of the optimal adjustment of each producer is based on the assumption of given prices paid for the factors and given prices received from the sale of the products. Definition of the levels of these prices necessary for overall optimality requires us to go beyond the adjustment for each individual firm.

Optimal Industry Adjustments

The preceding section was concerned only with the adjustment by the individual producer. Explanation of overall efficiency requires that the relationship among various producers be considered.

Intraindustry Adjustments.   A firm seeking to maximize profits is directly concerned with the relationship between marginal revenue product and the factor price and between marginal cost and marginal revenue (price). But production efficiency requires that the firm operate at the point of lowest long-run average cost.

This relationship will be attained as firms flow into and out of the industry. If price exceeds average cost, new firms will flow into the industry and the price will fall; if the price is less, firms will move out of the industry and the price will rise. After long-run adjustments have been completed, each firm will operate at the low point (or low segment) on its average cost curve, and price will equal both average cost and marginal cost at this level of output.

Overall Interindustry Adjustments.   All products are essentially rivals with all other products for resources. Hence, technical efficiency requires that factors cannot be reallocated among firms or industries in such a way that the output of one commodity can be increased without reducing the output of another. This will be achieved as long as the marginal rate of technical substitution between any two factors in any given industry is equal to their marginal rate of technical substitution in any other industry and that this common marginal rate of technical substitution is equal to the ratio of the prices of the two factors.

Given that factors are allocated as efficiently as possible so that Pareto optimality holds in production, the various possible patterns of output can be represented graphically by the transformation or product possibility curve, drawn for two commodities (X and Y), but valid for relationships among all commodities (Figure 2–1). Given resources and technology, the curve ab shows the maximum possible combinations of output of the two groups of commodities from sole production of a at one extreme to sole production of b at the other. Under the assumption of differing production functions for the two groups of

FIGURE 2-1

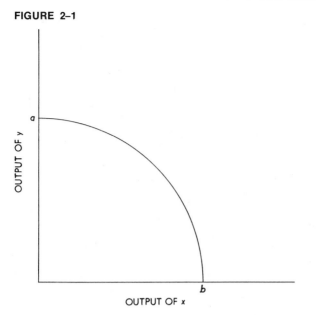

commodities and the law of diminishing returns, the curve is concave to the point of origin, showing that as the relative output of one commodity is increased, the sacrifice in the output of the other commodity will become progressively greater. The term *marginal rate of transformation* is given to the slope of the curve; it shows the number of units of one commodity that must be sacrificed to increase the output of the other by one unit. The marginal rate of transformation between each two commodities is equal to the ratio of their marginal costs, since the marginal cost shows the cost of producing another unit of the commodity in terms of the resources pulled away from the production of the other; the ratios of the two marginal costs—of the resources pulled away from the other—therefore is equal to the ratio of the reduction in the output of one that occurs with a one-unit increase in the output of the other.

Consumption Efficiency of the Individual

Having analyzed the requirements for technical efficiency or efficiency in production, we now analyze the requirements for efficiency in consumption. We will then consider the requirements for overall efficiency in consumption and production and outline the full requirements for Pareto optimality.

For efficiency in consumption, it is necessary that each consumer adjust his relative purchases of various goods in such a fashion that his satisfaction is maximized. Assumptions are made that (1) each consumer has a given money income, equal to the product of the price of the factor units he or she owns times the number of such units he or she owns; (2) each consumer has a pattern of relative preferences or tastes; (3) each consumer has adequate knowledge about the capacity of various goods to satisfy his or her wants. We assume the operation of the law of diminishing marginal utility, and thus indifference curves showing relative preferences as downward sloping and convex to the point of origin; the more of each commodity the person obtains, the smaller in the amount of the other commodity necessary to replace a unit of this commodity and maintain the same level of satisfaction.

Maximum satisfaction from consumption in view of the given budget constraint requires that each consumer adjust relative purchases of various goods in such a fashion that the marginal utility received from the last unit of money spent on each commodity is equal for all commodities, or in other words, that the marginal utilities are proportional to the prices. Alternatively the relationship may be stated as follows: Efficiency in consumption requires that the marginal rate of substitution between each pair of commodities—the number of units of one commodity that the consumer is willing to give up to get an additional unit of the other commodity and maintain the same level of satisfaction—is equal to the ratio of the prices of the two goods.[3] If this relationship is not attained, the consumer can increase satisfaction by increasing purchase of one good and reducing that of the other.

Adjustments for All Consumers

Each consumer must, under the assumption of the objective of maximizing satisfaction, adjust relative purchases of various goods, as described in the previous section. Provided the prices to which each consumer is subject are the same, then each consumer will adjust so that his or her marginal rate of substitution (MRS) is equal to the given price ratios, and, therefore, the marginal rates of substitution will be uniform for all consumers (the levels of satisfaction cannot be said to be equal for two reasons: Incomes differ; and satisfactions are not comparable among individuals). The relative amounts of various goods purchased by the different consumers will, of course, differ widely, as preferences and incomes differ. But for each, MRS equals the price ratios.

For this equilibrium to be obtained, therefore it is necessary that:

1.   All consumers are confronted by the same price, unaffected by the amount any one person buys.

---

[3] Stating the case more formally, we define the marginal rate of substitution between any two goods, a and b, as $MRS = -da/db$. For any given consumer, welfare will be maximized subject to the budget constraint when $MRS = da/db = MU_b/MU_a = P_b/P_a$, where MU_a and MU_b respectively represent the marginal utilities of a and b and P_a and P_b represent their respective prices.

2. Consumption by each person is noninterdependent; satisfaction of one person is unaffected by the consumption pattern of other persons.

3. Consumption benefits accrue individually and separately to each consumer, and the use of a good conveys no benefits positive or negative to anyone other than the purchaser. Thus, there are no consumption interdependencies or externalities.

Allocative Efficiency

Production efficiency and consumption efficiency, reviewed independently, must now be considered together. In summary of the discussion above:

a. *Technical efficiency* will be attained if for each firm:
   1. For all factors utilized, the marginal rates of technical substitution are equal to the price ratios, or, in other words, each factor is utilized to the level at which the marginal revenue product is equal to the cost of the factor.
   2. Optimal techniques are employed.
   3. Factor prices are uniform to all firms and equate supply of the factor with demand for it, with no unemployment of resources.
   4. There are no costs to society from the use of a factor or from production not reflected in the price paid for it.
   5. Each firm is operating at the lowest point on its long-run average-cost curve.
   6. Additional use of a factor conveys no benefits to other firms.
b. *Consumption efficiency* will be attained if:
   1. Each consumer adjusts his or her relative purchases in such a way that the marginal rates of substitution among all commodities are equal to the ratios of their prices.
   2. Prices of each product are uniform to all consumers.
   3. All consumption benefits are independent; consumption levels and patterns of one person do not affect the utility of others.
   4. Consumption benefits accrue separately and individually to the individuals acquiring the goods.
c. *Allocative efficiency* in the economy as a whole will be attained if:
   1. The rate of transformation between any two goods in production equals the marginal rate of substitution in consumption.
   2. In the absence of production and consumption externalities, outlined above, equality of price and marginal cost will ensure that for any two goods, $MRS = MRT$ and that Pareto optimality will occur, provided the following requirements are met:

Each consumer seeks to maximize satisfaction.

Prices for each factor are uniform to all firms and equate the supply of the factor with the demand for it.

Resources are fully utilized—all factor owners who wish to have their factor units employed at the prevailing factor prices are able to do so.

Under these circumstances, the marginal costs, to which product prices are equal, reflect the real opportunity costs for which the production of the given number of units of output of each good is responsible. Therefore the prices confronting each consumer reflect the real costs to society—in the sense of sacrifice of output of other commodities—resulting from his or her consumption of additional units of the commodity. The marginal rate of technical substitution— the number of units of one factor required to replace a unit of another factor and maintain output—will be equal to the ratio of the prices of the factors. No changes in relative factor combinations can increase output; no shifting of resources from production of one commodity to another can increase satisfaction.

Stated more formally, since consumers and producers face the same set of prices, consumers adjust relative purchases so that the marginal rates of substitution for any two commodities a and b, MRS_{ab}, are equal to the price ratios, P_a/P_b, and producers adjust outputs so that their marginal costs, MC_a, MC_b—which reflect marginal rates of transformation, MRT_{ab}—are equal to these prices. Since the marginal cost ratios, MC_a/MC_b, are equal to the marginal rates of transformation, MRT_{ab}, the marginal rates of transformation, MRT_{ab}, are equal to the marginal rates of substitution, MRS_{ab} for all consumers. Thus, given the pattern of income distribution, there is one overall efficient pattern of resource allocation of production, consumption, and factor utilization. At this point, the marginal rate of transformation—the sacrifice in output of one good necessary to produce a unit of another good—is equal to the marginal rate of substitution common to all consumers—given their incomes. The actual commodity and factor prices are those equating supply and demand. The product prices are equal to the marginal costs of producing the goods and to average cost. Each producer is operating at the lowest point on his average cost curve. In summary, therefore, for any two commodities (a and b) and any two factors (K and L):

$P_a = MC_a$ (Price equals marginal cost.)

$TC_a = rK_a + wL_a$ (Total cost equals the sum of factor prices times number of units of the factor.)

$P_a : S_a = D_a$ (Product prices equate supply and demand.)

$r = MRP_k$ (The price of each factor is equal to the margi-
$w = MRP_L$ nal revenue productivity of the factor in each use to which it is put.)

$r : S_K = D_K$ (Factor prices are such that supply and demand
$w : S_L = D_L$ are equal.)

$\dfrac{MC_a}{MC_b} = MRT_{ab}$ (The ratio of the marginal costs of the two commodities is equal to the marginal rate of transformation between them.)

$MRS_{ab} = \dfrac{P_a}{P_b}$ (For each consumer, for each set of commodities, the marginal rate of substitution is equal to the ratios of the prices of the two products.)

$MRS_{ab} = MRT_{ab}$ (The marginal rate of substitution between each pair of products, for each consumer, is equal to the marginal rate of transformation in the production of the two products.)

$P_a = AC_a$ (Price of each product is equal to average cost, and thus each firm is operating at the point of lowest average cost.)

$MRTS_{KL} = r/w$ (The marginal rate of factor substitution between each set of factors equals the ratios of the factor prices, r/w.)

Such efficiency or Pareto optimality will be obtained automatically, without governmental action, if the following conditions are met:

1. Universality of the maximization goal: profit maximization by each firm, income maximization by each factor owner, and utility maximization by each consumer, who should also be viewed as a factor owner.

2. Perfect competition in all factor and product markets.

Under perfectly competitive conditions and the goal of profit maximization:

All factor prices will adjust to the levels that equate supply and demand.

Each firm will adjust factor combinations so that the marginal revenue product of each factor is equal to the price of the factor.

The price of each product will equate the demand for the product with the supply forthcoming at that price.

Each firm will adjust output so that the marginal cost is equal to the product price (which also equals marginal revenue).

Each commodity price will equal marginal cost.

Each commodity price will equal average cost as resources shift among industries.

3.   Perfect knowledge on the part of consumers about the ability of various goods to satisfy their wants, of producers about available techniques and of the marginal product of various factors, of factor owners about the best opportunities for employment of their factor units.

4.   Attainment of full employment of resources.

5.   Absence of externalities in consumption or production that cause private valuations of costs and benefits to diverge from social valuations. Thus, satisfaction from goods accrue only to the consumers acquiring them, and the output price reflects the true opportunity cost of the good purchased.

The Failure to Attain the Requirements for Pareto Optimality

A major aspect of governmental activity has resulted from the failure of the economy to attain Pareto optimality or economic efficiency because the requirements outlined above are not fully met. Some of the deviations are more or less inevitable, such as the lack of perfect information on the part of consumers, factor owners, and firms; and government can take only limited steps to improve information. The major failures to be discussed in subsequent chapters can be noted briefly:

1.   Nondivisible goods, known as public goods. There are a number of goods for which persons have preferences but whose benefits do not accrue separately and indivisibly to individuals. If they are provided, they are available to all, since there is no feasible way to exclude anyone from gaining satisfaction from them. There is no way in which the market can allocate or price them; firms cannot produce them because they cannot sell them. Only society, through government, can provide them.

2.   Externalities in consumption and production. In the first case, utility functions are not independent and the consumption of some goods by a given individual will affect the utility of other individuals, either positively or negatively. In the second case, production by some firms may affect the costs of other firms, either positively or negatively, in a way that is not reflected in the price of the good. In either case, there is a divergence of individual and social costs. The production and/or consumption of certain products results in costs to society that do not enter into the costs of production and thus the prices of the products.

3.   Natural monopolies may exist where economies of scale, relative to the demand for the product, are sufficiently great that, at the level of output at which price equals marginal cost, average cost is greater than marginal cost. Since one firm can satisfy the demand of the entire market, competition is impossible, and this firm will only produce the product at a price greater than marginal cost in the absence of governmental intervention and subsidy.

4. Perfect competition may be absent in factor or product markets, apart from the case of natural monopolies. As a consequence, outputs will be less than the amount at which marginal cost is equal to price and firms may not operate at the point of lowest average cost. Prices may not be uniform to various consumers. Factor prices may not equate factor supply and demand; factor prices may not be uniform to all firms; and the quantity of a factor acquired by a firm may affect the factor prices. If it does, factor combinations will not be consistent with Pareto optimality.

5. The income distribution itself may be regarded as a "good"— the utility of individuals may depend upon the overall pattern of income distribution.

6. The economic system may operate in such a way that full employment is not attained; therefore factor prices do not equate factor supply and demand, even with perfect competition in the markets.

7. Information may be inadequate for consumers, factor owners, and firms to attain optimality.

INCOME DISTRIBUTION

Even if resources are organized in such a way that Pareto optimality prevails, the resulting income distribution may not be optimal from the point of view of society's preferences. In this case, governmental action will be needed to alter the distribution of income.

Under the assumptions of the competitive model outlined above, the pattern of income distribution is determined by the competitive equilibrium between firms and households that establishes the market-clearing quantities and prices of factors and commodities. Since the income distribution is determined by the prices and quantities of factors supplied by each household, any Pareto-optimal competitive equilibrium implies a unique income distribution.

Full economic optimality requires that the income distribution be viewed as optimal, given the restraints imposed by resources and technology. It, thus, not only requires that resources be organized in a Pareto-optimal fashion, but also that society, as organized through government, regards the actual distribution as conforming with that defined as optimal by society's social welfare function, which reflects the consensus of attitudes as expressed through the political process.

It is important to stress that for each Pareto-optimal allocation of resources there is a unique income distribution associated with it. It is highly unlikely that the income distribution resulting from the Pareto-optimal competitive equilibrium will be deemed optimal from the point of view of society's social welfare function. The determination of the optimal income distribution (or the choice among a number of income distributions determined by a number of different Pareto-optimal allocations of resources) can only be made through the political process. In a democratic society, as discussed in later chapters, the decisions made presumably reflect consensus in the particular society, or in other words, the social welfare functions. Thus, a second major source of governmental activity is that designed to bring the actual pattern of income distribution in line with that specified by the social welfare function.

DYNAMIC ASPECTS AND GROWTH: PRICE-LEVEL STABILITY

The analysis thus far is of essentially static nature, concerned with the optimal equilibrium, given resources and technology. But many elements change—factor supplies, production functions (with changing techniques), consumer preferences, and the like. The supply of capital goods inevitably—with full employment—increases if a portion of national income is saved. Not only do these changes result in inevitable lags of adjustments but also raise the question of optimality of growth—of increases in overall consumption-satisfaction levels. This question is of particular concern in the developing economies, in which a major objective of society is to raise per capita real incomes toward those of the most-developed countries. In other words, the actual rate of growth (which of course may be negative) may lag behind the rate regarded by the social welfare function of the particular society as optimal.

Furthermore, the general level of prices may fluctuate in a pattern regarded as undesirable by consensus of the particular society—partly for equity reasons, partly because of interferences with economic efficiency, partly because of a dislike of inflation, per se, even by persons not harmed and even benefited by it. Accordingly governments may act to stabilize the general price level. Such policy is, of course, closely related to that designed to eliminate unemployment—a source of loss of Pareto optimality.

SUMMARY

Governmental activity, therefore, involves in part the provision (although not necessarily the production) of various types of goods, primarily public goods; the regulation of various forms of activity, as, for example, the effort to lessen monopoly; the collection of taxes to finance the provision of these goods and to correct various distortions; activity to alter the pattern of income distribution dictated by the social welfare function, and to alter the rate of growth and the behavior of the general price level.

If the government is to secure the desirable results, the taxes to finance the activities (except to correct some types of distortions) and obtain the desired pattern of income distribution must be of a "lump-sum" nature; that is, the taxes and transfers must affect neither factor supplies nor the equilibrium conditions outlined above that are needed to insure Pareto optimality. While lump-sum transfers and subsidies must necessarily affect specific production and consumption decisions, they cannot affect the basic decision rules by which consumers maximize their utility and firms maximize their profits. If all of the conditions required for Pareto optimality are met before the imposition of lump-sum taxes or transfers, they will also be met after the imposition of these taxes or subsidies. Commodity taxes will not qualify, since they cause prices paid by consumers to diverge from those received by producers. Therefore commodity taxes drive a wedge between marginal rates of substitution and marginal rates of transformation. In a world of fixed-factor supplies, taxes or subsidies related to income would qualify as lump-sum taxes since they would not affect factor supplies or the marginal conditions required for Pareto optimality. Similarly, taxes or subsidies related to specific factors or factor incomes would also be lump sum in nature. In the real world, however, the supplies of different factors may be responsive to the income received. Thus, an income tax may affect work effort, causing marginal rates of substitution to diverge from marginal rates of transformation.

Consequently, the only true lump-sum taxes are poll or head taxes that are assessed on each individual. These cannot be used for redistributive purposes, however. Once certain kinds of factors or factor incomes are taxed or receive subsidies and others do not, factor supplies will be affected and the taxes will no longer have a lump-sum nature. In practice, therefore, society probably can never achieve a truly Pareto-optimal point because the taxes and transfers needed to reach this point are not operationally feasible. Hence, society will probably end up in a situation such that all objectives are not fully attained, sacrificing some Pareto optimality for preferred-income distribution. Pareto optimality, or efficiency, as such has no normative significance. An inefficient production and consumption point may be preferable to an efficient one when distributional considerations are taken into account.

REFERENCES

Bator, F. M. "The Simple Analytics of Welfare Maximization." *American Economic Review*, vol. 47 (March 1957), pp. 22–59.

Ferguson, C. E., and Gould, J. P. *Microeconomic Theory*. 4th ed. Homewood, Ill.: Richard D. Irwin, Inc., 1975.

3

Pure Public Goods

One source of failure of the market economy to obtain Pareto optimality is the existence of certain goods that cannot be divided among individuals. Unlike apples or automobiles, which can be purchased individually by different people, these goods can only be consumed collectively—that is, jointly and indivisibly—by society as a whole. These are known as public goods.

THE CHARACTERISTICS OF PUBLIC GOODS

The basic characteristic of public goods is nonappropriability. Thus once they are made available, they are equally available to all individuals. Consequently, the "consumption" of public goods by one individual does not reduce the amount available to others, and it is therefore not necessary for an individual to appropriate them to gain benefits from them. Thus in addition to nonappropriability, public goods have the following two related characteristics:

1. Nonrivalry in consumption. One person can increase his satisfaction from the commodity without reducing that obtained by others. In other words, the marginal cost created by an additional "consumer" of the product is nil. Thus, additional ships passing a lighthouse do not lessen the utility gained by the other ships benefiting from it. In a sense, public goods are not "consumed" in a using-up sense; they are enjoyed.

2. Nonexcludability. There is no feasible way of excluding anyone from gaining the benefits of a pure public good, as for example, from national defense.

National defense is the classic example of a pure public good; benefits in the form of protection from foreign invasion or seizure of foreign territory accrue indivisibly to the entire community, and no one can be excluded from the benefits. Thus the benefits accrue equally to all individuals, even though they may have very different preferences for these benefits. Although some people may obtain great satisfaction from defense expenditures, believing that they are essential to national security, while others may experience disutility from defense expenditures, believing that they are actually detrimental to the interest of society, all individuals are confronted with the same amount of national defense.

Since national defense and other public goods cannot be "packaged" and distributed separately to individuals and since no one can be excluded from their benefits, there is no way that a price can be charged for them. Furthermore, because of their nonrivalry feature, charging a price would lead to inefficiencies, even if it were feasible. Consequently, private enterprise cannot provide public goods to the public; they must be provided by government.

While pure public goods have characteristics of both nonrivalry and nonexcludability, there are some activities that have the former characteristic without the latter and vice versa. For example, additional patrons in a half-empty theater do not lessen the satisfaction of those already present, yet they can be excluded. But such a situation, while interfering with attainment of Pareto optimality under a market system, is not one of a public good in the usual sense; it is one in which marginal cost is less than average cost, as discussed in subsequent chapters. The situation of nonexcludability but rivalry in consumption—found in some aspects of police protection—may be regarded as a subvariety of public goods.

Voluntary Cooperation.   In limited situations, public goods can be provided by voluntary cooperation without governmental participation—but only under the following sharply constrained circumstances—a small group, willingness of some persons to take the initiative, similar preferences, and desire of all persons involved to avoid the ill will of their fellows. Early road improvements—not a pure public good but one with public good characteristics—were often made in this fashion, as well as fire protection in small villages (and in large cities in the past). But the inherent difficulties are obvious. There is always the likelihood that someone will not cooperate but cannot effectively be denied the benefits. As the number of persons involved increases, the danger of noncooperation increases sharply, under the basic characteristic of human behavior that the larger the group, the less responsibility each person feels for others in the group. In general, if there is strong desire for a public good, government, which represents the organization of society, must intervene, provide the service, and develop a method of financing.

THE OPTIMAL PROVISION OF PUBLIC GOODS

Because public goods are not divisible in consumption, consumers cannot add successive units of the good so that the point can be reached at which the marginal rate of substitution of this good with others is equal to the price ratios and therefore to the marginal rate of transformation in production. A person does not "add successive units" in any meaningful way because of the "nonpackageable" and nonappropriable nature of the activity; one does not add units of fire protection in the way one adds loaves of bread. Furthermore, increased satisfaction gained by one person from the service does not reduce the amount available for others. Thus there is no way the market can bring about equality of *MRS* and *MRT*—the basic requirement for Pareto optimality for private goods.

In the case of public goods, Appendix 3–1 shows that Pareto optimality requires that the *sum* of each individual's marginal rate of substitution between any public good and any private good must equal their marginal rate of transformation in production.[1] Stated more formally, Pareto optimality for public goods requires that

$$\sum_i MRS^i = MRT$$

where i ranges over all individuals.

In contrast, Pareto optimality for private goods requires that the marginal rate of substitution between any two private goods be equal for all individuals and equal to the marginal rate of transformation in production; that is

$$MRS^i = MRS^j = MRT$$

where i and j range over all individuals.

As indicated in Chapter 2, under perfect competition, market forces ensure that the marginal rates of substitution equal the marginal rates of transformation for private goods. An individual's demand curve for a private good represents the maximum price that he or she would be willing to pay for a given quantity of that good (assuming income and all other prices remain constant). Since total consumption represents the sum of individual consumption, the market demand curve is obtained by summing all individual demand curves with respect to quantity. Thus in Figure 3–1A, the total market demand curve D represents the *horizontal* sum of individual demand curves, d_1, d_2, and d_3. Under perfect competition, the equilibrium price is given by the inter-

---

[1] This proposition was first formally demonstrated by Samuelson. See P. A. Samuelson, "Diagrammatic Exposition of a Theory of Public Expenditure," *Review of Economics and Statistics,* vol 37 (November 1955), pp. 350–56. Other important contributions by Samuelson on the theory of public goods include: "Pure Theory of Public Expenditures," *Review of Economics and Statistics,* vol. 36 (November 1954), pp. 387–89; "Aspects of Public Expenditure Theories," *Review of Economics and Statistics,* vol. 40 (November 1958), pp. 332–38.

FIGURE 3–1A

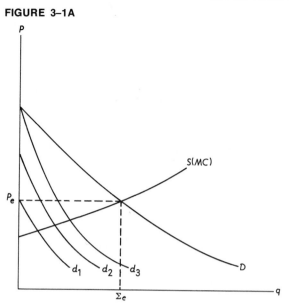

section of the market demand curve D and the market supply curve $S(MC)$, which represents the sum of all the marginal cost curves of all firms in the industry. Since all consumers face a common price, they each adjust their consumption to ensure that their marginal rates of substitution equal the relevant price ratios and, consequently, the relevant marginal rates of transformation. Thus market forces ensure the basic requirement for Pareto optimality is met with private goods.

This, however, is not true with public goods. Although we can define a Pareto-optimal point of production, there is nothing inherent in the market mechanism to move society toward that point. Thus let us define an individual demand curve for a public good as the amount of taxes an individual would be willing to pay to obtain a given amount of the public good. These are shown as the curves d_1, d_2, and d_3 in Figure 3–1B. Since, however, public goods are "consumed equally" by all individuals, it does not make sense to sum these curves horizontally. All people must consume the same quantity, in the sense that the same amount is available to all persons. Nevertheless we can ask what is the total amount that all individuals would be willing to pay for a given quantity of a public good. Thus by *vertically* summing the demand curves, d_1, d_2, and d_3, we can obtain the total demand curve for public goods, given by the curve D in Figure 3–1B. At this point the marginal rate of transformation in production is equal to the sum of the marginal rates of substitution of all consumers between this government service and all other goods, and Pareto optimality is attained. But since it is impossible to charge a price for public goods, there is no way

FIGURE 3–1B

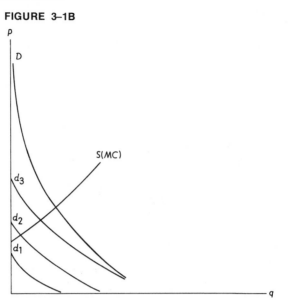

for the free market to ensure that this equilibrium will be reached. Thus Pareto optimality can only be attained if the government knows each individual's demand curve for public goods and charges a tax price that reflects each individual's preferences for public goods.

In practice, the relative charges imposed by the government upon various individuals to finance public goods reflect the political process and will not, in general, satisfy the conditions for Pareto optimality. Although a few individuals may find that their tax price correctly reflects their preference for public goods, this will not generally be true. One group of consumers would have preferred less service at the tax level established; another group would have preferred more. There is no possible adjustment an individual can make (except to move out of the jurisdiction) to attain a more preferred position. If preference schedules are very similar among most of the population, there will be general acceptance of the levels actually set; if there are wide differences, most consumers will be dissatisfied; and if the feelings are extreme—as over the Vietnam War—actual violence may develop as an expression of dissatisfaction. This is the basic explanation of why persons constantly complain about levels of governmental activity and why governments are often defeated in elections.

IS IT POSSIBLE TO OBTAIN EQUALITY OF THE *MRS* OF EACH INDIVIDUAL WITH *MRT*?

As noted, the basic solution involves overall equality of *MRS* of consumers as a whole with *MRT*, but not of each individual consumer.

Thus as long as the government is constrained to charge a uniform price (tax), many consumers will be dissatisfied, and there will be considerable pressures for change.

This leads one to ask whether it is possible to establish a stable equilibrium in which each individual is charged a different tax price. The work of Lindahl and Johansen (L-J) has sought to establish an equilibrium solution involving individual adjustments as explained in Appendix 3–2.[2] The government ascertains the preference schedule of each individual, and adjusts the charge (tax) on each individual to allow equality of MRS with the charge, at the same time determining overall output so that overall MRS equals MRT. The problem is, apart from determining preference schedules noted below, that there is no assurance that the desired results will be attained. In practice, the relative charges on various persons will reflect the political process noted below, rather than the optimum as defined.

Paul Samuelson has attempted to refine the Lindahl-Johansen approach.[3] Basically, he envisages the following kind of world. Assume that income is already distributed in an optimal fashion in the sense that the resulting market mechanism would take society to its preferred point in the absence of public goods or other sources of market failure. Assume further that there is an omniscient planner who not only knows each individual's preferences for private goods but also knows each individual's preferences for public goods as well. As long as there are no problems of externalities or production indivisibilities, as long as each person equates his or her MRS between any two goods to their price ratio, and as long as price equals marginal cost, the free market will allocate the private goods efficiently. This is the situation we described in Chapter 2. Thus, in the private market, for any individual i or j and for any two commodities (X and Y) $MRS_{XY}^i = MRS_{XY}^j = MRT_{XY}$.

In the case of public goods, however, there is no visible price mechanism. What the planner must do is set each individual's marginal rate of substitution between public and private goods equal to his or her appropriate tax share. Then the optimal amount of G will be given when $\Sigma MRS_{XG} = MRT_{XG}$, i.e., when the sum of each individual's marginal rate of substitution between the public good and the good X equals the marginal rate of transformation between the public

[2] Erik Lindahl, *Die Gerechtigkeit der Besteuerung* (Lund, 1919). The relevant section is printed in English in *Classics in the Theory of Public Finance*, ed. R. A. Musgrave and A. T. Peacock (New York-London, 1958). See also Lief Johansen, "Some Notes on the Lindahl Theory of Determination of Public Expenditures," *International Economic Review*, vol. 4 (September 1963), pp. 346–58.

[3] P. A. Samuelson, "Pure Theory of Public Expenditure and Taxation," in *Public Economics*, eds. J. Margolis and H. Guitton (New York: St. Martin's Press, 1969), pp. 98–123. For a somewhat similar treatment see Martin C. McGuire and Henry Aaron, "Efficiency and Equity in the Optimal Supply of Public Good," *Review of Economics and Statistics*, vol. 51 (February 1969), pp. 31–39.

good and the private good. This is entirely consistent with the L-J solution and is merely a more elegant and more general statement of it. If we know the preferences between X and G for each individual, and if we could charge each individual a price or tax share that equaled his or her marginal rate of substitution between a given public good and the private good, and if income were distributed in an optimal fashion, a market mechanism would exist that would lead to an efficient and optimal allocation of resources.

But, a little reflection will indicate that these exercises are of little use. Samuelson has made it abundantly clear that both his and the L-J solutions are really pseudosolutions. Granted that if there were an omniscient planner who knew each individual's preference map, the planner could charge each person a tax share or a price such that the person's MRS equaled his or her tax share; moreover, the sum of all individuals' marginal rates of substitution between public and private goods would equal society's marginal rate of transformation between these goods. But, the very essence of the public-good problem is that there is no way these preferences can be determined. Markets fail entirely with public goods. Pricing will not work, and any effort to determine them indirectly through polling or some such measures will fail because people will fail to state their true preferences as long as their tax payments depend upon their preferences. Thus, any solution analogous to the market is necessarily unsatisfactory.[4]

THE NATURE OF THE POLITICAL PROCESS

Actual outputs of public goods are determined by the government through the operation of the political process. Since this is a book about economics rather than political science, we shall only discuss the political process insofar as it relates to the provision of public goods or the determination of society's preferences for public goods. With the exception of the New England town meeting where every citizen has a direct vote and a right to speak, government in the United States is representative. Thus, there are basically three groups of actors on the political stage: the government officials who are in power; the elected representatives who vote on programs primarily proposed by the government officials; and the citizens. Since each of these groups

---

[4] Moreover, it is important to stress another assumption about the analysis; namely, that there is one public good, G. Typically government provides a range of public goods: national defense, natural resources or conservation, public health services, and so on. As soon as more than one public good enters the picture, it is necessary to allocate tax shares for each public good. In effect, this means that it is necessary to charge a price for each public good for each individual. In the context of Samuelson's pseudodemand curves, the problem is analytically tractable. We can simply assume that it is possible to set a price for each individual for each public good that equates the relative price of that public good and the numeraire commodity. But, again, we are caught in the dilemma, namely, how can we determine the proper price to charge?

has different attitudes toward public goods and their provision, let us consider their reactions to the problem of the provision and pricing of public goods. We then analyze how these preferences can be made known through the political process.

We shall assume that individuals as citizen voters, as representatives of voters, as government executives, or as bureaucrats are motivated by the desire to satisfy their own preference schedules. These reflect self-interest in large measure but also concern for the welfare of others, for particular activities of government per se, and for society. This behavioral assumption would appear more realistic than the alternate, that all persons in their capacities relating to government are motivated by the interests of society as a whole, whereas in other aspects of their life they are primarily motivated strictly by self-interest. Individuals in the governmental sector, while seeking to satisfy their own preferences, are subject to serious constraints by the need to bargain with others and the desire to obtain the favor of superiors, retain their positions, or be reelected. Thus their ability to act as they wish is greatly restricted.

THE CITIZEN VOTERS

Individuals are confronted with a range of possible public programs, with various possible levels of activity and various possible "prices" in the form of taxes that they must pay if the respective programs and levels are provided. The quantity that each individual prefers to have supplied depends on several elements—preference schedules, income, and the prices in the form of higher taxes that must be paid for public services. Before these determinants are analyzed, however, it is useful to discuss some of the differences between consumer decision-making in the public and private sector.[5]

Differences from Consumer Decision-Making for Private-Sector Output. Individual decision-making for public-sector output differs in several significant ways from decision-making for private-sector output.

Inability to Control the Amount Purchased. As explained above, a person decides upon the desired amount of a private good at the prevailing price and buys it. This he or she cannot do with a public good. The output of a public good and the tax price of this output are decided by government on the basis of overall preferences.

Nature and Knowledge of Benefits. Private goods are consumed individually and exclusively by an individual, who therefore is aware of the strength of his or her preference. Strict public goods are consumed collectively; the benefits, indivisible in nature, accrue to per-

---

[5] One of the few studies of this question is that of J. M. Buchanan, *Public Finance in Democratic Process* (Chapel Hill, N.C.: University of North Carolina Press, 1966). See also Roland McKean, *Government Spending* (New York: McGraw-Hill, 1968).

sons of the community as a group. Accordingly, the individual may not realize benefits at all, yet if the activity were not carried on, he or she might be worse off (or better off). A person may be unaware of public health measures designed to eliminate malaria, yet, if the activity were not undertaken, his or her family might become ill.

Uncertainty. There is an unusually high degree of uncertainty associated with public goods. Individuals may be highly uncertain about their benefits—the gain from additional spending on national defense, for example. They are also uncertain about the consequences of their own action for the actual determination of the level of government activity and about the actual tax price they will pay, that is, their share of various taxes, particularly with the corporate income tax (the distributional effects of which are not clear even to experts in the field) and progressive income taxes.

Finally, a person is uncertain about his or her ability to escape the tax by altering his or her activities (earning less or altering consumption patterns, for example) and the extent to which the tax price will be affected by the changes in activity by other persons.

Community Interest Motivation. The self-interest assumption does not preclude consideration of the interests of others either in the purchase of private goods or in decision-making for public goods. In the former, people do consider to some extent the welfare of others. They are encouraged to paint their houses because the neighbors appreciate it, and they contribute to private charity. In decision-making relating to public goods, broader motives may have greater significance. Individuals become concerned about the welfare of Indians or the preservation of forests, although they have no expectation of seeing an Indian or enjoying the forest preserves. Many attach substantial weight to the interests of future generations.

Furthermore, persons do frequently act as a group (e.g., labor union, civic club, farm organization, etc.) on matters of public goods; they consider the interests of the group and abide by its decisions rather than acting on the basis of narrow personal self-interest.

Mixture of Allocation and Distributional Activities. The provision of most governmental services of an allocational nature, those that increase outputs of certain goods relative to others, has distributional implications as well; given the nature of the tax structure, a net redistribution of real income results. Some goods with partial public-goods characteristics convey direct private benefits as well. Education, for example, conveys particular benefits to lower-income families but may be financed primarily by higher-income groups. Thus individual preference schedules for the service are influenced by attitudes toward the redistributional consequences.

Individual Preferences for Public Goods. Individual preferences for public goods are influenced by a number of forces.

Tastes. Individual preference schedules for public goods are influenced in part by the same forces that affect the demand for private goods. Individual preferences vary. To some persons, defense is important; to others, resource conservation. Since many are only partial public goods and convey some direct benefit to individuals as well as indivisible public benefit, those persons receiving the greatest direct gains will have greater preferences, other things equal. Thus families with several children to educate in public schools will have greater preference for education expenditures than childless couples or those preferring to send their children to private school.[6] Some persons have high preference for paying taxes to maintain national parks, while others prefer spending their incomes at Caribbean resorts.

Information. Since the benefits do not accrue separately to individuals, externally obtained information is necessary if the individuals are to have meaningful preference schedules. If the person has no knowledge whatever of the benefits of a particular government service, he or she can scarcely have a demand for it, and will therefore take no action on the proposal or will oppose any change because he or she knows nothing of the situation. For rational action a person must have information about costs and their distribution. For most persons optimal allocation of time and money dictates against scientific endeavor to obtain information necessary for a rational position on many issues relating to governmental activities. To the extent that the person does reach a position, he or she usually relies upon information readily available from the newspapers and similar sources, which may be neither accurate nor unbiased and will almost certainly flow in part from governmental news releases. A government inevitably seeks to defend the position it wishes to take and to provide information that will support that position.

There are several consequences of this information gap. Individuals frequently do not have opinions on various issues of governmental activity, and therefore the small group that does is in a position to dominate policy-making. Secondly, persons in higher-income groups are in a better position to gain information and are likely to have more influence on governmental policy than those in lower-income groups. Thirdly, many opinions are formed upon meager and biased information.

Degrees of Uncertainty. Preferences are affected by the certainty of the consequences of governmental activities on both benefit and cost sides.

In general, the more certain a person is about the attainment of benefits from government, the greater will be his or her preference at

---

[6] This is well evidenced by the tendency of residential areas with many elderly persons to vote against increased taxes to finance education.

any particular tax price. Preference, however, is also affected by his or her estimates of the relative possibilities of the benefits being more or less than anticipated. With national defense, the possibility that the benefits may be much greater than expected (in the event of attack which, while not expected, may occur), leads persons to favor higher levels of the service than otherwise.

Uncertainty about taxes has similar effects. If a person fears that there is greater chance that the tax cost to him or her will exceed the anticipated figure than be lower, he or she will prefer less of the service than he or she otherwise would.

Philosophy of Government.   Many persons have strong biases in favor of or against governmental activity generally. There is a correlation between income, wealth, and occupational activity and bias;[7] conservatism is typically found in higher-income business and professional groups. There are, of course, exceptions, and many persons in these groups strongly favor certain specific governmental activities.

Emotional Reactions.   Persons are conscious of the reactions of others to their attitudes on certain types of governmental activities and their decision-making relative to these activities is influenced thereby. National defense provides the most significant example. Few persons like to feel that they are open to the charge of neglecting national security. Thus, they can easily be led to support governmental activities that on the basis of more logical reasoning they might oppose. The argument that any difference of opinion favors the "enemy" and the charges of appeasement play a significant role in individual decision-making in this sphere.

Another example relates to morality; no politician likes to appear to be on the side of sin and against home, motherhood, and thrift. Thus, measures to enforce customary standards of morality may enjoy more support than measures to promote the use of birth control among lower-income families, even though the need for the latter is widely recognized and the former are not taken very seriously. A well-organized group may succeed in carrying through a program that a majority of the persons actually do not support but are reluctant to oppose publicly. The establishment of prohibition in the United States was an example.

Income Elasticity of Demand for Public Goods.   Income elasticity of demand for public goods, that is, the relationship between persons' incomes and their demands for public goods, may be positive or nega-

---

[7] With the exception that in some countries, including the United States, the persons generally unsympathetic to governmental activity favor high defense spending and the ones sympathetic to government prefer lower levels of defense activity. There are, of course, exceptions. The wealthy are, in a sense, seeking to ensure preservation of their wealth.

tive. As incomes rise, many persons will feel that they can afford more governmental services and they may wish higher standards of such services—better schools, varied curricula. For public goods regarded as inferior, the reverse will be true; as incomes rise, some persons will shift from public schools to private, from public parks to expensive resorts. Many persons become increasingly less sympathetic toward growth in governmental activity generally as they move into higher income levels, the "conservative bias" of the wealthy exercising greater influence on their behavior and reducing income elasticity of demand.

Closely related is the interdependence of demand for private and public goods. Relationships may be complementary; as more families have cars, their relative preferences for highways and national parks will increase. Others are of a substitute nature, particularly demands for governmental services that convey individual as well as community benefits. Thus increased availability or lower charges for private swimming pools will lessen preference for public pools.

The Relationship of the Tax Payment and Quantity Demanded.   As noted above, given a person's preference schedules, income, and the prices of other goods, the amount of the particular service that he or she wishes produced is a function of the tax price that he or she must pay for it; the lower the tax price, the greater the quantity he or she will prefer.

The actual tax price, given the tax structure, is affected by the ability of the person to escape the tax, legally or illegally. For example, if a person is willing to stop purchasing the article that is taxed to finance the service or does not use it at all, his or her demand for the service will be greater than if he or she is not able or willing to avoid the tax. Similarly, the convenience of the tax and the person's attitude toward its desirability, or toward the tax system as a whole if the service is not related to a particular tax, influence his or her demand.

Another significant aspect is the question of financing from a new tax or a tax increase, from growing revenue from existing levies, or from curtailment of other spending. Persons are much more willing, on the average—as borne out by empirical evidence—to support additional activities that can be financed without tax increases than ones requiring increases, even though, with the former, if the service were not increased, they could benefit from tax reduction or increases in other services. This is an aspect of the "threshold" or "displacement" phenomenon in taxation.[8] Persons become accustomed to a given level of taxes and will oppose increases in governmental services that require passage across the threshold. Only when shocked by some dras-

---

[8] See A. T. Peacock and J. Wiseman, *The Growth of Public Expenditures in the United Kingdom* (Princeton, N.J.: Princeton University Press, 1961).

tic event, such as a major war or a severe and prolonged financial crisis, will a country be able to pass the tax threshold. But once it has done so, a new tax plateau is reached, persons become accustomed to a higher level, and there is little pressure to move back below the original threshold. Thus World War II brought drastic changes in United States federal income tax rates and exemptions that would have been inconceivable before; the new threshold was obviously much higher after the war than before. The financial emergencies of the depression years of the thirties were responsible for establishing the sales tax in state finance in the United States and significantly raising the tax potential.

Some Consequences of the Nature of Public Goods Decision-Making. As previously noted, the failure of the market mechanism to determine the efficient levels of output of public goods or to allocate their costs makes it necessary for governments ot utilize other means to determine people's preferences for public goods and to reconcile the conflicts in preferences of various persons. Furthermore, since public goods are indivisible and since their costs are allocated among individuals through the political process, people can neither adjust the amount of a public good made available to them nor its tax price. An individual typically realizes that his or her participation in the decision-making process is not likely to influence the outcome and that decisions will be made about public goods whether he or she acts or not. Participation requires time and effort. Many persons, therefore, take no part in collective decision-making, preferring to delegate the task to others, and many even abstrain from voting to choose the representatives who will make the decisions. Or if they do participate, they do so in only a perfunctory fashion, choosing among candidates on the basis of general ideology rather than on any real understanding of the issues. One consequence is that small interested groups exercise primary influence in decision-making.

Another consequence is the disproportionate influence of the higher-income groups. While, in theory, all persons are equal in a democracy for purposes of collective decision-making, in practice their influence is not equal, with the higher-income groups exercising a disproportionate share. There are at least four reasons. First, the wealthy are in a much better position to acquire information about governmental activities and to participate in government. Secondly, because of their knowledge and stake in the protection of property, they are likely to have stronger desires for certain types of governmental services, and their biases toward governmental activity generally, although often adverse, may be stronger. Thirdly, they are in a position to buy influence; while votes cannot legally be bought and sold, persons contributing substantial amounts of money to political groups are in a position to receive favors in return. Fourth, the members of Congress are relatively affluent.

Political Parties and Revealing Preferences

Because individuals do not automatically reveal their preferences for public goods as they do for private-sector output, some system must be developed to ascertain the preference schedules. First, however, let us consider the basic question: Will individuals reveal their preferences at all? The answer is that they will so long as they know that their tax burden is not dependent upon the preferences that they indicate. So long as individuals know that the tax structure through which payments will be collected is not dependent upon their preference for expenditure levels, they have no reason to conceal their actual preferences. Even if their tax was affected they would still be willing to reveal their relative preferences among various kinds of expenditures at a given tax level.

What techniques may be employed to ascertain preferences? In a small community group, such as the New England and Swiss town meetings, individual voting on various measures is possible. Larger units of government may submit a few major issues to the voters on written ballots or utilize public opinion polls. This technique, however, is clearly not feasible for use on any scale. In the first place, in the modern complex society, far too much time and effort would be required to utilize the referendum technique on all issues.

Second, most individuals lack adequate information for reaching a decision about the various programs. Voting on the basis of complete lack of information cannot give results that reflect significant preferences. There is an observed tendency for persons to vote aginst any change on which they lack information, creating a built-in bias against a shift from present levels of activity.

Third, individual voters, either because of a lack of information or because they realize that their action will have little influence upon the overall outcome, may act irresponsibly, voting to increase expenditures and disapproving all proposals for financing them, for example.

Finally, voting by all individuals on proposed measures makes the logrolling necessary for recognition of the interests of minorities virtually impossible.

To meet these problems, institutions have developed through which individual preferences are ascertained and coordinated for the making of expenditure decisions.

Representatives. Typically, the voters choose legislators who will reflect their preferences in collective-goods decision making. Persons running for such an office will, under the assumption that they wish to attain and retain office, seek to estimate the preferences of their constituents for various levels of governmental activities (as well as other governmental policies) and establish a platform that in their belief most closely coincides with the preferences of the majority. The person elected is the one who most successfully estimates preferences, and once elected presumably will follow policies that reflect his or her estimate of the wishes of the constituents, under the assumption that he or she seeks reelection or, if ineligible, a person with similar views. Primary opportunity for logrolling and vote trading arises in the work of the legislative bodies, an activity that may bring the program of governmental activities more closely in line with individual preferences.

The representative system, while in a rough way bringing about policies that coincide with the preference schedules of the individuals in society, suffers from obvious limitations, arising primarily out of imperfect information. The candidates may seriously err in their estimates of individual preferences, and the voters may have little real choice; none of the candidates may take an overall position that coincides with majority preferences. Moreover, many voters lack information about the positions of candidates and do not trouble themselves to obtain it. Their votes, if cast at all, are based upon misinformation or upon purely extraneous considerations, such as the candidate's name. Finally, once elected, legislators may make little effort to ascertain the preferences of their constituents and may have great difficulty in doing so if they try. But imperfect as the system is, there is no feasible alternative in a democratic society.

Political Parties. At the national and state level, and to some extent at the local level, political parties play a major role in the decision-making processes.[9] The party may be defined as a group of persons with like interests seeking control of government. The goal of the party leaders is assumed to be the maximization of votes in order to gain and retain office. Accordingly, they seek to frame party platforms that most closely coincide with the preferences of the voters as a whole. Since voters regard additional governmental spending as favorable and taxes as unfavorable, the party will, in designing its program, attempt to expand each activity to the level at which the marginal gain from the activity is exactly equal to the marginal adverse response to the concomitant taxation. People will presumably vote for the party that they regard as maximizing their gain. Thus the parties serve as intermediaries, facilitating the functioning of the representative system by providing individual candidates of the party with a more or less common set of proposals and simplifying voting as particular parties come to stand for certain general positions, that is, to represent a particular ideology. The effectiveness of the system is higher to the extent that general consensus in society prevails on major issues. In fact, under these conditions, the positions of the two parties become very similar,

[9] See Anthony Downs, *An Economic Theory of Democracy* (New York: Harper & Row, 1957) for an analysis of the role of parties in decision making on governmental activities.

as each seeks to reach as closely as possible the median consensus position. The limited choice the voters have is not significant because of the high degree of consensus. If, on the other hand, there are several sharply divergent points of view on major issues, a multiparty system develops. Since no one party is likely to gain a majority, the consequence is instability of power and difficulty in deciding on and carrying through any consistent set of policies.[10]

The parties may not correctly estimate the preference schedules of the majority of voters on all issues of governmental activities. This is inherently an extremely difficult task, and any high degree of perfection is impossible. Accordingly, party leaders may substitute their own judgments for those of the community and seek to obtain popular support for them. Such a policy may cause parties to mislead their constituents about the merits of certain policies or the effectiveness of those carried out.

The Decision-Making Role of Executive and Bureaucracy

The chief executive in government is the leader of the governing party and as such has primary responsibility for interpreting the wishes of the public and developing, subject to legislative approval, and executing policies to meet the wishes of society. Capable executives can do far more than this, however; through their positions, they can exercise great influence in molding public opinion and thus shape the nature of individual preference schedules for public goods. This influence is made possible by the lack of information on the part of voters and their uncertainty about the outcomes of various policies. The net result is a complex interplay of executive and legislative interpretations of the preferences of individuals and executives' and legislators' own attitudes toward various governmental activities.

Great influence is likewise exercised over governmental programs by the administrative organization—the bureaucracy of government, the term not used in any derogatory sense. The administrative organi-

---

[10] Even with general consensus and a two-party system, neither party can usually remain in power for long periods, as the opposition has certain inherent advantages. First, it can obtain support of strong minorities whose policies are not acceptable to the majority; by bringing together minorities with intense preferences on various subjects, the opposition may bring about the downfall of the governing party. The latter's policy of seeking to follow majority preferences on all issues leaves in its wake a number of dissatisfied minorities, which may be united into a majority. This can be avoided only if the governing party is sufficiently successful in horse-trading with the minorities. Second, the government may encounter situations in which there is no clear-cut majority position. Since the government must indicate its position first, it is vulnerable to defeat, for a majority will oppose any policy that it adopts. Finally, voters appear to tire of the party in power, seeking change per se, even if the other party offers little prospect of meeting preferences more satisfactorily. How prevalent these problems are and how successful the opposition will be in utilizing them in elections determine their significance for stability in government.

zation not only influences the overall program of government but also, since it has responsibility for execution of the program, determines in large measure the manner in which it is carried out. At best the voters can influence only the general nature of an activity, while the bureaucracy determines the details.

What may be assumed about motivation of bureaucrats? The answer is not simple. As suggested by Downs,[11] no single motive can appropriately be assumed, since both purely personal motives as well as those relating to furtherance of the activity influence behavior. A reasonable assumption for strictly personal motivation is the desire to maintain position and gain promotion. Some persons seek to attain this goal primarily by performing their tasks with as little change as possible, aiming never to incur the enmity of anyone and to avoid policies that might fail and thus discredit them and their superiors. Others— the climbers, in Downs' terminology—emphasize the innovative role, seeking change and improvement to demonstrate their capacities to their superiors. This group is willing to take more risk and thus may move up very rapidly, on the one hand, or fail completely on the other. Both motives provide incentives toward efficiency and toward implementing as effectively as possible policies determined at higher levels. Unfortunately, they sometimes also lead to empire building: the attempt to secure as many subordinates as possible in the belief that the larger the empire, the higher the salary and the greater the chances for promotion.

The most casual observation of the functioning of governmental units (as well as those in larger businesses) suggests that other motives are frequently significant. Many persons become zealots for the activity with which they are associated. Preservation of wildlife or forests, strengthening of the Navy, building of more and better highways, improved standards of education become highly important goals to the persons.[12] While this phenomenon may further efficient operation of particular governmental units, it may also lead to expansion of activities beyond society's preferences. Without question, also, most persons in higher administrative tasks do become concerned with the interests of society as a whole and not alone with their immediate personal interests. Any economic analysis of government that fails to recognize this attitude will lead to inadequate and perhaps erroneous results.

With this dual motivation—the exact importance of each segment varying with the individual—the bureaucrats not only influence the manner in which governmental activities are carried out but also exer-

---

[11] See Anthony Downs, "A Theory of Bureaucracy," *Proceedings of American Economic Association for 1964*, pp. 439–46; and his *Inside Bureaucracy* (Boston: Little, Brown, 1967).

[12] See A. Wildavsky, *The Politics of the Budgetary Process* (Boston: Little, Brown, 1964), pp. 160–67.

cise influence upon the scope of various government programs. The chief executive and the legislators must rely heavily upon the bureaucrats for advice concerning benefits from expansion or contraction of each function, since they have on-the-spot knowledge of benefits and needs. Unfortunately both personal and activity motivation lead bureaucrats to favor continually higher levels of activity, which they seek to justify. The bureaucrats benefit, both personally and in terms of broader interests, from expansion of their activities but bear little of the additional costs. Thus legislative bodies must exercise independent judgment on their recommendations in terms of their estimates of the preference of individuals, considering both benefits and costs. The attitudes of those who bear costs as well as gain benefits must play a part in the decision picture.

To summarize briefly, this analysis envisages a situation in which the government makes proposals that it believes will maximize its vote-getting ability and the political leaders react in the way that they think will maximize their vote-getting ability. The citizens typically play a rather passive role and vote for the person or party they feel best represents their interests. Thus, different political leaders typically represent different socioeconomic groups. The art of politics is reaching a consensus that appeals to the majority of the voters or at least that is acceptable to them.

This process bears little resemblance to the formal models of the provision of public goods presented earlier in this chapter. Whether this process leads to more or less provision of public goods than that envisaged in these models is not clear. To the extent that bureaucrats push for their special interests or to the extent that various groups (or their elected representatives) trade votes on particular issues in such a way as to ensure majority support for programs of special interest to their constituents, an overexpansion of the public sector is possible.[13] In this way it is possible for every major group to receive special benefits without appearing to bear the burden of the cost. As long as no one major group feels exploited and as long as most groups feel that on balance they derive a net benefit from the actions of government (as represented by government officials and party leaders), the political system is viable.

It is interesting to note that while the formal models presented earlier in this chapter indicated that government would supply too few public goods because people would fail to reveal their true preferences, many of the political theories indicate that government may in fact produce too many in an effort to achieve a reasonable consensus and keep the major constituencies happy. While it is doubtful if the political process attempts to maximize anything, on the whole it seems to work in that the perceived benefits arising from government are usu-

---

[13] See J. M. Buchanan and G. Tullock, *The Calculus of Consent* (Ann Arbor, Michigan: University of Michigan Press, 1962), chaps. 10, 11, 12.

ally thought to be greater than the perceived costs by the relevant constituencies or socioeconomic groups. This is essential for the maintenance of a viable democracy.

RECONCILIATION OF CONFLICTING PREFERENCES

From the preceding discussion, it should be clear that various groups have different attitudes toward the provision of public goods. Not only do different individuals have different attitudes about the optimal provision of public goods, but there are often conflicts among the bureaucrats or administrators, the political representatives, and the citizen voters. How these can be reconciled by the political process will be considered in this section.

The Unanimity Rule

At one extreme, the unanimity or complete-consensus rule could be employed: Only those actions relating to output of public goods on which there is complete agreement can justifiably be undertaken. This rule is closely related to the Pareto criterion of economic welfare explained in Chapter 2. A change increases economic welfare only if one person is benefited without anyone suffering loss. Given rational behavior, any change in the output of public goods benefiting one or more persons and injuring no one will receive unanimous support, whereas changes not meeting this requirement will not. This rule, first developed and defended by the Swedish economist Wicksell,[14] avoids what may be called the "external cost" of change, that is, injury to persons who do not wish the change, and provides maximum protection of minority interests.

The proposal is not so rigid and extreme as it may appear, since various persons with divergent views will seek to compromise to obtain a solution acceptable to all. Since the group is confronted with a variety of issues relating to governmental activities, vote trading and compromise are feasible. Some persons will concede on certain issues to obtain approval of other persons on measures that they favor. Committees and small groups, so long as they are not segmented along ideological or representative-party lines, reach unanimity on most issues, even if there are substantial differences in preferences.[15]

---

[14] See Knut Wicksell, "A New Principle of Just Taxation," in *Classics in the Theory of Public Finance*, eds. R. A. Musgrave and A. T. Peacock (London: Macmillan, 1958), pp. 72–118 (article originally published in German in 1896).

[15] Even though members may have differing preferences, committees frequently reach unanimous decisions. In addition to the implicit "logrolling" consideration, committee members also seek to minimize the amount of time spent in reaching decisions and to present a united front to the larger group or higher authority, to increase the likelihood of acceptance of their decisions.

As a general rule for decision-making on governmental activities, however, the unanimity rule is unacceptable and in fact is never employed for this purpose. With modern complex governments involved in a wide range of activities, the time and effort that would be required to obtain unanimity through compromise and bargaining would be intolerable, even if decisions were made by a small representative group.

The unanimity rule gives small minority groups tremendous bargaining power to block change unless they receive concessions that are intolerable to the majority. Thus the status quo is tremendously favored. If literally complete unanimity is required, one person could block any change. Since society will not tolerate such dictatorship by the minority, the unanimity rule must give way.

Finally, the rule is unworkable for purely distributional (welfare) functions of government that move society along its utility possibility frontier, since these, by their nature, involve transfer of wealth from some persons to others, and some might never agree to the change.

Majority Decision-Making

Modern democratic society accepts the rule that conflicting preferences must be resolved by the rule of majority vote, with each adult vote counted equally. Acceptance of this rule involves, of course, a value judgment, but a judgment that is accepted in most societies in the world today. The rule is workable and does not block the interests of the many to protect the few. It presumably serves the interests of the largest number in society, but the claim cannot be made that it maximizes economic welfare, since benefits received and injuries suffered by various individuals cannot be compared.

The majority rule is not, however, so simple in its operation or so obviously desirable in its results as may first appear. While the political system appears to achieve a reasonably rational consensus that satisfies the bulk of the voters sufficiently to ensure political stability, Kenneth Arrow has raised a basic point about the collective rationality of the political process.[16] Stated most generally, Arrow has postulated that under certain plausible conditions that frequently describe the American political process, majority voting can fail to reflect the will of the majority. In specific circumstances, it is possible that a small minority (or even a single voter) could in effect dictate the outcome to the majority.

---

[16] Kenneth Arrow, *Social Choice and Individual Values* (New York: Wiley and Co., 1951). For a somewhat less difficult presentation of "Arrow's Paradox," see W. H. Riker, "Arrow's Theorem and Some Exmples of the Paradox of Voting," in *Mathematical Applications in Political Science*, ed. John M. Claunch (Dallas, Texas: Arnold Foundation of Southern Methodist University, 1965) pp. 41–60.

The paradox can be stated more clearly if the conditions necessary for majority voting to reflect the will of the majority are defined:

1.   Voters have transitive orderings; that is, if a voter is confronted with three alternatives, a, b, and c, and if he or she prefers a to b and b to c, he or she then prefers a to c. For example, if a person is confronted with a choice of 1, 2, or 3 fire engines for a city and prefers 1 over 2 and 2 over 3, he or she will also prefer 1 over 3.

2.   The voting procedure insures that transitive ordering of the individual voters will be reflected in transitive ordering for the society as a whole.

3.   All possible orderings are permitted.

4.   Any change in individual orderings will be reflected in a comparable change in society's orderings.

5.   Pairwise voting is used; the voter has only the choice between successive pairs of alternatives, with no possibility of point or weight voting or expressing preferences for a budget figure in a continuum of budget figures. This is the typical pattern in the United States.

Suppose, for example, there are three voters in a community, with orderings for the number of fire engines as follows:

Voter	Preferred number of fire engines
A	$1 \rightarrow 2 \rightarrow 3$ (i.e., 1 is preferred to 2, 2 to 3)
B	$2 \rightarrow 3 \rightarrow 1$
C	$3 \rightarrow 2 \rightarrow 1$

In this case there is no difficulty; there is a clear majority for 2 fire engines. Two engines are preferred over one; three are preferred over one; and two are preferred over three.

But suppose the preferences were given as follows:

Voter	Preferred number of fire engines
A	$1 \rightarrow 2 \rightarrow 3$
B	$2 \rightarrow 3 \rightarrow 1$
C	$3 \rightarrow 1 \rightarrow 2$

In this case, there is no positive majority; each option wins in a pairwise choice.

The trouble arises because of voter C; if voter C cannot have the three engines he or she prefers, voter C wants only 1 (perhaps under the belief that without 3 the city will burn if a fire starts, so the expenditures on fire engines should be minimized). There is a majority in favor of 1 over 2; of 2 over 3; but of 3 over 1. There is no stable majority solution since the outcome of the vote depends solely upon the order in which the vote is taken. If the first vote is on the choice between 1 and 2, 1 will win; then 3 will defeat 1 to be the winner. But if the first vote is between 2 and 3, 2 will win over 3 and then lose to 1, the final winner. If the first vote is between 1 and 3, 3 will win, only to lose to 2, the final winner.

On a more intuitive level, the possibility of the Arrow Paradox arises from two conditions: first, the comparisons must be pairwise; and second, any ordering is possible. If we think of the options as budget sizes, it is unlikely, but not impossible, that the paradox will arise. People who prefer a large budget will generally prefer a medium-sized budget to a small budget; and similarly for people who prefer a small budget. The problem only arises if a person who most prefers a large budget would have a second choice for a small budget. Similar considerations apply to other programs: housing, education, defense, and so forth. It is unlikely that people will hold these orderings, but not impossible. To the extent that people feel that if something is not done at their preferred scale, it should not be done at all, their preference ordering will not be regular. For example, a person may feel that if a large amount is not spent on national defense, nothing might as well be spent, since the country will be destroyed in any event.

The pairwise comparison is equally important. If the voters were permitted to select from a continuum—say the size of a budget—a consensus could be reached since this would imply some sort of point voting or rank voting. The alternative with the largest number of points would win. But, parliamentary rules usually follow the pairwise comparison. A motion is made, then an amendment is introduced. The amendment is then voted on (*yes* or *no*), which is in effect a vote between the amendment and the original motion. If the amendment passes, then the amended motion is voted on as a substitute for the initial motion on a *yes* or *no* basis. If it fails, the original motion is then voted for on a *yes* or *no* basis.

Although Arrow has proved that this problem can exist, it is not clear whether it is an important issue in terms of the political process. As we have pointed out above, certain intuitive standards of rationality indicate that it will not usually be a problem.[17] But its possibility does facilitate parliamentary maneuvering. In particular, while the possibility of the Arrow Paradox will probably never let the minority impose a program on the majority, it can enable the minority to thwart the will of the majority to prevent the passage of a program or activity the minority opposes.

---

[17] For example, in his interesting paper, Riker can only find two tentative examples. See Riker, "Arrow's Theorem and the Paradox of Voting."

Strategic Voting

A phenomenon closely related to the Arrow Paradox is strategic voting; when there are several sets of attitudes on a particular question, the proposal that would actually command the greatest support may be eliminated from consideration because those holding to one extreme vote initially for the other extreme to kill off the moderate proposal. For example, suppose that there are three proposals for improving transportation in an urban area:

Proposal A: Extensive expressway construction, no improvement in public transit; 30 percent of voters prefer.

Proposal B: Some expressway construction, some transit improvement; 40 percent prefer.

Proposal C: No further expressways, concentration on public transit; 30 percent prefer.

Under the assumption of the usual pairwise voting, B and C are voted on first, and by nonstrategic voting, B would win easily. But instead, the supporters of A vote for C, thus eliminating B from further consideration. Thus in the end the voters have the choice between the two extremes, and the A defenders hope to pull enough supporters from B to win over C. Thus B, the position preferred by the greatest number and the proposal that would win over either of the others with nonstrategic voting is defeated. This typically occurs in legislative bodies through amendments to the original moderate proposal to make it so extreme that it is killed.

This problem is obvious at the national level in the United States and may give a generally conservative bias to government activity and limit its scope to a level less than that desired by the majority. Insofar as the U.S. Congress is dominated by conservative parliamentarians who are aware of the possibilities of strategic voting, and insofar as the moderates tend to prefer the conservative position to the liberal position when confronted with a choice, the introduction of new programs can be severely curtailed. Thus Arrow's Paradox indicates that democracy as practiced in the United States may have a conservative bias, in that the conservative minority can prevent the will of the combined majority consisting of the moderates and liberals from taking even the actions preferred by the moderates. Thus there may be an inherent do-nothing bias built into Congress. When one considers the length of time it takes to get through Congress most major legislation that forms any sort of break with past traditions, there is some circumstantial evidence that Arrow's Paradox or strategic voting may be at work. But, it is possible only so long as the conservatives through the seniority system dominate the parliamentary proceedings and only insofar as they are aware of the possibilities of cyclic or strategic voting.

CONCLUSION

What then can we say about the problem of the provision of public goods? The question of what amount of public goods should be provided and how the costs of these goods should be borne is basically a political decision. The economists' search for solutions has been ingenious and often elegant, but not satisfactory in the sense of providing an operational framework to solve these two problems. The political process is primarily concerned with these two issues and, to the extent that it works, the solution it presents can be thought of as acceptable. Whether the solution is optimal in the sense that it would approach the economists' solution if their solution could be made workable is another matter. The answer to this question involves value judgments about the nature of the political process, the nature of the representatives, and whether the political process truly reflects individual preferences. Buchanan and Tullock have argued that the political process probably leads to provision of public goods beyond the optimum because of its logrolling nature. The possibility of strategic voting would lead one to argue that under certain plausible circumstances, the political process leads to less than an optimal provision of these goods. Unfortunately, as long as the optimal provision of public goods remains a nonoperational concept, whether the political process provides too many or too few of these goods must remain a matter of conjecture.

Nevertheless, whether the political process leads to an optimal provision of public goods or not, it is generally acceptable in the sense that it is usually able to reach a fairly wide consensus. One group may lose on one vote, but win on another. As long as a sufficiently large number of groups of voters ultimately feel that on the whole the net benefits of government activity are positive, the political system can be said to be workable; the provision of public goods and the determination of tax shares can be said to be acceptable. With some reservations, this seems to describe the American political system reasonably well.

APPENDIX A

PARETO OPTIMALITY AND PUBLIC GOODS

The problem of the optimal provision and financing of public goods can be graphically analyzed in a world which we assume to consist of two individuals, A and B; and two goods, a public good G and a private good X.[18] Since X is a normal private good, it is divisible in consump-

---

[18] See P. A. Samuelson, "Diagrammatic Exposition of a Theory of Public Expenditures," *Review of Economics and Statistics*, vol. 37 (November 1955), pp. 350–56.

tion; that is, the amount of X consumed by A cannot be consumed by B, and conversely. The total consumption of X must be divided between its consumption by A and its consumption by B. This can formally be stated by the condition that $X_a + X_b = X$, where X_a and X_b represent the amount of the private good X respectively consumed by A and B.

Since G is a pure public good, it is not divisible in consumption. Therefore, A's "consumption" of the public good G does not reduce the amount available for "consumption" by B. Because the amount of G that is made available cannot be divided between the members of society, A and B must collectively consume the amount of G that is made available. Moreover, since the total amount of G is equally available for consumption by each person, the total amount of G is in a sense consumed equally by each. This can formally be stated by the condition that $G_a = G_b = G$, where G_a and G_b represent the amount of G consumed by A and B respectively. Note that this statement does not imply that each person has the same preference for G or receives the same benefits from it. As noted above, the amount of G provided cannot be adjusted to the preference of both persons when these preferences differ; nor can each person adjust his or her consumption of G to the amount he or she prefers. Since each individual has to accept the amount of G made available on the basis of collective decision-making, we can say that the total amount of G must be equally consumed by each individual.

We assume that the tastes of A and B are given and that society's production possibility frontier is given. The problem at hand is to derive the conditions for Pareto optimality, that is, a situation in which it is not possible to increase A's welfare without reducing that of B. We do this by constructing the utility-possibility frontier, which shows the maximum welfare a given individual can achieve, given the utility level of the other individual. Let us choose a given level of B's utility and determine the maximum amount of utility A can achieve. In doing so, we will determine the conditions needed for efficiency and a given point on the utility possibility frontier. By choosing a different level of B's utility and repeating the exercise, we could derive a different point on the utility possibility frontier and thus eventually trace out the entire utility possibility frontier.

Figure 3A–1 gives A's utility map; Figure 3A–2 gives B's utility map; Figure 3A–3 gives society's transformation locus or production-possiblity frontier between X and G (TT'). Suppose that we assume B's level of utility to be at b_2 and determine the maximum utility A can achieve in view of this constraint. This can be done by first deriving A's consumption possibility curve, given that B is assumed to remain on a fixed level of utility reflected by b_2; and then by deriving A's utility-maximizing point of consumption, given the consumption-possibility curve.

FIGURE 3A–1
A's Utility Map

FIGURE 3A–2
B's Utility Map

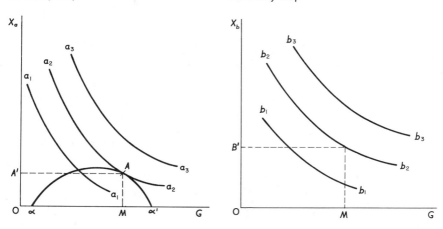

A's consumption-possibility curve can be derived by superimposing B's indifference curve b_2b_2 on the transformation locus as the line $b_2'b_2'$ in Figure 3A–3. This is permissible because we are dealing with physical magnitudes of the goods. By assumption, A and B consume identical amounts of G but different amounts of X. Let us determine how much of each good is available of A's consumption, if we take B's consumption of each good as given. For example, let us assume that B consumes at point B in Figure 3A–3, where B consumes OB' of X and OM of G. Because G is not divisible in consumption, if B consumes

FIGURE 3A–3
Society's Transformation Curve
Commodities X and G

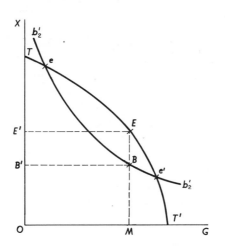

OM of *G*, A must also consume *OM* of *G*, and society must produce *OM* of *G*. If society produces *OM* of *G*, the production-possibility frontier *TT'* indicates that *OE'* is the maximum amount of *X* available. Therefore, given that *OM* of *G* is produced, society will be at point *E* on the production-possibility curve. If B consumes at point *B*, he consumes *OB'* of *X*, leaving *B'E'* of *X* for A to consume. Since A and B must consume identical amounts of *G*, the amount of *X* available for A's consumption, *B'E'*, must equal the vertical distance *BE* between the indifference curve $b_2'b_2'$ at point *B* and the production-possibility frontier at point *E*. Thus, at any point along $b_2'b_2$ (in Figure 3A–3), A's consumption possibilities can be derived by subtracting the amounts of each good implied by $b_2'b_2'$ *vertically* from the production-possibility frontier *TT'*. In this way, A's consumption-possibility curve, given B's consumption along the indifference curve b_2b_2 (or $b_2'b_2'$ in Figure 3A–3), can be derived. This is shown on the curve $\alpha\alpha'$ in Figure 3A–1. Note that the points α and α' in Figure 3A–1 correspond to points *e* and *e'* in Figure 3A–3. At points α and α' in Figure 3A–1, A's consumption of the private good *X* is zero since B's indifference curve $b_2'b_2'$ intersects the production-possibility frontier at points *e* and *e'* in Figure 3A–3.

A wants to maximize welfare subject to consumption-possibility curve $\alpha\alpha'$. This curve is tangent to A's indifference curve a_2a_2 at point *A* in Figure 3A–1. Given that B achieves a level of utility represented by indifference curve b_2b_2 ($b_2'b_2'$), A can achieve a level of utility given by indifference curve a_2a_2, where B will consume *OA'* of the private good *X* and *OM* of the public good *G*. Since both individuals must consume the same amount of the public good to utilize resources fully, society must produce at point *E* in Figure 3A–1 where *OM* of the public good *G* is produced and *OE'* of the private good *X* is produced. This must be equal to the sum of *OA'* of the private good *X* consumed (given as *B'E'* in Figure 3A–3) by A and *OB'* of the private good *P* consumed by B.

What can we infer about the conditions needed for efficiency at these consumption and production points? Inspection of Figures 3A–1 and 3A–2 indicates that at A's consumption point *A* and B's consumption point *B* the slopes of the indifference curves are not equal. Thus, when public goods are involved, efficiency does *not* require the equality of the marginal rates of substitution between consumers as it does in the case of private goods. Such equality is not possible unless their preferences are identical. Moreover, at point *E*, the slope of the production possibility curve is different from the slope of either A's or B's indifference curves at their point of consumption. Thus, the marginal rate of transformation does *not* equal the marginal rate of substitution of either consumer. It can be shown, however, that at point *E*, the marginal rate of transformation is equal to the *sum* of A's and B's marginal rates of substitution.[19]

The crucial difference between the conditions needed for efficiency in a world consisting only of private goods and in a world of private and public goods can be stated as follows:

1. For efficiency between private goods, $MRS = MRT$ and the MRS are equal for all individuals for any two goods.

2. For efficiency between a private good and a public good, $\Sigma MRS = MRT$ while the MRS are different for each individual.

The same point can be seen in Figure 3A–4. The line labeled MC is

FIGURE 3A–4
Optimal Output of a Public Good

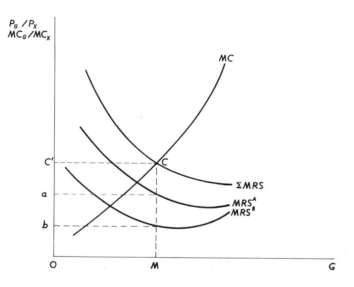

<hr />

[19] Note that A's consumption possibility curve $\alpha\alpha'$ was constructed by subtracting vertically the line $b_2'b_2'$ from the production-possibility frontier TT'. Thus, at any given point, the slope of A's consumption-possibility curve is equal to the difference between the slope of the production-possibility frontier TT' and the slope of the line $b_2'b_2'$. The slope of the production-possibility frontier at any given point is equal to society's marginal rate of transformation (MRT). Since $b_2'b_2'$ is B's indifference curve b_2b_2 superimposed upon the production-possibility frontier, the slope of $b_2'b_2'$ must reflect B's marginal rate of substitution (MRS^B). Thus, at any given point along A's consumption-possibility curve, its slope must equal the difference between the marginal rate of transformation and B's marginal rate of substitution, (i.e., $MRT - MRS^B$). A's optimal consumption point occurs when the consumption possibility curve is tangent to the indifference curve. At this point, the slope of the consumption-possibility curve must equal the marginal rate of substitution (MRS^A). Thus, in equilibrium, $MRS^A = MRT - MRS^B$, or $MRS^A + MRS^B = MRT$; the sum of A's and B's marginal rates of substitution between the private good X and the public good G must equal society's marginal rate of transformation between these two goods.

equal to the absolute value of society's marginal rate of transformation, which is equal to the slope of the production-possibility frontier in Figure 3A–3. Since the marginal rate of transformation is equal to the ratio of marginal costs, the line MC can be taken to reflect the marginal cost of producing the public good G in terms of the private good X, that is, the value of the amount of X that must be sacrificed when an additional unit of G is produced. The lines labeled MRS^A and MRS^B reflect the absolute values of A's and B's marginal rates of substitution along the indifference curve a_2a_2 and b_2b_2. Since these reflect the rates at which A and B are willing to exchange the public good G in terms of the private good X for different quantities of X and G, MRS^A and MRS^B are in effect A's and B's "demand" or preference curves for the public good G, indicating the amount of G they would prefer to see produced, if they had to sacrifice a unit of X to get an additional unit of G.

With private goods, each consumer regards prices as given and purchases sufficient quantities to equalize marginal rates of substitution with the given prices. Each individual's demand curve for a given private good shows the amount of the private good that individual is willing to purchase at the given market price. Since private goods are divisible in consumption and since two people cannot simultaneously consume the same physical output of the same good (e.g., the same apple), the market or total demand for a private good is obtained by horizontally summing the individual demand curves.

With public goods, each person cannot "buy" the amount he or she prefers; the total quantity is determined by collective decision-making through governmental action, and the person must accept that amount. Nevertheless, each person has a demand curve for a public good that measures the amount he or she would be willing to pay to get the amount of the public good available, if he or she had to pay to get it. The "total demand curve" for a public good, therefore, indicates the total amount people would be willing to pay for a given amount of G. This is derived by summing vertically the individual demand curves for the public good. Thus, the total demand curve for the public curve G is given by the line $\Sigma SMRS$ in Figure 3A–4, which represents the vertical summation of the lines MRS^A and MRS^B.

The optimal output of G is at the level at which the total amount society is willing to pay for the public good G equals the marginal cost or opportunity cost of producing the public good. In Figure 3A–4 this is given at point C where society produces OM of the public good G at a cost of OC'. This corresponds to the point E in Figure 3A–3. The curve MC represents the marginal rate of transformation. In equilibrium $\Sigma MRS = MC$, but $MC = MRT$. Therefore, $\Sigma MRS = MRT$ or, alternatively, $MRS^A + MRS^B = MRT$. Note that at the equilibrium point C in Figure 3A–4, A would bear Oa of the cost of the public good G while B would bear Ob of the cost of the public good G, if each individual had to pay a tax for the public good equal to his or her marginal rate of substitution, which represents the maximum amount he or she would be willing to pay to obtain the amount of the public good available. This indicates that at the equilibrium point C, which represents society's point of production E (Figure 3A–3), A's marginal rate of substitution is higher than B's, indicating that A values the public good more highly than does B. While payments for public goods cannot generally be related to each individual's marginal rates of substitution or marginal valuation of the public good, this analysis highlights a crucial difference between private and public goods. In the case of private goods, people face identical prices and adjust the quantities they purchase, while in the case of public goods, people face identical quantities and adjust their own internal prices or marginal rates of substitution in accordance with the quantities available.

It is important to note that the particular solution we derived was dependent on choosing a particular level of B's welfare. If we had chosen a different level of B's welfare, Say $b_1 b_1$, we would have derived a different consumption-possibility curve for A and a maximum attainable utility would have been chosen. Note that each point would be Pareto-optimal in the sense that it represents the maximum utility that A can derive, given B's fixed utility level. In each case, efficiency would require that $MRS^A + MRS^B = MRT$. But from a normative point of view, no one point would be preferable.

Thus, we can trace out the locus of alternative utility levels for A and B and plot them as the utility-possibility curve UU in Figure 3A–5. The point B represents, for example, the point given in our example where B is assumed to remain on $b_2 b_2$ and A then attains $a_2 a_2$. Alternatively, if we had set B's utility level at $b_1 b_1$, A's maximum utility could have been higher and the equilibrium could be represented by the point A. From the point of view of economic efficiency, A and B are equally desirable. Choosing among such points comes down to a purely ethical question of how welfare should be distributed among the different members of society.

This can be answered analytically only with the construction of a social welfare function WW, which we assume represents society's preferences as expressed through the democratic process. In the example given in Figure 3A–5, the maximum social welfare can be reached at point β^*, which happens to be intermediate between A and B. It is possible to determine B's indifference curve implied by this, and thus A's point of maximum utility and the amount of G and X produced.

Without the social welfare function or some other means of determining the desirable initial income distribution between A and B, the optimal solution cannot be found. Society may be producing efficiently, but there is no guarantee that this is society's preferred point.

FIGURE 3A–5
Alternative Equilibrium Outputs of a Public Good

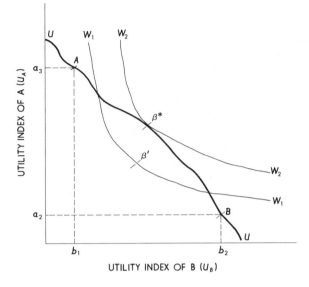

In fact, in Figure 3A–5, point β', which is inefficient, may be preferable to either point A or B, which are each efficient.

APPENDIX B

THE LINDAHL-JOHANSEN APPROACH TO THE STATEMENT OF ECONOMICALLY OPTIMAL LEVELS OF GOVERNMENTAL ACTIVITIES

The approach first used by Lindahl and recently revived by Johansen[20] assumes a fixed distribution of income between individuals who consume a private good X and a public good G. While easy to generalize to several individuals, the problem can best be seen by limiting the analysis to two individuals, A and B. Each person must bear a proportion of the total cost of G. The problem is to determine the following: How much G will be consumed collectively and how will the tax shares be allocated between A and B?

L-J start off with the usual assumption that each individual has a fixed-budget constraint and the usual indifference map between the

[20] Erik Lindahl, *Die Gerechtigkeit der Besteuerung* (Lund, 1919). The relevant section is printed in English in *Classics in the Theory of Public Finance*, eds., R. A. Musgrave and A. T. Peacock (New York-London, 1958). See also Johansen, *Public Economics;* and Johansen, "Some Notes on the Lindahl Theory."

private good X and the public good G. By using the fixed-budget constraint L-J are able to transform the usual indifference curves between X and G into indifference curves between G and h. These indifference curves are shown in Figure 3B–1 and are represented by the

FIGURE 3B–1
The Lindahl-Johansen Solution

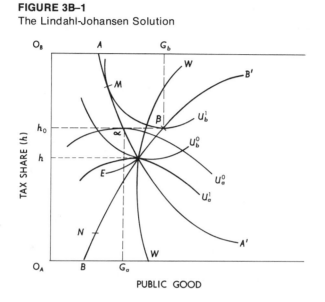

PUBLIC GOOD

curves U_a^0, U_a^1, etc. for A and by the curves U_b^0, U_b^1, etc. for B. These curves have the following characteristics. For A: Each indifference curve is convex from below and reaches a maximum at the tax share h; A's welfare increases as A's indifference curves move from top (where A bears the full tax share of G) to bottom (where A bears none of the tax share of G). For B: Each indifference curve is concave from below and reaches a minimum at the tax share $(1 - h)$; B's welfare increases as B's indifference curves move from bottom (where B bears the full tax share of G to top (where B bears none of the tax share of G).

Since each tax share represents the price of the public good G to A or B, we can derive A's and B's demand curves for the public good, by determining the maximum utility each individual can reach given a specific tax share. For example, when the tax share is equal to h_o, A bears h_o of the cost of G and B bears $(1 - h_o)$ of the cost of G. When the tax share facing A is h_o, can reach a level of utility denoted by U_a^0 where A would like to consume $O_A G_a$ of G. When the tax share facing B is $(1 - h_o)$, B can reach a level of utility denoted by U_b^1, where B would like to consume $O_B G_b$ of G. By changing tax shares, we can trace out the levels of G that each individual would like to consume, and thus derive demand curves for G for each individual, showing the quantities of the public good G they would prefer at various tax shares. These demand curves are shown by the line AA' for A and BB' for B. Since h represents the tax share A pays, A's demand for G rises as h falls. Since $(1 - h)$ represents B's tax share, B's demand for G rises as h rises.

The curve WW denotes the locus of all efficient consumption points where it is impossible to increase one individual's welfare without reducing that of the other. Graphically, this is determined by the points of tangency between the two sets of indifference curves in Figure 3B–1 where the marginal rates of substitution between h and G for A and B are equal. At any point along this contract curve, it can be shown that the sum of A's and B's marginal rates of substitution between X and G equal the marginal rate of transformation.[21] Thus all points along the curve are efficient consumption points.

The point E denotes that intersection of the two demand curves. Any point on the demand curve AA' represents a point where A's marginal rate of substitution between h and G is zero; and any point on the demand curve BB' represents a point where B's marginal rate of substitution between h and G is zero. Thus at point E, where the two demand curves intersect, the marginal rates of substitution must each be equal to zero and therefore equal to each other. Therefore, the point E must also be on the contract curve WW. Hence, at point E the two demand curves and the contract curve all intersect. Except for this one point, neither the line AA' nor the line BB' is on the contract curve WW, which represents the efficient consumption points. The solution E is efficient since it is on the contract curve and is stable since it marks the intersection of A's and B's demand curves. Thus, once this solution is achieved, both parties will be satisfied.

While this solution has a certain plausibility, there are several things wrong with it. First, the specific demand curves AA' and BB' depend on the initial income distribution. Unless the income distribution is deemed to be optimal, the resulting solution has no normative significance. Any given demand curve is one of an infinite number of demand curves that would exist with an infinite number of different distributions. Second, there is no market mechanism to ensure that society will end up at the intersection of the two demand curves. The determination of the relative tax shares essentially depends on the relative strength or bargaining power of each individual, who will try to minimize his tax share consistent with a solution that is acceptable to the other party. Thus society could easily end up at a point like M or N in Figure 3B–1. At M for example, B's indifference curve is tangent to A's demand curve, and B is imposing the major burden of the tax costs on A. This represents the greatest utility B can achieve consistent

---

[21] The contract curve WW denots all points where A's marginal rate of substitution between h and G equals B's marginal rate of substitution between h and G; $MRS_{hG}{}^A = MRS_{hG}{}^B$.

with A's demand curve AA'. Similarly, point N reflects the greatest utility A can achieve consistent with B's demand curve. While neither M nor N are efficient points, since there are alternative points on the diagram where A could be better off while leaving B no worse off or B could be better off while leaving A no worse off, there is no market mechanism to make this change come about. While less efficient than E, the points M or N offer equally plausible solutions. The actual output of G is not determined by any market mechanism, but by a political process that reflects A's and B's relative strengths.

More basically, the L-J solution never comes to grips with the essential problem. Individuals will hide their true preferences for public goods to minimize their tax shares. Although it is conceptually possible to visualize an indifference curve between X and G and to derive an individual's demand curve for G, this demand curve can never be determined; the person will not reveal it voluntarily or through a market mechanism. Unlike the private market where people are forced to make their preferences known through their purchase of goods and services, there is no market for public goods. And since people realize that once the good is made available they can enjoy its benefits whether they pay any of their tax share or not, there is no incentive to make them reveal their true preferences; the demand curves will never be observed.

REFERENCES

Breton, A. *The Economic Theory of Representative Government.* Chicago: Aldine, 1974.

Buchanan, J. M. "Public Finance and Public Choice," *National Tax Journal,* vol. 28 (December 1975), pp. 383–94.

Head, J. G. *Public Goods and Public Welfare.* Durham, N.C.: Duke University Press, 1974.

Johansen, Lief. *Public Economics.* Chicago: Rand McNally & Co., 1965.

———. "Some Notes on the Lindahl Theory of Determination of Public Expenditures," *International Economics Review,* vol. 4 (September 1963), pp. 346–58.

Mueller, D. C. "Public Choice: A Survey," *Journal of Economic Literature,* vol. 14 (June 1976), pp. 395–433.

Riker, W. H. "Arrow's Theorem and Some Examples of the Paradox of Voting," in John M. Claunch (ed.) *Mathematical Applications in Political Science.* Dallas, Texas: Arnold Foundation of Southern Methodist University, 1965, pp. 41–60.

Samuelson, P. A. "Diagrammatic Exposition of a Theory of Public Expenditures," *Review of Economics and Statistics,* vol. 37 (November 1955), pp. 350–56.

Samuelson, P. A. "'Pure Theory of Public Expenditures and Taxation," in J. Margolis and H. Guitton (eds.), *Public Economics.* New York: St. Martin's Press, 1969, pp. 98–123.

4

Externalities and the
Role of Government

The previous chapter discussed the problems posed by public or collective goods. Because they are indivisible in consumption once they are made available, they are equally available to all. Hence, there is no way the market mechanism can exclude persons from receiving the benefits from them, and they can be provided only by the government. There are other types of activities, however, that require governmental intervention if their output is to be optimal but do not require direct governmental provision. A major example consists of activities for which the exclusion is possible but which give rise to externalities; that is, their production or consumption gives rise to benefits or costs to persons other than those who acquire the goods. The activities are separable and divisible and can be sold to individuals, but the purchasers either do not receive the sole benefits or do not pay for all the costs for which the goods are responsible. In a sense, these may be regarded as partial public goods.

In somewhat different terms, externalities arise from interactions between the production functions of firms or utility functions of individuals that are not reflected in prices charged for the goods. If the output of one firm is purchased as an input by another firm and there are no externalities, the pricing system ensures an efficient allocation of resources.[1] With externalities, the need for governmental action arises because there is no market mechanism to ensure that the benefited party compensates the person or firm that is providing the benefits or to ensure that the damaged party receives compensation from the person or firm that creates the costs. Thus, private and social valua-

[1] This point will be expanded on pp. 59–60

tions diverge. Governmental action is needed to impose appropriate taxes or subsidies to equalize private and social valuations. But the government need not produce the goods, since the private market can allocate them efficiently once the government ensures that their prices reflect social marginal costs.

The nature of the divergence between social and private costs or benefits and the ways in which government can make them coincide is the subject of this chapter. The first section discusses consumption externalities while the second discusses production externalities. The closing section then analyzes some specific external diseconomies or spill-over effects, such as congestion and pollution, and discusses policies that the government could pursue to improve the allocation of resources in these areas.

Consumption Externalities

A consumption externality occurs whenever the welfare of one individual is affected by the consumption patterns of another individual.[2] Commodities such as apples or oranges do not create externalities since one's satisfaction is presumably independent of their consumption by others. However, activities such as house painting or lawn mowing do create positive externalities since one's well-being is increased by having a neighbor's property well-maintained. Similarly, entering a congested highway creates negative externalities since one slows down all other travelers and imposes additional costs upon them. In either case, private valuations fail to reflect the true social value of the activity. In the first case, the private valuation is less than the total social benefits received from the activity and there will be a tendency for too little of the activity to be undertaken; in the second case, the private costs are less than the social costs and too much of the activity will be undertaken.

Direct Negotiation

The policy implications of consumption externalities depend upon their pervasiveness and magnitude. The externalities one receives from one's immediate environment are not amenable to government intervention, and satisfactory solutions can in principle be obtained by direct negotiation. If, for example, John Jones builds a fence that casts a shadow on Mary Smith's vegetable garden, thus preventing the vegetables from growing, he imposes a cost on Smith. But Jones would not have built the fence if he had not derived some satisfaction from it.

---

[2] For a good discussion of consumption externalities, see R. A. Musgrave, "Provision of Social Goods," in *Public Economics*, eds. J. Margolis and H. Guitton (New York: St. Martin's Press, 1969), pp. 124–44.

Whether the fence should remain, in terms of the overall welfare of the two individuals, depends on whether Jones's psychic satisfaction from the fence is greater or less than Smith's loss from the ruined vegetables that no longer have sufficient sun. If Jones's gain is greater than Smith's loss, the fence should remain; if not, it should be removed. Although these changes in welfare cannot be compared directly, they could in principle be measured by the compensation each person would be willing to pay and the amount the other would demand. If, for example, Smith would pay Jones $100 to remove the fence, while Jones would gladly settle for $50, the fence should come down. Conversely, however, if the fence actually cost $200, and Smith would only pay $100 for its removal, the psychic satisfaction derived by Jones from having the fence is presumably greater than Smith's psychic loss, and the fence should remain.

Of course, compensation is rarely paid in situations such as this, as the resolution of the problem is largely based upon personal relationships. Nevertheless, as long as a payment could be made that would leave one protagonist as well off while improving the welfare of the other, the optimal solution can in principle be found. Thus in bilateral cases such as this, governmental intervention is impractical and is not usually necessary.[3]

This example indicates the reciprocal nature of many externalities. The building of a fence by Jones would not have created an externality if Smith had not had a vegetable garden located in a place where the fence would block its access to the sun. Thus, the proper solution to externalities and the determination of which person should pay the compensation is a matter of relative strengths of preferences and bargaining powers and cannot be determined by any purely objective criteria.

The Need for Governmental Intervention

When externalities impose costs or benefits on a few people the government usually does not intervene. There are many situations, however, in which the benefits or costs are so diffused that they cannot be captured without governmental intervention. Many goods offer significant and diffused benefits to others for which the persons buying the goods cannot be compensated; or they create diffused costs to others for which the purchasers cannot be held responsible. In all other respects, however, these goods have the characteristics of private goods. These include divisibility and salability of the goods, direct and separate benefits to the purchasing individuals, and the possibility

---

[3] There are numerous court cases dealing with similar problems that are usually settled with little economic rationale. For a good evaluation of similar situations, see R. H. Coase, "The Problem of Social Costs," *Journal of Law and Economics*, vol. 2 (October 1960), pp. 1–44.

of excluding individuals other than those purchasing them from the primary benefits arising from the goods.

Because of these external benefits and costs, the market cannot achieve efficient resource allocation since each individual adjusts his or her purchases according to the direct benefits he or she receives, which diverge from the total benefits that accrue to society. When the welfare of an individual is positively affected by the consumption of various goods and services by others, too little of these goods and services is produced; governmental action through subsidies, with or without actual provision by government, is needed to make private and social valuations coincide. When the welfare of some persons is adversely affected by the consumption of goods and services by others, too much of these goods and services is produced; governmental action through taxes or other means is needed to make private and social valuations coincide.

To the extent that people's welfare is dependent on the maintenance of certain minimum health, housing, educational, or income standards for all, governmental intervention is needed in the market to increase the quantity of these goods produced. By mobilizing resources collectively through its powers of taxation, the government ensures that any given individual's contribution will be matched by the contribution of other individuals. Therefore people are willing to subsidize certain activities collectively when they would be unwilling to do so individually. Basically, if certain kinds of activities simultaneously enter into a sufficient number of individuals' utility functions, efficient allocation requires government intervention. Medicare, Medicaid, education, and public housing can best be understood in this light. And even the welfare program, discussed in Chapter 6, can be regarded as of this character.

Production Externalities

Conceived in a broad sense, a production externality occurs when one firm's output enters as an input into another firm's production function. Since most firms use materials that are produced by other firms to produce their own output, externalities in the broadest sense exist in virtually every industry. As long as the output used as another firm's input is priced at marginal cost, however, the pricing system is capable of allocating goods efficiently.[4] In this respect, the distinction between a *pecuniary externality* and a *technological externality* is useful.[5]

---

[4] For a discussion of what happens when prices differ from marginal costs, see Chapter 5 below.

[5] This distinction was initially made by J. Viner, "Cost Curves and Supply Curves," reprinted in *Readings in Price Theory* (Chicago: Richard D. Irwin, Inc., 1952), pp. 198–232.

Pecuniary Externalities

A pecuniary externality arises from the interdependence of the production relations that exist in any economy. In an increasing-cost industry which has an upward sloping industry supply curve,[6] firms using the output of that industry are subject to pecuniary external diseconomies. As firms acquire more units of inputs from the increasing-cost industry, the price of the input rises. For example, as the output of textiles increases, the unit costs of textiles will rise because the cost of cotton rises as inferior land is used in cotton production.

Pecuniary economies occur whenever the price of an input falls as the scale of output increases. This can generally only happen when the input is produced by a natural monopoly, that is, if the scale of the efficient firm in the input-producing industry is sufficiently large that its average costs fall over the relevant range of output. If the natural monopoly is regulated so that its prices reflect costs, firms that use its output are subject to external economies. For example, aluminum production may be subject to pecuniary external economies if the cost of the electricity it uses falls as the utilization of electricity rises.

In either case, if the commodity that is used as an input is priced at marginal cost and firms cannot exercise any monopolistic pricing power, the resulting allocation of resources is efficient. Changes in demand or supply will lead to changes in the equilibrium output of goods and services, but each equilibrium will be equally efficient, or Pareto-optimal. In terms of pure efficiency, government intervention is unnecessary.

Technological Externalities

Technological externalities require governmental intervention. These occur whenever the producer of a given activity cannot realize all the gains or is not forced to bear all the costs that accrue to other firms or members of society as a result of his or her actions. Therefore, external economies or external diseconomies arise. With external economies, the social cost of an increase in output by any one firm is less than the costs to the firm because of the effect in lowering the cost schedules of other firms other than through reducing the price paid for inputs. An example is provided by the interdependence in the pumping of water from adjacent mines; the more pumped by one mine, the less water the others must pump. Fire-protection measures taken by one timber company will benefit nearby property owners by lessening the risk of fire spreading to their land. Since the firm cannot charge for

---

[6] In a perfectly competitive industry, this could arise from increasing factor costs and the like.

the benefits of these externalities, the total amount of the activity will be less than optimal.

A simple example of apple and honey production can help clarify the issues involved with technological externalities. Since the bees receive the nectar from the apple blossoms that enables them to produce honey, the apple orchard provides a positive externality to the beekeeper.

Assume that the orchard owner and the honey producer are different individuals. According to their individual rules of private profit maximization, they each employ labor until its marginal revenue product is equal to the wage rate. For the honey producer, there is no divergence between the private and social marginal revenue products. For the apple producer, however, there is, for he or she only takes into account the direct impact of labor on apple production and ignores the indirect impact of the labor he hires on honey production. Thus, there will be insufficient labor allocated to apple production and there will be a less-than-optimal output of apples and honey. The private valuation of the marginal product of labor in apple production is less than the social valuation. For optimal apple production one of two things must occur. Either the apple producer must be subsidized, or the externality must be internalized in the sense that the production of the two activities is taken over by the same individual who can take these interactions into account.

Technological externalities of these types are often found with water resources. For example, building a large upstream dam creates recreational, power, and flood-control benefits that the builders of the dam cannot typically capture. The benefits accruing to private developers of the dam will be less than the true social benefits. If left to the private market, the dam typically would not be built. Through governmental intervention, however, the dam can become feasible. While the government could subsidize the private developers, it typically chooses to build the dam itself, thus internalizing the externalities since it can take all of the costs and benefits into account in making its decision as to whether the dam should be built or not.[7] Similar considerations apply to irrigation projects, which are also typically financed by government.

Urban renewal has many of the characteristics of a technological externality.[8] For example, if a developer were to renovate a building in a run-down area, the developer would find that the entire area would benefit from the improvement; land values would rise, the neighborhood would become a more pleasant place, and so on. But there

---

[7] The nature of these cost and benefit calculations will be discussed at length in Chapter 7. Note that insofar as flood control is concerned, a public-good quality enters the problem.

[8] See O. A. Davis and A. Whinston, "Externalities, Welfare, and the Theory of Games," *Journal of Political Economy* vol. 70 (June 1962), pp. 241–62.

would be no way that he or she could capture the benefits of increased land values and amenities. If, however, the developer were given control over a sufficiently large area, he or she could then internalize these externalities and capture sufficient benefits arising from the improvement to make the venture profitable.[9] For this reason, the federal government has typically borne a major cost of assembling sites for private developers in urban renewal projects and thus given them sufficient subsidies to make private and social valuations coincide.[10]

Education also offers technological externalities since increasing the educational level of society increases productivity. Additional education results in improved efficiency in management and in more rapid technological and organizational change and thus more rapid economic growth and higher per capita real incomes. Therefore, the social benefits arising from a particular person's education are usually greater than his or her private benefits.

Whenever goods provide significant positive external benefits, the private market will undervalue these goods and too few of them will be produced. Some form of governmental intervention is needed to increase output. In some cases, such as elementary and secondary education and many water-resource programs, this may be accomplished by governmental provision of the activity. When the government actually undertakes activities that create positive externalities, it may either make them available for free, as it does with education, or it may price them at rates that reflect social marginal costs, as it does with some water-resource programs. Alternatively, the government may leave production in private hands and subsidize the private producer to enable it to charge a price that reflects social marginal costs instead of the higher private marginal costs. This occurs in some areas with commuter railroads and in some housing programs.

Whether the government actually provides the service or subsidizes private production depends largely upon the nature of the externality. When it is highly diffused and not easily appropriable, as in the case of education, the activity takes on many of the qualities of a public good, and governmental provision becomes necessary. If, however, the ex-

---

[9] An example of an attempt to do this is provided by the street railway companies around the turn of the century, when they simultaneously developed new subdivisions and built new car lines to serve them.

[10] J. Rothenberg in *Economic Evaluation of Urban Renewal* (Washington, D.C.: The Brookings Institution, 1967) has a good analysis of the nature of the costs and benefits of urban renewal. Recently, a large literature has developed concerning the essentially destructive nature of urban renewal projects, particularly with respect to the projects' impact on the poor. See, for example, A. Downs, "Uncompensated Non-Construction Costs of Urban Renewal," in *The Analysis of Public Output*, ed. J. Margolis (New York: Columbia University Press, 1970), pp. 69–113; Marc Fried, "Grieving for a Lost Home: The Psychological Costs of Relocation," in *Urban Renewal: The Record and the Controversy*, ed. James Q. Wilson (Cambridge, Mass.: M.I.T. Press, 1966), pp. 359–79; Martin Anderson, *The Federal Bulldozer* (Cambridge, Mass.: M.I.T. Press, 1964).

ternal benefits are easily recognized and appropriable, the market can allocate these goods efficiently if their price reflects marginal social cost. In this case the role of government is to ensure that the efficient prices are charged and to let the market provide the activity.

Negative Externalities and Spill-over Effects

In a period of ecological concern, the question of technological diseconomies or spill-over effects becomes important. The chemical plant that pollutes the water, making it unsuitable for recreation or consumption; the oil spills that ruin beaches and kill countless numbers of fish and wildlife; the pesticides that increase agricultural production while killing fish, wildlife, and occasionally people; the airports that generate excessive noise; the automobiles that congest the highways and impose costs on all other travelers and generate smog are all subjects that have received prominent attention in the news in recent years. We are constantly bombarded by noises, odors, delays, and other unpleasant phenomena over which we have no control. In each case, the producer (or offender) is concerned solely with his private costs. In each case, however, the social costs of the activity are considerably higher than the private costs. If the producers of the smoke emissions or the oil spills or the industrial waste were made to bear the social costs, less of the activity would be produced and, in some cases, it might cease altogether.[11]

How to deal with these spill-over effects is a difficult problem that has increasingly concerned economists, although the general principle that should be followed is relatively straightforward. The optimal level of pollution, congestion, and other spill-over effects is reached when the costs of further reductions equals the benefits accruing to society from further reductions. As a corollary, the means of reducing these spill-over effects must be achieved in the least costly way possible. The problem is complicated, however, by the reciprocal nature of externalities and by the difficulties associated with assuming the damages.

The Reciprocal Nature of the Problem[12]

It should be clear that it takes at least two to make an externality. To see the significance of this, let us consider the situation in which a

---

[11] For an excellent discussion of external diseconomies of this nature, see E. J. Mishan, *The Costs of Economic Growth* (London: Staples Press, 1967), and E. J. Mishan, "The Postwar Literature on Externalities: An Interpretive Essay," *Journal of Economic Literature*, vol. 9 (March 1971), pp. 1–28.

[12] For a good analysis of the reciprocal nature of the problem, see R. H. Coase, "The Problem of Social Cost," pp. 1–44. J. M. Buchanan and W. C. Stubblebine, "Externality," *Economica*, N.S. vol. 29 (November 1962), pp. 371–84.

physician moves his examining room next to a candy manufacturer.[13] The noise from the candy manufacturer's equipment makes it impossible for the physician to examine his patients. The physician consequently applies for an injunction to stop the candy manufacturer, claiming that the candy manufacturer prevents him from pursuing his practice of medicine. But an injunction would also make it impossible for the candy manufacturer to operate. Moreover, the candy manufacturer imposed no costs on society until the physician moved his office next door. This case is analogous to that of the fence we discussed in conjunction with consumption externalities. The efficient solution depends on who is damaged more. If the loss in income to the candy manufacturer is greater than the loss in income to the physician, the latter can be paid enough by the manufacturer to move. If the loss in income is greater to the physician, he can pay the manufacturer to move. As long as the gains to the remaining party are greater than the losses to the moving party, compensation can be paid leaving both parties at least as well off as before. With bilateral externality such as this, governmental intervention is not needed.

The problem is complicated, however, when the effects of the externality are diffused. Therefore the magnitude of the external effect of a given act may not only depend upon the decisions of the given actor, but also upon the actions of those who are affected. For example, the costs of smoke pollution may depend directly upon the number of people in the vicinity of a power plant. As the population near the power plant rises, the costs from its smoke pollution must rise. Since the number of people who move to the vicinity of the power plant is out of the control of the plant managers, a rule that makes the producers liable for the damage caused by the smoke emissions is neither unambiguous nor necessarily just. A power plant in a desert would impose no externalities while one in a densely populated city would. If, however, the power plant was there before the population now surrounding it, the causality of the externality is not completely unambiguous.[14]

In spite of these difficulties, the general principle to follow is clear. The spill-overs should be reduced until the marginal costs of further reduction equal the marginal benefits accruing to society from such a reduction. When few people lived near the power plant, the costs of pollution were relatively small and the costs of abating the pollution would have been greater than the benefits arising from abatement. As the population grew, the costs of pollution increased. At some point,

---

[13] See Coase, "The Problem of Social Cost," pp. 1–44.

[14] For a good exposition of this point and a summary of externalities, see W. J. Baumol, *Welfare Economics and the Theory of the State*, 2d ed. (Cambridge, Mass.: Harvard University Press, 1965), pp. 23–46.

the costs of abating the pollution became less than the benefits derived for such abatement. In the first case, no abatement is necessary, while in the second, it is.

Unfortunately, the benefits and costs arising from pollution abatement are likely to be large rather than marginal. The costs of reducing pollution to an acceptable level may be sufficient to cause the power plant to shut down its operations or to move, thus increasing costs of electricity throughout the area. Consequently, in assessing pollution, the total costs and benefits of pollution control must be taken into account as well as the marginal costs and benefits. Nevertheless, as long as the costs of pollution to society exceed the costs of removing the pollution to the firm, the level of pollution should be diminished.

Income Effects and Compensation

Because many changes are nonmarginal, they are apt to generate large income effects. The costs of reducing pollution of existing plants may be greater than the social benefits derived from such reductions, while the costs associated with new activities that create spill-over effects may be greater than the benefits derived from these activities. In the first case, the pollution will not be reduced, while in the second, the potential pollutant will not be introduced. Thus, the existence of large income effects may be such as to favor the status quo.[15]

In considering policy changes that affect persons welfare, there are two relevant magnitudes to consider. The first measures the maximum sum a person would be willing to pay to ensure that some beneficial change occurs. The second measures the minimum sum a person would require as compensation to acquiesce to a detrimental change. Economic theory indicates that for a wide range of goods or activities, the maximum sum a person would be willing to pay to experience a beneficial change is less than 'the minimum sum a person would require to undergo a detrimental change.[16] When the welfare changes are substantial, the maximum sum a person will pay for a beneficial

---

[15] This point was brought out forcefully by E. J. Mishan, "The Postwar Literature on Externalities," pp. 1–28. Mishan's point is essentially a restatement of Scitovsky's double criterion for a desirable change: namely, that a change is only desirable if (*a*) it would be possible to make some people better off without making everyone else worse off, and (*b*) it would be impossible by reversing the policy, to make everyone at least as well off. See T. Scitovsky, "A Note on Welfare Propositions in Economics," *Review of Economic Studies*, vol. 9 (November 1941), pp. 77–88. For a good summary of the connection between welfare theory and public finance, see J. G. Head, "The Welfare Foundations of Public Finance Theory," *Rivista di Diritto Finanziario e Scienza Della Finanze*, vol. 19 (May 1965), pp. 3–52.

[16] In technical terms, the first sum is called the compensating variation, while the second sum is called the equivalent variation. For a full discussion of these definitions see J. R. Hicks, *A Revision of Demand Theory* (Oxford: Oxford University Press, 1969), pp. 81 ff.

change must be limited by his or her available resources, while the minimum sum he or she would require as compensation for a detrimental change has no such constraint. For example, the sum a person is willing to pay for a lifesaving operation must necessarily be finite, but the sum he or she would require to forego the operation could well be infinite.[17]

There are several implications of this for ecological externalities. Consider a case where a pollutant exists. The removal of the pollutant will be beneficial to the recipient of the pollutant but detrimental to the polluter since it will increase his or her costs of engaging in the presently polluting activity. Insofar as the polluter requires more compensation to remain as well off than the recipients are willing to pay to get rid of the pollutant, no change will be made. Similar provisions apply to the introduction of a new polluting activity. The people who suffered no pollution may require a greater compensation for permitting the pollutants than the polluters will be willing to pay. Thus again, no change will be made.[18]

A few specific examples may help to make the implications of this analysis clear. Consider an airport that is already in existence, producing considerable noise, smoke pollution, and the like adversely affecting the nearby inhabitants, who would presumably be willing to make payments to remove the airport from their immediate environment. Removal of the airport, however, would impose considerable costs on other members of society: persons who use the airport but are sufficiently removed from it to avoid its negative externalities. Efforts to remove the airport or limit its flights would lessen the convenience of air travel and hence reduce the welfare of the people using the airport. Airplane travel is most certainly a normal good, and the beneficiaries from the airport are generally greater in number than those adversely affected by the airport. Consequently, the potential compensation those who are adversely affected by the airport would be willing to pay is almost certainly less than the compensation that would be required by the users of the airport if the airport were in fact removed.[19] Thus the airport remains and those who are fortunate enough to be able to leave the immediate environment of the airport do so.

Consider, alternatively, a proposed new airport. Here the situation

---

[17] For a full discussion of this point see Mishan, "The Postwar Literature on Externalities," pp. 18–19.

[18] In formal terms, those whose welfare is reduced must recieve an equivalent variation to reach their original level of welfare, while those whose welfare is increased will be willing to pay a compensating variation up to a level that would place them in their original indifference curve. If the good in question is a superior good, it is possible to show that the equivalent variation will generally be greater than the compensating variation. See Hicks, *A Revision of Demand Theory*, p. 81.

[19] Note that the actual payment of compensation is not required. These differential magnitudes are reflected in the political process to a large extent.

is reversed. Those who live near the proposed airport would be made worse off because of the increased noise and congestion, while others in society would be made better off because of reduced transport costs. Again, since the payments required by those whose welfare is reduced will generally be greater than the payments those who are better off will be willing to make, no action is taken. In this case, the airport is not built.

This analysis indicates that these considerations tend to favor the status quo. Once an airport is built, offshore oil wells are drilled, pesticides are approved for general use, and so forth, the potential compensation required by those who would be adversely affected by the removal of the sources of pollution are generally greater than the compensating payments society is willing to pay. Conversely, however, the same mechanism acts to limit further sources of pollution. To the extent that a new source of pollution lowers the welfare of the citizenry, the compensation they require is greater than the potential beneficiaries of the source of pollution are willing to pay. This partially explains why the SST was grounded, why it is almost impossible to find sites for new airports, why urban highways and large scale urban renewal schemes are facing increasing opposition.

Thus the picture is not entirely bleak. Some improvements can doubtless be made where people are willing to pay the charges required to equate private and social costs. As the citizenry becomes increasingly aware of the deterioration of the environment, the costs that they are willing to bear will doubtless increase. While the government has done relatively little to make private and social costs coincide, the increasing concern of the citizenry with ecological problems should encourage the government to move in this direction. In theory, the government can always make private costs coincide with social costs. In practice, whether this comes about is determined by the evaluation of the social costs. This is primarily a political problem, and, as we discussed in the previous chapter, there is some reason to believe that this also favors the status quo. Although environmental improvements may come about, for reasons discussed above and also in the previous chapter, they will probably be fairly slow in coming.

Corrective Actions

Given the difficulties associated with making corrective actions with regard to external diseconomies or spill-over effects, it is useful to discuss the range of alternatives open to the government: regulation, payments, or charges. In the first case the government imposes certain standards, sets zoning regulations, requires licenses, and so on. Activities of this type include the imposition of certain standards on auto emissions, the prohibition of certain pesticides, etc. Alternatively, the government may give firms a subsidy or payment not to engage in the offensive action; or, it may subsidize control devices, forgive local property taxes, permit accelerated depreciation, or give tax credits for investments in pollution-control devices. Finally, the government may impose charges, fees, or fines for the discharge of various pollutants. Similarly, it may prohibit the use of certain fuels that generate excessive pollutants or tax them more heavily.[20]

In a world in which the costs of pollution and the costs of abatement are known, it makes little difference which of these alternatives is used from the viewpoint of economic efficiency. Total social costs, which represent the sum of the pollution costs and the abatement costs, are minimized when the marginal costs of abatement equal the marginal costs of pollution, and it does not matter in terms of economic efficiency whether the solution is obtained by setting standards, imposing taxes, or providing subsidies.[21]

These considerations can be seen in Figure 4–1, which plots the

FIGURE 4–1
Marginal Costs and Benefits of Pollution Abatement

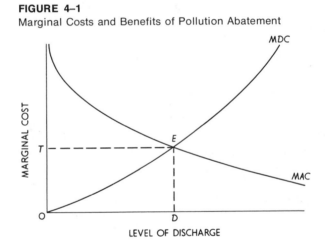

marginal cost of pollution abatement and the marginal cost of pollution against the level of discharge of the pollutant for a given level of output. The line marked *MAC* represents the marginal cost of pollution abatement and is drawn to portray the observed fact that pollution costs are relatively low for the removal of some discharge, but raise

---

[20] For a good discussion of these points, see E. S. Mills, "Economic Incentives in Air Pollution Control," in *Economics of Air Pollution*, ed. Harold Wolozin (New York: W. W. Norton, 1966), pp. 40–80.

[21] For a good discussion of governmental policy in the United States, see Allen V. Kneese and Charles L. Schultze, *Pollution, Prices, and Public Policy* (Washington, D.C.: The Brookings Institution, 1975).

rapidly as the pollutants are reduced toward zero. Depending on the industry and the specific pollutant, going from 90 to 95 percent removal may cost as much as the entire effort of going from zero to 90 percent, while going from 95 percent to 99 percent removal may cost as much as the entire effort of going from zero to 95 percent. The line marked *MDC* represents the marginal damage cost of the pollutants and indicates that costs rise slowly at relatively low levels of pollutants but then rise rapidly as the damage imposed by additional levels of pollution increases.

In Figure 4–1, the marginal abatement costs and marginal damage costs intersect at *E*, indicating that the level of discharge should be *OD*. This can be obtained by imposing standards requiring that no more than *OD* of the level of the pollutant can be permitted to be discharged, and is the approach used in the case of auto emissions. Alternatively, the government can impose a tax of *OT* per unit of discharge. For levels of discharge greater than *OD*, the marginal costs of abatement are less than the tax, and it pays firms and individuals to reduce pollution rather than pay the tax. For levels of discharge less than *OD*, however, the marginal abatement costs are greater than the tax, and firms and individuals would prefer to pay the tax than reduce the level of discharge. Thus given the tax of *OT*, they will voluntarily reach a level of discharge given by *OD*. Similarly, suppose the government granted a subsidy of *OT* for each unit of reduction in the discharge of the pollutant. For levels of discharge greater than *OD*, it would pay firms and individuals to reduce pollution, since the payments received would be greater than the costs of abatement. For levels of discharge less than *OD*, however, the subsidies received would be less than the abatement costs. Thus, again, firms and individuals would voluntarily produce a level of discharge given by *OD*.

Clearly, however, although the same level of pollution reduction may be reached by subsidies, taxes, or standards, the distributional implications of the policies are very different. In the case of subsidies, the general public pays the polluters to reduce pollution and the costs of pollution control are not reflected in the price of the commodity. Since, however, the polluters are imposing a real social cost upon society, it is desirable to have these costs reflected in prices and borne by the polluters. Thus subsidies appear to be an undesirable social policy. If the government sets standards, the polluters bear the costs of abatement directly, which presumably are reflected on commodity prices. Thus the users of these commodities should bear some of the costs of pollution abatement as well as the producers of the pollution.[22] This seems proper, since they are demanding goods that impose a

---

[22] For a full discussion of the condition under which these costs of pollution could be shifted forward to consumers, see Chapter 9, below.

social cost upon society and should presumably bear some of these costs.

Finally, if the government imposed taxes, the costs of pollution abatement would also be borne directly by the polluters, and indirectly by the users of the commodities produced by the polluters. In this case, however, the tax revenue could be used for general tax reduction or to compensate parties that are damaged by the remaining levels of pollution. In either case, welfare is increased over the case where standards are set. Thus, of the three forms of control, pollution taxes appear to be the preferable policy tool.

For maximum effectiveness, the taxes should be on the polluting activity rather than on some associated source. For example, the taxation of coal with a high sulphur content is less desirable than the taxation of the sulphur emissions directly, since it is the sulphur emissions that are undesirable rather than the use of the coal per se. Because, however, it is often administratively easier to tax certain types of fuel or certain polluting processes than to tax the pollutants directly, this form of pollution control is certainly an acceptable second-best solution to the problem.

The Level of Charges

It is important to stress, however, that this analysis has been based upon the simplified assumptions that the damage and abatement costs are known and independent of the level of output. In practice, however, the costs of pollution and abatement will typically vary with output, indicating that a single tax will not be sufficient. Instead, a schedule of taxes that varies with the level of output and the level of discharge must be imposed. While such a schedule may be theoretically feasible, in practice it is virtually impossible to implement.

Moreover, it is generally impossible to determine the actual functions representing the abatement costs and the damage costs. Thus, extremely difficult problems of measurement must be faced. While it is possible to measure increases in crop yields under various irrigation schemes, there is no scientific way to assess the costs of an oil spill that pollutes beaches, kills birds and fish, destroys shellfish beds, and so on. The costs are very real, but they are often subjective and nonquantifiable, except in an arbitrary way. The government usually copes with this problem by imposing certain standards and fining the offenders. But there are no real objective criteria on which to base the standards, and the fines imposed for failure to comply generally fail to reflect true social costs.

Nevertheless, certain kinds of externalities are amenable to the pricing system. The two most important relate to highway congestion and water or air pollution.

Highway Congestion. Once a highway has reached its point of maximum flow, the addition of one more vehicle will slow the flow and thus increase the travel time of all other vehicles. The marginal driver takes only his or her own private costs into account in deciding whether to use the highway or not and fails to consider the impact that his or her trip will have on all other drivers. Thus the true or social marginal cost is considerably greater than the private marginal cost of highway travel during peak periods.

These considerations can be seen in Figure 4–2 where the curve

FIGURE 4–2
Optimal Highway Use

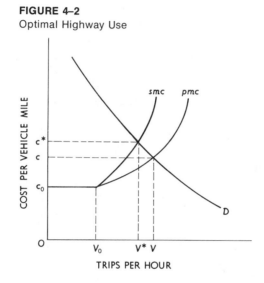

marked *D* reflects the travel demand for a given highway. The curve *pmc* represents the private marginal costs of using the highway to a typical driver and includes such items as gas, oil, and wear and tear. The curve *smc* represents the social marginal costs of using the highway and includes the costs that each driver imposes on all others. Note that *pmc* and *smc* coincide until V_0, which represents the number of cars per hour that could use the highway without congesting it. After V_0, private marginal costs rise because congestion typically increases gasoline and oil usage, wear and tear, time costs, etc. But social marginal costs increase at an even faster rate because the marginal driver increases gasoline, oil, time, and other costs to all other drivers. If drivers only consider their private marginal costs, *OV* trips will be made, while if they were made to pay a fee that would cover their social marginal costs, fewer trips would be made, measured by *OV**, and the highway would be less congested.

Several studies have been made on the social costs of highway congestion, and attempts have been made to measure these costs. For example, Walters has estimated that the tax needed to equate private and social marginal costs on congested highways would be at least 30 cents per gallon, which is approximately three times the actual taxes.[23] Imposition of user taxes of this order of magnitude would make enormous economic sense. They would ration the scarce highway resources and incidentally reduce air pollution considerably.

The problem is primarily one of enforcement. While several schemes have been devised to set up scanners or similar devices to impose charges during peak travel hours, none are very practical. Scanners are expensive and the means to make billing and collecting feasible are even more so. Stopping traffic to gather congestion fees would obviously be self-defeating. Thus, while much has been written about the need for congestion charges, virtually nothing has been done to implement them.

Nevertheless, the divergence between the private marginal costs of motor vehicles and the social marginal costs of motor vehicles during peak hours certainly contributes to the failure of mass transit to attract sufficient passengers to cover its fixed costs.[24] While it is unclear how much traffic would be diverted to mass transit if user charges were imposed to reflect social marginal costs, doubtless some diversion would occur. In this connection, the policy of most bridge or turnpike authorities with respect to commuter traffice is totally irrational. The use of commuter discounts makes no sense whatsoever and simply aggravates an already inefficient situation. One simple and effective step to reduce peak-hour highway congestion would be to charge higher fees for bridges and turnpikes during peak hours. However, efforts to institute these modest steps have met with little success.

Air and Water Pollution.   The problems posed by air and water pollution are similar. In both cases, the pollution is a by-product of the production process. Smoke containing noxious gases is emitted in producing electricity or transportation. Effluents are discharged in the production of many commodities: chemicals, paper, and so on. In the United States, the tendency has been to attack these forms of pollution by setting standards. The sulphur content of smoke is limited to so

---

[23] See A. A. Walters, "The Theory and Measurement of Private and Social Costs of Highway Congestion," *Econometrica*, vol. 29 (October 1961), p. 691. See also W. Vickrey, "Pricing of Urban and Suburban Transport," *American Economic Review, Proceedings*, vol. 53 (May 1963), pp. 452–65; and M. Beckmann, C. B. McGuire, and C. B. Winston, *Studies in the Economics of Transportation* (New Haven: Cowles Commission, 1955), pp. 80–86.

[24] There is considerable evidence, however, that the convenience and comfort differentials between automobiles and mass transit are such that massive subsidies would be needed to attract a significant number of passengers to mass transit. For a good discussion of this point see Leon Moses and Harold F. Williamson, Jr., "Value of Time, Choice of Mode, and the Subsidy Issue in Urban Transportation," *Journal of Political Economy*, vol. 71 (June 1963), pp. 247–64.

many particles per cubic yard; auto exhaust may have only so many hydrocarbons per cubic yard. Similarly, water pollution standards are set with regard to the kind of activities that the water can sustain: drinking, swimming, boating, and the like.

The problem with imposing standards is that they may fail to take the relative costs and benefits into account. For example, the Clean Air Act of 1970 established specific emission standards for automobiles that called for an effective 97 percent reduction in emissions by 1976 relative to uncontrolled conditions. While it is relatively easy to obtain a 90 percent reduction in emissions, it is increasingly difficult and expensive to obtain further reductions.[25] Thus there is some question whether the benefits from meeting the stringent automotive emission standards imposed by the Clean Air Act are worth their considerable cost. Similar problems exist with respect to water quality. The 1972 Water Pollution Control Act sets as goals that all discharge of pollutants into navigable waters be eliminated by 1985 and that by 1983, all waterways have a sufficiently high quality to support fish, shellfish, and swimming. As is true in the case of automotive emissions, however, the costs of reduction increases dramatically as one goes to zero discharge. For example, it has been estimated that removing 85 to 90 percent of all waterborne pollutants would cost $61 billion over the 1971–1981 decade. Increasing removal to the range of 95–99 percent of all discharge would increase costs by another $58 billion, and removing all discharge would increase costs by yet another $38 billion.[26] In view of the additional benefits derived from reducing discharges from 90 percent to, say, 100 percent, one can ask whether such high standards are worth the cost.

In addition to setting what appear to be excessively high standards, governmental policy with respect to pollution suffers from a number of other defects. First, because the standards are uniform, no account is taken of geographical differences. Automotive emissions in congested urban areas may have extremely different impacts from those in sparsely populated rural regions. Thus the standards do not seem to be sufficiently flexible to permit an efficient allocation of resources. Second, the federal government provides generous subsidies for the construction of waste-treatment plants by municipalities and industry. As indicated above, this policy is not desirable since it imposes the costs of treatment upon society at large rather than the specific polluters.

Present legislation attempts to deal with air and water pollution by imposing a wide range of direct regulations and subsidies. The problem with this approach is that it does not necessarily impose the costs

---

[25] See Henry D. Jacoby, John Steinbruner, et al., *Federal Policy on Automotive Emissions Control* (Harvard University, Environmental Systems Program, March 1973).

[26] See Kneese and Shultze, *Pollution, Prices, and Public Policy,* p. 78.

on the polluters and is excessively rigid.[27] The net result may be too much pollution reduction in some places, too little in others, and an inequitable distribution of the burden of the costs of pollution reduction.

As indicated above, taxes or charges are generally preferable to standards or subsidies because they create revenues, which can be used to compensate injured parties or for general tax relief. Moreover, once a system of pollution taxes is imposed, it may well be easier to adjust them to reflect changing costs, geographical differences, and so forth. Thus pollution taxes may well introduce more flexibility into the system than that provided by a central bureaucracy imposing uniform standards. By imposing effluent and emission fees and observing the response of the market, it should be possible to arrive at a socially acceptable set of effluent and emission charges that would bring private and social costs together where the marginal costs of abatement would equal its marginal benefits.

CONCLUSION

In conclusion, then, the existence of externalities can pose difficult problems for government. In the case of pecuniary external economies or diseconomies, the pricing structure reflects the benefits and costs of private production and no governmental intervention is needed. With technological externalities, however, private valuations diverge from social valuations and governmental action is needed for efficient resource allocation. Technological external economies occur whenever the production of an activity benefits someone who does not purchase the commodity. Examples include education, water-resource development, and urban renewal. In some cases, such as education, the government may actually provide the service, while in others, such as some urban renewal projects, it may subsidize private production. In either case, however, the goal of governmental action is to ensure that private and social valuations coincide and to increase the output of the activity that produces the external economy.

Technological external diseconomies occur whenever the producer of an activity does not have to bear all of the costs that the activity imposes on the purchaser or other members of society. The private costs fail to reflect social costs and too much of the activity that generates the technological externality is produced. Examples of technological external diseconomies include water and air pollution and transport congestion. In these cases, the goal of the government is to raise

---

[27] One of the obstacles to optimal policy in this area is the fact that the strong supporters of antipollution measures become zealots, insisting upon elimination of all pollution regardless of cost.

private costs of performing the damaging activity and thus to limit its output. This can be done by imposing direct taxes on the damaging activity or by imposing standards and letting the producer of the good in question choose the combination of controls and fines that it finds applicable.

REFERENCES

Bator, F. M.   "The Anatomy of Market Failure." *Quarterly Journal of Economics*, vol. 72 (August 1958), pp. 351–79.

Coase, R. H.   "The Problem of Social Costs." *Journal of Law and Economics*, vol. 3 (October 1960), pp. 1–44.

Freeman, A. M., Haveman, R. H., and Kneese, A. V.   *The Economics of Environmental Policy.* New York: Wiley, 1973.

Kneese, A. V., and Bower, B. T., eds.   *Environmental Quality Analysis: Theory and Method in Social Sciences.* Washington, D.C.: Resources for the Future, 1972.

Kneese, A. V., and Schultze, Charles L.   *Pollution, Prices and Public Policy.* Washington, D.C.: The Brookings Institution, 1975.

Mishan, E. J.   "The Postwar Literature on Externalities: An Interpretative Essay." *Journal of Economic Literature*, vol. 9 (March 1971), pp. 1–28.

Musgrave, R. A.   "The Provision of Social Goods," in *Public Economics*, eds. J. Margolis and H. Guitton. New York: St. Martin's Press, 1969, pp. 124–44.

5

Natural Monopolies, User Charges, and Imperfect Competition

In the last two chapters we have concentrated on two major sources of governmental intervention in the free market mechanism: public goods and externalities. The free market may also fail to allocate activities efficiently because the conditions of perfect competition are not met: A producer may have a sufficient share of the market that his output affects price (i.e., he is not a price taker). Therefore his profit-maximizing price will not equal marginal cost, and the conditions needed for efficiency and Pareto optimality are not met. This situation can come about from three major causes. First, the efficient size of the firm may be so large relative to the size of the market that it forms a natural monopoly. Second, the market may be characterized by oligopoly, in which a few sellers dominate the market. Third, there may be a large number of sellers, but each has sufficient market power that he faces a sloping, instead of a horizontal, demand curve. The policy implications of a natural monopoly differ from those of oligopoly or monopolistic competition, which pose rather similar policy problems. We therefore concentrate on the problems posed by natural monopolies and by noncompetitive pricing practices, whether they arise from oligopolies or imperfect competition.

When monopoly power is present, price generally exceeds marginal cost. Hence, one of the basic conditions for Pareto optimality is violated. Output is lower and price is higher than each would be in a perfectly competitive situation, which would lead to an efficient allocation of resources. Accordingly, when monopoly power exists, governmental intervention is desirable to increase efficiency in the utilization of resources. There are various forms this intervention can take. Government may seek to lessen monopoly power by antitrust laws that constrain the more obvious monopolistic practices; or it may regulate the prices of private firms. There are inherent limitations to these approaches, however, because of the continuing conflict between the government, which seeks to ensure that firms produce at socially desirable levels, and the monopolistic firms, which seek to produce at their profit-maximizing levels. In certain situations, the government may actually undertake the production of certain activities itself, just as it does with public goods or in the presence of certain externalities.

When the government supplies pure public goods, it cannot sell them to the users because there is no way to exclude anyone from the benefits of these goods if he or she does not contribute. Since the output of natural monopolies is divisible and has the characteristics of a private good, the government may sell it to the users if it wishes, rather than distributing it free of charge and financing production by taxation. Once the government has set the proper price, the free-market mechanism can allocate the output of a natural monopoly efficiently. The government's problem is complicated, however (as is its problem of the proper taxes or subsidies to apply in the case of externalities), by the existence of imperfect competition in the private market that makes prices diverge from marginal costs. Consequently, the problem facing the government is not only to find what price to charge in the case of natural monopolies, but, more generally, to determine what the proper relationship is between prices and marginal costs in government-controlled activities, given the imperfections in the free market. The problems posed by user charges, natural monopolies, and imperfect competition are the subject of this chapter.

The first part discusses the principle of user charges and outlines the general areas in which they are applicable. The next part analyzes specific cases in which user charges can and should be applied. The final part analyzes the problems posed by imperfect competition and discusses how the government's pricing policies should take market imperfections into account.

THE CASE FOR USER CHARGES

As we have pointed out, truly collective goods cannot be sold to the users. They cannot be packaged and distributed directly to individuals, and no one can feasibly be excluded from the benefits of the services. But many governmental services are not purely collective in nature. Services undertaken by governments because of externalities convey direct benefits to individuals, in the sense that the services are received separately by the individuals, and persons can be excluded from the benefits. Moreover, services provided by governments to avoid the undesirable consequences of monopoly, to ensure desired standards of quality, or to avoid collection costs necessary with private enterprise may yield no externalities, with all the benefits accruing to the persons who acquire units of the services.

Any governmental service yielding at least partial direct benefits can be financed by charges instead of general taxes or, if the use of charges per se is difficult, by a tax directly related to use. The key criterion for the possibility of use of a charge is excludability: the possibility that a person can be excluded, in a fashion tolerable to society, from benefits of the service if he does not wish to pay for it. Excludability necessitates direct provision of the service to individuals rather than in joint fashion to the community. Education, highways, parks, sewerage, among others, are activities for which charges can be imposed.

The Merits of Use of the Price System

The use of the price system offers significant advantages in terms of both resource allocation and equity.

Resource Allocation.   Financing by a charge instead of a tax allows the price system rather than the political process to determine the amount to produce. With user charges, output can be adjusted automatically to the amounts purchased at the established prices. Given the appropriate pricing policies, discussed below, an efficient allocation of resources can be attained. Accordingly, the complexities of political-process decision-making are avoided, with greater assurance that determination of output and resource use are in conformity with the preference of the community. The political process may result in serious resource misallocation because it may fail to interpret preferences correctly.

When the demand for a service is highly elastic the imposition of user charges prevents excessive utilization of the service. For example, pricing of electric power or water usage ensures that these services will not be used excessively or carelessly. When the demand for the service is inelastic, this consideration is less important since the failure to impose a sufficiently high charge will not lead to as much overutilization of the facility. Conversely though, the overpricing of services with a highly elastic demand will place a greater burden on society than the overpricing of services with an inelastic demand. Thus the social costs of improper pricing policies are greater in the case of services with an elastic, rather than an inelastic, demand.

In a short period of time, with demand in excess of a fixed quantity of a service available at a zero price (there are a given number of seats in a municipal auditorium for a concert), or over a longer period with unique resources (Yellowstone Park), the charging of a positive price rations available facilities among the users. Over a long-run period, with adjustable facilities, prices provide a key to decisions for expansion of investment.

Many governmental services are used for production purposes. Charging a price for these services, when the benefits are direct and exclusion is possible, facilitates the attainment of optimal factor combinations and optimal outputs of the commodities produced by firms using the services. If, for example, governments were to provide electric power free of charge to all users, production processes would use excessive amounts of electric power relative to other fuels, and output of commodities that are highly electricity-intensive in their production would be excessive. Failure to charge would result in prices that do not reflect all real costs for which production is responsible, and thus consumers would acquire relatively too much.

Constraints.   There are, however, constraints on the use of charges. The first is the cost of collection. With any service—just as with any sale by private-sector firms—some collection costs are incurred. Charges for electric service require meters, meter readers, billing, and action against persons who do not pay. Charges for rides on rapid transit lines require ticket sellers, turnstiles, and physical means to prevent access to trains without paying, while users are subject to the inconvenience of having to wait to make payment. Nevertheless, in both these examples, costs as a percentage of revenue are not high. But collection of tolls for use of city streets and rural roads, other than a few superhighways, would be extremely costly and a source of substantial nuisance to the users. If admission was charged to remote Forest Service camps and many state parks in off-season periods, the costs of collection would exceed the revenues.

With some services, high collection costs can be avoided by devising a tax that will operate as a charge; the user, instead of paying directly for the service, is taxed upon some action that is related to the gaining of benefits from the service. The gasoline tax, discussed later in the chapter, is the primary example. If collection costs are high and tax substitutes are not possible, the costs must be balanced against the gains from the use of charges to determine the desirability of imposing them.

The other restraint is the need to ensure that the charges do not cause loss of external benefits. If a charge is made on the basis of the ratio of direct benefits to externalities and the demand for the service is highly elastic, use will fall sharply and most benefits from the externalities will be lost.

Equity.   Use of charges also has merit on equity grounds. Except where special circumstances dictate otherwise, usual standards of equity dictate that persons pay for what they get. This is the rule of the private sector of the economy; and it can apply to governmental services conveying direct benefits to individuals. The question of the desirability of use of the rule involves a value judgment—but one that is widely accepted in a market economy and, in practice, in other economies as well.

Some services, however, are not regarded as suitable for sale on a pay-for-what-you-get basis because of distributional considerations and the desire of society that all persons receive the services as a matter of principle, even if not warranted by externalities—the so-called merit goods. This may be true, for example, of city parks or the direct-benefit portion of elementary education, as distinct from the externalities portion to be financed by taxation under all approaches. This equity question is the basic issue in the debate over tuition fees to state universities. Opponents of tuition argue that all qualified students are entitled to an education whether they can pay or not. The defenders of the use of tuition counterargue that abandonment of the price system is not necessary to meet distributional requirements. By establishing grants to cover tuition for those students with the necessary qualifications but lacking the funds to finance their education, the needs of persons in the lower-income groups can be met without loss of the advantages of the price system. This approach, however, requires means tests to determine eligibility for scholarships. The need to apply for assistance may be sufficient to discourage many qualified persons from seeking aid—whereas society wishes to encourage them to obtain the services.

In summary: Use of the pricing mechanism where possible instead of free distribution with financing by taxation is regarded as most justifiable when:

1. Benefits are primarily direct, so that charges will not cause significant loss of external benefits.
2. Demand has some elasticity, so that the use of prices aids resource allocation and eliminates excessive utilization.
3. Charges do not result in inequities to lower-income groups, on the basis of accepted standards.
4. Costs of collection of charges are relatively low, or alternate taxes measured by use can be employed.

Use of charges is more questionable when:

1. External benefits are significant and will be lost in part if charges are made.
2. Demand is perfectly inelastic, so that resource allocation is insensitive to the pricing system. Even so, charges may be regarded as warranted on equity grounds.
3. Equity standards require that the lower income groups be assured of obtaining the services.

4. Collection costs are relatively high and alternative tax measures related to usage cannot be devised.

Pricing Policy

If governments are to attain their objectives from the use of charges, several rules must be followed.

Charges to Cover Direct Benefits Only. Charges must cover only the direct private benefits as distinguished from the external social benefits; otherwise total output of the service will be too low in terms of optimal allocation of resources. If, for example, charges for education were set at levels to cover all costs, total output would be substantially less and society would lose the advantages of the externalities from the larger output. If rapid-transit facilities provide significant externalities in the form of reduced congestion and cost of urban expressways, rates set to cover all costs would sacrifice advantages of the externalities.

Implementation of this rule involves several problems. First is the determination of the externalities; how significant are these to the community? Some externalities can be calculated rather accurately, as, for example, the effect of rapid transit on reduction in cost of expressway construction and in congestion and accident rates on existing expressways. With other services, such as education, determination of externalities requires use of the political decision-making process to determine society's preferences for the external benefits: more rapid economic development, greater political stability, and broader cultural advantages of higher levels of education. Delineation of direct benefits to road users and benefits to property owners and others from roads has always been troublesome.

The other major question is the relationship between usage of the service and externalities. At one extreme, the externalities are produced by making the service available to the public, and the total external benefits do not vary with the amount of the service utilized. Society, for example, may regard the availability of a road to Alaska as of vital importance; the externalities relate only to the availability, not to the actual use. Accordingly, the users could, in terms of resource allocation, be charged tolls high enough to cover all costs (assuming that some toll level would do so), since reduction in usage would not lessen the total gain to society from externalities. At the other extreme, the externalities may be proportional to usage. The externality directly depends upon use of the service, with no decline in the marginal gains to society as more is used. Gains from education may be regarded as of this nature. Or externalities may be considered to decline, per unit of use, beyond a certain level of service. Once highway use is reduced to the point that congestion and pressure for new expressways have been eliminated, there may be no gain from diversion of additional traffic to public transport.

Whenever externalities depend upon usage of the service, to the extent that charges are imposed, some of the externality gains are lost. The problem, therefore, is to define the optimal level: The charge that, considering usage, behavior of externalities per unit of use, and economic effects of the taxes to finance the externality portion, is regarded by society as the optimum. While this decision can be made only on the basis of the political process, two economic relationships are significant for the decision: the behavior of the externalities as usage changes and elasticity of demand for the service. If the demand is highly inelastic, increases in charges will have little effect in reducing externality gains, while reduction in charges will accomplish little in increasing consumption and the magnitude of externality benefits.

Inclusion of All Costs. As pointed out in the previous chapter, in determining the sum of costs as a basis for establishing charges, all costs to society should be included, not merely those directly incurred by government in the production of the service. In establishing charges for highways (whether tolls or use-related taxes), indirect costs to society arising out of highway use must be included as well as costs of highway construction and maintenance. Spill-over costs include those caused other users by contributions of additional cars to congestion, those of air pollution, and the aesthetic effects of the noise and unsightliness of many urban expressways.

THE APPLICATION OF USER CHARGES

In the United States, user charges are applied most commonly in two situations: natural monopolies, such as public utilities, and highways. Each case poses certain analytical and policy problems.

Natural Monopolies

The problem posed by natural monopolies arises because the firm is subject to sufficient economies of scale relative to the market that its average costs fall over the entire range of potential usage. Only one facility is needed to provide the service in the given market, since sufficient duplication of the facility to ensure competitive behavior would result in excessively high costs. Figure 5–1 illustrates the problem. The demand curve D intersects the average cost curve (ac) on the declining portion of the latter. In this situation, efficiency dictates that one producer is sufficient.

If the situation were not regulated in some fashion, the firm would produce at Q_m, where marginal cost (mc) and marginal revenue (mr) intersect, and charge a price P_m. Its profits would be given by the area

FIGURE 5-1
Alternative Output Levels, Monopoly

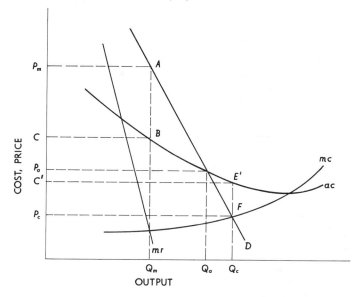

P_mABC. This solution is unacceptable, however. First, if resources are to be allocated efficiently, price must equal marginal cost in all sectors.[1] Thus, this solution violates one of the basic conditions of economic efficiency outlined in Chapter 2. Secondly, and probably more importantly, unregulated pure monopoly power is not considered to be ethically acceptable. Such a concentration of potential economic power in the hands of a given firm is thought to be excessive because the possibilities of exploitation on the part of the firm are too large.[2] Thus, on the grounds of both efficiency and equity, if a firm is a natural monopolist, it must be regulated or production taken over by the government. In either case, however, as long as the good is sold, a major question facing the government is the appropriate price to charge. The government has three choices: price at marginal cost, price at average cost, or price at a level that inversely relates the price to the elasticity of demand. The optimal solution depends upon the nature of the taxes available to government, but, in general, average-cost pricing is inferior to either of the other two pricing policies.

Average-Cost Pricing. If average-cost pricing is adopted the enterprise would charge a price equal to P_a and produce an output equal to

---

[1] Although, we shall soon see that price can rarely be made to equal marginal cost in the real world.

[2] For a discussion of this problem with respect to the railroad industry, see A. F. Friedlaender, *The Dilemma of Freight Transport Regulation* (Washington, D.C.: The Brookings Institution, 1969).

Q_a. It would earn no profits above those included in long-run average costs, but revenues would be sufficient to cover costs. Since the enterprise would break even and require no subsidies, this solution has a certain intuitive appeal. There is no monopoly exploitation of the consumer, and the enterprise is self-sufficient. But since price is not equal to marginal cost, marginal rates of substitution diverge from marginal rates of transformation, thus violating one of the basic conditions required for Pareto optimality and efficiency outlined in Chapter 2.

Marginal-Cost Pricing. If perfect competition and the marginal conditions required for efficiency exist elsewhere throughout the economy, economic efficiency requires that price should equal marginal cost in the natural monopoly. The enterprise should charge a price equal to P_c and produce an output equal to Q_c. But since marginal cost lies below average cost in this situation, the enterprise will suffer losses equal to $C'E'FP_c$. Thus, if it is to charge a price equal to marginal cost, it must be subsidized. In a world where lump-sum subsidies and transfers are possible that leave the marginal rates of substitution and transformation equal, the optimal solution is to charge a price equal to marginal cost and cover any losses from the revenues of general taxation. The marginal conditions needed for efficiency will be met throughout the economy and Pareto optimality will be achieved.

Nevertheless, some economists argue that average-cost pricing may be preferable to marginal-cost pricing since it provides an ex post facto check upon whether the facility should have been built or its capacity expanded.[3] Since marginal-cost pricing will lead to losses, it fails to provide an ex post facto evaluation of the investment. Although we discuss fully the problem of the proper investment criteria in Chapter 7, some aspects of it are relevant for the problem at hand.

To pose the problem in its clearest form, let us consider a pure natural monopoly that does not generate any externalities and whose output is divisible and therefore can be priced. The problem is to determine whether the investment decision should be based on a profitability criterion that states that the investment should be made if it yields sufficient revenues over costs or on some other criterion. With private goods, the problem is solved by the profitability criterion. Investments will only be undertaken if they yield at least some minimum return included in long-run average cost. The corollary for a pure natural monopoly is that it should also be able to yield a certain minimum profitability. Alternatively stated, to ensure that inefficient investments are not made, the government should only undertake investments that yield sufficient revenues to cover costs when the output is priced at long-run average cost.

Apart from the objections to average-cost pricing that we have al-

---

[3] See, for example, I. M. D. Little, *A Critique of Welfare Economics* (Oxford: Oxford University Press, paperback ed., 1960), pp. 182–83.

ready noted, this approach would prevent some desirable investments from being made. In principle, the proper investment criterion can easily be stated: The investment should be made if the aggregate willingness to pay for the facility is greater than its costs. This willingness to pay can be measured by revenues plus consumers' surplus and is illustrated in Figure 5–2, where the line *DD* reflects a typical de-

FIGURE 5–2
Consumers' Surplus

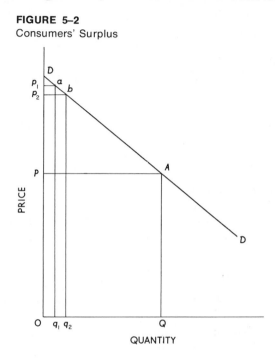

mand curve for a given good. At a price equal to Op_1 there would be some individuals who would be willing to consume a quantity Oq_1, while at a price Op_2 there would be individuals who would be willing to consume a quantity Oq_2. Note that this second group includes individuals who would have been willing to pay Op_1 and consume Oq_1; the incremental quantity consumed, equal to q_1q_2, is purchased by those persons brought into the market by the fall in price from p_1 to p_2. Those individuals who would have consumed Oq_1 at a price Op_1 are consequently receiving an extra benefit since they can consume Oq_1 at the market price Op_2. These individuals can be said to receive a consumers' surplus equal to the area p_1p_2ba. More generally, if the market price is given by OP, the total consumers' surplus is given by the area DPA and is equal to the difference between the area under the demand curve and the total revenues paid, which are given by the area $OPAQ$. The area under the demand curve reflects the total amount persons are willing to pay for the good in question, while the revenues reflect their actual payments; accordingly, the difference between the two reflects the consumers' surplus they receive from being able to obtain the good for less than they would be willing to pay.[4]

If the government were a perfectly discriminating monopolist, it could extract from each individual the maximum amount he or she would be willing to pay for consuming the service. The revenues received by the government would exactly equal individuals' willingness to pay. If, with this revenue, the return on the investment at least equaled the required return, the investment should be made. Alternatively stated, the project should be built if the aggregate willingness to pay is greater than or equal to the costs. This criterion is considerably more generous than the profitability criterion, which states that revenue should at least equal costs. In the first case, the measured benefits include any revenues received plus the consumers' surplus, while in the second case, they include revenue alone.

So long as lump-sum taxes, which have no distorting effects, are available to finance any deficits arising from marginal-cost pricing, the willingness-to-pay criterion is preferable to the profitability criterion. First, the profitability criterion will prevent some desirable investments from being made; and, second, on those investments that are made, the price of output will differ from marginal cost and losses in efficiency will result. Thus in determining whether to make an investment in the situation of a natural monopoly, the willingness-to-pay criterion should be employed.

Nevertheless, the willingness-to-pay criterion poses certain operational problems since the government cannot act as a discriminating monopolist. Suppose the government is trying to determine whether to build a hydroelectric plant. Unless it can correctly estimate the aggregate willingness to pay, it has no way of determining the optimal scale of the investment or whether the plant should be built at all.[5] Thus marginal-cost pricing and the subsidization of the facility gives no ex post facto way of determining whether the investment was in fact justified.

One solution to this is the so-called two-part tariff, in which the consumer pays a fixed charge for the privilege of using the facility and then pays a charge equal to the marginal cost of each unit consumed.[6]

---

[4] Strictly speaking, the area under the observed demand curve is only an unambiguous measure of consumers' surplus if the marginal utility of income is constant. If the good in question is a normal good, it will tend to overestimate the consumers' surplus for price reductions and underestimate the consumers' surplus for price rises.

[5] Some of the techniques that can be used to estimate willingness to pay will be discussed in Chapter 7.

[6] See Little, *A Critique of Welfare Economics*, p. 199; W. A. Lewis, "Fixed Costs," *Economica*, New Series, vol. 13 (November 1946), pp. 231–58; R. H. Coase, "The Marginal Cost Controversy," *Economica*, New Series, vol. 13 (August 1946), pp. 173–75.

But the optimality of this method depends upon the extent to which the fixed charge approaches the consumers' surplus. Since the charge must be identical to all users, some people will enjoy a consumers' surplus over and above the fixed charge while others will be excluded from using the facility who would use it if price only equaled marginal cost. Unless the fixed charge can be made equal to the consumers' surplus of each user, a two-part tariff is little better—though somewhat better—than average-cost pricing. Both provide an ex post facto check on the desirability of the investment and both ensure that only those who benefit from the facility pay for its use. But both exclude individuals who would use the facility if its service were priced at marginal cost and both might yield insufficient revenues to finance the project when total benefits are in fact greater than total costs.

Optimal Pricing and Distorting Taxes. If a deficit resulting from marginal-cost pricing can be financed by taxes that create no distortions in product or factor markets, the output of a natural monopoly should be priced at marginal cost and its losses should be made up from general revenues. But most taxes and transfers affect decisions at the margin and thus themselves violate the marginal conditions outlined in Chapter 2.[7] In general, any acceptable tax or subsidy affects relative prices and causes marginal rates of substitution to diverge from marginal rates of transformation. Thus, once market imperfections occur that make price diverge from marginal cost, it is unlikely that society can ever reach the efficiency frontier. The role of government is to structure the tax system in such a way that society maximizes its collective welfare as expressed through the political process, given the technological constraints facing it.

Thus policy-makers are faced with a dilemma. Either they must impose general taxes that distort economic activity in some way and subsidize the natural monopoly, letting it charge a price equal to marginal cost, or else they must let it charge a price different from marginal cost and let it cover long-run costs. In either case, the conditions required for efficiency and Pareto optimality are destroyed. At some point, wedges are driven between marginal rates of substitution and marginal rates of transformation. The question facing the policy makers is what solution maximizes welfare, given the constraint that the marginal conditions cannot universally be met.

If the government cannot impose nondistorting taxes to cover the losses from marginal-cost pricing, the optimum pricing policy of a

---

[7] Under certain conditions, other taxes can satisfy the condition of leaving decisions at the margin unaffected. For example, when the supply of labor is fixed, a proportional income tax is equivalent to a lump-sum tax and is thus neutral in the sense that it leaves relative prices unchanged. However, this assumption is as unrealistic as the assumption that lump-sum taxes and subsidies are possible. For a discussion of neutral taxation, see Chapter 9 below. Although head taxes are neutral, they are generally unacceptable on the grounds of equity.

public enterprise will generally be neither marginal-cost nor average-cost pricing; instead, the enterprise should cover long-run costs by charging a price that exceeds marginal costs by an amount inversely related to the elasticity of demand. If the demand for the good produced by the public enterprise is highly inelastic, little decline in output results from pricing above marginal cost, and there will be therefore little loss in consumers' surplus and relatively little reallocation of resources away from their efficient or Pareto-optimal configuration. If the demand is very elastic, small price differentials in excess of marginal cost can lead to large reductions in output and hence large losses in consumers' surplus and large misallocations of resources. Hence, the higher the elasticity of demand for the good, the smaller should be the departure of price from marginal cost.[8]

The Peak-Load Problem.   The pricing problem is further complicated by the peak-load problem, that is, the variations of demand and marginal costs over time. This problem creates difficulties in determining the optimal prices and the optimal scale of the facility. During off-peak hours, the cost of carrying an additional passenger on a subway or commuter train is virtually zero since the trains are scheduled to run and the work force has been hired. Similarly, as long as a highway is uncongested, the marginal cost of an additional automobile using the highway is essentially zero. Alternatively, as long as electric generators are running with excess capacity, the cost of an additional kilowatt hour is very low. More generally, if facilities have large fixed costs, as long as excess capacity prevails, the marginal cost of additional use is virtually nil.

When demand increases, however, optimal utilization of capacity may be exceeded. Additional buses or trains must be brought into use to carry the commuter passengers. Highway congestion increases the wear and tear on automobiles and increases travel time substantially. Additional electric generators must be brought into use. But, in addition to increasing the direct marginal costs of the facility, peak demands can make social marginal costs diverge from private marginal costs. Directly and immediately, an additional peak-load passenger causes inconvenience to other passengers by adding to overcrowding of cars and causing delays. The additional auto on the congested highway slows down all other autos and increases their wear and tear. Excessive demands on generators may cause the system to fail, creating blackouts, such as the one of November 1965 that plunged most of the East Coast into darkness for several hours.

---

[8] See in particular, W. Baumol and D. Bradford, "Optimal Departures from Marginal Cost Pricing," *American Economic Review*, vol. 60 (June 1970), pp. 265–83; and P. Diamond and J. Mirrlees, "Optimal and Public Production:1," *American Economic Review*, vol. 61 (March 1971), pp. 8–27. The reason why the price-marginal cost differential should be related to the elasticity of demand is straightforward and is detailed in the Additional Note at the end of the chapter.

Subject to the qualifications noted above, economic theory dictates that efficient utilization of resources requires that prices equal social marginal costs. Thus rates should vary over time to reflect changing marginal costs. This implies that transit fares should be high during peak commuter hours and that urban expressways should be subject to special charges during periods of peak congestion. These charges should not only reflect the higher private marginal costs but also the higher social marginal costs. Such pricing policies would be highly desirable. They would tend to even out the demand for the facilities by eliminating the casual users during peak hours and, hence, equalize costs over time. The revenues generated during the peak hours could be used to cover the losses in the nonpeak hours and, if total revenues exceeded total costs, the excess could be used to finance additions to capacity until the facility was in long-run equilibrium where revenues equaled long-run marginal costs.

Nevertheless, the introduction of peak-load pricing causes problems.[9] As we pointed out in the previous chapter, the implementation of congestion fees on urban expressways poses formidable practical obstacles. To date, it has been impossible to devise a collection scheme that is sufficiently inexpensive to be practical. While fares could easily be altered during peak hours on mass-transit facilities, the imposition of peak-load pricing on transit facilities without concomitant peak-load pricing on highway facilities would lead to an excessive utilization of already congested highway facilities. Thus, it would reduce rather than improve overall resource allocation.

Moreover, peak-load pricing may create problems of equity, particularly with regard to transit. Many rush-hour transit users are lower-income workers while many nonrush-hour users are higher-income shoppers. Thus, the imposition of peak-load transit fares might well lead to undesirable distributional results. The problem is less pronounced with highways, since many highway commuters are relatively affluent suburbanites. Thus in terms of equity, improved resource allocation might dictate congestion fees on highways and reduced fees on mass transit. To the extent that the demand for urban highways and mass transit is relatively inelastic, relatively little misallocation of resources should result from this policy.

In sum, economic theory dictates the use of higher charges for peak-load usage. While these may pose some problems with regard to equity and pose even greater problems with respect to implementation, the benefits in terms of improved resource allocation warrant their use.

---

[9] The telephone system employs peak-load pricing by lowering rates after 5 p.m. when demand is presumably lower. For an interesting proposed application of peak-load pricing to subways, see: W. S. Vickrey, *The Revision of the Rapid Transit Fare Structure of the City of New York*, Mayor's Committee on Management Survey of New York (New York: 1952).

Problems of Highway Finance

The provision and pricing of highway services provide an interesting example of the way in which government reacts to problems caused by indivisibilities and externalities. Highways are provided by the government for several reasons. First, and most obviously, except in periods of congestion (which we have discussed previously), the social marginal cost of using a highway is close to zero. My use of the highway generally does not interfere with your use. Thus once built, highways present elements of both natural monopolies and public goods until they become congested. The short-run marginal cost of using the highway is effectively zero, and there is virtually no rivalry in consumption. Second, to the extent that the marginal cost of using the highway differs from zero because of the wear and tear caused by automobiles and trucks, collection costs would be prohibitive except on a few major routes. Thus there is no effective way to exclude people from using most highways without intolerable costs. Third, in some instances, highways present elements of technological externalities. By providing cheaper transport they permit certain areas to develop that might otherwise have remained stagnant. This is particularly true with respect to less-developed countries, but also applies to a certain extent to the United States—Appalachia, for example.

Of all government programs, highway expenditures may achieve the most widespread support. The total expenditures on highways in the United States are over $20 billion a year, of which the federal government pays approximately one third. In spite of some recent studies that discuss the social costs of the automobile,[10] the highway lobby is capable of generating considerable support for these expenditures. The ubiquity of the automobile no doubt explains this widespread support. Good highways are appreciated by virtually all members of society.

Nevertheless, there appears to be considerable evidence that there is an inherent bias toward overinvestment in highways. The Federal Highway Administration (FHA) typically sets standards for highways to enable a certain number of cars to utilize the highway per hour at a given cost: usually the sum of the costs of gas, oil, wear and tear, and the like. When the actual costs rise above this level and the highway becomes congested, according to the FHA, this presents prima facie evidence that the highway capacity should be expanded.

This problem can be seen in Figure 5–3.[11] The line *DD* represents the demand for the highway per hour as a function of cost per vehicle

---

[10] See, for example, Donald Appleyard, Kevin Lynch, and John Meyer, *The View from the Road* (Cambridge, Mass.: M.I.T. Press, 1964).

[11] For a more rigorous discussion, see M. Bruce Johnson, "On the Economics of Road Congestion," *Econometrica*, vol. 32 (January–April 1964), pp. 137–50.

FIGURE 5–3
Demand for Highways

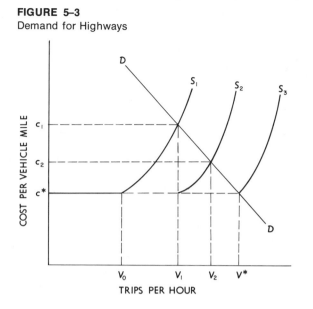

mile. The curve S_1 represents the existing supply or capacity curve, and measures marginal costs per vehicle mile. At V_0 these costs begin to rise, showing that as the number of vehicle miles per hour increases above this point, costs begin to rise. Since these curves represent private costs, the equilibrium use will occur at V_1 and users will bear a cost equal to c_1. When faced with this situation, the FHA then typically attempts to expand capacity to S_2, where costs will equal c^* at utilization levels V_1. This procedure does not take the interrelationships of supply and demand into consideration, and the new equilibrium will be at V_2 with a cost of c_2 which is still above c^*. Only if the highway capacity is expanded to S_3 will costs be at c^* in equilibrium—the goal of the FHA.

This approach to highway investment makes little economic sense. Setting a target cost for highway use and then expanding supply until the highways can be provided at this cost is a little like dictating that all cars should sell for a certain amount and having the government then ensure by subsidy that the supply of automobiles is such that there will be no excess demand for automobiles at this price. This approach obviously disregards the market forces of supply and demand.

A policy that does make economic sense is to charge users a price equal to social marginal cost, which will be greater than private marginal cost whenever congestion occurs. The revenues from these congestion user charges could then be used to finance new highway construction.[12] When the supply increases sufficiently to make highway revenues equal the long-run average costs of highway services, the system would be in equilibrium.

Unlike most government programs, highways are financed almost exclusively by user charges. All federal highway expenditures are made from the highway trust fund, which is financed by federal motor fuel, oil, tire, and truck taxes. In general, the use of these taxes leads to a pricing structure in which different vehicles are charged the long-run marginal costs they create for the highways, but not any additional charges for temporarily high short-run marginal costs or congestion costs.

The system of charges for long-run marginal costs appears to be relatively rational. All vehicles are made to bear a proportionate share of the costs of the basic roadway. Since heavier vehicles impose more wear and tear on the highways, trucks pay increasingly larger taxes as their size and weight rise. While the gradations are not perfect, these charges seem to approximate long-run marginal cost fairly well.[13] There is, however, evidence that the heavier diesel-using trucks are undercharged in terms of the costs they impose on the highways. If diesel fuel were charged a higher rate per gallon than gasoline because of its greater ton-mileage per gallon, as in Canada, the relative burden of the largest trucks would more nearly reflect long-run marginal costs.

As we have pointed out, once congestion occurs, the rational pricing of highway facilities breaks down completely. Social costs rapidly diverge from private costs, but no feasible means of imposing congestion charges has been developed. Moreover, the problems associated with spill-over effects discussed in the previous chapter may also apply here. The payments people are willing to make may be less than those needed to relieve the congestion. The automobile has such a sufficient advantage over other modes of transport in terms of comfort and convenience that the payments required to divert sufficient traffic to other means of transport may be prohibitive.[14] Moreover, as we have pointed out, the problem is further complicated by distributional considerations. If efficient user charges were imposed, the rich would probably be willing to pay them, while the poor (or less rich) would find that they could not. Without massive subsidies for mass transit, the poor might find themselves with no means of transport at all.

---

[12] For a full discussion of this point, see H. Mohring, "Urban Highway Investments," in *Measuring the Benefits of Government Investment Programs* ed. R. Dorfman (Washington, D.C.: The Brookings Institution, 1965), pp. 231–88.

[13] For a full discussion, see Friedlaender, *The Dilemma of Freight Transport Regulation,* and J. Meyer *et al., The Economics of Competition in the Transportation Industries* (Cambridge, Mass.: Harvard University Press, 1959).

[14] For a discussion of this point, see Leon Moses and Harold F. Williamson, "Value of Time, Choice of Mode, and the Subsidy Issue in Urban Transportation," *Journal of Political Economy,* vol. 71 (1963), pp. 257–64.

In conclusion then, government policy with respect to highways appears to have certain rational elements in that it attempts to equate user charges with long-run marginal cost. But because it neglects the difference between long-run costs and short-run costs and neglects the difference between social costs and private costs, it tends to price peak-period highway services at rates below their efficient levels and to provide more highways than economic efficiency alone would dictate. A rationalization of government policy would lead to fewer highways and higher user charges.

THE QUESTION OF IMPERFECT COMPETITION

Finally, markets may fail not because of natural monopolies per se, but because the efficient size of the firms is such that the relevant market can only support a limited number of producers. This is the typical situation in the United States economy, where most major industries are dominated by a relatively small number of major producers.[15] With imperfect competition, firms set prices above marginal costs and the marginal conditions needed for Pareto optimality are not met. In this situation, what pricing policies should the government try to implement with its own enterprises to achieve an efficient allocation of resources?

Once price differs from marginal cost in most industries, optimal resource allocation will not result by setting price equal to marginal cost in any one industry. This policy may actually decrease welfare rather than increase it. This is the famous theory of the "second best,"[16] which states that if price diverges from marginal cost in even one industry (and the divergence cannot be eliminated), price should also diverge from marginal cost in other sectors or industries. Thus government action to achieve the marginal conditions in any given industry may actually move society away from the efficiency frontier and reduce welfare. This is particularly true if individuals' utilities and firms' output are not separable, i.e., if the utility derived from driving automobiles is affected by the utility derived from watching television or if the output of automobiles is affected by the output of television sets.

If utility functions or production functions of broad bands of commodities are separable in the sense that output or consumption of one commodity does not affect the output or utility derived from the consumption of other commodities, the problem of the second best be-

---

[15] See Joe Bain, *Industrial Organization* (2d ed.; New York: John Wiley and Sons, 1968); C. Kaysen and Donald F. Turner, *Anti-Trust Policy: An Economic and Legal Analysis* (Cambridge, Mass.: Harvard University Press, 1959); A. E. Kahn, *The Economics of Regulation*, vols. 1 and 2 (New York: John Wiley and Sons, 1971).

[16] See R. G. Lipsey and K. Lancaster, "The General Theory of the Second Best," *Review of Economic Studies*, vol. 24 (December 1956), pp. 11–32.

comes more manageable.[17] The government can try to set prices equal to marginal cost within broad bands of separable commodities and thus improve the allocation of resources.

Moreover, if price differs from marginal cost by a certain amount in some industries and the difference cannot be eliminated, the government should attempt to make prices diverge from marginal cost by the same relative amount in similar industries. For example, if oil prices are substantially above marginal costs because of monopolistic pricing practices in the oil industry, setting electricity rates at marginal cost would lead to an excessive utilization of electricity for heating purposes. Difficulties arise when the price-marginal cost ratios vary radically from sector to sector. If these sectors are independent in consumption and production, efficiency is improved if all industries within a given sector have prices that bear the same relationship to marginal costs. But, as is usually the case, if sectors are interdependent in consumption and production and if the price-marginal cost ratios vary widely between sectors, the proper pricing rules to follow are not at all obvious.

Thus the policy-maker must remain largely agnostic. Often he or she simply does not have the information required to determine the proper pricing policy (or taxes or user charges) required to achieve efficiency. Moreover, even if the necessary information is available, it may be impossible to enforce these rules because society collectively feels that the benefits derived from the charges are not worth the costs imposed. Therefore, society may prefer an inefficient point of production to an efficient point, because efficiency per se may have undesirable distributional implications.

CONCLUSION

What then can we say about the proper pricing policies for the government to pursue with respect to natural monopolies or other governmental services sold to the users? If taxes and subsidies that do not affect economic decisions at the margin are available, the government should charge a price equal to marginal cost and make up any losses out of general revenues. If marginal rates of substitution and marginal rates of transformation are otherwise equalized throughout the economy, this policy will ensure that they are also equalized with respect to the governmental sector. Hence Pareto optimality can be achieved. Although marginal-cost pricing fails to provide an ex post facto check on the desirability of undertaking the investment, average-cost pricing to cover the cost of the facility is less desirable

---

[17] Ibid.; see also O. A. Davis and A. B. Whinston, "Welfare Economics and the Theory of the Second Best," *Review of Economic Studies*, vol. 32 (January 1965), pp. 1–14.

than marginal-cost pricing since it drives a wedge between producer and consumer prices, distorting resource allocation.

If, however, nondistorting taxes and subsidies are not available, taxes used to finance the natural monopoly will themselves cause a loss of economic efficiency. Nevertheless, average-cost pricing is still not desirable. A preferable policy is to set prices so that they are inversely related to marginal cost by the elasticity of demand. This policy, coupled with the constraint that the facility should generate sufficient revenues to cover long-run average cost, will lead to a better utilization of resources than average-cost pricing.

Finally, if imperfectly competitive pricing elements exist in major sectors of the private market so that prices diverge from marginal costs in these sectors, prices should probably exceed marginal costs in the government sectors. The optimal pricing policies in this situation depend upon the nature of the interactions between production functions of different commodities and the interactions of different commodities in people's utility functions. If broad bands of commodities are separable, resource allocation will be improved by trying to achieve the marginal conditions needed for Pareto optimality within that sector. If, however, such separability does not exist, the policy-maker has little to guide him or her in determining the proper pricing policies to pursue with respect to government-controlled or -regulated enterprises.

ADDITIONAL NOTE

The reason why the price-marginal cost differential should be related to the elasticity of demand is straightforward as illustrated in

FIGURE 5A–1

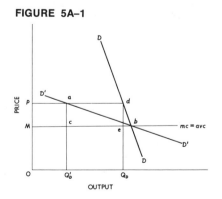

Figure 5A–1 where a constant marginal cost is assumed (i.e., $mc = avc$). DD represents an inelastic demand, while $D'D'$ represents an elastic demand. Let us assume that both firms charge a price equal to OP, which is in excess of marginal cost OM. The firm with the

demand curve $D'D'$ receives revenue equal to $aPOQ_D'$ while that with the demand curve DD receives revenues equal to the area $dPOQ_D$.

If price were set equal to marginal cost, consumers would receive an increase in consumers' surplus, while firms would experience a loss in revenue. Specifically, the firm facing the demand curve DD would experience a loss of $PdeM$, while its consumers would experience a gain of $PdbM$; the firm facing the demand curve $D'D'$ would experience a loss of $PacM$, while its consumers would experience a gain of $PabM$. If incomes are optimally distributed, any gain to consumers can be used to cancel out the losses to the producers. But the gain to consumers is greater than the loss to producers. The difference between the consumers' surplus and the producers' surplus reflects a deadweight loss to society from inefficient pricing at OP instead of at OM. For the firm with the elastic demand curve $D'D'$, this deadweight loss is given by the area acb, while for the firm with an inelastic demand curve this deadweight loss is given by the area dbe.

From this example, we can see that the more inelastic the demand curve, the smaller the deadweight loss resulting from pricing above marginal cost. In the limiting case where the firm faces a totally inelastic demand curve, the deadweight loss is zero. Thus, when demand is elastic, prices should be closer to marginal cost than when demand is inelastic.

REFERENCES

Baumol, W., and Bradford, D. "Optimal Departures from Marginal Cost Pricing," *American Economic Review*, vol. 60 (June 1970), pp. 265–83.

Brownlee, O. H. "User Price vs. Taxes," in *Public Finance: Needs, Sources, and Utilization.* New York: National Bureau of Economic Research, 1961, pp. 421–38.

Burch, Philip H. *Highway Revenue and Expenditures Policy.* New Brunswick: Rutgers University Press, 1962.

Friedlaender, A. F. *The Interstate Highway System.* Amsterdam: North Holland Publishing Co., 1965.

Hotelling, H. "The General Welfare in Relation to the Problems of Taxation and Railway and Utility Rates," *Econometrica*, vol. 6 (July 1938), pp. 242–69.

Lipsey, R. G., and Lancaster, K. "The General Theory of the Second Best," *Review of Economic Studies*, vol. 24 (December 1956), pp. 11–32.

Little, I. M. D. *A Critique of Welfare Economics.* Oxford: Oxford University Press, 1960.

Mohring, H., and Harwitz, M. *Highway Benefits.* Evanston: Northwestern University Press, 1962.

Mohring, H. *Transportation Economics.* Cambridge, Mass.: Ballinger, 1976.

6

Government and the
Income Distribution

In the absence of externalities and public goods, perfectly competitive markets will ensure that society reaches a Pareto-optimal equilibrium in which no change is possible that would increase the welfare of one individual without reducing that of another or increase the output of a commodity without reducing that of another. Nevertheless, it is highly unlikely that factor endowments, tastes, and technology will be such that the resulting income distribution is ethically acceptable to society. Hence, it is generally agreed that the government must take redistributive measures to ensure that society achieves an ethically acceptable income distribution.

If, however, the income distribution itself exhibits properties associated with public goods or externalities, the market mechanism may yield an inefficient solution, even if there are no other forms of market imperfections present. Consequently, the government may have to impose redistributive taxes or subsidies not only to ensure that society reaches its preferred point with respect to the income distribution, but also to ensure that society achieves efficiency in consumption and production.

While the formal analysis of the need for governmental intervention with regard to the income distribution is necessary if we are to understand all aspects of the role of government, it tells us relatively little about how the income distribution is actually determined in the United States, how it has behaved over time, and what policies the government has actually undertaken to change the income distribution from its market-determined structure. These questions are equally important for an understanding of the role of government with respect to the income distribution in the United States.

This chapter attempts to explore all of these issues. The first section shows why the government may have to undertake redistributive measures to achieve Pareto optimality as well as an ethically acceptable income distribution. The following section discusses the determination of the income distribution in the United States, both in terms of factor shares and income classes, and how it has behaved over time. The concluding section considers the actual redistributive measures undertaken by the government, showing how its tax and expenditure policies have altered the income distribution.

THE NEED FOR GOVERNMENTAL REDISTRIBUTION

As we have indicated, society organizes collectively through government for two purposes: to ensure that the market-determined allocation of goods and services is efficient and to enable society to reach an ethically acceptable income distribution. Externalities, public goods, and the like may prevent the market mechanism from being an effective allocative device, and even if the market allocation is efficient, it may not be ethically desirable. Both of these reasons for governmental intervention may arise with respect to the income distribution, creating a need for redistributive income taxes and transfers. We refer to the kind of redistribution that is needed to enable society to obtain production and consumption efficiency as Pareto-optimal redistribution, signifying that it is possible to make some redistribution that will make some members of society better off without making others worse off. We refer to the second kind of redistribution as ethical redistribution, signifying that this kind of redistribution can only take place by making some people better off at the expense of others. Society is presumably willing to make this kind of redistribution because in its social welfare function it gives more weight to the gainers than to the losers.

Pareto-Optimal Redistribution

While we do not usually think of the income distribution as a good or activity that can exhibit characteristics of public goods or create externalities, it can, in fact, exhibit these properties.

The Income Distribution as a Public Good. We have previously defined a public good to be a good that has the characteristics of total indivisibility and, hence, nonexcludability or nonrivalness in consumption. If the good is made available at all, it is made equally available to all individuals (even though they need not "consume" or share in its benefits equally). Clearly the income distribution has some of these characteristics. Each individual in a given society is subject to the environment of that society's income distribution, and no one individual can be excluded from its benefits (or costs). Thus, the income distribution meets the formal requirements of a public good: exclusion is impossible and consumption is nonrival.[1] Therefore, if the income distribution enters into individual utility functions, it must enter as a public good.

Insofar as the social welfare function is individualistic, the very existence of a social welfare function implies that the income distribution (or more precisely, the distribution of welfare among different groups) does, in fact, enter into individual utility functions. Since the social welfare function ultimately expresses the desires of the various interest groups of society with respect to the income distribution, it is difficult to see how social or collective welfare could depend upon the income distribution if individual welfare did not. It, therefore, seems reasonable to postulate that individuals' welfare is in some sense dependent upon the income distribution of society, as well as upon their own levels of consumption and income. This implies, however, that a redistribution of income through governmental intervention is needed to ensure that society reaches a Pareto-optimal equilibrium. In the absence of governmental intervention, no redistribution will take place because of the public good nature of the income distribution. Just as no person will voluntarily pay for national defense because a person knows that he or she can share in its benefits once it is provided, no one will voluntarily contribute to alter the income distribution. Because there is no incentive for people to reveal their true preferences or make voluntary income transfers, the political process must be used to make redistribution.

The Income Distribution as an Externality. Alternatively, the income distribution may be regarded as a source of externalities rather than as a public good. The utilities of different income groups may be interdependent in the sense that one's utility is not only dependent upon his or her own income level, but also upon the income level of different income groups. To be specific, the utility of the rich may depend to some extent upon the income of the poor, since, for example, a highly unequal income distribution gives rise to slums, a high incidence of crime, and political instability. In this situation, the rich will make some contributions to the poor, presumably through voluntary contributions and the like. But since a rich person's utility also depends upon his or her income, there is a limit to voluntary contributions.[2]

In this case, collective measures of redistribution through the gov-

---

[1] This section is based on an article by Lester Thurow, "The Income Distribution as a Pure Public Good," *Quarterly Journal of Economics*, vol. 85, (May 1971), pp. 327–36.

[2] This analysis is based in large part upon the paper of H. M. Hochman and J. D. Rogers, "Pareto Optimal Redistribution," *American Economic Review*, vol. 59 (September 1969), pp. 542–57; "Comments," by R. A. Musgrave, Robert S. Goldfarb and "Reply," by Hochman and Rogers, *American Economic Review*, vol. 60 (December 1970), pp. 991–1002. For a somewhat similar analysis see S. Marglin, "The Social Rate of Discount and the Optimal Rate of Investment," *Quarterly Journal of Economics*, vol. 77 (February 1963), pp. 95–112.

ernment can increase the total amount of contributions or transfers, thus making the poor better off without making the rich worse off. Let us assume that in the absence of governmental intervention, a given rich person would voluntarily contribute one dollar to be equally divided among the poor. Suppose, however, the government collects one dollar from every rich person through its powers of taxation and distributes this sum equally among the poor. Then each rich person is aware that if he or she gives up one dollar, all other rich persons must also give up one dollar and therefore that each poor person is receiving more than his or her own share of the dollar given up by the rich person. To be specific, suppose that there are N rich people and Q poor people in society. If a given rich person voluntarily gives up one dollar to be equally divided among the poor, each poor person receives $1/Q^{th}$ of a dollar. If all rich people give up one dollar collectively through the government, each poor person receives N/Q^{th} of a dollar. Since the rich person gives up one dollar in either case, his or her welfare loss is the same whether he or she gives up the dollar individually or collectively. But the welfare gain is greater if the rich person gives up a dollar collectively, since he or she knows that each poor person receives more income through collective transfers than through individual transfers. Consequently, there is apt to be more redistribution through a formalized government mechanism than through voluntary contributors alone.

Ethical Income Redistribution

In analyzing ethical income redistribution, it is useful to introduce the concept of the utility-possibility frontier, which shows the maximum amount of welfare a given individual can obtain, given some specified level of welfare for all other individuals. This is illustrated in Figure 6–1 for a society composed of two types of individuals, the rich and the poor. Since utility is an ordinal concept that cannot be measured or quantified, the shape of the utility-possibility frontier, denoted by the line U^*U^*, is somewhat arbitrary. Nevertheless, it is always downward sloping, indicating that one person's welfare can only increase at the expense of another's. Thus, the utility-possibility frontier denotes a Pareto-optimal equilibrium: no person can increase his or her welfare without reducing that of another; no more of no commodity can be produced without reducing the production of another.

Let us suppose that factor endowments, tastes, and technology are such that society ends up on a point like F on its utility-possibility frontier.

In the absence of any notion of how society collectively views the income distribution (or more precisely the welfare distribution), there is little we can say except that F is Pareto-optimal. Suppose, however,

FIGURE 6-1
Redistribution on the Utility-Possibility Frontier

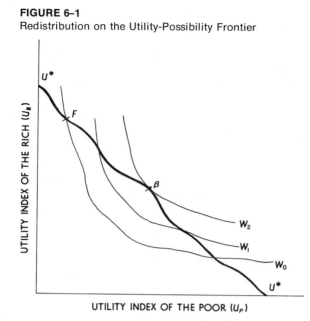

UTILITY INDEX OF THE POOR (U_P)

that society organizes collectively through government to create a social welfare function that expresses society's overall welfare as a function of the utility level of its members. We assume that this social
welfare function is individualistic and is responsive to individual
preferences, subject to the constraints imposed by majority rule. Consequently, insofar as both the rich and the poor are reflected in the
political process, the social welfare function should be such that society's preferred point is one like β, where the utilities of the members
of society are more equal relative to their maximum attainable levels.
It should be stressed, however, that this implies nothing about the
absolute utility levels of the members of society. Thus the point β does
not imply that the members of society are equally well off. The movement from F to β does imply, however, that the distribution of welfare is
made relatively more equal in terms of the maximum attainable utility
levels of the members of society.

Since the rich are typically in the minority, we might ask why more
redistribution does not take place. Why does not the nonrich majority
expropriate income from the rich until income is equally divided, or at
least more so? First, and most obviously, income is not divided among
rich and poor alone. Income is typically distributed along a continuum
so that class or income lines are not clearly drawn. Consequently, in a
society with upward mobility, there is bound to be some reticence in
taxing away too much income of the rich (or those richer than oneself)
because there is always the possibility that one will fall within that

higher-income class at a later date and does not want to be subject to that degree of taxation.

Moreover, there is another important political element constraining the degree of redistribution that will take place. In the United States, Congress is not composed of the poor, but is generally composed of the relatively (or very) affluent. Thus, members of Congress are not apt to vote for measures that would affect them too adversely. While members of Congress must necessarily be responsive to the wishes of their constituency, their own economic position undoubtedly influences their behavior. To the extent that the very poor are not represented in Congress, the actual social welfare function may fail to reflect their desires adequately, and society may fail to move very far from the market-determined equilibrium point. Nevertheless, insofar as all groups are represented in the political process (although doubtless to varying degrees), the social welfare function is so structured that it will probably cause society to move somewhat from the market-determined equilibrium point and redistribute income from the rich to the poor.

It is, of course, impossible to differentiate in practice between Pareto-optimal income redistribution that moves society to the utility-possibility frontier and ethical income redistribution that moves society along the utility-possibility frontier. Nevertheless, it is interesting to speculate on this question. Hochman and Rogers have attempted to make some crude estimates of this question by comparing the actual pattern of redistribution that takes place through the fiscal process with the one that would occur if all redistribution were Pareto optimal and was due solely to interdependence of income levels in utility functions.[3] If the actual redistribution to a given income group is greater than the estimated Pareto-optimal income transfer, it is likely that some ethical redistribution is taking place that moves society along its utility-possibility curve. Briefly stated, there seems to be considerable redistribution along the utility-possibility frontier to the income groups between $2,000 and $4,000 and from those over $10,000. Thus, the "rich" (those with incomes greater than $10,000) appear to transfer income to the "poor" (those with incomes between $2,000 and $4,000) along the utility-possibility curve since the respective transfers are greater than those indicated by interdependencies in the utility functions alone.

One interesting conclusion of the Hochman and Rogers analysis was that the "very poor" (those with incomes under $2,000) receive smaller transfers in relation to their income than the poor (those with incomes between $2,000 and $4,000). In terms of the social welfare function, this indicates that the very poor are not well represented in

---

[3] Hochman and Rogers, "Pareto Optimal Redistribution," pp. 542–57.

the political process. Their welfare is less heavily weighted by politicians than the welfare of the poor or moderately poor. Since the very poor are tyically uneducated and apathetic, it is likely that they are underrepresented in Congress; while their numbers may be large in certain districts, in terms of voter registrations their numbers are relatively small. While the hypothetical nature of the Hochman and Rogers analysis must be stressed, nevertheless, it is suggestive.

Income Distribution in the United States

In considering the income distribution, it is useful to distinguish between the distribution of income among different kinds of factors—labor, capital, and land—and the distribution of income among different income classes. Although considerable economic theory has been developed to explain the former question, relatively little has been developed to explain the latter. If is with the latter concept of the income distribution, however, that the policy-maker is ultimately concerned. Nevertheless, since economic theory can shed some insights on the nature of relative factor returns, it is a useful starting place. From that, we will then turn to a discussion of the income distribution by income class.

Distributive Shares and Wage Differentials

The distributive-share theory indicates that the ultimate allocation of income among factors (land, capital, and the various kinds of labor) depends upon the following: relative factor supplies, the nature of the production process, and the relative demands for the various goods and services. Since factor returns tend to be closely related to the marginal physical product of a given factor and the latter is closely correlated to factor proportions,[4] the most important element that determines relative factor returns is relative factor endowments.

More specifically the simple distributive-share theory indicates the following: First, the lower the marginal physical product of a factor, the lower will be its return; second, the more plentiful the factor relative to others, the lower will be its marginal product; third, if the plentiful factor is best suited for the production of commodities for which the demand is small relative to the supply and hence sells at a relatively low price, the return of that factor will be further depressed. This explains the plight of labor in the less-developed countries to a

---

[4] When the production function is subject to constant returns to scale, marginal physical products will be directly related to factor proportions. There is some evidence that, in the aggregate, the U.S. economy produces under constant returns to scale. For a full discussion of this point, see R. M. Solow, "Technical Change and the Aggregate Production Function," *Review of Economics and Statistics*, vol. 39 (August 1957), pp. 312–20.

large extent. These economies typically have a large labor supply relative to capital goods and concentrate their production on one crop, whose price often shows a secular downward trend in world markets. The combination of the low market price of the commodity and the low marginal product of labor in producing the commodity ensures that the real wage is quite low.[5]

In the United States, the situation is considerably more complicated. Nevertheless, the evidence concerning the relative factor shares is interesting in that, over the past 100 years or so, the relative total shares of income to labor and capital have remained essentially constant, with labor's share increasing somewhat during the past two or three decades. During this period, the capital-labor ratio has increased substantially. This implies that substantial technical change has taken place, which has caused the marginal product curves of both labor and capital to shift out. Because, however, labor's relative share has grown somewhat in recent years, it is likely that the rate of technical change with regard to capital has not quite kept pace with the degree of capital deepening, that is, the growth of capital relative to output or the increase in the capital-output ratio. Alternatively stated, there is some very sketchy evidence that the productivity of labor has grown somewhat relative to capital during the past few decades, causing labor's relative share to grow slightly during this period.

While useful to understand the behavior of the distributive shares in the United States, the previous discussion tells relatively little about the complex forces that affect the income distribution in the United States. As one step toward understanding this problem, it is useful to consider the forces that affect wage differentials. Clearly labor is not a homogeneous factor. There are many different kinds of labor with many different kinds of skills that receive widely varying payments. The most useful means of explaining these differentials lies in the concept of human capital, that is, education.[6]

If one views education and training as a process of individual capital accumulation, different types of labor become more clearly differentiated. In general, the greater the investment in human capital people make, the greater the relative scarcity of their skills and thus the greater their marginal product and hence the return they receive. Therefore the education and training (as well as the kind of physical capital) a person works with in large part determine his or her relative wage or income. The greater a person's education, the greater his or her training or experience, and the greater the amount of physical

[5] For a good discussion of this point, see J. E. Meade, *Efficiency, Equality, and the Ownership of Property* (London: George Allen and Unwin, Ltd., 1964).

[6] For a full discussion of the role of human capital, see Gary S. Becker, *Human Capital: A Theoretical and Empirical Analysis with Special Reference to Education* (New York: National Bureau of Economic Research, 1964).

capital an individual has command over, the greater will be his or her real wage. Since occupations reflect educational levels, in terms of occupations, per capita income tends to be distributed in the following order: professionals and managers, white collar, skilled operatives, laborers, and so on.

The importance of human capital leads one to expect a wide distribution of incomes in the market economy, not only among factors of production (i.e., land, labor, and capital), but within each class of a factor. The problem is further complicated by the existence of market imperfections and discrimination. Market imperfections can take many forms. Labor may not be mobile because of imperfect knowledge or transfer costs that permit substantial regional income differentials. Different types of labor may face different labor markets. For example, highly unionized labor in highly concentrated industries tends to have higher wages than labor in nonunionized, unconcentrated industries. Moreover, labor facing monopsonistic buyers who provide the sole source of employment in a given area tends to be exploited. Wages in company towns tend to be relatively low for this reason. Similarly, unorganized workers facing highly cartelized buyers (such as the California agricultural workers prior to their unionization) tend to have relatively low wages. In both cases, the monopoly powers of the purchasers of the labor permit them to pay labor less than its marginal revenue product and thus depress the wage. Moreover, many people have never been adequately trained or educated to participate fully in the labor market. These people form the so-called "secondary labor market,"[7] which is typified by unsteady, irregular employment at very low wages. These people are typically the last to be hired and the first to be fired. Finally, there is the element of discrimination: against Blacks, Puerto Ricans, Mexican Americans, Indians, and also against women. This leads to considerable wage and salary differentials that cannot be explained by differentials in human capital, the competitiveness of the labor and product market, and the like.[8]

From this brief discussion it should be clear that per capita income will not be evenly distributed among different factors of production or even among the same factors of production. Differences in endowments, production functions, and tastes will ensure that the returns to different factors will be different, with those factors that are relatively abundant receiving the lowest returns. Moreover, since factors are not generally homogeneous, there will be widely varying returns to different kinds of the same factor. We have discussed some of the most

---

[7] See Michael J. Piore, "Jobs and Training," in *The State and the Poor*, eds. Samuel H. Beer and Richard E. Barringer (Cambridge, Mass.: Winthrop, 1970), pp. 53–83.

[8] For a good discussion of the importance of discrimination, see Lester C. Thurow, *Poverty and Discrimination* (Washington, D.C.: The Brookings Institution, 1969).

obvious causes of wage differentials. Different kinds of labor typically work with different kinds of capital, have different amounts of education and training, work in different market situations, and so forth. But similar considerations apply to the other factors of production: capital and land. The returns to capital may vary with the degree of concentration in a given industry or the degree of risk in the industry. The returns to land will depend upon its fertility or productivity.

In a market economy, therefore, economic theory and empirical evidence indicate that there will be a wide range of factor returns or per capita income. How income is distributed among the population determines the extent to which the income distribution can be called equal or unequal. It is to this subject that we will now turn.

Income Distribution and Poverty

Although this chapter emphasizes the income distribution, it is important to remember that we are ultimately concerned about the distribution of welfare among the members of society. Because welfare is nonmeasurable, however, we must use some proxy that reflects economic welfare. Three obvious measures are consumption, wealth, and income.

Consumption measures the dollar value of goods and services actually consumed by individuals. The distribution of consumption expenditures therefore reflects the goods and services consumed by individuals during a given year. To the extent, however, that welfare depends on savings, consumption does not measure welfare accurately. For example, the miser who consumes very little and saves most of his income may have a high, if not higher, degree of satisfaction as the sybarite who spends all of his income on luxurious living. Since we cannot compare individuals' levels of welfare, there is no way that we can actually determine whether the sybarite or the miser is better off. But it should be clear that consumption alone does not reflect the full dimensions of welfare.

As usually defined, wealth measures the stock of one's net assets at a given period of time. These include stocks and bonds, real estate, personal property, etc., which can be denoted as physical wealth. Thus the distribution of physical wealth reflects how the stock of assets is distributed among the population. To the extent that physical wealth measures one's control over economic resources, physical wealth is obviously related to welfare. All other things being equal, a person with a large amount of physical wealth is apt to be better off than one with no assets. Nevertheless, because physical wealth does not generally reflect one's current and potential income earning ability, it fails to give a true picture of welfare. While this could be partially corrected in principle by redefining wealth to include assets in human capital or education, such data are not generally available. Moreover, even this definition of wealth would fail to encompass the person with a special talent who can earn economic rent on this talent: the star football player, the rock star, and so forth.

Income is usually considered to be the best proxy for welfare. Insofar as income reflects one's asset position and one's ability to control economic resources, its connection with welfare should be reasonably close. Nevertheless, because it cannot fully reflect one's asset position, it is an imperfect proxy for welfare. For example, the elderly couple who own their house and live off the proceeds of sales of their stocks and bonds are better off than their measured income level would indicate. Similarly, medical students with low current incomes but with prospects for high future incomes are better off than their current income levels would indicate. And conversely, individuals with large debts are worse off than their income level would indicate.

Welfare is closely related to one's control over economic resources. If wealth could be defined to include investments in education and one's control over scarce resources like the ability to be a star football player, it would probably be the best measure of welfare. Since, however, such measures are largely nonoperational, wealth fails to give a full picture of one's economic position. But, insofar as income neglects one's asset position, it too fails to give a full picture of one's economic position. Ideally we would like a measure of income-cum-wealth, but this is not available. Thus, on balance, income seems to be the best available proxy for welfare; but it is important to remember that it is not a perfect proxy.

In considering the income distribution, two questions are relevant. First, how equal or unequal is the income distribution? Second, how much of the population can be said to live in affluence or poverty? While connected, the two questions have different policy implications. Should it be the goal of government to equalize income differentials or to eradicate poverty or both? To pose the problem, let us consider two different societies. In one, income is evenly distributed among the population, but per capita income is at the subsistence level. In the other, income is very unevenly distributed, but society is sufficiently wealthy that its poorest members are comfortably off in terms of purchasing power or command over resources. If one were given the choice of living in the first society or of being among the poor in the second, one might well choose the latter option. But since poverty is a relative as well as an absolute concept, one might well be considered poorer in the second. This poses a problem for society since it is not clear whether, when collectively organized through government, it should be concerned with reducing poverty in an absolute or a relative sense. Typically, government is concerned with both. Before discussing the role of government, however, let us briefly discuss the nature of the income distribution and poverty in the United States and how it has behaved over time.

The Income Distribution. In discussing the income distribution we are ultimately concerned about the question of equality or inequality: Is income distributed relatively equally or relatively unequally in terms of some standard of total equality? This can be made operational by analyzing the distribution of income among the members of society to determine what percentage of the population receives what percentage of the income. To study this, the concept of the so-called Lorenz curve is useful, as shown on Figure 6–2. On the vertical axis,

FIGURE 6–2
Inequality of Distribution of Income, Consumption, and Wealth

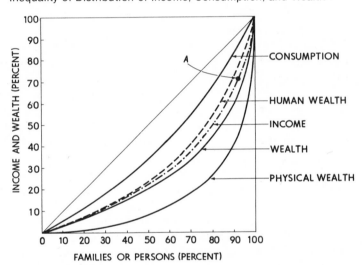

Source: L. C. Thurow, *The Impact of Taxes on the American Economy* (New York: Praeger, 1971), p. 11.

the percent of income cumulated from lowest to highest is plotted; on the horizontal axis, the percent of consumer units cumulated from lowest to highest is plotted. A given point on the income line shows what percentage of the population receives what percentage of income. For example, point *A* shows that the top 10 percent of the income recipients receive approximately 25 percent of all the income in the United States. If income were divided equally, the lowest 10 percent (or decile) of income recipients would receive 10 percent of the income, the next lowest 10 percent of income recipients would receive the next 10 percent of income, and so on. The Lorenz curve would be a straight line. The more uneven the income distribution, the more the curvature in the Lorenz curve.

Figure 6–2 also plots the distribution of other possible measures of welfare: consumption and various measures of wealth (human wealth or education, physical wealth, and some combination of the two). Consumption is more equally distributed than income, while wealth is less evenly distributed. Alternatively stated, one's command over the economic resources as measured by wealth is less evenly distributed than income, while one's actual consumption of economic resources is more evenly distributed than income. This finding is not surprising, since the income that is not consumed goes into the accumulation of wealth through savings.

Figure 6–3 indicates that, although income is not distributed par-

FIGURE 6–3
Lorenz Curves for the Distribution of Family Personal Income

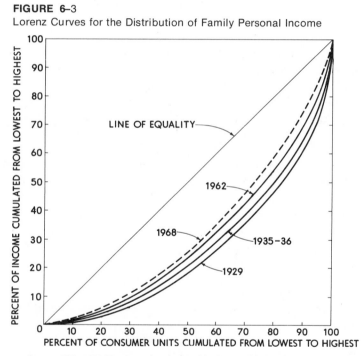

Source: 1929, 1935–36, 1962: Edward C. Budd, ed., *Inequality and Poverty* (New York: W. W. Norton & Co., 1967) p. xii; 1968, *Current Population Reports,* "Consumer Income." Series P–60, No. 66, November 1969, Table 8; 1974, *Current Population Reports,* "Consumer Income," Series P–60, no. 101 (January 1976), Table 22, p. 37.

ticularly evenly in the United States, there has been a secular trend toward increasing income equality. Nevertheless, the change is relatively small. This can be seen even more markedly in Table 6–1 and in the work of Gabriel Kolko.[9] Table 6–1 shows the income distribution by quintile (in terms of fifths of the population) from 1947 to 1974. If

---

[9] Gabriel Kolko, *Wealth and Power in America* (New York: Praeger, 1962), p. 14.

TABLE 6–1
Percentage Share of Aggregate Income, Selected Years, 1947–1974, Received by Each Fifth of Families, Ranked by Income

Year	Lowest 5th	Second 5th	Middle 5th	Fourth 5th	Highest 5th	Top 5 Percent	Percent of Total Families
1974.........	5.4	12.0	17.6	24.1	41.0	15.3	100.0
1970.........	5.4	12.2	17.6	23.8	40.9	15.6	100.0
1965.........	5.2	12.2	17.8	23.9	40.9	15.5	100.0
1960.........	4.8	12.2	17.8	24.0	41.3	15.9	100.0
1955.........	4.8	12.2	17.7	23.4	41.8	16.8	100.0
1950.........	4.5	11.9	17.4	23.6	42.7	17.3	100.0
1947.........	5.1	11.8	16.7	23.2	43.3	17.5	100.0

Source: *Current Population Reports,* "Consumer Income," Series P–60, no. 101 January, 1976), Table 22, p. 37.

these data are considered in conjunction with data extending back to 1910, they indicate that the share of the top income recipients has dropped over the past 50 years, while that of the bottom recipients has risen only slightly during this same period. For this latter group, most of the changes took place during the depression of the 1930s. Moreover, it is interesting to note that in 1910 the bottom 40 percent of the income recipients received 19.7 percent of the national income, while in 1955 this figure had dropped to 17.0 percent, and rose only to 17.4 percent in 1974 (see Table 6–1). Between 1947 and 1974, the share of income received by the top 5 percent of all income recipients dropped from 17.5 percent to 15.3 percent.

This indicates that whatever redistribution has occurred has primarily taken place at the upper half of the income distribution and that income has primarily been redistributed from the rich to the middle ranges rather than to the bottom ranges. Thus, while Figure 6–3 indicates that noticeable redistribution has taken place between 1929 and 1962, it is interesting to note that the lines only become differentiated above the bottom quintile. In general, the share of national income accruing to the poorest fifth of the population has remained distressingly constant during the past 50–60 years.

The Question of Poverty. Table 6–1 deals only with the relative incidence of poverty or the question of income inequality. From a policy point of view, however, the absolute incidence of poverty is probably more important, since it directly measures the standard of living of the poorest members of society.

Before the question of poverty is explicitly considered, however, it is useful to note the distribution of income by income class. In a growing economy, the percentage of individuals in any given low-income class should fall over time, while that in any given high-income class should rise. These trends are evident in Table 6–2. Between 1954 and

TABLE 6–2

Families, by Total Money Income, Selected Years, 1954–1974, in Constant (1974) Dollars

Percent of families with income	1974	1964	1954
Under $4,000	9.0	13.7	22.0
$4,000–5,999	13.0	16.1	22.5
$6,000–9,999............	13.8	17.9	24.4
$10,000–14,999	24.4	26.5	20.5
$15,000–24,999	28.3	20.4	8.6
Over $25,000	11.5	5.4	1.9
Total	100.0	100.0	100.0

Source: *Current Population Reports,* "Consumer Income," series P–60, No. 101 (January, 1976), Table 20, p. 34.

1974 the percentage of families with incomes (in constant 1974 dollars) in excess of $10,000 rose from 31 percent to 64.2 percent, while that of families with income under $4,000 fell from 22 percent to 9 percent.

For policy purposes, however, we are primarily interested in the question of poverty: What percentage of the population lies below some minimum acceptable standard of living? This, of course, is both a relative and an absolute problem. Compared to current standards, most people living in 19th-century America would be considered poor, while those who are considered poor today would probably have been thought of as extremely well off in the 19th century. Similar considerations apply to intercountry comparisons. The poor in the United States might be considered well off in many of the LDCs. Thus although poverty is typically measured in terms of absolute income levels, it is well to remember that the income level that is chosen to define this poverty is essentially a relative concept and in large part depends upon the general standard of living in the society under consideration.

Data have only been developed to analyze the incidence of poverty in the United States since 1959. The measures of the poverty level are based on the cost of basic food requirements, adjusted for family size, sex of family head, age of family members, and place of residence.[10] Table 6–3 indicates that between 1960 and 1974, the incidence of poverty has fallen steadily. In 1960, 22.2 percent of all families fell below the poverty line, while in 1974, only 11.6 percent did so. It is interesting to note that most of this decline took place during the decade of the 1960s, which was generally marked by buoyant growth.

---

[10] For a good discussion of different measures of the poverty line, see Joseph A. Kershaw with the assistance of Paul N. Courant, *Government Against Poverty* (Washington, D.C.: The Brookings Institution, 1970), chap. 1.

TABLE 6–3

Persons below the Poverty Level by Family Status, Selected Years, 1960–1974

	1974	1970	1965	1960
Total (thousands)	24,260	25,420	33,185	39,851
In families	19,440	20,330	28,358	34,925
Unrelated individuals	4,820	5,090	4,827	4,926
Total (percent)	11.6	12.1	17.3	22.2
In families	10.2	10.4	15.8	20.7
Unrelated individuals	25.5	34.0	39.8	45.2

Source: *Current Population Reports,* "Consumer Income," series P–60, No. 102, (January, 1976), Table 1, p. 13.

Between 1960 and 1970, the percentage of poor fell from 22.2 percent to 12.1 percent. Between 1970 and 1974, when the economy was sluggish, the percentage of poor has only fallen from 12.1 percent to 11.6 percent.

While sketchy, this evidence indicates that changes in GNP may in fact have more to do with the reduction of poverty than specific antipoverty programs. The period of boom, however, was also the period when the government launched its War on Poverty. Thus the relative roles of overt government action, such as the War on Poverty, and indirect government action through maintaining high employment levels, are difficult to disentangle. This is a subject to which we shall return shortly.

While the statistics of poverty reduction look impressive in terms of percent of the population living below the poverty line, it is important to realize that substantial numbers of persons are still below the poverty level. Moreover, even though the percentage of the poor may have fallen, the actual number of poor may have risen as a result of population growth, Table 6–3 makes this clear. While the percentage of poor has fallen by approximately 50 percent in the past 14 years, the number of poor has only fallen by 40 percent. Moreover, in 1974, there were still some 24.3 million people living below the poverty line. Of course, as we have pointed out, income does not reflect anticipated or actual wealth. Thus some of the poor include students with high-expected future earnings or elderly persons living off accumulated capital. Nevertheless, the bulk of the poor are likely to be counted as poor by any standard. These include the so-called hard-core poor—those with little education or training who live in areas where skilled jobs are not readily available. The untrained and uneducated blacks in the big-city ghetto; the hill-dwellers of Appalachia; the sharecroppers in Mississippi are all examples of the hard-core poor. They are effectively removed from the mainstream of American economic life. It is unlikely that increases in the national income of the economy will affect them significantly.[11]

Who, specifically, are the poor? Knowledge of their characteristics is important for policy purposes in developing programs to diminish the extent of poverty in the United States. Table 6–4 gives the information

TABLE 6–4
Number and Percentage of Poor Persons, by Selected Characteristics, 1974

| | *Family Status* | | |
	Unrelated	*In Families*	*Total*
Number of poor			
Total (thousands)	4,820	19,440	24,260
Male head			
White	1,200	8,238	9,437
Nonwhite	408	2,639	3,047
Female head			
White	3,212	8,563	6,852
Nonwhite	2,573	4,279	4,923
Poor as percent of population category			
Total (percent)	25.5	10.2	11.6
Male head			
White	20.4	6.5	6.0
Nonwhite	18.3	5.5	17.0
Female head			
White	26.5	27.6	27.2
Nonwhite	50.2	55.2	54.5

Source: *Current Population Reports,* "Consumer Income," series P–60, No. 102 (January, 1976), Table 1, p. 14.

needed to sketch in a poverty profile. For example, in 1974, 10.2 percent of all families were estimated to lie below the poverty line. However, 25.5 percent of single individuals were estimated to be poor. For any given category the incidence of poverty is greater for nonwhite than white families or individuals and still greater if the household is headed by a female rather than by a male. In 1974, the percentage living below the poverty line of total nonwhite families headed by a female was 54.5 percent, while that of families headed by a white male was 6.0 percent. In general, those groups with a poverty incidence substantially greater than the average include single individuals, nonwhite families with a male head, nonwhite families with a female head, and the aged. If the government is to develop programs to alleviate poverty, it should do so with these groups in mind.

---

[11] For a good discussion of this, see Michael Harrington, *The Other America: Poverty in the United States* (New York: Macmillan Company, 1963).

To summarize this discussion briefly, we have seen that poverty is both a relative and an absolute concept. In relative terms, the share of income going to the lowest income group has remained relatively constant, not only during the past decade but also during the past 50 years. In the postwar period, this share has remained virtually constant. In absolute terms, however, the past decade has seen considerable alleviation of poverty as the percentage of individuals falling below the poverty line has almost halved, while the number has fallen by somewhat more than a third. Thus in a very real sense, the incidence of poverty can be said to have diminished substantially in the past decade, although the income distribution has not become more equal in any meaningful sense.

THE ROLE OF GOVERNMENT AND THE INCOME DISTRIBUTION

The previous section generally ignored the role of government in discussing changes in the income distribution. Through its taxation and expenditure policies, the government can have a substantial impact upon the distribution of income and the incidence of poverty. This section discusses the way in which taxation and expenditure policies can affect the income distribution and attempts to assess government policies in the postwar period to determine whether government has played a significant role in equalizing incomes and reducing poverty.

Government can affect the income distribution in both absolute and relative terms in various ways: through its tax structure, through its specific expenditure programs, and through its macroeconomics policies to promote growth and full employment. As shown in Table 6–3, the incidence of poverty declined sharply during the buoyant decade of the 1960s and remained virtually constant during the sluggish period between 1970 and 1974. This certainly suggests that the maintenance of full employment and a high rate of growth of income may, in fact, have more impact on the incidence of poverty than specific antipoverty programs as such. Unfortunately, virtually no data exist to analyze this problem.

Since this section deals with microeconomic aspects of government finance, we concentrate on the impact of government expenditures and taxes upon the income distribution. Ideally we would like to know what would be the income distribution with and without government and what would be the incidence of poverty with and without government. Unfortunately, data do not exist to analyze the problem in these terms. Nevertheless, there are a number of studies that attempt to assess the fiscal incidence of taxes and government expenditures. These shed some light on the question of the impact of government upon poverty in a relative sense, or more precisely, on the income distribution. We then consider the impact of government on poverty in an absolute sense and assess its impact upon the incidence of poverty.

Government and the Income Distribution

In recent years there have been a number of studies that attempt to assess the fiscal incidence of government taxes and expenditures.[12] By fiscal incidence, we mean the difference between tax incidence and expenditure incidence. By tax incidence, in this context we mean the percentage of income paid in taxes per family by income class; by expenditure incidence, we mean the percentage of real income received from government expenditures per family by income class.[13] The tax structure is said to be progressive if the proportion of taxes paid rises with income and regressive if it falls. Similarly, the expenditure structure is said to be progressive if the proportion of expenditures or benefits received falls as income rises. Finally the total fiscal structure is progressive or regressive as the net benefits (expenditures received less taxes paid) fall or rise with income.

In assessing both tax and expenditure incidence, it is necessary to make a large number of essentially arbitrary assumptions regarding the ultimate payer of the tax or the ultimate recipient of the expenditure. These are discussed in Chapter 9. With income taxes, the question of incidence is relatively straightforward; the initial payer of the tax is assumed to be the final payer of the tax. But with other taxes, the question is not so clear. For example, there is considerable controversy about whether the corporate-profits tax is shifted forward to consumers, back to wage earners, or rests on the statutory tax base, corporate profits, and thus reduces retained earnings and the income of stockholders. If the tax is shifted forward to consumers or back to wage earners, the tax is proportional if not regressive; if, however, it falls on capital income, the tax is quite progressive. Similar problems exist with respect to the property tax. If the tax is shifted forward to tenants and consumers it is regressive, but if it falls on the owners of capital, it is progressive.

Since there is relatively little agreement concerning the incidence of the corporate income tax and the property tax, there is relatively little agreement concerning the ultimate progressivity of the tax struc-

---

[12] See W. Irwin Gillespie, "Effect of Public Expenditures on the Distribution of Income," in *Essays in Fiscal Federalism*, ed. R. A. Musgrave (Washington, D.C.: The Brookings Institution, 1965); Joseph A. Pechman and Benjamin A. Okner, *Who Bears the Tax Burden*, (Washington, D.C.: The Brookings Institution, 1974).

[13] It should be pointed out that this definition of incidence differs from that used in traditional economic analysis, which attempts to determine the relationship between the statutory liability of the tax and its ultimate liability. This subject will be discussed in detail in Chapter 9.

FIGURE 6–4

Effective Rates of Federal, State, and Local Taxes under the Most and Least Progressive Incidence Variants, by Adjusted Family Income Class, 1966

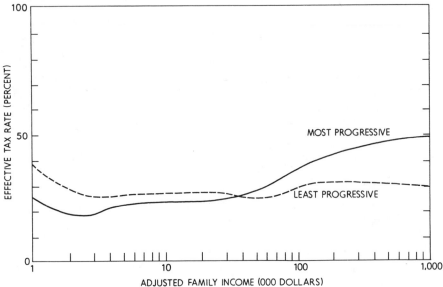

Source: J. A. Pechman and B. Okner, *Who Bears the Tax Burden?* Washington, D.C.: The Brookings Institution, 1974. Used by permission of The Brookings Institution.

ture. Figure 6–4 shows the progressivity of the entire tax structure (federal, state, and local) under two sets of assumptions concerning the incidence of the corporate income tax and the property tax. The most-progressive scenarios assumes that the taxes fall on capital income and hence are progressive, while the least-progressive scenario assumes that they fall on consumers and renters and, hence, are somewhat regressive. While the overall progressivity or regressivity of the tax structure is apparently sensitive to these assumptions, it is important to realize that the overall amount of redistribution involved is quite small. Pechman and Okner have estimated that under the most-progressive set of assumptions, taxes reduce income inequality by only 5 percent, while under the least-progressive set of assumptions, taxes reduce income inequality by only 0.25 percent.[14]

The problem of determining incidence is even more complicated with government expenditures. Typically, expenditures are divided into two categories: those whose benefits can be attributed to specific groups, and "public-good" expenditures which cannot be so attributed. In the first category are expenditures for education, highways, health, and the like, while in the second category are expenditures for

---

[14] See Pechman and Okner, *Who Bears the Tax Burden?* p. 64.

general government, national defense, space exploration, etc. Benefits from the first category are usually allocated according to some index of use, such as number of children in school by income class or usage of motor fuel by income class. The allocation of these benefits generally assumes that the initial recipients of these benefits receive the full benefits. But many of these goods are provided by the government because of the existence of externalities that cause private valuations to diverge from public valuations. Therefore, it is not theoretically justifiable to allocate these benefits entirely to the direct recipients. There is, however, no operational alternative. Even greater problems present themselves with the allocation of public goods since by their very nature these goods cannot be allocated to individuals. These goods are usually allocated on a number of different assumptions: by household, by the income distribution, and so on. The arbitrary nature of these allocations should be clear. Since the estimates of expenditure incidence are sensitive to the assumed allocation of public goods, they must necessarily be suspect. Nevertheless, studies of tax and expenditure incidence are useful since they give us some indication of the direction in which government actually redistributes income.

Table 6–5 indicates that the federal tax structure is generally progressive, while the state and local tax structure is generally regressive. It should be pointed out, however, that the income classes on which this analysis is based are quite broad. More detailed studies that consider the entire range of income levels indicate that the federal tax structure is not progressive at very high income levels,[15] particularly if it is assumed that the corporate and property taxes are not born by capital. Nevertheless, on balance, people with incomes above $15,000 pay a considerably greater proportion of their income in federal taxes than do those with incomes below $15,000. With the possible exception of the highest-income class, whatever progressiveness exists in the federal tax structure is generally counterbalanced by the regressiveness in the state and local tax structures. Thus, the overall tax structure is close to proportional until the highest-income bracket is reached, at which point it becomes progressive, except, possibly at the very top range. Both the federal and state-local governments have progressive expenditure structures, however, with the federal government being substantially more progressive than the state and local governments. Thus, on balance, there appears to be a net redistribution of income as a result of the fiscal structure since the poor and near-poor apparently receive considerably more benefits from government expenditures than they pay in taxes, while the rich pay more

---

[15] See Pechman and Okner, *Who Bears the Tax Buden?*; and R. Musgrave and P. Musgrave, *Public Finance in Theory and Practice* rev. ed. (New York: McGraw-Hill, 1975), chap. 15.

TABLE 6–5

Taxes and Expenditure as a Percentage of Total Income for All Families by Income Class, 1965

	Under $2,000	$2,000– 2,999	$3,000– 3,999	$4,000– 4,999	$5,000– 5,999	$6,000– 7,499	$7,500– 9,999	$10,000– 14,999	Over $15,000
Taxes:									
Federal	13.0	14.0	17.1	17.3	17.9	17.8	18.4	21.1	34.9
State and local	15.1	12.7	12.6	11.8	11.5	10.8	10.1	9.6	9.1
Total	28.1	26.7	29.7	29.1	29.4	28.5	28.5	30.6	44.0
Expenditures:									
Federal	79.3	46.0	31.6	21.2	18.2	15.6	13.8	12.7	11.0
State and local	29.7	19.0	19.4	12.5	11.2	9.8	8.3	7.3	5.2
Total	109.0	65.0	46.0	33.7	29.4	25.4	22.1	20.0	16.2
Fiscal structure **(expend.-taxes):**									
Federal	66.3	32.0	14.5	3.9	0.3	-2.2	-4.6	-8.4	-23.9
State and local	14.6	6.3	1.8	0.7	-0.3	-1.0	-1.8	-2.3	-3.9
Total	80.9	38.3	16.3	4.6	0.0	-3.2	-6.4	-10.7	-27.8

Source: Tax Foundation Inc., *Tax Burdens and Benefits of Government Expenditures by Income Class, 1961 and 1965*, Tables 7 and 8.

in taxes than they receive in benefits. Again, however, the arbitrary nature of the assumptions on which these conclusions are based must be stressed.

A study of the distributional pattern of the Canadian tax system by A. M. Maslove concludes that the overall system is highly regressive up to the $5,000–6,000 income range and roughly proportional over the income ranges above the level.[16] The real property tax is the most regressive; the personal income tax is the most progressive, but the overall federal tax structure is regressive, though less so than the provincial and municipal tax systems.

Government and Poverty

Since data on poverty are only available since 1958, it is impossible to assess the impact of government on the incidence of poverty prior to that date. Moreover, there are virtually no data available to assess anything other than the impact of the federal government upon the incidence of poverty. While the states obviously do engage in programs to alleviate poverty, such as welfare, the magnitude of their influence is unknown. Consequently, although the ensuing discussion will refer to the federal government, it is well to remember that the total impact of government is probably greater than this discussion indicates.

Although the federal government has always undertaken a wide range of activities aimed at income maintenance through the welfare and social security programs, relatively few of these have been aimed at the poor as such. In fact, only when the government launched the War on Poverty in 1964 did it undertake activities and expenditures that were specifically designed to eradicate poverty.

Table 6–6 gives estimates of federal aid to the poor for selected years, 1961–1969. This shows that the level of expenditures aimed at the poor more than doubled between 1964 and 1969, rising from $11.9 to $24.0 billion. While these figures look impressive, however, it is well to remember that they only represent between 30 and 40 percent of all expenditures on direct and indirect income maintenance. Thus, even during the war on poverty, considerable new funds were aimed at general income maintenance than on the poverty population alone.

The War on Poverty was relatively short-lived. Part of this was due to the Vietnam War, which absorbed resources that might otherwise have gone to the War on Poverty. Part of this was due to the change of administrations in early 1969 and the subsequent dismantling of the Office of Economic Opportunity, which directed the War on Poverty.

---

[16] A. M. Maslove, *The Pattern of Taxation in Canada* (Ottawa: Economic Council of Canada, 1973).

TABLE 6–6

Federal Aid to the Poor, Selected Years, 1961–69 (fiscal years, in billions of current dollars)

Category	1961	1964	1968	1969*
Education	0.1	0.1	2.3	2.2
Employment assistance	0.1	0.2	1.6	2.0
Health assistance	0.7	1.0	4.1	5.0
Income assistance	8.3	9.8	12.4	12.9
Other maintenance assistance	0.5	0.7	1.3	1.9
Total	9.8	11.9	21.7	24.0

Note: Figures are rounded and will not necessarily add to totals. It is well to stress that these sums are only those reaching the poor. Health expenditures, for example, were much higher than $4.1 billion in 1968; of the total expended, the poor received $4.1 billion.

* Estimated.

Source: J. A. Kershaw, *Government against Poverty* (Washington, D.C.: The Brookings Institution, 1970), p. 40.

Consequently, although the federal government presently undertakes numerous redistributive activities, none of them are explicitly aimed at the goal of eradicating poverty. Thus, we can view the War on Poverty as a brief experiment rather than as a fundamental change in government policy toward poverty and the poor.

Income Maintenance. The War on Poverty was largely predicated on the notion of providing services in kind to the poor: education, job training, health facilities, and so on, that would enable them to pass over the poverty threshold and into the mainstream of American economic life. It is certainly reasonable, however, to question the premise upon which this program is built. Instead of providing services in kind, why not give the poor sufficient income to let them cross over the poverty threshold and spend the income as they desire? This is essentially the proposal of the proponents of a negative income tax, who offer it as an alternative to the existing welfare programs and the kinds of programs encompassed in the War on Poverty.[17]

The existing income maintenance programs are a combination of social security and various forms of welfare. To qualify for social security one must be 65, have worked in some employment covered by social security, and earn less than a specified amount of income. Upon reaching 72, the income constraint is removed. The job coverage is sufficiently broad that most individuals are, in fact, covered. Although the bulk of the aged population receive some assistance in the form of social security, the disproportionate number of aged below the poverty line indicates that the payments tend to be inadequate. Social security payments alone are not yet sufficient to enable the typical aged indi-

---

[17] The notion of a negative income tax has been proposed by people with such diverse points of view as Milton Friedman and James Tobin. See Milton Friedman, *Capitalism and Freedom* (Chicago: University of Chicago Press, 1964); James Tobin, "On Improving the Economic Status of the Negro," *Daedalus* (Fall 1965), pp. 878–98.

vidual to live a life of decency and self-respect. While Medicare has helped in this respect, it too has been inadequate.[18]

The welfare program is composed of several parts: old age assistance, aid to the blind, aid to the permanently and totally disabled, and aid to dependent children (ADC). Until recently, old-age assistance was the dominant part of the welfare program. As social security benefits have increased and its coverage extended, old-age assistance has diminished in importance. Aid to the blind or disabled has never formed a major part of welfare payments. When one now thinks of welfare, one typically thinks of aid to dependent children and the mother who is deserted by her husband or who never had a husband and who must stay home to look after the children.

In recent years, there has been considerable disaffection with the welfare program in general and with ADC in particular. Part of this stems from the restrictions placed upon recipients with regard to income and husbands. For example, under current regulations in most states, as soon as a person earns more than a very nominal amount, all welfare payments are cut off. Thus the current welfare program typically imposes a "tax" of more than 100 percent on its recipients, thereby effectively eliminating any incentives to enter the labor market. Moreover, most states, which administer the welfare program, have requirements that the recipients have no husbands who are able or willing to support them and no other potential source of income. The result has been to a large extent the destruction of the nuclear family. The poor have incentives to stay unmarried and the husband has an incentive to desert the family.

There are other problems with the current welfare program. First, most programs involve a means test, which requires that considerable resources be spent on testing eligibility and policing it. Thus instead of helping welfare recipients, many caseworkers spend their time policing them. Second, because the welfare program is administered by the states, there is wide variability in the payments received throughout the country. New York and Massachusetts pay two to three times as much to recipients as, say, Mississippi or Alabama. Finally, the welfare program does not reach most of the poor. The 10 million people who currently receive welfare constitute only some 40 percent of the estimated 25 million poor. Thus some means must be found to expand its coverage.

All of these defects in the welfare program have brought increasing numbers of proposals aimed at eliminating it and substituting in its place some sort of a negative income tax. The principle behind a negative income tax is quite simple. Just as people must pay an in-

---

[18] For a good discussion of the social security program, see Joseph A. Pechman, Henry J. Aaron, and Michael Taussig, *Social Security: Perspectives for Reform* (Washington, D.C.: The Brookings Institution, 1968).

come tax on income earned above a certain level, they should receive a supplement on income below that level. From this, it is easy to postulate a certain minimum subsistence income level and then to pay families an amount based on the difference between their actual income and the minimum acceptable income level at some specific rate.

There are many advantages to a negative income tax. First, it bases the amount received purely on the difference between actual income and the specified minimum, thus removing the inequities and inefficiencies caused by the categorical assistance administered under the current welfare programs. Second, it can be administered relatively simply. Once the relationship between a family's given income and the minimum income level is set, the amount of money going to the family is easily determined.[19] Third, as long as the negative income tax rate is less than 100 percent, people have an incentive to work under a negative income tax program that they do not have under current welfare programs. For example, if the negative income tax rate were 33.3 percent, families could keep two thirds of any income earned.[20] Fourth, and most important, a negative income tax establishes a legal right of the poor to some minimum acceptable standard of living, regardless of their particular family situation. It consequently removes any stigma that is associated with receiving welfare. As such it marks a major departure from current categorical assistance programs that distribute funds not only on the basis of income but also on the basis of the recipient's age, health, family situation, and so forth. Under a negative income tax, being poor for whatever the reason is sufficient to receive the right to assistance.

The mechanics of a negative tax plan can be seen in Figure 6–5 in which disposable income is plotted on the vertical axis and preallowance (or pretransfer) income is plotted on the horizontal axis. If there were no taxes, disposable income and pretransfer income would be equal; the line *OA* would hold. But taxes do exist. Assume that the exemptions and deductions are such that a family of four pays no taxes until its income reaches $3,000. After that, its disposable income is less than its taxable income; the line *OEB* indicates the relation under the assumed tax laws.

There are three key elements in a negative income tax system: the

[19] For a good discussion of some of the technical problems associated with a negative income tax, see C. H. Green, *Negative Taxes and the Poverty Problem* (Washington, D.C.: The Brookings Institution, 1967).

[20] Nevertheless, a negative income tax will probably have disincentive effect upon work effort, since the income effect (which operates because people have more income) and the substitution effect (which operates because the return-to-work effort is reduced) act together to reduce work effort. Nevertheless, empirical studies indicate that a negative income tax would only have a small disincentive effect upon work effort. See, for example, Albert Rees and Harold Watts, "An overview of the Labor Supply Results," in *Work Incentives and Income Guarantees*, eds. J. A. Pechman and P. M. Timpane (Washington, D.C.: The Brookings Institution, 1975).

FIGURE 6-5

Relation of Preallowance Income to Disposable Income for a Family of Four

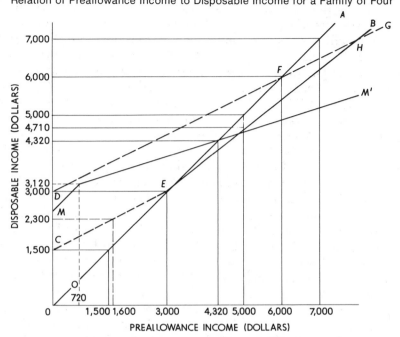

Note: Calculations are based on deductions, exemptions, and rates in the Revenue Act of 1964.
Source: J. A. Kershaw, *Government against Poverty* (Washington, D.C.: The Brookings Institution, 1970), p. 116.

minimum guaranteed income or what a family with no pretransfer income would receive; the break-even point at which a family neither receives transfers nor pays taxes; and the transfer rate, which is also called the negative tax rate. Once the minimum guaranteed income is set and the transfer rate chosen, the break-even point is determined. Alternatively, once the break-even point and the transfer rate have been determined, the minimum guaranteed income is also determined.

The break-even income level is often set at the minimum acceptable income level or the poverty threshold. Below this point, disposable income is greater than preallowance or taxable income. Suppose, for example, that a negative tax rate of 50 percent is adopted and that the breakeven point is set at $3,000, which is often thought of as the poverty line. Families with an income of $3,000 would receive no transfers and they would pay no taxes. For every dollar that family income falls below $3,000, the family receives the transfer from the government of 50 cents. This implies that the minimum guaranteed income is $1,500, a figure well below the poverty line. In this case, the appropriate line is *CEB* in Figure 6-5.

It should be clear from this example that as long as the negative tax rates are less than 100 percent and the break-even point is set at the minimum acceptable income level or the poverty line, a negative income tax will fail to take any given family beyond the poverty threshold. This can only be done setting the break-even point at some point beyond the poverty line. Suppose, for example, that a break-even point of $6,000 is adopted with a negative tax rate of 50 percent. Then the line *DFHB* would hold. A family of four with no income would receive an income of $3,000. Not until its income reached $6,000 would a family find that its disposable income equaled its taxable income. Only at point *H*, where its income was over $7,000, would a family be subject to the regular income tax rates.

This indicates the major problem with a negative income tax. There is a trade-off between the cost of the system to the Treasury, the transfer rates used, and the level of income to be guaranteed. Low transfer rates are important from the viewpoint of incentives. But low transfer rates impose considerable cost to the Treasury unless the minimum guaranteed income is very low. For example, with a $3,000 minimum guaranteed income, a transfer rate of 50 percent implies a break-even point of $6,000. The effective tax line *DFHB* lies considerably above the actual tax line *OEB*, indicating the cost to the Treasury. If, however, the transfer rate were reduced to 33⅓ percent, the break-even point would rise to $9,000 and the costs to the Treasury would rise. Alternatively, a transfer rate of 100 percent would make the effective tax line *DEB* at relatively little cost to the Treasury. But negative tax rates of 100 percent would effectively eliminate any incentives to work to move beyond the poverty threshold.

Some form of a negative income tax may eventually become a reality. In 1968 President Nixon proposed a family assistance plan, which was in effect, a limited negative income tax. This failed to pass in the session in which it was proposed, partly because the liberals thought it did not go far enough and the conservatives thought it went too far. A bill that passed the House in 1971 has met a similar fate.[21] A negative income tax program that succeeded in eliminating poverty would be extremely expensive and is probably not politically feasible. Never-

---

[21] The Social Security Amendment Bill of 1971 (the Mills bill) as passed by the House was, in effect, a negative income tax. It set a minimum income guarantee of $2,400, with a transfer rate of two thirds above the first $720 earned by a family. This creates a break-even point of $4,320. In Figure 6–5, the Mills bill is shown by the line *MM'*. It has been estimated that this program would have cost $6.5 billion at its inauguration if it had become law.

The provisions of the Mills bill were modest compared to a program proposed by the National Welfare Rights Organization, which envisaged a minimum guaranteed income of $5,500 for a family of four, and a negative tax rate of one half for income above the first $720 earned. Under this proposal, the break-even point would be $11,720; it was estimated that the total costs of this program would have been some $71 billion greater than the existing outlays for welfare.

theless, a more modest program to replace the existing welfare system with its many defects is periodically discussed and may become a reality in time. It clearly has many merits and warrants serious discussion.

CONCLUSION

This chapter has ranged over a broad range of subjects: the theoretical justification of government intervention with regard to the income distribution, the nature of the income distribution in the United States, and the impact of government upon the income distribution in both relative and absolute terms.

With regard to the first question, government intervention is justified under three circumstances. First, the income distribution may be regarded as a public good that enters all persons' utility functions; second, the income levels of the poor may enter into the utility functions of the nonpoor; and third, the general consensus as expressed by a social welfare function may indicate that, even if the market-determined solution is efficient, it may not be desirable from an ethical point of view.

With respect to the income distribution, differences in factor endowments, tastes, and technologies create income differentials among factors. Moreover, differences in education, training, and the like, as well as differences in market structures, create income differentials within any one factor group. Therefore, in a market economy such as the United States, a wide range of income should exist. This is, in fact, the case. Incomes are not only distributed unequally, but there has been relatively little movement toward increasing equality over the past 50 years. Thus in a relative sense, the incidence of poverty has remained substantially unchanged. In an absolute sense, however, poverty has been reduced substantially in the past decade, and presumably prior to that, although data are unavailable to measure this reduction. Nevertheless, in terms of a minimum standard of living, the incidence of poverty has doubtless dropped continually throughout most of the past 50 years (although the years during the depression of the thirties are probably an exception).

Finally, while government has done relatively little to affect the relative incidence of poverty, in recent years it has attempted to reduce the absolute incidence of poverty in the United States. The impact of government upon the relative incidence of poverty can best be seen by considering the incidence of the tax and expenditure structures. In terms of taxes, the structure is either neutral or slightly regressive when all levels of government are taken into account, while in terms of expenditures the structure is quite progressive. On balance, there appears to be some redistribution of income from the high to the low income classes. However, the arbitrary nature of the assumptions involved in this analysis makes these findings somewhat suspect.

Present programs specifically aimed at alleviating poverty are concentrated in the welfare programs, which represent catorical assistance to poor people who meet certain requirements concerning age, marital status, disability, means, and so forth. Although economists generally believe that the substitution of a negative income tax program for the existing welfare programs would be more equitable and more effective than present policies, there presently appears to be little political support for a negative income tax.

APPENDIX

INCOME REDISTRIBUTION IN CANADA

A recent study of the effects of taxes and governmental expenditures in Canada by W. Irwin Gillespie concluded that in 1969 the overall effect was to improve the position of the poor slightly, the progressive nature of the expenditures more than offsetting the tax structure that is regressive over the lowest third of the income units and in the top income classes. During the 1960s the tax and expenditure structure changed in such a way as to improve the position of the poor and the rich at the expense of the middle income groups. But during the 1970s the position of the poor has worsened. On the whole, therefore, the redistributive effects are not great and have not increased over recent decades.[22]

REFERENCES

Becker, Gary S. *Human Capital: A Theoretical and Empirical Analysis.* New York: Natural Bureau of Economic Research, 1964.

Budd, Edward C., ed., *Inequality and Poverty.* New York: W. W. Norton, 1967.

Current Population Reports, Series P-60, various numbers, "Consumer Income."

Gillespie, W. Irwin. "Effect of Public Expenditures on the Distribution of Income," in *Essays in Fiscal Federalism,* ed. R. A. Musgrave Washington, D.C.: The Brookings Institution, 1965, pp. 122–86.

Green, C. H. *Negative Taxes and the Poverty Problem.* Washington, D.C.: The Brookings Institution, 1967.

Harrington, Michael. *The Other America: Poverty in the United States.* New York: Macmillan Co., 1963.

---

[22] "On the Redistribution of Income in Canada", *Canadian Tax Journal,* vol. 24 (July–August 1976), pp. 417–50.

Hochman, H. M., and Rogers, J. D. "Pareto Optimal Redistribution," *American Economic Review*, vol. 59 (September 1969), pp. 542–57.

Kershaw, Joseph A., with the assistance of Paul N. Courant. *Government against Poverty*. Washington, D.C.: The Brookings Institution, 1970.

Musgrave, Richard A., and Musgrave, Peggy B. *Public Finance in Theory and Practice* 2d ed. New York: McGraw-Hill, 1976.

Pechman, Joseph A., and Okner, Benjamin A. *Who Bears the Tax Burden?* Washington, D.C.: The Brookings Institution, 1974.

Thurow, Lester C. *Poverty and Discrimination*. Washington, D.C.: The Brookings Institution, 1969.

Thurow, Lester C. "The Income Distribution as a Pure Public Good," *Quarterly Journal of Economics*, vol. 85 (May 1971), pp. 327–36.

7

Budget Systems and Cost-Benefit Analysis

We assume that governments in a democratic society seek to adapt their policies to the preferences of society, granting that in the process they exert substantial pressure upon the nature of these preferences. Given the lack of precise, clearly defined preference schedules and the difficulties of determining the schedules, society through government must determine the levels of various activities and the exact amounts to be spent on each activity. The basic power over expenditures rests with the legislative body as the representative of the voters, but of necessity, the chief executive and the administration exercise great influence both in guiding legislative action and in implementing policies within the framework of the broad guidelines established by the legislature. The government—in practice, primarily the executive and the administrative organization—selects the methods to be used to attain the goals of society, as, for example, the types of missiles to be developed or the mode of transport to handle mail.

BUDGET SYSTEMS

To facilitate annual (or, in many states, biennial) decision-making on expenditures, governments have developed budget systems, which provide for systematic presentation of recommendations for expenditures by the executive to the legislative branch of government. The budget systems, through appropriations legislation and control of expenditures, also provide a basis for ensuring that actual expenditures

128

conform with the law. A budget may therefore be defined as a financial plan that serves as the basis for expenditure decision-making and subsequent control of expenditures.

Nature of Budgets

Budgets usually contain financial data for the previous year (or years), estimated figures for the current year, and recommended figures for the coming year, for both expenditures and revenues. Most of the space in the budget, however, is devoted to expenditures.

Several questions arise about the exact coverage of a budget, and differences in approaches to them led for a time to three separate budget totals for the federal government. One major issue relates to trust funds, to which certain revenues are allocated and from which certain specified expenditures are made. For many years the social security and highway trust fund expenditures and revenues were omitted from the federal budget figures. The budget totals frequently quoted, therefore, were much less than the actual expenditures. Unification of the budget system in 1968 resulted in inclusion of these funds in the totals. Another issue relates to government lending. The totals were long included in the budget, thus including expenditure items that involved the granting of loans. Since 1968, totals have been shown with and without lending to provide a clearer picture. A third issue is the use of cash versus accrual reporting. The federal budget has always been on a cash basis rather than an accrual basis, but figures of the national income accounts place government activity on an accrual basis.

Another question of coverage relates to governmental activities of essentially commercial nature with large revenues from the sale of services, such as Tennessee Valley Authority. The typical practice is to include only the net earnings or deficit figure plus capital expenditures, rather than the gross expenditures and revenues. This same rule has been used since 1969 for additional market-oriented activities, such as sales of timber from national forests. These receipts are deducted from the expenditure figures of the respective agencies and only the net is shown. At the municipal level, similar practices are usually followed. To include the gross figure gives a misleading picture of government-induced reallocation of resources and therefore is less useful for purposes of decision-making relative to governmental activities. The revenues of the governmental commercial projects serve primarily to cover the expenses of operation, and the governmental operation replaces private operation; there is no change in resource allocation except insofar as pricing policies differ. The gross expenditures of some cities on their utilities exceed their strictly governmental expenditures.

The Budget Cycle

The budgetary process in larger governmental units involves four steps: preparation of the budget and submission to the legislative body, enactment of authorization and appropriations legislation, execution, and audit. Responsibility for preparation of the budget usually rests with the executive branch of government, with a special budgetary agency in larger governments to handle the work of preparation, under the jurisdiction of the chief executive. In the United States the Office of Management and Budget (OMB), formerly the Bureau of the Budget, an independent agency (independent, that is, of any department), has this responsibility. Congress is aided in its action on the budget by the Congressional Budget Office, created in 1974. The fiscal year of the United States federal government traditionally extended from July 1 to June 30. But the difficulty experienced by Congress in enacting appropriations legislation by July 1 led to a shift in the fiscal year as of 1976–77 so that it now begins on October 1. Fiscal years are designated by the final of the two years; for example the 1977–78 fiscal year is known as f/y (fiscal year) 1978.

The United States federal budget cycle is outlined briefly below:[1]

A.   Preparation.

1.   Preparatory work for the budget is commenced about 18 months before the beginning of the fiscal year involved; that is, for the fiscal year 1977–78 which begins October 1, 1977, work began in January 1976. At the agency level, preliminary estimates are made of needs for the year and submitted to OMB. At the same time, officials of OMB, the Treasury, and the Council of Economic Advisers prepare tentative budget guidelines.

2.   In late spring the Director of OMB discusses the proposed figures with the President and his advisers, who also have information available about general economic conditions. The President then establishes budget guidelines in conformity with his general plans for governmental activities and fiscal policy.

3.   OMB then requests formal detailed estimates from all departments in conformity with the guidelines.

4.   The requests are then submitted to OMB and studied intensively by the Bureau's examiners, with discussion with personnel of the agencies involved.

5.   The recommendations of the examiners are then discussed with the director of OMB, and the final figures are reviewed with the President.

---

[1] For greater detail, see Ira Sharkansky, *The Politics of Taxing and Spending* (Indianapolis: Bobbs-Merrill, 1969).

6.   Agencies are notified of the amounts to be recommended for them and they prepare statements to justify these amounts.

7.   The budget document itself is then prepared and in early January is presented by the President to Congress with the Budget Message, summarizing the proposed changes.

B.   Enactment.

The enactment process was altered by the Congressional Budget and Impoundment Act of 1974, designed to strengthen the hands of Congress in the budgetary process. In addition to establishing the Congressional Budget Office, the legislation established Budget Committees in the House and the Senate, made up of influential members of other key committees.

The enactment process is now as follows:

1.   No later than May 15 of the year in which the new fiscal year begins, Congress, on the basis of the President's budget, reports on budget estimates from the major committees and a general fiscal policy report from the Budget Committee, and adopts a concurrent resolution establishing expenditure and revenue targets, as a guide to the action on the appropriations measures.

2.   Next, the actual appropriations legislation is enacted. By tradition all appropriations measures originate in the House and are initially considered by the House Appropriations Committee. This committee is divided into 13 subcommittees organized on functional lines (national defense, agriculture, and so on). The subcommittees carefully review the recommendations, with hearings in which officials of the agencies testify, and may change items upward or downward. The recommendations of each subcommittee are considered and merged by the Appropriations Committee, frequently with little change. The appropriations measures are then voted on by the House (usually with little change) and sent to the Senate.

3.   The Senate follows a similar but less lengthy and detailed review.

4.   Differences are ironed out by a Conference Committee and the bill sent to the President. He can only sign or veto it; he cannot change particular items. The appropriations measures authorize the expenditures of certain amounts; the authorizations may extend beyond the current year. Frequently congressional action was not completed by July 1, and expenditures on the basis of the previous year's appropriations were extended on a temporary basis.

5.   By September 15, Congress enacts a second concurrent resolution providing budget ceilings, by program and activity, either confirming or amending the figures in the May resolution. The resolution may contain recommendations to the various committees for changes in authorization legislation, revenues, or debt.

C. Execution.

1. The funds authorized are released to the agencies by OMB, usually with allotments by quarter of the year and with reserves kept for emergencies.

2. Expenditures are made by the agencies in conformity with the authorizing legislation. The appropriations are allotted by agency, but with considerable flexibility in the use of the funds.

3. Under the 1974 legislation noted above, the administration cannot "impound" or refuse to spend funds appropriated by Congress—a common phenomenon prior to 1974 that led to a series of court cases, which in general denied the President the power to impound. The legislation specifically denies this power.

4. Checks are written by the disbursing officer of the agency, and payment made through the Treasury.

D. Audit.

Post audit is made by the General Accounting Office to ensure that funds are spent in conformity with the law. The Comptroller General, who heads the GAO, is appointed by and responsible only to Congress.

Operation of the Budgetary Process

A budget is designed to facilitate determination of governmental activities in light of the preferences of society by ensuring the comparison of conflicting programs and methods in the attainment of the goals. The budget system should also aid in attaining greater efficiency in the use of governmental resources. The task, especially for the federal government, is an extremely complex one—particularly in establishing priorities among competing goals. How are the relative priorities for defense and the elimination of poverty to be estimated—even if the relative preference schedules of society for the attainment of these goals are known? How are the relative advantages of deterrent atomic power versus larger armies, and of various equal opportunity programs, to be compared as relative means of attaining the objectives? The task for a state or a city may be somewhat simpler, but the complexities and need for value judgments remain.

As a consequence of these complexities, the operation of the budgetary process has inevitably developed many shortcuts in order to be workable—just as business firms develop shortcuts to pricing since calculation of marginal revenues and marginal costs for all products is neither economical nor feasible. These take several forms:

Specialization. The various agencies play a key role in determination of actual expenditure levels; each is concerned only with its own specialized work, with which its officials are familiar. In OMB, detailed examination of requests is made by examiners specialized by type of work. The appropriations subcommittees, which play the dominant role in congressional action, are likewise specialized by activity. Each of these groups feels justified in considering only the direct needs of the particular activity, since other groups are considering other needs.

Fragmentation. The overall budget is fragmented into small pieces for most of the work, both at the level of preparation and at the congressional committee level—and even at the level of overall action by Congress, since there are a number of appropriations bills rather than one.

Incremental Nature of Action. Existing programs are not reviewed in detail each year. In preparing the budget, no one considers annually such questions as: Are we to continue antitrust regulation? Are we to maintain consulates and embassies abroad? The presumption is that existing activities will continue unless there is strong evidence that their existence should be reconsidered, and the principle that new appropriations should be similar to the existing ones is accepted with little question. If the Indian Service spends $400 million one year, no thought is given to the possibility of its spending $4 million or $4 billion next year. Consideration is given only to incremental changes from the present figure—and usually, of course, upward changes. Consideration is likewise sequential; if this year's figure turns out to be undesirable in terms of the goals, correction can be made next year or even in a supplemental appropriation this year.

While there is occasional talk of adopting zero-budgeting procedures, that is rejustifying all existing activities on the assumption of a zero initial level of funding, in practice this is never instituted because of its complexity and expense.

Thus the budgetary process becomes manageable. But is there any coordination or central review at all? What prevents rapid expansion of some agencies, far exceeding any reasonable level of expenditures in terms of the goals, while others, lacking dynamic leadership, wither? What prevents agencies whose work has become obsolete from continuing forever?

The basic coordination is provided by the competition of the various programs for funds in face of strong legislative resistance to continuous increases in taxes—the struggling of various agencies for money. The department head—the Secretary—exercises some restraining influence over the divisions, so that the overall requests of the department will not appear completely unreasonable. The OMB, representative of the Chief Executive, seeks to hold down overall spending, and the congressional committees do likewise. Despite the absence of direct, centralized decision-making about the relative activities, there is downward pressure on all—and particularly on those that appear to conform least with estimates of society's preferences. Each unit, each subcommittee of appropriations, is well aware of the overall contraints and makes its own decisions in light of them. The chief pressure to eliminate obsolete activity is the desire of the agency or department to use the funds for expansion of other activities.

Roles

Each element in the expenditure decision-making process comes to exercise a certain primary role—a role to which there are exceptions, of course.

The agencies are the *advocates* of additional activity, seeking virtually always to expand their activities, the strength of their pressure to do so depending upon their estimates of needs and the attitudes of the agency heads.[2] As specialists in their fields, they are most familiar with the contributions that the activities make; and they are inevitably enthusiastic about their activities. The agency head may also be influenced by the more direct considerations of pure and simple empire building. Expansion typically conveys benefits to the agency heads without direct costs to them; the pressure is always toward more, never toward less.

The question of how much to ask for is answered partly by the belief of the agency head about the need for the activity, and in part by considerations of strategy. The tendency is always to ask for more than is expected, partly because the heads believe in the activities, partly because they expect to be cut in the face of the general constraints against all increases and the competition of other agencies, partly because they think that higher authority believes they pad their requests. In a sense, padding strengthens the hand of OMB and Congress, which can point to the reductions they have made in the requests as evidence of their drive for economy. To pad too much, however, is to generate loss of confidence.

There are several techniques that agencies use in their efforts to get higher figures.[3] One is to cultivate a clientele—farmers, truck operators, chambers of commerce, clergymen—any group that will bring pressure on the administration and Congress to provide additional funds. The agencies that suffer are those that lack an organized clientele. A second is to build confidence by all means possible with higher echelons and with congressional subcommittees—a long-range subtle endeavor. Closely related is the technique of seizing every

---

[2] W. A. Niskanen, Jr., *Bureaucracy and Representative Government* (Chicago: Aldine-Atherton, 1971).

[3] See Aaron Wildavsky, *The Politics of the Budgetary Process*, 2d ed. (Boston: Little, Brown, 1974).

opportunity to propagandize the activity; if current attention is centered on elimination of poverty in urban centers, all agencies will seek to relate their work to this activity—even if this work is education of the Navajos.

When agencies fail to obtain approval of the desired amounts from their department or the OMB, they may seek to influence the appropriations subcommittee that deals with their activity. Many attempts have been made by the Executive to prevent this runaround, but doing so is difficult. Officials of the agency may develop close personal relationships with subcommittee members, who are themselves sympathetic to the activity and will not infrequently heed the pleas of the agency.

The role of the OMB is that of the *President's representative*, one that reviews the requests in light of the overall preferences of the President for expansion or contraction of certain activities and for general expenditure-level trends. OMB inevitably has a bias toward cutting requests, because of the advocacy nature of the agencies themselves and their well-known tendency to pad demand figures—in the face of the usual desire of the President to hold down overall expenditure and tax levels. OMB cannot make a careful review of benefits and costs of all budget requests; it can merely give them a broad review in terms of apparent merits—given the estimates of what society wants and in light of its estimates of congressional attitudes—and look for excessive padding. OMB is reluctant to come up with a total 20 percent higher than last year when it knows that Congress is seeking to hold the line at existing figures, or to approve a large increase for a certain activity to which it knows Congress to be most unsympathetic. OMB's actions are based on political considerations as much as or more than on economic considerations, as well they should be in view of the goal of adjusting expenditures in light of community preferences.

The House Appropriations Committee and its subcommittees play the primary role of *guardian of the Treasury,* reflecting the common desire of society to hold taxes down. The Committee therefore has a strong bias in favor of cutting requests, and in fact cuts far more than it increases.[4] There are exceptions, in which the subcommittee supports the agency and overrules OMB, or may even raise the figure over the agency request. But these represent a minority of cases.

The Senate, particularly the Senate Appropriations Committee, serves primarily as a *court of appeal* from reductions made by the

---

[4] One extensive study showed that of 443 measures over a 12-year period, the Appropriations Committee left 74 unchanged, cut 342, raised 27. See Wildavsky, *The Politics of the Budgetary Process.*

House. Traditionally the Senate tends to be more liberal, raising many House-approved figures, the final figures therefore being compromises between the two.

Proposals for Greater Coordination and Broader Evaluation

Many studies have been made of federal budgetary procedure over the years and most have called for the same general type of reform: more effective overall review of expenditures for various purposes, that is, for lessened emphasis on the shortcuts noted earlier in the chapter. The existing system has been criticized for unnecessary fragmentation, especially at the congressional level. Each expenditure is considered independently, with little or no attempt—either by OMB or Congress—to weigh relative merits of various activities against one another, except in the crudest fashion. Attempts to remedy this situation by establishing expenditure ceilings by Congress prior to enactment of appropriations legislation and to employ a single appropriations bill failed in the late 1940s; it proved impossible to agree on ceilings and the single bill proved to be too cumbersome. In 1974, however, as noted above, Congress made a new attempt to improve coordination, by establishing the congressional budget office to provide technical assistance, and in providing for the resolutions establishing ceilings. Whether the new approach will be any more effective than that of the 1940s remains to be seen. The inherent problem is the complexity of the federal expenditure program, which makes the necessary overall comparison very difficult.

As stressed by Wildavsky, the present decentralization of expenditure decision-making is a reflection of the nature of the political process in the United States; no group has the political power to make all of the basic decisions about expenditures. The system is inherently one of checks and balances, and the distribution of political power has been such that no group can completely dominate. In a country with the parliamentary form of government, domination by the majority party and strict adherence to party policy, much greater centralization in decision-making is possible. But the United States situation is not of this character, and no change in budgetary processes can make it so.

The present fragmented structure, it is true, may not make overall review and balancing of relative needs of various activities completely effective. Those activities having strong clienteles—pressure groups—behind them may succeed in pushing their activities beyond what might be regarded as reasonable. Inertia may restrict readjustment of activities for long periods and preserve obsolete activities. But the system is workable; it ensures pressure to expand useful activities on the one hand, and provides general constraint on the other. It may not be ideal, and, as subsequently noted, improvements in budget structure and better evaluation of benefits are possible. But the overall system is much better than its critics have made it out to be.

State and Local Budget Systems[5]

Much of this discussion is also applicable to state and local activities. On the whole, the processes are simpler and the benefits of many of the activities are easier to measure. In most states the governor has responsibility for preparation of the budget, with an agency to assist. The legislature, in enacting appropriations measures, makes less detailed inquiry into the activities than does the House Appropriations Committee. Many of the activities are less controversial and less complex, and programs change less frequently. On the other hand, budget restraints are sometimes more severe because of the lesser scope of potential tax resources and constitutional restrictions on borrowing. Local budget systems differ in one major respect. Typically legislative and executive branches are not sharply distinguished, and thus responsibility for both preparation and enactment rests upon the legislative agency (city council, school district trustees, and so forth).

Earmarking and Expenditure Determination

The federal government has never allocated particular taxes to specific functions—a practice called earmarking—by constitutional provision; by congressional action, certain taxes have been allocated to the trust funds. In a number of states, however, the revenues from various taxes are constitutionally earmarked for certain functions. The gasoline tax is the most common example, but some states have carried earmarking much farther. At the local level, the same effect as earmarking is produced by the formation of special districts, with the taxes imposed by these districts allocated to the specific activities of the districts (schools, mosquito control, and so on).

Earmarking reflects in part the desire to make a particular tax more palatable to the public by allocating its revenues to a purpose for which there is strong popular support; motorists may support a gasoline tax used solely for road purposes but may oppose one if used for general state activity. A sales tax proposal may gain organized support if it is to be used solely to finance education. Some persons argue that it is easier to undertake and expand an activity having strong support by this means than by incorporating it in the general

---

[5] A. Schick, *Budget Innovation in the States* (Washington, D.C.: The Brookings Institution, 1971).

budget. Buchanan has argued that earmarking gives the individual voter and representative greater choice in expressing his attitudes about various forms of government spending.[6]

The primary objection to earmarking is the reduction in budgetary flexibility that results; the hands of the legislative body are tied so far as the earmarked funds are concerned, and relative allocation may differ sharply from present legislative preferences. Flexibility in adapting to changing conditions and preferences is greatly reduced.[7] Long delays in making constitutional changes may perpetuate arrangements that have become obsolete as a result of changes in circumstances. To the extent that representatives have an opportunity to express preferences on various segments of a budget, earmarking gives them no greater choice and in fact lessens their freedom. The income elasticity of demand for the service and that of the earmarked tax may differ widely, complicating the attainment of optimal output levels and tax structures. The best case for earmarking is that for highway financing, with taxes justified as user charges. These taxes have, by usual standards, little justification as sources of general governmental revenue.

PROGRAM BUDGETS AND PPBS

A primary function of the budget system is to facilitate evaluation of proposals and to compare the relative merits of various requests. Unfortunately the traditional presentation of material in budget documents has not facilitated the fulfillment of this task.

First, the usual budget is organized on the basis of agencies, without regard to interdependencies among various agencies or the conduct of closely related work by other agencies. As a consequence, all costs of particular activities are frequently not revealed and the estimation of benefits is made difficult. Second, the budgets are organized in such a fashion as to stress inputs—purchases of various types of items, hiring of various classes of personnel (typists, filing clerks, and so forth)— without reference to the activities or outputs produced with them. Accordingly, relationships between inputs and accomplishments are not established, and no basis is provided for comparing the relative effectiveness of programs from year to year or between jurisdictions or of various alternative means to attain the same end products. Such comparisons are presumably made within the agency in developing its work program and its budget requests, but the information does not show up in the budget. Not infrequently there is no reference to end product at all.

[6] J. M. Buchanan, "The Economics of Earmarked Taxes," *Journal of Political Economy*, vol. 71 (October 1963), pp. 457–69.

[7] W. W. McMahon and Case M. Sprenkle, "A Theory of Earmarking," *National Tax Journal*, vol. 23 (September 1970), pp. 255–62.

Finally, the typical budget is on a strictly one-year (or, often with the states, two-year) basis, without regard to future prospects or commitments arising out of the proposals included in this year's budget.

Program Budgets

These deficiencies have been recognized for decades. Many suggestions have been made for remedying them, and some attempts have been made to do so. The principal approach, in terms of budget structure, is the replacement of the traditional agency and input emphasis by the performance or program budget. The local governments and to some extent the states have also been introducing program features into their budget systems.

The program approach stresses the end product, such as eliminating poverty in urban core areas or providing a retaliatory striking force of a certain magnitude, relative to the goals of governmental activity, rather than the inputs of various types of materials and manpower. The approach is designed to consider the pursuit of policy objectives of government in light of all economic costs of the programs.

Secondly, program budgeting stresses the relationship between various outputs or programs and the inputs necessary to produce them. The work of each department is classified into programs, which are broken down into subcategories. Programs include all work seeking to attain the same objective. This in turn facilitates use of PPBS (Planning-Programming-Budgeting Systems) and cost benefit analysis, discussed later in the chapter.

The primary advantage of the program budget structure is obvious from its nature: It provides a more useful basis for evaluation of agency requests by department, OMB, and Congress by concentrating on end products instead of inputs and by providing better information on costs and benefits. Use of this structure forces the agencies in preparing budget requests to stress product and input-to-output relationships and to give attention to a wider range of benefits and costs.

Planning-Programming-Budgeting Systems (PPBS)

The program budget, per se, is merely a form of budgetary presentation—a particular type of budget document. Accompanying its introduction has been growing use of Planning-Programming-Budgeting Systems (PPBS), first introduced into the Defense Department and subsequently extended to other sectors. These systems seek to integrate long-range planning of governmental activities and programming of specific activities with annual budgeting, making use of the program-budget structure and of various quantitative techniques, with quantification of costs and benefits to aid in the selection of the best alternatives. Programming involves the statement of the relationship of inputs and outputs, under various alternatives, to accomplish the desired objectives. This approach seeks to aid in defining the goals and in choosing among the goals, in specifying alternative programs to attain the goals, in choosing the best alternatives, and, subsequently, in measuring performance. Stress is placed on trade-offs within and between programs. Cost analysis stresses marginal relationships rather than mere overall or average figures. Planning is extended forward for several years, rather than focusing attention on the current year, with reconsideration of the overall plan at frequent intervals as the specific budget for each year is developed. Because of the long-range approach, advance planning is possible, and a better picture is given of all costs and benefits over a period of several years. Accordingly, use of the foot-in-the-door technique on the part of subordinate agencies—starting a program with a small sum of money without calling attention to the large sums that will eventually be necessary to complete it—is made more difficult. PPBS seeks to cut across agency lines to consider overall programs in light of objectives, even though several agencies are involved.

Limitations.   One of the greatest difficulties centers around the specification of outputs. With many governmental activities, the outputs are services not clearly distinguished from the activities involved in the production of them (e.g., education, police protection) and not easily defined or measured. The ultimate objective of police protection is to reduce crime, but this accomplishment is not easily measured or compared. The result is to use a proxy measure, such as the number of arrests—yet maximization of these is of course not the ultimate objective at all. Or, more commonly, a measure of the conduct of the activity—man-hours of patrol duty—is used as an imperfect substitute, but this does not actually measure accomplishments. By the nature of public goods, output does not consist of discrete, separate units. Even with activities that appear to have discrete units there are difficulties of measurement. "Miles of streets paved" is not made up of homogeneous units, since some streets require much more expensive paving than others. Many activities, such as public health, involve a number of subproducts (improved maternity care, lessened infant mortality, health care of the aged, and so on). Not only are the outputs of the subcategories not easily measured but there is no obvious basis for comparison or weighting. In other words, particular activities serve more than one objective.

Secondly, apart from the measurement of output is the problem of defining objectives and establishing priorities of objectives. These decisions require value judgments and are not susceptible to scientific determination. PPBS is primarily useful in choosing among various alternative subordinate programs—various ways of accomplishing secondary objectives, such as selection of alternative means of lessening traffic congestion. Even for these, consideration of all alternatives—all possible tradeoffs—is impossible, and the exact structure of the budget determines which ones will be stressed and which are largely ignored. PPBS suffers from the inherent limitations of cost-benefit analysis discussed below. Actual costs are often difficult to ascertain even with the best methods and involve arbitrary allocations of overhead or common costs. Benefits from various activities in the face of uncertainty—of particular importance in the national defense and foreign policy fields—cannot be estimated with any degree of accuracy. In other words, program budgeting is not capable of solving many of the basic issues of determining optimal government activities; it merely facilitates decision making.

Another criticism is the charge that PPBS tends to centralize decision-making in government, thereby lessening innovation and concentrating power. To some observers, the promoters of the overall PPBS system seek to eliminate political review from decision making as much as possible, with decision-making on grounds of economic efficiency alone and the ultimate aim that decisions be made by computers. Only political review involving conflict resolution can ensure consideration of the relationship of the various programs to community preferences—which cannot be defined in such a way that they can be programmed for computers. Significant value judgments must be made. There is some danger that persons will attach too much significance to the quantitative magnitudes produced by PPBS techniques and that systems techniques will further depersonalize the relations of programs with the people they serve.

Another obstacle to effective PPBS is the lack of adjustment to the existing administrative organization. While the approach seeks to take into consideration elements in programs in a number of administrative agencies, implementation of the programs may be seriously restricted by the structure of the administrative organization—yet change in the organization may be strongly resisted. In departments in which the bureaus are traditionally strong and largely autonomous (e.g., U.S. Treasury), any administrative change or greater centralization of power may be virtually impossible in practice. Furthermore, there may be no single organizational structure that will be entirely satisfactory for implementation of program budgeting. A particular activity, by its very nature, may necessitate participation by several departments, and concentration of the activity in any one department to facilitate program budgeting might seriously impair, rather than improve, the overall attainment of the objectives. Yet failure to concentrate the activities may prevent implementation of programs.

On the whole, program budgeting and PPBS may make very significant contributions to rational decision making about governmental activities and expenditures, but they cannot solve all problems; they do little to define objectives in light of preferences of society for various public goods or to lessen the uncertainties about the benefits from many governmental activities. But they do increase the rational element in governmental decision making.

COST-BENEFIT ANALYSIS

An essential element of PPBS is the careful comparison of benefits and costs of various programs and alternative means of attaining the objectives. Quite distinct from this general comparison of benefits and costs is the technique that has come to be specifically designated as cost-benefit analysis, which developed independently of PPBS although now used as an element in it. Cost-benefit analysis, in this technical sense, involves the ascertainment of the economic desirability of a government investment project—a project yielding its return over a period of years—with analysis of costs and benefits over the entire economic life of the investment. Cost-benefit analysis first developed in the field of water resources and has emphasized investment in physical resources; but to an increasing extent it is being applied to investment in human resources (education, among others). Like PPBS, cost-benefit analysis seeks to take all benefits and costs, direct and indirect, into consideration and to evaluate alternative approaches as well as the overall project in light of objectives.

The Elements in a Cost-Benefit Study

Cost-benefit studies are typically undertaken within a particular government department as a preliminary to budget preparations or as a continuing program to determine efficient expenditure patterns and budget recommendations. Or, they may be undertaken by persons outside government, such as the pioneering work of Otto Eckstein in the water resources field.[8] A study involves several major steps.

Statement of Objectives. Obviously, the goals of the particular programs must be defined: What does the activity seek to attain, in conformity with the overall objective of society of seeking the highest possible level of welfare? The goal may be very specific, such as that of an irrigation project, with the immediate objective of bringing 2,000 acres under cultivation by providing adequate water. The longer-range objective, to increase the country's potential food supply, may be much less well defined, especially in a situation of crop surpluses. Other projects have multiple goals; dams may have flood control, irrigation, navigation, and recreational objectives. Others may have goals

---

[8] Otto Eckstein, *Water Resource Development* (Cambridge, Mass.: Harvard University Press, 1958).

much more difficult to define specifically. The more sharply the goal can be defined, the greater the contribution that cost-benefit analysis can make to decision-making. The priority status assigned to a goal is not a question for cost-benefit analysis to answer, but one of general governmental decision-making relating to priority of goals.

Statement of Alternatives.   With many types of activities, there are various alternative ways of attaining the goals: different locations for irrigation facilities, different timing for parts of the project (one large dam now versus many small dams built successively over a period of time), different methods of construction. Cost-benefit analysis seeks to determine relative benefits and costs of the major alternatives. Obviously, all possible alternatives (such as building irrigation canals by pick and shovel or dams of brick) are not considered, since many are so clearly inferior that they do not warrant attention. Cost-benefit analysis is itself costly, and the number of alternatives considered must be held to a tolerable number.

Analysis of Benefits.   With the objectives defined and alternatives established, analysis proceeds to a consideration of the benefits, which may be defined as the present value of the time stream of contributions to the objective. Determination of benefits involves two major questions: Which benefits are to be included and how are the benefits to be valued?

Direct and Indirect Benefits.   With many projects there are two types of benefits: those accruing directly to the users of the service provided and the indirect benefits or externalities—those accruing to others. For example, a new rapid-transit line offers direct benefits to those who use it and externalities to others, such as reduced congestion for those who continue to drive on less-crowded streets.

Obviously the direct benefits to the users must be included; the problems center around the indirect benefits. Should they be taken into consideration, and which indirect benefits are relevant? The answer to the former question is that evaluation of the undertaking requires that all appropriate indirect benefits be considered, although in practice the inclusion must be restricted to major categories. The answer to the second aspect of the question is more complex. In general, only real or technological benefits, those increasing output potential of society other than through direct use of the activity, are relevant, whereas strictly pecuniary benefits are not. Included in real benefits are reductions in outlays and resource use for other governmental activities, such as those for highways when new rapid-transit lines are built.

If the building of an irrigation dam reduces flooding or provides more pleasant scenery for tourists driving past the lake created by the dam, these are real externalities and should be included in the measured benefits. The building of a subway, by lessening the traffic on expressways, saves time for persons continuing to use their cars and reduces accidents, air and noise pollution, and investment in expressways and parking structures. These benefits alter the physical conditions of production or consumption for persons other than those directly using the activities.

Pecuniary benefits in the form of lower input costs or increased volumes of business and land values arising through the use of the service are not real externalities and should not be included. Many are distributional in nature, benefiting some persons at the expense of others. The values involved are derived from the direct benefits and are reflected in their values. For example, the building of a rapid-transit system may increase the business of stores located near transit terminals and the value of property in these areas, but these are only pecuniary externalities; they are by-products of the use of the subway, and income and property values of others are reduced.[9] Lower production costs due to better highways are not indirect benefits to be calculated separately, as the benefits are reflected in highway usage through lower input costs for producers. With irrigation facilities, the additional revenues and profits received by the firms purchasing and shipping the farm produce, the railroads and trucklines from hauling it, or the farm equipment companies from selling more equipment to the farmers are not real externalities, as the values involved are reflected in the values of the farm produce itself. All economic activity results in this form of "benefit" and those "attributable" to government investment projects therefore should not be included as benefits from the projects.

Valuation of Benefits. The direct benefits to the users of many services can be calculated on the basis of the amounts the users are willing to pay, or in other words, the revenue that would be obtained from the sale of the services with perfect discrimination. As pointed out in Chapter 5, this measures the consumers' surplus, or the difference between aggregate willingness-to-pay and the costs of the project. With electric power plants and city water systems the amounts can be calculated accurately in advance on the basis of experience elsewhere. In other instances, however, only a rough estimate is possible. An irrigation dam will provide a certain amount of water, which will allow cultivation of a given number of acres of land; output of the most profitable crops can be estimated and valued at expected prices. Other costs are then subtracted to determine the benefit from the provision of the irrigation water. Other activities are more difficult to value, as for example, recreational activity. How does one measure the amount a person is willing to pay for spending a day fishing on a lake or camping in a forest preserve, if similar facilities are not actually sold

---

[9] From an equity standpoint, however, those benefiting from higher land values may be required to pay a portion of the costs of the subway construction.

to the users? The number of users of a recreational project can be counted once the project is in operation, and advance prediction may be feasible. But there is no real way of assessing monetary benefits to the projects. Similarly valuation of human life always involves arbitrary assumptions.

Another valuation problem arises from the lack of perfect competition in the market for the activity or in the markets for the products produced as a result of the program. If the government charges for the service and prices on a monopoly basis, total revenues and thus the measure of benefit will differ from the competitive market figure. Or, if the benefits are measured indirectly on the basis of the revenue from the sale of the products produced with the aid of the governmental activity (farm produce grown on the irrigated land), the sales may not be made in perfectly competitive markets or may be made at prices held artificially high by government support programs. Alternatively, particularly with major projects in developing economies, the government project may have such great impact upon the whole price structure that valuation of benefits at either old or new prices gives a misleading picture of the actual benefits.

Apart from valuation difficulties, estimation of benefits is always colored by uncertainties about future conditions.[10] Benefits from irrigation facilities will depend upon future trends in population and farm outputs. If we are to have many decades of farm surpluses, the gains from additional irrigation facilities are much less than they would be if in a few years surpluses will be exhausted and farm product prices will rise. The uncertainties with some activities are so great that any precise conclusions are impossible.

Valuation of externalities encounters even more difficult problems. This task is not impossible with such benefits as reduced expressway congestion resulting from improved rapid transit; it is much more difficult with such benefits as reduced air, water, and noise pollution. With purely public goods the task is particularly difficult, since there is no accurate way of estimating what the community as a whole is willing to pay for the services.

Costs.   Costs of the project may be defined as the present value of resources that will be used in the project, valued at their opportunity cost, that is, the amount that would be paid for them for alternative use. Analysis of cost involves the same type of problem as that of benefits, although costs are more easily calculable. The direct costs include capital costs and operating and maintenance costs over the years. Indirect costs include those created for other governmental agencies (for example, more manpower for OMB, if the program is a major one) and

---

[10] An advanced analysis of the significance of uncertainty is presented by K. J. Arrow and R. C. Lind, "Uncertainty and the Evaluation of Public Investment Decisions," *American Economic Review*, vol. 60 (June 1970), pp. 364–78.

overall costs to society not directly borne by the government. These are in a sense negative benefits. Additional expressways in urban areas will increase air pollution by increasing motor traffic; they may aggravate traffic congestion in downtown areas and increase delays and accidents in these areas; they make the continuation of public transportation more difficult and necessitate subsidies to ensure its continued operation or losses to persons who would wish to use it. Without cost-benefit analysis, indirect costs are often not taken into consideration. There are obviously measurement and valuation difficulties, just as there are with benefits. Air pollution provides an excellent example.

The Need for Discounting

Cost-benefit analysis is primarily employed for long-range projects. Costs will be incurred currently and in the future; benefits will be obtained over a number of years. Because of time preference, benefits in subsequent years are of less importance than benefits in the current year; costs incurred now are more significant than costs incurred in later years because of the existence of interest. Some method, therefore, must be used to adjust benefit and cost figures on the basis of the year in which they occur. This process is referred to as discounting.

Choice of Method of Evaluation

Three types of decisions may be involved in the final evaluation of a project. First, is a particular project warranted or not, under the assumption that funds will be available for all projects that are economically justifiable under the criteria employed? Secondly, if two mutually exclusive projects are being considered, both of which are justified under the criteria, which of the two is to be selected? For example, two alternative reservoir systems to irrigate a particular area are under consideration; only one will, of course, be built. Thirdly, if several projects of a nonmutually exclusive nature are under consideration and funds are not available for all of them, what criteria should be used in establishing priorities?

There are several alternatives approaches:

1. Determination of the present value of the project, by discounting the net excess of benefits over costs $(B - C)$ for each year back to the present year. A project having a positive current value is justified; if funds are available, all such projects other than ones alternative to one another should be undertaken.

2. Determination of the ratio of the present value of total benefits to the present value of total costs (B/C) with the same discounting procedure as in the first method. All projects that are not mutually exclusive with a benefit-cost ratio in excess of 1 are justified.

3. Internal rate of return. Since the first two methods require explicit use of a social discount rate, emphasis has long been given to the use of the internal rate of return method, commonly used by private business. The internal rate of return is the rate of discount that will equate the net benefits over the life of the project with the original cost. While this method ranks various projects, it does not indicate which ones are justified except by comparison with a social rate of discount; use of the latter is therefore not avoided.

If there are no capital constraints and no projects are mutually exclusive, all three criteria give the same answer about the justifiability of various projects. Under the present-value criterion, all projects will be undertaken whose discounted benefits exceed or are equal to the discounted costs $(B \geq C)$. Under the benefit-cost ratio criterion, all projects will be undertaken whose benefit-cost ratio is greater than or equal to 1 $(B/C \geq 1)$. Under the rate-of-return criterion, all projects will be undertaken as long as their rate of return is greater than or equal to the social rate of discount. Inspection of the first and second criteria indicates that they are equivalent for the marginal investment $(B = C$ implies $B/C = 1)$. Some reflection will indicate that they are also equivalent to the third. The internal rate of return is that rate that makes the discounted benefits equal to the discounted costs. If the rate of return just equals the social discount rate, the discounted benefits equal the discounted costs $(B = C)$ at the social rate of discount, which is equivalent to the first two criteria.

But capital is usually not available in unlimited amounts, and projects are often mutually exclusive. Thus it becomes necessary to choose among projects. In this case, the best procedure is to maximize the discounted net benefits $(B - C)$ subject to the existing capital constraint. This criterion can be shown to be formally equivalent to the criteria of choosing all projects whose benefit-cost ratio is greater than some constant, whose value is greater than 1. But the value of this constant is not generally known, and is in fact part of the solution to the first problem. Choosing the wrong constant can lead to inefficient results. Maximizing the discounted net benefits subject to a capital constraint will always ensure that the most efficient combination of projects is chosen.

The rate-of-return criterion will generally give the wrong answer in this situation. This can be shown by considering Figure 7–1, which plots two net present value curves (i.e., the discounted benefits minus the discounted costs) against the interest rate (r). When the interest rate is zero, the investment I_1, whose present value is represented by the line I_1I_1, clearly has a present value greater than that of the investment I_2, whose present value is represented by the line I_2I_2. In fact, for all interest rates that lie between 0 and e, I_1 has a greater present value than I_2. At point e, they each have the same present value, while to the

FIGURE 7–1
Rates of Return from Alternative Projects

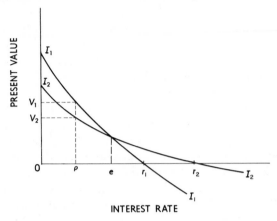

right of point e, I_2 has a higher present value than I_1. The internal rate of return of each investment is that interest rate that makes the net present value of each investment equal to zero. Graphically it is depicted by the point where each present value line intersects the horizontal axis. Thus we can see that I_2 has a higher rate of return than I_1, since the interest rate (r_2) at which I_2's present value is zero is greater than the interest rate (r_1) at which I_1's present value is zero. Suppose the social rate of discount is given by ρ. When the projects are discounted at the interest rate ρ, I_1 has a higher present value than I_2, i.e., V_1 is greater than V_2. Since r_2 is greater than r_1, the rate-of-return criterion tells us to choose I_2 since I_2 has a higher rate of return than I_1. Nevertheless as long as the social rate of discount remains at ρ, the policy-maker should choose I_1. In doing so, by appropriate reinvesting of the net benefit stream resulting from I_1, he can reproduce the net benefit resulting from I_2 and have some funds left over for further reinvestment or consumption. Thus, unless the social rate of discount happens to equal the rate of return of the marginal project, the present value criterion will always lead to a choice of alternative investments that will yield a higher discounted income stream than will the rate-of-return criterion.

The Discount Rate[11]

The benefits from projects that lend themselves to cost-benefit analysis, such as water and transport development, will be obtained

[11] S. A. Marglin, "The Social Rate of Discount and Optimal Rate of Investment," and "The Opportunity Costs of Public Investment," *Quarterly Journal of Economics*, vol. 77 (February and May 1963), pp. 95–111 and 274–89; M. S. Feldstein, "Net

over a period of years. Some of the costs will be incurred at the time the program is undertaken while others will be incurred in subsequent years. But a dollar of benefits now is worth more than a dollar in benefits 10 years from now because interest can be earned on money. In order to evaluate a particular project and to compare alternatives, therefore, a discount factor must be used to determine the present value of benefits and costs.

There are several possible alternative rates:

The Marginal Productivity of Capital in Private Investment. The opportunity cost may be defined as the amount the funds would earn in private investment—the typical earnings rate of money capital in new private investment. This approach is favored by persons who seek to minimize government investment activity, since it produces the highest of the alternative discount rates and therefore allows justification of a minimum of governmental activities. It may also provide maximum pressure toward efficiency in the use of resources in the project. Currently the relevant before-tax figure may be 15 percent or more. But there are several objections. First, risk is greater with private enterprise; if the project is unsuccessful, the owners may lose their entire investment and control of the firm. In contrast, the government, and thus society as a whole, face no similar risk, particularly in view of the wide range of projects being undertaken. It is true that any particular government project does involve some risk of failure, in the sense of waste of the resources, but this is of a different order of magnitude than the risk facing the business firm. Moreover, government projects are backed by the full taxing power of the government. Second, capital markets are by no means perfect. Third, the use of this discount rate is based on the assumption that the resources taken by government are diverted from private investment. But this is not necessarily valid; if the project is tax or user charge financed, the resources are in part diverted from consumption, not investment, and the opportunity cost of use in the investment sector is not relevant.

Social Rate-of-Time Preference. This consideration leads to the second alternative: that the discount rate should be the figure of the rate-of-time preference, the compensation necessary to induce consumers to refrain from consumption and save. This figure would be equal to the marginal productivity of capital in private investment in a riskless world with perfect capital markets but in fact is substantially lower than the actual marginal productivity of capital. The only feasi-

Social Benefit Calculation and the Public Investment Decision," *Oxford Economic Papers*, vol. 16 (March 1964), pp. 114–31; E. J. Mishan, "Criteria for Public Investment: Some Simplifying Assumptions," *Journal of Political Economy*, vol. 75 (April 1967), pp. 139–46; W. J. Baumol, "On the Appropriate Discount Rate for Evaluation of Public Projects," in *The Planning, Programming, Budgeting System: Progress and Potentials* (Washington, D.C.: Government Printing Office, 1967).

ble method is to ascertain the current government bond rate which reflects riskless investment. If, on the whole, persons are willing to purchase the existing issues of bonds at 6 percent, presumably this figure reflects the time preference—the amount that the person must be paid to induce him to save instead of consume. But there are several problems. From all indications most saving is made for reasons unrelated to compensation for time preference and thus the figure is of no particular significance; it measures the compensation necessary to induce persons to forego liquidity and buy bonds rather than to forego present consumption. The actual bond rate is dependent in large measure upon monetary policy, reflecting the current objectives of the Federal Reserve System to expand or contract the supply of money capital. It may also be higher than the figure allowing full employment. The bond rate also involves in part a compensation for risk that is not relevant for time preference.

A variant of this objection maintains that the unadjusted government borrowing rate is unsuitable as a measure of social rate-of-time preference because it does not take into consideration the neglect by individuals of the welfare of persons living in the future. Society as a whole should, therefore, give additional weight to the interest of future generations; accordingly, the social-rate-of-time preference is less than the borrowing rate. If individuals would save more (provided other individuals were also saving more) in the interest of more rapid economic growth, thus giving savings social goods characteristics, the argument would have some validity. But there is no evidence that this is true. Since future generations will presumably—if not polluted to death—have higher real incomes than present ones, there seems little need for formal consideration of their interests relative to those of present generations. Furthermore, if the government wishes to increase the overall rate of real saving, it may do so by encouraging private investment as well as public investment.

Government Borrowing Rate without Reference to Time Preference. The complexities and inadequacies of these approaches suggest the use of a simple rule: the rate of interest at which the particular government can borrow, without any effort to justify this figure on a time-preference basis. In a sense this is the direct cost to the government of obtaining the funds and thus the risk element involved is that of the government, not of lending to private enterprise. Admittedly it is an artificial figure because of the influence of monetary policy on the rate, and it is substantially lower than the figure of marginal productivity of capital on an equity basis in private enterprise. But given the risk element and the fact that government investment is in large measure competitive with private consumption, not private investment, use of the figure is perhaps the most logical. Certainly it is the simplest. This approach would currently produce a discount rate of around 5 percent and thus justify a much greater range of government projects than the 15 percent or so rate of return on private equity investment.

Merits and Limitations of Cost-Benefit Analysis

There are several limitations to the effectiveness of cost-benefit analysis; like PPBS it does not solve all problems of determination of governmental investment expenditures. In evaluating programs of relatively broad scope and in comparing programs with different objectives, cost-benefit analysis is of limited usefulness; it does not solve the problem of optimal outputs of social goods. It does not assist in the establishment of priorities for various goals (national defense versus education, for example). The problems of measurement of benefits and uncertainties are so great with many of the programs that quantification is almost impossible. This is particularly true with public goods, but the problem of complex interrelationships is encountered with other activities as well. The technique tends to overemphasize those benefits and costs that can be quantified compared to those that cannot. Many of the programs have redistributive effects, benefiting some persons at the expense of others, and cost-benefit analysis makes no contribution toward the establishment of the social welfare function that provides society's answer about the relative desirability of various patterns of income distribution.[12] It may, however, aid in measuring distributional effects of alternative programs.

REFERENCES

Burkhead, J. *Government Budgeting*. New York: Wiley, 1957.
A detailed examination of budget systems and practice.

Burkhead, J., and Miner, J. *Public Expenditure*. Chicago: Aldine, 1971, chaps. 6 and 7.
A relatively advanced analysis.

Chase, Sam B., Jr., ed. *Problems in Public Expenditure Analysis*. Washington, D.C.: The Brookings Institution, 1968.

Dorfman, R., ed. *Measuring Benefits of Government Investments*. Washington, D.C.: The Brookings Institution, 1965.
Case studies of benefits and costs of governmental activities in several fields.

---

[12] Solutions to this problem are discussed in A. M. Freeman, "Income Distribution and Planning for Public Investment," *American Economic Review*, vol. 57 (June 1967), pp. 495–508; B. A. Weisbrod, "Income Redistribution Effects and Benefit-Cost Analysis," in *Problems in Public Expenditure Analysis*, ed. S. B. Chase (Washington, D.C.: The Brookings Institution, 1968), pp. 177–223; and R. A. Musgrave, "Cost Benefit Analysis and the Theory of Public Finance," *Journal of Economic Literature*, vol. 7 (September 1969), pp. 797–806.

Haveman, R. H., and Krutilla, J. V. *Unemployment, Idle Capacity and the Evaluation of Public Expenditures*. Baltimore: Johns Hopkins Press, 1968.
A theoretical and empirical analysis with reference to water resources.

Hovey, H. A. *The Planning-Programming-Budgeting Approach to Government Decision Making*. New York: Praeger, 1969.

Marglin, S. A. *Public Investment Criteria*. Cambridge: M.I.T. Press, 1967.

McKean, R. N. *Public Spending*. New York: McGraw-Hill, 1968.
A study of governmental decision-making.

National Bureau of Economic Research. *Public Finances: Needs, Sources, and Utilization*. Princeton, N.J.: Princeton University Press, 1961.
A series of papers on budgeting and decision-making.

Prest, A. R., and Turvey, R. "Cost Benefit Analysis: A Survey," *Economic Journal*, vol. 75 (December 1965), pp. 683–735.
A survey of the literature in the field, with an extensive bibliography.

Steiner, P. O. *Public Expenditure Budgeting*. Washington, D.C.: The Brookings Institution, 1969.

Wildavsky, Aaron. *The Politics of the Budgetary Process*, 2d ed. Boston: Little, Brown, 1974.

Wildavsky, Aaron. *Budgeting: a Comparative Theory of Budgetary Processes*. Boston: Little, Brown, 1974.

8

Government Expenditure Patterns and Tax Structures

The previous chapters have discussed the reasons for governmental intervention in the private market. The existence of public goods, externalities in consumption or production, indivisibilities, market imperfections, problems of the income distribution, and so forth prevent the private market from allocating goods efficiently or equitably. Thus the government must intervene. Part of this intervention can take the form of taxes to ensure that social benefits and costs coincide with private benefits and costs. But part of this intervention must involve the governmental provision of goods and services, either directly or through subsidies to the private market.

In this chapter, we discuss the magnitudes of governmental activities, the patterns of governmental expenditures and some of the major issues involved with them, and the overall structure of the tax system. Primary emphasis is placed on the United States.

PART I
EXPENDITURES

GOVERNMENT EXPENDITURES: AN OVERVIEW

Table 8–1 shows the amount of government expenditures in fiscal 1975 by level of government. Government plays an important role in the economy. In fiscal 1975, government accounted for 37 percent of gross national product (GNP). Of this, the federal government ac-

TABLE 8–1

Government Expenditures, by Function, Fiscal 1974 (all levels of government)

	Amount (*billion dollars*)	*Percent*
Total	556	100
National defense and related	96	17
Education	95	17
Highways	23	4
Interest on debt	33	6
National resources	16	3
Welfare	39	7
Social security	106	19
Health and hospital	25	5
Postal Service	13	2
Veterans' benefits	8	1
Police and fire	13	2
Sanitation	7	1
Other	81	16

Source: U.S. Bureau of the Census, *Governmental Finances in 1974–75* p. 7.

counted for 19 percent of GNP, the state governments accounted for 7 percent, and the local governments accounted for 11 percent.[1]

For all governments, in total, welfare, social security, and health expenditures are the most important (31 percent of the total), followed by defense and protection (19 percent) and education (17 percent). The breakdown for the various levels of government is somewhat different. Welfare and health expenditures and defense expenditures dominate the federal budget, respectively accounting for 41 percent and 26 percent. For the state governments education, welfare and health, and transport and communications are the most important, accounting respectively for 35 percent, 33 percent, and 11 percent of the total state budgets. Education dominates the budgets of the local governments, with 45 percent of the total.

The functions of each level of government are different, as in other countries with a federal system of government. The national government concentrates on defense and welfare expenditures that have a national impact. The local governments concentrate on purely local matters, such as education and the various local public services: police, fire, sanitation, and the like. The states occupy an intermediate position and finance expenditures that affect the inhabitants of the states, such as higher education, health and welfare, and highways, and provide substantial aid for local education and other functions.

---

[1] Note that these figures represent direct expenditures. Because of intergovernmental transfers, the federal and state governments actually have budgets larger than indicated by these figures. Intergovernmental transfers are eliminated to avoid double counting.

The appropriate activity for each level of government to undertake essentially depends on the scope of the activity and the geographic dispersion of its beneficiaries, as discussed in Chapter 19. The broader the dispersion of the beneficiaries, the higher the level of government that provides the service.

THE FEDERAL GOVERNMENT

Table 8–2 shows the behavior of the federal government by major activity for selected years, 1945–76. It indicates that although national defense has consistently taken a high proportion of the federal budget, this proportion has varied considerably and fallen in recent years. It is highest in war years and lowest in periods when the external threat seems relatively small. Defense expenditures accounted for 48 percent of the budget in 1965 at the beginning of the escalation of the Vietnam War. Since then, they have declined steadily as a proportion of the budget and account for a proposed 26 percent of the budget in 1977. As defense expenditures have been falling, those on income security have been rising. In 1977, these accounted for 41 percent of the budget. After defense and income security, no one activity dominates. Interest on the federal debt, expenditures on transportation and commerce, and various veterans' benefits are the major categories after defense and income security. None of these, however, exceeds 10 percent of the budget.

Defense and Related Expenditures

National defense is the classic case of a pure public good. Once it is provided, there is no way anyone can be excluded from its "benefits." Thus it is indivisible in consumption, and its benefits are equally available to all persons; benefits to one person do not reduce the benefits available to others. These characteristics similarly apply to space research and the operation of foreign affairs, which can all be classified together under the general heading or national defense.

Table 8–3 gives the breakdown of defense, space, and foreign expenditures by category for the fiscal years 1967 and 1975 through 1977, as well as the percentages of these expenditures in the total budget. Military personnel, operation and maintenance, and procurement comprise the bulk of defense expenditures. The bulk of expenditures on foreign affairs goes for military and supporting assistance and development assistance. Expenditures on manned space flights dominate the space program.

In assessing the trends in these expenditures, we see that defense expenditures have comprised a shrinking proportion of the total federal budget. In 1963, defense expenditures accounted for 47 percent of

TABLE 8-2
Federal Expenditures by Function, Selected Years 1945–1976

	Billions of Dollars					Percentage of Total Expenditures				
	1945	1955	1965	1970	1976	1945	1955	1965	1970	1976
National defense and related	84.9	42.3	59.0	87.6	102.8	89	62	48	44	26
Income maintenance and health	1.4	9.4	27.4	56.8	160.7	1	14	23	29	41
Agricultural aid	1.6	4.0	4.8	6.2	2.9	2	6	4	3	1
Veterans' aid	1.1	4.5	5.7	8.7	19.0	1	7	5	4	5
Interest	3.5	6.0	10.4	18.3	34.8	4	9	9	9	9
Transport and communications	4.1	1.1	7.4	9.3	19.6	4	2	6	5	5
Education	0.2	0.6	2.3	7.3	18.9	neg.	1	1	4	5
Natural resources and community development	0.1	0.5	2.4	5.6	18.1	neg.	1	2	3	4
General	0.8	1.2	2.2	3.3	6.9	1	2	2	2	2
Revenue sharing	—	—	—	—	7.2	—	—	—	—	2
Total	95.2	68.5	118.4	196.6	373.5*					

* After deduction of offsetting receipts. Percentages figured on gross amount ($391 billion).
Source: *Budget of the United States Government, Fiscal Year 1977.* This is the source for Tables 8-2 through 8-9.

TABLE 8–3

Defense, International, and Related Expenditures 1967; 1975–1977 (dollars in billions)

Category	1967	1975	1976	1977 est.
Defense related:				
Defense	67.5	85.0	89.8	99.6
Military assistance	0.9	1.0	1.4	0.5
Atomic energy	1.3	1.5	1.6	1.8
Total defense related	69.1	86.6	92.8	101.1
International:				
Assistance	4.0	3.7	5.0	4.7
Conduct of foreign affairs	0.4	1.0	1.2	1.3
Total	4.7	4.4	5.7	6.8
Space and technology:				
Space research	5.3	2.9	3.2	3.3
General science research	.9	1.0	1.1	1.2
Total	6.3	4.0	4.3	4.5
Total, three categories	80.1	95.0	102.8	112.4
Percent total expenditures	51	28	26	27

Note: In this and succeeding tables, "other" items, including negative ones, have been omitted and, therefore, the columns do not add to the totals indicated.

the budget; in 1973, 32 percent of the total budget; in 1977, 25 percent. Even during the peak year of the Vietnam War in 1968, defense expenditures took a smaller share of the federal budget (45 percent) than they did in 1963 (47 percent). Similarly, international affairs have played an increasingly small role in the budget. From a peak of nearly 4 percent in 1963, they have fallen to their current levels of 2 percent of the federal budget. Finally, the share of space research has also fallen in recent years. In 1966, space research accounted for 4 percent of the federal budget, but only 1 percent in 1977.

Few, if any, would question that defense and related services must be provided by the government if they are provided at all. Clearly the private market cannot provide national defense, space exploration, foreign aid, and similar items. Since there is no way people can be restricted in benefits received from these activities on the basis of their contribution, they will not make their preferences known voluntarily through the market mechanism. But there is considerably less agreement about the proper scope and size of the defense budget. The efforts in recent years to reduce the size of military expenditures, the effort to divorce military aid from economic aid in the foreign-aid bill, the cutback in the moon program, and the defeat of the SST all indicate a fairly widespread questioning about the importance of defense expenditures and a shifting of society's priorities away from national defense.

As we discussed in Chapter 3, the proper scope of government activity can only be determined through the political process. While this may be an imperfect mechanism of allocating government expenditures, it is at least workable. Because the exclusion principle does not operate with respect to public goods, the free-market mechanism is totally unworkable in allocating these activities. But because of the nature of defense activities, there is bound to be wide diversity among reasonable men about the proper scope of national defense. Most of this diversity depends upon perceptions about the nature of the external threat, national honor, and so on. Thus in times when the external threat is clearly seen by all, as in World War II, virtual unanimity prevails on the scope of national defense.

The current period, however, is one when the question of the external threat is not so clear-cut. Those who view the world situation in terms of a continual power struggle between the United States and the Soviet Union (and to a lesser extent between the United States and China) and believe that detente is proving to be meaningless support large defense expenditures, large amounts of military aid, and large expenditures on space exploration (the latter partly because of its military implications and partly because of prestige). If the deterence of a nuclear attack on the United States and the resulting nuclear holocaust depends upon the United States maintaining sufficient nuclear stockpiles, sufficient armed forces in Western Europe and Southeast Asia, and sufficient retaliatory forces to ensure that any strike will be met by equal or greater force, one must be led to the conclusion that the maintenance of a large defense establishment is essential. Certainly this view of the problem prevailed during the cold war in the 1950s.

If one accepts the principle that detente, despite its ups and downs, does lessen the chances of nuclear war, and that Soviet defense spending is influenced by our own levels of defense spending, the case for reducing such spending is strengthened.

Income Maintenance

In terms of dollars spent, income maintenance is now the most important function of government. This consists of the various social security and welfare programs and the farm price support program to maintain farm incomes. Table 8–4 indicates that in fiscal 1976 these programs totaled $132 billion or 33 percent of the total federal budget. The bulk of these expenditures go for social security payments and other forms of social insurance, unemployment, and other retirement programs. The remainder is spent on public assistance and farm support programs. Table 8–4 indicates that the importance of income maintenance has risen markedly in recent years.

The social security, unemployment, and retirement payments can be regarded as a form of insurance. Thus, to some extent they reflect repayments for earlier contributions to the various retirement and un-

TABLE 8–4

Federal Income Maintenance Expenditures, 1967, 1975–1977
(dollars in billions)

Category	1967	1975	1976	1977
Retirement and disability:				
Old age*	22.8	69.4	77.2	87.4
Employee retirement	2.0	7.0	8.3	10.0
Unemployment	2.5	13.5	19.4	16.9
Public assistance:				
Supplementary security	na†	4.8	5.2	5.9
Grants, states	na	5.1	5.9	6.2
Housing assistance	na	2.0	2.5	3.1
Food stamps	na	4.6	5.6	4.7
School lunch	na	2.0	2.6	3.1
Total, public assistance	3.4	18.8	23.6	22.9
Overall total	30.8	108.6	128.6	137.1
Percentage	20	32	33	33
Agricultural assistance:				
Income stabilization	2.5	0.8	1.9	0.7
Research	.5	0.8	1.0	1.0
Total	3.0	1.6	2.9	1.7
Percentage	2	1.5	0.7	0.4

* Including railroad retirement.
† na: not available.

employment trust funds. It should be clear, however, that the transfer is not perfect. High-income people typically pay more into the various trust funds than they receive, while low-income people receive more. Thus, in addition to providing a cushion to income losses resulting from retirement, disability, unemployment, and the like, the social security program serves as a means of transferring income.

Public assistance covers areas where social security fails—mothers of young children and unable to work, the blind, the disabled, and the elderly who are not covered by social security or unemployment insurance.

Although the farm program is, in a sense, aimed at maintaining farm incomes, its administration and goals differ substantially from the other income-maintenance programs. While social security, unemployment compensation, and welfare payments are aimed specifically at ensuring that individuals have sufficient income to live their lives in a certain dignity and without excessive hardship, the farm program is primarily aimed at ensuring that farming is sufficiently profitable to maintain a strong agricultural sector. With agriculture relatively prosperous, this program has declined in recent years. Because, however, the farm program is directly aimed at keeping farm commodity prices high rather than farm incomes high, there generally is little correlation between the income of the recipients and the payments they receive from the federal government. In fact, it has been well documented that most money paid out goes to large agricultural producers with relatively high incomes rather than to small, impoverished farmers. Thus the primary goal of the farm program appears to be the maintenance of a strong agricultural sector rather than the maintenance of farm incomes above some minimum socially acceptable level.

The difference in emphasis between the farm program and the other income-maintenance programs highlights a basic difference in the reasons for making income transfers. One relates primarily to efficiency, the other to equity. If the income distribution as a whole enters into people's utility functions or if individuals' utility depends upon the income levels of other members of society, governmental intervention is needed in the form of income transfers to ensure that resources are allocated as efficiently as possible. The externalities created by the income distribution or the public-good quality of the income distribution as a whole require that the government make income transfers that will lead to an increase in welfare on the part of both the giver and the recipient of the transfer. Equity considerations may also require that the government make further income transfers that will increase social welfare, although these transfers reduce the welfare of the specific giver while increasing the welfare of the recipient. Because society values the marginal gain in welfare to the income recipient more than it values the marginal loss in welfare of the giver, social welfare will increase as a result of the income transfer.

The redistribution caused by the farm program can probably be explained in terms of economic efficiency. If a strong farm sector is deemed to have social benefits in excess of those measured by the profitability of farming alone, society will choose to subsidize the farm industry, as it does through the farm support program. In contrast, the other income-maintenance schemes can be explained primarily in terms of equity. Society redistributes income from the well-to-do to the poor because the loss in social welfare arising from the income payments of the rich is assumed by society to be less than the gain in social welfare arising from the income received by the poor.

Interest and Veterans' Services

Veterans' payments and, in part, interest payments are related to defense since they primarily reflect costs incurred in fighting past wars. The $19.0 billion spent on veterans' services in fiscal 1976, shown in Table 8–5, clearly reflects payments for past defense-related services, while the interest payments of $34.8 billion primarily pay for debt incurred to finance wars. Both have remained remarkably constant as a percentage of total federal spending.

Unlike the defense expenditures on military personnel or hardware, veterans' and interest payments are transfers and as such do not reduce the goods and services available for private consumption. Inter-

TABLE 8–5

Veterans' Benefits and Interest Payments, 1967, 1975–1977 (dollars in billions)

	1967	1975	1976	1977
Veterans				
Income security	4.7	7.8	8.4	8.3
Readjustment benefits	0.3	4.6	6.0	4.2
Health	1.4	3.7	4.1	4.5
Total	6.9	16.6	19.0	17.2
Percentage of total	4	5	5	4
Interest	12.6	31.0	34.8	41.3
Percentage of total	8	9	9	10

est payments are contractual obligations akin to private-market transactions. When the government chooses borrowing rather than taxes or printing money to finance its expenditures, society presumably make a decision that its welfare will be higher if expenditures are financed by bonds rather than by taxes or printing money. But this decision is usually based on macroeconomic considerations of economic welfare relating to economic stability rather than the microeconomic considerations of welfare that we have discussed in this book thus far.

While the payments of veterans' benefits can doubtless be explained in terms of consumption externalities in the sense that persons are sensitive to the income and health levels of veterans, these payments have a slightly different rationale from those dictated by pure economic efficiency. Veterans' benefit payments are related to the services that veterans performed for their country. In effect, veterans are singled out as being socially meritorious because they incurred specific costs while in the service. At the very least, these costs reflect losses in income and career opportunities; at the most they reflect losses in life. Thus veterans' benefits are designed to compensate for the inadequate payments received by the veterans when they were serving in the armed forces. The payments, therefore, can be explained in terms of equity as well as economic efficiency.

Interest payments have risen rapidly in the last decade as interest rates have gone up and government debt has increased.

Health

With the inception of Medicare and Medicaid, health expenditures have become a major activity of the federal government (Table 8–6). Health expenditures have risen from $1.1 billion in 1963 to $38 billion in 1972. While they comprised little more than 1 percent of the federal budget in 1963, they comprised 7.2 percent of the budget in 1972 and 8 percent in 1977. The bulk of these expenditures go for Medicare and

TABLE 8–6
Federal Expenditures on Health, 1967, 1975–1977 (dollars in billions)

Category	1967	1975	1976	1977
Medicare	3.1	14.8	17.8	21.9
Medicaid	1.1	6.8	8.1	9.3
Health research	1.6	1.8	2.1	2.2
Other	0.9	4.2	4.1	1.0
Total	6.8	27.6	32.1	34.4
Percentage of total	4	8	8	8

Medicaid, which respectively accounted for $17.8 and $8.1 billion of the total health expenditures in 1976. The other large item in the health budget ($2.1 billion) went for the development of health resources.

Clearly, some health expenditures have a public-good quality. The benefits from basic medical research or the prevention and control of health problems are pervasive and not readily excludable on the basis of monetary payments. Unlike apples or oranges, public health cannot be distributed in proportion to payments made. Because the exclusion principle cannot apply to public health or basic research, the government must support these activities.

In contrast, the expenditures on Medicare and Medicaid are primarily income transfers in kind. Musgrave uses the term "merit goods" for the wants such goods satisfy, in recognition that society views adequate health standards as sufficiently meritorious that it is willing to ensure that the poor and the elderly have access to them. But as Musgrave and others have pointed out, the concept of merit goods is nothing more than another way of expressing the fact that the health levels of the poor or the elderly affect the utility levels of others in society. Thus merit goods reflect the existence of consumption externalities. Because the consumption of certain goods and services on the part of certain groups in society affects the welfare of the other members of society, the private market mechanism fails to provide a sufficient amount.

Transportation and Communication

During the past decade, expenditures on commerce and transportation have remained relatively stable as a percentage of the federal budget although they have grown in absolute size (Table 8–7). In fiscal 1963 these expenditures accounted for 5.2 percent of the federal budget while in fiscal 1976 they accounted for 5.0 percent. The largest portion of these expenditures is made for ground transportation and in particular for the federal highway program. Air transport accounts for

TABLE 8–7
Federal Expenditures on Commerce and Transportation, 1967,
1975–1977 (dollars in billions)

	1967	1975	1976	1977
Surface transport				
Highways	ns	4.8	6.6	7.0
Mass transit	ns	0.9	1.5	1.8
Railroads	ns	0.5	1.2	1.2
Total	4.1	6.5	9.5	10.1
Air transport	1.0	2.4	2.7	2.8
Water transport				
Shipping	ns	0.5	0.6	0.7
Coast guard	ns	0.9	1.0	1.2
Total water	0.8	1.4	1.7	1.9
Total transport	ns	10.4	14.0	14.9
Postal service	1.1	1.9	1.7	1.5
Plus nonbudget	—	1.1	1.8	1.4
Total	9.2	16.0	17.8	16.5
With nonbudget	9.2	17.1	19.6	17.9
Percentage	5	5	5	4

ns: not separately stated.

the next largest element of the transport budget. The $2.7 billion in fiscal 1976 primarily reflects federal subsidies to airports. The expenditure on waterways is primarily made to extend and maintain the inland waterway system, to pay subsidies to the maritime fleet and maintain the Coast Guard.

Governmental activity in all of these areas reflects the existence of production externalities or indivisibilities. In the case of highways, airports, or waterways, only one facility is typically needed. If it were provided by private firms, there would be danger of monopolistic exploitation. Collection costs on highways would be substantial. A network of roads serving all points is also regarded as essential for national unity and a nationwide market, even though many roads would not cover their costs.

In the last three years, for the first time in a century, federal funds have been provided to the railway industry to facilitate rehabilitation of lines, and reorganization of the eastern railroads following the collapse of the Penn Central. This action reflects recognition of the externalities of the preservation of an efficient rail transport system.

Mass Transit. A major issue in domestic ground transport development today is the relative emphasis to be given expressways and rapid-transit facilities in urban areas. While a few cities undertook development of rapid-transit facilities at an early date, primarily public transport has been provided by private companies—local transit systems and commuter railroads. Thus public funds concentrated entirely on expressways while public transport deteriorated. This trend in turn increased still more the demand for expressway construction. The lag in expressway construction behind needs, its tremendous expense, its external diseconomies in terms of carving up cities and adding to noise and air pollution finally brought renewed interest in improvement and extension of rapid-transit facilities, including commuter-railroad operation. Moving persons in congested areas by rapid transit is far more economical and less expensive than continued expansion of expressways, and limited federal aid is now being provided for the purpose. Rarely can these facilities be operated profitably, but the externalities in the form of lessened need for expenditures on expressways and lessened congestion on streets warrant operation of these transit facilities at less than full cost. Unfortunately certain interested groups, particularly automobile associations, have resisted expansion of these transit facilities—probably shortsightedly so—and some transportation experts have questioned the ability of rapid transit to pull persons from the highways. One aspect of urban development has admittedly made the task of providing rapid transit more difficult: the tendency toward decentralization in urban areas, which disperses traffic flows. Los Angeles is the extreme example. But with growth in metropolitan-area traffic there may nevertheless be many instances in which the volume of traffic will be adequate to make rapid transit, at least separate bus lanes on expressways, advantageous. The field of urban transit has provided the worst instance of misallocation of resources attributable to the location of one form of transportation in private hands, the other—highways—in public hands.

Water Transportation. Traditionally, in the United States the federal government has undertaken improvements in navigable waterways. Many of these have been essential for important transport routes. Others, unfortunately, have taken the form of "pork barrel" expenditures benefiting limited areas at substantial cost to society. Few areas of governmental activity have come under greater fire over the years. The problem is compounded by the failure to charge the firms using improved waterways for any portion of the costs. More recently, substantial subsidies have been paid to the owners of the American merchant fleet to keep the vessels in operation in competition with lower-cost foreign vessels. Needless to say, questions have been raised about the desirability of this policy, which can be defended only on grounds of international prestige and national defense.

Air Transportation. In recent decades, the federal government has provided funds to develop airport facilities in conjunction with municipal governments. The air-transport firms are charged for use but in insufficient amounts to cover all costs. In addition, the federal government subsidized the air-transport industry to enable it to get started. The trunk carriers have in recent years been able to operate profitably without aid, but the secondary carriers still receive subsidy—a questionable policy if continued indefinitely. Subsidization of one form of transport when others are not can lead to distortion of resource use and indirectly benefits users who are in no need of financial assistance.

The most pressing problem facing air transport is the growing congestion of air space in and around metropolitan airports, a natural facility that cannot be expanded. The consequence has been increasing delays and costs of operation and accident hazards. Construction of more airports does not increase air space unless they are well separated from the old airports; if they are, the other problem of air transport, the long period required to get from terminal to the downtown area, is aggravated. Improvement of connecting ground transport has long been neglected.

The air congestion and the airport-to-downtown problem have revived interest in better and faster rail passenger service between major cities under 400 miles apart. For these distances the overall time-saving for air travel is small, and if much of this travel can be returned to rail transport, the air congestion problem can be significantly reduced. Rail passenger service, however, has been unprofitable for some years; in 1971, the federal government established AMTRAK, a semigovernmental enterprise, to preserve a basic rail passenger network. Deficits are met from federal funds. Corridor service between major cities under 400 miles or so can be justified because of congestion of road and air space; it is difficult to justify preservation of longer-distance rail passenger service given the availability and economy of other forms of transport.

The most discouraging aspect of this sphere has been the continuing rise in deficits of the postal system. When Congress transferred the system from government agency to separate status in 1970, it intended that the system cover its costs. But this has not occurred. Postal rates have risen sharply, yet losses have not been cut. The problem is complicated by the fact that some types of mail do not pay the costs for which they are responsible while first-class mail more than covers costs, but political pressures make readjustments difficult.

Other Activities

Education and Manpower. Since the passage of the education act in the mid-1960s, federal expenditure on education and manpower has comprised 4 to 5 percent of the federal budget (Table 8–8). In fiscal 1976, these expenditures totaled $18.9 billion. A large portion went for federal aids to vocational, secondary, and elementary education and manpower training.

Some of these expenditures can be explained in terms of consumption externalities and merit goods, some in terms of production exter-

TABLE 8-8
Federal Expenditures on Education and Related Social Services 1967, 1975-1977 (dollars in billions)

Category	1967	1975	1976	1977
Elementary, secondary	2.6	4.6	4.6	4.4
Higher education	1.2	2.0	2.7	2.3
Other	0.4	0.9	0.8	0.9
Training programs	1.2	4.0	6.9	5.0
Social services	.6	3.3	3.6	3.7
Total	6.0	15.2	18.9	16.7
Percentage of total	4	5	5	4

nalities. To the extent that persons are sensitive to the quality of education available to the disadvantaged members of society or to their job opportunities, federal aid for education or manpower training can be justified on the consumption-externalities basis. To the extent that the overall level of productivity and income in society is dependent upon an educated and skilled work force, federal aid for education or manpower training reflects the existence of production externalities that cannot be captured by the private market. In addition, income-distribution considerations play a major role; better education for the poor increases job opportunities and breaks the self-perpetuating chain of poverty.

Natural Resources. Expenditures on natural resources in fiscal 1976 reached a level of $11.8 billion, or 3 percent of the federal budget (Table 8-9). Major items are water resources, energy development and pollution control. Because of concern over petroleum prices and shortages, the federal government is embarking on a crash program to increase energy resources—an externality type of activity.

A relatively new element is the providing of large grants to the states and local governments for pollution control.

Recreation, flood control, and forest management are other elements in the program.

All of these are subject to externalities, and private developers would fail to capture all of the benefits arising from their provision. This is easiest to see in the case of flood or pollution control, since the benefits are diffuse and not generally subject to capture by the market mechanism. Hydroelectric developments have elements of natural monopolies. The output necessary for lowest average cost is so great that the usual market will not allow full attainment, and governmental provision is required for efficient production. Also to the extent that the development of some regions is dependent on cheap electric power, hydroelectric projects can create significant externalities. This was certainly true in the case of TVA, and it doubtless plays a role in most power projects.

TABLE 8-9

Federal Expenditures on Natural Resources, Community Development, Revenue Sharing, and General Government, 1967, 1975–1977 (dollars in billions)

Category	1967	1975	1976	1977
Natural resources				
Energy research	na	1.4	2.0	2.7
Energy, total	.8	1.6	2.6	3.4
Pollution control	.2	2.5	3.1	4.4
Water resources	1.8	3.3	3.8	3.9
Forest and land management	.7	1.3	1.3	1.0
Recreation	.3	0.8	0.9	1.0
Total	3.7	9.5	11.8	13.8
Percent of total	2	3	3	3
Nonbudget				
Energy, rural electrification	—	0.5	0.5	1.1
Law enforcement	0.6	2.9	3.4	3.4
Percent	0.4	1	1	1
Community and regional development	1.4	4.4	5.8	5.5
Percent	1	1	1	1
General government	1.6	3.0	3.5	3.4
Percent	1	1	1	1
Revenue sharing	0	7.0	7.2	7.4
Percent	0	2	2	2

Community Development and Housing. Community development and housing accounts for 1.4 percent of the federal budget. Most consists of grants for community development.

The expenditures on community development and housing also reflect a combination of consumption and production externalities. To the extent that the housing levels of the poor affect the welfare of the other members of society, governmental intervention is needed to provide an adequate amount of housing services. Expenditures on community planning and development probably reflect externalities created by these expenditures that could not be captured by the private market. The Model Cities program is aimed at upgrading wide regions of the central cities to make them more attractive places to work or live. Water and sewer grants are needed because of the indivisible nature of these facilities. Thus, a large portion of these expenditures reflects the divergence between the social and private benefits arising from activities related to the housing, sewerage, water supply, and other needs of urban areas.

General Government. Table 8–9 indicates that expenditures on general governmental services accounted for only 1 percent; law enforcement adds another 1 percent of the federal budget. These include such services as central fiscal management, operation of the executive department, law enforcement and justice, and others. These activities clearly fall into the realm of public goods. The provision of legal, tax, and administrative functions is a prerequisite for a smoothly functioning government. The benefits from these activities are diffuse and intangible, but very real. Like national defense, there is no way to allocate these activities by a market mechanism, and they must be provided by the government. The total is a very small fraction of the budget.

Revenue Sharing. New since 1972, revenue sharing—block grants to the states and local governments—constituted 2 percent of the budget.

STATE AND LOCAL GOVERNMENTS

Just as with the federal government, the activities of the state and local governments are based on considerations of economic efficiency or equity. Their programs are either necessitated by failure of the private market to allocate goods efficiently or they are designed to increase the equity of income distribution. The main difference between activities undertaken by the federal and state and local governments lies in their geographical area of impact. The federal government undertakes activities that are national in scope, such as defense, or that involve a large number of geographically dispersed but nationally interdependent projects, such as highways. In contrast, the state and local governments undertake activities of limited geographical impact. State government direct expenditures are concentrated in higher education, highways, and welfare; grants to the public schools are significant intergovernmental budget elements. For the local governments, expenditures are concentrated in elementary and secondary education and a wide range of local services.

State Governments

Table 8–10 shows that outside of its general and protective expenditures, which comprised approximately 5 percent of the total state expenditures in fiscal 1975, the state governments spend relatively little on purely public goods. In fiscal 1975, the largest two items of state expenditures were education, 35 percent, and welfare, 27 percent. Education expenditures were partly for aid to local schools, partly for state higher education. The next most important categories of direct expenditures were highways and health services.

A portion of the states' expenditures for education goes to higher education, which is supported by government because it creates externalities and can most efficiently be provided on a statewide basis. The greater his or her education, the higher a person's productivity. Thus, by making higher education readily available to the residents of the states, the state governments are not only trying to ensure that all

TABLE 8–10
State Expenditures by Function, 1975

Category	Amount (billions of dollars)	Percentage
Education		
Grants, primary and secondary	31.1	20
Higher education	17.8	12
Total	54.0	35
Welfare	43.2	27
Highways	17.5	11
Public health	10.1	6
Resources	3.6	2
Police, correction	3.6	2
General	3.9	3
Interest	3.3	2
General support, local government	7.4	5
Other	9.6	7
Total	156.2	

Source: U.S. Bureau of the Census, *State Government Finances in 1975.*

qualified persons have access to higher education but also are recognizing that higher education creates significant external benefits and, therefore, should be made available to all.

Just as higher education creates benefits to the inhabitants of a state, so does a highway system. Thus, the state governments spend 11 percent of their total budgets on highways. These expenditures are in recognition of the fact that highways must be the responsibility of government and that a free interchange of people and goods is beneficial to a state. While the federal government concentrates upon highways that are national in scope, such as the interstate system, the state governments concentrate on the state highway systems and the relevant portions of the federal highway systems to ensure a free flow of commerce within the states.

The expenditures on public welfare that are made by the state governments are largely in response to incentives provided by the federal government, which gives matching grants for state welfare expenditures. These expenditures are also made in recognition that the poor in any state are considered to be the responsibility of the people in that state. Rapid increases in welfare expenditures are placing a severe financial strain on the states and leading to demands for increased federal aid or federal assumption of all welfare costs.

Table 8–11 shows the trend in the relative importance of major expenditure categories 1962–75. Education rose, fell, and then has been rising again, but has remained close to 40 percent of the total for a decade. Highway expenditures have steadily declined, relatively; welfare has risen, though not significantly, percentagewise, since 1970, while health has remained at essentially the same level.

TABLE 8–11

Distribution of State General Expenditures by Major Function, 1962–1975 (percent)

Year	Educa-tion	Highways	Public Welfare	Health and Hospitals	All Other
1975	39.1	12.6	18.5	7.4	22.4
1974	39.1	13.2	18.8	7.1	21.8
1973	38.5	13.9	20.1	6.8	20.7
1972	37.7	16.2	19.3	6.8	20.0
1971	38.1	17.1	18.2	6.8	19.9
1970	39.1	17.4	17.4	6.8	19.4
1969	39.9	18.4	16.0	6.9	18.8
1968	40.2	19.6	14.3	7.0	18.9
1967	39.9	21.2	13.5	6.9	18.9
1962	34.3	25.5	13.7	7.5	19.0

Source: U.S. Bureau of the Census, State Government Finances, 1975.
Social security trust expenditures are omitted.

Local Governments

By far the largest expenditures of the local governments are made for elementary, secondary, and vocational education. In the 1975 fiscal year, as shown in Table 8–12, $65 billion were spent by the local

TABLE 8–12

Local Government Expenditures by Function, 1975.

	Billions of dollars	Percentage of total
Education	65.0	45
Streets and roads	8.3	6
Welfare	9.7	7
Health, hospitals	9.9	7
Police and fire	10.5	7
Sewage and sanitation	7.4	5
Housing, urban renewal	3.0	2
Parks and recreation	3.5	3
Finance, general administration	5.4	4
Interest	5.5	4
Other	14.9	10
Total	143.1	100

Source: U.S. Bureau of the Census, *Governmental Finances in 1974–75.*

governments on education, 45 percent of their total spending. No other item approached this figure.

Until recently it has seemed logical that local governments provide elementary and secondary education. Governmental provision of these services reflected the benefits of education over and above those directly received by the recipient. Certainly an educated workforce increases the overall productivity of the economy. The provision of these services by local governments reflected the view that the people of each community should essentially have local option about the quantity and quality of education they provided their children—that areas preferring high levels of education should be free to provide such levels and those preferring lower levels should be free to do so.

It was recognized long ago, however, that this freedom could not be absolute because a certain minimum education was regarded as essential throughout the state. Accordingly, the states have for decades exercised some control over the levels of education and provided some financial assistance in the form of state grants to the school districts, in part to equalize the financial position of rich and poor districts. As will be explained in Chapter 19, in recent years there has been increased concern about the remaining inequalities in the ability of various school districts to finance an adequate level of education. As a consequence of changing attitudes and a series of court cases noted in Chapter 19, it is possible that the states may assume most of the costs of school financing.

After education, the local governments spend the greatest amount on various public services: fire, police, sewerage and sanitation, general control, parks and recreation, and so on. All of these are public goods in the strict sense of the word. Once they are provided, there is no feasible way of excluding anyone within a given jurisdiction from their use. Thus the rich and the poor living within a given city have equal access (in theory) to the benefits of police and fire protection, although given practical considerations, they do not always have it.

Government expenditures by function in Canada are shown in Table 8A–1 in the Appendix to this chapter.

PART II
REVENUE STRUCTURES

OVERALL REVENUES

In the fiscal year ending June 30, 1975, governments as a whole in the United States received $517 billion in revenue, of which $76 billion involved net increases in debt. Of the total, the federal government received $303 billion, the states $98 billion, the local governments $117 billion (excluding intergovernmental transfers). The total can be broken down into several classes:

1. General revenue—all revenue other than that included in the three special categories below.

General revenue is primarily made up of taxes, which totaled $332 billion: $190 billion at the federal level, $80 billion at the state level, $61 billion at the local level. Charges and miscellaneous revenues yielded $71 billion: $32 billion at the federal level (primarily postal receipts, sales of surplus farm products, etc.), $17 billion at the state level, $23 billion at the local level.

2.   Public-utility revenue, at the local level, yielded $11 billion. Similar items at the federal and state levels are included as general revenues.

3.   Liquor-store revenue, primarily state, yielded $2 billion.

4.   Insurance-trust revenue, yielded a total of $100 billion, of which $81 billion was federal (primarily payroll taxes for the old-age annuity system), $17 billion at the state level (primarily unemployment-insurance payroll taxes), and $2 billion at the local level.

This classification may not appear to be entirely logical but is presented because data are most readily available on this basis, following Bureau of the Census classifications.[6]

BREAKDOWN OF TAX REVENUES

Table 8–13 provides the breakdown of tax revenues by type, in total, for all levels of government for 1975. The income tax, yielding

TABLE 8–13
Tax Revenues, by All Levels of Government (1975 fiscal year)

	Billions of Dollars	Percent of Total Tax Revenue
General taxes:		
Income:		
Individual	143	34
Corporation	47	11
Total	191	45
Property	51	12
Consumption related:		
Customs	4	1
Sales and gross receipts	29	7
Excises	38	9
Total	71	17
Other	18	4
Payroll taxes	95	22
Total	427	100

Source: U.S. Bureau of the Census, *Governmental Finances, 1974–75.*

$191 billion, or 45 percent of total tax revenues, was the primary single source. The federal government collected $163 billion of this total; the states $25 billion, local governments $2.6 billion. The individual income tax is far more productive than the corporate tax in total.

---

[6] U.S. Bureau of the Census, annual series: *Governmental Finances; State Government Finances; State Tax Collections; City Government Finances.*

The second major levy consists of the payroll taxes of the social security program (including payments into government employee retirement systems, which are the equivalent of the social security levies). These are primarily federal, financing old-age annuities, health, disability, and survivors' insurance; the state figure is primarily for unemployment compensation; the local government figure is almost solely for retirement for their own employees. These payroll taxes yielded $95 billion in fiscal 1975.

The consumption-related taxes yielded $71 billion, or 17 percent of total tax revenues in fiscal 1975. The federal excises, primarily on liquor, tobacco, and motor fuel, constituted the chief element, $17 billion, while the state and local sales taxes provided $29 billion.

Finally, the property tax, now almost solely a local government revenue, yielded $51 billion, or 12 percent of total tax revenues. This item exceeded any one of the consumption-related tax categories but is less than the total of these categories.

FEDERAL REVENUES

At the federal level, as shown in Table 8–14, the personal income tax is by far the chief source of revenue, yielding 43 percent of total fed-

TABLE 8–14
Federal Tax Revenues (1976 fiscal year)

	Billions of Dollars	*Percent of Total Tax Revenue*
Personal income taxes	130.8	43
Corporate income taxes	40.1	13
Social security payroll taxes	92.6	31
Excise taxes	16.9	5
Estate and gift taxes	5.1	2
Customs duties	3.8	1
Miscellaneous	8.3	3
Total	297.5	100

Source: *The Budget of the United States*, fiscal year 1977.

eral tax revenues fiscal 1976. The structure of the tax is outlined in Chapters 10 and 11.

The corporate income tax yielded 13 percent of the total tax revenue in fiscal 1976; thus the two income taxes together yielded 56 percent of total federal tax revenues. As noted later in the chapter, this is a relatively high figure compared to many other countries.

The payroll taxes, primarily for the financing of old-age annuities and health, exceeded the corporate income tax, yielding 31 percent of total revenues; this element has been growing steadily.

The excise taxes yielded only 5 percent of total tax revenue for the 1976 fiscal year. The major excises are those on liquor products ($5.4 billion), cigarettes and tobacco products ($2.1 billion), and motor fuel ($4.1 billion). The revenue from the motor fuel tax is earmarked to the highway trust fund.

The other sources are relatively minor. Estate taxes yielded $5.1 billion, or 2 percent of the total; customs duties $3.8 billion or 1 percent. The estate-tax yield is limited because of very high exemptions and numerous opportunities for escaping the tax via gifts. The United States does not use customs duties deliberately for revenue purposes, the yield being incidental to the protective function.

The pattern of federal tax revenues has not undergone major change over recent decades, as shown in Table 8–15 below. Income taxes

TABLE 8–15
Relative Federal Tax Revenues by Major Source, Selected Years

	Percentage of Total Tax Revenues						
	1929	*1939*	*1949*	*1959*	*1969*	*1971*	*1976*
Personal income tax	31	19	44	50	47	46	43
Corporate income tax	35	21	28	22	20	14	13
Total income taxation	66	39	72	73	67	60	56
Excise taxes	15	32	19	13	8	9	5
Estate and gift taxes	2	6	2	2	2	2	2
Payroll taxes	...	14	6	11	22	26	31
Customs duties	17	6	1	2	1	1	1

Source: Tax Foundation, *Facts and Figures on Government Finance 1971; Budget of the United States.*

have been declining relatively, as have the excises, as the payroll taxes have jumped sharply.

STATE REVENUES

In 1975, the states received $38 million in intergovernmental grants (most federal) and $80 million in taxes (except payroll), $17 million in charges and interest, $18 million in insurance-trust revenue; the total, including miscellaneous, was $154.6 million.

Table 8–16 shows overall state tax revenue by major source for the 1975 fiscal year. Sales taxes have become the major single revenue source, yielding 31 percent of total state tax revenues. These taxes have grown steadily in use and importance since their introduction in the 1930s.

The second major source of general state tax revenue is the individual income tax, now in use (January 1977) in 44 states. The corporate income tax is of less importance, providing 8 percent of the total; it is

TABLE 8–16

State Tax Revenues, 1975 Fiscal Year

	Billions of Dollars	Percent of Total Tax Revenue
Sales taxes	24.8	31
Motor fuel	8.2	10
Motor vehicle and operators licenses	3.9	5
Alcoholic beverages......................	2.0	3
Tobacco products........................	3.3	4
Special business taxes	5.1	6
Personal income.........................	18.8	24
Corporation income......................	6.6	8
Other general corporate taxes	1.0	1
Property	1.5	2
Death and gift	1.4	2
Severance	1.7	2
Other...................................	0.4	1
Total	80.1	100

Source: U.S. Bureau of the Census, *State Tax Collections in 1975.*

used in 46 states. The two income taxes together yield slightly more than the sales tax. Another $1 billion, or 1 percent of the total, comes from other general corporate levies, such as capital stock taxes, used in some states in addition to or in lieu of corporate income taxes.

The third important category consists of the taxes imposed to finance highways, the motor fuel tax yielding $8.2 billion, or 10 percent of the total; motor vehicle license fees, $3.9 billion, or 5 percent of the total in 1975. Both of these categories are used in all states; in most states the revenues are allocated to highway use. They have declined in relative importance in recent years, partly because the rates are specific, unrelated to motor fuel prices.

Taxes on tobacco products and alcoholic beverages combined yielded 7 percent of the total in 1975. There are also special levies on insurance companies and public utilities. This tax is in a sense an extension of the sales tax to public utilities by separate levy, whereas many states apply the sales tax itself to these industries. State property taxes, now of significance only in a few states, yielded 2 percent of the total, and severance taxes on the output of petroleum and other natural resources, 2 percent.

Historically, the major changes include the decline of the state property tax, especially during the thirties when exclusive use was given to the local governments in most states; the rise of the motor fuel taxes in the twenties; the revival of income taxes in the twenties and thirties; and the growth of sales taxes from 1932 on.

The overall figures are reasonably typical of many states, which rely on both sales and income taxes. But there are exceptions. One group of states, five in number, still resists use of the sales tax and instead relies heavily upon income taxes; Oregon, with income taxes much higher than the national average and heavy reliance on property taxation at the local level, is the prime example. At the other extreme, another group of states still resists the income tax; this group included, until the late sixties, such major industrial states as Michigan, Ohio, Illinois, and Pennsylvania. But one by one, fiscal pressures have forced these states to impose the tax, and, as of January 1977, only six states (Florida, Nevada, South Dakota, Texas, Washington, and Wyoming) do not use personal income taxes. The tax in New Hampshire, however, is of very limited scope (this is the only state not to use either a general sales or income tax), and the taxes in Connecticut and Tennessee are limited in scope. In general, the trend has been toward use of both of these major levies. In such states, therefore, the primary tax issues center around the question of the relative reliance on one form or the other.

LOCAL GOVERNMENTS

As shown in Table 8–17, in 1975 local governments received 40 percent of their revenues from intergovernmental grants; 38 percent

TABLE 8–17
Local Government Revenues, 1975

Revenue Sources	Billions of Dollars	Percentage of Total Revenue
Taxes	61.3	38
Charges and utility revenues	33.9	21
Insurance trust revenues	2.2	1
Intergovernmental revenue	62.0	40
Total	159.7	100

Source: U.S. Bureau of the Census, *Government Finances in 1974–75.*

from taxes, 21 percent from charges, public utility revenue, and other nontax sources. Table 8–18 shows that in 1975, 82 percent of the tax revenues came from the property tax; 7 percent from local sales taxes, 3 percent from local excise taxes, 4 percent from local income taxes, and 4 percent from miscellaneous tax sources. These figures relate to all local governments. Cities, which are the primary users of local sales taxes, receive 11 percent of their revenues from these taxes, whereas school districts receive nothing from this source in most states. Municipal income taxes are limited to 11 states and are of substantial importance only in Pennsylvania, Ohio, Michigan, Kentucky, and the counties of Maryland and Indiana. Local sales taxes are almost universal in California, Illinois, New York, Texas, Oklahoma, and Utah and wide-

TABLE 8-18
Local Government Tax Revenues, 1975

Tax	Billions of Dollars	Percent of Total Tax Revenue
Property	50.0	82
Income	2.6	4
Sales	4.3	7
Excises	2.1	3
Other	2.3	4
Total	61.3	100

Source: U.S. Bureau of the Census, *Government Finances in 1974-75*.

spread in a number of other states. In general, the only significant change in local financing over the years has been the slow growth of nonproperty taxes (sales and income) and the growing importance of intergovernmental grants. These trends are almost certain to continue as a result of objections to the property tax.

INTERNATIONAL COMPARISONS

Precise comparisons of tax structures among various countries are always difficult, in light of varying allocation of functions by level of government, different nomenclature, and varying treatment of social security and other semitax revenues. Some rough comparisons can be made, however.

Canada

Tables 8-19 through 8-21 show the relative importance of various revenues at federal, provincial, and local levels in Canada for 1975. Major contrasts with the United States include the following:

1. The much greater reliance on indirect taxes at the federal level. The federal sales tax, which has no counterpart in the United States, yielded 13 percent of the total revenue in 1975 (including social security revenue), customs duties yielded 6 percent, and excises yielded 4 percent for a total of 23 percent. The somewhat greater reliance on customs duties reflects in part the greater importance of foreign trade in the economy.

2. The absence of municipal sales and income taxes. Local governments in Quebec did impose sales taxes but these were merged into the provincial tax in 1964.

In general, however, the tax structures of the two countries are very similar.

TABLE 8–19

Tax Revenue, Canada, All Levels of Government, 1975*

	Billions of Dollars	Percent of Total Tax Revenue
Income taxation:		
Personal	17.4	37
Corporate	6.0	13
Sales tax	7.2	15
Excises	2.8	6
Customs	1.8	4
Death duties	negl.	—
Property taxes.....................	4.1	8
Health insurance premiums	0.7	1
Business taxes.....................	0.4	1
Payments to pension systems	3.9	8
Other............................	3.3	7
Total	47.6	100

* The social security supplements to the major taxes are included in the figures as given.

Source: Canadian Tax Foundation, *The National Finances, 1975–76,* and *Provincial and Municipal Finances, 1975.*

TABLE 8–20

Dominion Tax Revenue, Canada, 1975 Fiscal Year

	Billions of Dollars*	Percent of Total Tax Revenue
Income taxation:		
Personal	11.7	41
Corporate	4.8	17
Nonresident...............................	0.4	1
Sales tax	3.9	13
Excise taxes and duties	1.1	4
Customs	1.8	6
Oil export charges	1.7	6
Pension and unemployment fund premiums	3.4	12
Total	28.9	100

* These figures include old-age security tax revenue:

Personal income tax	1.6
Corporation income tax	0.6
Sales tax	1.0
Total	3.2

Source: Canadian Tax Foundation, *The National Finances, 1975–76.*

TABLE 8–21
Provincial and Municipal Tax Revenues, Canada

	Billions of Dollars	Percent of Total Tax Revenue
Provincial, 1975 fiscal year		
Income taxation:		
Personal	5.3	38
Corporate	1.4	10
Sales tax	3.3	24
Excises	1.7	12
Death duties	0 1	1
Health insurance premiums	0.7	5
Social insurance	0.5	4
Other	0.8	6
Total	14.2	100
Municipal, 1974 fiscal year		
Property taxes:		
Real property	3.9	87
Special assessments	0.2	4
Business taxes	0.4	9
Total	4.5	100

Source: Canadian Tax Foundation, *Provincial and Municipal Finances, 1975.*

Other Industrial Countries

Data for a group of industrial countries (members of OECD) are presented in Table 8–22.

Several features of these systems warrant brief reference:

1. The very heavy reliance on payroll taxes for social security purposes, particularly in France, West Germany, and Italy (and other EEC countries as well). These are collected from both employer and employee and constitute a major supplement to the wage bill.

2. The relatively greater reliance on excises and sales taxes compared to the United States.

Further breakdown of the data not shown in the table shows two additional features:

1. National sales taxes are important in all of the countries except Japan and the United States.

2. The relatively small reliance on wealth taxes, which are primarily levies on net wealth. The property tax, per se, is very much an Anglo-Saxon tax, limited primarily to the United Kingdom, the United States, and countries of the British Commonwealth.

The fact that relative reliance on income taxes is less in these countries does not demonstrate that income tax rates are lower. While comparisons are difficult, it does not appear that United States income taxes, personal or corporate, are in fact heavier than those of most other industrialized countries; this is indicated by the data of ratios of income tax collections to GNP.

TABLE 8–22

Major Tax Revenues—OECD Member Countries, 1973

	Taxes on Goods and Services as a Percent of		*Taxes on Income and Profits as a Percent of*		*Social Security Contributions as a Percent of*	
	GNP	*Total Taxes*	GNP	*Total Taxes*	GNP	*Total Taxes*
Australia	7.3	30.7	12.6	53.0	0	0
Austria	13.8	37.6	9.5	25.9	9.5	26.0
Belgium	11.2	30.6	13.3	36.3	11.0	30.0
Canada	11.4	33.5	15.5	45.9	2.9	8.6
Denmark	15.1	34.2	24.0	54.4	2.3	5.3
Finland	14.1	38.4	16.6	44.9	5.3	14.5
France	12.5	33.9	6.3	17.0	15.2	41.1
Germany	9.9	26.7	12.8	34.3	12.9	34.5
Ireland	16.1	49.7	9.4	29.0	3.1	9.5
Italy	10.0	34.1	5.7	19.4	12.1	41.2
Japan	4.3	19.0	10.8	47.7	4.1	18.3
Luxembourg	8.2	22.2	15.6	42.1	10.3	27.8
Netherlands	11.1	25.5	15.1	34.5	16.0	36.6
New Zealand	7.2	23.9	19.8	66.0	0	0
Norway	17.6	38.4	13.5	29.3	13.4	29.3
Portugal	8.3	36.9	5.2	23.0	6.0	26.9
Spain	7.0	31.5	4.4	19.9	9.3	42.1
Sweden	13.0	29.8	19.4	44.7	8.7	20.0
Switzerland	6.2	23.3	10.9	41.2	7.2	27.3
United Kingdom	9.2	27.9	13.4	40.7	5.5	16.8
United States	5.3	18.8	12.5	44.6	6.1	21.9

Source: *Canadian Tax Journal*, March–April 1976, p. 155. Used by permission of the Canadian Tax Foundation.

APPENDIX

TABLE 8A–1

Government Expenditures by Function as a Percentage of Total Expenditures, Canada 1975–76

Function	*Federal 1976*	*Provincial 1975*	*Municipal 1975*
National defense	8	0	0
Debt charges	10	6	7
Unconditional intergovernmental grants	8	6	—
Education and manpower	6	24	42
Health and welfare, pensions	35	38	17
Veterans	2	0	0
Transportation and communication	6	9	13
Agricultural aid	2	0	0
Public works, development	5	8	—
General	12	3	4
Protection	*	3	8
Miscellaneous	*	6	9
Payments, oil importers	6	0	0

* Included in other categories.
Source: Canadian Tax Foundation, *The National Finances, 1975–76; Provincial and Municipal Finances, 1975.*

REFERENCES

Bird, R. M. *The Growth of Government Spending in Canada.* Toronto: Canadian Tax Foundation, 1970.

The Budget of the United States Government, annual.

The Budget in Brief, Annual.

Canadian Tax Foundation, annual publications:
The National Finances.
Provincial and Municipal Finances.

Setting National Priorities, Washington, D.C.: The Brookings Institution, annual volumes. Authors differ from year to year.

U.S. Bureau of the Census, annual publications:
Governmental Finances.
State Tax Collections.
State Government Finances
City Government Finances.

PART II

Allocation and Distribution:
Taxation

9

Revenue Structure
Decision-Making

Governmental activity requires the transfer of resources from the private sector of the economy to the governmental sector or, with distributional activities, from some persons to others. Governments could make the transfer by commandeering physical resources. This was done for local road-building activity in the past and more recently, in the form of the draft, for personnel for the military. With respect to income redistribution, governments could snatch clothing off the backs of the rich and give it to the poor. But such action is neither efficient nor, by usual standards, equitable and is strongly resisted by the persons adversely affected. In practice, governments find it much more efficient to obtain command over money and use the money to acquire the desired resources or transfer it to the beneficiaries of welfare activities. The problem of obtaining command over resources, therefore, becomes the problem of financing governmental activities. Under conditions of full employment the financing methods have the dual function of providing the government with the means to acquire the resources and at the same time reducing private-sector purchasing, so that the government may obtain the resources without competing with private-sector demand and driving up prices. In periods of less than full employment, only the first function must be fulfilled; as explained in later chapters, use of financing methods that minimize the second function—that do not reduce private sector purchasing—will aid in the elimination of unemployment. This chapter is concerned, except for incidental references, with periods of full employment.

The Concept of Burden. The reduction in private-sector output that is necessitated by governmental use of resources is called the *direct burden* of the governmental activities. This burden is, of course, more than offset by the gains from the governmental programs if the latter are established on the basis of the preferences of the community, with a net gain from the activity as a whole. The concept of burden refers only to the effect on private-sector output of governmental use of the resources. For simplicity in terminology, we usually refer to the burden as pertaining to the tax or other revenue source used to finance the program. But actually it is appropriately attributable to the governmental expenditures.

The Decisions. There are several types of decisions that must be made relating to financing of governmental activities.

Are methods not directly compulsory, such as borrowing or the creation of money, to be preferred? Is it possible and desirable for governments to charge for the services, thus using the same method of financing employed by firms in the private sector of the economy? Shall taxation be used, that is, shall persons be required to give up a portion of their incomes to finance the governmental activities? If taxes are used, what criteria are to be employed in the selection of the taxes and the establishment of the precise tax structure?

In a democratic society, the decisions are presumably made by legislative bodies in such a fashion as to reflect the preferences of contemporary society. Economic analysis can facilitate decision-making by indicating the requirements that the revenue structure must meet if optimal economic efficiency is to be attained. It may also be able to establish the economic consequences of various alternative policies. But it cannot establish the criteria, which involve value judgments about equity and relative weighting of equity and economic efficiency considerations. These can be determined only on the basis of attitudes of the majority in the society. Legislative bodies presumably base their policies—in a very crude and uncertain way—on these preferences.

MONEY CREATION

National governments have an "easy" way to finance their activities—namely, by money creation, either by printing money or by borrowing from the central banking system.[1] There appears to be no direct burden; the method appears to be entirely painless since the government gets its funds without anyone giving up anything. Why do persons not universally favor this method in preference to taxation or in preference to borrowing, which necessitates payment of interest?

---

[1] Such "borrowing" is essentially money creation, not true borrowing. Amounts are simply credited to the government's account with the central bank. The government then draws on this account.

From an economic standpoint, the basic objection is that creating money fails to fulfill the second function of financing government; it does not reduce private spending in monetary terms. In fact, by increasing commercial bank reserves,[2] borrowing may actually increase private spending as well as finance government spending. The consequence, under conditions of more or less full employment, as societies long ago learned by experience, is inflation. Inflation is disliked for several reasons. The burden of the transfer of resources from the private sector rests upon those persons whose incomes lag behind the increase in the general price level and those whose assets, such as bonds, decline in real value. Persons whose incomes rise with the price level and who own no fixed-dollar-value assets escape any contribution to the costs of government. Inflation is also disliked for other reasons: the fear that incomes will lag behind prices; the labor strife generated; the lessened willingness to buy bonds; the uncertainty and disorganization introduced into the economy. Financing by money creation would also remove the direct restraint on government spending and prevent attainment of optimal levels of governmental activity.

As a consequence, governments typically avoid money creation as a source of financing. Unfortunately, however, the reasoning and the experience that are applicable to full employment periods are carried over into periods of unemployment, when, as will be explained in Chapter 21, there is strong justification for the use of money creation to avoid reducing private spending.

GOVERNMENT BORROWING

A second alternative for financing government is borrowing. In its usual form the provision of the funds is strictly voluntary; persons currently give up purchasing power in exchange for bonds, which will ultimately be repaid.

Borrowing and Capital Formation

The primary difference between borrowing and taxation is that the former allows each person greater freedom in choice of time for downward adjustment of private-sector consumption. With taxation a person must make the adjustment immediately; with borrowing, he or she may make it now if he or she wishes (reducing spending and using the funds to purchase bonds and thus offset the liability for public debt) or may defer his or her reduction in spending to a later period, when taxes are higher because of interest and principal payments. If a

---

[2] As the government draws on its account with the central bank and the persons who receive the checks deposit them in their accounts, the deposits of their banks with the central bank are increased.

person follows the former alternative, borrowing offers no advantage. But the borrowing technique alone gives the alternative of postponement. Theoretically, if capital markets were perfect and risks uniform, the person could accomplish the same result by borrowing privately to meet his or her tax liability and curtailing consumption at some date in the future. In practice, the government can borrow more cheaply than individuals because of lesser risk.

A major consequence of this difference is that consumption is reduced much less and, under conditions of full employment, investment is reduced much more relative to financing of the activities by most forms of taxation, which in practice compel many persons to curtail consumption immediately. Under conditions of full employment, borrowing, like taxation, does reduce private-sector spending as smaller sums are available for consumption or investment; the difference is the greater impact upon investment relative to consumption. Only if otherwise idle funds are borrowed by government will total private-sector spending not be reduced by the amount of the governmental spending. In this instance, the velocity of money increases, with effects the same as those of money creation.

The heavier relative reduction in investment results, in a sense, in a portion of the burden of current governmental activities being transferred forward to future generations, since these generations will inherit fewer capital goods and per capita output will be less. This reasoning is valid only with full employment; as explained in later chapters, with unemployment, financing of governmental activities may increase total spending in the economy because the funds would not have been used either for consumption or investment; thus both investment and consumption may increase through absorbing unemployed resources.

Direct Shifting of Burden to Future Generations

It is commonly argued that borrowing results in a much more direct transfer of burden from present to future generations than through its effect upon investment and capital formation. As persons often view borrowing, its use allows society to avoid any burden now—since no taxes are collected—while future generations must pay the taxes to cover interest and principal on the bonds. This argument is not valid, however, for internal borrowing if burden is defined, as above, as a reduction in private-sector output due to the transfer of resources to the governmental sector. With this definition, the burden (assuming full employment) of the governmental activities is borne at the time the expenditures are made, whether the expenditures are financed by taxation or borrowing. Thus, in this sense, the cost of World War II was borne during the war through reduced output of goods for civilian use,[3] as resources were diverted from the manufacture of automobiles and other civilian goods to national-defense items. The burden was borne at the time regardless of use of taxation or borrowing; borrowing did not permit a shift of resources from future periods to the war period.[4] In turn, persons in subsequent generations have no fewer resources available because of the borrowing, and real private-sector GNP is not reduced. The future generations inherit both the bonds and the obligations that they represent. When interest and principal payments are made, funds are merely transferred from some persons to others in the same generation, a transfer that may have some adverse effects on the economy.

Given these definitions and assumptions, there is no shifting of real costs and future generations are burdened with the expenditures of the present only through the effects of the frictional effects of the taxes in the future and the effects of borrowing in reducing the current rate of capital formation more than taxation does. There are, of course, distributional implications: The distribution of burden among individuals will be different with borrowing than with taxation. The argument does not apply to external borrowing, which gives the jurisdiction command over resources from the outside and requires transfer of resources (through a surplus of exports over imports) when interest and principal are paid.

If, however, as argued by Buchanan, burden is defined as the reduction in personal satisfaction resulting from the financing of governmental activities, no burden is incurred at the time the money is borrowed.[5] The bondholders purchase bonds voluntarily, exchanging liquid wealth for them and presumably increasing, not decreasing, their satisfaction. The taxpayers pay no tax currently for the activity and suffer no burden. Bondholders have either given up consumption voluntarily to buy the bonds, or, more likely, have purchased the bonds in lieu of other assets. At the time the debt is retired, the tax collected from the taxpayers places burden on them and reduces their consumption or saving. The bondholders, on the other hand, experience no gain; they merely exchange their bonds for money, which in turn they may place in other assets. A net burden has been placed upon the

---

[3] That is, output of goods was reduced below potential levels. Since there was substantial unemployment when the war began, little overall cutback in civilian production was required. Much of the burden was borne from use of idle resources and, indirectly, by persons serving in the armed forces instead of in preferred occupations.

[4] Burden suffered by future generations from more rapid depletion of natural resources is not related to the use of the borrowing method of financing.

[5] J. M. Buchanan, *Public Principles of Public Debt* (Homewood, Ill.: Irwin, 1958); and the collection of articles in J. M. Ferguson, *Public Debt and Future Generations* (Chapel Hill, N.C.: University of North Carolina Press, 1964).

future generations, shifted forward from the borrowing generation. If the debt is not repaid, no burden is created except from the payment of interest; if governments borrow in perpetuity, no one bears burden other than interest charges.

The significant issue on the question of shifting of burden is the relative usefulness of the alternative definitions of burden. The first, of more general applicability, stresses that borrowing does not enable one generation to pull resources from another to use in conduct of its activities, although by reducing the rate of capital formation it will reduce the potential real income and consumption of future generations. The difference between the effects of taxation and borrowing on capital formation is one of degree, but the difference may be substantial. The definition related to individual satisfaction, on the other hand, is useful in analyzing individual decision-making relating to borrowing and debt retirement and the distributional implications. Thus borrowing does shift burden to future generations, as individuals view the burden, but it does not shift resources to the present and it does not reduce future real income and consumption except through its effect on the rate of capital formation.

Shifting to Future Generations and the Preference for Borrowing

The belief—valid as the individual sees borrowing and in part for the community as a whole—that borrowing permits the shifting of burden to the future plays a major role in shaping popular attitudes toward borrowing. To what extent do persons wish to shift the burden to the future? With a narrow concept of self-interest, it would appear that they would always wish to push burden off on to others. But this viewpoint is by no means universal. First, to the extent that persons regard their heirs as extensions of their own lives, they will consider the interests of their heirs as well as their own. To many persons, the shifting of burden of current governmental activity to future generations is inherently unfair.

Second, attitudes are influenced by the expected time distribution of benefits. If benefits will be spread over a number of years, persons will regard the use of borrowing to spread burdens forward as justifiable. The best example is nonrecurrent expenditure on major capital improvements that will last for a number of years. Long life of a particular item of capital equipment does not in itself make borrowing desirable. If a large city spends $1 million each year on new school buildings and is expected to do so in the future, there is no long-range gain from borrowing, as the annual amortization payments will soon equal the annual expenditures, even though each school building will last for a long period. The nonrecurrent character of expenditures makes borrowing attractive as a means of spreading costs forward.[6] Other nonrecurrent expenditures yielding benefits over a period of years include those for "crash" programs to raise standards of education or public health and for conduct of major wars. With all these activities, a widely accepted view is that since the activities convey benefits to persons in the future, the present generation is justified in passing a portion of the costs forward. If governments could not borrow, voters would be biased against any projects yielding their benefits over a period of time.

Other Influences on the Choice of Borrowing

Borrowing introduces a much greater degree of uncertainty about peoples' ultimate tax liability. If the current tax approach is used, uncertainty is lessened but not entirely removed. The significance for their decision will depend upon their estimates of future tax liabilities. If they believe that they are likely to pay less in the future than they would pay now, they will have greater preference for borrowing. This attitude may be found on the part of persons close to retirement age. On the other hand, if people expect their tax liability to rise, as would younger persons expecting increases in their incomes, they will be less sympathetic toward borrowing. Buchanan argues that a prime reason persons oppose borrowing is their fear that other persons will not prepare themselves for payment of their share of the debt, and thus one who succeeds will bear a disproportionate amount.[7] Accordingly they prefer taxes, which others cannot escape.

A final influence that affects the choice between borrowing and taxation is the concern that many persons have for the interest burden created by the borrowing and the significance of both the interest and the debt for the functioning of the economy. The interest is an obvious phenomenon. While any individual may escape his or her share of the interest cost by reducing his or her consumption immediately—as the person would do if he or she were taxed—and buying bonds, most persons appear not to consider this alternative. The more sophisticated citizen is also aware that a debt may have adverse consequences for economic development. Taxes necessary to pay interest charges may retard investment, and fear of the debt, per se, may be a confidence-reducing influence on the economy. At the subordinate levels of government, persons may fear that a heavy outstanding debt may deter establishment of new industry. Finally, many persons, reasoning by

---

[6] J. M. Buchanan, *Public Finance in Democratic Process* (Chapel Hill, N.C.: University of North Carolina Press, 1966), chap. 17.

[7] Buchanan, *Public Debt*.

analogy with the individual, regard borrowing as inherently undesirable if it can be avoided.

In summary: Persons will be most inclined to favor borrowing in preference to taxation:

1.   When financing by taxation would require a sharp temporary curtailment in consumption.

2.   When they expect their own tax liabilities to be less in the future than at present.

3.   When they feel that shifting of burden to future generations is desirable, either as a simple device to escape tax or because the expenditures will yield benefits in the future.

Their preference for borrowing will be greater:

1.   The lower the interest rate level and, thus, the interest burden.

2.   The less the fear that borrowing and the debt will have undesirable consequences for the economy.

3.   The weaker their emotional bias against debt.

Government versus Individuals

While we assume that democratic governments seek to follow the wishes of the people and that their decisions relative to borrowing reflect the preferences of the voters, governments nevertheless exercise considerable influence over voter choices. Governments, per se, may take different attitudes toward the desirability of borrowing than the typical voter and thus disregard or seek to alter voter preferences. There is presumably some disposition on the part of legislatures and administrations in an unsophisticated society to have stronger preferences than voters for borrowing, since by this means they can provide services (which voters like) without taxes (which they dislike). The provision of governmental services becomes very painless—so long as no thought is given to the future. This attitude was common on the part of local governments in the United States in the last century. Today the typical voter has learned to consider the future as well as the present, and borrowing thus has somewhat less appeal to government. On the other hand, governments may understand the consequences on the economy of borrowing better than the average voter and may be less willing to use it.

In summary: Apart from use in periods of unemployment as an instrument of fiscal policy, borrowing is primarily confined to:

1.   Financing of local government capital investment projects believed to be of a nonrecurrent nature, yielding their benefits over long periods of time.

2.   Financing of wars or sudden increases in spending on defense or on other activities that would necessitate very sharp increases in tax rates and drastic curtailment of consumption.

3. Financing deficits when governments are subjected to strong demands for services yet equally strong opposition to tax increases. Such borrowing does not usually continue for long periods.

CHARGES FOR GOVERNMENTAL SERVICES

As explained in Chapter 5, certain types of governmental services can be sold to the users; the case for doing so was outlined in that chapter. But, as noted, most governmental services cannot be sold at all because they are public goods. Others offer externalities, and charging an amount sufficient to cover all costs would defeat the purposes of governmental undertaking of the activities. With other services, such as education, distributional considerations dictate against charging or charging in full. Strictly distributional activities, by their nature, cannot be sold to the users. Accordingly, charges do not represent a viable alternative for financing most governmental activities.

TAXATION: ATTITUDES TOWARD USE OF TAXES

Governments, representing the community as a whole, may require the members of the community to contribute to the support of governmental functions through the payment of taxes. In a sense, these represent charges paid by the community to government to cover the costs of the collective goods the community obtains. But from an individual standpoint they differ sharply from charges, in that the individual has no choice about paying them if he or she is liable under the law, and payment of the tax, as such, does not enable him or her to obtain more governmental services than he or she otherwise could. Taxes, in general, serve both functions of a revenue system: They provide funds and they reduce private consumption and investment spending. Because of the limitations of the other methods of financing, taxation is the normal method.

Persons typically regard taxes as necessary evils, ones that they must accept in order that desired governmental services can be provided without the use of even less acceptable methods of financing. Attitudes toward the general level of taxation and tax increases are dependent, of course, on attitudes about the desirability of the governmental programs and attitudes toward the government itself. Persons opposed to expansion of activities will fight tax increases or the use of new taxes that will facilitate additional spending.

Levels of Taxation

Popular attitudes toward existing levels of taxation may be substantially different from those toward significant increases. Persons may accept existing tax levels or small annual increases with little resistance but oppose strongly any sharp increases. In part, this reflects the usual resistance to curtailment of living standards, in part a purely psychological reaction to higher taxes, per se. This phenomenon has been called the threshold effect; only some drastic financial emergency, such as a major war or widespread closing of schools for lack of funds, may jolt voters into accepting a major new tax or sharp rate increases. The federal income tax rates introduced in 1941–42 to finance the war would have been regarded as intolerable in 1939. While there was pressure to reduce rates after the war, there was no thought of lowering them to prewar levels. Thresholds appear to develop on certain particular taxes; in many states today there is strong resistance to increases in sales tax rates beyond 5 percent, although increases up to this figure encountered nominal resistance. In many states, breaking past such a threshold or introduction of a major new tax—such as the income tax in Michigan, Illinois, and Ohio or the sales tax in Wisconsin—occurred only because of a dire financial emergency. Desired functions could no longer be financed by existing taxes, and since the power to borrow was restricted, drastic curtailments in functions would have been necessary had the tax thresholds not been broken.

Attitudes toward Structures

Attitudes toward relative reliance on various forms of taxes and the precise structures of these taxes are influenced—under the usual maximization assumption—by a person's desire to minimize the tax he or she must pay;[8] thus a person prefers tax adjustments that will reduce his or her burden and increase that of other persons.[9] Under a narrow self-interest interpretation of the maximization assumption, the majority in society would favor the enactment of taxes that placed the entire burden on the minority—a consequence that the wealthy minority sometimes fears, despite their greater political strength. Actually, this is far too narrow an interpretation of motivation. A more realistic interpretation is that persons favor those taxes that will place upon themselves no more burden than they regard as essential, consistent with the attainment of the objective, namely, the financing of the services. In other words, persons recognize that they cannot expect to escape

---

[8] That is, that each person seeks to maximize his or her satisfaction.

[9] Note the study by Elizabeth Likert David, "Public Preferences and State-Local Taxes," in *Essays in State and Local Finance*, ed. H. E. Brazer (Ann Arbor, Mich.: University of Michigan Institute of Public Administration, 1967), pp. 74–106. David concludes that self-interest considerations explain most of the variations in individual attitudes toward alternative tax measures.

payment if the governmental services are to be provided and financed; they recognize that placing all the costs on a small minority is impossible, and thus they must make some contribution themselves. They are also influenced by concepts of fairness; few persons seek to place upon others all of the costs of services from which they benefit. Persons will oppose taxes that they feel strike them "unfairly" and allow others to escape a "reasonable" burden, and they will favor taxes they expect to concentrate on others, especially when the "others" are nonhuman persons, such as corporations—thus the popularity of the corporate income tax—but they do not seriously hope to avoid all payment. There is frequently a strong bias in favor of existing tax structures; uncertainty is minimized, as well as the need for decision-making about new proposals. Any change offers the danger of heavier burden.

Ideological biases play a more significant role in influencing attitudes toward taxation than those toward most governmental expenditure programs. Organizations come to support certain taxes or tax features and fight others, without reconsideration of changing conditions, and partisans of these groups accept the position without serious evaluation. They fear disapproval of fellow members if they do not and they accept the group position as a shortcut to decision-making. Labor unions typically oppose sales taxes and favor income taxes, although many of their members may pay more under the latter than under the former with given total revenue yield. Political parties become committed in like fashion. There are curious instances of strong biases about particular taxes acquired by a large part of the population of a state without any obvious reason—the long-standing bias in Oregon against sales taxation.

A person's preference for a tax may be increased if the tax—or an increase in it—is tied directly to expenditures that he strongly favors. Many persons would approve a property-tax increase to allow elimination of overcrowding of schools but oppose one for a general increase in local government spending. The gasoline tax is one of the least unpopular taxes because it is so closely tied to the financing of highways. Finally, attitudes toward choice of taxes and tax structures are greatly influenced by various standards or criteria—often called principles—of taxation that have come to be widely accepted. The principal standards are reviewed later in the chapter.

The Advisory Commission on Intergovernmental Relations, a joint federal-state-local agency, has had surveys made in recent years of attitudes toward various taxes. Table 9–1 reproduces the results of these surveys for 1972, 1973, and 1974, the latest available. The decline in acceptance of the federal income tax is undoubtedly a result of increased awareness of loopholes allowing escape by the wealthy. The increased popularity of the property tax reflects somewhat less re-

TABLE 9–1
Public Attitudes toward Various Types of Taxes, United States, 1972–1974

	Percent of Total U.S. Public			
The Major Types of Taxes	*March 1972*	*May 1973*	*October 1973**	*April 1974*
Which do you think is fairest?				
Federal income tax	36		29	26
State income tax	11		11	13
State sales tax	33		24	24
Local property tax	7		15	14
Don't know.............................	13		21	23
Which do you think is the worst tax— that is, the least fair?				
Federal income tax	19	30	25	30
State income tax	13	10	13	10
State sales tax	13	20	17	20
Local property tax	45	31	31	28
Don't know.............................	11	11	16	14

* The October 1973 responses are from a poll conducted by Opinion Research Corporation for H. & R. Block, Inc.

Source: *Changing Public Attitudes on Government and Taxes,* Washington, D.C.: Advisory Commission on Intergovernmental Relations, 1974.

liance on it, relatively, and various property-tax relief measures discussed in subsequent chapters.

TAX INCIDENCE—THE DISTRIBUTIONAL EFFECTS OF A TAX

As noted at the beginning of the chapter, the burden of governmental activities arises from the transfer of resources from the private sector to the governmental sector. Thus the "burden" is attributable to the expenditures, not the revenue sources. But the type of tax used determines the pattern in which this burden is distributed among various persons, or in other words, the distributional effects of the tax. These distributional effects are often referred to as the incidence of the tax.

There are several approaches to distributional patterns. One is with reference to factor groups, labor and capital, or labor, capital, and land. A second approach stresses the distinction between taxes that reduce real income in relation to consumption in total or by category versus those reducing real income in relation to income received. The third approach is concerned with distributional patterns by income group; these can be ascertained, of course, only on the basis of assumptions about initial distributional effects on various income receivers and consumers. Detailed analysis of the distributional effects of each tax will be presented in the chapters dealing with the various taxes; this section is concerned only with broad issues. Distributional effects by income class were considered in Chapter 6.

Sources versus Uses of Income

The distributional effects, or relative changes in real income, resulting from the tax, may impinge upon persons in several ways. First, the person's factor income may be reduced; a tax on an employer on the basis of his payrolls may result in a reduction in money wages to employees. Second, the tax may appear as a reduction in disposable income relative to factor income. An income tax collected by withholding does not reduce the factor payment for work, but not all of this payment reaches the worker in the form of disposable income to use. The distributional effects may be directly correlated with income received on a proportional or progressive (or even regressive) basis, or they may not be correlated to income but to wealth owned in total or of a certain type. A property tax borne by the property owners reduces disposable income, but in a pattern related to property owned, not income. Distributional effects that affect factor income or disposable income are designated as effects on the sources-of-income side.

Alternatively, the distributional effect may impinge on persons relative to their consumption of goods and services—or in other words, on the uses-of-income side. Thus, an excise tax that raises the price of gasoline, other prices and factor incomes remaining unchanged, has distributional effects relative to consumer expenditures on the taxed product. A given sum of disposable income will buy fewer goods and services than before. If a 10-cents-per-gallon tax is imposed upon gasoline formerly selling at 40 cents a gallon, and price is raised by 10 cents, $5 will buy only 10 gallons instead of 12½ gallons.

The overall redistributional effects of a tax include the effects on the sources of income side as well as the uses-of-income side.

Changes in the Level of Employment

Changes in governmental expenditures and/or taxes may raise or lower the level of employment and the level of national income. Such changes will inevitably affect the distribution of income. But they are not attributable to the particular tax, as such, but to the overall fiscal policy—the relationship between governmental expenditures and revenues. To avoid confusing the distributional pattern of the particular tax with that attributable to the fiscal policy, the differential approach to incidence is used; the analysis assumes that when one tax is substituted for another, the level of aggregate real demand remains unchanged, and therefore the level of employment and GNP are unaffected.[10]

The differential approach requires the use of some standard for comparison; the usual standard is a tax that has a distributional pattern that is actually proportional to income.

Relative Price Changes

Distributional effects of taxes depend upon changes in relative prices in the economy, not upon absolute changes, per se. Thus if all prices rise by 10 percent as a result of the levying of a 10 percent sales tax, but all incomes also rise by 10 percent, and all persons spend all their income, the tax has not been "shifted to consumers," nor borne in relation to consumer spending. The relevant changes are those in the relative prices of various factors and various consumption goods.

The Problem of Analysis of Distributional Effects

While analysis of incidence of taxes has played a major role in economics for two centuries, it is generally agreed that the present state of knowledge in the field is unsatisfactory. So far as the analytical approach is concerned, the inherent problem is that of selecting a model that has sufficiently realistic assumptions as to produce relevant answers, yet is not so complex as to be unmanageable. Simple models are manageable but may give erroneous answers because the assumptions are unrealistic and oversimplified. Yet if the model attempts to take into consideration all possible influences and reactions, it becomes unmanageable, the results not subject to empirical testing. Econometric analysis of the actual influences encounters the usual problems of such analysis in extreme form: the impossibility of excluding other influence affecting prices.

The traditional approach is based upon partial equilibrium theory—the effects of the tax upon a particular price being analyzed under the assumption that all other commodity and factor prices re-

---

[10] Clarification of this question was attained in the work of Richard Musgrave, *The Theory of Public Finance* (New York: McGraw-Hill, 1959), chap. 10. One approach, emphasized by Earl Rolph (*Theory of Fiscal Economics*, Berkeley: University of California Press, 1954), maintained that only the effects of the tax itself should be considered, without the assumption of a given level of employment or aggregate demand. As a consequence, the prices of the factors will fall in response to any tax because total factor-demand falls. This approach, called specific incidence, is not useful for purposes of analysis because it confuses the effects of the tax with those of the relationship of total expenditures and revenues. A third approach (balanced-budget incidence) uses the assumption that when a tax changes, government expenditures change by the same amount. This approach merges the distributional effects of the taxes and expenditures and is, therefore, less useful for analytical and policy purposes.

main unchanged. This clearly does not bring all reactions to the tax into the picture, and, therefore, various attempts have been made in recent years to use a general equilibrium approach. The latter does recognize all possible reactions—but it is manageable only with highly simplifying assumptions and in usual form does not give meaningful answers. The general equilibrium model that has, with modifications, come into most general use is the Harberger model, developed by Arnold Harberger of the University of Chicago.[11] It is based upon several simplifying assumptions:

1. Fixed (perfectly inelastic) factor supplies. The quantity of labor, for example, is not affected by wages received.

2. Perfect factor mobility; factor units will move in response to differential rates of return and thus the after-tax rate of return in all fields will equalize.

3. Perfect competition in all product and factor markets.

4. Closed economic system, international and interregional adjustments disregarded.

5. Constant cost conditions; increases in capital and labor inputs produce proportional increases in output.

6. Marginal propensities to consume uniform among all consumers.

7. No assets with value and income fixed in money terms.

8. All income is consumed; there is no net current savings.

9. All consumers have the same factor endowments.

The analysis is in terms of two factors and two products.

With the greatly simplifying assumptions, some of the basic results are obvious. A tax on all wages, for example, will be distributed strictly in relation to wages. Since the supply of labor is assumed to be fixed and all markets are perfectly competitive, obviously the tax cannot be shifted to anyone else. A tax on all income will remain on the income receivers. A tax on some forms of capital will be distributed in relation to all capital income because of the perfect factor-mobility assumption.

The difficulty is that the assumptions are questionable, to put it mildly—as for example, the assumptions of perfect competition, perfect factor mobility, and given factor supplies (perfectly inelastic supply schedules). Some of these assumptions can be dropped and the analysis modified accordingly. But others cannot be without seriously affecting the overall results. By ruling out any current net saving, the model is of no use for analyzing dynamic effects involving savings, investment, and growth. The model is useful only as a first step in incidence analysis.

---

[11] A. C. Harberger, "The Incidence of the Corporation Income Tax," *Journal of Political Economy*, vol. 70 (June 1962), pp. 215–40. Note also the article by C. E. McLure and W. R. Thirsk, "A Simplified Exposition of the Harberger Model," *National Tax Journal*, vol. 28 (March 1975), pp. 1–28.

Excess Burden[12]

As stressed above, the direct burden to society arising from governmental activities—hopefully more than offset by the benefits—is appropriately attributable to governmental use of the resources rather than to the taxes, which merely control the pattern of distribution. But the taxes, being compulsory levies, may alter economic activity and produce what may be called *excess burden* or deadweight loss, a reduction in economic efficiency, or in other words, a shift away from Pareto optimality, below the level attainable with an optimal tax with no distorting effects—a lump-sum tax. In other words, the taxes cause loss of the equality of *MRS* and *MRT*. If the economy had attained Pareto optimality prior to the tax, the changes would inevitably lessen economic welfare. In practice, it is always difficult to determine the extent to which the optimum had been attained, but there is an a priori case against change in economic behavior except in those instances, such as air pollution, where there is deliberate desire for change.

Excess burden takes these principal forms:

1. *Change in factor supplies.*[13] If factor supplies are not perfectly inelastic, any change in the real income of factor owners will alter the number of units of the factor available. If one tax reduces net wages more than the optimal tax, for example, and as a consequence some workers drop out of the labor market or work fewer hours, total output falls and economic welfare is reduced. Similarly, if the tax causes persons to work more rather than less, economic welfare falls—even though output rises—since persons are moved away from their preferred work-leisure choice, unless this change is desired as a matter of deliberate social policy. If this is the case, the change does not constitute an excess burden.

2. *Loss of allocative efficiency.* If Pareto optimality has been attained, taxes that alter consumption patterns and, therefore, production patterns will reduce economic welfare by causing loss of allocative efficiency. Any tax that alters the relative prices of various goods will inevitably have this effect. Consumers will shift from the higher-priced goods to the lower-priced ones and relative outputs will shift; the consumers will lose satisfaction and no one will gain. If Pareto optimality was not attained, taxes may be used to produce changes to move closer to the optimal position. If so, there is no excess burden.

Excess burden may be illustrated graphically. Let us assume that all markets are perfectly competitive and all factor supplies perfectly in-

---

[12] The article by D. B. Johnson and M. V. Pauly, "Excess Burden and the Voluntary Theory of Public Finance," *Economica*, vol. 36 (August 1969), pp. 269–76, explores the question of excess burden.

[13] In a sense, this is merely a special case of item 2. It is noted separately for purposes of emphasis.

elastic. Under the former assumption, for each commodity, the marginal rate of substitution between each set of commodities will be equal to the marginal rate of transformation in the production of the two commodities or, in other words, shifting of resources from one commodity to another will not increase want satisfaction. This relationship is illustrated by the tangency between the transformation curve (*TT*) and the social indifference curve (*DD*). On Figure 9–1, the curves are

FIGURE 9–1
Excess Consumer Burden of an Excise Tax

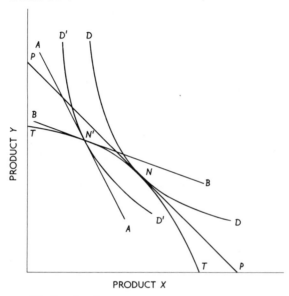

PRODUCT X

TT: Transformation curve.
DD: Equilibrium social-indifference curve, with income tax.
D'D': Equilibrium social-indifference curve, with excess tax.
PP: Price ratio, before excise tax.
AA: Price ratio confronting consumer, after excise tax.
BB: Price ratio, net of tax, to producers after excise tax.

tangent at *N*, indicating attainment of optimal welfare with given resources. *PP* indicates the ratio of prices of the two goods.

If a tax is levied uniformly on all commodities, on total income, or on a per capita (poll tax) basis, the equilibrium adjustment is not disturbed so long as factor supplies are fixed, although the level of consumption of each commodity will be reduced because of lower disposable income. If, however, one commodity is taxed and another is not, one commodity will now be more expensive than the other, relative to input costs, regardless of the absolute direction of change in prices. Thus, equality of marginal rate of transformation and marginal rate of substitution is lost. In a sense, a tax wedge has been inserted between the market price and the factor cost of one commodity but not of the other; the consumer bases decisions on the market price, the producer on price net of tax. Thus relatively too little of the taxed commodity and too much of the untaxed commodity will be consumed and produced. On Figure 9–1, when an income tax is replaced by an excise, the new equilibrium is at N', on a lower indifference curve, which is tangent to the price ratio curve after excise tax *(AA)* but not to the transformation curve, since producers' decisions are based on price relationships net of excises. Thus Pareto optimality is lost.

3. *Loss of technical efficiency.* Taxes may also reduce economic welfare by reducing output below optimal levels by distorting choice of methods of production and organization, provided that optimal technical efficiency has been attained prior to the tax. If a tax makes one method of production more expensive than another or, for example, alters the relative advantage of the corporate form of organization, output from given resources will be reduced.

CRITERIA OF TAX STRUCTURES: PARETO OPTIMALITY

There has developed over the years a set of standards of taxation that has received widespread acceptance—although with widely varying interpretations—and has constituted a major influence upon actual tax policy. As any criteria of "good" or "bad," these standards have no scientific validity; they merely reflect attitudes in a particular society. But they nevertheless have great influence in crystallizing views of individuals and as guideposts to legislative action in the tax field. The criteria fall into two general classes—those relating to Pareto optimality and those relating to equity. This section is concerned with the former.

In nontechnical terms, the principle that more goods are better than fewer goods and that goods persons most want are better than ones less preferred is, for obvious reasons, widely accepted. Contemporary society regards attainment of Pareto optimality—consistent with preservation of an acceptable environment—as a goal of primary importance. This view is not universal; groups rebelling against the establishment regard a simple life as ideal—as have utopian groups throughout history. But they remain exceptions. Initially it is assumed that income distribution is optimal in terms of accepted standards; equity aspects will be considered subsequently.

In simple terms: Adjustment of the tax structure to facilitate attainment of Pareto optimality requires that taxes *(a)* move the economy toward Pareto optimality when this has not been attained, as explained in Chapter 2, and *(b)* produce a minimum shift away from Pareto optimality when it has been attained or, in other words, create minimum excess burden. Unfortunately, it is impossible to ascertain

Pareto optimality; the best that can be done is to estimate whether a particular tax is likely to shift the economy toward optimality or away from it, particularly since other sectors of the economy have not necessarily attained optimality. Major aspects of possible change are noted below.

Resource Allocation

If the private sector fails to attain equality of *MRS* and *MRT*, taxes may be imposed in such a way as to improve allocation by reducing output of goods that are produced in excess and increasing output of those produced in inadequate amounts. Likewise, if private and social costs differ because of externalities, taxes may move the economy closer to optimality. But if the market attains equality of *MRS* and *MRT*, then any tax that alters *MRS* and thus destroys equality with *MRT*—that is, that makes one commodity more expensive relative to others—will distort allocation away from the optimum and create excess burden.

Factor Supplies

Taxes may alter the relative supplies of various factors. The change may improve attainment of the objectives of society. If, for example, a society wishes to induce additional persons to enter the labor market, as many developing economies do, a substantial flat-sum tax unrelated to actual income may force persons to seek jobs instead of living off subsistence production. If a society wishes, as a matter of policy, to encourage wives to stay out of the labor market, it can do so by adjustment in tax structures. If a country wishes to alter the birthrate it may, at least theoretically, do so by adjusting the system of income tax allowances for dependents. But if present factor supplies are at levels regarded as optimal, any effect of a tax in decreasing or increasing the supply creates excess burden and prevents the attainment of the optimal level of real income.

Production Efficiency

Taxes may stimulate businesses to greater efficiency in production. This is particularly likely when the firm has been dominated by the satisfactory profit motive and actual profit is reduced below the satisfactory figure by the tax. But to the extent that the private sector attains maximum efficiency—and there are strong pressures in this direction—taxes may lessen efficiency and thus produce excess burden. Taxes taking a high percentage of net profit may lessen the efforts of firms to attain maximum efficiency. Taxes favoring one technique of production or distribution structure over another may lead to use of less efficient methods; for example, multiple-stage sales taxes may artificially encourage integration.

Collection

Resources used in the administration of taxes, in compliance with them and in devising methods of escaping from them, are not available for use in the production of goods and services. All taxes require some resources for these purposes; the less the extent to which resources are so used, the less is the sacrifice of resources from other uses. The fewer resources used in enforcement, however, the greater will be the evasion; a balance must be struck between resources used in enforcement and effectiveness of enforcement. Maximum convenience to taxpayers in calculating tax liability, in making payment, and in timing of payment aid in minimizing use of resources.

Stabilization

Stabilization of the economy is controlled by overall fiscal and monetary policy, but taxes vary in the extent to which they facilitate stabilization policy through their revenue elasticity and their adaptability to adjustments that will aid in the attainment of stability. By revenue elasticity is meant the percentage change in tax revenue that results from a given change in GNP. If a 5 percent increase in GNP produces a 7.5 percent increase in tax revenue, the coefficient of revenue elasticity is 1.5. Income taxes with exemptions and rate brackets fixed in monetary terms and progressive rates have a revenue elasticity greater than one. Levies with specific rates applied to commodities with little income elasticity will have revenue elasticity much less than one. Likewise, some taxes are more efficient than others, per dollar of revenue, in checking inflation because they provide incentive to curtail spending. Some, by the nature of their structures, facilitate various types of stabilization objectives. With a corporate income tax, for example, the depreciation allowances can be speeded up in years of inadequate total demand and reduced in inflationary periods. A tax on transfer of property at death, on the other hand, offers little or no possibility of adjustments; to vary the rate frequently would penalize the heirs of persons dying in high-rate years.

Taxes may affect the rate of economic growth, by affecting the rate of capital formation and other determinants of growth.

CRITERIA: EQUITY

As noted above, the structure of taxation determines the manner in which the real costs of governmental activities—the reductions in real income in the form of privately produced goods—are borne by various persons in society. Thus inevitably the question of equity—of "fairness" of distribution of this burden—arises. What is "fair" or equitable in taxation is inevitably a value judgment; no scientific specification of an equitable distribution pattern is possible. Such a pattern can be specified only on the basis of a consensus of attitudes of persons in the contemporary society. There are two principal elements in the question of equity: equal treatment of persons in equal circumstances and acceptable relative treatment of persons in different circumstances. The former requires definition of equal circumstances; the latter, of the nature of an acceptable relative treatment.

Benefit Received or Generalized User Charges

In the private sector of the economy, persons pay for private sector output in relation to what they are getting—and thus in relation to benefits. The same rule is used in the governmental sector when persons are charged for governmental services provided or when taxes, such as the motor fuel levy, are designed as substitutes for outright charges. Particularly in past years, the benefit principle was carried over into the field of taxation, based in part on the contract theory of government and the exchange idea of the provision of governmental services. "Equal circumstances" were defined in terms of equal benefits, and taxes should therefore vary among individuals in relation to benefits received. All taxes were thought of essentially as prices designed to facilitate attainment of optimal allocation of income by individuals and optimal levels of output of governmental services and in so doing were providing an equitable distribution of burden.

While this principle is clearly applicable for taxes, such as the motor fuel levy, that are levied as substitutes for prices, as a general basis for determining the distribution of the costs of governmental activities it is in part unworkable, in part unacceptable on an equity basis. The amount of benefits received by individuals from truly public goods or alternatively, the costs of providing the services to individuals, cannot be determined. This is also true of the external benefits of goods yielding partial externalities. Any specification of benefits is purely arbitrary; the costs of government are not actually distributed on the basis of benefits—which cannot be determined—but on the basis of an arbitrary measure of benefits. Secondly, the approach is unworkable for distributional activities of government, which have the deliberate objective of increasing the real incomes of some persons while reducing those of others. The basis is likewise unacceptable to society for financing functions from which the lower-income groups particularly benefit, such as education, because of the heavy burden that would be placed on these groups. Lower-income families would either be unable to pay for the benefits or would suffer reduction in their ability to attain minimum living standards. In effect, universal use of the benefit principle simply does not conform with consensus in modern society about the nature of an equitable distribution.

Ability

Except for those governmental services of such nature that individual benefits are easily determined and the use of the benefit basis does not contradict usual concepts of equity, the generally accepted equitable principle of distribution of tax burden is ability—that persons should pay tax on the basis of their relative ability. This principle, of course, has no scientific foundation; it has merely become widely accepted as reflecting a reasonable general statement about equity.

Measures. The rule is, of course, not a workable one without further elaboration. The first issue is the measure of ability—what indicates ability to pay? In a broad sense, the term refers to economic well-being: how well off a person is in an economic sense. One primary measure of economic well-being is income, which more than any other variable determines relative levels of living of various persons. There are many problems involved in the precise definition of income and in possible adjustments in it for tax purposes, as will be explained in the next chapter, but there is widespread acceptance of the rule that income is the most suitable single measure.

A second alternative is somewhat narrower—consumption expenditures, either in total or for specified categories. This approach will be considered in Chapter 14. For most families, consumption is less than income, but the ratio of consumption to income varies widely among families.

The third major alternative is wealth, either a net amount or the total value of certain types of property. Accumulated wealth influences the level of living a family can enjoy at a given income level; in fact, if a family has enough wealth, it can enjoy a high living standard indefinitely without earning any income at all. Yet income is the more significant of the two criteria, in the sense that variations in living levels are correlated, in modern society, more closely with income than with wealth.

In practice, all three of the measures are used, but opinions differ over the relative desired emphasis on each of the measures.

Progressivity. Granted the use of a particular measure, there remains the question of the appropriate relative tax on persons with different income, consumption, or wealth; most of the issues center around the relationship to income. There are three possible relationships of tax to income: regressive, proportional, and progressive. The relationship is regressive if the ratio of tax to income declines as income rises; it is proportional if the tax constitutes the same percentage of income at all levels; it is progressive if the percentage rises as income rises.

The defense for progression was long built upon the principle of diminishing marginal utility of income; as incomes rise, marginal utility falls, it was assumed, and therefore the taking of a larger percentage in tax would cause no more sacrifice than taking a smaller percentage from persons in lower-income levels.[14] There are, however, several serious objections to the defense of progression on this basis. There is no significant evidence that the law of diminishing marginal utility—which is obviously valid for consumption of pancakes at breakfast—applies to income as a whole. As a person's income rises, it may be argued that his desires rise as fast or faster. Even more fundamentally, the use of the law—even if valid for income—to justify progression requires interpersonal utility comparisons (the assumption that a dollar of income yields the same utility to all persons with the same income). With the present state of knowledge, the assumption of interpersonal utility comparison is not a valid one; there is no possible way of comparing satisfactions among various persons.

Progression can be satisfactorily justified on equity grounds only on the basis of consensus in society that in the absence of progression, income is distributed in an excessively unequal and, therefore, inequitable pattern. Progression, by lessening inequality, lessens inequity. The basis is simply that of consensus of popular attitudes, or in other words, the social welfare function.

There are also defenses for progression on grounds other than equity. Lessened inequality reduces the percentage of national income saved and the deflationary gap, for example, although it may aggravate inflationary pressures.

Some persons without question favor progression because it results in less burden on themselves and more on others. While some wealthy persons strongly oppose progression, others take a broader point of view, regarding progression as inherently fair or as essential for preservation of the market economy and a democratic society. Without progression, they fear greater strength for revolutionary movements. Other persons wish to shift their own tax burden from the present,

---

[14] As developed in the last century, there were several versions of the sacrifice doctrine relating to equity. Some writers argued for a tax that would cause the same absolute sacrifice at all income levels; a second group argued for burden proportional to income; a third for equi-marginal or least aggregate sacrifice—a burden such that total sacrifice would be minimized. Such analyses rest on interpersonal utility comparisons—the ability to compare satisfactions gained by various persons. Since such comparison is impossible, the sacrifice analysis is useless. Apart from this problem, the lack of knowledge of the rate at which marginal utility of income falls as incomes rise—if it falls at all—would prevent implementation.

when their incomes are low, to the future, when their incomes are higher.

Despite widespread acceptance of progression, a substantial element in society, primarily in the higher-income groups, opposes it. In part the opponents, disliking progression because of the heavier tax they would pay and the fear that the tax would ultimately confiscate their incomes, characterize it as unfair. They stress the lack of any scientific basis for establishing the degree of progression. Most of the attack, however, rests not on equity grounds but on charges of adverse effects upon investment, real capital formation, work incentives, and efficiency. These charges are discussed in subsequent chapters.

CONFLICT OF STANDARDS

In practice, as a tax structure is framed or revised, conflict among various standards is almost inevitable. If society seeks a high degree of progression for reasons of equity, the consequence may be a significant reduction in the rate of savings, investment, and economic growth. Provisions that increase equity may complicate administration and compliance to such an extent that evasion becomes substantial. To resolve such conflicts, society must weigh the importance of the various conflicting considerations. These conflicts are apparent in any analysis of a tax structure as a basis for reform.

ATTITUDES OF GOVERNMENTS

Governments—we assume—seek to frame tax policy in terms of the overall preferences of society. The problems of doing so are similar to those encountered in developing expenditure programs. Preferences are not well defined and not easily ascertained, and there may be no majority position. Preferences may even be contradictory; majority support may be obtained for a balanced budget but not for any combination of taxes that will permit it. Not infrequently, as happened in 1966 in Nebraska, voters will turn down all alternative tax measures offered. The preferences relate to overall objectives and types of taxes, not to detail.

Accordingly, society gives to governments the responsibility for devising means to carry out the major objectives and to develop the precise tax structure that will best fulfill the preferences. Society in turn is typically willing to accept the structures unless they appear to be highly objectionable; if they do, the government may be defeated in its attempt to gain reelection. But too many issues enter into the voters' decisions for tax considerations alone to control the outcome. Thus, governments have broad discretion in fulfilling this responsibility. As a consequence the views of persons in the executive and legislative branches responsible for determination of tax legislation play a major role in framing the tax structure.

Governments sometimes have an unfortunate tendency to devise tax structures that conceal the actual tax burden from the public. This policy has been less popular in the United States than elsewhere,[15] but even in this country it plays a part in the strong support in the administration and Congress for the corporation income tax, the burden of which is well hidden from consumers, stockholders, and others who experience reduction in real incomes. Support for the manufacturers sales tax in Canada rests primarily upon concealment from the public, whereas the principal alternative, the retail sales tax, is clearly evident to the customer. Some European countries prohibit vendors from showing sales taxes separately from prices in order to keep the public unaware of the actual burden. Such a policy, while understandable, can be criticized on the grounds of making reasonable appraisal of the tax structure by the voters more difficult.

Governments, and particularly legislative bodies, not only give some attention to preferences of the public about particular taxes but also are subject to strong pressure groups. Tax policy is not made in a vacuum, but by human beings in the context of a particular environment. Powerful truck lobbies, not adverse, it is rumored, to sharp threats, have substantial influence over tax legislation affecting their members. Groups not infrequently warn of dire consequences if certain tax legislation is passed, including threats of firms to close down and move out of the state if tax rates are increased. Farm groups, chambers of commerce, educational associations, labor unions often have substantial influence on legislatures, and, to some extent, on Congress. But organizations that develop doctrinaire positions may lose most of their influence; the otherwise influential National Association of Manufacturers in the United States, for example, has little impact on tax legislation because of its rigid positions.

In the framing of legislation, there is always danger that small groups with unusually strong bargaining power may distort tax structures to their own benefit, contrary to the interests of society as a whole. The unusually favorable treatment of oil producers through liberal depletion allowances under the federal income tax was an example. As with other legislation, the higher-income groups have disproportionate influence on tax structures compared to their numerical importance. In the United States actual progression is very much less than it appears to be on the basis of rate tables because disproportionate political strength of the higher-income groups prevents adequate taxation of capital gains.

---

[15] Legislation in 1970 required that the tax on air fares be concealed in the price of the ticket. Strong complaints led Congress to repeal the requirement later the same year.

APPENDIX I—THE PROCESS OF ENACTMENT
OF TAX LEGISLATION

In the United States, as in many countries, the route of revenue legislation is different from that of expenditure legislation. The budget document itself contains only a summary of revenue forecasts with existing taxes, prepared for the Office of Management and Budget by the Treasury; it does not contain detailed plans for changes in taxation.

Preparation of Recommendations[16]

Primary responsibility for preparation of the recommendations on taxation rests with the Treasury. On major issues of policy, however, and particularly on those relating to the level of taxation compared to expenditures (the deficit or surplus position), the responsibility is shared with OMB and the Council of Economic Advisers. The President and his economic advisers may also play a major role in the decisions. The Treasury has a permanent staff to make studies of the tax structure and to consider objections to features of taxes raised by taxpayer groups or others, or noted by the Internal Revenue Service in the administration of the tax laws. If the Treasury is convinced that major reform measures are needed, the Secretary will consult with the President on the possibility of a tax measure; if he obtains approval, the details of the proposal will be developed by the Treasury staff. At the later stages of preparation the proposals will be discussed with OMB, the Council of Economic Advisers, and the President. On matters of fiscal policy, such as a general increase in taxes to lessen inflationary pressures, the initiative for the proposal may come from the Council or from the President himself, but the Treasury will undertake the task of preparing the specific recommendations. With agreement on the proposals, the President may make some general reference to them in his State of the Union message, and again, in more detail, in the budget message; if the proposed changes are significant, he may present a separate tax message to Congress following the transmission of the budget, outlining the proposals and the justification for them in detail.

Congressional Consideration

By constitutional requirement, all revenue measures must originate in the House. The proposals go to the Ways and Means Committee, the most powerful committee of the House, for hearings. The Secre-

---

[16] See J. A. Pechman, *Federal Tax Policy* (rev. ed.; Washington, D.C.: The Brookings Institution, 1971), chap. 3.

tary of the Treasury presents a detailed statement of the proposals to the committee, accompanied by substantial supporting evidence, and is subjected to questioning. The committee over the next several months receives statements from numerous groups and individuals favoring or opposing particular changes. After the hearings, the committee reviews the evidence and statements, obtains assistance from the staff of the Joint Committee on Internal Revenue Taxation[17] and from the Treasury, reaches a position on the various major issues, and produces a tax bill. While voting on some issues tends to be along party lines, on many issues substantial consensus is reached. The measure is sent to the House and debated under rules limiting debate, with amendments usually barred, and the committee's proposal is almost always approved.

The bill next goes to the Senate and is first considered by the Senate Finance Committee, with procedure comparable to that of the Ways and Means Committee, but briefer. The committee then considers the various provisions in the measure and almost always makes some changes from the House version. Debate is unrestricted on the Senate floor, and amendments to the committee proposal are frequently approved.

Since the House and Senate versions inevitably differ, a Conference Committee works out a compromise and the amended version is almost automatically approved by each house. The measure then goes to the President for signing. On a few occasions, the measure has been so distorted from the original proposals that the President vetoed it (none since 1969). Typically, at least six months elapse from the President's message until the measure is signed. Needless to say, the administration seeks through its key supporters on the two committees and in the Senate to obtain approval of the provisions it regards as important and to keep out undesirable ones, but it is not always successful; the final bill always differs substantially from the original proposal.

Legislation in 1974, which created the congressional budget committees, introduced a new element in the picture; the concurrent resolutions on the budget each year may contain recommendations about revenue changes. The extent to which these influence actual tax legislation remains to be seen. The initial effect was to create a power struggle between the Senate Finance Committee and the Senate Budget Committee.

A few incidental features of the process should be noted. While appropriations measures must be enacted annually, general revenue measures are considered at less-frequent intervals; there were 15 between 1948 and 1977, and not all these were major. Individual members of Congress may introduce tax measures; virtually never do these

---

[17] Ibid.

bills get out of committee or even receive committee attention. The Ways and Means Committee has tremendous power, subject to potential overrule by action of the House, to prevent action on tax proposals, and, in turn, the chairman has great influence over committee action. No one person in the United States has more influence over tax legislation than the chairman of the Ways and Means Committee.

Thus the process of development of tax legislation involves a combination of influences: taxation experts, especially on more technical aspects of the law; the economists of the Council of Economic Advisers; the Treasury, especially on questions of fiscal policy (deficits and surpluses); the President; and members of Congress, particularly of the two key committees. Both the administration and Congress are subject to substantial pressure by interested groups; presumably Congress is somewhat more directly responsive to attitudes of the public than are the technical experts of the administration. Perhaps the most serious criticism that can be advanced against the procedure is the excessive influence on the tax structure of a relatively few persons in key positions, whose attitudes may not reflect more widely accepted ones. Small pressure groups may likewise exercise disproportionate influence.

Another difficulty has been the separation of consideration of expenditure and revenue measures, which in the past have been handled by separate committees, with measures voted on at different times. While this is still true of actual appropriations and tax legislation, the congressional budget committees are concerned with both expenditures and revenues and hopefully will bring better coordination of the two sides.

State Tax Measures

The enactment of tax legislation at the state level is similar but much simpler. Initial recommendations usually come from the governor, who may get them from a variety of sources. Only a few states have agencies that give continuing study to tax questions. Some major proposals are products of the work of state tax-study commissions. The legislative committees give much briefer attention; their members are typically much less expert in the taxation field than members of the congressional committees and the influence of outside pressure groups is likely to be stronger. Several states have encountered serious financial crises because of inability of the legislature and the governor or of both houses of the legislature to compromise on a mutually accepted tax program.

Since local governments rely primarily on the property tax, they make no continuing review of the tax structure, but occasionally consider new tax sources.

APPENDIX II—CONSTITUTIONAL RESTRICTIONS:
UNITED STATES

In the United States and some other countries, constitutions place restrictions upon the taxing powers of the legislative bodies. These in large part reflect an inherent distrust of legislatures by the persons responsible for the framing of the Constitution. In part, this arises from legitimate fear of discrimination against minorities (British Columbia once had a special tax on Chinese) but, in part, it reflects a fear by the framers of the Constitution that legislatures will be swayed by transitory influences and will be excessively "liberal" in taxing the rich and favoring the poor. To the extreme conservatives, strict constitutional provisions that can be changed only with popular vote well in excess of a majority are essential to preserve the interests of the rich minority. Experience suggests that this last-named fear is groundless—but it is nevertheless widely held.

Major constitutional provisions are explained below.

THE FEDERAL GOVERNMENT[18]

Section 8 of Article I of the Constitution gives Congress specific power to levy taxes: "The Congress shall have Power to lay and collect Taxes, Duties, Imposts, and Excises, to pay the Debts and provide for the common Defense and general Welfare of the United States . . . ." This power is subjected, however, to certain limitations, some by specific provisions of the Constitution, others by court interpretation of other sections of the Constitution.

Specific Limitations

1. *The Uniformity Clause.* Section 8 concludes with the statement: "but all Duties, Imposts and Excises shall be uniform throughout the United States." This section has been interpreted to mean that any federal tax regarded by the courts as an indirect tax shall be levied at a geographically uniform rate, the rate being the same in all states. In earlier years the use of progressive rates was contested as a violation of the uniformity clause, but this argument was overruled by the Supreme Court when it upheld the use of exemptions and progressive rates with the inheritance tax. The term *excise* has never been clearly defined by the courts. Taxes on sale of commodities, plus death taxes and the original corporation income tax, have been held to be excises. The personal income tax has been held to be a direct tax.

---

[18] See S. Ratner, *American Taxation* (New York: Norton, 1942) for a historical review.

2. *The Apportionment Clause.* Section 9 of Article I states: "No capitation, or other direct Tax shall be laid, unless in Proportion to the Census or Enumeration herein before directed to be taken." Under the terms of this provision the amounts to be collected from any tax interpreted to be direct would have to be apportioned among the states according to population rather than be collected at a uniform rate throughout the country. Thus, if $10 billion were to be collected from a property tax and 6 percent of the population of the United States were in Illinois, the federal property tax rate in Illinois would be set at such a level that the amount collected in the state would equal 6 percent of $10 billion, or $600 million. Thus the federal tax rate would be high in states with low per capita wealth and low in states with high per capita wealth. Because of the inequity of this rule, any tax interpreted to be a direct tax is effectively barred from federal use.

A major issue was encountered with the attempt of the federal government to levy an income tax, namely, whether, at law, the income tax was direct or indirect. In 1872 the Civil War income tax was held to be indirect and thus valid. But portions of the income tax of 1894 were held to be direct and therefore unconstitutional because the tax was not apportioned among the states according to population. As a consequence, the 16th Amendment was enacted (1913), providing that "the Congress shall have power to lay and collect taxes on incomes, from whatever source derived, without apportionment among the several states, and without regard to any census or enumeration."

Implied Restrictions

1. *The Welfare Limitation.* If a tax is interpreted by the courts to be levied for purposes other than the general welfare, it may be held invalid. In a very few instances, taxes were interpreted to be regulatory rather than revenue measures: the special tax on industries using child labor and the processing tax of the Agricultural Adjustment Act. Other taxes imposed with the primary aim of regulation have been upheld.

2. *The "State Instrumentalities" Doctrine.* The Supreme Court has held that the basic division of power between federal and state governments requires that each level of government be prevented from taxing the "instrumentalities"—the property, securities, and activities—of the other, to ensure that the taxing power would not be used to weaken the powers of the other level of government. Thus the federal government has been denied the right to tax interest on state and local bonds and sales to the states under federal excises. The attitude of the courts has shifted somewhat on the interpretation of this doctrine over the years, and the Supreme Court might uphold taxation of state and local bond interest, were Congress to change the law to

make such interest taxable, as it did with wages and salaries of state and local employees.

3. *The Due Process Requirement.* The federal government is prohibited from depriving persons of "life, liberty or property without due process of law." This provision prevents completely arbitrary classification for tax purposes and retroactive (past the current year) imposition of taxation and ensures the right of appeal to the courts from the decisions of tax-administering agencies.

THE TAXING POWERS OF THE STATES

The states, with residual sovereign powers, possess full powers of taxation without specific designation by the federal Constitution. However, the Constitution does specifically restrict their taxing powers, and other limitations have arisen out of the interpretation of provisions of the Constitution not directly relating to taxation. In addition, the states hve imposed limitations in their own constitutions on the taxing powers of their legislatures.

Specific Federal Restrictions

The federal Constitution specifically prohibits use by the states of three types of taxes: (1) import duties, (2) export duties, and (3) tonnage duties (levies upon ships for the privilege of entering or leaving a port). These restrictions were designed to ensure for the federal government complete power over foreign commerce.

Implied Restrictions

1. *Federal Instrumentalities.* In order to protect the powers of the federal government, the states (and their subdivisions) are denied the right to tax federal instrumentalities. Thus, property taxes may not be applied to federally owned property or federal securities, and sales to the federal government may not be taxed under states sales and excise taxes, at least if tax liability is on the purchaser.[19]

2. *The Due Process and Equal Protection Clauses.* The states, by provision of the 14th Amendment, are prohibited from depriving persons of life, liberty, or property without due process of law. This prohibition ensures the taxpayer the right of appeal to the courts from the action of tax-administration agencies and protects against arbitrary procedures. In addition, it has been interpreted to mean that a state

---

[19] For a century, the states were drastically restricted in their power to tax national banks, which are privately owned but federally chartered. These restrictions were removed by federal legislation in 1969.

may apply a tax only within its territorial jurisdiction. In very rare instances, the courts have held taxes to violate due process on the ground that they were confiscatory but usually the courts have taken the position that the question of the height of a tax is one within the discretion of the legislative body.

The 14th Amendment also requires that no state shall "deny to any person within its jurisdiction the equal protection of the laws." This clause has been interpreted by the courts in such a manner as to invalidate some state taxes, such as certain ones on chain stores, on the basis of arbitrary classification and thus denial of equal protection. In practice, however, the courts will not interfere with classification unless it is extremely arbitrary. On the basis of this clause, in 1971 the California Supreme Court held local property taxes to finance schools to be invalid because with this system, educational opportunities were not equal for students in poor and wealthy districts.

3. *Discrimination against Citizens of Other States.* Closely related is the prohibition of discrimination against citizens of other states; residents and nonresidents must be treated equally. Thus, property owned by nonresidents cannot be taxed at a higher rate than that owned by residents. This provision applies only to citizens, not to corporations, and thus a state may apply heavier taxes to businesses incorporated outside the state than to those incorporated in the state. This is common in the insurance field.

4. *Interstate Commerce.*[20]   Some of the most significant restrictions on state taxing powers arise out of interpretation of the clause of the Constitution that gives control over interstate commerce to the federal government. States cannot levy discriminatory taxes against goods brought into the state from other states and cannot directly tax interstate sales as such under sales or excise taxes, although they may apply use taxes to goods bought outside the state and brought in. Businesses engaged in interstate commerce can be taxed on their gross receipts or net profits only if the totals are allocated on a reasonable basis. Taxation of railroads is complicated by their interstate character. The powers of the states to tax interstate motor carriers are considerably broader because of the states' proprietary interest in the highways.

Legislation in 1976 prohibits the states from tax discrimination against railroads.

5. *Miscellaneous Restrictions.* State taxation must not violate treaties made with other countries by the federal government. The states may not tax in such a manner as to impair contracts. For exam-

---

[20] An exhaustive study of this question is to be found in the October 1960 issue of the *Virginia Law Review,* "A Symposium on State Taxation of Interstate Commerce," and in *State Taxation of Interstate Commerce,* Report of the Special Subcommittee on State Taxation of Interstate Commerce of the House Judiciary Committee, 3 vols. (Washington, D.C.: U.S. Government Printing Office, 1964).

ple, interest on bonds issued free from state income tax cannot subsequently be taxed.

Restrictions Imposed by State Constitutions

The state legislatures are subject to restrictions imposed by the state constitutions as well as by those of the federal Constitution. The exact degree of restriction varies widely. In a few states, legislatures have complete freedom. In others, they may levy any type of tax they wish subject to certain general requirements, such as uniformity of treatment. These uniformity clauses have been interpreted differently in various states, sometimes to prevent the use of progressive taxation. Other legislatures are permitted to levy only certain specified types of taxes, and in a few states, such as Louisiana, virtually the whole tax structure is prescribed directly by the state constitution.

The significance of these restrictions depends to a great extent upon the ease of amending the constitution. If amendment is relatively simple, as in California, the restrictions do not prevent readjustment in the tax structure. If amending is very difficult, as it long was in Illinois, the tax structure may be essentially frozen for long periods.

THE TAXING POWERS OF THE LOCAL GOVERNMENTS

The local governments, as creations of the states, are subject to the same restrictions imposed by the federal Constitution as are the states themselves. Furthermore, they can levy only those taxes that are specifically authorized for them by the states, since they have no inherent taxing powers of their own.

The taxing powers of the localities may be established by provisions of the state constitution or, more commonly, by general state law, and by provisions of municipal charters. Virtually all local governments are given the right to levy property taxes. Many, such as school districts and townships, have no other taxing powers. Cities are frequently given powers to impose various forms of license taxes and, in some cases, sales, excise, and income taxes.

APPENDIX III—CONSTITUTIONAL TAXING POWERS: CANADA[21]

Under the British North America Act, which is the Canadian Constitution, the provinces have only those powers specifically au-

---

[21] See G. V. La Forest, *The Allocation of Taxing Power under the Canadian Constitution* (Toronto: Canadian Tax Foundation, 1967); V. C. MacDonald, "Taxation Powers in Canada," *Canadian Bar Review*, vol. 27 (October 1941), pp. 75–95; J. H. Perry, *Taxtion in Canada* (3d ed.; Toronto: University of Toronto Press, 1961), chap. 8.

thorized, while the Dominion retains the residual powers. This is the reverse of the United States situation.

Federal Taxing Powers. The Dominion government is given unlimited taxing powers, being authorized to make laws relating to "the raising of money by any mode or system of taxation." The primary restriction prohibits taxing provincial lands and property, interpreted to mean also purchases by a province for governmental use. Otherwise, there is no provincial instrumentalities doctrine, and interest on provincial bonds may be taxed. If a tax is levied for attainment of *ultra vires* purposes rather than for revenue, it may be held invalid.

The Provincial Powers. The powers of the provinces are more limited than those of the states. The provinces are given the right to levy only direct taxes, and the taxes must be levied for the purpose of "raising a revenue for provincial purposes."

Substantial difficulty arose over the meaning of the term *indirect taxes*, particularly when the provinces required gasoline and sales tax revenue. In their usual form these taxes are indirect, in terms of the definition formulated by John Stuart Mill and generally accepted by the Canadian courts, since they are ordinarily shifted from the taxpayer to the purchaser. By the guise of imposing these taxes on the consumer, the vendor being required to collect and remit the taxes as an agent of the province, the provinces have succeeded in making them acceptable as direct taxes in the eyes of the courts.

The taxing clause limits taxation to persons or property within the province. This clause has been interpreted very broadly; a resident may be taxed on his or her entire income, for example, even though it is earned outside the province. Dominion companies, however, may be taxed only in a fashion nondiscriminatory as compared to other corporations. Only property with situs in the province may be taxed.

Taxes must be levied for the purpose of raising revenue, being invalid if levied in order to gain control over activities that are not within provincial jurisdiction.

In addition to the power to levy direct taxes, the provinces are authorized to impose "shop, saloon, tavern, auctioneer, and other licenses in order to the raising of revenue for provincial, local or municipal purposes." Only limited use is made of this power.

The provinces are not subject to a federal instrumentalities doctrine comparable to that in the United States, although they are not permitted to tax federal property or direct purchases by the federal government. Likewise, they are not subject to restrictions on taxation comparable to those arising out of the interstate commerce clause in the United States except insofar as they are prohibited from levying duties on the importation of goods from other provinces. They can, for example, tax an out-of-province purchaser on an article bought in the province for out-of-province delivery. Their power to compel out-of-province vendors to collect sales taxes for them is less than the power of the states in the United States.

Local Governments. Local governments have no inherent taxing powers, but only those which the provinces give them by terms of general laws or charters. The provinces may delegate to them any taxing powers which they themselves possess.

APPENDIX IV—TAX LEGISLATION IN CANADA AND OTHER COMMONWEALTH COUNTRIES

Countries, such as Canada, with the parliamentary form of government have somewhat different procedures for the enactment of tax legislation, because of the lack of a sharp distinction between executive and legislative branches of government. Proposals for tax changes are developed by the Cabinet on the basis of recommendations of the Department (Ministry) of Finance, which prepares the detailed recommendations. The Cabinet will debate the proposals, obviously taking into consideration attitudes of the public in light of the desire of the party to gain reelection. Once the Cabinet reaches agreement, the proposal is presented to Parliament, having been kept secret up to this point. Extensive debate ensues, with opposition members attacking the proposals and government members defending them. There are no committee hearings. The Cabinet will sometimes modify the proposals as a result of debate. At the conclusion of discussion, enactment is almost automatic, since party discipline is strong and failure of the House of Commons to approve the tax measure would result in fall of the government and a new election.[22] Action by the Senate is a formality, as is approval of the Governor General; there is no executive veto power, by the nature of the parliamentary form of government. Many of the proposals will have become effective the day of their presentation to Parliament, subject to subsequent ratification.

Use is also made of the government-appointed Tax Committees or Royal Commissions on Taxation. The group, made up of persons familiar with the field, assembles a staff for detailed study and prepares a report. The recent Royal Commission on Taxation in Canada, appointed in 1961, carried on an extensive study of the Canadian tax structure as a whole and prepared a six-volume report, issued in 1966, calling for drastic changes in the tax structure.[23] Only a few were actually made. Similar studies have recently been made in most of the

---

[22] In February 1968, a bill in Canada to apply a 5 percent income tax surcharge was defeated in the House of Commons by two votes, with a large number of absentees. The government would have fallen had it not succeeded in winning a subsequent vote of confidence. A modified version of the proposal was then enacted.

[23] See *Report of the Royal Commission on Taxation*, 6 vols. (Ottawa: Queens Printer, 1966).

provinces.[24] Traditionally governments pay substantial attention to the recommendations of these commissions, but they are not necessarily accepted if the government is convinced that there is strong popular opposition to them or that the proposals are unwise.

REFERENCES

Blough, Roy. *The Federal Taxing Process*. New York: Prentice-Hall, 1950. Out of date, but one of the few general studies of the question.

Break, George F. "The Incidence and Economic Effects of Taxation." In *The Economics of Public Finance*, by Alan S. Blinder et al. pp. 122–38. Washington, D.C.: The Brookings Institution, 1974.

Buchanan, J. M. *Public Finance in Democratic Process*. Chapel Hill, N.C.: University of North Carolina Press, 1967.

Pechman, Joseph A. *Federal Tax Policy*. Rev. ed., especially chap. 3. Washington, D.C.: Brookings Institution, 1971.

---

[24] See, for example, *Ontario Committee on Taxation Report* (Toronto: Queens Printer, 1967); *Rapport de la Commission royale d'enquête sur la fiscalité, Gouvernement du Quebec* (Quebec City, 1965).

10

The Structure of Income Taxation I: The Concept of Income

As we have discussed in Chapter 8, no one tax can be considered to be "optimal" in the sense that it will simultaneously satisfy the goals of economic efficiency, the desired income distribution, the proper degree of stabilization and growth, and so forth. While it may be conceptually feasible to devise an optimal tax structure that takes all of these goals into account, in the real world, problems of incomplete information and political constraints make the achievement of such an optimal tax structure impossible. We must rely on a limited number of taxes and hope that they will at least approximate this optimal tax structure if not achieve it.

In this respect, the income tax has substantial merit and is widely used in the United States and other economies. First, although theoretically it can distort the work-leisure and savings-consumption choices and other decisions, the evidence suggests that unless extremely high progressive rates are used, the income tax creates relatively little substitution of leisure for work effort or other alterations in behavior. Thus it is relatively neutral with regard to allocational efficiency. Second, it is the most effective tax vehicle for attaining equity in distributional patterns and in bringing about income redistribution, particularly if it is a progressive tax. Third, a progressive tax serves as a strong built-in stabilizer, by enabling the government to collect relatively more revenues as income rises and relatively less as income falls. Fourth, by adjusting the tax burden the government can, in effect, influence the savings ratio throughout the economy and thus the growth rate. Thus the income tax simultaneously satisfies a number of the goals of society—albeit imperfectly.

Of course, the income tax as structured in the United States is a far cry from an optimal income tax. Various exemptions and deductions have crept into the tax structure over the years that vitiate its impact with respect to the goals that have been outlined above. This chapter and the next are concerned with two primary issues: What is the nature of an optimal income tax structure and how does the actual income tax structure in the United States correspond to this optimum? In general, we shall see that the current tax structure is seriously deficient in achieving the general goals of efficiency, equity, stabilization, and growth. Thus, a large portion of the next chapter is devoted to proposals to reform or change the income tax structure. But despite its limitations, the income tax is widely regarded as preferable to other levies.

GENERAL REQUIREMENTS

As we have pointed out throughout this book, government cannot, in general, fully achieve all of its goals simultaneously. Taxes to redistribute income or to stabilize the economy will typically distort various consumption or production choices and thus conflict with the goal of economic efficiency. Similarly, policies to increase savings and investment and growth must necessarily distort some private decisions and may well have an adverse effect upon income distribution. All of these problems are encountered with the income tax. Nevertheless, it is generally agreed that an optimal income tax should have the following characteristics:

1. All income should be treated uniformly, regardless of source, in view of the equal-treatment-of-equals or horizontal-equity rules. All dollars of income should be accorded equal tax treatment, regardless of the source. If income is accepted as the measure of ability to pay, then any variation in tax by source of income results in discrimination. Differential taxation of income from different sources will, in general, distort resource allocation. One exception is the situation in which taxation of some types of income will cause greater change in factor supplies than taxation of other types, and thus departure from Pareto optimality will be less if the tax rates are different on different types of income. Such a system would be very difficult to implement and would be contrary to usual equity standards. Another exception occurs if externalities or other circumstances exist that cause the market to fail to allocate resources efficiently. It may on occasion be desirable to relax this rule and treat different sources of income differently. There are usually more efficient ways, however, of correcting these market imperfections through regulation, explicit taxes, or subsidies. Once the notion of horizontal equity is abandoned in specific cases, it quickly

becomes abandoned in general (as is true of the U.S. tax structure) and the resulting structure must necessarily create considerable inefficiencies and inequities.

2.   Just as equals should be treated equally, unequals, should be treated unequally, in a pattern consistent with accepted goals of equity. Thus, the rule of vertical equity is as important as horizontal equity. Questions of income differentials, family size, medical expenses, and so forth must be taken into account to ensure that the tax burden placed upon different families meets the distributional goals outlined in Chapter 7.

3.   The tax structure should be sensitive to changes in economic activity in order to dampen the changes. This problem will be discussed more fully in Chapter 23, but the evidence suggests that the U.S. federal income tax structure is relatively good in this respect. As a related matter, the tax structure should be reasonably elastic, so that it will generate sufficient revenues to finance needed programs without frequent rate revisions. Again, this problem will be discussed more fully in Chapter 23, but the evidence again suggests that the U.S. income tax performs reasonably well in this matter.

4.   The structure of the tax must be designed, for efficiency reasons, in such a fashion as to facilitate ease in compliance and in enforcement, consistent with attainment of the other objectives. Furthermore, a tax structure that is difficult to enforce will almost certainly lose equity because of evasion. No matter how equitable a tax structure may appear to be, it will not in fact attain the desired equity objectives unless it is enforced with a high degree of effectiveness.

Design of an income tax to fulfill these requirements is not a simple task, because of inadequate knowledge about shifting of tax from some persons to others and about effects upon economic efficiency of various policies. Do highly progressive rates actually reduce the supply of managerial and professional talent, for example, and if so, by how much? The determination of society's preferences about the degree of progressivity and the extent to which persons in the lower-income groups should be free of tax is impossible in any precise way. There are a number of problems of definition and delineation that defy easy solution. These questions will be considered in subsequent sections.

THE DEFINITION OF INCOME

The initial basic step in the establishment of an income tax structure is the definition of income. In a broad sense, income consists of any economic gain a person has experienced during the period. More precisely, under the definition of Henry Simons[1], one widely accepted for

---

[1] Henry Simons, *Personal Income Taxation* (Chicago: University of Chicago Press, 1938). This is a classic work on the income tax.

purposes of analysis though not of law, a person's income during the period, in an economic sense, consists of the algebraic sum of:

1.   The value of consumption during the period financed from factor income or transfer income (e.g., gifts) flowing to the person during the period or from accumulated wealth, plus (*a*) goods produced by the person for his or her own use, and (*b*) the value of the use of durable consumer goods possessed, such as homes.

2.   Net increase in personal wealth during the period, whether from accumulation of net savings during the period or increases in the value of property held. This sum may of course be negative, so that income is less than consumption.

This definition may be expressed as follows:

$$Y = C + \Delta W$$

Logically this is the most satisfactory definition of income in light of the objectives, but it is not the approach used in tax laws. The usual approach is in terms of flow of money and, to a limited extent, of commodities to a person. This is a concept somewhat easier for the noneconomist to understand; it is in agreement with the everyday notions of income, and it is a workable approach. Use value of owned durable goods and unrealized increases in assets are not included, in part for compliance and administrative reasons, but primarily because these elements are frequently not thought of as income. Major differences between the Simons definition and that commonly employed and various borderline questions encountered under any definition require further attention.

Nonmonetary Transfers

Persons may be paid in kind as well as in money; they may be provided commodities, meals, housing, use of a company car, a vacation at company expense; they may receive free health service, parking space, discounts on purchases, and the like. Under the Simons definition, the values of all of these are incomes—but there are serious problems of valuation. A person receives a "luxury" meal at a company banquet—at a cost of $20 to the company—but he would never buy it if he had to pay for it; he would eat at home at a net cost of perhaps $2.00. Clearly, to include the full commercial value in income is unfair—and doing so would lead persons to avoid receiving the income. This problem was pointed out decades ago by the German economist Kleinwachter in the case of the aide-de-camp who received free tickets to all operas which he had to attend with his superior officer—but unfortunately he detested operas. The logical rule would be to value these services at the figure the person would pay for them voluntarily, but this is unworkable.

In practice, in the United States, in part as a result of these problems, only outright payment in commodities is taxable (at their commercial or "fair" market value) plus the value of housing provided when not essential to the performance of the work. Thus, if a university provides free housing for faculty, the value of this housing—the amount for which it would rent—is taxable income. But housing provided an employee at a power plant high in the mountains, where he must live to perform his duties and where no alternative housing is available, would not be taxed. Most, but not all, services provided, such as parking space, are not taxable. The distinctions are fine and there have been many controversies. The general exclusion of free benefits in the form of services encourages firms to provide these in lieu of equivalent money payments, particularly to executives. As a consequence, some distortion of resource allocation results, as well as discrimination in favor of persons who receive these services compared to ones who do not. But to do otherwise encounters the valuation problem noted above.

Self-Produced Goods

In modern society, most persons gain their incomes through the monetary sector of the economy, but persons may produce some goods for their own use. Farmers may use their own produce in the household; persons grow vegetables and flowers in their gardens; persons may repair their cars or paint their houses. These are all items of income by the Simons definition, but they are excluded from taxable income, partly for administrative reasons; it is difficult to discover these activities if persons do not report them. But there are also serious problems of delimitation and valuation. If farmers use some of the butter they produce for their own use instead of selling it all and buying an equivalent amount, the item is obviously income by the Simons definition. But some of the activities are primarily designed to utilize leisure time; the persons are not as much interested in the product as in the fun of growing it, and the output may be far greater than they would ever buy. This type of activity is probably extremely vulnerable to taxation; if persons had to pay tax on the value of all the garden produce they grow, they might well quit producing it. Apart from this element, valuation is difficult, particularly with such items as flowers.

As a consequence of these problems, in general, such self-produced goods are not taxed at all. But this practice goes too far in the opposite direction; persons are encouraged to produce their own goods and services instead of buying them. Persons gain by taking a week off from work and painting their houses because they would have to pay tax on the income they would otherwise earn to pay the painters.

Presumably greater efficiency is obtained if they work at their regular jobs and hire a professional painter to paint the house.

The most serious question arises with the work of the housewife (or househusband). This is obviously a portion of total real income of society (though not included in measures of GNP). If the wife obtains a job and hires the work done, her income is fully taxed; if she devotes her time to housework, no tax liability is created. Inevitably some distortion of work patterns results. Yet to include the value of housework in taxable income is not only impractical but a potential source of inequity. And of course, housework does not generate money income with which taxes must be paid. Any adjustment must be along the lines of allowing deductions of expenses of having housework done, since that is a cost of earning income. But the distinction between expenditures to earn the income and purely consumption expenditures, as discussed below, is not a clear one.

Owner-Occupied Housing

Use of the flow approach to income rather than the Simons approach results in exclusion from tax of the use value of all owner-occupied housing and, in so doing, gives rise to serious inequity and economic distortions (in addition to the inequity created by deductibility of interest and property taxes discussed below). Compare the situation of two families, each with $40,000 accumulated wealth and salary incomes of $20,000 a year. One buys securities yielding $2,400 a year and pays rent with this amount. The other invests the $40,000 in a home, thus escaping rent. The costs associated with the house are much less than the rental figure. The first pays tax on the $2,400 at its marginal rate; the second pays nothing. The consequence is to create serious discrimination aginst the tenant and to provide strong artificial stimulus to purchase a home rather than renting and making other investments. Some of the advantage may be lost, of course, if increased purchasing of houses drives up housing costs, and there is some evidence that this has occurred. The imputed return on homeowners' investments in their homes is very low.[2]

The present treatment may be justified on the grounds that society wishes to encourage home ownership, but there are other far more efficient ways of doing so than by tax discrimination. It is possible to require persons to include imputed rental values—what the homes would rent for if they were rented—in their incomes. Compliance and administrative problems would be serious but not insuperable. But the principle of freeing these imputed incomes is so widely accepted—despite the inequity and the distortions—that change is

---

[2] R. Goode, *The Individual Income Tax*, rev. ed. (Washington, D.C.: The Brookings Institution, 1976), p. 122.

most unlikely. Any such change would necessitate increased federal aid to local government, since resistance to property taxes would be increased. Great Britain originally did tax imputed rentals, but this rule was eventually eliminated. One study concluded that the real cost of exclusion of rental value of owner-occupied housing in the United States is about $500 million a year, in the sense of the loss in consumer surplus from the production of the additional housing instead of other goods.[3] While this figure cannot be taken too seriously because it involves interpersonal utility comparisons, it does suggest a magnitude of some importance. A study by Henry Aaron shows that homeowners, as a whole, pay from $7 to $9 billion less income taxes—17 to 22 percent of what they pay—as a result of the exclusion of imputed rent (about $4 billion of the $7 to $9 billion tax savings) and other concessions. Aaron concludes that consumption of housing is perhaps 20 percent greater than it otherwise would be.[4] More seriously, the gain from the exclusion is highly regressive.[5] The very poor typically do not own their homes and get no benefit; the income elasticity of demand for housing is apparently well above 1, and the wealthy are given more incentive to acquire additional housing because of their high marginal tax rates. The result is to lead to increased supply of housing for the wealthy compared to that for the low-income groups—hardly a policy in conformity with usual social values.

In some degree, this favor to homeowners is offset by the favorable depreciation treatment allowed owners of rental housing.[6] If these benefits are passed on to tenants, who concentrate in the lower-income groups, the discrimination against them is lessened to some degree. A study of Canadian practice concluded that in that country the gains to tenants, as a whole, through the depreciation allowances, may be as great as that to homeowners—but that the wealthy homeowners gain relative to the poor.[7]

Legislation in 1975 added, at least temporarily, a new concession to homeowners; a tax credit of 5 percent of the purchase price, up to $2,000, was allowed the purchase of new residences between March 12 and December 31, 1975.

---

[3] D. Laidler, "Income Tax Incentives for Owner Occupied Housing," in *The Taxation of Income from Capital*, eds. A. C. Harberger and M. J. Bailey (Washington, D.C.: Brookings Institution, 1969), pp. 50–76.

[4] T. H. Aaron, "Income Taxes and Housing," *American Economic Review*, vol. 60 (December 1970), pp. 789–806.

[5] Ibid.; *Shelter and Subsidies: Who Benefits from the Federal Housing Policies?* (Washington, D.C.: The Brookings Institution, 1972).

[6] Laidler, "Income Tax Incentives."

[7] F. A. Clayton, "Income Taxes and Subsidies to Homeowners and Renters: A Comparison of U.S. and Canadian Experience," *Canadian Tax Journal*, vol. 22 (May–June 1974), pp. 295–305.

Gifts and Bequests Received

Under a strict definition of income, any sum received as a gift or bequest would be taxable income. These elements are, however, excluded from income by specific provision of the law in the United States and most countries.[8] In part, this results from the use of separate taxes on bequests, namely, the estate or inheritance taxes, plus a related levy on gifts imposed upon the donor. Taxation of bequests in the United States is older than income taxation; bequests were regarded as particularly suitable objects for taxation because of their windfall character, and the taxes were regarded as means to lessen concentration of wealth. Special treatment is also justified on the basis of their irregularity, which would require special treatment under the income tax, and because the tax capacity involved is considered to depend in part on the relationship of the heir to the decedent. Widows and minor children are essentially no better off because title of property has passed to them, since they had previously enjoyed the use of the property, whereas a person left $10,000 by an uncle he or she has never seen has gained just as much as if he or she had won this in a lottery or worked for it. Use of a separate levy, therefore, allows adjustments for these special circumstances without distorting the income tax structure.

Taxation of gifts was largely introduced to check avoidance of the estate tax. To include all gifts as taxable income would encounter several problems. Many are hard to discover. Some involve support of dependents, or in other words, use of the income within the family unit. Others involve partial support of relatives who are not dependents, essentially sharing of income. Gifts in kind—Christmas presents and such—would not only create valuation problems but difficulties for the recipient comparable to those encountered in any taxation of income in kind. The recipient might be hard pressed to find the money with which to pay tax, and might prefer not to receive the gift at all. Taxation of Christmas presents is to many a little like shooting Santa Claus.

The exclusion of gifts, while not seriously affecting the equity of the tax structure, does lead to some borderline questions—the watch given a retiring employee by the employer, the distinction between a fellowship for a graduate student (a gift and not taxable) and an assistantship (a payment for a service and therefore taxable, with some exceptions). Thus a graduate student pays tax if he works for the money; he does not if he does not work for it.

All in all, however, it is hardly practicable to tax all gifts, while to tax

---

[8] The Canadian Royal Commission proposed taxation of bequests and gifts beyond a specified exemption as income. Those within the family unit would be exempt.

only larger ones would result in splitting large ones into smaller pieces; separate treatment of gifts and bequests is usually regarded as preferable.

Life Insurance Proceeds and Annuities

Life insurance is a major outlet for saving and a source of substantial income. Life insurance proceeds contain three elements: return of amounts paid in; earnings on the amounts of premiums paid in; and pure insurance compensation, arising from deviation from standard mortality. The heirs of a person who dies sooner than the life-expectancy figure gain; the heirs of a person who lives longer than the expectancy lose. The first of these three elements is clearly not income but merely the return of savings; the second is income; the third one is income, in a broad sense of that term. The problem centers around the second and is basically a question of who is going to pay tax on the gain and when. In practice, the earnings, in the United States and most countries, are not subject to tax, except when the holder of the policy realizes on the policy himself, as under an endowment policy, where the amount in excess of premiums paid in is subject to tax. There is no pure insurance element involved. The present system results in substantial escape of tax and distorts investment policies of wealthy persons wishing to leave property for their heirs; life insurance offers great tax advantages since all the earnings until death will be free of tax. The gains are less for the very wealthy than other alternatives such as state and local bonds; they are particularly attractive to the upper-middle-income groups. The only workable approach is to require each person to include in his or her income each year *(a)* policy dividends received or credited to his or her insurance, and *(b)* an allocated amount of the share of the profits earned on investment from policyholder funds during the year. The companies would be required to report these amounts. This proposal has rarely been taken very seriously, although it was proposed by the Canadian Royal Commission. In part, the dividends are regarded simply as overpayments of premiums and thus return of the person's own money—which in fact they may or may not be. The most significant portion, the year's share of earnings, involves taxing persons on sums they cannot realize on, either easily or at all, and thus is a type of item that Congress is reluctant to tax. Yet failure to do so perpetuates serious discrimination and distortion in the tax structure.

Annuities represent a particularly troublesome type of payment because of their mixture of capital and earnings. A person retires at 65 and commences to draw on a lifetime annuity. If the person lives only a few years he or she will not get back all that was paid in, so all of the payments received are return of capital. If the person lives to be 95, he or she will get back the capital and much more as well. But in any one of the earlier years the determination of the nature of the payment is not possible. Accordingly, an arbitrary rule is used: The amount received is divided into two parts on the basis of the life expectancy at the person's age, and the part held to be income is made taxable. This is arbitrary, but there appears to be no better alternative.

The tax treatment of retirement income generally is essentially a question of timing of tax liability rather than of exempt status and will be considered later in the chapter.

THE DEFINITION OF INCOME: CAPITAL GAINS

Most incomes that persons receive are factor incomes—wages and salaries paid for work done, interest and dividends on capital, profits from the operation of a farm or small business. But one additional type is large in overall importance but unevenly distributed by individuals, namely, capital gains—increases in the value of property held. A substantial portion of the total—half or more—arises on corporation stock—which has, on the average, over the years tended to appreciate at the rate of 7 percent a year, although with much variation among individual companies.[9] These gains, in turn, primarily reflect earnings retained in the business, although in shorter periods they may arise from temporary acquisition of a monopoly position, speculation, and other causes. The other major segment arises from increases in real property values resulting from growth of population and economic activity, which push up the demand for land.

Are Capital Gains Income?

The argument is sometimes advanced that capital gains are not income at all; that, to use an analogy common in the literature, they reflect growth in the size of the tree rather than fruit produced by the tree. This argument in its extreme form has no validity whatever. If I bought stock for $50 a share in 1965 and sell it this year for $100, I can spend the $50 gain in exactly the same fashion as $50 earned from giving a lecture. Basically, capital gains do represent economic gain; they fall within the Simons definition noted above.

There are two elements in capital gains about which legitimate questions can be raised. First, in part, gains may reflect increases in the general price level. But other elements in income are also affected by general price level shifts; corporations profit from increases in the value of inventories and from using older equipment purchased at a lower price when competitors are using more expensive equipment.

---

[9] M. J. Bailey, "Capital Gains and Income Taxation," in *The Taxation of Income from Capital*, eds. Harberger and Bailey pp. 16–17.

In general, persons making capital gains during a period of inflation fare much better than those holding fixed-income assets (bonds and the like). Since it is not feasible to adjust all income for the effects of price level changes there is little justification for seeking to eliminate inflation-caused elements in capital gains, the recipients being, on the whole, beneficiaries of inflation.

Secondly, some capital gains result from reductions in the interest rate. If the market rate falls, outstanding bonds rise in price. If the person uses the gains to buy consumption goods, he has experienced a gain. If he buys other securities, in a sense he has not, yet he must pay tax. But the second case cannot be distinguished easily from the first—and in general, since these existing security holders benefit from lower interest rates, there is little need for special adjustment for them. Adjustment for all consequences of interest rate changes for income tax purposes is hopeless.

A major issue is whether the income should be taxed each year as it accrues, as under the Simons definition, or when it is realized through sale of the property. In practice the realization basis is used; the accrual alternative is discussed later in the chapter.

Peculiarities of Capital Gains

While capital gains are income, there are certain differences between capital gains and other incomes that have affected tax treatment of them. First, they are less regular than most incomes, because they are particularly affected by changes in business activity and, when taxed at the time of realization, they may have accumulated over a number of years. Secondly, unlike most income, when they are taxed on a realization basis, persons have control over the timing and, in fact, tax can be avoided throughout the person's lifetime, the property being passed on to heirs. Thirdly, there is a relatively high degree of convertibility between capital gains and other income, as explained in a later section. For one simple example, the principal owner of a small corporation may take the profits out of the business for his own use in the form of dividends or he may retain them in the business and sell his holdings, realizing on them as capital gains. Fourthly, persons may treat capital gains differently from other income and make decisions about consumption versus savings on a somewhat different basis. Finally, unlike most incomes, gains may be negative as well as positive, since property unfortunately declines in value as well as rises.

Special Treatment

Capital gains have from the beginning of the income tax in the United States law been singled out for special treatment, with substantial changes being made in 1969. As the situation now stands, under the personal income tax, capital gains are taxed as follows:

1. Short-term gains, on property held less than one year (nine months in 1977, previously six months); fully taxed.

2. Long-term gains, on property held over one year (nine months in 1977); one half of the capital gains can be excluded from income; thus the top effective marginal rate is 35 percent instead of the 70 percent figure on other property income.

3. Capital gains are taxed only when realized, that is, when the property is sold; transfer at death is not subject to income tax but the beneficiary, when ultimately selling, calculates his gain on the basis of the donor's purchase price.

4. Capital losses are deductible (short-term, in full; long-term, to the extent of one half) against capital gains and against other income up to the amount of $3,000, with carry-forward provisions allowing the same treatment of successive years, until all has been deducted.

5. The one half of capital gains excluded from other income, along with certain other preferential treatment income, is subject to a flat 15 percent rate on the amount of such income in excess of the sum of $10,000 or half the taxpayer's regular income tax, whichever is greater.[10]

The net result is to tax capital gains less heavily than other income at the highest income levels, while the deductibility of capital losses is significantly restricted. A large portion of accrued capital gains existing at any one time has not been taxed. Before the minimum tax rule, as much as half escape tax completely; about one fifth escape at death.[11]

Canada did not tax capital gains until 1972, when a system comparable to that in the United States was introduced.[12] Great Britain, which traditionally did not tax capital gains, began to do so in a series of steps in the sixties. Some other British Commonwealth countries still do not tax them.

The reasons for the special treatment follow from the characteristics noted above:

Irregularity. Particularly because capital gains are taxed at the time of realization, they are highly irregular. Thus to apply regular progressive income tax rates would seriously discriminate against

---

[10] Suppose a taxpayer has capital gains of $200,000 and no other "preferential" income and owes tax of $18,000. He includes one half of the capital gains with other income. On the $100,000 not included, he owes tax of $13,500 (15 percent of $90,000).

[11] Bailey, "Capital Gains."

[12] One half of capital gains are included in taxable income and taxed at regular rates. One half of capital losses may be subtracted from the taxable gains or deducted from other income to the extent of $1,000. Nondeducted losses may be carried back one year and forward indefinitely. Realization is deemed to occur at death.

gains just as it would against other irregular income, in the absence of a general system of allowing persons to spread their incomes over a period of years for tax purposes. Capital gains constitute a major form of irregular income and thus attention was given them prior to other irregular incomes. This problem could, of course, be avoided by general averaging.

Safety Valve for Investment and Economic Growth. There has been widespread feeling—but little evidence—that the high income tax rates deter risk-taking and investment, particularly in new and growing businesses. The low rate on capital gains has been regarded as an important escape hatch to prevent the income tax from having devastating effects on the economy. This reason, probably more than any other, has helped to perpetuate the favorable treatment, which was first introduced apparently because of irregularity.

Investment Markets. Since the tax is imposed upon realization, investors may be "locked in" to their investments, that is, they defer selling securities upon which the tax will be due. The lower rate lessens this effect.

Inflation. The favorable treatment has been encouraged to some extent by increases in the general price level and the consequent belief that the gains are in part fictitious.

Special Circumstances. Capital gains treatment has been extended to certain specific transactions of a lump-sum nature—sale of timber; royalties from patient rights, iron ore, and coal; and farm livestock. To some extent, pressure of interested groups was responsible for these special concessions.

Objectionable Features

The present system is seriously defective in a number of respects, in terms of the objectives of the income tax structure.

Nonuniformity. One form of income, that arising from increases in asset values, receives more favorable treatment than other forms of income, particularly for persons in the higher-income levels. By one estimate, the effective tax rate on capital gains as a whole was only 8 percent in the pre-1970 period.[13] The treatment favors the stock speculator over the person gaining profit from a proprietorship or dividends from a corporation. It favors property income generally over labor income; the action of Congress in 1969 in lowering the maximum rate on earned income to 50 percent was in large part due to this consideration. It makes the tax much less progressive than it would appear to be from the rate tables, because the capital gains concentrate so heavily in the high-income groups. There is a strong positive corre-

---

[13] Bailey, "Capital Gains."

lation between income and the percentage of income consisting of capital gains. Whereas capital gains constitute (1970) .9 percent of the income of persons with incomes from $5,000 to $10,000, they constitute 8 percent in the $50,000 to $100,000 range, 40 percent in the $200,000 to $500,000 range, and 62 percent in the $1 million and over group.[14]

If capital gains were made fully taxable, the income tax liability of persons in the $5,000–10,000 range would rise by 1.7 percent, of persons in the $50,000–100,000 range by 7.5 percent, of persons with incomes over $1 million, by 60.8 percent.[15] Since the 1976 legislation, the increase would be somewhat less.

The nonuniformity is objectionable on grounds of economic efficiency as well as equity. The favorable treatment without question alters investment patterns toward those special categories receiving capital gains treatment (e.g., livestock fattening) and toward the types of investments that will generate capital gains rather than other income. The venturesome type of enterprise is favored over the more stable income-yielding investment, such as public utilities. As noted below, this encouragement to risk-taking may be of some advantage, but the existence of a net gain is by no means clear. The corporate form of organization is artificially encouraged so that persons can realize on earnings via capital gains as frequently the capital gains advantage more than offsets the corporate income tax liability. Firms— particularly closely held ones—are given strong encouragement to retain earnings in the business so that the owners can receive capital gains treatment. The fact that liquidating dividends are taxed as capital gains encourages continuous creation and dissolution of corporations.

Conversion of Other Income into Capital Gains. The objectionable equity and economic-efficiency consequences are compounded by the constant pressure to convert regular income into the legal form of capital gains. In addition to compounding effects on equity and economic efficiency, substantial resources are utilized to find ways to make the conversion. Owner-managers of smaller corporations hold down their salary payments and accumulate larger retained earnings, which will increase the value of the stock; thus even wage income is converted into capital gains. There is constant pressure to sell rights to future incomes for a capital sum. Congress and the tax advisers have waged a running battle for years over collapsible corporations. A corporation is formed by a contractor to put up an apartment building; the building is then sold and the corporation liquidated, the profits of the venture being paid out as liquidating dividends at capital gains rates.

---

[14] Goode, *Individual Income Tax*, p. 188.

[15] George F. Break and Joseph A. Pechman, *Federal Tax Reform* (Washington D.C.: The Brookings Institution, 1975), p. 49.

Deferral and the Lock-In Problem. Because capital gains are taxed at realization and not at death, and since persons can control the time of realization, there is substantial incentive to defer the sale of property on which gains have accrued. If the property is sold and the money reinvested, the net earnings will be reduced as a result of the tax payment. This effect, of course, costs the government revenue and is unfair to persons who cannot defer realization of income, and it also lessens the fluidity of capital markets.

It should be stressed that deferral and lock-in are not a result of the favorable treatment given capital gains, per se; it would be worse if they were fully taxable. It is a result of the use of the realization basis and the failure to tax capital gains on property held till death except when the property is sold by the heirs.

Administration. The provision of special treatment to one form of income requires the delimitation of that form of income from other types. Capital gains are particularly hard to delimit, and as a consequence, many of the interpretative questions and court cases generated by the income tax arise on capital gains questions. If all income can be treated in the same manner, these borderline interpretative questions can be avoided.

Lost Revenue. In 1972, loss of revenue from untaxed accrued capital gains totaled about $17 billion; considering other exclusions of capital gains, the loss was from $26 billion to $29 billion.[16] Changes in the tax laws since that date have reduced the relative loss somewhat.

Reforms within the Present Structure

The unsatisfactory nature of the present treatment of capital gains—not only in the United States but in most other countries as well—has led to numerous suggestions for change. These fall into two general categories: changes within the present framework, designed to lessen the severity of some of the most objectionable features, and a broad revision of the entire system. Several significant changes were made in 1969 and 1976.

A number of individual reforms have been proposed:

Eligibility. The special type of transaction, such as various royalty incomes, brought within the capital gains category by the law could easily be removed. The treatment of livestock, for example, is a completely unnecessary concession to agriculture and a source of substantial tax avoidance by wealthy persons who buy farms as hobbies and tax-escape devices or directly invest in cattle they never see. This has the further social disadvantage of reducing the role of the small inde-

---

[16] J. A. Pechman and B. A. Okner, "Individual Income Tax Erosion by Income Class," in *The Economics of Federal Subsidy Programs,* Joint Economic Committee (Washington, D.C.: 1972), pp. 13–40.

pendent farmer. Stock options were denied capital gains treatment in 1976.

A more drastic change would deny capital gains treatment to holdings in closely held businesses, where the greatest leakage now occurs. Capital gains arising out of overdepreciation of real property (the gain at the time of ultimate sale getting capital gains treatment) could likewise be given full tax treatment. A strong case can be made, in fact, for full taxation of all increases in land values, which reflect a type of "unearned" income and often result from speculation of a type harmful to optimal land-use development.

Holding Period. On the basis of the philosophy that special treatment is required for capital gains because they accrue over a period of years and are realized in one year, there was no possible justification for use of an eligibility period under one year. Finally, in 1976, Congress raised the holding period to one year (commencing in 1978).

Capital Gains on Gifts and Bequests. One of the worst sources of revenue leakage, inequity, and adverse economic effects has been the exclusion from the tax of gains not realized until death.[17] The fact that the estate tax applies does not at all compensate for failure to tax the gains; the estate tax exemptions are high, property on which no untaxed gains have been made being treated in the same fashion as that on which gains have accrued. Similarly, on gifts, there is merit in applying tax to the gain at the time the gift is made, with adjustments for transfers within the family. Since the 1976 legislation the accrued gains will be taxed when realized by the heirs.

Until 1969, when a person made gifts to charitable and other organizations of property on which gains had accrued, he was allowed to deduct the current value of the property as a charitable contribution without having to pay tax on the capital gains that had accrued. The result was a great incentive to give such property instead of money, and large tax savings were possible for such persons. When large capital gains had been made, the person would have more money left over after giving the property to a charitable organization than if he sold the property and paid tax on it, despite favorable tax rate on such gains, plus having the satisfaction of making the contribution. The 1969 legislation restricted this privilege somewhat; only property subject to long-term capital gains treatment is eligible, and the deduction is limited to half the value on gifts to certain types of organizations. There is still substantial room for tax avoidance, however, and further restriction is desirable.

---

[17] According to one estimate, the revenue loss is about $2 billion a year. Peter Eilbott, "The Revenue Gain from Taxation of Decedents' Unrealized Capital Gains," *National Tax Journal*, vol. 22 (December 1969), pp. 506–15.

Roll-Over. A reform aimed solely at the lock-in problem, and in fact one that would liberalize the overall treatment still more, is the authorization of roll-over; that is, if a person sold one property and purchased another, he would not be subject to capital gains tax. This rule is now applied to owner-occupied homes. The change would, of course, lessen the lock-in effect. But it would result in substantial deferment of tax and complete escape in many instances unless gains accrued at death were taxable. The rule would substantially complicate operation of the tax when a person did extensive trading over a long period of time. There are also difficulties with losses; if losses were currently deductible, but gains could be rolled over, there would be still more escape from tax. On the whole, this offers no basic solution to the major disadvantages of the present treatment. Furthermore, the significance for the economy of the lock-in effect, particularly if the death rule were eliminated, is not at all clear.

Basic Reforms—The Accrual Approach

The need for special treatment and the lock-in effect are in large measure products of taxation of capital gains at the time of realization. If all taxpayers were subject annually to tax on the gains that accrued during the year, as under the Simons concept of income, the irregularity would be greatly reduced (but not eliminated; gains do not necessarily accrue on a uniform basis year by year). All incentive toward lock-in would be eliminated, as well as to deferment of tax; there would be no large accumulation of gains to be taxed (or escape tax) at death. Special rules for owner-occupied homes, forced sales of property, and the like would be unnecessary.

There are, however, serious limitations to the use of the accrual basis. One is administrative. Many types of property are not easily valued. Taxpayers would be put to substantial trouble and expense to periodically value all property, and the tasks of IRS would be tremendous if effort were made to check the reported valuations. If this were not done, taxpayers would adjust the value figures in particular years to minimize tax. The task would be most difficult with closely held businesses and with some types of real property.

Secondly, persons would frequently be in the position of lacking liquid assets with which to pay tax. In periods of rapid increases in prices of stocks many persons would be unable to meet their tax payments without sale of stock and forced liquidation would to some extent replace the lock-in effect. Persons owning small businesses or real estate might be squeezed even more severely since they could not easily sell portions of their holdings.

Thirdly, a substantial amount of wasted effort would result. Stock prices rise in one year, fall in another, and rise again, with consequent taxation of gains and deduction of losses. It is not at all clear whether the net effect of accrual taxation would be stabilizing or destabilizing. There would also be serious transitional problems in moving from realization to the accrual basis.

These problems, coupled with the merits of the idea, led the Canadian Royal Commission to propose taxation on an accrual basis only of shares in publicly held companies, on a five-year basis. These securities—which account for a substantial portion of capital gains— are easy to value, and persons can sell some shares to obtain needed funds if required. Use of the accrual basis on those types of assets most difficult to value would be avoided. The liquidity problems of holders of large blocks of stock would remain, however, and the use of one system for one type of property and of another system for other types would inevitably lead to distortion in investment and in corporate organization decisions. The Canadian government did not accept the proposal. It is questionable whether in practice the accrual basis is workable at all without unacceptable effects.

Basic Reform: Proration or Averaging

The initial impetus for special treatment of capital gains arose from their irregularity. The accrual basis would lessen this problem; it could be eliminated completely by some form of spreading or averaging capital gains over a period of years. One simple technique is proration—to allow the gains to be taxed at a marginal rate based on the number of years the property was held. In simple form: If the property were held 10 years, the person's marginal tax rate would be applied to one tenth of the gain and this sum multiplied by 10 to get the total tax due on the gain. This approach would in many respects be an improvement over the present system or over full taxation of gains in a particular year. But it would encourage persons to time their capital gains to minimize tax and it would provide a permanent tax advantage for persons with recurrent capital gains.

The most inclusive approach to the capital gains problem is some form of general averaging, as discussed in the next chapter. If all taxpayers were allowed to average, that is, spread out their incomes over a period of time to avoid adverse effects of progression upon irregular incomes, capital gains could be treated like all other income. If a compound interest feature were included, as subsequently discussed, all incentive to defer realization would also be eliminated. The principal difficulty is one not confined to capital gains but to all averaging— the need for records on previous years' incomes and for recalculation of previous returns. These are not insurmountable tasks, but they are by no means negligible. This approach would allow the treatment of capital gains in exactly the same fashion as other income and avoid all interpretative questions. It would not eliminate the lock-in effect, of course; only the accrual basis can do this. If coupled with taxation of gains at death, however, the system would reduce the lock-in effect compared to the present situation.

Defense of Preferential Treatment

The slowness of Congress to act to lessen the preferential treatment given to capital gains illustrates the degree of support that such treatment has. Most of the argument for preferential treatment—and for the more extreme position of no tax at all—centers around the safety-valve feature of the low taxation of capital gains, encouraging risk-taking and increasing the amount of internal capital available for expansion and perhaps even increasing the percentage of national income saved. Various interview studies have shown that the capital gains treatment encourages many wealthy persons to place more funds in growth stocks than they would otherwise.[18] Certainly the present tax treatment encourages closely held businesses to retain larger portions of earnings in the business, and there is considerable evidence that firms are more willing to expand with internal funds than from sale of additional stock or bonds. The lenient treatment lessens, it is argued, adverse effects that progressive income taxation may have upon the propensity to save. Alternatively, the capital gains treatment may be regarded as a political safety valve, which allows Congress to place heavy nominal taxes upon the incomes of the wealthy without leading to violent protests or serious deterring effects on the economy.

The capital gains treatment probably does lead to more risk-taking and real investment than would occur with full taxation of capital gains, other elements in the tax structure, such as tax rates, being given. But if capital gains were fully taxable, the high-level income tax rates could be substantially lower than they are, with the same or greater tax burden on the wealthy as at present but more equitable distribution among individuals, and the net effect might not be significantly different from the present.

The present inadequate taxation of capital gains is a serious source of loss of equity in the income tax structure and of loss in revenue at given tax rates. It is a major source of economic distortions and administrative complications. The price paid for limited stimulus to risk-taking and real investment is very great. Progress was made in the Tax Reform Act of 1976; the holding period was increased to one year, the minimum tax rate was increased, and heirs are taxed, at realiza-

[18] R. Barlow, H. E. Brazer, and J. N. Morgan, *Economic Behavior of the Affluent* (Washington, D.C.: The Brookings Institution, 1966).

tion, on the gains accruing prior to inheritance; but capital gains are still favored.

ITEMS EXCLUDED FROM INCOME BY SPECIFIC PROVISIONS OF THE LAW

In the United States, as in many countries, certain other items of income are specifically excluded from tax for various reasons of economic and social policy, not because of any inherent problems in taxing them.

Welfare, Social Security, and Various Veterans' Benefits

While there is no general justification for excluding transfer incomes from taxable income, the United States does in practice exempt social security and various welfare payments. The original reasoning appears to be that most persons receiving these payments would owe no tax anyway (especially with income tax exemptions of the thirties) and that such payments were not appropriate for taxation. But many persons do draw social security payments along with other income (investment income) and some welfare recipients may be subject to tax. There is no possible objection to including the items in the former case; in the latter, the taxation would necessitate higher welfare payments, but would make clearer the actual cost of the welfare program, avoid discrimination against the poor not obtaining welfare, and avoid distortions in the tax structure. The most serious distortion has been the effect of the social security exemption in leading Congress to reduce tax on other types of retirement income, and, in 1976, on all income of the lower-income elderly.

Exemptions of this type add to the complexity of the tax returns and tax calculations and lead to continuing demands for further extension of the exemption.

Interest on State and Local Bonds

One of the most significant exclusions in the United States income tax law, one rarely found in other countries, is that of interest on state and local bonds (commonly called municipals). These were originally excluded for constitutional reasons—the belief that taxation of them would be rejected by the United States Supreme Court, as occurred in 1896. Until 1938 wages and salaries of state and local employees were likewise exempt under court interpretation; the Supreme Court reversed its attitude on wages and salaries in that year and very possibly would do so on interest. But Congress, under the political pressure of the states and local governments, has not acted to eliminate this exemption from the law and made no changes in the reform legislation of 1969.

There are several significant objections to the exemption. First, the exemption provides a major avenue of tax avoidance for persons in the higher-income groups. A married couple with $100,000 taxable income would pay $45,180 (1976); if this entire income were obtained from state and local bond interest, it would pay nothing. At the most, the yield might be $20,000 less than could be obtained from other securities of comparable risk. In other words, in the higher-income levels, the differential in yield due to the tax-exempt status is much less than the tax saving; even in middle-income levels there is advantage. Low-income groups, of course, cannot afford to buy state and local securities because of the lower yield.

A second consequence is to divert investment patterns of wealthy groups in the direction of greater holdings of municipals, thus lessening the amount they place into greater-risk equity investments. Yet the wealthy are the ones in the best position to take risk. At the same time, nontaxable entities, such as retirement funds, avoid these investments. Over 70 percent of the interest from municipals owned by individuals goes to persons with a marginal rate in excess of 50 percent. About half of all municipals are owned by commercial banks.

Third, the federal government loses far more revenue (about $2 billion annually) than the states and localities gain (an estimated $1.3 billion), for the same reason that the wealthy gain from buying the securities. If all municipals were purchased by persons in the highest tax bracket, there would be little net revenue loss, but this is not so; they can be absorbed in the market only over a considerable income and tax-rate range. On holdings by persons above the break-even range of tax rates, the federal government loses more than the states and local governments gain. Finally, the subsidy may increase relative state-local reliance on borrowing compared to taxation because of the "subsidy" element.

To compound the undesirable effects, various local governments commenced to finance facilities for business firms from tax-exempt municipals, in order to lure industries to the community, thus, in effect, providing the firms with tax-free capital. This has at least been restricted; securities issued for this purpose are not tax exempt if the issue exceeds $1 million.

The obvious overall solution is to make interest on all future issues taxable, even if existing issues are left tax free in view of the expectations on the part of the holders at the time of purchase and the sharp decline in bond prices that would occur. The obstacle to the basic reform is the strong opposition of the states and localities because of the higher interest cost they would have to pay. There is some objection to increases in the costs of these units in view of the many pressing urban problems and limited tax resources. A compromise measure has been suggested: to make the interest taxable, with the federal government sharing a portion of the interest cost. More recent proposals suggest that states and local governments be given the option of issuing taxable securities in exchange for a federal subsidy of a portion of the interest. A study shows that such a policy will cost the federal government much less than the interest saving to the states and local governments and will improve equity by greatly reducing the volume of tax exempts issued; a 50 percent subsidy would eliminate all exempt issues.[19] Some offset will result from the rise in the price of existing municipals (primarily benefiting the wealthy), but there is a net gain in equity, so long as the subsidy rate is not excessive. If the subsidy rate exceeds the corporate income tax rate, however, corporations will shift investments to these municipals, and the cost to the treasury will rise rapidly.[20] Some state and local officials are sympathetic to this program in the desire to attract institutional tax-exempt investors, while others fear the conditions that might be attached to the subsidy grants.

GROSS VERSUS NET INCOME: THE EXPENSES OF GAINING INCOME

Regardless of the approach used to the definition of income for tax purposes, a distinction is required between production expenditures—those necessary to gain the income—and consumption expenditures, which involve use of income. With the Simons definition, consumption, which is a part of taxable income, must be distinguished from production expenditure, which is not. With the flow approach to income, expenditures to gain the income must be identified to permit this deduction.

In the United States, the term *adjusted gross income* (AGI) is given to the figure of gross income minus the cost of earning the income.

Most production expenditures—costs of materials, wages paid employees, and the like—are clearly identifiable. The problem arises with expenditures for items that may be used for either purpose and dual items acquired partly for one, partly for the other, purpose.

Minimum Living Expenditures

In a sense, basic living expenditures are necessary to earn the income, since a person must eat to work. Rather than allow actual deductions, however, the policy is to provide a minimum exemption for the

[19] P. Fortune, "The Impact of Taxable Municipal Bonds," *National Tax Journal*, vol. 26 (March 1973), pp. 29–42.

[20] H. Galper and G. E. Peterson, "The Equity Effects of a Taxable Municipal Bond Subsidy," *National Tax Journal*, vol. 26 (December 1973), pp. 611–24.

taxpayer and his or her dependents, as explained in the next chapter, because of the problem of identifying actual necessary amounts for each individual case.

Education[21]

Educational expenditures are essentially dual in character, with the relative role of the two objectives varying in individual cases. In part, persons seek education to increase their lifetime incomes and attain more desired occupations, but in part, they do so for purposes of personal satisfaction unrelated to future income. There is no effective way that the two elements can be separated. If any deduction at all is to be allowed, choice must also be made between the parent and the student as the recipient of the deduction. To allow the parents to make the deduction (except when the child is self-supporting) should encourage them to provide more education for their children and allow them more funds to finance it. Current deductibility for the students against current income would often be of little benefit to them. Alternatively, if the granting of the allowance to the students rather than their parents would have greater effect in encouraging persons to obtain higher levels of education, authorization for deduction of the capital sum against income in subsequent years on a depreciation basis might be the most satisfactory answer. There are also questions of the amounts to be allowed. Obviously, cost of tuition and books would be deductible but should living costs, often the largest item, be included, in view of the fact that the person must live anyway? Actually the largest opportunity cost is that of income foregone during the years of education, yet deductibility of this item would create intolerable administrative problems, persons are foregoing current income voluntarily in order to gain greater income in the future and the foregone income of course is not taxed. There are also questions about which education to include—graduate and professional as well as undergraduate, for example.

At present, in the United States, deductibility is rigidly limited to education a person must obtain to continue to qualify within a particular occupation. The principal example is the cost of education public school teachers must obtain on a periodic basis to retain their certificates. Various efforts have been made in Congress to increase the coverage of the deduction, primarily on the grounds of the need to encourage persons to obtain or provide for their children a higher level of education. It is often charged that the tax structure favors physical capital (on which depreciation can be deducted) over human capital. Other motives include the desire to increase opportunity for

---

[21] The article by J. K. McNulty, "Tax Policy and Tuition Legislation: Federal Income Tax Allowances for Personal Costs of Higher Education," *California Law Review* vol. 61 (January 1973), pp. 1–80, provides a detailed review of the question.

education and to aid private education in its struggle against cheaper public education. But Congress has been unwilling to act—partly because of the problems noted above, partly because of the belief that the upper-income groups would gain most of the benefit. Other forms of assistance to higher education appear to be much more equitable and efficient.

Expenses for Child Care and Housework, Particularly for Working Wives

If the wife remains in the home, no taxable income is created. If she takes a job and hires a baby-sitter and other personal help, she must pay taxes on her income. Should she be allowed to deduct these expenditures, which have been necessitated by the earning of the income? The problem is most acute when the wife is the principal or sole wage earner. In recent years, Congress has greatly liberalized the child-care deduction, and, as of 1977, converted it to a credit against tax, equal to 20 percent of the amount paid for child care, up to $400 for one dependent, $800 for two. The children must be under 15. Disabled spouses are also eligible. There is no longer an income limitation for eligibility. The principal issue is that there is no clear line of delineation between costs necessary for the wife or husband to work and additional consumption expenditures.

Commuting and Moving Expenses

Given the place of residence, a person must incur certain costs in getting to and from his or her place of work. This is a necessary expense, of course, but presumably a basic minimum is covered by the personal exemption. If persons choose to commute at a greater than usual distance, they do so because they prefer to do so, and the additional expense is essentially of consumption nature—to enable them to enjoy lower rent, more pleasant living conditions, better schools for their children, and so forth.

Moving expenses are of somewhat different character, since they arise only when a person is considering taking another job. In a sense, they likewise are voluntary, but failure to allow their deduction interferes with labor mobility. Accordingly, the United States has greatly liberalized the law to allow moving expenses to be deducted under most circumstances.

Travel, Entertainment, Hobby, and Related Expenditures

The dual character of expenditures is particularly evident with certain types of travel, entertainment, hobby, and related activities. A family travels to Florida to look over income-yielding property they have in that state but also spends two weeks on the beach at Miami. Persons may subscribe to the *Wall Street Journal* partly as a source of general information, partly to improve their financial investment decisions. Doctors' conventions are frequently held in the Canadian Rockies or on Caribbean cruises. Expenses of entertaining customers may be necessary to obtain the client's business, but there are important luxury spending elements—both for the person and the customer— involved as well. Farmers raise show horses as a hobby and deduct the expenses for tax purposes. This activity may or may not be closely related to the basic farming activity. A farmer or small businessman buys equipment more elaborate than necessary for the task, simply because he enjoys using such equipment or wishes to impress his neighbors; he depreciates the entire cost for tax purposes.

No perfect solution to this problem is possible; delineation between necessary and nonnecessary expenses is administratively hopeless. To disallow all travel, convention, and entertainment expenditure, as proposed by the Canadian Royal Commission in an effort to stop abuses, would prevent the deduction of legitimate expenditures. Without question, doctors abuse the convention travel deductibility, yet attending conventions is presumably important in keeping them up with developments in the profession. The present liberal treatment in the United States does favor certain groups relative to others, particularly those with nonsalary income and corporate executives, and stricter control might be feasible. New restrictions on foreign convention travel were introduced in 1976.

REFERENCES

References for this chapter are found at the end of Chapter 11.

11

The Structure of Income Taxation
II: Adjustments in
Income, Reform

For the typical family, income is a stream commencing at the time the first dollar is earned, continuing till ended by death or other cause.

But the income stream is segmented into periods, usually annual, for purposes of defining tax liability. If the stream were identical in character for all taxpayers and none had ability to delay receipt of income for tax purposes, the segmentation would not be significant. But this is not the situation. Some persons have relatively regular incomes, others highly irregular ones; some can defer income and others cannot.

Irregular Incomes and Averaging

The use of fixed-dollar exemptions, which cannot be carried forward from one year to another if unused, and progression in rates place a penalty on persons with irregular incomes. With 1976 rates, a single person earning $10,000 a year for 10 years would pay a total of $20,900 tax over the 10 years; a person earning $100,000 in one of the years and none in the other nine would pay $53,090 in tax. There is similar discrimination against such persons as professional ball players whose lifetime incomes concentrate in a relatively few years of their lives. Apart from these extreme cases, much more common variations in lifetime earning patterns will result in substantially different amounts paid, as demonstrated in a recent article by A. J. Robinson.[1]

The solution to this problem is the authorization of some form of averaging of incomes, as mentioned above in the discussion of capital gains. If persons with irregular incomes are permitted to average out their incomes over a period of years, the penalty will be lessened. While originally the United States law had virtually no concessions of this type, there has been a gradual liberalization, particularly in 1969. The rules are complicated, but, in effect, if a person's income for one year is substantially above the average of the four preceding years, he or she may use a lower marginal rate than that indicated in the tax tables.[2]

There are several defects with the present system. As summarized by Martin David, "the drafters . . . labored mightily and brought forth a monstrous mouse." As David shows, in 1966 only 0.55 percent of taxpayers used the averaging provision.[3] It is incredibly difficult to understand the provisions. The adjustment applies only when income rises, not when it falls, and provides only limited averaging at best. David proposes a modification of the present system that is based on three years only, with eligibility if the current year's income either exceeds or is less than the average of the two previous years' income by $1,000. He stresses the need for adjusting when income falls.[4] Another alternative is the Canadian block system; all persons (originally only farmers and fishermen) can recalculate their incomes on five-year intervals, averaging the income over that period. Such a plan was proposed for all income by the Canadian Royal Commission, but not accepted by the government. This version, if allowed all taxpayers, is more general and easier to understand than the U.S. system, but suffers from the defect that once the taxpayer chooses a particular block of five years, the decision is irrevocable. If in the sixth year income jumps or falls sharply, the taxpayer has to wait till the end of the next five-year block for an adjustment.

All these approaches suffer from several basic defects. They require substantial effort to retain records and data from previous years, and the block systems require recalculation of past years' returns. Secondly, they provide only partial solution for irregularity and little or none for the persons whose incomes are concentrated in relatively

---

[1] "Lifetime Averaging," *Canadian Tax Journal*, vol. 22 (November–December 1974), pp. 595–601.

[2] Specifically as of 1976, if income for the current year exceeds by more than $3,000 the figure of 30 percent of total income of the four preceding years, the person may use the marginal tax rate that would apply to one fifth of this excess.

[3] M. David, H. Groves, R. F. Miller, and E. A. Wiegner, "Optimal Choices for an Averaging System," *National Tax Journal*, vol. 23 (September 1970), pp. 275–97.

[4] Ibid.

short periods of their lives. Thirdly, they do not meet in any way the problem of deliberate deferment of income, encouraged because of the interest gain. Also, with the usual approaches to averaging, even the more complete ones, there is strong incentive to defer income to retirement years when income will be lower.

These problems can all be met by some form of cumulative averaging, as proposed three decades ago by William Vickrey.[5] Each year, taxpayers would add their incomes for the year to the cumulated total of incomes over past years, and then calculate total tax on the cumulated sum from special tables based on the number of years over which the accumulation had occurred. The next step would be to subtract the total paid in previous years (plus compound interest) from the tentative tax to determine tax liability for the year. The cumulative averaging and compound-interest features would ensure equal treatment of fluctuating and regular incomes and eliminate gain from postponing income realization, as well as the need for recalculation under the block averaging system with its chance element. Adoption of a general averaging system would constitute a major step toward satisfactory taxation of capital gains at regular tax rates. The proposal would have one adverse stabilization effect: As national income rises, tax payments would lag and the anti-inflationary effect would be lessened. The major limitation is the apparent complexity of the proposal, which has prevented it from receiving serious attention.

For the lower-income groups, a simple system of allowing carry-over of unused exemptions would mitigate much of the present inequity.

Full carry-over of business losses is highly important to minimize adverse effects of the tax on risk-taking and on the establishment of new businesses, which often incur losses in their earlier years. At present, firms are limited to carry-back of three years and carry-forward of seven years, a rule that discriminates against new firms lacking the three-year carry-back option.

Acceleration of Expenses for Tax Purposes

Without a system of cumulative averaging, taxpayers have incentive to deduct expenses in as early a period as possible and thus to defer taxable income as long as possible (except when in a situation without averaging they expect their incomes or the tax rates to be higher in the future). This is equally true for the personal and corporate income taxes. With most expenses of gaining an income, little acceleration is

---

[5] W. Vickrey, *Agenda for Progressive Taxation* (New York: Ronald Press, 1947); "Cumulative Averaging after Thirty Years," in *Modern Fiscal Issues*, eds. R. M. Bird and J. G. Head (Toronto: University of Toronto Press, 1972), chap. 7.

possible; one cannot deduct wages to be paid next year from this year's income. But with the cost of capital equipment, substantial variation is possible. The equipment is acquired in one year for use over a period of years.

The entire cost is obviously an expense of gaining the income received over the life of the equipment. The amount chargeable to any one year should, logically, equal the decline in value of the equipment for the year or, in other words, the amount necessary to maintain intact the capital of the firm. This figure cannot be ascertained, however, and so the figure chosen is arbitrary. The manner in which the total is allocated over the years of use affects the timing of the government's tax receipts and, in an expanding economy, the total receipts. Taxpayers usually find it advantageous to depreciate for tax purposes as quickly as possible; the faster the depreciation, the sooner they recover their money capital tax free and the less total tax they will pay if they continue to expand. The risk of not being able to deduct the entire costs of the equipment because of a series of years of losses is also reduced.

Governments initially approached the problem from the standpoint of maximizing tax revenue within the constraint of allowing complete depreciation over the life of the equipment. Long periods of estimated life and straight-line or other depreciation techniques that prevented concentration of depreciation in early years were required. Gradually, however, under pressure from business groups, increased awareness that rapid depreciation aids investment, and increased concern for maintaining adequate investment, the rules have been materially relaxed, permitting acceleration of deductions. The net result is to reduce the tax liability on an expanding business year after year so long as expansion continues. While the total deduction on any one piece of equipment is not increased by acceleration of depreciation, the total tax liability of the firm is reduced so long as it is expanding and, in an expanding economy, the government will get less revenue at given tax rates. Whether this is desirable or not must be decided on the basis of fiscal policy considerations. Deliberate adjustment of depreciation rules for stabilization purposes will also be considered in Chapter 13, since the primary impact is on corporations.

Argument has been advanced in periods of inflation to allow firms to recover tax free an amount equal to replacement cost rather than original cost in order to facilitate purchase of new equipment. Equity requires only the tax-free recovery of the original sum; owners of equipment bought in low-price periods benefit from its use in a high-price period and are scarcely in need of special tax favors. If tax adjustments are to be made for anyone in an inflationary period, they should favor those persons who are injured by inflation. Business firms with good profit prospects usually have no trouble in raising additional funds and there is no justification for taxpayers providing funds for them.

Retirement Income

A different type of timing question arises with retirement income. The pattern in the United States provides an excellent example of how one concession leads to another. As noted, when the Social Security System was established, all benefits (including old-age annuities) were exempted, in part because the amounts were small, given the income tax exemptions of the period, and there was some feeling that they were not appropriate bases for taxation, given the overall objectives of the program. Employees were not permitted to deduct the payroll tax which their employers withheld and paid into the system for them. Incomes from other pension systems, however, were fully taxable except for the return of the amount the worker had paid in. Therefore, with private pension systems, the portion of the pensions arising from the employers' share and the earnings on all amounts paid in was subject to tax, whereas under social security these amounts were not taxable. This ultimately led Congress to provide a tax credit for private pension-system retirement income of 15 percent of the amount of the retirement income. In 1976, however, this provision was replaced by one giving a general tax credit for all persons 65 or over, on earned income, at 15 percent, subject to a specified limit. The credit is phased out as AGI rises, being eliminated when AGI reaches $12,500 for a single person, $17,500 for a married couple.

There is no simple solution. There are several alternatives to the present compromise approach:

1. Make all retirement income taxable, including social security, in excess of the amount paid in by the employee. This would ensure equal treatment of social security and private pension recipients, but it complicates the tax returns and creates problems of determining the portion of the pension reflecting the employee payments into the system.

2. Make all retirement income fully taxable but allow deductions for employee payments into the pension systems. This also would provide uniform treatment for all systems, but it would allow deferment of tax to the future, when incomes are lower, and would particularly benefit the higher-income groups.

The issue is complicated still more by the inability of the self-employed, without special provisions of the act, to defer payment of tax on the equivalent of the employer's payments into the pension fund, as occurs with employed persons. To meet this problem, Congress permitted the self-employed to exclude up to a specified limit from tax amounts paid into pension systems.

In summary: The present treatment is haphazard and complicated, but Congress shows little interest in moving to a simplified, generalized system.

THE TAXPAYING UNIT

Since the income tax is a personal levy collected from individuals on the basis of returns, specification of the taxpaying unit is necessary. If the taxes had proportional rates and no exemptions, the selection of the unit would be of little significance. But the use of exemptions and progressive rates results in substantial differences in tax liability with one method compared to another. The various alternatives reflect different philosophies about income-earning and spending decision-making.

Individual Persons

One approach, which is traditional in Canada but in few other countries, is to regard each individual as a taxpayer, taxing the person on his or her own income regardless of family status. This requires, in the definition of dependency, a cutoff point; if the person has income of more than a certain amount, he or she ceases to be a dependent for tax purposes.

In a sense, this approach is the simplest one. But there are several objections. First, the tax liability of a family depends upon the earnings pattern; it will be substantially less if both husband and wife are earning substantial incomes than if either alone is earning the same total amount. Limited differential might be justified because of added expenses when a second person in the household works, but the magnitude of the difference is so great that it can hardly be regarded as warranted by the expense difference. Much more seriously, with this system persons with property income can reduce tax liability by placing property in the spouse's name, whereas persons with salary and wage income cannot do so. Attempts to prevent this in Canada have led to complications and little success—as have the various rules relating to payment of a salary to the wife for working in the family business.

Pooling of Income: Husband and Wife

An approach more in accord with the typical decision-making practices in the family is that of treating the family, rather than the individual members, as the unit and taxing the combined income under one of various approaches. Typically, the basic decisions about spending are made by the husband and wife jointly on the basis of the combined income, even though each may retain substantial discretion. Certainly, in a financial emergency, income is pooled. The great advantage of this approach is that the liability is not dependent upon whether the income is earned by one person or by both, and property income receives no preference.

There are several approaches to implementation, and the consequences differ. First, husband and wife may be required to pool their incomes and to pay tax on the basis of a single rate table also used for single persons. This is the British tradition and is still used in some Commonwealth countries. While it is not without some merit—under the assumption that the incomes really are pooled for decision-making purposes in the usual family—it encounters some objections. If a couple making comparable incomes marry, their tax liability will rise as a result. This may be defended on the grounds that two persons can live together more cheaply than the combined expense of their living separately. But to many persons it appears unfair, and legislators have feared that it would encourage persons to dispense with a marriage ceremony.

There is also the danger that such a policy will discourage the wife from working, because her income will be taxed at the marginal rate of her husband's income.

A second alternative, as established in the United States in 1948, is to allow pooling of the income of husband and wife but then in effect to divide it equally between them and apply the basic rates to one half of the income (and multiply by two). In other words, income is split evenly between husband and wife and the tax rate determined by the amount of each share. This avoids the evils of mandatory pooling as well as those of separate taxation of individuals; there is no longer incentive to put property in the wife's name. The procedure alters tremendously the relative burden on single and married persons, especially in the middle-income groups. The tax advantage from marriage is greatly increased, to the complaint of single persons. Inequity was obvious with unmarried heads of households, since if the wife died, the husband experienced a sharp increase in tax, although necessary household costs (of child care and the like) might rise. This led ultimately to special provisions for these persons, adding to complications in the tax returns. Finally, in a series of steps, Congress modified this system to provide separate tables for single and married persons set up in such a way that the tax on a single person will not be more than 20 percent greater than for a married person, other circumstances being the same. Thus the tax penalty on being unmarried has been drastically reduced. But this change causes at least partial loss of the advantages of the splitting system. Marriage may now increase total tax liability of two persons and methods can be devised to allocate property to lessen tax liability, an avenue not open to persons with salary income.

Income of Children

Even more difficult than the husband-wife problem is that of the treatment of income of children. The United States rule is simple: The income of children is not aggregated into the family income, but the child must pay tax on the income if it exceeds the figure of the exemption. This income is taxed separately, without regard to the magnitude of the parents' income, and the parent does not lose the child as a dependent, if other dependency requirements are met and the child is under 19 or a full-time student. The basic difficulty with this treatment is that it encourages families to place income-yielding property into the names of minor children. This practice lessens tax in two ways: a double exemption (for the child and for the parent) is obtained and progression is checked. The practice is very widespread. Parents do not lose control over the property until the child becomes of age, and the gifts offer estate tax advantages as well.

The most drastic alternative is to require that the income of the children be included in the family income. As used in France, this system involves automatic income-splitting among the children on the basis of a formula that treats a child as a partial partner. As proposed by the Royal Commission in Canada, there would be no splitting at all; a single rate table would be used. The French system avoids penalty on larger families where several persons are gaining incomes and lessens pressure on persons to escape from the family unit for tax purposes. But it does require the use of arbitrary weights for children in the formula and provides great tax concessions for large families. The very drastic Canadian proposal, which the government did not accept, would eliminate the evils of the present system, but it involves potential inequity against persons essentially self-supporting but living in the family and would encourage these persons to leave home— obviously an undesirable social consequence in many instances. The high marginal rate applied to earnings of children in higher-income families would discourage the children from part-time and summer work.

Since drastic change along the French lines is unlikely, the only possible avenue of improvement is by some tightening of rules under the present system. The main difficulty relates to transferring property. If some workable means could be found to include in family income the earnings on securities transferred to the children by the parents, the worst abuses of the present situation would be eliminated without impossible problems, although admittedly there would be some borderline cases and some inequity.

EXEMPTIONS FOR THE TAXPAYER AND DEPENDENTS

One of the inherent advantages of the income tax is its ability to adjust tax payments on the basis of personal circumstances affecting tax-paying capacity and to exclude from tax those persons who have no such capacity, under the standards established.[6] A major instrument used to attain this objective is the personal exemption or credit for dependents. Under United States law, for a number of years (1948–1970) the exemption was $600 per person; in the 1969 legislation it was raised in a series of annual steps to $750. This exemption accomplishes several objectives. It removes from the tax rolls families with incomes so small that they are considered to have no taxpaying capacity, including children with nominal incomes. On those subject to tax, it adjusts the total amount of tax according to the number of dependents and thus brings the tax more closely in line with tax capacity. It creates progression in the tax structure for persons just over the minimum at which liability for tax is incurred; in fact an income tax with high exemptions and proportional rates, such as that of Illinois, has a substantial degree of progression over an extensive range of incomes.

While the granting of personal exemptions is generally accepted despite the very large revenue loss that results, there are several questions about their precise nature.

Height of Exemption

Presumably the intent of the exemption, under usual standards of equity, is to exempt those persons with incomes so low that they have no tax capacity. The exemption figure, therefore, should be sufficiently high as to exclude all persons with incomes less than the bare minimum poverty level. In fact, however, the figures have been set largely on the basis of revenue needs, given the rates regarded as tolerable. The real value of the exemption has continued to decline as the price level has risen. The 1969 Treasury Tax Study showed that one fourth of single persons and married couples without children below the poverty income line (as defined by the Department of Health, Education, and Welfare) paid some income tax.[7] As a conse-

---

[6] L. H. Seltzer, *The Personal Exemptions in the Income Tax* (New York: Columbia University Press, 1968) explores this question at length.

[7] *Tax Reform Studies and Proposals*, U.S. Treasury Department, Joint Publication, Committee on Ways and Means of the U.S. House of Repesentatives, and Committee on Finance of the U.S. Senate (Washington, D.C., 1969), p. 74.

quence, Congress took two actions. First, it raised the exemption figure in annual steps to $750, being reluctant to go farther because of large revenue losses and the gains to persons in the higher-income groups. Secondly, it modified the minimum standard deduction into a low-income allowance; all taxpaying units, single or married, are free of tax if their income is less than $1,700 single, $2,100 if married.[8] This system is used to reduce the tax gain to the wealthy that arises if exemptions are increased. The taxpayer has the choice of the low-income allowance or the standard deduction (or itemizing deductions). The net effect of these changes has been to exclude from the tax large numbers of taxpayers below or close to the poverty line.

Commencing in 1975, a tax credit was also introduced. As of 1976, the figure is $35 per taxpayer and dependents, or 2 percent of the first $9,000 of taxable income, whichever is greater. The aim was to reduce tax on the lower income group.

Exemption versus Credit

The federal exemption takes the form of a deduction from income in calculating tax liability. Thus the tax saving from an additional dependent rises as the income rises; the tax gain from the birth of another child is $105 in the first income tax bracket, $525 in the top bracket (1976 rates). This is often criticized as an unwarranted reduction in tax at the higher levels; critics propose the tax-credit system used by some states, whereby the exemption is a specified amount of tax (perhaps $100, roughly the beginning rate times the present exemption) regardless of the tax level. In defense of the present treatment is the argument that, in practice, dependents require the spending of larger sums of money in the higher-income levels than in the lower, given customary living patterns. But the present system does sacrifice revenue unnecessarily to accomplish the basic objective. In 1975, Congress took one step toward the credit system, providing a credit against tax for each dependent, in lieu of increasing the exemptions. As noted, the figure is $35 per dependent or 2 percent of taxable income, whichever is greater.

Uniformity of Exemption or Credit

The United States income tax provides the same exemption for the taxpayer and each dependent, $750, as of 1977. This has been done mostly for simplicity, particularly for withholding tables. There is

---

[8] Except a person who is a dependent of another taxpayer. A dependent becomes liable for tax on income in excess of $750.

some feeling as well that tax legislation should encourage adequate care of dependents. But in terms of objective measures of cost, successive additional dependents do not add proportional amounts to the figure of expenditures necessary for a given level of living; in other words, there are economies of scale within the family. Various studies suggest that at bare-subsistence incomes, with an index of 100 for a married couple without children, the cost figure (for a given living standard) is 78 for a single person, 119 for the couple and one child, 151 for a family of four, 202 for a family of six.[9] Thus present income tax treatment, especially before the low-income allowance, taxes small families relatively more heavily than large families. These figures suggest a diminishing credit for additional children—a rule supported by those who fear excessive population growth and regard the present treatment as an unwarranted stimulus to larger families. The significance of tax exemptions for size of families has never been ascertained; it is doubtful at best, given actual exemption figures. Some countries do limit the number of dependents for tax purposes; four is a common figure in Commonwealth countries of Africa.

Definition of Dependents

The establishment of a simple yet equitable definition of dependents has proven difficult. There are several elements in the definition:

1. *Relationship.* In order to prevent wealthy persons from multiplying dependents for purposes of tax avoidance, dependency status is limited to persons defined by the act to be related, plus, in the United States, unrelated dependents who are members of the household, but excluding unrelated persons other than adopted or foster children (the latter added in 1969) not living in the household.

2. *Portion of support.* In general, the taxpayer must provide more than half of the dependent's support; there is an exception that allows one person to take the exemption when several jointly support a dependent, as when children jointly support a parent.

3. *The dependent's income.*[10] The person claimed as a dependent must receive less than $750 in gross income during the year; this gross-income test is not applied if the dependent is under 19 or is a full-time student. The gross-income rule has long been a defect in the law, incredibly unfair to a person supporting an elderly relative who owns real property with gross income above the dividing

[9] J. Pechman, *Federal Tax Policy*, rev. ed. (Washington, D.C.: The Brookings Institution, 1971), p. 72.

[10] There are two other requirements; one relates to citizenship or residence of the dependent while the other denies the exemption status to a child who is married and filing a joint return with a spouse.

line but little net income; adjusted gross income is the appropriate figure.

These rules are without question somewhat arbitrary, but this is necessary if they are to be workable; wherever the border is drawn, some inequity results.

A primary defect in the present system is the double deduction for children who earn income; the taxpayer receives a $750 exemption and the dependent receives a $750 exemption as well. The net effect is to free substantial income from taxation. This concession benefits the wealthy much more than the poor, because of the higher marginal rates that apply to the income.

OTHER ADJUSTMENTS: PERSONAL DEDUCTIONS

By the personal nature of the income tax, the tax liability of different persons can be adjusted in terms of circumstances in a fashion that is impossible with most other taxes. First, the tax liability can be adjusted to reflect other types of expenditures that are considered to reduce tax capacity. Secondly, the liability can be adjusted to encourage increases in certain types of spending. The deductions are, of course, determined through the political process, reflecting the relative political strength of groups seeking the various deductions (e.g., charitable organizations, homeowners), and the attempt to adjust the overall income tax structure to the different preferences of various persons, in part influenced by the outlays of these persons on the various items. Thus persons with heavy medical expenses will have a relatively low demand for government services unless they are allowed to deduct these expenses.[11]

Medical Expenses

Heavy medical expenses drastically reduce tax capacity out of a given income, and they are unevenly distributed among various families. Despite modern health-insurance systems, many families are hit hard by high medical bills. Accordingly, there is strong justification for allowing deduction of those expenses in excess of a minimum that is typical for the average family. The United States rule of the deductibility of expenses in excess of 3 percent of adjusted gross income is a reasonable one. The deduction expressed as a percentage of adjusted gross income falls sharply as income rises, from 19 percent for nontaxable returns to 0.3 percent for those over $100,000.

As with any exemption, however, various problems are created,

---

[11] C. M. Lindsay, "Two Theories of Tax Deductability," *National Tax Journal*, vol. 25 (March 1972), pp. 43–52.

primarily of an interpretative nature. Does a vacation trip taken on the advice of a physician for one's health constitute deductible medical expenses? Whiskey recommended by your doctor? Toothpaste? The general answer in these cases is no—the expenditure must be directly related to an immediate health problem and be made for purposes of a medicinal character—but the borderlines nevertheless are serious. Like all exemptions, some abuse is possible, although reasonably close check is possible by requiring receipts. Another difficulty is that medical expenditures contain a substantial discretionary element. A person may visit a local general practitioner or the most expensive doctors in Rochester; he or she may choose a private hospital room or a bed in a ward.

Despite these problems, however, the deduction is, by usual standards of equity and improved medical care, highly justifiable.

Casualty Losses

Losses from theft, fire, accident, and other casualties in excess of insurance compensation represent essentially negative income, reducing the person's net wealth and income, in the Simons sense. The United States permits deduction of such losses in excess of $100. Deductibility does favor the person who fails to take out insurance—but this would not appear to be a controlling objection.

Interest Paid

The payment of interest on funds borrowed for production use is obviously an expense of gaining the income and, therefore, is appropriately deductible as a business expense. But interest paid on loans made for personal purposes is another matter. The United States allows the deduction of all such interest; Canada and most other countries do not. There are several arguments for the deduction. First, there are potential difficulties in distinguishing between loans for business purposes and those for consumption purposes; a farmer, for example, may mortgage the farmland to build a new house. Secondly, it is argued that some loans are a product of adversity—of illness or unemployment. Thirdly, the deduction equalizes somewhat between persons having large equities in their home and those having little equity.

These arguments are of limited significance. Other countries have found that separation of personal and business interest is feasible. Low-income borrowers can be aided more effectively in other ways; the deduction does not aid the low-income tenant. A very large portion of the total borrowing by individuals is made for purchase of homes or cars; the borrowing is voluntary and there is no more justification for allowing deduction of interest than of a portion of the expenditures on the goods. In general, the limited aid given to the poor by the deduction does not warrant the substantial revenue loss and the additional incentive given to home ownership.

As with the other deductions, interpretative problems arise, particularly with charges that involve both interest and carrying charge for handling the account. An arbitrary division between the two is now permitted—a rule adding one more complication to tax returns.

Taxes Paid

Since taxes constitute an obligatory payment, they may be considered to reduce tax capacity. In part on this basis, in part from the desire to lessen somewhat the financial problems of the states and local governments, the United States law provides for deduction of virtually all state and local taxes (excluding excises, except on motor fuel, estate and inheritance taxes, motor vehicle license fees, and special assessments, which are technically not taxes). The effect is presumably to reduce somewhat the resistance of state and local taxpayers to increases in state and local taxes. In the higher-income levels, half or more of any increases will be absorbed out of reduced payment of federal taxes. Since, as explained in Chapter 18, the state and local governments have relatively limited taxable capacity relative to the federal government, the deduction helps to meet one of the most pressing problems of intergovernmental fiscal relations. How effective this approach is, however, is not known; do taxpayers, in contemplating state and local tax increases, actually take into consideration the partially offsetting reduction in federal taxes? It is very doubtful that many do. In any event, this is not the most effective method of meeting intergovernmental fiscal problems, as noted in Chapter 18, but it is a method that has more political appeal than many others.

The deduction of state and local income taxes is justifiable, as it avoids any danger of combined marginal rates exceeding 100 percent. This is not possible currently, but it was when the federal marginal rate was 92 percent and the top state rate, 11 percent. There is particular merit, by usual standards, in encouraging the states to introduce income taxes. Deductibility of the sales tax—of necessity based on estimates—accomplishes little; it erodes the tax base still farther and reduces progressivity. The property tax deduction is one further bonus to property owners and a further source of discrimination against tenants in favor of homeowners. Only the desperate financial plight of urban areas can justify the property tax deduction, and this is not the most sastisfactory approach to the urban fiscal problem, as explained in Chapter 18. There is least justification for deduction of the gasoline tax, essentially a charge for the use of the roads. Nothing is gained in equity and substantial revenue is lost.

Empirical data show that tax deductions are nearly proportional to income at all income levels except the very low ones, where they are higher.

Contributions

In the United States and many but not all countries, the point of view is widely accepted that contributions should be deductible for tax purposes in order to encourage persons to provide funds for charitable, religious, and related institutions. Many of these organizations perform activities, such as education, hospital service, and welfare, comparable to those of governments. The greater extent to which these organizations provide the services, the less money the government must spend. Preservation of educational and research activities independent of government and of welfare activities not subject to governmental rules is widely regarded as meritorious. Contributions to religious institutions per se, as distinct from their educational and other functions, are somewhat different, given traditional attitudes in the United States of separation of church and state. Over half of total contributions are made to religious organizations. But there appears to be substantial consensus that, while the government should not finance religion directly, it can appropriately do so indirectly via the tax deduction privilege. Certain groups, of course, strongly object to this philosophy, but they constitute a minority.

The United States rule is relatively liberal. Contributions to charitable, religious, educational, scientific, or literary institutions are exempt up to 50 percent of adjusted gross income (limited to 20 percent for certain types of organizations). Presumably the deduction privilege stimulates giving to these organizations; a person subject to a 70 percent rate bears only 30 percent of the amount of contributions.

Earlier studies suggested that the tax did not have much actual effect in stimulating contributions. But a recent econometric study by Martin Feldstein concludes that the effects are substantial; elimination of the deduction would cost the organizations more than the treasury would gain in tax revenue.[12] Elimination of the deduction would reduce individual giving by an estimated 20 percent—but this would affect various organizations differently. Religious organizations would lose 14 percent, while gifts to educational institutions and hospitals would fall by roughly 50 percent. There are two explanations: Gifts to churches are concentrated more heavily in the lower- and middle-income groups subject to lower tax rates than are gifts to other groups, and many persons feel more compelled (that is, have higher relative preference) to continue to give to churches than to other organizations.

---

[12] M. S. Feldstein, "The Income Tax and Charitable Contributions," *National Tax Journal*, vol. 28 (March and June 1975), pp. 81–100; 209–226; M. S. Feldstein and C. T. Clotfelter, "Tax Incentives and Charitable Contributions in the United States," *Journal of Public Economics*, vol. 5 (January–February 1976), pp. 1–26.

Unfortunately, however, the system is not without objection. The deduction as a percentage of income rises as incomes rise except at the lowest levels, making the tax structure less progressive. The deductibility privilege gives wealthy persons tremendous freedom over the manner in which the dollars that would otherwise go for taxes are spent; a real question can be raised about the extent to which the government can appropriately forego tax revenue in order to allow individuals freedom to allocate the money as they wish.

Questions can also be raised about the legitimacy of various organizations, contributions to which are eligible for the deduction. Some religious organizations, for example, are primarily right-wing propaganda machines operating under the guise of religion—yet distinguishing these from straight propaganda mills is difficult. Some foundations are established to propagate a particular point of view, a fact not necessarily evident to IRS. Just how far does society wish to go in aiding in the financing of organizations for the conservation of ragweed, chicory plants, or field mice? The trouble is that the distinction between censorship and legitimate evaluation is a very fine one. In recent years, IRS was subject to sharp criticism when it indicated possible loss of tax-exempt status of certain conservation organizations and ones providing legal aid for the poor.

Even more serious, various organizations, particularly foundations, have served as devices for tax avoidance. A wealthy businessman gives the physical assets of his business to a foundation or charity and rents them back; the earnings received are invested by the foundation in additional assets for the firm. Thus the firm receives tax-free funds for additional investment. Various restrictions have been imposed in recent years to lessen this activity and foundations are now subject to tax at 4 percent on their investment income. But the avenues for escape are still substantial.

The Optional or Standard Deduction

In order to simplify tax returns, taxpayers are given the alternative of deducting a minimum or standard deduction even if their actual personal deductions do not reach this amount. Prior to 1970, this figure had been 10 percent of adjusted gross income, up to $1,000. When the provision was introduced in the 1950s, more than 80 percent of all taxpayers used the standard deduction; by 1969, the figure had fallen to 57 percent. Rising prices and incomes had resulted in more and more taxpayers having actual deductions in excess of the $1,000 limit. As a consequence, the percentage has been raised to 16 percent, the maximum figures to $2,400 for a single taxpayer, $2,800 for a married couple. But the range of applicability is still quite limited, because of the low-income allowance alternative on the one side and the dollar limitations on the other.

TABLE 11-1

Itemized Deductions as a Percentage of Adjusted Gross Income, by Adjusted Gross Income Classes, Federal Individual Income Tax Returns with Itemized Deductions, 1968

Adjusted Gross Income Class (Dollars)	Total	Contri- butions	Interest	Taxes	Medical	Other
Nontaxable returns						
Under 1,000[a]	103.8	13.8	18.8	30.0	31.3	7.5
1,000–3,000	60.3	7.3	8.7	15.5	24.8	3.5
3,000–5,000	49.1	5.8	11.3	11.9	15.7	3.7
5,000 and over	58.8	10.2	14.5	8.7	16.5	7.1
All nontaxable	56.9	8.1	12.0	11.8	18.7	5.1
Taxable returns						
600– 1,000	12.5	[b]	0	[b]	[b]	[c]
1,000– 3,000	28.5	5.2	3.0	8.0	9.1	3.0
3,000– 5,000	24.5	4.0	4.1	7.3	6.2	2.7
5,000– 10,000	20.6	2.9	5.6	6.6	3.3	2.0
10,000– 20,000	17.4	2.5	5.3	6.5	1.6	1.5
20,000– 50,000	15.6	2.7	3.9	6.6	1.1	1.3
50,000–100,000	15.4	3.4	3.4	6.4	0.6	1.6
100,000 and over	18.8	6.7	3.7	6.1	0.3	2.1
All taxable	18.1	2.9	4.9	6.5	2.0	1.7
All returns	18.8	3.0	5.0	6.6	2.3	1.7

Note: Figures do not add to totals because the total column includes small amounts for which the type of deduction was not specified.

[a] Excludes returns with no adjusted gross income or deficit.

[b] Not shown separately because of high sampling variability, but included in total.

[c] Less than 0.05 percent.

Source: Reproduced from J. Pechman, *Federal Tax Policy*, rev. ed. (Washington, D.C.: The Brookings Institution, 1971), p. 300, by permission of The Brookings Institution.

TABLE 11-2

Deductions Reported on Federal Individual Income Tax Returns, 1972 (billions of dollars)

Deduction	Amount
Itemized	92.0
State and local taxes	35.1
Interest payments	26.1
Medical and dental expenses	8.7
Charitable contributions	12.8
Other[a]	9.2
Standard	50.8
Percentage deduction	23.9
Low-income allowance	26.9
Total	142.8

Source: U.S. Department of the Treasury, *Statistics of Income— 1972, Individual Income Tax Returns* (1974), tables 1.4 and 2.4, pp. 20 and 92. Figures are rounded.

[a] Includes deductions for child care, casualty losses, alimony payments, work-related expenses, expenses of earning investment income, and deductions not specified on tax returns.

Source: J. Pechman, *Federal Tax Reform*. (Washington, D.C.: The Brookings Institution, 1975), p. 23.

From the standpoint of simplification, the standard deduction has merit. But, in a sense, it contradicts the basic intent of the deductions: to adjust tax in light of personal circumstances and to encourage certain types of spending. This standard deduction does compensate to a limited degree for some discrimination, especially against tenants, arising from the actual deductions. A far better approach, however, would be to modify the deductions to lessen discrimination and allow persons to deduct only amounts in excess of specified percentages of income—with, of course, lower tax rates. But Congress has on various occasions rejected this approach when presented by the Treasury; it appears to believe that persons prefer the system in which they are getting concessions via the deductions rather than lower tax rates.

Table 11–2 gives some indication of the magnitude of the various deductions, as of 1972.

The Tax-Rate Structure

The U.S. federal tax-rate structure, as of 1977, is reproduced in Table 11–3. The basic rule should be noted, that each successive rate applies only to the income in excess of the bracket figure, and therefore a person can never become worse off by gaining additional income. The degree of progression in the rate structure is very substantial, particularly at the lower-middle-income levels; for a single person, the 50 percent rate is reached at \$32,000 taxable income. The optimal degree of progression, reflecting consensus of thought in the particular society about equity, cannot be selected on any scientific basis. Studies suggest, however, that the tax is in practice much less progressive, relative to actual income, than the rate tables would indicate, because of the greater ability of persons in the higher-income groups to escape tax.

Adjustments for Inflation

When the general price level rises, the exemptions and the brackets figures decline in real terms; more persons are brought within the scope of the tax and taxpayers are pushed into higher brackets and pay more tax even though their real incomes have not increased. In periods of temporary inflation, this feature has always been regarded as advantageous from the standpoint of fiscal policy; the effect is to raise government revenues at a faster rate than the price-level increase and thus dampen aggregate demand.

In the continuing inflation of recent years, however, increased question has been raised about the failure to make adjustment for price-level changes through indexing. There are several objections to failure to adjust. The progression in the tax structure is altered from the

TABLE 11–3
U.S. Federal Income Tax Rates, 1977, Married
Taxpayers Filing Joint Returns

Income*			Of the Amount Over—
Over—	But Not Over—		
$1,000	$2,000	$140+15%	$1,000
$2,000	$3,000	$290+16%	$2,000
$3,000	$4,000	$450+17%	$3,000
$4,000	$8,000	$620+19%	$4,000
$8,000	$12,000	$1,380+22%	$8,000
$12,000	$16,000	$2,260+25%	$12,000
$16,000	$20,000	$3,260+28%	$16,000
$20,000	$24,000	$4,380+32%	$20,000
$24,000	$28,000	$5,660+36%	$24,000
$28,000	$32,000	$7,100+39%	$28,000
$32,000	$36,000	$8,660+42%	$32,000
$36,000	$40,000	$10,340+45%	$36,000
$40,000	$44,000	$12,140+48%	$40,000
$44,000	$52,000	$14,060+50%	$44,000
$52,000	$64,000	$18,060+53%	$52,000
$64,000	$76,000	$24,420+55%	$64,000
$76,000	$88,000	$31,020+58%	$76,000
$88,000	$100,000	$37,980+60%	$88,000
$100,000	$120,000	$45,180+62%	$100,000
$120,000	$140,000	$57,580+64%	$120,000
$140,000	$160,000	$70,380+66%	$140,000
$160,000	$180,000	$83,580+68%	$160,000
$180,000	$200,000	$97,180+69%	$180,000
$200,000	—	$110,980+70%	$200,000

* For income not over $1,000 the rate is 14 percent.

pattern deliberately established by Congress. Some persons below minimum subsistence levels will be required to pay taxes and will be pushed farther below the poverty line. Lower-income groups, squeezed by the diminished real value of the exemptions, are those most likely to suffer. The increased income tax revenues will encourage growth in government spending beyond the levels that would be selected by deliberate action.

In the United States, Congress has given little serious consideration to the problem, partly because of revenue implications, partly for fiscal-policy reasons, partly because of the dislike of recognizing the fact that continued inflation will occur. The more indexing that occurs in the economy, the more cumulative inflation becomes and the less resistance there is to it.

Canada, however, introduced indexing for the income tax in 1974; exemptions and bracket figures are automatically increased each year by the index of the general price-level change. The January 1, 1975 adjustment was 10.1 percent, that a year later 11.3 percent. A number of other countries have introduced similar plans.[13]

Tax Shelters

In the last decade, substantial attention has been given to tax shelters—devices that shelter current income from taxation. These universally involve deferment of tax liability to the future—thus yielding an interest saving. They often involve "leverage"; the gain is increased if part of the funds are borrowed. Frequently, when taxable income is finally realized, it receives advantages of the favorable treatment of capital gains. Examples, as indicated in the work of Stanley Surrey and others, have included:[14]

1. Treating as a current expense the following capital investment items:

    a. The "intangible" costs of drilling oil wells—75 percent or more of the total cost of drilling.

    b. The costs of raising livestock later sold or held for breeding. This, plus the capital gains treatment of the proceeds from sale of the cattle, has led large numbers of wealthy persons to invest in livestock they never see—in a few cases with disastrous results as the ventures have failed.

    c. Cost of developing orchards and vineyards; land-clearing and drainage and other costs to improve farmland. Large enterprises are now required to capitalize these costs.

    d. Interest and real estate tax costs in the construction of a new building. Under the 1976 legislation, these must be depreciated.

2. Accelerated depreciation, as discussed below—allowing deduction of a higher percentage of capital costs in the early years after the investment is made.

The net effect is to distort investment patterns of higher-income persons—toward financing cattle feeding, for example—instead of economically rational types and at the same time barring nontaxable entities from legitimate investments in these fields, because the yield is reduced by the flow of funds to the field.

---

[13] A. H. Petrei, "Inflation Adjustment Schemes under the Personal Income Tax," *I.M.F. Staff Papers*, vol. 22 (July 1975), pp. 539–64: V. Tanzi, "Adjustment of Taxation for Inflation," *I.M.F. Paper*, May 1975; J. Bossons and T. A. Wilson, "Adjusting Tax Rates for Inflation," *Canadian Tax Journal*, vol. 21 (May–June 1973), pp. 185–99; H. J. Aaron, ed., *Inflation and the Tax Structure* (Washington, D.C.: The Brookings Institution, 1976).

[14] S. S. Surrey, *Pathways to Tax Reform* (Cambridge, Mass.: Harvard University Press, 1973), chap. 4.

Congress has been concerned with the shelters and introduced some restrictions, particularly with regards to capital gains treatment when the gain is realized, and the 1976 tax reform act significantly curtailed them, partly by specific restrictions on various types, partly by introduction of the "at risk" rule, by limiting loss deductions in certain situations to the amount of capital the investor has at risk. But the shelters are still very important.

In recent years, shelters have been created for labor income, whereby persons are allowed to place a percentage of their incomes into tax-sheltered annuities, avoiding tax now, and paying on the gains in subsequent years when their incomes will be lower.

COMPREHENSIVE INCOME TAX PROPOSALS

The existing income tax structure in the United States, like that of many countries, has evolved over a long period of time, and the evolution has brought about a rather complex structure characterized by exceptions and special rules and deductions and means of escaping tax. It is widely argued by the critics of the present structure of the tax that an optimal income tax structure is one that applies to all income in a comprehensive and uniform fashion with deductions and exclusions limited to those for which a compelling case can be made. To do otherwise results in inequity, administrative problems, and potential economic distortions. While a system of differential income tax rates, high on incomes of the owners of factor units whose supply schedules are inelastic (that is, the tax will have little effect on the numbers of units they are willing to supply) and low where supply is elastic might maximize economic welfare, such a system is not feasible of implementation. Any differentiation that is employed is very likely to reduce economic welfare.

As a consequence of the noncomprehensiveness of the present tax and numerous questionable means of escaping—often called loopholes—there have been a number of proposals for a completely comprehensive tax that would apply uniformly to all incomes.

The Canadian Royal Commission Proposals

The Canadian Royal Commission on Taxation—the Carter Commission—proposed one of the most complete and carefully developed plans for a comprehensive system in its report of 1966.[15] While imputed rental on owner-occupied homes and unrealized capital gains would remain outside the scope of the tax, the coverage would

---

[15] Canada, *Report of the Royal Commission on Taxation*, vol. 3 (Ottawa: Queens Printer, 1966).

be very broad to include all realized capital gains (at regular rates), gifts and inheritances, social security and retirement benefits, and income now excluded because of special concessions to certain industries. On the other hand, rates would be lowered and broad averaging permitted. Unfortunately, these proposals encountered serious objections from interested groups. When the legislation was finally enacted in 1971, it did little more than make half of capital gains taxable.[16]

United States—The Defects

For the last two decades a number of proposals for more comprehensive income tax structures have been made, particularly by Musgrave, Surrey, Pechman, and others. Complaints about loopholes did result in a request by Congress in 1967 for a detailed study by the Treasury of the coverage of the tax. This report was made to Congress in 1969,[17] but the recommendations were essentially of a piecemeal nature rather than for a comprehensive reform and greatly broadened coverage. Congress, after a year of discussion, enacted the Revenue Act of 1969, which tightened the law in some respects, but even less broadly than the Treasury proposed.

The principal changes included the raising of the maximum tax rate on capital gains to 35 percent, placing of some restrictions on deductability of contributions, reduction in the depletion allowance, and limitations on the deductability of farm losses and establishment of the minimum tax. This is a levy on certain tax-preference incomes, those receiving favorable treatment, over and above the regular income tax.

Continued concern resulted in the Tax Reform Act of 1976, aimed primarily at the loopholes. Major changes included:

a. Increased coverage of the minimum tax. The following items are subject to this tax:

1. The half of capital gains excluded from regular income.
2. Accelerated depreciation on real property—the excess of actual depreciation allowed over straight-line depreciation—and on leased equipment.
3. Gains from exercise of stock options given corporate executives. Corporations frequently give their executives the right to exercise an option to buy stock at a specified price; if the market price of the stock rises, the option is exercised and the gain taxed on a capital gains basis.

---

[16] M. Bucovetsky and R. M. Bird, "Tax Reform in Canada: A Progress Report," *National Tax Journal*, vol. 25 (March 1972), pp. 15–42.

[17] *Tax Reform Studies and Proposals*, U.S. Treasury Department, Joint Publication, Committee on Ways and Means of the U.S. House of Representatives, and Committee on Finance of the U.S. Senate (Washington, D.C. 1969).

4. Depletion allowances—the excess of the depletion allowances over actual depreciation.
5. The excess of interest paid on funds for investment over the net investment income. This rule is designed to prevent tax avoidance by borrowing money to buy stock on which capital gains are made, the interest being deductible, while the capital gains get favorable treatment.
6. Intangible drilling costs of oil wells, in excess of the depreciation allowance.
7. Excess of personal deductions (except medical expenses and casualty losses) over 60 percent of AGI.

Minimum tax at 15 percent applies to the income from these sources minus *a*) $10,000, or *b*) half the regular income, whichever is greater.

b. Elimination of several tax shelters.
c. Increasing the holding period for long term capital gains to one year, but liberalizing the deductibility of capital losses.
d. Broadening of the retirement income credit to a credit for the elderly.
e. Conversion of the child care deduction to a tax credit.
f. Tightening of tax on income earned abroad.

Between 1971 and 1977 the principal steps taken to improve coverage were to eliminate the depletion allowance on petroleum products in 1975, and to broaden the minimum tax and eliminate some tax shelters in 1976.

The Defects as of 1977

There is still widespread feeling that the tax does not accomplish the desired results—that large numbers of wealthy persons escape tax they should legitimately pay, while the typical wage or salary worker cannot escape. The primary defects today include:
1. The ability of the wealthy to use some tax shelters, as noted above, arising primarily out of the privilege to write off various capital expenditures as current expenses and then gain capital gains treatment when the profits are finally realized. The range of tax shelters has been materially reduced, however.
2. The continued exemption of state and local bond interest.
3. As late as 1976, the ability of some very high-income persons to pay little or no tax despite the minimum tax, which is not fully effective; and to give very large amounts of contributions tax free.
4. The continued favorable treatment given capital gains—though substantially less favorable than prior to 1970.
5. The favorable treatment given homeowners compared to tenants; to farmers; and other groups.

As a result, one point of view presses for very broad inclusion of all income and elimination of most or all exclusions, and deductions, except those necessary to gain the income and credits for dependents. In turn, the basic tax rate could be materially reduced. Stanley Surrey has argued for replacement of all concessions—including contributions—and use of outright subsidies for the various activities, which would avoid the present concealment and eliminate the present greater gain to high-income groups. But Surrey well recognizes the political obstacles to such an approach. Others, such as B. I. Bittker of the Yale Law School[18] and Roger Freeman of Stanford[19] object to the basic approach of calling the various concessions "loopholes," maintaining that while some are certainly defective, on the whole they reflect the preferences of society for various types of concessions in the public interest, and that to attack them all makes more difficult the only type of reform that is feasible and desirable—changes in particular items to prevent abuses that are contrary to the intent of Congress.

The Pechman Study

A recent paper by Joseph Pechman stresses the limited coverage of income under the income tax and the lack of substantial progressivity.[20] While the study is based on 1967 data, the current picture is not very different. Pechman's study was based on a sample of 30,000 families for which detailed income data were collected for the 1967 *Survey of Economic Opportunity* and on income tax returns for the same families. The adjusted income used as a basis for analysis of the tax payments is a very broad one, including all usual forms of income, imputed rent, and the individual's share of undistributed corporate earnings (as a proxy for accrued capital gains). His major conclusions are as follows:

1.   The overall income tax burden is not heavy—for all families, 13 percent of total income.

2.   The maximum paid by any income class is 29 percent.

3.   The federal personal income tax is progressive except at the over $1 million bracket, but to a much lesser degree than the tax rates imply, reaching a maximum of 21 percent. There is little progression beyond $50,000 income.

---

[18] B. I. Bittker, "Income Tax Loopholes and Political Rhetoric," *Michigan Law Review*, vol. 71 (May 1973), pp. 1099–1128.

[19] R. A. Freeman, *Tax Loopholes* (Washington, D.C.: American Enterprise Institute, 1973).

[20] "Distribution of Federal and State Income Taxes by Income Classes," *Journal of Finance*, vol. 27 (May 1972), pp. 179–91. Note also the study by J. A. Pechman and B. A. Okner, *Who Bears the Tax Burden* (Washington, D.C.: The Brookings Institution, 1974). Thus study is concerned with the burden of all forms of tax.

4. The burden on income from labor earnings is much heavier than that on property income.

5. The corporate tax, if not shifted to consumers, is much more progressive than the personal income tax.

6. Drastic tax rate reductions would be possible if the income tax base were made comprehensive.

Various reforms since the study should have made the tax more effectively progressive.

CONCLUSION

The experience with comprehensive tax reform in both Canada and the United States in the late sixties shows very clearly the difficulties in obtaining effective reform.

While it is easy to get widespread nominal support for a "comprehensive" income tax, it is difficult to enact such a plan. The special interests benefiting from the present preferential treatment fight the change to the bitter end, and there is no equivalent group to fight for the reform. Even though the tax rate would be lowered, the persons now benefiting would experience some increase in taxes and others would have their taxes reduced—but the latter group is not always aware of this and is not organized to fight for the change. The problem is aggravated by legitimate differences of position over just how far the tax should go in the way of comprehensiveness and how to treat some of the basically difficult items noted earlier in these chapters. Once some exceptions are made—for administrative or political reasons—it becomes politically difficult to avoid making others. A truly comprehensive levy, despite its attraction, is not likely to be attained. But some improvement over the present tax is not impossible.

APPENDIX–CANADIAN INCOME TAX RATES, 1976

TABLE 11A–1

Federal Income Tax Rates, 1976

Taxable Income Bracket	*Rate Percent*
First $654	6
655– 1,307	18
1,308– 2,614	19
2,615– 3,921	20
3,922– 6,535	21
6,536– 9,149	23
9,150–11,763	25
11,764–14,372	27
14,373–18,298	31
18,299–31,368	35
31,369–50,973	39
50,974–78,420	43
78,421+	47

TABLE 11A–2
Combined Federal and Provincial Personal Income Tax
Marginal Rates, 1976

Taxable Income	1976
1	1.83
655	5.49
1,308	5.80
2,615	26.10
3,922	27.41
5,227	27.41
6,536	30.02
7,840	30.02
9,150	32.63
10,453	32.63
11,764	35.24
13,063	33.08
14,378	37.98
15,680	37.98
18,299	42.88
19,600	42.88
31,369	50.90
32,667	50.90
50,974	56.12
52,266	56.12
78,421	61.34
115,184	61.34
158,052	61.34
280,594	61.34
495,041	61.34

Source: Canadian Tax Foundation, *The National Finances, 1975–76,* p. 40.

REFERENCES

Break, G. F., and Pechman, J. A. *Federal Tax Reform: The Impossible Dream?* Washington, D.C.: The Brookings Institution, 1975.
Alternatives to reform.

Goode, Richard. *The Individual Income Tax.* rev. ed. Washington, D.C.: The Brookings Institution, 1976.
A thorough examination of income tax issues.

Pechman, J. A. *Federal Tax Policy.* rev. ed. Washington, D.C.: The Brookings Institution, 1971.

Simons, H. C. *Personal Income Taxation.* Chicago: University of Chicago Press, 1938.
The classic work on the concept of income for tax purposes.

Surrey, Stanley S. *Pathways to Tax Reform.* Cambridge: Harvard University Press, 1973.
Emphasis on tax shelters and the need to eliminate them.

Vickrey, W. *Agenda for Progressive Taxation.* New York: Ronald Press, 1947.
The first exhaustive study of various aspects of income tax structure.

U.S. Treasury. *Tax Reform Studies and Proposals.* Washington, D.C.: Government Printing Office, 1969.
A study of defects in the income tax structure.

Canada

Bucovetsky, M., and Bird, R. M. "Tax Reform in Canada: A Progress Report," *National Tax Journal,* vol. 25 (March 1972), pp. 15–42.

Report of the Royal Commission on Taxation. 5 vols. Ottawa: Queen's Printer, 1966.

"Symposium on the Report of the Royal Commission on Taxation," *National Tax Journal,* vol. 22 (March 1969), pp. 1–178.

12

Economic Effects of Income Taxation

Evaluation of the role of income taxation in the tax structure is dependent upon a knowledge of the various economic effects that the tax may have. Many of the complaints against the tax are made on grounds of economic effects; are these effects as drastic as sometimes claimed? Does the tax lessen capital formation and destroy incentives, for example? Does the tax actually reduce income in the pattern in which it is imposed? Unfortunately the answers are by no means entirely definitive.

The Basis of Analysis

To facilitate analysis, let us assume that the economy is in equilibrium, in the sense of having adjusted to the various determinants:

1. Given factor supply schedules that relate quantities of labor and other factors available at various factor prices.
2. Given production functions, which relate inputs of various factors to outputs of various commodities.
3. Consumer preferences, which show relative consumer preferences for various goods.
4. A given rate of capital formation, such that magnitudes of planned savings and investment are in equilibrium.
5. A given pattern of market relationships.

With these assumptions, an equilibrium of commodity and factor prices, levels of output, rates of utilization of factors, and rate of growth develops. The price structure, given the constraints, determines both the pattern of resource allocation and the pattern of income distribution. The equilibrium changes, of course, as the determinants change.

Next, let us introduce government into the picture. The governmental activities alter the pattern of resource allocation, as governmental services replace some private sector output. Some factor-supply schedules may be altered; free governmental services replacing ones formerly purchased, for example, may reduce the hours that persons are willing to work at given wages. Educational activities may reduce labor supply temporarily while children are in school and permanently increase the supply of skilled workers and reduce the supply of unskilled workers. But we are primarily concerned, at this point, with the effects of the various forms of taxation, and initially the income tax, upon the adjustments in the economy.

With the governmental activities, real income from the private sector is reduced, in one fashion or another, under the assumption of full employment. The objective of the analysis is to compare the reactions to this reduction with various alternative forms of taxation. The simplest initial standard to use as a basis for considering the effect of the income tax is a lump-sum poll or head tax, imposed at a uniform rate on all persons (or at least all adults). Such a tax is hopelessly objectionable from an equity standpoint, but it is a convenient standard for comparison of efficiency effects because it produces no substitution effect. Since the amount of tax is independent of the income earned or other aspects of economic behavior, it gives no incentive to alter behavior at the margin. Like any reduction in real income, it will produce an income effect; it will presumably lead persons to attempt to increase their incomes in order to maintain living standards. But it has no marginal or substitutional effect.

In the remainder of the chapter, it is assumed that a personal income tax is introduced in lieu of the hypothetical poll tax, the level of governmental activities remaining the same. We shall ignore in this chapter the significance of differential impact of the corporate income tax, assuming that the income tax applies uniformly to income regardless of the legal form of business organization. The significance of the corporate income tax will be considered in Chapter 13.

INCOME TAXES AND CAPITAL FORMATION

Income taxes may affect capital formation in two ways: by altering the quantity of savings at full employment and thus the maximum possible rate of capital formation (the supply function) and by affecting the willingness to undertake investment and thus the actual level of real capital formation (the demand function).

Income Taxes and Savings: The Maximum Rate of Capital Formation

As explained in greater detail in Chapter 20, the real rate of capital formation cannot exceed the level of savings at full employment. Thus the impact of taxes on savings will ultimately determine the impact of taxes upon the level of capital formation. Both theoretical considerations (which we discuss fully in Chapter 20) and empirical evidence suggest that for a given individual, savings are positively related to income and possibly to the return to savings. A head tax or poll tax reduces all persons' incomes by the same amount but is not related to the return from savings. Thus a poll tax has only an income effect, which will tend to reduce the level of savings both for each household and for the economy as a whole.

A proportional income tax differs from a poll tax in two ways. First, the income effect will tend to be greater with an income tax than with a poll tax; and second, an income tax has a substitution effect that affects savings adversely, which a poll tax does not have. Both considerations imply that there will be less savings under a proportional income tax than there would be under a poll tax. Each warrants brief attention.

In terms of the income effect, a proportional income tax reduces all individuals' incomes proportionately while a poll tax reduces all individuals' incomes by the same amount. Thus high-income individuals will have a greater reduction in income under a proportional income tax than under a poll tax. Even if savings were proportional to income, savings would be lower under a proportional income tax than under a poll tax. But there is considerable evidence that savings increase as income rises, resulting in an even lower level of savings with a proportional income tax.

The income tax also reduces the return to savings and, hence, alters the relative advantage of savings as opposed to consumption. Consequently, the substitution effect of a proportional income tax reduces the amount of savings. The net effect on savings depends upon the functional relationship between the volume of savings and the net after-tax interest return available. If the relationship is highly inelastic, as it may be because many persons save for motives unrelated to the return from savings, changes in the net return will have little adverse affect upon savings; if it is highly elastic, change in the net return will have substantial adverse effect upon savings. Unfortunately, the sensitivity of savings to the return to savings is an empirical matter, upon which there is limited information. It has been widely believed that the elasticity is relatively low, but a recent study by M. J.

Boskin, under the auspices of the United States Treasury, using time-series data, concludes that there is a substantial positive response of savings to the rate of return—an elasticity of .3 to .4 percent.[1]

A progressive income tax will increase the negative impact of taxes upon savings as compared to a proportional tax. Under a progressive income tax, people with high incomes pay relatively more than those with low incomes. Since savings rises more than proportionately with income, the income effect associated with a progressive income tax will have a larger adverse effect upon savings than that associated with a proportional income tax. Similarly, a progressive income tax reduces the return to savings as the return rises. Consequently, the substitution effect associated with a progressive tax will be greater than that associated with a proportional tax. Thus both the substitution and income effects that affect savings adversely will be greater with a progressive income tax than with a proportional income tax, which in turn has a more adverse affect upon savings than a poll tax.

In summary: While no definitive answers can be given about the precise effect of an income tax on the percentage of national income saved—the S/Y ratio—almost inevitably the ratio will be reduced, compared to the situation with a poll tax, because families will absorb more of the tax out of savings. The magnitude is not known nor is any precise comparison between the income tax and other taxes possible. Upon what appear to be reasonable assumptions, a progressive rate structure will reduce the savings-income ratio more per dollar of revenue than a proportional tax.

One study suggests a difference of about 5 percent in the S/Y ratio.[2] Whether the total real private and governmental savings in the economy will fall from a governmental program financed by an income tax is dependent upon governmental use of the funds, a question beyond the scope of this chapter. Typically, governments have a lower savings ratio (ratio of government capital expenditures to total government expenditures) than the taxpayers as a whole, if saving is defined narrowly to exclude outlays on education and health.

The Investment Schedule and Capital Formation

The actual level of investment depends upon the relationship of the savings schedule (supply of investible funds) and the investment schedule (demand for investible funds). The demand for

---

[1] M. J. Boskin, *Taxation, Saving, and the Rate of Interest*, OTA Paper no. 11 (Washington, D.C.: U.S. Treasury, 1976).

[2] G. Break, "The Incidence and Effects of Taxation," in *The Economics of Public Finance*, A. S. Blinder, *et al.* (Washington, D.C.: The Brookings Institution, 1974), pp. 192–93, based on the work of R. D. Husby, "A Nonlinear Consumption Function Estimate from Time Series and Cross Section Data," *Review of Economics and Statistics*, vol. 53 (February 1971), pp. 76–79.

investment—the schedule of real investment at various interest-rate levels—is dependent on the marginal productivity of the investment.[3] The effect of alternative taxes upon the actual amount of investment therefore depends upon how the tax affects the savings schedule and the investment schedule. Let us assume initially that the government pursues a policy to ensure that full employment is always maintained, regardless of the tax imposed. Therefore savings is a function only of the rate of interest, that is, the return to savings alone, and not of the level of income, which is assumed as given.

While a poll tax reduces aggregate private savings, the investment schedule is unaffected, because a poll tax does not alter the after-tax return of an investment. The actual level of private capital formation must fall to equal the lower value of private savings.

An income tax will alter the investment schedule by reducing the after-tax return to investment. But, if the savings schedule at full employment has no elasticity with respect to the return from savings, the volume of capital formation is not affected by the nature of the investment schedule—the schedule of demand for real capital goods at various levels of rate of return—since the volume of investment must adjust to the given volume of savings for full employment to be maintained. The investment schedule will affect the equilibrium after-tax rate of return, however. This relationship is illustrated in Figure 12–1A; the volume of capital formation is at ON before and after tax for attainment of full employment. After tax, the gross rate of return is R (the same as before tax), and after tax rate of return R'.

If the savings schedule has some positive elasticity with respect to the rate of return at full employment, however, the rate of capital formation will be dependent upon the investment schedule, as indicated in Figure 12–1B. As the rate of return is reduced by the tax, the volume of savings falls and the savings schedule shifts to S'. Moreover, the investment schedule will also shift to the left, since the tax reduces the after-tax return to investment; once adjustments are complete, investment will be somewhat lower than before the tax and the before-tax rate of return (R') will be somewhat higher than the rate of return (R) prevailing before the tax was introduced. The net rate of return after tax $(R'-t)$ is lower than the old rate of return, but not by the full amount of the tax. The greater the extent to which savings falls in response to the decline in the rate of return, the greater will be the decline in capital formation and the greater the increase in the before-tax rate of return. If invest-

---

[3] Formally, the marginal efficiency of investment measures the internal rate of return that can be earned at each level of investment. The internal rate of return is that rate of interest which compounded makes the discounted value of the investment just equal to the cost of the investment. As long as the return from an investment is greater than the interest rate, the firm will make the investment.

FIGURE 12–1

Effects of Income Tax on Capital
Formation (full employment)

A Proportional Income Tax, Perfectly
Inelastic Supply

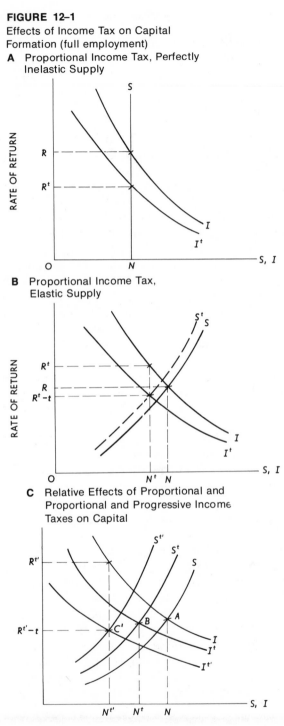

B Proportional Income Tax,
Elastic Supply

C Relative Effects of Proportional and
Proportional and Progressive Income
Taxes on Capital

S: Savings.
I: Investment before tax
I': Investment after tax, proportional income tax.
I'': Investments after tax, progressive income tax

ment is highly unresponsive to changes in the rate of return, there will be little decline in capital formation; if investment is sharply reduced by the lower rate of return, capital formation will be reduced substantially.

A progressive income tax will have a greater adverse affect upon investment than a proportional income tax since it will tend to shift the savings and investment schedules more than a proportional income tax. That is shown in Figure 12-1C. The schedules S'' and I'' represent the savings and investment schedules under a progressive income tax, while the schedules S' and I' represent the schedules under a proportional income tax. Under a progressive income tax, N_t of investment is forthcoming, with an after tax return of R and a before-tax return of $R_{t'} - t$.

Risk-Taking

In addition to being related to the after-tax rate of return, the demand for investible funds and supply of money capital may be related to individuals' willingness to take risk. If an income tax affects risk-taking, the previously discussed shifts in the savings and investment schedules may be altered somewhat. Reduction in willingness to take risk will necessitate a somewhat higher rate of return for full employment to be attained; it will alter somewhat the character of investment and it will make the government's task of maintaining full employment more difficult.

The question of the effect of taxes on risk-taking has been debated extensively.[4] The income tax reduces the return from risk-taking. But whether this increases or reduces the total amount of risk undertaken is not as easy to answer as might appear. As with any tax there is an income effect, which encourages persons to take more risk in order to maintain their incomes. But the income tax also has a substitution effect, by lessening the gain from taking risk relative to the danger of the loss of the money; this leads in the opposite direction. The net effect is impossible to predict, but various influences on it can be noted.

First, the existence of a loss offset is important because with it the net risk involved from an investment is reduced. If there is full offset, any loss from an unsuccessful investment can be deducted against other income, with refund of excess of loss over income. With a proportional tax and full loss offset, the tax would reduce yield and potential loss by the same amount. So long as the taxpayer recognizes this fact, there is no incentive to shift in the direction of less risk. There is only

---

[4] A good review and analysis is provided in the paper by M. J. Roberts, *Portfolio Models and the Impact of Taxation on Investment,* Discussion Paper 213 (Cambridge, Mass.: Harvard Institute of Economic Research, 1971).

the income effect, which encourages persons to take more risk.[5] This conclusion is valid, however, only if taxpayers do recognize the significance of the loss offset, which they may not do if they are eternally optimistic and consider only the possibility of gain.

Furthermore, loss offsets are in practice by no means complete. No tax refund is granted when losses exceed other income and carry-back and carry-forward of losses are limited. In the United States, capital losses, as distinguished from operating losses, can be deducted from other income only to the extent of $3,000 a year (with unlimited carry-forward) and operating losses can be carried back or forward for limited periods only. Accordingly, the possibility of an increase in risk-taking is lessened.

Second, the rate structure presumably has some significance for the reaction; with a progressive rate, the government shares in the losses to a lesser extent than it shares in the gain, since, other things equal, the taxpayer's rate bracket will be lower. With a proportional tax, the tax savings from a loss and tax increase from a gain will be the same per dollar.

Third, the lenient treatment given capital gains by most countries almost certainly increases the willingness to take risks. Bonds and stock in secure companies yield dividends subject to full tax rates; the yield of growth stocks—typically in expanding industries—largely takes the form of capital gains subject to the lower rate. The fact that common stock has constituted a growing element in portfolios is evidence. The Brookings study on investment decisions concluded, on the basis of interviews, that the capital gains treatment does have significant influence in leading to increased relative investment in growth stocks.[6] About two thirds of all persons interviewed in the study indicated preferences for growth stocks over income stocks, and a third of these indicated tax considerations as a primary reason; the proportion doing so was much higher in the top income levels than in the lower levels.

Other Provisions of the Tax Laws. The differentially favorable treatment given, at least in the past, to oil and mineral production—

---

[5] This conclusion, based on the work of E. D. Domar and R. A. Musgrave, "Proportional Income Taxation and Risk Taking," *Quarterly Journal of Economics*, vol. 58 (May 1944), pp. 388–422, was long accepted. In recent years it has been questioned on the basis of the applicability of the assumptions. Specifically, the conclusions are valid only if there is available a truly riskless asset (and money is not riskless in an inflationary economy), if risk aversion rises as incomes rise, and if investors have a peculiar quadratic utility function such that the standard deviation of the expected return serves as a measure of risk. See M. S. Feldstein, "The Effects of Taxation on Risk Taking," *Journal of Political Economy*, vol. 77 (September-October 1969), pp. 755–64; Roberts, "Portfolio Models"; and the summary by Lester Thurow in *The Impact of Taxes on the American Economy* (New York: Praeger, 1971), p. 40.

[6] R. Barlow, H. E. Brazer, and J. N. Morgan, *Economic Behavior of the Affluent* (Washington, D.C.: The Brookings Institution, 1966), p. 38.

among the more risky investments—presumably increases total risk-taking in the economy. This is not a desirable effect, however, as investment is concentrated in the direction of one form of risky activity.

A few features encourage taxpayers to move away from the more risky investments—the tax exempt status of state and local bonds, the favorable treatment provided life insurance, and encouragement given to establish trusts for minor children.

The Net Effect. The net effect on risk-taking is difficult to assess, but it appears reasonable to conclude that it is not very great and the capital gains treatment may well tip the balance in the direction of greater risk-taking. Thus the supply of money capital and investment demand are altered less than they would be if they were independent of risk-taking. The optimal amount of risk-taking in the economy is not easy to define—"more" is not necessarily better than "less." Obviously, society does not seek to maximize risk-taking, to concentrate investment in the most risky endeavors. To do so would result in gross misallocation of resources. What is required is sufficient willingness to take risk that the volume of investment required to ensure full employment—given other variables—will be attained. Complete absence of willingness to take risk would stagnate the economy; a wild passion for extremely speculative ventures would cause serious economic losses and misallocation of resources.

Nonfull Employment: Effects of the Tax

Supply of Funds for Investment. With the assumption of full employment dropped, the relevant supply is no longer the total amount of savings made during the period, but the schedule of the amounts of money capital that persons are willing to make available at various rates of return. This schedule is not identical with the schedule of savings since amounts of personal wealth may simply be held rather than being made available to others. Thus the schedule depends upon not only the volume of savings during the period at various interest-rate levels, but also the willingness of persons to invest this in their own businesses or make it available to others.

An income tax, therefore, may affect the supply in three ways: by altering the quantity of new savings, by altering the willingness to forego liquidity preference, and by altering the willingness to take risk. The previous discussion suggests that the first and third determinants are not significantly affected by changes in the rate of return; the second may be affected to a greater extent, giving the schedule some positive elasticity, as suggested in Figure 12–2.

Demand. On the demand side, the considerations are in part the same as with full employment. While a poll tax does not alter the rate

FIGURE 12–2
Effects of Income Taxation on Capital Formation, Less than
Full Employment

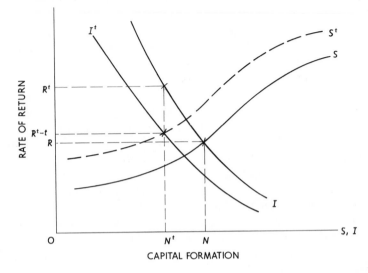

of return from investments, an income tax reduces the net return and
therefore reduces the amount of investment businesses are willing to
undertake. With the assumption of full employment dropped, however, another effect of the two taxes in reducing investment must be
noted: Both poll taxes and income taxes curtail the total amount of
consumption expenditures made at given interest-rate levels. Without
question the volume of consumption goods sales is a primary determinant of the volume of investment. The more uniformly distributed poll
tax is likely to have greater effect per dollar of revenue than the income tax, which concentrates more heavily in the higher-income
levels.

Net Effect. The net effect of the income tax upon actual capital
formation is impossible to determine with any degree of accuracy. The
tax, by reducing the gains from foregoing liquidity, will reduce the
supply of money capital somewhat even if it affects neither the volume
of savings (at given levels of national income) nor the willingness to
take risk. The tax, by reducing gain from investment, may deter investment to a somewhat greater extent than a poll tax. Therefore, the
total volume of capital formation may be reduced, the level of GNP
and personal income reduced, and unemployment increased in the
absence of government intervention. The lesser effect of the income
tax compared to the poll tax (or, in fact, other levies) in reducing
consumption per dollar of revenue, however, offsets this effect to some
extent.

The effect of the tax on the level of investment may be offset by fiscal and monetary measures. If these are successful in restoring the old level of employment, the same considerations apply as with full employment. To the extent that the income tax does reduce the percentage of national income saved at full employment, it makes the task of maintaining full employment easier. To the extent that it does significantly reduce the willingness to undertake real investment, it makes the task more difficult. There is no conclusive evidence of the net effect, but there is no reason to believe that the tax has substantial effects on investment, as compared to alternative taxes. The net effect, therefore, may well be a somewhat lower rate of full-employment capital formation but a somewhat greater ability to attain that level compared with other forms of tax.

THE INCOME TAX AND THE SUPPLY OF LABOR

A proportional income tax is equivalent to a proportional reduction in wages and salaries. A 10 percent proportional income tax, for example, has the same impact upon real incomes of workers as a general 10 percent cut in labor incomes, other prices remaining the same. Therefore, just as a wage change, the tax will produce both substitution and income effects.

The Indifference-Curve Analysis

The indifference-curve analysis can be used to illustrate the possible reactions. On Figure 12–3 each indifference curve (A^1, A^2, A^3)

FIGURE 12–3
Income–Leisure Equilibrium

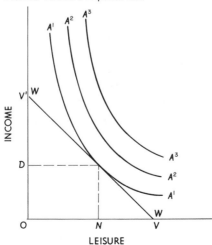

shows the relative combinations of work (income) and leisure that yield the same satisfaction for a family. Each curve flattens out on the ends; beyond a certain point, physical limitations prevent further substitution of work for leisure; in the other direction, a person is unwilling to substitute additional leisure for work—unless he or she has nonlabor income—as more leisure ceases to be enjoyable without income to spend. The curves presumably vary among individuals; to some there is limited substitutability, as they have strong preference for a certain income and a certain amount of leisure; others have a high degree of substitutability, or, in other words, the marginal rate of substitution falls slowly as one is substituted for the other. The former situation produces an indifference curve with a sharp bend; the latter, a gentle curvature. Successive AA curves on the diagram show successively higher levels of income and leisure and, therefore, higher (but unmeasurable) levels of satisfaction. Variation in labor hours may reflect changes in hours worked by the principal wage earner or by other members of the family.

Curve WW indicates the wage rate, or in other words, the marginal cost of substituting leisure for work and vice versa. The curve is drawn as a straight line on the assumption that the wage rate is independent of the hours worked. If the person worked 24 hours a day with no leisure, the income would be OV'; if he did not work at all income would be O (and leisure OV). The point of tangency of the wage curve with an indifference curve indicates the optimum—the highest level of satisfaction a person can reach, given the wage rate. Thus on the diagram income will be OD, leisure ON, and the person will work the number of hours a day (NV) that will produce this income under the assumption that the person seeks to maximize satisfaction.

Reactions to Taxes

A poll tax reduces the person's disposable income by a constant amount, thus pushing the WW curve to the left on the diagram, parallel to the old curve. This change produces only an income effect, since the tax liability is not dependent upon the amount earned and thus the person will work either the same amount or more, so long as income is a superior good, as shown in Figure 12–4.

An income tax introduces two major differences. First, the relative tax on various persons will be substantially different. The lowest-income groups, the ones most likely to increase their work effort in response to a tax, will be freed of tax, and much greater relative amounts will rest on persons in the high-income levels. The income effect may be very different for these persons—but there is no way of predicting with any degree of certainty.

Secondly, with the income tax the amount of tax is dependent upon

FIGURE 12–4

Response of Work and Leisure to a Poll Tax

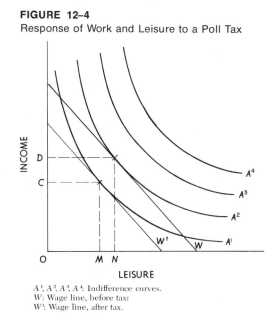

A¹, A², A³, A⁴: Indifference curves.
W: Wage line, before tax.
Wᵗ: Wage line, after tax.

the amount earned, and thus there is possibility of a substitution effect. Figure 12–5 shows the income and substitution effects; the new income curves no longer parallel the old. Therefore the amount of work is almost certain to be somewhat less than with the poll tax for any given person paying the same amount under the two taxes. The decline in labor effort will take several forms. Absenteeism will be greater; the person will be less willing to work overtime or to moonlight; the wife or children may drop out of the labor market. With the wife working, there are often nondeductible expenses associated with the work; the reduced gain may no longer be sufficient to warrant these expenses and the loss of time from housework, shopping, and so forth. Persons with substantial nonlabor income are among the groups most liable to reduce labor. There is an intermediate situation, of course, in which the two effects balance and the same work is performed as before.

The actual magnitude of the effect is quite another matter; there is reason to suspect that it is not very great. One reason is the limited control many persons have over hours of work. They must work a certain number of hours if they are to hold the job, and there is no opportunity for overtime or moonlighting. The wife and children work (or do not work) regardless of the tax. The likelihood of failure to adjust is increased by the importance of nonmonetary motives, especially among those persons, such as professional men, in the best position to alter their work patterns. Persons are influenced not only by the desire

FIGURE 12–5

Response of Work and Leisure to a Proportional Income Tax

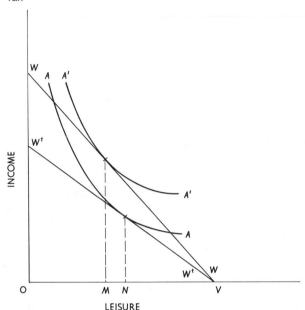

for income but also by such goals as satisfaction from accomplishing a task, sense of responsibility, power and prestige, diversity in life, and freedom from boredom that work provides. Especially in the higher-income levels, many wives work because of strong professional aspirations and the sense of satisfaction in work and because they find housework, women's clubs, and similar activities boring.

The Spite Effect. We have assumed thus far that the worker reacts to a tax increase in the same fashion as to a wage cut. But this is not necessarily valid. Richard Musgrave has stressed the possibility of a "spite" effect—the person may so dislike income taxes that he deliberately curtails work whereas he would not do so in response to an ordinary wage cut. Conversely, the person may regard the tax as a payment for government service and therefore not change his work behavior at all; this may be called the purchase effect.

Progression

The use of progressive rates increases the likelihood that any particular individual will work less rather than more with a particular tax level. The fact that the rate is progressive increases the relative influence of the substitution effect, because additional dollars earned lead to progressively greater sacrifice of leisure for income; the net gain from additional hours of work grows progressively less. If the marginal rate reaches 100 percent, as it in fact is with some welfare programs, the person will not work beyond the number of hours at which this rate is reached, because there will be no further gain so long as he has positive preference for leisure. If he does not—if he prefers work to being bored—this rule is not valid. The progressive rate situation is shown on Figure 12–6; the after-tax wage curve is no longer straight

FIGURE 12–6
Response of Work and Leisure to a Progressive Income Tax

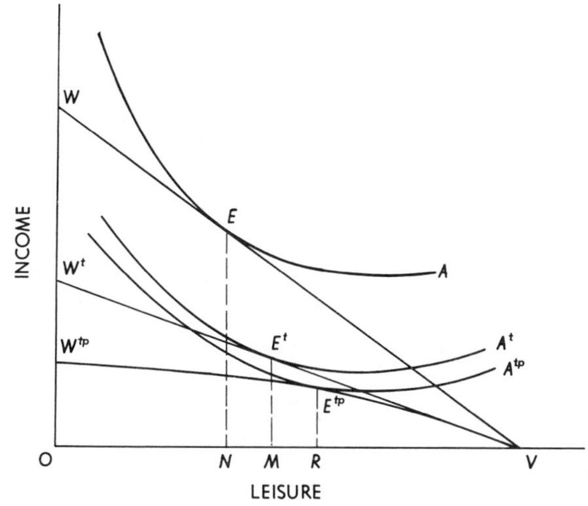

but bends down to the left horizontal axis and the tangency with the indifference curve (E^{tp}) is of necessity to the right of the one with a proportional rate collecting the same amount of tax from the person; that is, leisure will be greater and work less. This does not prove that work will be less than without an income tax at all, but merely that it will be less with a progressive tax than a proportional tax for any one person, giving usual relative preferences for work and leisure. When comparison is made in terms of labor as a whole, the net difference between the two forms of tax is less clear; the proportional tax places a heavier relative burden on the lower- and lower-middle-income groups; the progressive tax a higher burden in the upper levels. The reactions of the two groups will not necessarily be the same.

Empirical Studies

Economic analysis outlines possible reactions and avenues for empirical study, but can provide no answers about the actual direction or magnitude of effects of present income taxes upon factor supplies.

There are two approaches to empirical analysis. One, reflected in work by Thurow, is based on aggregate data.[7] Thurow notes that during the sixties, per capita disposable income was rising 3.5 percent per year, while labor supply (in hours) was falling 0.24 percent a year due primarily to shorter workdays. Accordingly, he concluded that the income effect is dominant, and therefore, if the relationship is reversible, a reduction in income taxes would reduce the labor supply, specifically by 3 percent if all federal income taxes were eliminated. Using an estimated aggregate production function, he concludes that GNP would have been 2.5 percent more if there were no taxes. The precise figures cannot be taken too seriously, but the study suggests that the taxes are not having a drastic effect on labor supply.

A number of econometric studies have been made in recent years of labor-supply functions, but the results as yet contribute little to our knowledge of tax influences.[8]

The other approach is based on interviews of relatively small samples of persons, primarily in the higher-income levels, to ascertain the effects of taxes on their work behavior. On the whole, the studies show very low sensitivity of quantity of labor available to changes in wage rates, whether due to taxes or other forces. Thus, without exception they conclude that present taxes are not having significant effects upon the overall supply of labor or the supply of executive and professional man-hours available to society.

1.   A study made for Brookings Institution by R. Barlow *et al.*[9] utilized interviews with a selected sample of 957 persons in the upper income levels. Only 12 percent of the sample indicated that taxes had any effect upon their incentives to work, and even these were, from all indications, working hard despite the taxes. The group as a whole averaged a 48-hour workweek, 50 weeks a year. The study concluded: "The implication of these findings is that the loss of annual output due to work disincentives caused by the progressive income tax is of negligible proportions."[10] The small group reporting adverse tax effects was not usually in the highest marginal rate bracket, but in those from 50 to 59 percent; this range may be the peak of the spite effect.

2.   An extensive survey of wage earners in 1962, with interviews with 2,997 families, showed a negative relationship between the wage rate and hours worked; an income tax would, therefore, increase the number of labor hours available, though not necessarily as much as a poll tax.[11]

---

[7] Thurow, *The Impact of Taxes*, pp. 25–27.

[8] Break, "Incidence and Effects," pp. 186–90.

[9] Barlow, *et al.*, *Economic Behavior of the Affluent*.

[10] Ibid. p. 3.

[11] J. N. Morgan, M. H. David, W. J. Cohen, and H. E. Brazer, *Income and Wealth in the United States* (New York: McGraw-Hill, 1962), pp. 76–77.

3. An earlier study by Sanders of executive behavior, with interviews of 160 executives, concluded that there was no significant influence of the tax upon the supply of executive talent, although behavior was affected in some respects.[12] A few executives reported that the taxes caused them to work harder; a few, to work less hard.

4. Break's study of 306 solicitors and accountants in Great Britain in 1956—a group having more control over hours worked than many—showed that over half reported no tax influence whatever; of the remainder some reported working more, some working less. Break concluded that he could not ascertain the magnitude of influence or even net direction of change, but indications were strong that the overall effects were not great.[13] A followup study by D. B. Fields and W. T. Stanbury showed a somewhat greater negative incentive effect–19 percent vs 13 percent in the Break study.[14]

5. An extensive study in England by C. V. Brown and E. Levin, involving some 2,000 weekly paid workers, showed that the income taxes did not effect the willingness of most workers (74 percent of the men, 93 percent of the women) to work overtime. Of those that did indicate an effect, more said that they worked more overtime because of the tax than the number indicating that they worked less. The authors conclude that the net effect on the labor supply could not exceed 1 percent.[15]

Long-Run Supply

The long-run supply of labor is primarily dependent upon the rate of population growth. While theoretically the income tax may influence the birthrate, there is grave doubt about any serious influence. The exemptions for dependents may reduce the cost of having children, as does deductibility of medical expenses. Gains from income splitting may have some impact on decisions to marry, but, given the other motives, the significance of the effect is very doubtful.

Relative Supply of Labor in Various Occupations

To the extent that relative supplies of labor in various occupations are affected by money income considerations, a tax will alter relative

---

[12] F. H. Sanders, *Effects of Taxation on Executives* (Boston: Graduate School of Business Administration, Harvard University, 1951).

[13] George Break, "Income Taxes, Wage Rates and the Incentive to Supply Labor Services," *National Tax Journal*, vol. 6 (December 1953), pp. 333–52.

[14] D. B. Fields and W. T. Stanbury, "Incentives, Disincentives, and the Income Tax: Further Empirical Evidence," *Public Finance*, vol. 25 (1970), pp. 381–415, and "Income Taxes and Incentives to Work," *American Economic Review*, vol. 61 (June 1971), pp. 435–43.

[15] C. V. Brown and E. Levin, "The Effects of Income Taxation on Overtime," *Economic Journal*, vol. 84 (December 1974), pp. 833–48.

supplies. A poll tax, with only an income effect, will push persons toward higher-paid occupations. While the income effect of an income tax has this effect, the substitution effect operates in the opposite direction. If the tax is progressive, there is greater likelihood, compared to a poll tax, of reducing the supply flowing into the high-pay occupations as the differential is curtailed in progressive fashion.

The significance of this effect may be questioned because of the importance of nonpecuniary motives in leading persons into higher-pay occupations. Prestige, more favorable working conditions, greater stability of income, and tax-avoidance devices available to the high-income groups are major attractions leading persons into relatively high-pay professional and managerial work. The same considerations apply with respect to persons offered more responsible positions; even if the income tax does reduce the differential substantially, other motives may lead the person to take the position.

Differentials in tax treatment of various forms of income may also have some influence on relative labor supplies. The penalty on irregular incomes and on incomes concentrating in a few years of a person's life may reduce the relative supplies in these fields, if persons calculate the pecuniary gain carefully. Any occupation with high non-monetary nontaxable gain appears relatively more attractive compared to others—the work of the housewife, for example, or, at least in the past, university teaching. The flow of labor is also increased into those occupations where evasion is relatively easy—an increasingly uncommon phenomenon in the United States, but important in many countries.

The Empirical Evidence.   There is very little empirical evidence about the effects upon relative supplies of various factors. The studies indicated above suggest that there is little impact on the hours persons in higher incomes seek to work; this conclusion suggests that the tax may have little impact on the willingness of persons to enter these occupations in the first place. The Sanders study found a few isolated instances in which persons refused more responsible jobs because of tax considerations, but in total these were not significant.[16]

DISTRIBUTIONAL EFFECTS

The use of resources by government necessitates, with full employment, a reduction in private-sector output; the provision of transfer payments to some persons in the economy necessitates a reduction in real income of others. The particular taxes used to finance the governmental activities determine the pattern of reduction in real incomes or "burden" that the activities necessitate. For an extreme

---

[16] Sanders, *Effects of Taxation.*

example, if the entire tax was collected from one very wealthy person, this person alone would suffer reduction in real income. If a $5 poll tax was collected from each person, the dollar reduction in real income would be the same for all persons if the tax had no effect on factor supply. Actual taxes are, of course, more complex in their distributional effects.

The Differential Approach

The pattern of reduction in real income arising from the particular tax is distinct from two other redistributional effects of the government program: the distributional pattern of the benefits and the pattern of changes in incomes arising from a change in the level of employment produced by the expenditure and tax program. The latter is best regarded as an effect of the overall fiscal policy employed. For example, a new expenditure program is introduced and an income tax is levied to finance it. Suppose aggregate demand in the economy falls and unemployment develops because the tax reduces aggregate demand more than the government spending increases it. As a consequence, incomes fall. This effect is appropriately attributable to the overall relationship of taxes and expenditures, not to the use of the income tax per se.

The most satisfactory approach to distributional effects is to compare the actual distributional pattern with one proportional to income.

A Proportional Income Tax

If a tax is levied at a proportional rate on all incomes in lieu of a poll tax, the actual distributional pattern will be proportional to incomes only if all markets are perfectly competitive and factor supplies are perfectly inelastic.[17] With perfect competition, individual factor owners have no control over price. With a perfectly inelastic factor supply, the net reduction in income due to the tax will not alter the number of factor units available and the factor price cannot rise, given the demand for the factor. If the factor supply is not perfectly inelastic, however, the tax will alter the quantity of units available and the factor price will change. A poll tax could have some effects on factor supply because of the income effect; almost certainly the net effect would be to increase quantity of labor available and depress, not increase, wages. An income tax would have both income and substitution effects.

The Actual Reactions. The actual typical pattern is difficult to ascertain. As explained early in the chapter, the total supply of labor is

---

[17] Or if by sheerest accident, all have similar demand and supply curves.

believed to be relatively inelastic and possibly even backward sloping; that is, at higher wages a smaller quantity will be available. Since all incomes are being taxed, a worker cannot escape by shifting from one occupation to another, and therefore the elasticity of the overall supply of labor is the relevant consideration. Because of the role of the substitution effect, however, the labor supply may be less than with a poll tax and a portion of the tax may pass off of workers on to others.

Total savings in the economy are likewise believed to be relatively inelastic to changes in net return, but a reduction in net return may reduce the willingness of persons to provide it for real investment; as a consequence, the rate of return may have to rise for the old level of employment to be restored. That is, if a certain profit rate is required for a given level of investment, the after-tax return must rise to avoid loss in employment—unless, of course, offset by fiscal policies. The supply of land is by definition perfectly inelastic in perfectly competitive markets.

Over a long period of time, the supply schedules may be somewhat different. As discussed, the total supply schedule of labor may be different over a long-run period than in a short period. Relative supplies of different types of labor may also react differently. The reduced wage differential may reduce the number of persons going into the highly paid occupations and thus bring some reallocation of tax.

Nonperfectly Competitive Markets. Few markets approach the perfectly competitive model. Labor markets are frequently characterized by employer domination, by bargaining by unions and by individuals at higher levels. The markets for goods, which influence changes in the rate of profit, are characterized by imperfections of various kinds, and especially oligopoly. In general, in imperfect markets suppliers will seek to maintain their real incomes in the face of the tax by obtaining higher prices, if they can do so. Whether they can depends on market circumstances. Individual workers, except at executive levels, typically have no direct influence on wages; they either take the job or not at the going wage. But unions exercise substantial impact on wage determination. To the extent that unions take income taxes into consideration in their wage demands and the wages they are willing to accept, the tax may be shifted off of the worker onto the business firm and therefore, in all likelihood, into the prices of the goods produced. Higher-level employees may well be able to bargain directly with the employer to obtain a higher salary to offset the increased tax. Professional men who set their own fees may raise fees in response to a tax that reduces their real incomes. Had they already obtained the income-maximizing level of fees it would not be advantageous to do so—but methods of fee-setting suggest that this is probably not the usual case. Interest and dividend receivers have less direct influence since the money capital markets are more nearly perfectly competitive. The behavior of business firms in readjusting selling prices in response to an income tax will be considered in the next chapter in the analysis of corporate income taxation.

In Summary.   A tax levied on incomes at a proportionate rate will almost certainly not be distributed in proportion to incomes. Only if all factor supplies were perfectly inelastic and all markets perfectly competitive would this be true—and while there is reason to believe that many of the schedules, such as those of labor, are relatively inelastic, it is almost impossible that all of the schedules would be perfectly inelastic. Certainly all markets are not perfectly competitive. To the extent that factor prices change as a result of the tax, the original intent of the tax is not attained; the tax does not reach persons in a fashion proportional to income and the equity is partially lost. Some persons, by getting higher factor prices, are relieved of any share in the cost of the governmental activities. This share must go on to others; it either results in reduced profits or, more likely, in higher prices for consumption goods—with a distributional pattern comparable to that of a sales tax, discussed in Chapter 14. Actual measurement of departure from a proportional pattern is impossible; it may not be too great, given the apparent relative inelasticity of factor-supplies schedules. But there is certain to be some.

A Progressive Income Tax

An income tax levied at progressive rates is not necessarily progressive relative to incomes, as U.S. experience noted in the previous chapter has shown. First, modifications in factor prices as described in the previous section may occur. Secondly, in the U.S. income tax structure, numerous escape hatches, in the form of special exclusions from income, capital gains treatment, deductions, and the like, are relatively much more advantageous to persons in the higher income levels than in lower levels. As a consequence, the tax is progressive only to $100,000 income, then regressive. [18]

The use of an effective progressive tax instead of a proportional tax to raise the same amount of money produces a different initial pattern of income reduction; more tax is placed on the higher-income groups—owners of businesses, executives, professional men—and less on lower- and middle-income workers and farmers. The relative ability of the higher-income groups to shift the tax to someone else may be greater; executives are in a better bargaining position; professional

---

[18] The Pechman-Okner study shows some progression, though at a slow rate, up to the $100,000 to $500,000 bracket, and regressivity beyond. The $100,000–500,000 bracket had an effective burden of 15.3 percent of income, the $500,000 to $1 million of 14.1 percent, and the over-$1 million of 12.4 percent. These figures include state income taxes. J. A. Pechman and B. A. Okner. *Who Bears the Tax Burden* (Washington: The Brookings Institution, 1974).

men have substantial discretion in setting fees. On the other hand, unionization, one of the chief sources of forward shifting, is less significant at the higher levels.

In one respect, progression lessens the likelihood of further shifting of the tax, since the amounts of tax on various individuals in similar occupations will differ according to their actual incomes. A union, for example, may include workers subject to marginal rates ranging from 14 to 20 percent; no uniform increase in wage rates can pass forward the exact amount of the tax. Professional men will have widely differing ratios of tax to gross fees collected, and, therefore, even with uniformity of action and collusion, passing forward of the differentially higher amounts is almost impossible.

ECONOMIC EFFICIENCY

In the absence of an income tax, a general equilibrium is reached in the selection of factor combinations, relative prices of factors and commodities, organization of economic activity, selection of forms of business organization, and other variables. If all markets are perfectly competitive and other requirements for Pareto optimality noted in Chapter 2 are met, this initial equilibrium will be Pareto-optimal. It will be optimal from the standpoint of society's social welfare function, however, only if income is distributed in accordance with society's preferences. Of course, to the extent that markets are not perfectly competitive, the initial equilibrium will not be Pareto-optimal. Nevertheless, the profit motive and the price system, coupled with at least some competition, do provide substantial pressure toward Pareto optimality. This is particularly true in the selection of factor combinations and forms of organization of economic activity—since the most efficient way is the cheapest way, apart from pollution and other externalities already discussed.

Effects of the Income Tax

The introduction of an income tax inevitably produces some alteration in resource allocation and organization of production. These changes can reasonably be presumed to lessen efficiency unless there is evidence to the contrary in particular instances. The distortions take several forms:

1. *Differential tax treatment.* As noted, investments in several industries, particularly owner-occupied housing, livestock, and some real property construction, receive favorable treatment, and outputs are excessive in the favored industries. This may be justified on the basis of general policy for housing, but it is difficult to justify the others.

2. *Relative factor prices.* To the extent that factor supplies are elastic, relative prices of factors will be altered by the tax. The effect is to alter factor combinations. Fewer of the more expensive types will be used and more of those now relatively cheaper. The changes in factor prices likewise will alter resource allocation. If doctors are in short supply because the income tax discourages persons from entering the profession, fees will be higher and less medical service will be acquired. If it is assumed that the combinations are initially optimal, the changes caused by the tax lessen economic welfare.

3. *Favored income.* As noted, the income tax by its limited coverage of monetary items encourages persons to produce goods and services for their own use instead of working for additional money income and hiring the work done. Women are discouraged by the tax from working outside the home, for example.

4. *Incentives to maximize efficiency.* As considered in greater detail in the next chapter, a tax on the net profit of any business may lessen the pressures toward efficiency, since the government bears a portion of the cost of inefficiency—to the extent of 70 percent with the personal income tax for a business owned by a person in the top income bracket.

As subsequently discussed, other taxes also produce distortions, some apparently being far more serious than those of the income tax.

OVERALL EVALUATION OF INCOME TAXATION

The case for income taxation rests primarily upon equity considerations and upon the avoidance by the tax of some of the worst adverse economic effects of other levies.

Equity

The primary justification for the income tax rests upon equity grounds. Under usual standards of equity and the ability principle for taxation, income is regarded as the most acceptable basis for distribution of the cost of government, since income is the primary determinant of economic well-being. A tax imposed upon income is much more likely, it is assumed, to be distributed in relation to income than a tax imposed upon proxies for income, such as luxury consumption. Only the income tax allows complete exclusion of the lowest-income groups from tax, as is regarded as desirable under accepted standards of taxation.

Second, only the income tax can be adjusted on the basis of various personal circumstances considered to affect tax capacity, as outlined in the previous chapter, such as numbers of dependents and medical expenses. Finally, only the income tax can be made effectively progressive. As noted, the present system in the United States has been seriously defective in this regard at the higher income levels, but this is a fault of the structure, not of income taxation per se.

Criticism on equity grounds rests in part on the claims of some persons that consumption rather than income is the best measure of taxpaying capacity, as noted in Chapter 14. Primarily, however, the critics stress the difficulties of devising an income tax structure that fully attains the objectives. Some of these difficulties, as noted in the last chapter, are inherent in the problems of defining and delimiting income and handling certain borderline elements (home-produced goods). Others arise out of simple defects in the law and out of political pressures that prevent adaptation of the structure to the forms regarded by society as optimal. In some countries, much of the criticism centers around complications in compliance and evasion from inadequate administration. Compliance ease remains a problem in the United States, but there is apparently little serious leakage from evasion. Much of the equity criticism of the tax over the years has been advanced against the progressive rates, which to some are inherently inequitable.

Economic Efficiency

The defense for income taxation on economic efficiency grounds is based on the distorting effects of other taxes. A perfectly designed income tax does not create excess burden by distorting consumer choices and thus resource allocation. While it may alter factor supplies, particularly the work–leisure choice, so may other taxes, and there is little evidence that, in fact, that tax has serious distorting effects. In practice, as noted, there is some departure from uniformity of treatment of all income, with consequent adverse effects, but again these are in large part a fault of the structure of the tax.

Much of the controversy over the effects of the tax centers on issues of investment and growth. The opponents of the tax have long based their attack on the argument that the tax not only dries up the supply of money capital in the hands of those who would invest it but also gives strong disincentive to take risk and to undertake real investment since the government shares in a progressive fashion in the returns. At the same time, the tax reduces the S/Y ratio more than other taxes, per dollar of revenue, and thus reduces the potential rate of capital formation. There are two principal answers to these claims. First, there is little evidence of any kind that the tax actually reduces risk-taking and willingness to undertake investment. The loss offset provisions and the capital gains treatment (although objectionable in many ways) reduce any adverse effect on risk-taking and may result in greater willingness to undertake risky investments.

Secondly, it may be argued that the tax, while reducing the potential rate of capital formation, facilitates the attainment of full employment, compared to other levies, and therefore permits a higher actual rate of economic growth. The tax avoids any incentive to curtail consumption and it has relatively greater income impact on the upper-income groups, who save higher percentages of their income. The net relative effect on growth of the income tax and other levies, therefore, depends in large part upon the nature of the investment function: the relative influence of the greater adverse impact of the income tax on the supply of money capital and upon the direct return from investment on the one hand, and the lesser effect of the tax compared to other levies upon the level of aggregate consumption demand, on the other.

An important property of income taxation is the high revenue elasticity; as total income rises, the yield of the income tax rises at a more rapid rate. This is due to the use of fixed-dollar exemptions and rate brackets; as per capita income rises, more persons become subject to the tax and persons move into higher rate brackets. This feature has two important advantages: It provides a built-in stabilizing effect against inflation and it lessens the danger that governmental revenues will lag behind expenditures, given the tendency of the latter to rise more rapidly than national income. The only difficulty is the danger of fiscal drag; if revenues rise too rapidly relative to expenditures, aggregate demand will fall below full-employment levels and tax reductions—which Congress may be slow to enact—will be needed.

The actual revenue elasticity figure is open to some debate. A study by Pechman suggests a figure of 1.113 (that is, an increase of 10 percent in GNP would lead to an increase of tax revenue of 11.3 percent.[19] Work by Tanzi suggests a figure of 1.09 with respect to GNP, 1.4 with respect to adjusted gross income.[20]

Administration and Compliance

The income tax requires substantial time and effort and cost for preparation of income tax returns and considerable cost for administration and enforcement. The complexity of the present federal levy greatly increases the compliance nuisance, and the existence of various potential escape hatches results in the devotion of much high-level manpower to find ways to escape. No good estimates are available of costs of compliance; the overall costs of enforcement for 1969–1970 were 0.45 percent of revenue–a relatively low figure but involv-

[19] J. A. Pechman, "Responsiveness of the Federal Individual Income Tax to Changes in Income," *Brookings Papers on Economic Activity*, vol. 2 (1973) pp. 385–421.

[20] Several studies by Vito Tanzi are summarized by R. Goode, *The Individual Income Tax*, rev. ed. (Washington, D.C.: The Brookings Institution, 1976), pp. 276–77.

ing a substantial sum of money in total. The figures for the states, with their lower rates and yields, run somewhat higher.

CONCLUSION

The income tax is in many respects the most acceptable type of tax, in terms of usual standards. It yields, at tolerable rates, very substantial sums of money; to raise equivalent amounts from other taxes would create tremendous problems and adverse effects. It most successfully meets accepted standards of equity and it has a high degree of revenue elasticity; it may lessen the problem of maintaining full employment; and it does not appear to have significant adverse effects on efficiency or economic growth. The present tax is defective in many respects—but it is still the most acceptable form of tax. Many of the present defects could be removed by appropriate legislation.

REFERENCES

Barlow, R., Brazer, H. E., and Morgan, J. N. *Economic Behavior of the Affluent*. Washington, D.C.: The Brookings Institution, 1966.

Break, G. F., "The Incidence and Effects of Taxation," in A. S. Blinder, *et. al.*, *The Economics of Public Finance*, Washington, D.C.: The Brookings Institution, 1974.

Goode, R. *The Individual Income Tax*, rev. ed. Washington, D.C.: The Brookings Institution, 1976.

Musgrave, R. A. *The Theory of Public Finance*. New York: McGraw-Hill, 1959, chaps. 11–14.

Thurow, L. C. *The Impact of Taxes on the American Economy*. New York: Praeger, 1971.

APPENDIX—PAYROLL TAXES

A payroll tax is a levy upon wage payments, typically upon both the wages received by the employee and upon the total amount paid out by the employer. The former portion is deducted from the wages; the latter is presumably borne by the employer. These levies are universally used for the financing of social security programs. The United States, as virtually every other industrial country in the world, imposes such a tax, primarily to finance old-age annuities, but also to finance unemployment compensation and medical care for the aged. More specifically, in the United States as of 1976, a tax of 5.85 percent is applied to the wages received by the employee and the wages paid by the employer, to finance old-age annuities and medical care for the elderly. Both portions apply only to wages up to $14,100 per year; amounts in excess of this figure are not taxed. The tax also applies to self-employed persons, at a rate of 7 percent. It does not apply to non-labor income. In the countries of Western Europe, the figures are much larger—40 to 50 percent of wages in Italy. The states impose similar levies, usually on the employer only, to finance unemployment compensation systems and low-rate taxes on employers to finance workmen's compensation (in the event of injury on job).

The payroll tax rates in the United States have been steadily increased since their inception in the 1930s, in response to demand for higher social security benefits. In the 1976 fiscal year, the tax yielded $92.6 billion to the federal government, 31 percent of total tax revenue, and second in magnitude to the personal income tax.

Distributional Effects

The traditional popular view upon which policy has been based is that the portion of the tax deducted from the employee's pay is on the employee and the portion on the employer is borne by the firm and thus by the owners. Thus the progressivity of the latter portion is assumed to offset the regressivity of the former. This naive view is obviously open to serious question.

Application of the Harberger model to shifting produces a very different result. Under the assumptions of (1) perfectly inelastic supply of labor, or, alternatively that the workers regard both employer and employee shares as a part of their wages, so that the tax does not reduce their wage, (2) a given supply of capital, (3) perfect competition in all markets, and (4) perfect factor mobility, the tax will rest entirely on labor, as illustrated on Fig. 12A–1. Under these assumptions the total real compensation for a given supply of labor is fixed and cannot be altered by a tax. There are several possible ways in which the employers' share may shift to the workers: a lag in wages behind the increases that would otherwise occur; an actual reduction in money wages; increases in the prices of the products, ultimately shifting all burden to labor.[21]

Empirical confirmation for this conclusion was found by John Brittain.[22] One approach involved a cross-section analysis among countries of the relationship of the marginal productivity of labor and wages; he found a better fit with the assumption that the entire wage was borne by the employees. A time-series analysis utilizing United States data tended, at least weakly, to confirm this result, showing that the fit

---

[21] Any initial burden on capitalists via price increases on their purchases will lead to subsequent increases that will transfer all burden ultimately to labor.

[22] John A. Brittain, "The Incidence of Social Security Payroll Taxes," *American Economic Review*, vol. 61 (March 1971), pp. 110–25; and *The Payroll Tax for Social Security*. (Washington, D.C.: The Brookings Institution, 1972).

FIGURE 12A-1

Effect of a Payroll Tax on Wage Rates, Perfectly Inelastic
Supply Curve of Labor

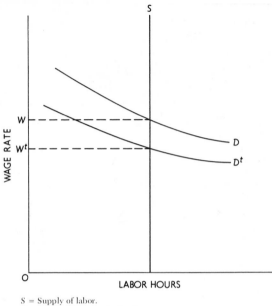

S = Supply of labor.
D = Demand for labor before tax.
D' = Demand for labor after tax.

of wage changes to productivity changes was better with the full burden on labor assumption than others.

This conclusion about shifting has important implications for policy. The tax is far more regressive than otherwise; it is a very poor economic stabilizer; unions should consider in collective bargaining that the employer share is borne by the worker; and countries with high social security levies are at no disadvantage in competing in world markets.

Several questions can be raised about this model.

1. The tax is not uniformly imposed upon all labor—for example, the uncompensated work in the household—and mobility of labor is not perfect.

2. The oversimplified model ignores fixed-income receivers. If the shifting takes place via price increases, a substantial portion may rest upon these persons in their capacity as consumers—a consequence ignored by the structure of the Harberger model.

3. Labor supply may not be perfectly inelastic in response to changes in payroll taxes, especially on the part of "marginal" workers—wives, children, retired persons, etc.

4. The validity of the perfectly competitive assumption can be

questioned. Collective bargaining in wage determination and oligopolistic product markets make the outcome theoretically indeterminate and increase the likelihood that the tax will not fully shift to the workers.

An empirical study by Jane Leuthold, using United States quarterly time series wage data, concludes that there is strong evidence that the tax is not fully shifted to employees.[23] Profit maximization, but not perfect competition, is assumed in the model. The absence of short-run shifting, of course, does not necessarily mean that long-run shifting, arising out of substitution of capital for labor, does not occur.

Other Economic Effects

Under the assumption that the taxes are borne entirely by labor, there would be no significant repercussions on factor combinations. If the tax does raise the cost of labor compared to the cost of capital goods, there would be some effect in encouraging the replacement of labor by capital goods. Such an effect is particularly disadvantageous in a developing economy with a relative surplus of labor and acute shortage of capital goods. In the United States, with the possibility that in some industries the tax may not be fully reflected in lower wages to employees, there may be some net influence in encouraging greater relative use of capital. In nonperfectly competitive markets, if businessmen think that increases in payroll taxes make labor more expensive relative to capital goods, they may shift toward more capital intensive processes even though after all adjustments have taken place there is no net increase in the cost of labor relative to capital goods.

Equity

If the taxes are borne entirely or primarily by workers, they are highly regressive and place a substantial burden on the lowest-income groups. Since there are no exemptions, the lowest-income worker is subject, while the tax does not apply to the portion of earnings in excess of the specified figure. Only labor income is taxed; other income is more progressively distributed. Not only is the tax regressive, but it places a very heavy absolute tax burden on the low-income workers, far exceeding income tax payments at the lower incomes. The situation has been growing steadily worse, as the payroll taxes continue to rise while income taxes go down. The net effect is to increase inequality of income and wealth. Basically, what the system does is to require the working poor to contribute very heavily to the retired

---

[23] J. H. Leuthold, "The Incidence of the Payroll Tax in the United States," *Public Finance Quarterly*, vol. 3 (January 1975), pp. 3–13.

group. Furthermore, the system is set up in such a way as to produce significant discrimination against women—a feature that is certain to change.

The tax thus violates the most elementary notions of equity. The explanation of the use of such a tax goes back to the philosophy of the social security system as it was established. The framers of the system sought to emphasize the "insurance aspect"—that workers and their employers were simply making payments into a fund from which benefits would ultimately be paid. Essentially the payments were not regarded as taxes at all (although legally they were) but as compulsory insurance-premium payments. Several advantages for this approach were stressed. The insurance aspects would, on the one hand, avoid the appearance of charity, the benefits being simply returns of amounts paid plus interest. At the same time the system would lessen the demand for larger and larger benefits out of public funds. Any potential adverse effects of the tax would be avoided by the emphasis on the insurance-premium payment aspect.

Serious questions can be raised, however. The system is not true insurance at all; many persons receive benefits all out of proportion to the amount they have paid in and others receive much less for reasons other than those relating to probability. The levy is essentially a tax, and no amount of argument to the contrary is likely to influence behavior. There is increasing recognition, as noted in Chapter 6, of the inadequacy of the whole system. A strong case can be made for the argument that the system should never have been established in its present form—that some form of negative income tax system, financed from general revenues, would have been far simpler and more adequate. While the system is not likely to be abandoned, modification of the taxes to reduce the burden on the very poor is a minimum change to make the system tolerable.

Alternative Reforms

There are several approaches to reform. First, the inequity could be greatly reduced by providing an exemption and removing or greatly increasing the ceiling. Secondly, the tax could be eliminated, the financing of old-age security being provided by the income tax. Basic reform, however, receives little popular support. First, roughly a 40 percent increase in income tax would be required, with a very substantial shift in overall tax burdens and, some persons fear, serious adverse effects upon saving. Secondly, it is feared that if the so called "insurance" feature is dropped, benefits will rise without limit. In any event there is no strong movement to make drastic changes; Congress simply proceeds to continue to raise the rate, the ceiling, and the benefits.

In Canada, initially, the old-age pension program was not financed by payroll taxes but entirely from special supplements to the personal and corporate income taxes and the sales tax. There was no attempt to link individual benefits and payments. In 1972, the tax supplements were incorporated into the basic tax rates and the separate fund discontinued; benefits are thus paid from general governmental revenues. In 1963, however, a supplementary pension fund was established, financed from payroll taxes, 1.8 percent on employer and employee and 3.6 percent on self-employed. These are low rates compared to those in most countries, but it can be argued that the establishment of this system was a backward step in the financing of old-age security.

REFERENCES

Brittain, J. A. *The Payroll Tax for Social Security*. Washington, D.C.: The Brookings Institution, 1972.

Pechman, J. A., Aaron, H., and Taussig, M. K. *Social Security: Perspectives for Reform*. Washington, D.C.: The Brookings Institution, 1968.

13

Corporation Income Taxation

The analysis of Chapter 12 was based upon the assumption that all income is earned directly by the persons supplying factor units for use in production. But the existence of the corporation form of business organization interferes with universal attainment of the rule. This chapter seeks to explore the issues created for optimal income tax structures by the existence of the corporation and considers present and alternative approaches to the problem.

The Significance of the Corporation

The corporation is a legal entity existing between the individuals who own the enterprise—the stockholders—and the initial earning of the income; the income accrues initially to the corporation. There are several primary tax consequences of the existence of the corporation:

1. The corporation may not pass the earnings on to the individual stockholders but use them for reserves or expansion, giving rise to capital gains.

2. The existence of the corporation, itself a creation of government, and the division between initial earning of the income and subsequent payment of dividends encourages governments to tax both the corporation and the dividends received whereas no similar policy is followed with other income.

3. The division between ownership and control in the large corporation, the ownership being spread out over thousands of stockholders,

the control resting in the hands of top management and perhaps a few large stockholders, may cause the reactions to the tax to be different from those to the personal income tax.

The Present Tax

The corporate income tax in the United States is typical of such taxes as used in most countries. Tax applies to the net earnings of corporations (other than certain nonprofit institutions), without, of course, personal deductions or credits to dependents, except contributions to charitable and similar organizations. Operating losses may be carried back three years and forward seven years—a feature that sometimes makes the purchase of a corporation with large accumulated losses advantageous. Capital gains receive favorable treatment, but capital losses can be deducted only from capital gains. Dividends paid by one corporation to another are excluded from income of the recipient corporation entirely if the firms are affiliated and to the extent of 85 percent otherwise.

The basic rate is 48 percent on profits in excess of $50,000, with a reduced figure of 20 percent on the first $25,000, and 22 percent on the second $25,000. This concession is not based on usual concepts of ability to pay but on the desire to lessen the impact of the corporate income tax on new growing businesses that must expand primarily with reinvested earnings.

Corporate income taxes are now in use in 46 states. Only one large state, Texas, does not use the tax. The rates are much lower than the federal, typically 4 percent to 6 percent; six states have significant progression in the rates (Arizona, for example, from 2.5 percent to 10.5 percent), despite the lack of any rationale for such progression. Large corporations may be owned by large numbers of small stockholders, smaller ones by one or a few wealthy individuals. Income of firms doing an interstate business is allocated among the states on the basis of formula, normally employing three elements—payrolls, property, and sales—within the state as a percentage of total.

THE DISTRIBUTIONAL PATTERN OF THE TAX

The first and basic question to be raised about the corporation income tax is whether it actually results in a reduction in real incomes of the stockholders (through reduced dividends and/or reduced amounts added to reserves and therefore lower selling prices of the stock) or is shifted forward in the form of higher prices of the products of the corporation or possibly backward to labor. There is a widespread belief, especially in the business community, that the tax is fully shifted forward to consumers. But much of the criticism of the tax—also from the business community—is based on the assumption that the tax does reduce the real income of the stockholders.

The Traditional Approach

Economists long maintained that a tax on net profit could not be shifted forward and, therefore, must reduce the incomes of the owners of the business. This conclusion is valid under conditions of perfect competition in the market for the products, at least in a short-run period of time with the assumption of given investment and other factors. The rate of return on capital is reduced by the tax—but since the reduction is universal there is no escape from it; therefore supply of the various products will not fall and price cannot rise. The individual sellers in perfect competition have no control over market price; they have only the options of selling at the market price or holding the commodity, and price cannot rise unless the supply falls. Given the assumptions, there is no way that they can shift the tax to labor. Over a longer period of time, some shifting might occur if the total supply of money capital and real investment were reduced by the tax, as discussed in the previous chapter.

Similarly, under complete monopoly conditions, the seller cannot profitably shift the tax if he was previously maximizing profit. For a monopolist, some one price ($MC = MR$ output level) will yield the greatest amount of profit, given the demand and cost schedules. While this profit will be reduced by a tax on profits, so would the profits obtainable at all other prices. If a series of figures is reduced by a common percentage, the one that was highest before the change will still be highest.

Application of the Harberger Model

As explained in Chapter 9, the Harberger model of shifting of taxes is based upon several assumptions, four of primary importance; perfect competition in all markets, perfect mobility of all factors among sectors; a given stock of capital and labor, independent of the rate of return, and constant cost conditions. This model can, of course, be applied to the corporate income tax:

1. Capital will flow from the corporate sector to the noncorporate sector to equalize the rate of return to all capital.

2. Prices of products in the corporate sector will rise and those in the noncorporate sector will fall.

3. Labor will flow from the corporate to the noncorporate sector.

Accordingly, if the elasticity of substitution between capital and labor is the same in the two sectors, and is equal to the elasticity of substitution in the consumption of the products of the two sectors, the entire burden will rest on the owners of all capital. The overall rate of return to capital will be reduced equally in the corporate and noncorporate sectors.

If, however, the elasticity of substitution between capital and labor is not the same in the two sectors, some burden may shift on to labor. This will occur if the corporate sector is labor intensive and the elasticity of substitution of labor for capital is relatively low. In this instance, workers released from the corporate sector would not find employment in the noncorporate sector until wage rates had fallen.

If all persons had the same tastes and factor endowments, as is assumed in the Harberger model, there can be no burden on consumers as such, since the relative price effects resulting from the tax will operate only on the sources of income side, not on the uses of income side. Since, however, persons do have different tastes and factor endowments, the relative price effects caused by the tax will have an impact on the uses side. Persons having relatively greater preference for corporation-sector products will experience a loss in real income, offset by the gain to those persons having high preference for noncorporate-sector products.

Serious questions can be raised, however, against both the "traditional" conclusion and those of the Harberger model, centering around the assumptions—directly specified in the Harberger model.

Nonperfectly Competitive Conditions

Over recent decades, increased recognition has been given to the importance of nonperfectly competitive conditions (NPC). The assumptions of the NPC model appear to resemble the conditions of actual markets more than do those of either perfect competition or complete monopoly. Unfortunately there is no single theory of NPC markets; it is generally recognized that there is a wide variety of possible relationships, varying according to the exact degree of interdependence (oligopoly) among the firms and the strength of differentiation of product. There are also questions about motivation, particularly of corporate management. The profit-maximization assumption, typical of economic analysis in the past, has been supplemented by various alternatives: maximization of gross sales, maximization of rate of growth of the firm, attainment of a "reasonable" or target rate of return, and so forth.

Under the framework of NPC conditions, it is not difficult to develop a model that will indicate substantial forward shifting of the corporation income tax.[1] The assumptions include:

1. Pursuit of the objective of a "target return" or satisfactory rate of

---

[1] Note also S. Bruno, "Corporate Income Tax, Oligopolistic Markets, and Immediate Tax Shifting," *Public Finance*, vol. 25, no. 3 (1970), pp. 363–80.

profit, with the long-range, often ill-defined objective of maximization of the profits for the firm as a group.

2. Substantial interdependence among firms, with consequent uniformity of pricing policy. The uniformity is not necessarily complete, however.

3. Use by the firms of the markup or average-cost approach to pricing, average cost or markup including the "satisfactory" rate of profit the firm seeks to get. Significant increases in average costs experienced by all or most firms lead to increases in prices, subject to some constraints imposed by elasticity of demand.

4. Despite much uniformity of policy, substantial variation in ratios of profits to sales exists among the various firms in an industry. The more successful, frequently the larger, ones will have more favorable profit ratios than the smaller firms with higher cost per unit of output or those suffering from management inefficiencies.

With this model—which may be reasonably applicable to many industries—the corporate income tax will be shifted forward, at least in part, in the form of higher prices for the products if the following conditions are met:

1. The firms treat the corporate income tax as an expense for purposes of price determination.

2. The ratio of tax to sales among the various competing firms in the industry is reasonably uniform, or, alternatively, the low-profit firms follow the prices set by the high-profit firms.

3. The firms as a group are not maximizing joint profits; as a whole, they could earn more profit if they could make necessary adjustments.

Under these conditions, when a corporate income tax is imposed or the rate is increased, the firms will estimate the ratio of tax to sales and increase selling prices by this amount; so long as all follow the same pricing policy, they will pass the tax forward to the consumers.

There are, however, almost certain to be significant exceptions to complete shifting:

1. *Variations in ratio of tax to sales.* Firms having higher than average ratios of tax to sales—the most profitable firms—are likely to find shifting of the differential over the typical figure in the industry impossible, unless the less profitable firms are willing to follow their prices.

2. *Nonuniformity of action.* Some firms in an effort to increase sales will not make the price increases, and therefore others will lose sales substantially if they attempt to raise.

3. *Relatively high elasticity of demand for the product.* The firms will find that they will be worse off if they try to increase prices.

If the tax does shift forward into the prices of the products, the distributional pattern will be comparable to that of a sales tax, considered in Chapter 15. But the tax-induced price increases, as a percentage of selling price, will differ in various fields because of variations in ratios of profits to sales. Presumably over time the ratios of profits to capital investment tend toward uniformity after adjusting for risk differences. But, since capital-output ratios differ widely, the ratios of tax to sales will also vary. Thus consumers will experience greater reduction in real income relative to purchase of some commodities than relative to purchase of others. As the owners of some businesses shift the tax and those of others do not, an inequitable pattern of distribution develops, one that may be eliminated slowly over time by shift of investment from some lines to others but may be very significant in a shorter period.

What actually happens? The preceding analysis has merely shown that under the typical nonperfectly competitive conditions, the tax may be shifted forward. Whether it does or not, theory cannot tell us; only empirical studies of actual responses to the tax can do so. As in so many aspects of economics, this is not easy to do; there are so many variables affecting profit behavior and prices that any attempt to trace through the distributional effects by econometric techniques has not been highly successful.

Backward Shifting

There is always some possibility that the corporate income tax may be shifted backward to the owners of other factors—and particularly labor. Given the importance of labor unions in present-day labor relationships, any direct wage reduction as a result of increase in the tax appears unlikely. But the magnitude of profits does play a part in wage negotiations. If profits are reduced by a corporate income tax that is not shifted forward, unions may get somewhat smaller wage increases than would otherwise be possible.

Restricted Capital Mobility

The Harberger model also assumes perfect capital mobility between the corporate and noncorporate sectors. This assumption is open to question. Many investors will not shift from corporate securities to participation in partnerships or to proprietorships, and many institutional investors cannot, for legal and practical reasons. The tax structure itself is a barrier to transfer of capital through increased payments of dividends to stockholders, who invest the money in noncorporate undertakings. If the difference in the average rate of profit in the corporate sector is substantially greater than that in the noncorporate sector, because of greater efficiency or oligopolistic elements, etc., reduction in the net return due to the corporate tax may lead to little or no shifting.

Econometric Studies—Behavior of the Rate of Return [2]

. The aim of the empirical studies is to develop a model that will allow separation of the influences of the corporate income tax from those of other determinants of corporate earnings; this model can then be tested with empirical data to show whether or not the tax was actually shifted. But the establishment of such a model is a very difficult undertaking. The earliest empirical studies essentially used no model at all but merely examined profits in the corporate sector over a period of years, with no effort to eliminate the effects of other influences.[3] The conclusions, therefore, were of little significance. Since 1960, there have been two general approaches. One centers on the behavior of the rate of return on capital as the corporate tax rate has changed, under the argument that if the rate of return after adjustments for changes in other determinants has remained the same, the tax has been shifted. The other, noted below, stresses the behavior of the share of corporate profits as a percentage of total income originating in the corporate sector. If this figure remains unchanged after adjustments for other variables, it is argued that the tax has been shifted.

Krzyzaniak–Musgrave. The first serious effort to employ a model and econometric techniques was that of Marian Krzyzaniak and Richard Musgrave (hereafter referred to as KM). They sought, in the early sixties, to analyze the problem by an extensive econometric study designed to ascertain the influence of the corporation tax variable on the rate of return.[4] By the use of a profit-behavior model and multiple-regression techniques, they sought to isolate the effects of the corporate tax rate from other exogenous variables influencing the rate of return, comparing the actual return in the 1935–59 period with the figure that would have prevailed without it, other determinants being unchanged. This was strictly a short-run analysis, seeking to determine the effects of the tax year by year, by comparing actual behavior with the behavior that the model suggests without the tax element.[5]

The primary conclusion was that the entire corporate tax (not merely

---

[2] A good summary is provided by W. H. Oakland, "A Survey of the Recent Debate on the Short Run Shifting of the Corporation Income Tax," *Proceedings of the National Tax Association for 1969*, pp. 525–46.

[3] E. M. Lerner and E. S. Hendriksen, "Federal Taxes on Corporate Income and the Rate of Return on Investment in Manufacturing, 1927 to 1952," *National Tax Journal*, vol. 9 (September 1956), pp. 193–202.

[4] M. Krzyzaniak and R. Musgrave, *The Shifting of the Corporate Income Tax.* (Baltimore: Johns Hopkins Press, 1963).

[5] The other elements in the model are: (1) increase in consumption, expressed as a percentage of GNP, for the previous year; (2) ratio of inventory to sales in manufacturing for the previous year; (3) current-year ratio to GNP of all federal, state, and local taxes (excluding the corporation income tax and deducting transfer payments and grants-in-aid to the states).

the differential over the personal income tax) was fully reflected in prices and thus did not reduce after-tax income of the corporations; in other words, the rate of return on capital was maintained at the level that would have prevailed without the tax. The study also reveals a "ratchet" effect; when the tax is reduced, the rate of return rises rather than remaining constant. The basic study shows not only full shifting but overshifting to the extent of 34 percent.[6] The authors grant that these results overstate actual shifting, partly because of the lag of capital value figures in the face of inflation and partly because of the correlation between the tax rate and government expenditures produced by the stimulative effect of the latter upon profits. Even with adjustments made for these two considerations, the authors find that the tax is at least fully shifted.[7] A study by Robert W. Kilpatrick of the relationship between increases in rates of return and the concentration ratios in a number of industries during the Korean War period, when the corporate income tax rate rose from 38 percent to 52 percent, showed a very high correlation, thus substantiating the shifting thesis.[8]

The Krzyzaniak-Musgrave (KM) work has been subjected to substantial criticism. One question centers around the adequacy of the model as a means of isolating the tax influences from those of other variables. In the period under study, there were a number of forces that tended to produce a correlation between tax rates and profit levels; tax rates tend to be high in periods in which forces in the economy make profits high. Operation at a high level of capacity and strong economic pressure, that is, a high level of aggregate expenditures at full employment, were two such forces. The KM model sought to exclude these other forces, but many critics believe that it did not do so adequately. Goode and Slitor, introducing a "pressure variable" of the relationship of actual to potential GNP into the Musgrave model, showed that shifting was in fact much less than KM indicated.[9] Also working within the KM framework but introducing a cyclical variable

---

[6] Lester Thurow argues that this figure does not show overshifting but rather a decline in the percentage of national income saved due to the tax; this reduces the supply of money capital and raises the rate of return. See his *The Impact of Taxes on the American Economy*. (New York: Praeger, 1971), p. 63.

[7] A study by Karl W. Roskamp of the reactions to the West German corporate income tax, 1949–62, using the KM model, produced similar results. See "The Shifting of Taxes on Business Income: The Case of the West German Corporation," *National Tax Journal*, vol. 18 (September 1965), pp. 247–57.

However, a simpler economic model developed by Gerald Brannon in 1960 showed that the corporate tax had very little influence on before-tax profit behavior. This study was presented to the Econometric Society in 1960, as "Some Investigations on the Incidence of the Corporate Income Tax" (unpublished).

[8] Robert W. Kilpatrick, "The Forward Shifting of the Corporate Income Tax," *Yale Economic Essays*, vol. 5 (Fall 1965), pp. 355–422.

[9] R. Slitor, "Corporate Tax Incidence," and R. Goode, "Rate of Return, Income Share, and Corporate Tax Incidence," in *Effects of Corporation Income Tax* ed. M. Krzyzaniak (Detroit: Wayne State University Press, 1966), pp. 136–206 and pp. 207–45.

(the employment rate) and a dummy variable to represent wartime mobilization, John C. Cragg, Arnold C. Harberger, and Peter Mieszkowski reached the conclusion that the tax is not shifted but rests entirely upon capital owners.[10]

KM deny the validity of the criticisms, on the grounds that use of pressure variable measuring the level of business activity captures part of the effect of the tax and the results do not show failure to shift. They also point out that even if these criticisms are granted, there is still a substantial degree of shifting, at least under the Goode and Slitor approaches.

Another question is the lack of any similarity between the KM profit behavior model and those developed for other purposes in recent years; several of these appear to explain profit behavior adequately in the period without reference to the corporate tax rate at all.[11]

The Gordon study, noted below, also uses the rate-of-return approach in part.

The Factor-Shares Approach

One basic question raised about the KM analysis is that of the appropriateness of behavior of rates of return on capital as a measure of redistributional effects of the tax. A constant after-tax rate of return does not demonstrate shifting of the tax if changes in capital-output relationships were tending to raise this ratio during the period. If the marginal productivity of capital goods was rising rapidly because of technological change, the rate of return on capital should be rising; if it remains constant, the tax has not been shifted. This problem led to use of the alternative factor-shares approach, based on the assumption that shifting of the tax from corporate owners occurs only if the pretax share of profits in income originating in the corporate sector increases. If it does not, the tax is not shifted, regardless of the behavior of the rate of return.

The first of these factor-share studies, made by M. A. Adelman and published in 1957,[12] concluded that in the period between the twenties and 1946–55, the ratio of total corporate profits (before payment of tax) to GNP originating in the corporate sector remained constant. As a consequence, he concluded that the tax was not shifted; shifting would require that the ratios *after tax* remain constant.

---

[10] John G. Cragg, Arnold C. Harberger, and Peter Mieszkowski, "Empirical Evidence of the Incidence of the Corporation Income Tax," *Journal of Political Economy*, vol. 75 (December 1967), pp. 811–21.

[11] Goode, "Rate of Return," pp. 220–21.

[12] M. A. Adelman, "The Corporate Income Tax in the Long Run," *Journal of Political Economy*, vol. 65 (April 1957), pp. 151–57.

In the sixties, Challis Hall, Jr.,[13] under National Bureau of Economic Research auspices, undertook an econometric study of the behavior in the 1919–59 period of relative factor inputs, factor outputs, and income shares, seeking to determine whether the corporate tax altered these relationships. He employed highly simplifying assumptions: a Cobb Douglas production function,[14] constant cost conditions, and technological neutrality, that is, that technological change had not altered the relative marginal productivity of capital and labor. He concluded that the actual data agree more closely with those of a nonshifting model than with those of a shifting model. In other words, Hall concluded that the tax does not alter input-output relationships among the various factors and that profits receivers do not escape from the tax, but his assumptions are very restrictive.

The Gordon Study

A study by R. J. Gordon sought to reconcile the two approaches.[15] He used a model based on constant markup-pricing techniques and included changes in productivity of capital as an input in the analysis. With this model, his analysis shows that the tax was not shifted, on the whole, as determined by either the rate-of-return or share-of-income approaches, although some shifting occurred in particular industries. Essentially, firms with markup pricing were able to maintain their profit margin as the tax increased. The rate of return remained relatively constant but for reasons other than tax shifting; without the tax the rate would have risen. The productivity of capital rose rapidly during the period and the capital-output ratio fell, less capital being needed per unit of output. Accordingly, the ratio of after-tax profit to income originating in the corporate sector fell even though the rate of return remained constant. Firms were able, through the markup technique, to maintain the ratio of profits to sales, but the rising pretax ratio of profits to assets was offset by the tax. Firms were not able to go farther and shift the tax as well, and the after-tax share of corporate income fell. Gordon argues that the KM conclusions are wrong because of the use of a defective model, which resulted in the conclusion that maintenance of the old rate of return on capital was attributable to tax shifting whereas actually it was attributable to other sources, particularly the rapid growth of productivity of capital.

The Gordon model has itself been subjected to criticism, especially

---

[13] Challis Hall, Jr., "Direct Shifting of the Corporation Income Tax in Manufacturing, 1919–59," *Proceedings of American Economic Association for 1963*, pp. 258–71.

[14] That is, as output increases, the relative shares of capital and labor remain fixed.

[15] R. J. Gordon, "The Incidence of the Corporation Income Tax in U.S. Manufacturing, 1925–1962," *American Economic Review*, vol. 57 (September 1967), pp. 731–58.

on the grounds that various assumptions he made bias the results in the direction of no shifting.[16] His results are based on the assumption of a constant ratio of profits to sales; while this assumption is not an unreasonable one, it is not necessarily valid, and thus his conclusions lack the universality that he claims. But he made a significant contribution in showing the weakness in KM's analysis of ignoring the effects of changing productivity.

It should be noted that even if the rate of return is partially maintained in the corporate sector, this may be offset by a decline in the return in the noncorporate sector as capital shifts to the latter sector.

Other studies continue to appear, and with equally conflicting results. Richard Dusansky concluded that the U.S. tax is shifted in full, using the rate-of-return approach,[17] whereas a study by Oakland found zero short-run shifting.[18]

A study by David Reaume, stressing analysis of pricing behavior, concluded that the firms try to shift from 70 to 100 percent but competition cuts the figure about one fourth, so that in practice about half the tax is shifted.[19] The study shows that actual prices are typically less than the joint profit-maximization level, thus allowing shifting to be profitable. A study by J. M. Davis for Great Britain concludes that there is no evidence, from time-series analysis, of shifting.[20]

Canadian studies include one by R. J. Levésque showing 70 percent shifting, using both approaches; Spencer, using the KM model, concluded that short-run shifting was 118 percent; Dusansky showed shifting between 65 and 90 percent, using a rate-of-return approach different from KM.[21]

In conclusion: With the present state of knowledge, we do not know whether the tax is shifted or not; there is certainly no conclusive evidence that it is fully or primarily shifted. But the possibility of shifting

----

[16] F. D. Sebold, "Short Run Tax Responses in a Utility Maximization Framework," *National Tax Journal*, vol. 23 (December 1970), pp. 365–72. See also in the same issue, R. J. Gordon, "Specification Bias and Corporate Tax Incidence," pp. 373–78.

[17] R. Dusansky, "The Short Run Shifting of the Corporate Income Tax," *Oxford Economic Papers*, vol. 24 (November 1972), pp. 357–71.

[18] W. H. Oakland, "Corporate Earnings and Tax Shifting in U.S. Manufacturing," *Review of Economics and Statistics*, vol. 54 (August 1972), pp. 235–44.

[19] David Reaume, "Production Functions, Demand Functions, and the Incidence of the Corporate Income Tax, 1948–1970" (Paper presented at the 1973 Winter meetings of the Econometric Society, New York City).

[20] J. M. Davis, "An Aggregate Time Series Analysis of the Short Run Shifting of the Company Tax in the United Kingdom," *Oxford Economic Papers*, vol. 24 (July 1972), pp. 259–86.

[21] R. J. Levésque, *The Shifting of the Corporate Income Tax in the Short Run*, Studies of the Royal Commission on Taxation, No. 18 (Ottawa: Queen's Printer, 1965); B. Spencer, "The Shifting of the Corporate Income Tax in Canada," *Canadian Journal of Economics*, vol. 2 (February 1969), pp. 21–34; R. Dusansky and J. E. Tanner, "The Shifting of the Profits Tax in Canadian Manufacturing," Working Paper No. 59, State University of New York at Stony Brook, 1972.

must be kept in mind in analysis of economic effects and policy proposals.

Long-Run Shifting. All of the empirical analyses are essentially short-run studies, concerned with the direct responses to changes in the corporate tax rate. Over a longer period, there are obviously more possibilities of shifting. Capital may flow from the corporate to the noncorporate sector not subject to the differentially high burden, thus reducing the rate of return in the latter and raising it in the former. Accordingly, a portion of the burden may be shifted to investors in the noncorporate sector. There are other possible ramifications arising out of effects of the reduced return upon the percentage of national income saved; if the percentage falls, the rate of return from savings will rise and the tax, therefore, will be shifted away from capital owners. With immediate full shifting, no further adjustments will occur as the rate of return on savings is not reduced.

OTHER ECONOMIC EFFECTS

The economic effects of the corporate income tax per se are those that occur with use of the corporate tax as compared with a tax structure in which the equivalent amount of money is raised from a personal income tax applying equally to all income, including undistributed profits of corporations.

Effects upon Factor Supplies

Savings-Income Ratio. The corporate income tax has conflicting effects upon the ratio of savings to income. On the one hand, because it concentrates more of the relative burden on the earnings from investment in the corporate field than otherwise, and thus on the higher-income groups, it is likely to have more adverse effect on private savings than the personal income tax. The tax may also reduce the amounts the corporations have to retain as reinvested earnings. But, on the other hand, the tax gives an incentive to corporations to pay less out as dividends and increase reinvested earnings.[22] This is particularly likely to occur with corporations controlled by very wealthy persons. The net effect is impossible to determine.

Real Investment Decisions. With the corporation, the real investment decisions are made by corporation management, and, thus, in the larger corporation, by persons other than those providing the funds. The effects depend upon the determinants of the investment decisions by management, about which there is substantial controversy.

---

[22] M. Feldstein, "Tax Incentives, Corporate Saving, and Capital Accumulation in the United States," *Journal of Public Economics*, vol. 2 (April 1973), pp. 159–71.

1.   *Rate of return.* A 50 percent corporate income tax, if not shifted, reduces the return from a 10 percent yield project to 5 percent; the before-tax yield must rise to 20 percent if the old 10 percent net return is to be earned. As compared to the personal income tax, it may be argued that management is not subject to an income effect from the tax since the executives do not share personally in the gains from a successful expansion of the investment project. Since the tax lessens the net gain, the substitution effect discourages management from undertaking the investment. But there is an effect somewhat equivalent to the income effect: Management knows that it is judged by the profitability of the enterprise, and therefore it does associate its own welfare with that of the earnings of the company, even though the management may not directly share in the higher profits. This income effect will tend to offset the substitution effect and help to prevent a decline in real investment.

The exact net effect reflects the elasticity of the investment function relative to the rate of interest: what percentage of total investment projects lie between the before-tax and after-tax rate of return—still assuming that the tax does not shift forward? No definitive answer can be given. Several studies have been made of the question; two show that a 1 percent cut in the corporate tax rate would have no effect on investment; others show increases of from $300 million to $800 million. An average of these figures shows an elasticity of 0.2; the 1 percent reduction in corporate income taxes would increase investment 0.2 percent.[23]

For the closely held corporation, the significance is different. By incorporating, owners can reduce the tax below their personal income tax marginal rate if the latter is high and if they are willing to retain the earnings in the business; thus the net gain from additional investment is greater than it would be with the personal tax applicable to all income.

2.   *Availability of money capital.* Real investment is dependent not only upon the returns from the investment but upon the availability of money capital as well. In some instances, if the corporation maintains dividends at the old level and absorbs the tax from funds that would otherwise be available in the business, its ability and willingness to undertake real investment will be reduced. But the evidence suggests the opposite: the income tax structure as a whole encourages businesses to add more to retained earnings rather than less, and thus the funds available for real investment are increased.

The availability of money capital is affected by the tax treatment of depreciation, as noted later in the chapter. The more liberal the per-

---

[23] Summarized in Thurow, *Impact of Taxes,* p. 33.

mitted depreciation deduction, the more money capital the firm can accumulate out of given gross receipts.

3. *Loss deductibility.* Finally, the privilege of deductibility of losses may be more significant for the corporation. For the individual, there are severe restrictions on the deductibility of losses from other income; with the corporation, with its greater diversity, there is much greater likelihood that losses on one investment will be fully deductible from the gains from others.

In summary: The ratios of total savings to national income and real investment are undoubtedly less with a corporate income tax than they would be if corporation earnings were not taxed at all at the corporate or personal level. This is obvious, on the bases of both availability of funds and net returns from investment. But this is not a reasonable comparison. If the present system is compared with one in which corporations are not taxed per se, the funds being raised from a personal income tax including undistributed profits in the base, the net difference is by no means obvious, if the corporate tax is not shifted. The present tax may reduce available undistributed profits of larger, widely held corporations and the net return from investment in such businesses to a greater extent than the alternative would. But it has less direct tax impact on the closely held businesses, where the corporate tax is less than the personal income tax, and gives great incentive to retain earnings. There is evidence that even the large corporations increase retained earnings as a result of the tax. In a sense, the corporate tax allows some tax avoidance, but in doing so, the impact upon real investment is reduced. If the corporate tax is shifted, its effects are comparable to those of a sales tax analyzed in Chapter 15.

Economic Efficiency

The corporate income tax may influence the efficiency of the functioning of the economy in several ways.

Choice of Form of Business Organization. Given the structure of the personal and corporate income taxes and the prevailing rates, the choice between corporate and noncorporate forms of business organization is altered. The most significant effect, in all likelihood, is in encouraging wealthy persons to incorporate their businesses when they would not otherwise do so, in order to take advantage of a corporate rate lower than the top marginal personal rate to which they are subject. They then realize on the undistributed profits through capital gains treatment—with no tax at all if the gains are not realized until death. When a person wishes to use the earnings primarily for expansion, as is often true, the corporate form offers significant advantage.

On the other hand, if the earnings of the businesses are to be used personally by the owners and if the rates to which the owners are subject are similar to or lower than the corporate rate, tax will be saved by not using the corporate form.

The relative magnitude and significance of these two influences cannot be ascertained. The overall size of the corporate sector, in relative and absolute terms, has been growing over several decades. Any net adverse effect of the use of the corporate form is therefore not likely to be great. The percentage of business income originating in the corporate sector has continued to rise steadily.[24]

Suitability of Various Forms.   Related to the question of the choice of form of business organization is that of the relative suitability of each form in various types of production. Large-scale manufacturing and other fields virtually necessitate use of the corporate form; agriculture and housing—particularly investment in owner-occupied housing—do not. There is, therefore, likely to be some relative shifting of resources from the corporate-dominant sector to the housing and agriculture sectors. There is also likely to be some shifting away from capital to greater relative use of labor in production. Arnold Harberger attempted to measure the costs of these diversions, concluding that they would range between $0.5 and $1.5 billion a year, but the assumptions involved in reaching these conclusions are such that not too much significance can be attached to the results.[25]

Splitting of Corporations. In an effort to lessen the adverse impact of the tax upon smaller, growing businesses, Congress provided for a lower rate on such enterprises. Similar policies are followed in Canada and some other countries. The result has been to encourage closely held businesses to split into a number of separate enterprises— sometimes into several hundred. Some types of business can split much more easily than others—chain stores, for example, compared to manufacturers. Not only did such practices reduce tax liability but they distorted the choice of the form of business organization as well.

Some restrictions were imposed on the practice in the Revenue Act of 1964. The 1969 Act provided for much more drastic control, affiliated companies (those under common ownership) being limited to one exemption only. Proposals by the Carter Commission in Canada to eliminate the lower rate on smaller corporations led to violent opposition; once a low-rate provision is placed in a tax law, strong political pressures build up to preserve it— and this occurred in Canada.[26]

[24] J. A. Pechman, *Federal Tax Policy,* rev. ed. (Washington, D.C.: The Brookings Institution, 1971) p. 114.

[25] "The Corporate Income Tax: An Empirical Appraisal," U.S. House of Representatives, *Tax Revision Compendium* (Washington, D.C.: 1959), pp. 231–50.

[26] A 25-percent rate applies to the first $100,000 income of Canadian-controlled companies, compared to the basic rate of 46 percent (20 percent and 40 percent for manufacturing concerns).

Methods of Financing. In the United States and elsewhere, interest paid on borrowed money is deductible in determining income tax liability, whereas dividends paid to stockholders are not. Accordingly, the borrowing method is made relatively more attractive. With a tax rate of 50 percent and the cost of borrowing at 8 percent, the cost (in the sense of dilution of interest of stockholders) of obtaining funds from sale of stock is 16 percent.

How great the actual effect is, is difficult to say. Many firms will not finance by borrowing under any circumstances and others seek to minimize it because of the greater risk. While borrowing will result in greater net gain for the stockholders if all goes well, it increases the danger of bankruptcy and loss of control in periods of losses. Data are by no means conclusive; debt financing as a percentage of total financing has risen in recent decades; for manufacturing the ratio was 15 percent in the late twenties, while it has been around 25 percent in recent years.[27] But it is by no means obvious that the tax treatment has been responsible. In any event, tax considerations have not led to massive shift to debt.

Incentives toward Efficiency. One of the complaints commonly advanced by critics of the corporate income tax is the effect it may have in reducing efficiency of operation and encouraging certain types of marginal expenditures. With a 50 percent tax rate, the government bears one half the cost of any inefficiency or any losing activity the firm continues to conduct. It is argued, therefore, that so long as a firm is earning profit, the pressure to weed out inefficiencies is less, since the government bears half the cost. Continued operation of various parts of the business which the executives personally dislike discontinuing is facilitated, as is increased expenditure on marginal advertising.

The significance of this influence is difficult to state. Traditions of efficiency are dominant in the thinking of many businessmen. Modern theories of business behavior stress the objective of a target rate of profit. If the actual profit is below this, the firm will seek to attain it and will not be deterred from doing so by the tax. If it is above, the tax admittedly may lessen the attention the firm pays to weeding out inefficiencies. Empirical evidence is lacking.

Location Effect. Differentials in corporate income tax rates may affect choice of location, particularly of manufacturers. A chief example in the United States is that of Puerto Rico, where industry has grown rapidly in the last two decades because firms can ship into the United States free of customs duties, yet are not subject to U.S. income tax, and have typically been freed of Puerto Rican taxes for a period of time. Within the continental United States, where all firms are subject to the federal corporate income tax, state corporate taxes differ; a few

---

[27] Pechman, *Tax Policy*, p. 120.

states still do not use the tax, and rates vary among the others. Opponents of the use of the tax or of an increase in rates always charge that the tax discourages the development of industry in the state. There is little evidence of this; differences in taxes are usually not great enough, apparently, to outweigh other factors influencing location decisions.[28] But they could be if the differentials were greater—and the argument is often highly effective with state legislatures, more so than similar arguments against the personal income tax.

The Corporate Income Tax as a Built-in Stabilizer

The revenue elasticity of the corporate income tax is relatively good as profits tend to keep pace with increasing GNP. It is not as good, however, as the personal income tax because of the lack of personal exemptions and the proportional rate (except for the lower figure on the first $50,000 of corporate profits).

Furthermore, even though the tax revenues vary with business conditions, the corporate tax may not be highly effective in stabilizing consumer and investment spending. Dividend payments do not always respond quickly to changes in profits and therefore the stabilizing effect of changes in tax payments on profits has less relevance for consumer spending. The tax payments do affect the amount of internal funds available for expansion, but this is only one of several determinants of actual investment and may be a rather minor one. If business activity and sales fall sharply, investment will fall despite the cushioning effect of the tax decline on funds available for expansion—but by less than without the tax cushion.

THE ROLE OF DEPRECIATION

In the previous section we pointed out that if the corporate income tax is not shifted and, hence, is borne entirely by the corporation, after-tax returns will be reduced by the amount of the tax. Consequently, investments will be adversely affected by the corporate income tax. It is important to realize, however, that even if the corporate income tax is borne fully by the corporation, its adverse effects upon investment are mitigated by certain elements in the tax laws that permit the firm to deduct depreciation allowances from taxable income.

Corporations as well as other businesses acquire capital equipment that has a life extending beyond one year. The capital, therefore, is used to produce goods in more than one income period. Over the life

---

[28] Advisory Commission on Intergovernmental Relations, *State-Local Taxation and Industrial Location* (Washington, D.C.: 1967).

of the equipment, the entire cost of the equipment is a legitimate expense for tax purposes; logically the amount allocated to each year should reflect the actual decline in value of the equipment during that period—in other words, the amount necessary to maintain intact the capital of the business. Unfortunately, however, this amount cannot be determined, and therefore, a somewhat arbitrary depreciation charge must be established for the period. The manner in which this charge is determined is of major significance for the business firm and for tax revenue.

The Formal Analysis

The way in which the corporate income tax and depreciation allowances can affect investment can be seen by considering the following simplified model of the firm's investment decision. We assume that the firm initially is not subject to any tax whatsoever. A firm will make a given investment as long as the present value of the stream of revenues equals the cost of the investment. To make the marginal investment the firm requires that the following equality holds:

$$C = \frac{R_1}{1+r} + \frac{R_2}{(1+r)^2} + \cdots + \frac{R_T}{(1+r)^T} \qquad (13-1)$$

where

C = the initial cost of investment
R_n = the net return in year n
r = the rate of interest

If the annual returns are all equal, this expression can be simplified to read:

$$C = RA \qquad (13-2)$$

where

C = the cost of the investment
R = the annual return from the investment
A = the present discounted value of payments of $1.00 for the life of the investment, for example,[29]

$$A = \sum_{h=1}^{T} \frac{1}{(1+r)^h}.$$

If a profits tax is introduced and is not shifted, the return after tax is reduced. But for tax purposes, firms are allowed to deduct deprecia-

---

[29] For computation of the present discounted value, see Additional Note 1 at the end of the chapter.

tion from their taxable income. Consequently, their tax liability is reduced by their depreciation reserves. Specifically, the after-tax equilibrium conditions are given by

$$C = \frac{R_1(1-t) - tD_1}{1+r} + \frac{R_2(1-t) - tD_2}{(1+r)^2} + \cdots + \frac{R_T(1-t) - tD_T}{(1+r)^T}$$

(13–3)

where

D_h = the depreciation reserves accumulated in period h

t = The tax rate, which is assumed to be maintained throughout the life of the investment.

If the returns are equal in every year and if straight-line depreciation is followed (under straight-line depreciation $D_h = C/d$: depreciation in any one year is equal to the cost of the investment [C] divided by the taxable life [d] of the investment), the present value formula can be simplified to read

$$C = R(1-t)A + \frac{tC}{d}B$$

(13–4)

where

B = the present value of payments of \$1.00 for each of d years

d = the taxable life of the investment.

Therefore, the adverse effect of the unshifted corporate income tax upon the firm's investment decision largely depends upon the nature of the allowable depreciation reserves; and this depends upon the following: the permissible sum to be depreciated, the rate of depreciation, the length of life of the investment for tax purposes, and the allowable depreciation formula.[30]

The Sum to Be Depreciated. By standard practice, for both internal accounting and tax purposes, a firm is permitted only to deduct the original cost to it of the capital items. It is sometimes argued that in an inflationary period, depreciation charges based on original cost are not adequate because replacement cost is greater. This argument has little merit. Firms using capital equipment purchased at a lower price in the past have a competitive advantage over those using more costly equipment acquired more recently and, in general, benefit from inflation. There is no possible need to compound the difference by allowing the firms to depreciate on a higher basis. The firms will, of course, require additional money capital to replace the equipment over and above earned depreciation charges. But this will be available—so long as earnings prospects warrant—from other sources. Provision of de-

---

[30] In Chapter 22 we discuss how changing government policies with respect to depreciation, tax rates, etc. can affect investment.

preciation allowances in excess of replacement cost could be justified only as a deliberate effort to increase the funds available for reinvestment, and there is no indication of pressing need to do so.

The Rate of Depreciation. The actual speed at which firms are able to write off capital equipment and plant for tax purposes depends on two elements: (1) the service life of the equipment—the length of time over which depreciation charges must be spread; and (2) the formula for depreciation—the basis for allocating the total among the various years. A reduction in the life period used and a shift to a formula concentrating more of the depreciation charges in the early years, known as accelerated depreciation, increases the amounts deductible in the early years of the life of the equipment. In general, business firms seek freedom to depreciate as rapidly as possible in light of the advantages. First, rapid depreciation returns the money capital tax free earlier than otherwise, thus not only saving interest but increasing the amount of internal funds available for expansion. If the entire amount were made deductible in the year of purchase, the firm would in effect be getting a tax-free loan from the government, as taxable income would be reduced by the amount of the cost of the capital equipment. In this case, the corporate income tax liability would precisely be offset by the depreciation allowance and the tax would have no affect on investment.[31]

Secondly, the risk of never being able to deduct fully the amounts for tax purposes, in the absence of a full loss offset system, is reduced. The more that can be deducted in early years, the less is the danger that some of the cost may never be deducted for tax purposes because of a series of years of losses. Thirdly, and in a sense the most important, the more accelerated the depreciation for tax purposes, the lower will be the actual tax on the income of the firm, so long as the firm continues to expand. On any one piece of equipment, the firm eventually "catches up"; with larger sums deductible in the early years, less is deductible in the later years, and other things being equal, the tax will be greater in those years. But so long as the firm continues to expand, it will pay less tax, year after year, to infinity.[32]

By contrast, and for obvious reasons, the governments of the United States and most countries have long sought to restrict firms in depreciation deductions for tax purposes in order to protect government revenues.

Length of Life. Theoretically, the length of life permitted should be that of the actual usage. But this cannot be determined at the time

---

[31] This can be seen in the context of our simplified model as detailed in Additional Note 2 at the end of the chapter.

[32] When accelerated depreciation was first proposed as a deliberate policy in the early fifties, this elementary fact of arithmetic was vehemently denied by many persons, particularly in the field of accounting.

the equipment is introduced or in subsequent years up to the final one. A few capital goods items have limited lives in usage, storage batteries or truck tires, for example. But even these may become obsolete before they are exhausted. With many types of equipment the actual length of life cannot be predicted with any accuracy—like railway steam locomotives or ferry boats, they may last with continued repair and patching for a century or they may be rendered obsolete in a few months.

Since 1942, the Internal Revenue Service has established guidelines for depreciation on a wide range of capital items. These were materially liberalized in the early 1970s.

Depreciation Formulas. Traditionally, for tax as well as other purposes, the straight-line method, whereby the capital sum is divided equally over the estimated years of life, was the most common practice, and, until 1954, the IRS was reluctant to allow firms to use other methods. The business community long complained that the straight-line method was unrealistic—that the decline in value was much greater in the earlier years than in the later ones. In 1954, legislation was enacted that permitted firms to switch to accelerated depreciation methods enabling them to increase the amount of depreciation claimed in the early years of the investment. Specifically, the government permitted firms to utilize one of two forms of depreciation: sum-of-the-years'-digits or double declining balances. Under the sum-of-the-years'-digits method, the deduction for depreciation declines linearly over the lifetime of the asset, starting at twice the corresponding straight-line rate (e.g., $200 instead of $100),[33] under the double declining-balance method the deduction drops exponentially starting at twice the straight-line rate (again at $200 instead of $100). Because the asset will never be fully depreciated under double declining balances, the firm has the option of switching to straight-line depreciation at any point.

These depreciation methods are illustrated in Figure 13–1 where the investment is assumed to have a life of 10 years. Both the sum-of-the-years'-digits method and the double declining-balance method permit depreciation to start out at twice the straight-line rate. Since the depreciation deduction declines exponentially under the declining-balance method, the initial depreciation deductions are less than those under the sum-of-the-years'-digits. At the fifth years, the depreciation allowance is the same under all three methods. After that the straight-line depreciation is greater than that of the other two methods.

Since the depreciation allowances are greater in the early years under accelerated depreciation than under straight-line depreciation,

---

[33] The number of years of life are added (for a 10-year life, $10 + 9 + 8 \ldots \ldots = 55$, and the depreciation allowed each year is determined by the ratio of the number of the year to the total; for the first year, 10/55, the second 9/55, etc.).

FIGURE 13–1
Relative Annual Depreciation Charges under Various Formulas

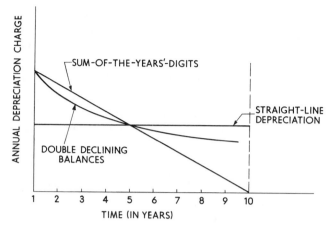

the present value of the tax credit on depreciation is greater under accelerated depreciation than under straight-line depreciation. Moreover, since the depreciation allowances in the early years are greatest under sum-of-the-years'-digits, this will give the firms the largest present value of the depreciation deductions. While authorization of these methods can be justified on the basis of their relationship to actual depreciation, they do have the effect of reducing the effective rate of tax.

Various countries have, at times, provided initial allowances, an unusually large depreciation deduction the year of acquisition of new equipment, but one that reduces the subsequent permissible deductions. This is, of course, merely one further step in the direction of acceleration of depreciation and can be justified only as a deliberate effort to encourage investment.

The Investment Credit

The investment credit system, used by a number of countries including the United States from 1962 to 1969 (except for a five-month suspension) and reinstated in 1971, provides credit against tax over and above normal depreciation allowances. This has the effect of further mitigating the adverse effect of an unshifted corporate income tax upon investment. This can be seen by extending our simplified investment model to allow for the impact of the investment credit. An investment credit allows the firm to receive a tax credit equal to α times the cost of the investment, where α is the rate of the tax credit. Thus, the introduction of an investment credit alters the firm's present-value formula on the assumption that the firm utilizes straight-line depreciation to read

$$C = (1 - t)RA + \frac{tC}{d} B + \alpha C \qquad (13\text{--}5)$$

where

C = the initial cost of the investment

R = the annual stream of returns, which are assumed to be constant over the life of the investment

A = the present discounted value of payments of \$1.00 for each year of the life of the investment

B = the present value of payments of \$1.00 for each of d years, which represents the taxable life of the investment

t = the tax rate

α = the rate of the tax credit.

If the tax rate and depreciation formulas are unchanged from those given in equation 13–4, the present value of the investment will be increased by the term αC. Note that in this formulation, the tax credit is not subtracted from the amount of depreciation to be claimed. If the tax credit is subtracted from the amount of the deduction to be claimed, the present value formula will read

$$C = RA(1 - t) + \frac{tC(1 - \alpha)}{d} B + \alpha C. \qquad (13\text{--}5a)$$

Thus, the present value of a given investment will be greater if the investment tax credit is not deducted from the amount of allowable depreciation than if it is.[34]

As used in the United States, firms are authorized a deduction from taxable income equal to 10 percent of the cost of new capital equipment in the year of acquisition and then are allowed to depreciate the full cost. The effect is similar to that of accelerated depreciation, but the system does not disturb normal depreciation procedures. The credit reduces tax revenue by several billion dollars a year. The purpose is, of course, to provide deliberate encouragement for additional capital investment in order to aid economic growth and lessen unemployment.

The investment credit is usually considered superior to accelerated depreciation for several reasons. It is simpler to understand and more likely to affect investment policy; it avoid readjustments in usual depreciation rules; it provides the same credit, as a percentage of investment, for all firms regardless of tax rate (providing, of course, they are earning profit). The credit increases the after-tax rate of return in

---

[34] The significance of the specific formulation of the investment credit will be discussed in more detail in Chapter 22 below.

much the same fashion as a reduction in the actual tax rate, but since the impact is concentrated on new investment, the effect should be greater in encouraging investment than a rate reduction involving the same revenue loss.

The credit has been criticized on several grounds: as an unnecessary reduction of tax on business income; as providing an artificial stimulus to replacement of manpower by machinery; and as a stimulus to additional inflation. For this last-reason, it was eliminated by Congress in 1969; it was then reinstated in December 1971 as a move to lessen unemployment, and the rate was increased from 7 to 10 percent in 1975 to stimulate investment. The investment tax credit system as it stands suffers from several defects that produce distortions—as for example the distinction made between short-run and long-run investment and the lower rate allowed public utilities.[35]

Empirical Studies of the Effectiveness of Changes in Depreciation Policy

Several studies in the United States have concluded that accelerated depreciation and the investment credit have had substantial impact on investment. Norman Ture concluded that in 1959, business investment was increased by the accelerated depreciation rules by at least $1.3 billion, and perhaps as much as $5.7 billion.[36]

An econometric study by R. E. Hall and D. W. Jorgensen employed a model that sought to isolate the effects of changes in tax policy upon investment from the effect of changes in other determinants of investment in the post-World War II years.[37]

The conclusions are summarized below:

1. Accelerated depreciation was found to have a significant impact upon real investment; the authors attribute 17.5 percent of all investment in manufacturing equipment and 15.4 percent of the investment in nonfarm nonmanufacturing equipment in the 1954–1969 period to changes in rules that permitted faster depreciation. In 1956, nearly a third of all manufacturing equipment investment was attributable to the changes. It is important to note, however, that each particular change tends to lose effectiveness after several years; the primary ef-

---

[35] Note the article by E. M. Sunley, "Toward a More Neutral Investment Tax Credit," *National Tax Journal*, vol. 26 (June 1973), pp. 209–20.

[36] Norman Ture, *Accelerated Depreciation in the United States* (New York: National Bureau of Economic Research, 1967), pp. 95–96.

[37] R. E. Hall and D. W. Jorgensen, "Application of the Theory of Optimal Capital Accumulation," in *Tax Incentives and Capital Spending*, ed. G. Fromm (Washington, D.C.: The Brookings Institution, 1971) pp. 9–60. See also R. E. Hall and D. W. Jorgensen, "Tax Policy and Investment Behavior," *American Economic Review*, vol. 57 (June 1967), pp. 391–44. The significance of these changes in depreciation policies for stabilization and growth will be discussed in Chapter 24 below.

fect is to speed up investment in the years immediately after the change. The changes in leading to a permanently larger capital stock do produce a continuing higher level of reinvestment, even though the effects on new investment dampen down.

2. Liberalized depreciation guidelines had a lesser but measurable effect on real investment.

3. The investment credit provided a substantial stimulus to investment. In 1965, the credit was responsible for 28.4 percent of manufacturing equipment investment and 36.8 percent of nonmanufacturing, nonfarm investment (1964). The suspension of the credit resulted in a sharp drop in investment.

In summary, Hall and Jorgensen conclude that changes in tax policy do have substantial effect upon investment; the investment tax credit had, in the last two decades, the most significant impact. Changes that increase the returns from capital have their primary impact in the first several years following the change; eventually the total capital stock catches up with the level the tax change makes desirable. But gross investment remains permanently higher because of the greater capital stock and the greater replacement demand. On the other hand, they conclude that the change in the corporate income tax rate in 1964 had very little impact on investment, relative to that of the other changes.

A study by Charles Bischoff, using a somewhat less-restrictive model, reaches similar conclusions, but a study by Robert Coen, using a slightly different model, shows very limited impact, much less than the magnitude of the tax reduction.[38]

One empirical study of somewhat limited scope, relating to large California farms, concludes that the present tax leads to greater risk-taking and output.[39]

Thus, the answers available are by no means entirely satisfactory; the trouble, as always, arises out of the great difficulty in isolating the effects of the taxes from other influences and the lack of an adequate knowledge of the nature of the investment function. Debate continues over the relative influence on investment of the major variables, particularly changes in the level of output and the availability and cost of finance. A summary analysis by Jorgensen reaches the conclusion that changes in real output appear to be the primary determinant of

---

[38] Charles Bischoff, "The Effect of Alternative Lag Distributions" and Robert Coen, "The Effect of Cash Flow on the Speed of Adjustment," in Fromm, *Tax Incentives*, pp. 61–196.

A study by T. M. Stanback, Jr., *Tax Changes and Modernization in the Textile Industry* (New York: National Bureau of Economic Research, 1969) showed that tax changes had considerable influence on investment decision-making in the textile industry, but the effect was restricted by the failure of many executives to note the significance of accelerated depreciation for the rate of return.

[39] W. F. Lin *et al.*, "Producer Response to Income Taxes: An Empirical Test within a Risk Framework," *National Tax Journal*, vol. 27 (June 1974), pp. 183–95.

changes in investment.[40] To the extent that this thesis is valid, tax changes have less impact than they otherwise would, except insofar as they affect the overall level of GNP. But nevertheless, availability of money capital is found to be a significant secondary determinant. Cost of capital appears to be more significant, on the basis of recent empirical studies, than availability of internal funds—contrary to earlier beliefs.

EVALUATION OF THE PRESENT CORPORATE INCOME TAX

Defense

The present corporate income tax is defended on several bases.

Productivity. The tax is the third largest federal revenue source. The yield averages about 30 percent of that of the personal income tax.

Equity. Despite defects subsequently noted, the tax is widely accepted, in Congress and outside, on equity grounds. The direct impact is on the corporation; a small number of large corporations pay a substantial portion of the total tax. To persons who regard the large corporation as a source of taxpaying ability in itself, distinct from that of the stockholders, this tax is particularly appropriate. The typical corporation accumulates large sums of wealth over which individual stockholders have no direct claim and which would not be reached effectively by other levies.

Political Appeal. Closely related is the political appeal; the tax appears to be attractive all out of proportion to its actual justification on equity or other grounds because of widespread acceptance of the belief that a tax on business or, specifically, corporations is not borne by people—and corporations do not vote. As noted, the actual distributional effect is difficult to ascertain; the majority of the voters may feel that the "wealthy corporation" will pay the tax and, therefore, the distribution of wealth and income is improved.

Supplement to Personal Income Tax. Without some form of tax on earnings of corporations, the portion not distributed as dividends would escape current taxation entirely. The consequences would include serious inequity, a tendency to hold earnings in closely held corporations to an even greater extent than at present, and much greater pressure to incorporate. The tax leakage would be tremendous.

Progressivity. If the tax is not reflected in higher prices, the overall distributional pattern is almost certain to be progressive, in view of the relatively progressive distribution of stockholdings—although with a

---

[40] D. W. Jorgensen, "Econometric Studies of Investment Behavior: A Survey," *Journal of Economic Literature*, vol. 9 (December 1971), pp. 1111–46.

great many individual variations from the typical pattern. If the tax is shifted in large measure, it will not be progressive.

The Benefit Basis.   Some attempt is made to defend the corporate income tax, particularly at the state level, along benefit lines. The privilege of incorporating, granted by government, offers very significant advantages in operation over other forms of business organization. This argument has only limited significance at best, however, since presumably competitive forces prevent firms from making a higher rate of return with corporate than noncorporate forms of organization. A related argument does have merit at the state level—a corporation operating in one state does receive benefits from that state, yet may be owned entirely by persons living outside the state. Without some form of a corporate income tax, the state would receive no tax revenue, all of which would accrue to the state of residence of the owners.

The Primary Criticisms

One set of major criticisms is based upon the assumption that the tax is not reflected in higher prices of the goods produced by the corporation. Under this assumption, the tax is condemned on both equity and economic efficiency grounds. Dividend income is taxed more heavily than other income, since the corporate tax applies and then the amount paid out as dividends is taxed again under the personal income tax, whereas all other income in the income stream is taxed only once. While the receipt of dividends is, as a whole, progressive relative to income, there is great individual variation and a substantial sum of dividends is received by persons in the lower-income groups. The equal-treatment-of-equals rule is violated. A case may be made for taxing all property income more heavily than labor income—but it is difficult to justify taxing dividend income more heavily than interest and other property income. On the other hand, undistributed profits are taxed less heavily than they would be under the personal income tax for persons whose marginal income tax rates are higher than the corporate tax rate.

As noted, the double taxation of dividend income is charged with lessening the S/Y ratio and the incentive to undertake real investment. Commencing in 1974, this argument has been stressed by those persons maintaining that the country faces a serious capital shortage, and that recovery from unemployment and further growth will be restricted drastically unless tax measures are undertaken to increase the percentage of national income saved. The U.S. Treasury has been stressing this point of view, as well as many business groups. In 1976, the point has been showing up frequently in corporate reports to stockholders. Closely related is the "crowding out" argument, that governmental borrowing will further deter investment by lessening funds available to other borrowers. To others, capital shortage is a sheer fiction—the apparent capital shortage is a result of a monetary policy that tightens the money supply in the face of substantial unemployment in the belief that inflation can be controlled by this means.

Thirdly, the tax is charged with creating numerous distortions in the economy and thus loss of economic efficiency: with regard to choice of form of business organization, methods of financing, division of corporations into smaller ones, and other changes. As noted, in a sense the tax places an umbrella over the inefficient firm, which pays little or no tax, and checks the growth of the more efficient firm. This argument is likewise open to doubt: The no-profit firm may be a new firm struggling to get started; the high-profit firm may be one with a semi-monopoly position rather than maximum efficiency.

Finally, the tax is criticized on the grounds that it is not, in fact, borne by the stockholders but is shifted forward to the consumers of the products, as noted. It appears almost certain that the tax is shifted to some extent. When the tax is shifted it does not, of course, discriminate against dividend income or lessen investment. But the distributional pattern becomes similar to that of a sales tax. Not only is it regressive, but, unlike a retail sales tax, the burden varies widely among commodities according to the ratios of profits and sales and the actual extent of shifting, with the consequent objections noted in Chapter 15.

These objections, which in total are potentially serious, have led to proposals for reform of the tax.

REFORM PROPOSALS—INTEGRATION OF THE CORPORATE AND PERSONAL INCOME TAXES[41]

Much of the present difficulty arises out of the failure to coordinate the personal and corporate income taxes. Each is a separate levy (although with many common rules), the corporate income tax applying to the entire sum of corporate net profits whether retained or paid out as dividends, the personal income tax treating dividends in the same fashion as other income. The corporation is essentially treated as a separate entity with tax capacity of its own, quite distinct from the persons who own it—the stockholders. Essentially, this reflects the philosophy that a corporation possesses tax capacity of its own, as measured by its net profits, without regard to the distributional effects the tax may have on the individual stockholders, consumers, or workers.

---

[41] This issue is reviewed in detail in the NTA–TIA Symposium volume, *The Taxation of Income from Corporate Shareholding*, the September 1975 issue of *National Tax Journal*, vol. 28, no. 3.

Under the rule noted at the beginning of Chapter 10, equity and economic effects of income taxation can be optimized only if all income is treated in exactly the same fashion, regardless of the form in which it is earned. Attainment of uniformity of treatment of income earned through the corporation and other income requires abandonment of the rule that the corporation has tax capacity of its own and integration of personal and corporate taxes in such a way that both income not distributed by the corporation and that paid out as dividends are taxed in exactly the same fashion as earnings with noncorporate forms of organization. There are various approaches to integration.

The Partnership Approach

Complete attainment of the goal of equality of treatment of income earned through the corporation is possible only if the corporation is treated as a partnership for tax purposes, the corporation as such being freed of tax and stockholders being taxed on the dividends received plus their share of the company's undistributed profits. These would be reported by the corporation to each stockholder, just as dividends paid during the year are reported at the end of the year for tax purposes. This is the treatment provided partnerships and is authorized for small corporations—those with 10 stockholders or less.

The great merit is that income earned through the corporation would be treated in exactly the same fashion as other income and all distortion arising from the differential treatment eliminated. But there are two serious limitations. First, with complex capital structures, exact determination of the appropriate share of each type of stockholder of the undistributed profits requires arbitrary decisions. Frequent changes in ownership complicate the ascertainment of pro rata shares. More seriously, some stockholders would be hard-pressed to pay tax on stock of companies earning substantial amounts and paying out little or nothing as dividends. Some stockholders would have to sell securities to pay tax; larger stockholders would pressure the company to pay out more in dividends, thus lessening funds for expansion.

Dividend Received Credits

The second approach seeks to lessen the double taxation of dividend income by reducing the impact of the personal income tax on dividend income, which has been already subjected to the corporate tax. There are several possible systems varying in completeness. Under the system long used in Canada and to a limited extent in the United States from 1954 to 1963, a given percentage of dividends [42]

---

[42] The Canadian system requires that an amount equal to one third of dividends received be added to income (as well as the dividends themselves) and then a credit of four fifths of the one-third figure is given against tax.

received constitutes a credit against personal income tax, thus reducing the double tax impact. This version fails to provide any credit for low-income stockholders, who have been subjected to the corporate income tax on their dividends whereas they would not be subject to personal income taxes. The credit is worth more to high-income stockholders than to low-income stockholders. This defect is avoided by a more completely integrated system, long used in Great Britain but abandoned in recent years and proposed by the Carter Commission in Canada, that regards the corporate income tax as a withholding device for the personal income tax. The corporation reports to the stockholder the tax paid on the dividend income; the stockholder includes this tax and the dividends in his or her income, calculates the income tax liability, and then subtracts the tax reported on the dividends from the tax due, in the same fashion as a person deducts tax withheld from wages during the year from his or her income tax liability for the year. Persons having no income tax liability receive a cash refund, as they do with withholding on labor income. The withholding approach is more complete and more equitable than the Canadian system, but of course, causes greater revenue loss. Both systems do reduce the double impact of the tax and both confine the reduction to domestic stockholders.

The dividend-received credit approach in any form suffers from three basic defects. First, to the extent that the corporate income tax is shifted, the stockholder has not been subjected to a double burden and he or she receives an unwarranted refund. An interesting phenomenon in the United States is that groups that argued strongly for this approach are the same ones that argue equally strongly that the corporation income tax is shifted forward to consumers. Second, since the tax remains intact at the corporate level, any adverse effects the tax may have on real investment decisions by management, methods of financing, and the like are not eliminated. Finally, the tax on undistributed profits is not the same as that on the income of noncorporate business.

Dividend-Paid Credit

The third alternative is to retain the corporate income tax but to apply it only to undistributed profits, by allowing the corporation to deduct dividends paid in the same fashion that it now deducts interest. This approach does not provide perfect integration, as the tax on undistributed profits will not be the same as the personal income tax on the incomes of the owners. But it avoids some of the worst evils of the dividends-received credit approach. Since the tax on the dividend portion is not collected at the corporate level, shifting of the tax by the corporation would appear to be impossible and stockholders would not receive an unwarranted refund. Since the tax will not be collected at the corporate level, any influence on corporate policy would be avoided; there would be no effect on choice of methods of financing, for example.

Despite the relative advantages of this approach, it has little political appeal. One fear commonly expressed is that firms would be encouraged to pay out a large portion of profits as dividends in order to minimize the tax liability of the corporation per se. Such a policy is not necessarily advantageous to the larger, often dominant, stockholders, however. If there are good investment opportunities for the funds, it would not appear rational for management to pay out the funds merely for the purpose of reducing corporate tax liability. Furthermore, reduced corporate saving would be offset in substantial part by increased private saving, although there might be some decline in real investment on the part of firms whose investment policies are greatly influenced by the amount of money capital on hand.

A related argument is the relative discrimination against new, growing businesses; since they need additional capital in the business, they would pay more tax per dollar of sales than established competitors. This argument is likewise of doubtful significance; at a given tax rate, they would pay no more than they now do, and the fact that established competitors are paying less per dollar of sales is not necessarily a source of competitive disadvantage.

The main obstacle to this alternative is a purely political one; making the change at the corporate level does not directly affect the individual stockholders' tax liability, whereas it appears to make important tax concessions to business. A change that directly reduces the tax paid by large numbers of persons is obviously more popular.

General Evaluation of Reform Proposals

All of these avenues of reform will reduce tax revenues substantially. Under the assumption that the tax is not shifted to consumers, the net effect of the change would be to reduce the relative tax burden on owners of corporations—a change that not only lacks political appeal but may be considered contrary to usually accepted standards of equity. The same overall distributional pattern by income class could be obtained with much greater equity by treatment of corporate earnings in the same fashion as other income and with a higher rate on all property income than on labor income. But even this type of reform seems to have little appeal.

If the corporate tax is shifted forward, the whole picture changes. A shifted tax is not an effective means of reaching the higher income groups at all, but a haphazard and regressive sales tax, passing much of the burden to labor. Reform is dictated much more urgently than under the assumption of nonshiftability, by usual standards. But Congress has, in general, been unwilling to face up to this assumption of shifting. If the change is made under this assumption, the adjustment must be made at the corporate level—via use of the dividend-paid credit approach, and this has, as noted, the least political appeal.

Thus the tax remains largely unchanged, despite criticisms from a wide range of sources. The small step taken by the Eisenhower administration in 1954 to integrate the taxes was eliminated by the Democrats, in part because of use of the defective dividend-received credit approach, and there has been no strong effort to make significant changes since. In Canada, the Carter Commission proposed full integration of the two taxes so far as dividends were concerned (stockholders to receive full credit for corporate tax paid on the amounts distributed) and provision of an option to corporations to allocate undistributed profits to stockholders, with equivalent tax treatment.[43] This system would provide complete integration on dividends and on undistributed profits when corporations chose the option, but incomplete integration on the undistributed portion otherwise. The government, however, was unwilling to go this far, partly for revenue reasons, and the system finally adopted in 1971 provides a tax credit of roughly one third of the dividends received.

The issue of integration of the personal and corporate income taxes, dormant for a decade, was suddenly revived in the United States in the summer of 1975, primarily by the Treasury and business groups, as a consequence of the concern with shortage of capital. Congress, however, shows no disposition to act on the proposals.

ADDITIONAL NOTES

1. The present discounted value of an annual payment of $1.00 over the life of an investment lasting for T years represents the amount that an individual would be willing to pay today to receive annual payments of $1.00 over the life of the investment of T years. Suppose that the market rate of interest is r. Then if an individual invests $1.00 today, he or she will receive ($1.00)(1 + r)$ at the beginning of the following year. This implies that an individual would only pay $1.00/(1 + r)$ for the right to receive $1.00 next year. By investing that amount today, he or she would have exactly $1.00 at the beginning of next year. Hence, the present value of $1.00 to be received next year is $1.00/(1 + r)$. If we assume that the interest r is constant and can be compounded, it follows that the present value of $1.00 received in two years' time is $1.00/(1 + r)^2$. Consequently, the present value of payments of $1.00 next year and the following year must be $1.00/(1 + r) + $1.00/(1 + r)^2$. By extending the argument for T periods, it

---

[43] G. F. Break, "Integration of the Corporate and Personal Taxes on Income," *National Tax Journal*, vol. 22 (March 1969), pp. 39–50.

follows that the present value of annual payments of $1.00 for T periods must be equal to

$$\sum_{h=1}^{T} \frac{1}{(1+r)^{h}}.$$

2. If instantaneous depreciation were granted so that the firm could deduct the entire cost of the investment in its year of purchase, the taxable life of the investment equals 1 (i.e., $d = 1$) and the present value of a dollar of a depreciation deduction must also equal 1 (i.e., $B = 1$). In this case, it is clear that the initial present value formula (equation 13–1) is not altered. This can be seen by substituting $d = 1$ and $B = 1$ into equation 13–4 to yield

$$C = R(1 - t)A + Ct \qquad (13\text{--}4a)$$

or

$$C(1 - t) = RA(1 - t)$$

or

$$C = RA$$

which is equal to equation 13–1. Thus, by permitting the firm to deduct the entire cost of the investment in the year of purchase, the government effectively gives it a tax-free loan whose value is precisely equal to the reduction in returns caused by taxes. The net effect is to offset the taxes so that the present value of the investment is not affected.

APPENDIX—BUSINESS TAXES[14]

Business firms are subject to a wide range of taxes also applying to individuals. The property tax is the most important, with business firms paying directly more than half of total property tax collections. Firms are also subject to federal personal and corporate income taxes and they pay sales tax and excises on many purchases of commodities. They also serve, in effect, as collecting agents for governments for various sales and excise taxes. Distinct from these levies, however, is a group of taxes frequently known as "business taxes," designed to place a tax burden on business per se in compensation for governmental services. There are no federal taxes of this type (the federal corporation income tax is regarded as a part of the overall income tax structure). But they are used by a number of states and by some municipal governments.

---

[14] Tax Institute. *Business Taxes in State and Local Governments.* Lexington, Mass.: Lexington Books, 1972.

There are two varieties: the general levies imposed upon all forms of business and specific levies on particular industries.

General Business Levies

The great majority of states today, 46, employ a corporation income tax, essentially in a dual capacity, as a complement to the personal income tax to reach undistributed profits and as a general business tax to make corporations operating in the state contribute to the state in compensation for benefits received. [45] Without such a levy, even if all dividends were distributed to stockholders, the particular state would get no revenue from the activity if the stockholders lived in other states. The income tax form of general corporate levy is generally regarded as the most satisfactory form in terms of usual standards of equity, since each corporation is required to pay in relation to the profits earned from operation in the state and the tax offers the advantage of complementing, even in a somewhat imperfect way, the personal income tax.

Several states, however, use a gross receipts tax, either in conjunction with a corporate income tax (Alaska, West Virginia, Delaware, at low rates) or as an alternative, firms paying whichever is higher (Indiana), or in lieu of a corporate income tax (Washington). The nonretail portion of the sales tax in Hawaii could also be regarded as a general business levy. These gross receipts taxes resemble sales taxes, which are also essentially levies on gross receipts. But they differ in several respects. Rates are typically fractional. The legislative intent is that the tax be paid by the business firm, not directly collected from the customer. The taxes are not—and in Washington State cannot be by law—quoted separately to the customer. The distributional impact is likely to be similar to that of sales taxes, but the legislative intent and the level of rates differ. Furthermore, the taxes are not confined to retail sales, but apply, in general, to all types of business.

These gross receipts taxes are highly objectionable in many ways. Like turnover taxes, they foster integration of businesses, discriminating against the small nonintegrated business. They favor firms selling out of the state, since receipts from such sales are constitutionally not subject to tax. Where a wide range of rates is used, as in Washington, there is no possible logic for selection of the rate differences.

Another group of states uses capital stock taxes, usually in addition to the corporate income tax or other levy. In only two states are these significant revenue sources. The capital stock is usually valued in some rather arbitrary fashion that bears no relation whatever to any

---

[45] The Michigan tax, since 1975, applies not only to corporate profits, but also to wages, dividends, royalties, and some other items paid, and thus resembles a value added tax, discussed in Chapter 15.

measure of tax capacity. Except at nominal rates these levies have no justification whatever and are highly discriminatory among various business firms.

Concern with the possible effects of high corporate income taxes on business location and desire to broaden the base of the tax has led to proposals for use of value added taxes, explained in Chapter 15, as state business taxes, and actual introduction of such a levy in Michigan in 1975 (that state also used a value added tax in modified form in the 1960s). The principal argument used for this form of business tax is that value added is the most suitable measure of the value of state services received. The opponents argue that corporate profits are a better measure of tax capacity, and that the value added tax duplicates in large part the personal income tax and/or the sales tax.

On the whole, general business taxes, other than the corporate income tax used as a part of the overall income tax structure, make little sense and may have seriously objectionable results. As previously noted, the concept of tax capacity has little significant meaning distinct from the individuals involved—employees, consumers, stockholders, and the like. States may be justified in taxing the income of corporations doing business in the state, particularly when the owners do not live in the state. But to use another levy in addition to the corporate tax or in lieu of it has little justification and may have significant adverse effects. Because the limitations are well known, there has been no tendency to increase the rates of these levies, or for other states to add them. But inertia and the problems of raising the equivalent revenue have led the states imposing them to continue to do so.

Some cities also impose gross receipts taxes; the same arguments apply. The levies may tend to drive economic activity outside the city limits.

Special Levies

Various states impose special levies on certain types of businesses:

1. Severance taxes on the output of mineral resources and petroleum, used in several states to ensure that the state obtains some payment in compensation for the exhaustion of its resources.

2. Taxes on insurance gross premiums. For a variety of reasons, insurance companies are difficult to reach satisfactorily by either income or property taxes; therefore, most states impose separate levies on the gross premiums received as a crude measure of tax capacity.

3. Taxes on motor carriers. These are essentially elements in the highway finance system.

4. Taxes on public utilities. Some of these levies are merely substitutes for the sales tax on these services and therefore regarded as elements in the sales tax structure. Others, however, are levied in

addition to other types of taxes, justified on the basis of special benefits received. Since they are likely to result in higher rates, they become in effect levies on the consumers of the utility services and, therefore, are open to serious question in terms of equity, except as a part of a general sales tax.

5. Occupational license taxes. Frequently cities impose flat sum occupational license taxes on various types of businesses, especially those considered to represent sumptuary or luxury activity—taverns, movie theaters, and the like. The flat rate makes administration easy but discriminates against the smaller businesses. As essentially fees related to police activity the levies have justification; as sources of general revenue they suffer from the defects of the general excise tax type of levy.

REFERENCES

Canada. *Report of the Royal Commission on Taxation.* vol. 4. Ottawa: Queens Printer, 1966.

Goode, R. *The Corporation Income Tax.* New York: Wiley, 1951.
Now badly out-of-date, but one of the most complete studies of the corporate income tax.

Holland, D. *The Income Tax Burden on Stockholders,* and *Dividends under the Income Tax.* Princeton: Princeton University Press for National Bureau of Economic Research, 1958 and 1962.

Pechman, J. A. *Federal Tax Policy.* rev. ed., chap. 5. Washington, D.C.: The Brookings Institution, 1971.

14

Approaches to Consumption Taxation; Excise Taxes

The second principal approach to taxation is based upon the measure of consumption—the portion of income spent for consumption purposes rather than being saved: $C = Y - S$. The total base, therefore, is less than that of income taxation since total savings is a positive magnitude. There are two types of approaches to use of the consumption base: the "direct" approach of the spendings tax, whereby individuals pay on the basis of returns in the same fashion as they pay the income tax; and the "indirect" or excise and sales tax approach, whereby the tax is imposed upon sellers of goods and services and presumably shifted forward to the consumers of the products.

THE RATIONALE OF CONSUMPTION TAXATION

Equity

The equity argument for the use of the consumption base for taxation centers around the philosophy that satisfaction is gained only from consumption, not from saving, which involves postponement of consumption, and therefore, C, rather than Y (i.e., $C + S$) is the appropriate measure of equity in taxation. It is argued that a person's economic well-being during the period is measured by the amount he or she consumes, not the amount of income that the person earns. This was first emphasized by the 17th-century English philosopher Hobbes and stressed in the work of Irving Fisher.[1]

---

[1] Fisher confused the issue by emphasis on terminology; he defined income as equal to consumption. To Fisher, income does not include the amounts saved, and taxation of both income saved and the subsequent earnings from the savings would constitute double taxation. This is a futile type of argument—but it did emphasize the possible desirability of the consumption approach.

Like all equity arguments, the issue can be resolved only upon value judgments; the more common point of view is that equity requires taxing total income—that persons save because they prefer to do so, and that amounts saved reflect tax capacity as well as amounts consumed. One cannot conclude that the latter argument is more valid scientifically than the former, but the income measure would appear to have much broader support.

The primary objections to consumption taxation center around equity considerations and will be developed at greater length in the succeeding chapters. The chief objection is the difficulty of avoiding regressivity of the taxes, heavy absolute burden on the lowest-income groups, and discrimination among consumers on the basis of their relative preferences for various goods. In terms of the typical life cycle of a family, the consumption type of tax hits relatively heavily in the earlier years of formation of the household and in the years of retirement, and less heavily, relative to income, in the years of highest earning capacity. It is difficult to design consumption taxes in such a way as to avoid these effects, because most forms cannot be adapted to the personal circumstances of the individual taxpayer. There is also inherent discrimination in favor of the family which prefers to save a high percentage of its income.

Economic Efficiency

The principal case for the consumption basis rests upon arguments relating to economic efficiency rather than to equity. There are several aspects.

Labor Supplies. The basic distinction between income and consumption levies is that persons can escape the income levy only by earning less income, whereas they can escape the consumption levy by saving rather than consuming their income, while changing their income does not, in itself, affect their tax liability. The general argument is therefore advanced that consumption-related taxes are less likely to reduce total supplies of labor and relative supplies of highly paid labor than is a tax related to income. This argument has validity, of course, only if consumption and savings are substitutable. If income were desired only for consumption or if all persons have fixed ratios of savings and consumption to income, the effects of the two taxes will be the same. But this is not the situation. The potential difference is reinforced in practice by the progressivity of income taxes on the one hand and the regressivity or at least proportionality of consumption levies on the other hand. This latter element is not an inherent difference between the two forms of taxes but is in practice a significant difference.

Another potential difference between the effects of the two types of taxes on labor supply arises from the money illusion—the apparent tendency of many persons to react to monetary changes in their incomes to a much greater extent than to changes in their real incomes caused by price changes.[2] The indirect form of consumption tax hits the individual in the form of an increase in prices of goods purchased rather than as a charge against income.

Closely related is the potential difference in the *spite effect*, noted in Chapter 9; if persons are unaware that a price increase is due to the tax, the potential spite effect is avoided—but so is any "purchase" effect working in the opposite direction.

The overall significance of the labor-supply argument for consumption taxes depends upon the actual effects of income taxes upon factor supplies. As explained in Chapter 12, the actual effect, at least at present, does not appear to be great, and, therefore, the potential advantages of consumption-based taxes are likewise limited. They would be much greater if income tax rates were substantially higher and had demonstrable effect on labor supply.

Relative Effects on the Rate of Capital Formation—The Savings/ Income Ratio. A primary argument for the consumption approach is based on considerations relating to the rate of capital formation and therefore the supply of capital goods and the level of employment and national income.

Other elements given, consumption-related taxes should ensure a higher overall S/Y ratio than income-related taxes. There are two aspects of the difference.

1. The income effect. Consumption-related taxes concentrate to a greater extent on those persons consuming high percentages of their incomes than does an income tax, particularly a progressive tax. Persons consuming all of their incomes and unable or unwilling to go into debt must curtail consumption by the amount of any tax. The income tax places a relatively greater burden on persons saving higher percentages of their incomes and therefore having greater potential for paying the tax from funds that would otherwise be saved. It must be recognized that a tax measured by consumption is not necessarily absorbed through reduced consumption; it too may be absorbed from savings. But consumption taxes place a heavy burden on those persons consuming all or most of their incomes and having no option.

2. The substitution effect. The consumption-related taxes provide incentive to consume less and save more, since the person can escape current tax liability by reducing spending, whereas the income tax does not do so. If the person saves for the purpose of consuming in the future and the tax is expected to be permanent, the only gain from saving more is to delay payment of tax, so long as the person reacts

---

[2] Labor unions will usually strike against a reduction in money wages, but will pay little attention—except in subsequent bargaining—to increases in the cost of living.

rationally. When the person is saving for other purposes, however, or the tax is expected to be temporary, there appears to be a net tax saving from consuming less. The effects in increasing saving will be greater if:

1. The person believes that the tax will be temporary. If so, the person can lessen total tax that he or she will pay by saving now and consuming later after the tax has been repealed.
2. The person saves for purposes other than consumption purchases in the future—as for example, a reserve or to accumulate a sum to give to heirs.
3. A type of spite effect is present. The person may save more to reduce tax without regard to prospective future tax liabilities. This is a form of irrational behavior reflecting strong adverse reactions to taxes.

The actual differences between a consumption tax and an income tax yielding the same revenue cannot, so far as incentive effects are concerned, be ascertained. The conclusion that the consumption-related tax will result in a higher overall S/Y ratio and permit higher rate of growth is a reasonable one—but the actual difference cannot be specified; the answer depends in part on the rate structures and upon the nature of the response of households to changes in the net return from savings.

Actual Capital Formation. Given the S/Y ratio, the relative effects of a consumption tax and an income tax on the actual rate of capital formation, and thus on the supply of capital goods as well as the level of employment, are dependent upon the nature of the investment function: the determinants of the volume of real investment at various rates of return. A consumption-related tax, unlike the income tax, does not reduce the net money return the owners of the business obtain from a given before-tax profit. The real purchasing power—the ability to buy consumption goods—is reduced, but there is little evidence to suggest that investors give serious attention to this effect. From this standpoint, one stressed by the defenders of consumption taxation, therefore, the rate of investment should be greater with the consumption-related taxes. The exact difference depends on the precise nature of the investment function. The same conclusion applies to the availability of money capital; the consumption-related taxes, per dollar of revenue, will have less effect in reducing willingness to supply money capital than either personal or corporate income taxes.

There are, however, offsetting considerations. In the first place, the differences are of no significance if investment is adequate to ensure full employment anyway. Under such circumstances, a change in the tax structure that will increase real investment beyond that permitted by the higher S/Y ratio will simply generate inflation unless adequate fiscal and monetary techniques are employed to cut the investment back.

Secondly, since a consumption tax will reduce consumption more and savings less than an income tax, the use of the consumption basis may make the task of obtaining full employment more difficult. The higher potential rate of capital formation permitted by the higher S/Y ratio with the consumption tax will necessitate a higher level of real investment to ensure full employment. The lower level of consumption with the consumption tax makes the attainment of such a level more difficult, as the sale of consumption goods is the major determinant of investment.

In summary: A shift from an income basis to a consumption basis permits a higher rate of capital formation and economic growth in the economy by increasing the percentage of national income saved. But by making the attainment of full employment more difficult, the shift may actually lead to a lower level of capital formation (and more unemployment). Theoretically, appropriate fiscal and monetary policy measures can offset this influence of the tax, but these measures themselves offer certain disadvantages (e.g., popular fear of the deficits and growth of the debt) and there may be serious political obstacles to the use of the appropriate measures.

Other Economic Effects. Consumption-related taxes avoid various distortions in the economy created by personal and corporate income taxes in their present form, such as choice of form of business organization, debt versus equity financing, subsidization of oil production, and the like. The income tax dilemma created by the corporation would be eliminated by exclusive use of consumption taxation. A corporation does not, itself, consume; spending from dividend income and spending based on higher values of securities resulting from retention of earnings would be reached by consumption taxes. Unfortunately, however, consumption related taxes—particularly of the sales and excise variety—create a whole host of distortions of their own, as subsequently discussed.

Administrative Considerations

The consumption approach avoids the problems that arise in the definition of income and the delineation of income from related payments. The troublesome issue of capital gains is completely avoided; to the extent that capital gains increase consumer spending, they lead to higher tax payments; if they do not affect spending, no problem of taxation arises. As subsequently noted, the problems do not vanish completely, since there are serious problems in delimiting spending for consumption and production purposes, the counterpart of the delimination of consumption and production expenses with the income tax. But at least some of the problems are avoided.

The consumption approach offers the possibility of collecting tax from a relatively small number of business firms instead of from large numbers of individual income receivers. This consideration is of great merit in many developing economies but of little importance in the United States.

THE SPENDINGS (EXPENDITURE) TAX[3]

The idea of a tax on consumption expenditures of a direct nature, collected from individuals on the basis of returns, has been considered for several decades. Such a tax was proposed to Congress by the U.S. Treasury in 1942 as a wartime anti-inflationary measure. The tax was actively promoted by the British economist Nicholas Kaldor in the 1950s, used for short periods by India and Ceylon on Kaldor's advise, and considered now and again in other countries.[4] The tax is normally referred to as a spendings tax in the United States, an expenditure tax in Great Britain.

The Nature of the Tax

The spendings tax would be collected from individuals on the basis of returns; in fact, all that would be required is an additional page on the income tax returns. Withholding could be used as with the income tax, although with less precision. Various deductions would presumably be permitted, as at present: exemptions for dependents, medical expenses, contributions, possibly expenditures for education and other items not considered suitable for taxation. The basic difference from the income tax would be the deduction of net realized increases in savings—that is, increase in net wealth (other than from unrealized capital gains) during the year. By this deduction, the figure of actual consumption expenditures would be obtained $(C = Y - S)$ without the hopeless task of actually cumulating consumption spending items. Thus the tax base would be the C of the Simons income definition, rather than $C + \Delta W$. Let us take an example. A person has total income of $20,000. He has four credits for dependents at $750, or $3,000; contributions and other deductions also allowed for income tax of $1,200; deductions for additional items, such as education, authorized for the spendings tax, $800; and net increase in accumulated savings,

---

[3] A recent study is *The Expenditure Tax; Concept, Administration, and Possible Applications* (Washington, D.C.: Advisory Commission on Intergovernmental Relations, 1974). Note also R. E. Slitor, "Administrative Aspects of Expenditures Taxation," in *Broad Based Taxes*, ed. R. A. Musgrave, (Baltimore: Johns Hopkins, 1973), pp. 227–66.

[4] N. Kaldor, *An Expenditure Tax* (London: Allen and Unwin, 1955).

as evidenced, for example, by additional sums in his savings account, of $3,000. His net taxable consumption expenditures would be $20,000—$8,000 or $12,000. The rate structure could be proportional or progressive; if the tax was designed as a temporary fiscal measure to check inflation, the rates could be run to very high figures—to perhaps 1,000 percent, for example. Such a rate would mean that in the top expenditure bracket, each additional dollar spent would create tax liability of $10. As a permanent element in the tax structure, rates would of course be much lower.

The tax could be used as a replacement for the income taxes, but usually the tax is regarded as a supplement for the income tax, perhaps in lieu of a value added or other form of sales tax. It could be applied to the mass of taxpayers, or to a small number of very high-income taxpayers.

The Advantages

Clear distinction must be made between temporary use of the tax as an anti-inflationary measure and more permanent use. With steeply progressive rates and certainty that the tax is temporary, the levy should drastically reduce consumer spending, and some administrative problems intolerable from a longer-range standpoint would be acceptable for an emergency period. On the other hand, the problems of setting up and operating a new tax for a short period are so great as to suggest that this method of fighting inflation not be used except in a major war of some duration.

As a permanent element in the tax structure, the spendings tax offers the advantages of the consumption basis of taxation without the major difficulties, particularly the inequities, of the indirect type of tax— excise and sales taxes. The levy would be adjusted to the personal circumstances of the taxpayer; low-income groups could be excluded completely; and the tax made progressive. Persons spending large sums from accumulated wealth, favored under the income tax, would make more adequate contribution to the government. A person who inherits $1 million, for example, and does not invest it at all, merely living off the capital, could spend $20,000 a year for 50 years with no tax liability under the income tax.

The tax, substituting in part for the income tax, should stimulate savings for reasons noted above and increase the S/Y ratio, and therefore, so long as full employment is maintained, increase real investment and economic growth. It should reduce any adverse effects the income tax may have on work incentives. Primarily the argument centers around the use of the tax as a deliberate instrument to increase the rate of capital formation in the economy. The strength of the case for the tax, therefore, depends in part on the extent to which the income tax reduces the S/Y ratio and investment incentives—effects that in practice are probably not very great. But the case also depends on the importance to the economy of obtaining a higher rate of capital formation; in the United States, as noted in Chapter 24, the case is not strong, since a very substantial change in the S/Y ratio would have limited impact on the rate of economic growth. But in countries in which the S/Y ratio is very low and additional capital formation is urgently required for economic growth, the case becomes much stronger—provided the administrative problems noted below can be solved.

Some other more incidental advantages are claimed. If the tax were used in lieu of income taxes, the problems of capital gains and integration of the personal and corporate taxes would be solved.[5] But these problems would still exist if the tax were used as only a partial replacement for income taxes, as usually planned.

The Problems

The primary question usually raised about the spendings tax relates to implementation, but there are also questions about economic effects.

The Precise Base of the Tax. While the spendings tax may avoid some of the problems of the income tax, it does not escape others and encounters some new ones. Only the major are noted below.

1. *Homeowner versus tenant.* Equality of treatment of homeowner and tenant is particularly difficult to attain. If rent payments of tenants are included in expenditures, tenants are discriminated against compared to owners of existing homes, even if the purchase price of new homes is included in expenditures. The only alternative is to include an imputed rental figure for homeowners, but this encounters all of the problems noted in reference to the same issue with income tax. This problem is particularly acute if the rates are high.

2. *Durable goods.* When a person purchases a home or consumer durables lasting over a period of years, some spreading of the purchase is imperative if progressive rates are used—yet doing so adds to complications of the tax.

3. *Home-produced goods.* The same problem exists as with the income tax, but of much greater magnitude if the tax rates are high.

4. *Consumption versus production expenditures.* With rates of any magnitude, persons are given even greater incentive than under the

---

[5] Capital gains would not directly enter the tax base until realized and then only if the amounts were spent on consumption, but accrued capital gains would affect tax liability if they resulted in higher levels of consumption. The lock-in problem would be avoided.

income tax to treat essentially personal expenditures as business expenses.

Administrative and Compliance Aspects. Without question the tax is more complex for the taxpayer and for the government than the income tax. The difficulty centers around the ascertainment of the net savings during the year. This is not easily ascertained by the individual, let alone checked by the government.

First, it would be necessary to add in items of income not covered by the income tax, such as interest on state and local bonds as well as gifts in cash, as it would be intolerable to let expenditures from these sources go tax free or to allow persons to deduct savings built up from these sources.

Second, it would be necessary for the taxpayer to keep records of net increases in savings during the period. This is not easy to do and not easy to check, particularly with extensive sales and purchases of securities. Net borrowing would have to be reported as well as conversion of assets into cash in turn used to finance spending.

There are related problems of outright evasion. Persons would have great incentive to hoard cash when the tax was introduced and then bring it forth in subsequent years as evidence of saving. Foreign bank accounts would provide additional sources of evasion; they would provide funds to make expeditures without showing evidence of decline in savings. Expenditures abroad financed from income earned outside the country would never be caught, and incentive would be given to use this method to escape tax.

Economic Effects and Equity

In the discussion above of the merits of the tax, the point was noted that the tax—as any consumption tax—would make the task of attaining full employment more difficult. Theoretically this can be overcome by adequate fiscal and monetary adjustment, but in practice this may be difficult to do. Much of the argument centers around the effect on the overall ratio of savings in the economy to national income. There is adequate evidence in the United States that changes in this ratio have relatively little impact on economic growth, even if full employment were maintained.

One of the most objectionable features of the introduction of the tax would be the loss in built-in revenue flexibility. When incomes fall, consumption falls less rapidly, and thus the decline in revenue would be less than with the income tax. But more seriously, once full employment is lost, the tax becomes a destabilizing force because it encourages greater savings and reduced consumption. Thus when a recession begins, Congress would need to suspend or reduce the tax and action may be slow. One of the greatest advantages of the income tax is the sharp drop in revenue that occurs as business activity falls. There are also serious potential "announcement" effects. If Congress debates introduction of the proposal at length, persons will accelerate their purchases to escape the tax; if removal is being considered, consumer spending will be deferred.

The principal equity objection is that of favoring persons at each income level spending relatively small percentages of their income, and particularly the person building up a large fortune and spending little. This is difficult to justify under any usual standards of equity and is contrary to the social objective of lessening excessive inequality of wealth.

Experience

India employed a spendings tax from 1957 to 1966 and Ceylon, 1959–63.[6] Both taxes were aimed at luxury spending of the high-income groups, and exemptions were liberal; there were only 8,000 taxpayers in India and 2,000 in Ceylon. Rates initially ranged from 10 percent to 100 percent in India. The administrative experience was not satisfactory, partly because of defects in the taxes, and the taxes were repealed. The yield was very small (less than one tenth of 1 percent of the total tax revenues in India, 1.1 percent of internal tax revenue in Ceylon) partly because the exemptions were so liberal and the rates so low. The experience, however, is by no means conclusive, given the problems of taxpayer compliance and tax administration generally in these two countries.

THE INDIRECT OR COMMODITY TAX ALTERNATIVE

The traditional form of consumption tax, one of the earliest forms and one used in virtually all countries of the world today, is the indirect type, collected at importation or on business firms on the production or sale of commodities or services.

There are three basic forms of commodity or indirect consumption taxes: customs duties, excises, and sales taxes. The first is not designed to be a revenue measure in the United States; the small amount of revenue actually derived is incidental to the protective function. But customs duties are highly important in developing economies, as they were in the United States a century ago, and discussion of them is deferred to Chapter 25. Excises are levies imposed upon particular commodities, services, or closely related groups of commodities or

---

[6] O. Prakesh, "An Indian View of the Expenditure Tax," *Manchester School of Economic and Social Studies*, vol. 26 (January 1958), pp. 48–67; R. Goode, "New System of Direct Taxation in Ceylon," *National Tax Journal*, vol. 13 (December 1960), pp. 329–40; P. L. Kelley, "Is an Expenditure Tax Feasible?" *National Tax Journal*, vol. 23 (September 1970), pp. 237–54.

services. Traditionally they were imposed at specific rates, that is, specified amounts per physical unit (by weight, dimensions, or single units), but in recent years a number have been given ad valorem (percentage of value) rates. In the British Commonwealth countries there are still traces of the earlier idea that excises must have specific rates. Likewise, traditionally excises were imposed only upon domestic products, customs duties applying to imports. Currently, however, many countries apply their excises to both imported and domestic products. Sales taxes are imposed upon all or a wide range of goods, of necessity at ad valorem rates, and frequently, particularly in the United States and Canada, at a uniform rate.

These commodity taxes are consumption-related taxes if they are shifted forward to the purchasers of the products, raising consumption goods prices relative to factor incomes. To the extent that this assumption is realistic, the tax reduces real income in relation to expenditures on the taxed commodities. If liquor is taxed and liquor prices rise by the amount of the tax, other prices and factor incomes being given, persons who do not purchase liquor will experience no reduction in real income and thus escape any contribution to the governmental activities financed by the tax. To the extent that they do purchase liquor, their real income is reduced in proportion to their purchases, since they pay more for each fifth of whiskey, while their money income is unchanged. They may, of course, escape some of the tax by reducing their purchases. To the extent that they do so, the reduction in their real income is lessened but they suffer an "excess burden" or "deadweight loss," in the sense that they shift from a preferred commodity (Scotch) to a less preferred one (milk).

The same considerations apply to a tax on sales of all commodities. If all prices rise by the amount of the tax while incomes remain unchanged, real incomes fall in proportion to total consumer expenditures made. Such a levy is equivalent to a proportional rate spendings tax without exemption. In this instance, likewise, persons may reduce total purchases by amounts in excess of the tax element; if they do so, they suffer an excess burden from the tax.

The major question involved, therefore, is: Are taxes imposed on the sale of goods actually consumption levies in the sense that they reduce real incomes in relation to consumer spending rather than in relation to the amount of income? Do they actually raise the prices of consumer goods relative to factor incomes, so that persons can vary their tax burdens by altering their consumption but not be altering their income, given the level of consumption? In other words, what is the nature of the distributional impact? We shall use the differential incidence approach, comparing the distributional pattern of sales and excise taxes with that of a tax proportional to income, aggregate demand in the economy remaining unchanged.

SALES TAXATION: SHIFTING

Let us consider first a general retail sales tax applying to all consumption goods and services—all purchases for personal consumption.

Complete Shifting Models

There are two models of price determination under which a tax of this sort will be fully and exactly reflected in higher consumption-goods prices.

Perfect Competition. Let us make the following assumptions: (1) All markets are perfectly competitive; (2) the supplies of all commodities are perfectly elastic within the relevant ranges, or in other words, all goods are produced under conditions of constant cost and output could be increased immediately; and (3) all factor supplies are perfectly inelastic relative to changes in real income caused by higher consumption goods prices.[7] With these assumptions, when a sales tax is introduced, all consumption goods prices would rise by the amount of the tax, while all factor prices would remain unchanged. As noted, we are employing the concept of differential incidence; the height of the tax is assumed to be such as to maintain aggregate factor demand at the same level as that of an alternative tax proportional to income. Essentially the tax drives a wedge between the price received by the seller and the price paid by the consumer. Supplies of all goods will fall until prices have risen by the amount of the tax, under the assumption of perfectly elastic supplies of all goods and unchanged quantities of factors available for use in production. The tax is, therefore, identical in distributional effects to an expenditure tax.

Imperfect Competition with Oligopoly. A second, and more realistic, type of model will also produce full and immediate shifting. Let us assume, as in the analysis of shifting of the corporate income tax: (1) oligopoly, with substantial interdependence of the firms and uniform pricing policies; (2) immediate objective of a satisfactory or target rate of return, with an ill-defined hope of "maximum" profits over a longer period; (3) use of markup-pricing techniques; and (4) constant average cost in the range of operation for the firm and constant-cost conditions for the industry. Under these assumptions a tax on sales, which constitutes a direct and uniform increase in average cost for all firms, will lead to immediate price increases by the amount of the tax. So long as all follow the same pricing policy, all will benefit from the increase. The major difference between a sales tax and a corporate income tax is that the former constitutes a uniform percentage of the sales price

---

[7] The assumptions are consistent with one another only if all outputs employ the same factor combinations.

for all firms whereas the latter does not. Total sales of all commodities are, of course, less, but this is offset, in terms of aggregate factor demand, by the avoidance of the alternative levy, an income tax proportional to income.

Modifications from the Uniform Pattern

Modifications from this uniform pattern are obvious if the assumptions are relaxed.

Conditions Other than Constant Cost—Specialized Factors. Obviously constant-cost conditions cannot prevail over a wide segment of the economy because of scarcity of specialized resources in various fields, e.g., land best suited for wine grapes, even if aggregate factor demand is unchanged. The conclusions of complete shifting would still be valid if relative outputs did not change as a result of the use of the sales tax in lieu of an income tax—that is, if with the two taxes the consumption patterns would be the same. This is most unlikely. Therefore, under more realistic assumptions, some shifting of prices of factors specialized to certain industries, such as land for wine grapes, will occur with modifications in the pattern of distribution. Some factor owners will gain; others will lose.

Elasticity of General Factor Supplies. While under the assumptions aggregate factor demand remains unchanged, almost certainly the pattern of demand for major groups of factors will be different with a sales tax than with the alternative income tax. Since factor supplies are not, in fact, perfectly elastic, the shifting in relative demands will alter their prices, with consequent redistributional effects. The nature and magnitude cannot be predicted. Total factor supplies may be affected by the form which the reduced real income takes, since persons may react differently to reductions in real income affecting them through price increases than they do to ones involving reduction in diposable income.

Since the overall net effect of the use of a sales tax in lieu of an income tax is presumably to shift resources from consumption to investment, some reduction in the overall rate of return to capital may be expected.

Taxation of Capital Goods. In practice, sales taxes are often not confined to consumption goods, but apply also to final capital goods—industrial machinery, building materials, office supplies, and the like. Thus additional money capital is required to acquire a given quantity of capital goods. With an inelastic supply of money capital, the return to the owners of money capital would be reduced, consequently reducing the return on savings. Thus, if the tax applied to all consumption goods and to all final-product capital goods with perfect competition in all markets, the former would reduce real income in proportion to consumption and the latter in proportion to savings, leading to the same overall distributional effect as a proportional income tax. If the supply of money capital is perfectly elastic, however, return to savings will not fall.

With the nonperfectly competitive model, the firms, it may reasonably be assumed, will regard the tax as an element in the cost of the capital goods, and depreciate the larger sum (or treat the tax as a current expense). As a consequence, the element will be reflected in higher prices of the consumption goods produced with the capital goods and be passed forward to consumers, but in a very uneven fashion, as various industries differ in the degree of capital intensivity. Under these circumstances, there is no necessity that the overall return on money capital will fall; the portion of the tax on capital goods is not necessarily distributed in relation to saving.

Exemptions.   In practice, sales taxes virtually never apply to all goods and services. Exempted commodities will not rise in price; relative outputs will increase as consumption shifts to these goods, with consequent alteration in relative prices of factors specialized to the industries losing and gaining output. Persons consuming relatively high percentages of tax-exempt goods will, of course, experience less tax burden than with a universal tax, and others will pay relatively larger amounts.

Exceptions Relating to the Nature of Competition.   A major question relates to the applicability to actual markets of the two models that allow complete shifting.

The perfectly competitive model is not a useful one for analyzing the reactions to taxes in the modern economy because the assumptions are too far removed from those of the real world. While the nonperfectly competitive model may be more realistic, the precise assumptions employed in the analysis above are not likely to be universally realized.

1. *Failure of some firms to increase prices.*   It is possible in nonperfectly competitive models that some of the firms will not raise prices in response to the tax. They may seek to increase sales at the expense of their competitors; in doing so they may make price increases unprofitable for all firms. Or the firms in an industry may decide, individually or collectively, that the demand for the product is sufficiently elastic that an increase will not be profitable—or in other words, they believe they have already been maximizing profits for the firms as a group and that full increases will be unprofitable. This is not too likely a situation, however, since the usual concept of demand elasticity is not relevant when all prices are rising. There is less danger of loss of sales to substitute commodities. In other words, even if firms were maximizing profits for the group in the old pattern of prices, they will no longer be doing so after other prices have risen.

Whenever some prices do not increase, the burden of the tax will not be distributed in relation to overall consumer spending. Purchases of some goods will give rise to tax liability; purchase of others will not. At the same time, the owners of factors in some lines of production will experience declines in their real incomes. This will lead ultimately to movement of these factors out of the industry and thus to greater shifting over a long-run period than occurs immediately after the tax is imposed, as noted below.

2. *Tax-free competition in geographically limited jurisdictions.* In some instances, firms are subject to competition of firms located in nearby areas in which there is no tax or the rate is lower. Merchants in northern Maryland and southern Pennsylvania, for example, are subject to competition of Wilmington merchants not subject to sales tax. Under such circumstances, direct shifting may prove to be impossible, and departure of some firms is necessary to allow the remaining ones to operate with larger volume and cover all costs. If the supply of retailing service were perfectly elastic, the retailing would vanish in the taxed area. But, of course, it is not, and departure of some firms will allow the remaining ones to cover costs. But in the process land values will fall, and some of the burden will rest on landowners.

Separate Quotation of Tax

The tendency to shift forward is increased in the United States and Canada by the practice, required by law in the provinces and in many states and followed in all, by retailers of adding the tax separately to the price at the time of payment rather than readjusting prices. This rule was introduced under the pressure of the retailer groups. These groups sought it for several reasons: They wished to avoid blame for price increases; they believed that it would facilitate uniformity of action by all firms; and it avoided the necessity of adjusting large numbers of prices and departure from established price lines (e.g., prices ending in 95 cents, traditional sale of neckties at prices ending in even dollar or half-dollar figures).

Without question, separate quotation does increase uniformity of action and facilitates shifting in NPC markets.[8] If prices were actually readjusted, firms would be uncertain as to the precise adjustment others would make, particularly because of the price-line phenomenon. Also, there is less likelihood of firms considering demand aspects

---

[8] As subsequently noted, price increases by retailers by the exact amount of the tax involve complete shifting of tax only if average cost remains constant in the relevant range of sales. If it does not, a price increase by the amount of the tax results in overshifting if average cost is less at the lower output, in undershifting if average cost is greater at the lower output.

since with the practice of treating all goods uniformly at the cash register, individual prices are not adjusted at all. The typical consumer probably tends to react to the quoted price (except on very expensive items) rather than to the price-plus-tax figure, and, therefore, demand elasticity may be less than otherwise; the retailer may not consider the question at all in his treatment of the tax.

Nonretail Taxes

The assumption has been made thus far that the tax is imposed on the retail sale. Sales taxes in many countries, however, are imposed prior to the retail level. There are several differences with nonretail taxes.

Successive Shifting. Since several successive price changes will be necessary, almost inevitably there is greater danger of deviation between the tax and consequent price increases.

Pyramiding. Wholesale and retail merchants frequently establish prices on the basis of percentage markups; a given percentage is applied to purchase price to determine the selling price. Thus the markup is applied to the tax element, and the price increase to the consumer exeeds the tax received by the government. Competition should in time eliminate the excess, but traditional pricing methods are so strongly entrenched that readjustment may be very imperfect—particularly if the per unit costs of the firms rise as their sales fall.

Longer Period Adjustments

Over a long-run period, the price reactions suggested by various imperfectly competitive models and the perfectly competitive model are similar. If firms are no longer covering all costs, some must leave the business and the remaining firms will again be able to cover costs, either through greater volume or ability to raise prices. Price must at least cover average cost, regardless of the nature of competition. If there have been excess profits, however, some of the tax may be borne by the owners of the business for long periods.

There are also dynamic influences arising out of the change in the S/Y ratio produced by the tax.

Empirical Studies

Few attempts have been made to study the actual effects of changes in sales tax rates on prices. When the state taxes were first introduced Robert Murray Haig and Carl Shoup of Columbia University supervised an extensive interview study, which inquired of retailers in New

York, Illinois, and Michigan about their responses to the tax.[9] They found that most retailers in Detroit were shifting (92 percent), about half (47 percent) in Chicago, and a much lower percentage in New York where the rate was low and the tax thought to be temporary. Separate quotation of tax was much less common in the early period of the taxes. In more recent years, casual observations suggest that retailers almost universally add the tax to the price, except in some instances on large value items where the tax becomes an element in bargaining, and apparently do not make noticeable changes in pretax prices when the tax is raised. Therefore few persons have bothered to examine the question scientifically. A study by Nancy Sidhu sought to test the shifting hypothesis, using Bureau of Labor Statistics price data in eight metropolitan areas.[10] The results showed substantial forward shifting in three fourths of the instances, but little shifting in the other fourth. There was clear evidence that proximity to a border reduced the ability to shift; shifting was least in Chicago, Detroit, and Washington, D.C. Elimination of other influences on prices is difficult in studies of this type.

It should be noted, of course, that price increases by the exact amount of the tax do not demonstrate exact shifting of the tax; they do so only under the assumption of constant average cost in the relevant output ranges. If average cost is less at the lower sales volume but prices rise by the full amount of the tax, the tax has been overshifted and profits are increased; the reverse is true if average cost is higher at the lower sales levels.

EXCISE TAXES: SHIFTING

Next let us consider an excise tax levied upon the production or sale of a particular commodity. The consequent price readjustments and therefore distributional effects will depend upon: (1) the nature of competition in the markets for the product, (2) the nature of the cost conditions under which the product is produced. These in turn may differ somewhat according to the time period considered.

Perfect Competition

With the perfectly competitive model, individual sellers have no control over price; price can change in response to the tax only if supply (or demand) schedules shift. There are three possible relevant cases, illustrated on Figure 14–1.

---

[9] R. M. Haig and C. S. Shoup, *The Sales Tax in the American States* (New York: Columbia University Press, 1934).

[10] Nancy D. Sidhu, "The Effects of Changes in Sales Tax Rates on Retail Prices," *Proceedings of National Tax Association for 1971*, pp. 720–32.

FIGURE 14–1
Response of Commodity Price to Excise Tax

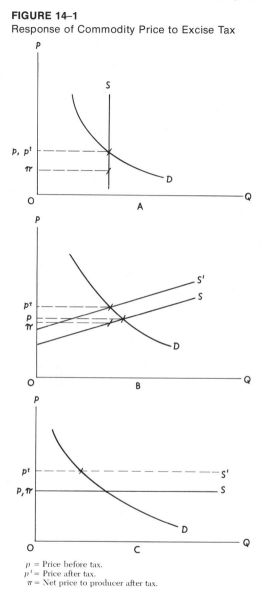

p = Price before tax.
p^t= Price after tax.
π = Net price to producer after tax.

Perfectly Inelastic Supply. If the supply of the commodity is perfectly inelastic (Figure 14–1A), as that of a perishable commodity already produced in a short period of time, the tax cannot affect price. Price remains at p; the net price to the producer is π. Market supply, by definition, is given; individual sellers have no control over price. The tax will reduce the real income of the owners of the business or of other factors used in production.

Partially Elastic Supply. The more realistic assumption is that the supply has some elasticity, as shown in Figure 14–1B. This is the typical market and short-run situation and the long-run supply situation in an increasing cost industry. Accordingly, when the tax is imposed, the supply curve at market prices (S′) shifts to the left on the chart (less will be supplied at each price because of the tax); price will rise to p' as output falls; the exact amount of the change depending on the relative slopes of the supply and demand curves. The price to the producer after tax is π. Thus the tax is shared between the consumers of the products and the factor owners. In a short-run period, if supply prices for the various factors are given regardless of the quantity used, the burden not shifted forward will rest upon the owners of the firms. But over a period of time, if the industry is one of increasing cost conditions and thus the long-run supply curve is also upward sloping, the reduced output of the commodity will reduce the prices paid for the factors of production specialized to the industry and they will share in the burden. The owners of the business per se will escape from the burden (in their capacity as owners) through flow of firms out of the field. Let us pursue the wine example noted above. Suppose that a tax is imposed on the sale of wine. As a consequence, the price of wine rises and output declines. But as it does, the demand for and the rental price of land best suited for wine grape growing (but not equally well suited for anything else)[11] will decline. A portion of the burden, therefore, will rest upon the owners of the land used in the production of wine grapes. The remainder will rest upon the consumers of wine. The relative division between consumer and factor owner depends upon the exact nature of the cost schedule and the demand elasticity.

Perfectly Elastic Supply. There is also a third possible case, namely, that in which the supply over a long-run period is perfectly elastic (Figure 14–1C). This was the one used in the initial model employed to analyze the reaction to a sales tax earlier in the chapter. If the industry is one of constant-cost conditions—as it could be over some range of output for an industry using only a small fraction of the total supply of each factor—price must rise by the full amount of the tax, as firms will continue to flow out of the industry until the average profit rate is restored.

There are other possible influences upon shifting of an excise tax as compared to an income tax. For example, the supply schedules of various factors may be somewhat different, as persons react differently to a reduction in disposable take-home pay than they do to higher prices for certain goods purchased. The persons involved are somewhat different as well; consumers of fur coats, as a class, may react

---

[11] This is in fact the case; much of the land used in producing wine in California, the source of most of the U.S. wine output, has low productivity for other purposes.

differently to a reduction in real income than do payers of income taxes as a group.

Complete Monopoly

The situation of a complete monopolist is different. If the firm is maximizing profit prior to the introduction of the tax and thus marginal revenue equals marginal cost, it will find, typically, some increase in price advantageous, because marginal cost is increased by the amount of the tax (Figure 14–2).[12] But under what appear to be

FIGURE 14–2
Response of Price to Excise Tax, Monopoly

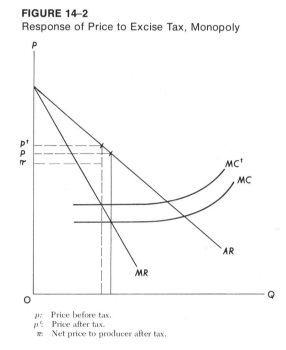

p: Price before tax.
p': Price after tax.
π: Net price to producer after tax.

reasonable assumptions, the seller will raise price by less than the tax. The seller will reduce output to reequate marginal cost and marginal revenue; therefore marginal revenue will be increased by the amount of the increase in marginal cost. But the slope of the average revenue (demand) curve is much less steep than that of the marginal revenue curve, and thus the increase in price (p to p') will be less than the cost increase. Exception to this rule will arise only out of peculiar curvature of the demand curve.

---

[12] A specific rate tax is assumed, for simplicity.

Nonperfectly Competitive Models

Neither the perfectly competitive nor the perfect monopoly models are adequate for analysis of distributional effect of a tax. The conditions in few industries approach those of the assumptions of the perfectly competitive model and excises are rarely imposed on the outputs of these industries. Complete monopoly is relatively rare. Unfortunately there is not—and probably cannot be—a single workable model of the vast range of conditions that lie between perfect competition on the one hand and complete monopoly on the other. For purposes of anlaysis, however, the model presented above in the analysis of a general sales tax will be used.

When an excise tax is imposed on the product of such an industry, all competing firms experience a uniform increase in average cost per unit of product. A tax increase of 2 cents a gallon for gasoline, for example, hits all competing firms equally per gallon sold; a tax of 20 percent on television sets strikes all firms equally per dollar of sales. Under the pricing assumptions employed in the model, the reaction will be to increase the price of the product by the amount of the tax. So long as all follow the same policy, all will gain from the increase, provided the original price was less than the price that would have maximized the profits of the firms as a group—essentially the complete monopoly price. Output of course will be reduced, since less can be sold at the higher prices. Under the differential concept of incidence employed, aggregate demand in the economy will be maintained; the reduction in factor demand due to the higher prices will be equivalent to that created by repeal of the alternative proportional income tax.

Deviations. There are likely, however, to be deviations from this standard pattern. First, the firms may realize that the demand for the product is sufficiently elastic that the price increase will reduce the profits of all firms; in other words, the previous price was the optimal one for the firms as a whole. This is much more likely than with a sales tax because other prices are not rising. There is some evidence that movie theaters were not fully shifting the tax on admissions prior to the repeal of the tax in 1965 because of high demand elasticity arising out of the development of television.

Second, especially in periods of overcapacity, some firms may not go along with the increase in an effort to raise sales volume. As a consequence, other firms will find the increase impossible because of loss of sales.

Third, changes in the prices of specialized factors may occur, as with the perfectly competitive model. A tax on wine selling in an NPC market, for example, will reduce the sales of wine and lessen the demand for wine-grape land. This is a true increasing-cost industry, and a portion of the tax will be borne by the landowners—the owners of the specialized resources. This could be offset by increased purchasing made possible by elimination of the alternate income tax, but this is unlikely since the greater spending is likely to spread over many goods.

Finally, the use of the markup system of pricing leads distributors and retailers to raise prices by more than the amount of a tax imposed prior to the retail level. A manufacturer has been selling a product at $100; the retailer (to keep the example simple) applies a markup of 40 percent of cost and sells at $140. A tax of 10 percent is imposed on the manufacturer, who raises the price to $110. The retailer applies a 40 percent markup to $110 (and thus to the tax) and raises the price to $154; the government has received $10 tax, but the consumer is paying $14 more for the merchandise.

Longer-Period Considerations. An immediate price increase by the amount of the tax does not necessarily indicate that the tax is shifted to the consumer over a long period of time. First, all firms may experience loss of sales. With very tight oligopoly but failure to maximize profits of the firms as a group, a secondary set of price increases to shift forward the increased per unit cost at the reduced sales volume is possible; this is similar in effect to pyramiding. But uniformity of action to bring this about is unlikely. Alternatively, the reduced volume may lower specialized factor prices sufficiently to offset the effects of lower volume. Or some firms may leave the industry, allowing the remaining firms to restore their old volume of output and profit margins.

If the firms are unable to shift fully immediately after the tax is imposed, there will be no further adjustments if they were previously earning sufficiently more than the average rate of return to cover the tax element. If they are not, some firms must sooner or later leave the field. When they do, there are two alternatives: The remaining firms may be able to raise prices again because of lessened competition, or they may benefit from greater sales volume and earn a normal profit without further price increases. As with pyramiding, if this policy does lead to higher rates of profit, presumably either competition of existing firms or entry of new ones will eliminate the additional profit, although not necessarily reduce prices. But if it does not, if the higher price merely serves to offset the decline in volume and higher average cost, the pyramiding may remain more or less indefinitely, since the firms are not earning more than an average rate of profit.

Empirical Studies of Price Responses to Excise Taxes

Empirical studies of price reactions to commodity taxes have been relatively rare, even though initial attempts were made as early as the 1880s. The technique is simple: Prices of taxed commodities are compared before and after a tax change. This technique measures only immediate commodity price adjustments and not factor price or longer-period adjustments. The major limitation is the inability to isolate the tax influence from other sources of price change. Statements made by business firms at the time of excise tax changes often suggest that the tax has served as a stimulus to make changes that had previously been under consideration; thus the actual change reflects not only the tax influence but that of other accumulated forces as well.

Analyses were made of responses of prices of electrical appliances to 1954 legislation that reduced the tax rate from 10 to 5 percent. The studies utilized list prices of manufacturers; while by no means all sales were made at list, the behavior of these prices was probably a reasonably good measure of overall behavior. A study made at the time with information supplied by manufacturers and mail-order houses indicated that of 274 models, prices were immediately reduced on 94 percent. In addition, the data showed strong evidence of pyramiding, especially on larger appliances; the median reduction was 4.8 percent of the retail price, although the tax alone constituted only about 2.5 percent of the price. [13] A study made a decade later by H. L. Johnson [14] with more complete data and a larger number of models (676) showed generally similar results, although with a somewhat smaller percentage of price changes (91 percent of small appliances, 76 percent of larger) and somewhat less tendency toward pyramiding. The extent of pyramiding was shown to be related to the degree of concentration in the production of the particular type of appliance.

Further evidence of the reaction is provided by a study of Bureau of Labor Statistics data of changes in prices of various items affected by the 1954 reductions, using actual, not list, prices. Although the overall price index rose slightly between March and June 1954, during the period in which the reduction became effective, the indices of the taxed items fell in all instances and with several types of appliances by percentages in excess of the price reduction.

Following the reduction in excise taxes in 1965, the Council of Economic Advisers requested the Bureau of Labor Statistics to collect detailed information on price responses to tax reductions. A series of reports were issued; one of September 22, 1965 showed that for 99 percent of the sellers involved the tax reduction had been reflected in lower prices. On a number of items, such as women's handbags, reductions by the amount of tax were universal. Manufacturers of a few items raised their prices to offset the tax reduction (pens, pencils,

---

[13] John F. Due, "The Effect of the 1954 Reduction in Federal Excise Taxes upon the List Prices of Electrical Appliances," *National Tax Journal*, vol. 7 (September 1954), pp. 222–26.

[14] Harry L. Johnson, "Tax Pyramiding and the Manufacturer's Excise Tax Reduction of 1954," *National Tax Journal*, vol. 17 (September 1964), pp. 297–302.

matches), but these were of minor consequence in the overall picture. While most retailers passed the tax reduction forward, from 30 to 50 percent of those of electric ranges, movie cameras, and television tube replacements did not do so. Table 14–1 summarizes the changes.

TABLE 14–1

Approximate Percentage of Sellers Who Passed on Federal Excise Tax Cut by August 1965

	Retailers*			Percentage of Manu-facturers
	Completely Passed on Tax Cut	Partially Passed on Tax Cut	Did Not Pass on Tax Cut	Who Passed on Tax Cut
Retailers' excise tax				
Women's handbags	100	†	—	—
Men's wristwatches	100	†	—	—
Home permanent kit	95	—	5	—
Manufacturers' excise tax				
New automobiles	100	—	—	100
Optional auto equipment (factory-installed)	100	—	†	100
Air-conditioners	80	†	20	100
Television sets	80	†	20	100
Refrigerator-freezers	75	†	25	100
Ranges	60	5	35	100
Movie cameras	60	5	35	95
Typewriters	95	5	†	100
Adding machines	95	5	†	100
Small TV replacement tubes	40	5	55	100
Phonograph records	n.a.	n.a.	n.a.	‡
Gold equipment	n.a.	n.a.	n.a.	30
Pens and mechanical pencils	n.a.	n.a.	n.a.	0
Matches	n.a.	n.a.	n.a.	0
Stamp tax				
Playing cards	30	15	55	100

* Based on a nationwide sample of retailers.
† Less than 5 percent.
‡ Excise tax was partially passed on by all major manufacturers.
n.a.—Not available.
Source: *Report to the President on Excise Tax Reduction from the Council of Economic Advisers,* September 23, 1965.

Subsequently, two detailed studies were made of the immediate reactions of prices of commodities on which excises had been reduced in 1965. The more extensive study, by O. Brownlee and G. L. Perry, examined Bureau of Labor Statistics price data by commodity class over the period in which the excise reduction became effective.[15] The

---

[15] Oswald Brownlee and George L. Perry, "The Effects of the 1965 Federal Excise Tax Reduction on Prices," *National Tax Journal,* vol. 20 (September 1967), pp. 235–49.

study concluded that prices of commodities subject to retail excises fell immediately by the amount of the tax, except for admissions and club dues. Prices of goods subject to manufacturers' excises also fell immediately, with a few exceptions, typically by the amount of the tax with little evidence of pyramiding. The failure to find extensive evidence of pyramiding may be attributed in part to greater encouragement for price increases that other determinants of pricing were giving in 1965 than in 1954. An alternative explanation is that the additional 11 years of operation of the tax may have resulted in squeezing out of more pyramiding. Finally, the earlier studies were based on list prices, the 1965 study on actual prices, and less pyramiding would be expected.

The second study was confined to automotive accessories and replacement parts, utilizing price schedules developed and used in the industry.[16] The analysis showed a peculiar result. Prices of about half the items, primarily accessories, were reduced by the pyramided amount of the tax reduction. A group of items periodically replaced, such as spark plugs, showed some downward adjustment. The prices of irregularly replaced parts remained unchanged. Demand for these items without question is inelastic and the sellers saw no reason, therefore, to reduce prices at all. This reaction illustrates one of the exceptions noted in preceding sections to the basic NPC shifting model: Demand elasticity may affect shifting in some instances. The firms may have been charging the maximum joint profit price before tax was imposed; they made no increases in prices when the tax went on and did not reduce prices when it was repealed. Or, alternatively, they saw in the tax reduction the possibility of moving closer to the maximum joint-profit level.

CONCLUSION

Thus in conclusion, given the typical market conditions in the economy of the United States and most countries:

1.   An excise tax may be regarded as a tax related to consumption of the taxed commodity, and a sales tax as one related to consumption generally. Both taxes represent additions to cost that tend to be reflected, usually rather quickly, in higher prices. Accordingly, real incomes are reduced in relation to purchase of the taxed goods. This conclusion is based on the differential approach to taxation, aggregate factor demand being assumed as given.

---

[16] F. O. Woodard and Harvey Siegelman, "Effects of the 1965 Excise Tax Reduction upon the Prices of Automotive Replacement Parts," *National Tax Journal*, vol. 20 (September 1967), pp. 250–58.

On the whole, the forward shifting of the taxes is more likely to be complete over a long-run period than directly after the tax is imposed, but even in the immediate market period, shifting is likely to be substantial.

2. There are certain to be exceptions. With complete monopoly or oligopolists already maximizing joint profits, some of the tax will be absorbed from excess profits. In the short run, the owners of firms may find it necessary to absorb the tax because demand conditions do not permit price increases, or costs per unit rise when sales fall. In increasing cost industries, prices of factors specialized to the industries losing sales will decline. Prices of major factor groups may possibly rise if the reduced real income reduces the quantity available on the market but effects may be less than with income taxes because of the price illusion; workers are less prone to react to consumption goods price increases than to declines in disposable income.

EXCISE TAXATION—STRUCTURE AND EVALUATION

The remainder of this chapter is concerned with excise taxes—their structure and evaluation—the following chapter with sales taxes.

Tables 14–2 and 14–3 shows the relative use of excise taxation in the United States with a breakdown of major types. The number of excises used at the federal level was sharply reduced in 1965 when a number

TABLE 14–2

State Excise Tax Collections, United States, 1975

Tax	Total Revenue (millions of dollars)
Motor fuels	$8,256
Liquor	1,958
Tobacco products	3,286
Parimutuel betting	676
Amusements	99
Other	794
Total, excises*	15,069

* Taxes on utilities and insurance companies excluded.
Source: U.S. Bureau of the Census, *State Tax Collections in 1975.*

imposed during World War II or earlier were repealed, and the automobile excise tax was repealed in 1971.

Excise taxes fall into three distinct patterns, with different objectives and criteria of evaluation.

TABLE 14–3
Federal Excise Taxes in the United States 1976

Tax	Rate	Revenue 1975 (millions of dollars)	Revenue as Percentage of Total Excise Tax Revenue
Liquor:			
Distilled spirits	$10.50/proof gal.[1]	3,865	22
Wine	Varies with alcoholic content	177	1
Beer	$9 barrel[2]	1,308	8
Total, including miscellaneous		5,351	31
Tobacco:			
Cigarettes	$4 per thousand[3]	2,261	13
Cigars	Various	51	1
Total, including miscellaneous		2,315	14
Highway trust fund:			
Gasoline	4¢ gal.	3,980	24
Diesel fuel	4¢ gal.	370	2
Tires	10¢ lb.	698	4
Trucks and parts	10%, 8% of price	659	4
Oil	6¢ gal.	91	1
Truck use tax	$3 per yr. per 1,000 gross over 26,000 pounds	208	1
Total		6,006	36
Airway user taxes:			
Passenger	8% fare	751	4
Freight	5% charge	47	1
Total, including miscellaneous		851	5
Telephone service	6%	2,024	12
Sugar		104	1
Firearms, fishing rods	10%	84	1
Coin operated gaming devices	$250 per yr.	12	neg.
Total, including miscellaneous		16,848	100

[1] Thus, for example, $2 per fifth of 85 proof.
[2] About 2.7¢ per 12 oz. can.
[3] 7¢ per pack.
Source: U.S. Treasury Bulletin, May 1976

Excises Designed to Improve Efficiency in the Use of Resources (Sumptuary Excises)

As explained in Chapter 2, optimal use of resources requires that the marginal rates of substitution (*MRS*) be equal to the marginal rates of transformation (*MRT*) among all commodities. If this situation is not attained, shifting of resources from production of one commodity to that of another to bring equality of *MRS* and *MRT* will result in greater overall satisfaction from the use of resources, given the pattern of income distribution. But, as also noted in Chapter 2, various circumstances may result in failure to attain this optimal position. In brief, these circumstances include, in addition to pure public goods:

1. Differences in competition with various industries, with greater monopolistic power in some than in others; differences in the degree of monopoly power by labor unions in some fields compared to others; differences in prices paid for factors in various fields.

2. External economies in the production and use of some commodities. In such instances the real gain to society exceeds the gain realized by the producers.

3. External diseconomies in the production or use of the commodities; thus all of the costs to society do not appear as costs to the producers, and therefore prices are artificially low relative to real economic costs; output of these goods will be excessive compared to that of others.

As explained in Chapters 3, 4, and 5, there are various means by which society can deal with these problems: preventing monopoly power and undertaking or subsidizing the production of goods with significant externalities, for example. A major method usable in some instances is the placing of an excise tax on those goods whose prices are uneconomically low and output excessively great because of external diseconomies—the creation of costs to society that do not appear as costs to the producer. These may be called sumptuary excises, designed to restrict consumption to economically justifiable levels.

Pollution Taxes. One of the best current examples, one receiving attention only in recent years,[17] relates to pollution, as noted in Chapter 4. A manufacturing plant dumps wastes into a river and pollutes the water supply, makes swimming impossible, and kills the fish, and it pours pollutants, odors, and noise into the air as well. These are real costs to society that are not borne by the producers; the prices of the products, therefore, are too low, and production is excessive. Pollution of the air by motor vehicles is another; car users do not pay for these costs. There are two alternative solutions—to set limits on the permissible levels of pollutants, or to impose an excise tax on the product. Setting standards may be criticized as using unnecessary force; it is arguable that the market mechanism may be employed to accomplish the result through excise taxes that place all costs on the consumer. The excise alternative allows the firms to continue to operate but requires consumers to cover all costs for which the production is responsible. Decisions on taxation versus setting standards must be based on a weighing of alternative considerations relating to the seriousness of the particular pollutant and the relative feasibility of direct control and taxes. If a tax is used, the objective is to establish the tax rate suffi-

---

[17] As a consequence of laissez-faire Victorianism, for decades person could freely pollute a river with wastes from their factory but could be arrested for swimming nude in the river.

ciently high as to fully cover the costs to society arising from the pollutant—an objective not easily attained because of the problems involved in measuring pollution costs.

Liquor and Tobacco Taxes.   The other field in which the objective of offsetting costs of external diseconomies has played a role in justification of excises, although not the primary reason for their use, is taxation of liquor and tobacco products.[18] Use of liquor to excess obviously creates external costs that are not included in the prices of the products: automobile accidents, broken homes, lost time from work, illness, and the like.[19] The link between cigarette smoking and lung cancer has by now been well established. Essentially, without governmental intervention the prices of these products are too low and consumption too great, since the users are not paying all of the costs for which the use of the products is responsible. As a consequence, an excise tax to cover these external costs is warranted.

The great popularity of these taxes and the use of very high rates, often as much as 100 percent of price net of tax, clearly unrelated to any measure of external costs, indicates that other considerations as well play a part in the actual excise tax structures. There is a substantial carryover of Victorian notions of sin—that people should not really use these products, which is in some sense "immoral," and therefore if they wish to do so they can justifiably be made to pay a high tax as a type of penalty. Society has moved a long way from the fanatical antiliquor attitudes of the turn of the century but the old reasoning still influences legislative bodies. The attraction of the levies is increased by their high productivity of revenue, the belief that demand is inelastic, and the relative absence of complaints. But clearly they have reached heights that are unwarranted on an external costs basis. Experience with alcoholic beverages provides an excellent example of the evils of attempting to prohibit the use of a good because of its external costs; prohibition in the United States was an unmitigated failure because a large portion of the population, probably a majority[20] opposed the ban on use of the product, although persons were willing— as witnessed by the acceptance of the very high tax rates—to pay high taxes to cover these external costs. Control of marijuana might possibly better be attained through taxes than prohibition. On the other hand, most of society would agree that the external diseconomies of use of heroin are so great that prohibition is necessary, even if difficult to enforce.

---

[18] Carl Shoup designates these as addictive or habit-forming commodities. *Public Finance* (Chicago: Aldine, 1970), pp. 271–72.

[19] For evidence, see the study, *Beer, Wine and Spirits: Beverage Differences and Public Policy in Canada* (Toronto: Alcoholic Beverage Study Committee, 1973).

[20] The prohibition movement was an excellent example of how a well-organized fanatical minority group can obtain passage of legislation in all likelihood opposed by a majority of the people.

Nature of Liquor and Tobacco Taxes. With minor exceptions, liquor and tobacco taxes are imposed with specific rates and thus upon physical units rather than on an ad valorem basis. Rates are shown in Table 14–3. There are several reasons. One, historically the primary explanation, is ease of application. No valuation is required; only the physical quantity need be ascertained. Avoidance of the valuation problem is particularly important because of the high rates of tax. But related has been the principle—partly arising from the sumptuary nature of the levy—that the amount of tax should be uniform per unit of the product or constituent element of it, that the "tax penalty" a person should pay for using the goods should be related to physical quantity. Another consideration of more recent concern is the desire to avoid distorting effects upon distribution channels that arise with ad valorem taxes at the manufacturing level, as explained in detail next in the chapter. The distortion would be potentially very severe because of the high rates of duty.[21] Finally, the specific rate has the political advantage of obscuring the actual ratio of tax to selling price, which is often 100 percent or more of price exclusive of tax.

The specific rates are the source of some complaint, particularly discrimination against the cheaper brands of the commodities, such as cigarettes, which distorts resource allocation by lessening relative use. Also, since the cheaper brands are used primarily in the lower-income groups, the taxes are more regressive than otherwise. The purchaser pays no more tax on the most expensive top-quality whiskey than on the cheapest; thus the relative after-tax price differential is lessened.

The units to which tax applies are often constructive rather than actual units of the product. With distilled spirits the tax is usually applied on the basis of a 100-proof gallon, or 50-percent alcohol by volume.[22] The aim is to make the tax uniform on the basis of the ultimate object of the tax—the alcohol involved. Beer is taxed on the actual gallons of output. With wine, rough adjustments to alcoholic content are made, typically with two rates: one for table wine, with actual alcoholic content under 12.5 percent, and the other for dessert wines (port, sherry, etc.) with over 12.5 percent alcohol (these wines are typically about 20 percent alcohol). Champagne and other sparkling wines draw a much higher figure, often comparable to that on distilled spirits. Tobacco products are more frequently taxed on physical units.

Control measures in the liquor, beer, and tobacco tax fields are typically very drastic compared to those with other taxes. Rigid licens-

---

[21] This consideration alone led the Canadian Royal Commission on Taxation to conclude that the Canadian excise levies should not be converted to an ad valorem base. *Report of the Royal Commission on Taxation*, vol. 5 (Ottawa: Queen's Printer, 1966), pp. 87–88.

[22] Thus, if a particular whisky were 80 percent proof, the tax rate applied would be 80 percent of the basic tax rate.

ing requirements are established; firms cannot produce the commodities without specific authorization, and physical inspection is intensive.

Objections to Liquor and Tobacco Taxes.   Several objections can be advanced against the sumptuary excises as they exist today in the United States and most countries:

1.   There is no attempt to adjust the rates on the basis of social costs for which the products are responsible, and the high figures in part reflect simply their high revenue productivity because of the inelasticity of demand and the sin attitude. To the extent that the figures exceed the external costs, these levies have the same undesirable consequences as the general revenue excises noted below.

2.   Because of the inelastic demands, the tax may be paid out of funds that would otherwise be used to provide necessities of life for the family, particularly in the lower-income groups. It is particularly difficult to gauge the extent of this reaction; interview surveys about liquor consumption patterns are useless as persons will not report correctly. Families are not going to admit that their children go without milk so that they can buy liquor.

The actual elasticity of demand is open to some question. A study in Canada suggests that the price elasticity of demand for beer is $-.6$, but for distilled spirits is -1.6, and for wine -1.0.[23]

3.   On equity grounds, while these goods may be regarded as luxuries, they are widely consumed in the lower-income groups. As a consequence, the absolute burden is likely to be significant on the lower-income groups, and the burden may well be regressive. This is particularly true of cigarettes and beer.

Few studies of distributional effects of excise taxes by income class have been made except in the U.S. Treasury, and these have not been published. Such evidence as is available from the work of Musgrave and a recent article by T. S. Kalmus[24] suggests that the tax on cigarettes is extremely regressive, the expenditures constituting only one fifth as great a percentage of income in the higher-income brackets as in the lower. Taxes on beer are somewhat progressive in the lower-income brackets and regressive in the higher. Liquor taxes appear to be progressive relative to income. A Canadian study shows that the tax on beer is highly regressive above $10,000 income, but slightly progressive up to $6,000 and proportional to $10,000. The tax on distilled spirits is regressive to $5,000 income and progressive above; the tax on wine is proportional to $10,000, progressive above.[25]

---

[23] *Beer, Wine and Spirits*, p. 179.

[24] T. S. Kalmus, "The Burden of Federal Excise Taxes by Income Classes," *Quarterly Review of Economics and Business*, vol. 10 (Spring 1970), pp. 17–24.

[25] *Beer, Wine and Spirits*, p. 138.

4. The very high rates encourage illegal production, particularly of distilled spirits, often of poor quality. The rates sometimes lead to smuggling, particularly among states where rates differ and between the United States and Canada.[26]

Despite these limitations, the liquor and tobacco taxes do have a legitimate role in the tax structure, and they have a strong degree of acceptance, beyond what might logically be expected. This, plus their high revenue productivity, lead to greater relative reliance on them than logic would suggest.

Excise Taxes in Lieu of Charges

The second category of excise taxes consists of those that are essentially substitutes for charges for governmental services. The most important, in the United States and many countries, is the motor fuel tax, plus the related motor vehicle license taxes (often called fees). Taxes on plane tickets and air freight are of comparable nature. Similar taxes could be used for inland water carriers but are not in the United States.

Major excises of this type in use in the United States and Canada are shown in Table 14–3 and the Appendix to this chapter.

Justification. The motor fuel tax, by far the most important, will serve as the basis for the defense for this type of levy, but similar reasoning applies to the others.

The provision of highways is essentially a "commercial" type of governmental activity, that is, it is not a true public good since persons can easily be excluded from receipt of the benefits. Externalities are limited, since most of the indirect benefits accrue through the use of highways and, therefore, are not true externalities. As noted in Chapter 5, under these circumstances, charging the users for the service offers several major advantages. First, adequate charges limit the use of the roads to those who are willing to pay prices equal to marginal costs and, therefore, prevent "waste," in the form of traffic congestion and distorted locational decisions. If transport is artificially cheap, industry will locate too far away from markets and resources. Second, charging the users facilitates investment decision-making by government. If roads are free and become overcrowded, governments will be inclined to pour additional investment into them. This is not economically warranted since the existing roads would not be overcrowded if persons were paying appropriate costs. Third, user charges facilitate optimal allocation of traffic between roads and railways (and other carriers). If railways must cover all costs from their own revenue

---

[26] Per capita sales of cigarettes in Montgomery County, Maryland, adjoining the low-tax-rate District of Columbia, are only half those in Baltimore, K. L. Wertz, "Cigarette Taxation by the American States," *National Tax Journal*, vol. 24 (December 1971), pp. 487–92.

but roads are largely financed by general tax levies, commerical road transport is artificially favored.

Fourth, the financing by user charges avoids the distorting effects of other taxes and the draining of revenue away from other high-priority functions. In fact, the widespread support for user taxes in the United States primarily reflects the belief that only by this means could funds be obtained for rapid expansion of the highway system. Finally, from an equity standpoint, there is little justification, by usual standards, for making the general taxpayer pay for a service that yields direct and immediate benefits to certain individuals, when user charges do not result in unacceptable burdens on the lowest-income groups.

Direct charges in the form of tolls have several disadvantages. They are a nuisance to the user and a source of substantial expense to collect per dollar of revenue, on all except the most heavily traveled routes. Accordingly, in the twenties, as road construction expanded, a substitute or proxy for tolls was developed—a tax on motor fuel used for highway operation, plus a license fee for the privilege of operating on the highways.[27] These taxes are inexpensive to collect and, at least so far as automobiles are concerned, are as good or better measures of usage than tolls would be. They vary not only with mileage traveled but also, at least to a limited extent, with the weight of the car. Motor fuel taxes were made possible by the correlation between motor fuel consumption and road usage; should the electric car develop, the simple system would break down as there would be no equivalent base for taxation.

The height of the charge is determined through the political process, although in a rough way reflecting the preferences of road users for road construction and their willingness to pay for the roads. Decisions are also influenced by a very powerful lobby of highway contractors, petroleum producers, automobile manufacturers, truck operators, and automobile associations. Actual expenditures on roads are dictated largely by the amount of tax revenue received at the rates set. The system worked very well in earlier years, in part because it was strongly favored by the road-using groups who saw it as the only means of getting suitable highways built relatively quickly. This is one of the few taxes in history that was sought by the persons who were going to pay it.

Problems of Implementation.   Several problems arise in the implementation of the principle of user charges. One is the exclusion from tax of motor fuel used for nonhighway purposes. Fortunately gasoline has few such uses, the principal one being for farm purposes. A refund system is typically used, although with some evasion by

---

[27] Historically, license fees came first, initially being regarded merely as charges to finance the issuance of licenses for regulatory purposes.

persons claiming refund on fuel used on highways. The development of the diesel truck complicated the problem because diesel fuel and its close relative, stove or fuel oil, are widely used for other purposes, and some evasion is almost inevitable.

The diesel vehicle created another complication: Since mileage per gallon is greater for diesel fuel than for gasoline, a higher tax per gallon is necessary. The users of diesel fuel fight this differential, arguing for equality of rates, whereas equality does not mean equity. The states have been very slow to introduce necessary differentiation and the federal tax is uniform on the two types of fuel. Studies show that the rate on diesel fuel should be about 40 percent greater than that on gasoline. Several Canadian provinces employ a substantial rate differential.

The most serious problem of implementation of the principle arises generally with larger vehicles. Regardless of the approach employed, presumably larger vehicles should pay higher per mile charges than passenger automobiles. They are responsible for substantially greater highway maintenance and construction costs than automobiles, for slowing traffic on mny highways, for noise pollution, and for increasing accident hazards. Appropriate charges are particularly important because the larger vehicles are directly competitive with other forms of transport. The necessary rule for optimal pricing is adjustment of charges in conformity with the added highway costs for which the heavy vehicles are responsible. Unfortunately these are very difficult to calculate, although a number of studies have been made over the years, including an exhaustive federal study published in 1961.[28] More frequently, relative burdens have been compared on a ton-mileage basis, under the assumption that in the absence of better knowledge, a uniform charge per ton mile is a reasonable rule. In practice, the relative charges have been based upon guesswork and political considerations as much as on anything else. The studies show that the larger trucks pay inadequate amounts on a ton-mileage basis.

The license fees are flat annual amounts and accordingly are unrealted to mileage, thereby favoring the commercial vehicles that travel extensively and discriminating against those used relatively little. Accordingly, some states have supplemented the other levies by a ton-mileage tax, based upon the number of miles traveled. This form of tax is much more satisfactory in terms of pricing principles but it is more difficult to enforce.

---

[28] U.S. Department of Commerce, Bureau of Public Roads, *Final Report of the Highway Cost Allocation Study*, House Doc. 54, 87th Cong., 1st sess. (Washington, D.C.: U.S. Government Printing Office, 1961).

A good summary of the approaches and issues is found in the article by R. W. Harbeson, "Some Unsettled Issues in Highway-Cost Allocation," in *Public Finance and Welfare: Essays in Honor of C. Ward Macy* (Eugene, Ore: University of Oregon Books, 1966).

Excises for General Revenue

Third, governments frequently make some use of excises for general revenue purposes, as a measure of ability to pay. The excises of this character are typically imposed upon goods regarded as luxuries, in the sense that they are not essential for a basic living standard and have a relatively high-income elasticity of demand, that is, as persons' incomes rise, they purchase progressively greater amounts of the taxed items. In practice, the items are often selected haphazardly, without careful study of expenditure patterns. These levies are not designed to attain a more suitable allocation of resources; rather, the purchase of the taxed goods is regarded as a proxy for income as a measure of ability to pay. The only excise of this type in the United States today is that on telephone service, regarded as a temporary levy. A number introduced during World War II were repealed in 1965 and the tax on automobiles and light trucks in 1971.

In part, the support for such levies in developed economies rests on the general argument for at least partial use of the consumption basis of taxation. Excises, if not too numerous, provide a simple means of accomplishing this result without the potential inequity of sales taxes, with their general coverage, discussed in Chapter 15, and without a large number of taxpaying firms. The luxury excises used in the United States for two decades prior to 1965 were introduced in part for a second motive: to reduce consumption of scarce goods during World War II in order to check inflationary pressures and the need for rationing. But they were kept on for two decades after this argument was no longer relevant.

Objections. There are several primary objections to the use of excises as ability-based general revenue measures; all of these objections played a part in the repeal of most of the United States excises of this character in 1965.

1. *Economic efficiency.* As indicated in Chapter 9, an excise tax, by raising the price of one commodity relative to others, distorts the adjustment between the transformation curve and the indifference curve away from the optimum and, if the optimal position was attained before, causes an excess burden or deadweight loss. In nontechnical terms: The price of the taxed good has been made artificially high compared to untaxed goods. Therefore, persons shift consumption from the taxed good to the untaxed ones. When they do so, they lose satisfaction—they are buying goods that they prefer less—but the government gains no revenue from them. This contrasts with a properly used sumptuary levy, which is designed to reduce comsumption of those goods that are being used in excessively large quantities because the prices do not cover all social costs. Excess burden, however,

will be created by sumptuary levies if they exceed the external costs for which the commodity is responsible, thus raising the prices too high. Excess burden will be created also by user charge excises if the excises exceed the social marginal costs for which the users are responsible.

2. *Equity.* Luxury general revenue excises are criticized on equity grounds, for discriminating against consumers on the basis of individual preferences. Properly adjusted sumptuary and user-charge excises cannot be condemned on this basis, since they merely require consumers to cover costs for which they are responsible. But luxury excises inevitably suffer from this weakness. For example, in the recreation field, admissions to movies and plays and operas may be taxed; other forms of recreation, such as reading, are not usually taxed. As a consequence, those persons who prefer movies to books are required to bear a disproportionate share of the costs of government.

In practice, many such excises used in the past were also regressive, particularly those on radios and television sets, light bulbs, matches, toilet preparations, and telephone service (still in use). Those on furs, musical instruments, sporting goods, club dues, and motor vehicles were progressive.[29]

Administration. The administrative advantages of excises are gradually lost as more and more are introduced; each excise has to be handled separately, and the nuisance problems multiply as more and more are added. There are frequent problems of interpretation as to exactly what is covered and what is not, and constant check is required to ensure that vendors are reporting sales of the taxed items correctly. So long as the excises are collected from the manufacturer, the administrative task is relatively simple in most fields because the number of manufacturers is small. But any tax on the manufacturing level encounters the pyramiding effect discussed in the previous chapter; prices to the consumer will frequently rise by more than the amount of the tax. Yet to use the retail level as was done with four U.S. excises during the 1942–65 period (furs, cosmetics, jewelry, luggage) creates almost insuperable administrative problems, since it is very difficult to get retailers to keep accurate records of sales of particular commodities.

Miscellaneous Excises

Occasionally, governments looking for additional revenue, but being unwilling for political reasons to raise major taxes, turn to levies on various commodities or transactions when there is no logic what-

---

[29] Kalmus, *Burden of Federal Excise Taxes*, p. 20.

ever for doing so. Thus, the United States prior to 1965 imposed a tax on office machines and prior to 1954 on freight transport. Taxation of any goods used in production is inherently objectionable, except as a user charge or a sumptuary tax, because of the consequent distortion of selection of methods of production with inevitable loss of production efficiency.

SUMMARY

1. Excises designed to make consumers cover all costs for which production and use of a good are responsible aid in attainment of more efficient utilization of resources and therefore attainment of objectives of society. This argument applies equally to the so-called sumptuary levies, so long as the rates are properly adjusted, and to the user charge type of excise, particularly for highway finance. The actual sumptuary excises in use may be regarded as excessive relative to external costs; they reflect in part the very high revenue potentiality and the widespread acceptance of the "penalty" notion—a carry-over from Victorian days.

2. Luxury excises, ones designed to distribute the costs of government on the basis of ability as measured by consumption of items regarded as luxuries, are basically objectionable because of the distortion of consumption patterns and consequent excess burden they create and their discrimination among individuals on the basis of relative preferences. Such taxes are unnecessary in a highly developed economy to attain progression in the tax structure.

3. The occasional fondness of governments for applying excises to goods or transactions where there is no possible justification except revenue is one of the most unfortunate phenomena in the tax field.

APPENDIX—CANADIAN FEDERAL EXCISE TAXES, 1976.

Tax	
Automobiles	Related to weight
Gasoline	10 cents per gallon
Boat motors, private aircraft, jewelery, watches, matches	10 percent
Liquor	$16.25 per proof gallon
Beer	$0.42 per gallon
Wine	27½ and 55 cents per gallon, according to alcoholic content
Cigarettes	$5 per thousand: plus $6 per thousand plus 20½ percent
Longs	$6 per thousand
Cigars	$2 per thousand
Air fares	8 percent

Source: Canadian Tax Foundation, *The National Finances*, 1975–76.

REFERENCES

The Expenditure Tax: Concept, Administration and Possible Applications. Washington: Advisory Commission on Intergovernmental Relations, 1974.

Kaldor, N. *An Expenditure Tax.* London: Allen and Unwin, 1955.
A strong defense of the expenditure tax.

Recktenwald, H. C. *Tax Incidence and Income Redistribution.* Detroit: Wayne State University Press, 1971.
A detailed review of tax-incidence analysis.

15

Sales Taxation

As noted, sales taxes are applied to all or a wide range of commodities and services, as distinguished from excises imposed upon particular goods or classes of goods. Sales taxes are used today in all countries of Western Europe, all other industrialized countries except Japan, and by at least half of the less-developed countries.

Table 15–1 indicates worldwide use of sales taxation. In the United States, sales taxes constitute the largest single source of state revenue, yielding 31 percent of state tax revenue in fiscal 1975. They are employed by 45 states and are used as a source of local government revenue in over half the states. The local levies are much less important in terms of revenue, yielding 7 percent of total local revenue. Table 15–2 summarizes the state levies. Comparable taxes, with somewhat higher rates but broader exemptions, are used in nine of the Canadian provinces. The U.S. federal government has never imposed a sales tax; the movement for one is discussed in Appendix II.

Merits of Sales Taxation

The case for sales taxation is in large measure the case for consumption taxation generally and the argument that the sales tax form offers certain advantages over the alternative forms of consumption taxation. As compared to the spendings tax, it offers much greater ease of administration since it is collected from vendors rather than individual consumers. As compared to excise taxes, sales taxes offer much greater revenue potentiality at feasible rates because of the broad coverage. A sales tax also offers administrative advantages compared to an extensive system of excises since the tax applies uniformly to all transac-

tions. A truly universal sales tax avoids both of the major objections to
excises: the excess burden arising out of shifting of consumption from
taxed to untaxed goods and the discrimination among individuals on
the basis of their relative preferences. The only situation in which a
system of excises could produce less excess burden than a uniform
sales tax is one so designed that the tax was concentrated on those

TABLE 15–1
Major Sales Tax Systems*

Country	Year Introduced	Basic Rate, 1974[4]
Manufacturers sales tax[1]		
Canada, federal	1923	12
Colombia	1965	4
Ghana	1965	11.5
Kenya	1973	10
Uganda	1968	10
Tanzania	1969	12
Malaysia	n.a.	5
Pakistan	1951	20
Brazil (federal)	n.a.	8
South Africa	1969	10
Greece	n.a.	7
Turkey	n.a.	various
Indonesia[6]	1950	10
Guyana	1969	various
Philippines	1936	7
Wholesale sales tax[2]		
Australia	1930	15
New Zealand	1933	20
Switzerland	1941	4
Portugal	1966	7
Retail sales tax		
Canada, provinces	1935–	5–8
United States, states and localities*	1932–	3–7
Iceland	1960	20
Paraguay	1969	3
Nicaragua	1972	5
Honduras	1964	4
Costa Rica	1967	5
Barbados	1975	10
Finland[5]	n.a.	12.4
Turnover taxes[3]		
Spain	1964	2
Mexico	n.a.	4

* This table is designed to provide a general view of the use of various forms of sales taxation. Often more than
one rate is used; the rates given are not necessarily current, as changes are frequent.

  1. Plus several ex-French countries of west and equatorial Africa.
  2. Israel applies a wholesale tax to a number of commodities.
  3. Plus Taiwan, Ethiopia, Sri Lanka, South Korea, some Indian states.
  4. Many of these taxes use more than one rate.
  5. Retail and wholesale dual tax.
  6. Some multiple application.

TABLE 15–1 (continued)

Value-Added Taxes

Country	Year Introduced	Rates, 1976[1]	Features
EEC countries			
France	1955	20; 7, 17.6, 33.3	Through retail level since 1968
Germany	1968	11; 5.5	Through retail
Netherlands[3]	1969	16; 4	Through retail
Luxembourg[3]	1970	10; 2.5	Through retail
Belgium[3]	1971	18; 6, 14, 25	Through retail
Italy	1973	16; 6, 30[4]	Through retail
Ireland	1972	20; 10, 35, 40	Through retail
United Kingdom	1973	8	Through retail
Denmark	1967	15	Through retail
Other European countries			
Sweden	1969	17.65; 3.09, 9.89	Through retail
Norway	1970	20	Through retail
Austria	1973	16; 8	Through retail
Latin America			
Chile	1975	20	Through retail
Brazil[2]—state	1967	16.3 to 19	Through retail
Uruguay	1968	14; 5	Through retail
Ecuador	1970	4; 9	Through retail
Argentina	1975	13; 21	Through retail
Bolivia	1973	5	Through retail
Peru (partial)[5]	1972	15; 3, 7, 10, 25	Through wholesale only
Africa (levies known as value-added taxes, but primarily limited to the manufacturing sector)			
Senegal	1966	10; 4.25; 33	Primarily on manufacturers
Malagasy Republic	1969	13.6; 6.4	Through wholesale
Ivory Coast	1960	10; 20; 23.9	Optional beyond manufacturing
Algeria	n.a.	25; 42.9	Primarily on manufacturers
Morocco	1961	14.6; 18.6; 25	Primarily on manufacturers
Tunisia	1955	17.8	Primarily on manufacturers

Rates shown are effective rates, adjusted to a tax-exclusive basis if imposed tax-included.
1. Basic rate given first.
2. The federal tax has value-added features but is confined to the manufacturing sector.
3. The Benelux countries agreed in 1973 on a uniform basic rate of 16 percent, with a 4 percent reduced rate on necessities.
5. The credit for tax paid on purchases is severely limited in the manufacturing sector.
Source: S. Cnossen, "Sales and Excise Systems of the World," *Finanzarchiv*, vol. 33, no. 2 (1975), pp. 177–236, and other sources.

TABLE 15–2
State Sales Taxes, January 1, 1977

State	State Sales Tax Rate (percent)	Tax Revenue as Percent of Total State Tax Revenue, 1975	Food Exemption
Alabama	4	32	
Arizona	4	42	
Arkansas	3	35	
California	4.75	32	x
Colorado	3	31	
Connecticut	7	40	x
Florida	4	43	x
Georgia	3	36	
Hawaii	4	46	
Idaho	3	27	
Illinois	4	34	
Indiana	4	33	x
Iowa	3	27	
Kansas	3	34	
Kentucky	5	29	x
Louisiana	3	24	x
Maine	5	37	x
Maryland	4	23	x
Massachusetts	3	11	x
Michigan	4	34	x
Minnesota	4	19	x
Mississippi	5	49	
Missouri	3	37	
Nebraska	3	33	
Nevada	3	34	
New Jersey	5	37	x
New Mexico	4	42	
New York	4	22	x
North Carolina	3	22	
North Dakota	4	36	x
Ohio	4	31	x
Oklahoma	2	18	
Pennsylvania	6	27	x
Rhode Island	6	29	x
South Carolina	4	35	
South Dakota	4	50	
Tennessee	4.5	42	
Texas	4	35	x
Utah	4	44	
Vermont	3	14	x
Virginia	3	22	
Washington[1]	4.6	43	
West Virginia[1]	3	15	
Wisconsin	4	24	x
Wyoming	3	47	

[1] Excluding gross receipts tax.
Source of revenue data: U.S. Bureau of the Census, *State Tax Collections in 1975*.

goods that are complementary to leisure, thus minimizing distorting effects on labor supply to a sufficient degree as to offset the excess burden arising out of substituting untaxed goods for taxed goods. But given the inability to design and implement such a system, the case for uniformity is strong. In practice, however, sales taxes are not universal in coverage and, therefore, suffer from the same defects as the excises to some degree. But the degree is typically less, and there is the possibility of universality.

A second major advantage is the provision of an autonomous source of revenue for the states in a federal system. National governments inevitably dominate the income tax field and limit the potential revenues to the states from this source. The states also fear that high income taxes will drive business and wealthy persons out of the state. The sales tax provides an autonomous revenue source, one from which there is relatively little fear of loss of economic activity. Sales taxes are often politically much more acceptable to state legislatures than income taxes; state spending would undoubtedly be much less than it now is were it not for the additional revenue potential offered by the sales tax. John Kenneth Galbraith argues for greater reliance on sales taxation on this basis; the tax will allow financing of urgently needed state and local activities.

The Objections

Sales taxes are subject to objections common to all consumption-related taxes: the discrimination in favor of persons who save high percentages of their incomes, the lower elasticity of revenue relative to changes in national income, and the effect of the higher S/Y ratio is making more difficult the attainment of full employment. The significant objections, however, arise from the nature of the sales tax as compared to other forms of consumption-related taxes.

Equity. Because of the impersonal nature of the sales tax—its collection from vendors rather than individuals—adjustment of the tax in conformity with the personal circumstances of individuals is impossible. There are two major consequences. First, a broad-based sales tax is almost certain to be regressive relative to income, that is, the percentage of income paid in taxes is greater in the lower income levels than in the higher. The basic reason is the lower average propensity to consume in the higher income levels. A smaller percentage of income is spent on consumption goods. In addition, in practice most sales taxes do not apply to a wide range of services with use concentrated primarily in the higher-income groups—expensive education, foreign travel, personal service, and the like.

The regressivity of the sales tax has been demonstrated in a number of studies, and particularly in the work of David Davies.[1] Most studies show the tax to be regressive relative to income if food is taxed, more or less proportional, except at low- and high-income levels, if food is exempt (Figures 15–1A and 15–1B). A study by Darwin Johnson, however, shows a high degree of regressivity both with food taxed and with food exempt, as shown on Figure 15–2.[2] The significance of these studies has been questioned by supporters of the Friedman "permanent income component" doctrine, that many persons are only temporarily in low-income brackets and that consumption patterns are dictated by average lifetime incomes, not by the income of the particular year. Thus, many of the persons who are in the lowest income levels are young persons expecting higher incomes in the future, older persons deliberately using up capital, and persons temporarily out of work. It is, therefore, argued that the distributional pattern noted above is not significant; if sales tax payments are expressed as a percentage of permanent income, the pattern is not regressive.[3] But question can be raised about this argument; taxes in general must be paid from current income or wealth, and even though a person expects his or her income to be higher in the future, he or she still has to pay tax out of this year's income. Furthermore, studies of poverty show that there is a very substantial group of persons in the country who are permanently, generation after generation, at low-income levels, just as many families remain in the highest income levels. Studies do show that many persons in the lower-income groups have substantial net worth, and thus with a broader concept of tax capacity than income, the regressivity is less. But many of these persons have little wealth except their homes, and another large segment of the poor has no significant net wealth at all.

As subsequently discussed, various adjustments can be made in the structure of the sales tax to lessen regressivity, but only with loss of

[1] The studies include: D. G. Davies, "An Empirical Test of Sales Tax Regressivity," *Journal of Political Economy*, vol. 68 (February 1959), pp. 72–78; G. N. Rostvold, "Distribution of Property, Retail Sales, and Personal Income Tax Burdens in California," *National Tax Journal*, vol. 19 (March 1966), pp. 38–47, which summarizes the work on the question in California by W. H. Hickman; J. F. Due, *Provincial Sales Taxes*, rev. ed. (Toronto: Canadian Tax Foundation, 1964), pp. 105–8; H. M. Somers, *The Sales Tax*, California Assembly Interim Committee on Revenue and Taxation (Sacramento: 1964); O. E. Nelson, "Progressivity of the Ontario Retail Sales Tax," *Canadian Tax Journal*, vol. 18 (September–October 1970), pp. 411–15. D. G. Davies and D. E. Black, "Equity Effects of Including Housing Services in a Sales Tax Base," *National Tax Journal*, vol. 28 (March 1975), pp. 13–38.

[2] Darwin G. Johnson, *Distribution of the Illinois Tax Burden* (University of Illinois Ph.D. dissertation, 1971), pp. 49, 52.

[3] See D. G. Davies, "Commodity Taxation and Equity," *Journal of Finance*, vol. 16 (December 1961), pp. 581–90; D. C. Morgan, Jr., *Retail Sales Tax* (Madison, Wis.: University of Wisconsin Press, 1963), chaps. 3, 4.

FIGURE 15–1A

State of Maryland: Sales Tax Payments as Percent of Money Income by Income Classes, 1961 (food exempt)

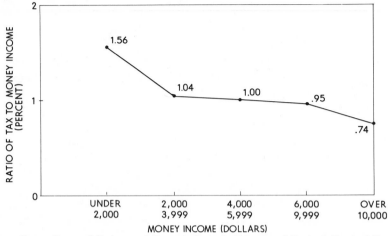

Source: Bureau of Business and Economic Research, University of Maryland, *Maryland Tax Study* (College Park, Md.: 1965), p. 81.

FIGURE 15–1B

Sales Tax Payments as Percentage of Income by Income Class, Papke-Shahen Study

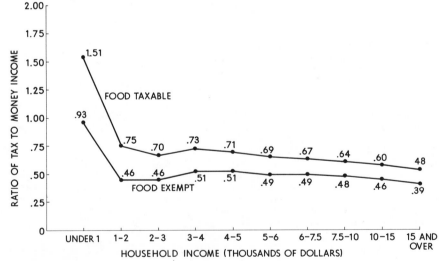

Source: J. A. Papke and T. G. Shahen, "Optimal Consumption Base Taxes," *National Tax Journal*, vol. 25 (September 1972), pp. 479–87.

FIGURE 15–2

Distribution of Illinois Sales Tax Burden by Income Class, 1960–1961 Data

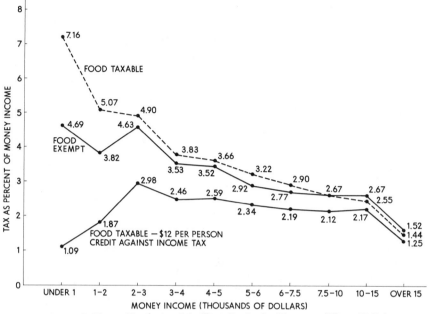

Source: Darwin G. Johnson, *Distribution of the Illinois Tax Burden* (University of Illinois Ph.D dissertation, 1971), pp. 49, 55.

substantial revenue at given tax rates, administrative complication, and economic distortion.

Distinct from the question of regressivity, which is a matter of relative tax burdens, is that of the absolute magnitude of taxes on the lowest income groups, families that may be considered to have no taxpaying ability. The use of income taxes in a tax structure, together with sales taxes, can eliminate the regressivity but it cannot eliminate the absolute burden on the poorest groups.

In addition to regressivity, the distributional effects are undesirable in other respects as well. The tax tends to be capricious and perverse, placing disproportionate burden on all families whose circumstances require them to spend higher than average percentages of their income on taxable goods. Studies by Reed Hansen[4] and others show discrimination against large families compared to small, against younger couples acquiring consumer durables compared to older ones with the same incomes, families suffering misfortunes, city dwellers compared to those in rural areas, and residents of high-cost areas generally.

[4] Reed R. Hansen, "An Empirical Analysis of the Retail Sales Tax with Policy Recommendations," *National Tax Journal*, vol. 15 (March 1962), pp. 1–13.

Inequities arise not only from expenditure patterns but from shifting difficulties as well. As noted in the previous chapter, it is not likely that a sales tax is always fully and precisely shifted forward. Some may rest in an inequitable fashion on the owners, particularly of smaller businesses, and some may be shifted backward to the owners of specialized factors. No generalizations are possible about the relationship of these unshifted and backward transferred burdens and the incomes of the persons involved.[5] All that can be said is that the distributional pattern is likely to be very haphazard and unrelated to any accepted measures of tax capacity.

Economic Efficiency.   The tax is also subject to criticism on economic efficiency grounds.

The most serious losses in economic efficiency from the sales taxes result from defects in the structure of the tax, as noted later in the chapter. Some of these defects are products of inherent problems in the drafting of the tax; others result from illogical design. One of the most serious is the failure to exclude all producers goods from the tax, thus interfering with efficiency in the organization of production.

Stabilization.   Clearly the tax, lacking progression, is inferior to the spendings tax as a means of promoting additional saving or checking inflationary pressures, if these are primary goals. The low-revenue elasticity compared to the income tax was noted above; consumption changes less rapidly than income as income changes and the tax is not progressive in relation to consumption. The Advisory Commission on Intergovernmental Relations estimate of revenue elasticity for the state sales taxes is 0.97, compared to 1.65 for state personal income taxes.[6] Other estimates range from 0.8 to 2.27.[7]

On the whole, the sales tax is definitely inferior on equity grounds to the income tax and to the spendings tax, which can be made progressive and adjusted to personal circumstances. The tax offers little apparent advantage over the income tax in terms of incentives. It is by no means clear that a higher S/Y ratio is beneficial to the economy; a higher ratio could easily make the task of attaining full employment more difficult. The sales tax does offer significant equity and efficiency advantages over a widespread system of general excises.

---

[5] If these unshifted burdens rested on monopoly profits, there would at least be some justification.

[6] Advisory Commission on Intergovernmental Relations, *State-Local Finances* (Washington: 1971), p. 212.

The elasticity figure for the California sales tax is estimated to be only 0.77. See H. S. and George Break, "Tax Reform in California," *Public Affairs*, Report, Institute of Governmental Studies (University of California, Berkeley, February 1971).

[7] Advisory Commission on Intergovernmental Relations, *State-Local Finances*, 1972 edition (Washington, D.C.: 1972), p. 301.

The Case for the Tax. The primary case for the sales tax is to be found in the following circumstances:

1. As a major revenue source for the states in the United States and equivalent units in Canada and other federal systems. Given the limitations to high income taxation at the state level, the sales taxes allow the states to carry on functions at higher levels than would otherwise be possible and lessen their financial dependence on the federal government.

2. As a supplemental element to the national income tax, should the latter get so high as to have demonstrable effects upon incentives. There is no evidence that this situation has even been approached in the United States.

3. As a key element of the tax structure of LDCs and in other countries in which effective operation of high income taxes is difficult, as explained in Chapter 24. In these countries, administrative considerations preclude raising substantial revenue from the income tax and an increased S/Y ratio is highly important for economic growth— whereas it is not in the United States.

Optimal Structure of a Sales Tax—Form of the Tax

If a sales tax is to conform most fully with the objectives of the tax and the accepted standards of taxation, several requirements must be met:

1. The tax must be reflected fully and exactly in higher prices of all consumer purchases so that the distributional pattern will be the same as that of a proportional spendings tax without exemptions. This condition, in turn, requires that the tax rate is uniform on all goods and services bought by consumers, that the tax is shifted forward fully by the firms from which it is collected, that production is carried on under constant cost conditions in the relevant ranges, and that factor prices remain unchanged.

Any deviation from this rule will produce the twin evils of luxury excises: consumer excess burden and discrimination against families on the basis of their relative preferences for various goods; and it may give rise to compliance and administrative complications. The only exception is a variation that lessens the adverse effects of the tax on factor supply to a sufficient degree to offset the excess burden from the "excise" effect.

2. The tax must accord as closely as possible with accepted standards of equity; this, in turn, requires, by usual standards, avoidance of burden on the very poor and at least a proportional pattern over other income levels.

3. The tax must not cause loss of efficiency in the use of resources

by distortion of choice of methods. This, in turn, requires that the tax be neutral as among various methods of organization and conduct of production and distribution.

4. Costs of compliance and administration must be minimized, consistent with effective enforcement, as is true with any tax.

Complete attainment of these objectives is obviously impossible. No sales tax is ever completely general on all consumption purchases. Shifting is not likely to be complete and exact, as noted, and there may be no effective way of keeping the burden off the poor except by exemptions, which violate the first requirement. The objective, therefore, is to attain the requirements as closely as possible, with optimal trade-offs when necessary among competing requirements.

Sales taxes can be imposed at a number of possible levels in production and distribution: the retail sale, that is, the sale to the final consumer; the sale to the retailer (the wholesale form of tax); or the sale by the manufacturer. These are known as single stage sales taxes. Or it can be applied to all sales through which commodities pass, either in the turnover tax form on total price or, under the value-added tax, on value added by each firm.

The Retail Sales Tax. Of these forms, the requirements can be most fully attained only if the tax applies to the retail selling price—to the sale to the final consumer and only to this sale. The optimal form is a retail tax (and a value-added tax extending through the retail level).

1. *Shifting.* The retail sales tax is the type most likely to bring about immediate price increases by the amount of the tax. While this reaction does not ensure exact shifting if cost per unit changes when output falls, it does indicate shifting apart from cost changes. The tax requires only one price adjustment; others require several price changes in the production and distribution structure, with greater likelihood of variation. The practice of separate quotation and the uniformity of the tax facilitate shifting, as previously noted. The possibility of pyramiding through application of percentage markups is avoided.

2. *Ratio of tax to consumer expenditures.* Only the retail sales tax, with complete shifting, can constitute a uniform ratio of tax to consumer expenditures. Taxes imposed prior to the retail level and thus not covering all distribution costs will produce varying ratios of tax-induced price increases to consumer expenditures, in view of differences in distribution activities and margins. A fully shifted 10 percent manufacturers sales tax will constitute 5 percent of the retail price and thus of consumer expenditures on a commodity with a 50 percent distribution margin, 7½ percent on one with a 25 percent margin. Thus the tax is lower, relative to consumer spending, on luxury goods (e.g., jewelry), which tend to have higher margins, than on necessities (e.g., food), which have low margins. Turnover taxes will vary for another

reason as well, namely differences in numbers of taxable transactions through which commodities pass on the way to the final consumer.

3. *Economic neutrality.* Only the retail tax is neutral among various distribution systems and therefore does not alter selection of methods. Taxes levied at manufacturing and wholesale levels favor firms that transfer distributional activity forward beyond the impact of the tax in order to minimize the taxable price figure. Thus a manufacturers tax discourages forward integration by manufacturers, favoring firms performing a minimum of distributional functions and selling to wholesale distributors. Wholesale sales taxes favor the backward integrated retailer buying in large quantities at low cost. Both favor the private brand distributor, who performs many functions normally carried on by the manufacturer (research, advertising) and thus is able to buy cheaply.

4. *Imported versus domestic goods.* Only the retail form of tax can provide equal treatment for domestic and imported goods (except in the relatively rare instances of importation by the final consumer, where equality is difficult with any tax). The problem is particularly severe with a manufacturers sales tax since the tax applies to most imported goods at a later stage of distribution than that at which domestic goods are taxed.

5. *Administration.* From an administrative standpoint, the retail form of tax has many advantages. For subordinate units of government, no other form is feasible because of jurisdictional problems. A much higher percentage of retail sales is made within a taxing jurisdiction than the percentage of sales by manufacturers and wholesalers, and the task of enforcement against outside firms is less troublesome. In many other repects the retail tax is the simplest form of sales tax to operate. "Retail sale" is an easier concept to define in workable fashion than "manufacturer" and "sale by a manufacturer" or "sale to a retailer." Treatment of transportation and other incidental charges creates less uncertainty and discrimination with the retail tax. The retail tax also avoids the troublesome adjustments in taxable price with wholesale or manufacturers taxes designed to lessen discrimination against certain distribution channels.[8]

6. *Yield.* The retail tax yields a substantially greater revenue with a given tax rate—nearly twice as much as a manufacturers tax. Accordingly, pressure to evade and resistance on the part of the taxpaying firms are lessened.

7. *Separate quotation.* Only with the retail tax can the consumer be made aware of the amount of tax he or she is paying, a consequence of merit for attainment of levels of governmental activities optimal in

---

[8] This has been demonstrated by Canadian experience. See *Canada, Report of the Royal Commission on Taxation,* vol. 5 (Ottawa: Queen's Printer, 1966), pp. 13–16.

terms of the preferences of society. With the typical quotation of retail tax separate from selling price of the commodity, the taxpaying vendors may be more likely to regard themselves as tax collectors rather than as taxpayers and therefore less likely to seek to evade tax.

The Manufacturers and Wholesale Taxes.[9]   Single-stage taxes levied prior to the retail level offer only one advantage over the retail tax: The number of taxpaying firms is much smaller and these firms are typically large enough to have adequate record systems. The one significant limitation of the retail sales tax is the large number of small retailers, many with limited record systems. In the United States, this has proven to be only a minor nuisance, although there are about 4.1 million taxpaying firms under the state sales taxes. In a country in which most retailing is of a small-scale nature, the enforcement of a retail tax is much more difficult and costly, and the case for a manufacturers or wholesale tax is stronger. Otherwise, the preretail taxes have no merit whatever compared to retail taxes, as has been demonstrated very conclusively by Canada's 40-year experience with the manufacturers sales tax. Failure to attain neutrality among various distribution channels, uncertainty, and complications in the operation of the tax, and unequal burden on various consumer purchases led the 1966 Royal Commission to recommend its replacement by a retail tax.[10] In 1975, a governmental report offered a provisional recommendation to shift the tax to the wholesale level (sale to the retailer), primarily to provide more uniform treatment of imported and domestic goods and reduce the instances in which adjustment of tax to avoid discrimination against certain forms of doing business is necessary.[11]

The Turnover Tax.   The turnover tax, applying to each sale through which a commodity passes in production and distribution channels,

---

[9] If a country is unwilling to use a retail sales tax, the choice between the manufacturers and wholesale taxes is not a clear-cut one. The wholesale tax (which applies to sales to retailers, whether by manufacturers or wholesale distributors) is subject to the defects of preretail taxes to a lesser degree, since the tax is closer to the final retail level. Ratios of tax to final consumer expenditures will differ less, since only variations in retail margins are relevant. Possible effects on choice of distribution channels are also less. The wholesale tax is advantageous if imports are significant, since equality of tax on imported and domestic goods is easier to attain with it than with a manufacturers tax. The wholesale tax has one major limitation compared to the manufacturers tax: When retailers integrate backward and buy cheaply at the manufacturing level, the price adjustments necessary for tax purposes to lessen discrimination are upward ones—called *uplift* in Great Britain. The firms will inevitably resist this type of adjustment more than downward adjustments permitted competitors with the manufacturers tax. The wholesale tax would be more difficult to administer in a country with large numbers of small wholesalers.

[10] *Royal Commission on Taxation*, vol. 5.

[11] Canada, Department of Finance, *Discussion Paper: Federal Sales and Excise Taxation* (Ottawa: 1975). Note also the papers on the subject presented at the 1975 Annual Conference of the Canadian Tax Foundation, published in the 1975 *Conference Report*, pp. 188–227.

does not warrant serious consideration. The discrimination against nonintegrated firms and the effects in encouraging integration produced by the "cascade" nature of the tax lessen economic efficiency, lead to strong complaints, and bring modifications that complicate the taxes beyond the possibility of effective administration. The nonuniformity of burden on various consumer expenditures is substantial, and burden pattern by income group is indeterminate. Elimination of the exact amount of tax from exports is impossible, and imported goods are often favored over domestically produced goods. The only advantage of the tax is the lower rate required to raise a given sum. Germany, the originator of the turnover tax in its modern form, abandoned it January 1, 1968 in favor of the value-added tax, and the other European Common Market countries have now done so. Latin American countries, except Mexico, have also made the change.

THE VALUE-ADDED TAX

The newest form of sales tax, and one whose use has expanded rapidly in recent years, is the value-added tax.

The Nature of the Tax

The *value added* by a business firm is the difference between the receipts from the sales of the firm's product and the sum of the amounts paid by the firm for produced goods purchased during the period, and therefore is equal to the sum of the factor payments made by the firm (including the profits of the owners). For a very simple example: A newsboy pays 8 cents for a newspaper and peddles it on the street corner for 10 cents; he has added 2 cents of value to the paper; the value added attributable to him is 2 cents.

A value-added tax could be operated by requiring each firm to calculate value added in the manner indicated above, either by subtracting the costs of goods purchased from sales or by adding together the various elements that make up value added—payments for wages, interest, profit, and so forth.[12] As the value-added taxes usually operate, however, with the tax credit method, vendors at each level of production and distribution are subject to tax on purchases; when they calculate their own tax liability they apply the tax rate to their figure of taxable sales and deduct the total amount of tax they have paid during the period on their purchases to ascertain their net tax liability. With a 10 percent rate, sales of $300,000, purchases of taxable goods of $80,000, and therefore tax paid on purchases of $8,000, a vendor

---

[12] This is the method used in the Michigan business tax, essentially a value-added tax.

would subtract $8,000 from $30,000 and pay $22,000 tax to the government. The net effect is the same as if each firm calculated value added and applied the tax rate. The tax credit method is considered to be simpler and to facilitate cross-check in audit, since tax reported as deducted by firm B should show up as tax paid by firm A, from which B has purchased.

The tax takes several forms. Most of the levies are extended through the retail level, but they may not apply beyond the last wholesale transaction. A tax using the value-added principle but confined to the manufacturing sector is usually referred to as a type of manufacturers sales tax. The value-added taxes also, like other sales taxes, differ in the extent of taxation of producers goods; in the usual form, called the consumption form, credit is allowed for all tax paid on purchases for business use, and, therefore, multiple taxation of the final product is completely eliminated. Some of the Latin American value-added taxes, however, restrict the deductability of tax paid on industrial machinery, supplies, etc.

In effect, a value-added tax extending through the retail level is identical, basically to a retail sales tax, except that the tax is collected in increments throughout the production and distribution channels, instead of entirely from the retailers. With a given tax rate and coverage, the revenue yield will be the same as that of a retail sales tax.

Use of the Tax

The value-added approach was discussed as early as 1918, but first came into use in France in 1954. It was adopted as the standard form of sales tax for the European Common Market countries and is now used by all of them, and by several other European countries as well. Extensive use is now made in Latin America. Table 15-1 indicates the extent of use. The tax has been proposed on various occasions in the United States and Canada.

Evaluation of the Value-Added Form of Sales Tax

The value-added tax offers several potential adantages:

1. For many countries, the possibility of avoiding the adverse consequences of the turnover tax without concentrating the impact of the tax at any one stage in production and distribution. The value-added tax produces no economic distortions or loss of efficiency if properly designed. The advantages of the retail sales tax are fully attained, yet a large portion—more than half—of the revenue is collected at preretail levels. This is of no great importance in the United States but is of great merit in many countries, in which retailing is small scale and retailers strongly resist paying taxes.

2. The greater ease in excluding producers goods from tax. As explained below, a sales tax should, in principle, apply only to purchases for consumption use. Under other forms of sales tax, exclusion of sales for business use requires check upon both the seller and the customer. With the value-added tax, all sales among business firms are taxable; the purchaser takes credit for the tax paid on purchases, and therefore check must be made only upon the purchaser, not upon the supplier. The difference should not be exaggerated; there still remains the problem of determining whether the firm has actually used the goods for business or personal use. But the check may be somewhat easier. In practice, value-added taxes do free far more business purchases from tax than do the typical retail sales taxes.

3. The cross-audit check. Tax reported as paid by one firm to its suppliers, for which it takes credit against its own tax liability, should appear as tax paid to the government by the supplier. This cross check is not automatic—but it can be made, by auditors, or ultimately, by computers. Somewhat similar checks are made under retail sales taxes; if there is doubt about the correctness of the sales reported by a retailer, check is made upon the retailer's purchase records and if necessary with the retailers' suppliers. But the cross check is easier with the value-added tax.

On the other hand, the value-added tax is somewhat more complex than the retail sales tax, particularly in concept. The number of taxpaying firms is somewhat larger, since not only retailers but all manufacturers and wholesale firms must be registered and must file returns. The tax is somewhat less adaptable to exemptions than other sales taxes, since the exemptions must be handled throughout production and distribution channels. Farmers pose a serious problem; to register them all as taxpaying firms would greatly add to administrative and compliance tasks, yet if they are not registered, there is no way for them to receive credit for the tax paid on purchase for farm use. Some form of special rule is required—(such as outright exemption of major purchases for farm use) and thus the operation of the tax is complicated. Because of the interrelationship of tax on all firms, a value-added tax works best if it applies at a uniform rate to all businesses without exemptions, but doing so may be contrary to other objectives of government policy and may create some administrative complications of its own.

On the whole, the value-added form of sales tax offers few advantages for countries such as the United States and Canada, in which the retail sales tax can be operated successfully. The defects of the present sales taxes can be corrected in large measure without the added complexities of the value-added tax. But it is undoubtedly the ideal form of sales tax for many countries.

Structure of a Sales Tax

For a sales tax structure to be optimum in terms of the objectives, several structural aspects are important: The tax must apply only to final sales for consumption use (either directly or through the value added technique), and it must apply to all consumer expenditures at a uniform rate, except as exceptions are strongly justified to allow attainment of greater equity.

The Tax Treatment of Producers Goods–Purchase for Production rather than Consumption Use. We usually think of a sales tax as a levy on final consumption goods. But, in fact, this is not necessarily the case; the state sales taxes typically apply to a number of purchases for business use. The sales taxes of many states exclude from tax only sales for resale, defined to include sales of materials and parts becoming physical ingredients of the finished products, and farm feed, seed, fertilizer, and livestock. Thus all industrial and distribution equipment, supplies, and the like, are taxed. Some of the industrial states of the northeast, however, extend the exclusion from tax to industrial machinery, fuel, and goods consumed in production processes but not becoming physical ingredients. Only a few states seek to exclude most producers goods. In many states, as much as 25 percent of the tax revenue comes from sales for business use—despite the basic objections to this practice:

1.   Taxation of business purchases results in multiple taxation of the final product, under the assumption of forward shifting; one consequence is an obscure and haphazard distribution of a portion of the burden of the tax and excise-type excess burdens.

2.   Factor combinations will be distorted; taxation of some inputs and not others will cause loss of economic efficiency. Particularly, firms will be given incentive to produce taxable goods and services within the firm, because by doing so the tax liability will be reduced. The danger is greatest if tax is applied to services rendered to business firms, as the firms will hire employees to do the equivalent work.

3.   Investment may be deterred because of the increase in the cost of investment activity.

4.   The country will be placed at a disadvantage in foreign markets at given exchange rates, since exports will contain a tax element that is not refunded at export. Imports will be artificially favored. This problem has been aggravated by the shift of European countries to the form of value-added tax under which virtually all purchases for business use are freed from tax.

Complete exclusion of producers goods, however, is difficult. Many sales are made by the same vendors for both consumption and business purposes, sometimes by the same purchasers. It is difficult for vendors to apply the tax correctly, and audit is difficult. There is danger that many sales will be made tax exempt when then they really are for consumption use. The trouble may be less under a value added tax but is still present.

Beyond this problem, the failure to confine sales taxes to consumption purchases is largely a result of political considerations—of the attractions of taxing sales to firms, instead of placing all the burden on sales to individuals (even though the tax on businesses may well result in the end in higher consumption-goods prices.

Exemptions of Consumption Goods. There is a strong case against introducing exemptions of consumption goods into a sales tax, except when there is overwhelming specific justification. First, exemptions erode the base and reduce revenue, and each exemption leads to demands for additional exemptions. Second, loss of complete coverage gives rise to excise tax effects: It discriminates in favor of those persons having relatively high preferences for exempt goods and leads to reallocation of resources and to consumer excess burden. Third, the ability to shift the tax forward may be lessened if some products are exempt. Fourth, in virtually all cases, compliance and administration are made more difficult because vendors must distinguish between taxable and exempt goods at the time of sale and in their records, audit is made more complicated, and chances for evasion are increased.

While most state sales taxes are relatively broad in coverage of commodities, nevertheless a number of states have introduced some exemptions, either to make the distributional pattern more acceptable or to meet certain administrative problems or to avoid so-called "double taxation." The Canadian provinces have provided a much wider range of exemptions.

Food Exemption. To meet the complaint against regressivity and the absolute burden on the lowest income groups, two general approaches have been followed: the exemption of food and medicine and, in a few states, certain other items; and the provision of a credit against income taxes representing tax paid on basic necessities. Each approach will be considered. As of January 1977, 20 states of the 45 using sales taxes exempted food—an increase from 15 in 1972. Food is exempt in all Canadian provinces. The exemption covers all goods for human consumption except, in most states, candy and soft drinks—although these are exempt in some. No state exempts all meals from taxation, although cheaper meals are exempt in several.

Food exemption without question accomplishes the objective of lessening regressivity and the absolute burden on the poor, because such a high percentage of family expenditures in the lowest income groups is made for food. This has been ascertained empirically in a number of studies, which uniformly show that a sales tax with food taxed is regressive; with food exempt, much less so.[13] Figure 15–2 above shows the picture for Illinois; the tax is regressive even with food taxed. Some studies suggest that the tax is more or less proportional with food exempt.[14] Of perhaps even greater advantage is the importance of the exemption in reducing the absolute burden on the poor. Food exemption also lessens discrimination against large families compared to smaller ones.

Food exemption, however, has a number of objectionable features:

1.   Revenue. Food exemption causes a loss in revenue between 15 and 20 percent of the total; thus a state with a 5 percent rate must increase the rate by one percentage point to obtain more or less equivalent revenue.

2.   Major administrative problems are created. First, questions of interpretation are numerous and some are hard to solve. Several relate to whether certain items are food or not—vitamin tablets, for example. The most serious questions relate to the exclusion of candy and soft drinks and of meals from the exemption.

Quite apart from interpretative matters is that of ensuring that the tax is applied correctly at the cash register and is reported correctly.

3.   Food exemption is discriminatory in favor of those families that prefer to concentrate their luxury spending on expensive foods. Many foods are in no sense necessary for a minimum living standard; many families spend substantial amounts on expensive cuts of meat, fresh fruit out of season, exotic seafoods, and other items. There is no necessity whatever of exempting these purchases—nor in fact is there need to exempt any food expenditures of higher income families. As noted, any deviation from uniform coverage of a tax is inherently objectionable on grounds of inequity and possible excess burden, and exemption of food is no exception to this rule.

At the same time, food exemption leaves substantial absolute burden on the lowest income groups; the tax with food exempt is still regressive at the very lowest levels. Restaurant meals are almost never exempt yet many older persons must eat in restaurants for lack of cooking facilities.

Other "Necessities."   Exemption of medicines and drugs has spread rapidly in recent years; as of January 1977, most states exempted prescription drugs and several of these exempted all drugs and medicines.

This exemption not only reduces the burden on the poor, but it also

---

[13] For example, J. M. Schaefer, "Sales Tax Regressivity under Alternative Tax Bases and Income Concepts," *National Tax Journal*, vol. 22 (December 1969), pp. 516–27; H. M. Somers, *The Sales Tax* (California Assembly Committee on Revenue and Taxation, Sacramento, 1964); Reed Hansen, "Empirical Analysis of the Retail Sales Tax," *National Tax Journal*, vol. 15 (March 1962), pp. 1–13.

[14] Somers, *The Sales Tax.*

avoids a heavy burden on those who are unfortunate enough to require heavy expenditures for medicine. These costs are very unevenly distributed over various families. Control is not difficult so long as the exemption is confined to prescriptions.

Complete or partial exemption of clothing is provided in several states and Canadian provinces. This exemption is particularly unjustified. It produces the usual undesirable consequences: discrimination in favor of persons spending large amounts on clothes; numerous interpretative, compliance, and audit problems; and reduced revenue. At the same time, it makes the tax more, not less, regressive—contrary to the usual intent, for clothing expenditures as a percentage of income rise as incomes rise.[15] Experience of the Canadian provinces with clothing exemption has been equally unsatisfactory.

Credit against Income Tax. An alternative to food exemption is the provision of a credit against income tax (with a refund if no income tax is due) in lieu of a food exemption. The amount, which may be either flat or diminish as income rises, is set by law, designed to equal the tax on food expenditures of the typical family. This is a far more satisfactory approach than food exemption; the revenue loss is much smaller, exemption of luxury foods is avoided, and the compliance and audit problems created by food exemption are avoided. As of 1976, seven states[16] used this system (although two also exempted food) and one additional used it in lieu of exemption of medicine. Three states that had used the system, however, discontinued it. There are some technical problems in the operation of the system, the number of income tax returns with no tax owing is increased, and some low-income persons fail to file and take advantage of the system. But the main disadvantage is political; voters tend to prefer the food exemption, which they see as benefiting all persons (although ignoring higher sales tax rates made necessary), whereas the income tax credit, particularly if diminishing as income rises, appears to benefit only a few persons.

Other Exemptions. Several other categories are frequently exempted:

1. Newspapers, primarily because of the low unit price and sale through newsboys.

2. Articles subject to excises, particularly motor fuel, but frequently cigarettes and, in some states, liquor. This exemption makes no sense, costs substantial revenue, and complicates operation of the tax. It is mainly a product of a misguided notion that applying two taxes to the same good is objectionable double taxation. It is actually

---

[15] J. M. Schaefer, "Clothing Exemptions and Sales Tax Regressivity," *American Economic Review*, vol. 59 (September 1969), pp. 596–99.

[16] Colorado, Hawaii, Nebraska, Utah, Idaho, Vermont, Massachusetts, plus the District of Columbia.

simpler to apply both taxes than to exempt the goods from the sales tax.

3. Sales to religious, charitable, and related institutions. This exemption is based on social policy considerations but complicates operation of the taxes.

Services. Under the principle of the sales tax as a levy on consumer spending, a sales tax should apply to services as well as to commodities. Failure to do so inevitably favors consumption of services, thus producing "excise" effects in distorting consumption patterns and favoring those persons with relatively high preferences for services. If all services were taxed, the distributional pattern would be less regressive, as service expenditures as a percentage of income are greater for persons in high-income levels than those in lower. Finally, inclusion of services would facilitate administration of the tax in certain respects, by eliminating the need for distinguishing between "service" and "commodity" on the part of various establishments, such as repair shops, providing services in conjunction with the sale of goods. Obviously, only those services rendered to consumers should be taxed, not those for business use, or those services provided by employees to employers, which are not consumption goods.

Only a few jurisdictions, including Hawaii and New Mexico among the states, come close to including all services. Most states initially did not tax services at all, and while some have been added, the coverage is still limited. There are several obstacles in the way of complete taxation of all services:

1. Carry-over of the old view that a tax on services is in some sense a tax on labor, whereas it is almost certainly a tax on the consumer.

2. The difficulty of distinguishing between the rendering of services to business firms and to individuals; legal service, for example, is provided widely to both groups.

3. The objection, from the standpoint of general social policy and equity, of taxing a wide range of major services—hospital, medical, dental, educational, legal and the like.

4. Administrative problems, of taxing personal service in the home, foreign travel, education abroad, and the like.

5. With housing service, the desire to avoid additional burden on the poor, and the great difficulty of providing equitable relative treatment of tenants and homeowners.[17]

As a consequence, when services are taxed, the usual practise is simply to list a group of services, primarily those provided by commer-

---

[17] Inclusion of all housing service would apparently make the present state sales taxes more regressive, as shown in the study by D. G. Davies and D. E. Black, "Equity Effects of Including Housing Services in a Sales Tax Base," *National Tax Journal*, vol. 28 (March 1975), pp. 135–38.

cial establishments (as distinguished from the professions, individuals, etc.), in a relatively narrow range of activity, such as hotel, motel, repair, dry cleaning, and the like. But this group will not add more than ten percent to the base of the tax, and evidence suggests that taxation of them, while not adding greatly to the burden on the poor, does not lessen regressivity, whereas taxation of all services would do so. Taxation of utility services would make the tax more regressive. The general conclusion reached in two studies of the question shows that the usual taxation of services has little impact on the distributional patterns.[18]

The Special Problem of Interjurisdictional Sales

As noted, there is particular justification for use of sales taxes by the states. Since most retailing is an instate activity, most of the revenue can be collected without encountering jurisdictional problems. But some sales are interstate in nature; a person living in one state orders a good from a vendor in another state for delivery by mail or a person drives across the state border and buys goods in the other state. The courts have long held that a state cannot apply sales tax per se to an interstate transaction, one where delivery occurs across a state line. But they do permit the states to employ supplemental use taxes, applying to initial use in the state of a good purchased in another state.[19] All sales tax states now employ these levies. But the taxes cannot be enforced against many such transactions as, for example, when a person orders by mail from a store in another state or when a resident of Boston drives to Concord, New Hampshire, to buy a new television set. They are enforced against purchases from the large mail-order houses, which do business in most states; purchases of motor vehicles, which must be registered; and purchases by business firms subject to audit in the state.

Since the use taxes are not fully effective, some incentive is given to buy outside the state, buying either tax free when delivery is made across the state line or the other state does not have a sales tax, or at a lower rate. The states have long feared the problem, but most states are now convinced that it is not serious, although studies in the last

---

[18] David Davies, "The Significance of Taxation of Services for the Pattern of Distribution of Tax Burden by Income Class," *Proceedings of the National Tax Association for 1969*, pp. 138–46. A similar conclusion was reached by O. E. Nelson, "Progressivity of the Ontario Retail Sales Tax," *Canadian Tax Journal*, vol. 18 (September–October 1970), pp. 411–15, using Canadian data; a study by S. M. Ghazanfar concludes that including services other than utilities and housing would make the Idaho sales tax slightly less regressive. "Equity Effects and Revenue Potential of Sales Taxation of Services" *Public Finance Quarterly*, vol. 3 (April 1975), pp. 163–90.

[19] The Canadian provinces use similar levies.

decade have shown that there is a measurable loss to merchants in border communities.[20]

The danger is particularly great when the major shopping center for the region is in the other state (e.g., Memphis for northern Mississippi). But there is no simple way, short of federal assistance, that will allow the closing of this loophole, and Congress has considered legislation that would reduce still further the power of the states to force out-of-state vendors to collect and remit use tax.

While many transactions across state lines have escaped tax, some transactions have been taxed twice: by the state of original sale on an across-the-counter sale, and by the state of residence when the person brought the good home. Primarily, business firms were affected. Virtually all states now, however, provide credit for the tax paid the other state.

CONCLUSION

Sales taxes are inherently inferior relative to income taxes, basically because they cannot be adjusted in terms of the personal circumstances of the individual families. The primary objection to them is the regressiveness and the absolute burden on the poor; these can be lessened by food exemption, but only at the expense of other inequities and economic distortions. The best solution is the provision of a credit for sales tax paid on minimum purchases against income tax liability.

The primary justification for sales taxes is to be found for the states in a federal system where the national government dominates the income tax field and legislators fear adverse effects of income taxation on development of their state.

Unfortunately, however, the state levies leave a great deal to be desired in terms of structure. They do have the merit, with a few exceptions, of uniform rates and broad coverage of consumer goods. But by excluding services they omit a broad range of consumer expenditures; by providing commodity exemptions they introduce to some degree the evils of excise taxation, and by including some producers goods within the base of the taxes they bring about unequal burdens and cause economic distortions. For the most part, the structures have not been carefully examined in light of the objectives of the taxes. This is even more true of the provincial sales taxes, with their more extensive exemptions and higher rates.

---

[20] Harry E. McAllister, "The Border Tax Problem in Washington," *National Tax Journal*, vol. 14 (December 1961), pp. 362–74; William Hamovitch, "Effects of Increases in Sales Tax Rates on Taxable Sales in New York City," *Financing Government in New York City*, Graduate School of Public Administration of New York University Report to the Temporary Commission on City Finances (New York: New York University, 1966), pp. 619–34; John L. Mikesell, "Central Cities and Sales Tax Rate Differentials," *National Tax Journal*, vol. 23 (June 1970), pp. 206–13.

APPENDIX I—CANADIAN SALES TAXES

Federal: Manufacturers sales tax, 12 percent, with a rate of 5 percent on building materials.

Exemptions: food; electricity; fuel; insulation materials; drugs; clothing and footwear; bicycles; materials; manufacturing, farming, and mining machinery; commercial-transport equipment; construction equipment.

The government has thus far not acted on proposals to move the tax to the retail or wholesale level.

Provincial: All provinces, except Alberta, employ retail sales taxes, comparable in many respects to those of the states. Rates are shown in the table below.

Exemptions are broader than in the United States: food, prescription drugs, most books, farm machinery, feed, seed, and fertilizer are exempt in all provinces; most provinces exempt children's clothing and fuel.

There are numerous other exemptions.

Province	Rate (July 1, 1976)	Sales tax Revenue as Percentage of Provincial Revenue from Own Sources
Newfoundland	10%	28
Prince Edward Island	8%	25
Nova Scotia	8%	24
New Brunswick	8%	22
Quebec	8%	16
Ontario	7%	21
Manitoba	5%	19
Saskatchewan	5%	18
Alberta	no tax	—
British Columbia	7%	16

APPENDIX II—PROPOSALS FOR A FEDERAL SALES TAX IN THE UNITED STATES

While the United States has never used a sales tax at the federal level, there have been a number of proposals—in the early 1920s, during the depression year of 1932, during World War II, in the early 1950s, and in the late 1960s and early 1970s. The early proposals called for a manufacturers sales tax, either to lessen reliance on income taxes or to gain additional revenue. The more recent proposals call for a value-added tax.

Proposals for a Value-Added Tax to Replace the Corporate Income Tax

In the United States, the drive for a value-added tax began in the late fifties and gained considerable support during the sixties, in large measure from the same groups that had previously, without success, fought for a federal sales tax.

Balance of Payments

The argument that received greatest attention from 1965 to 1971 centered around foreign trade considerations and the persistent U.S. outflow of gold.

The basic argument, stressed particularly by D. T. Smith[21] and Richard Lindholm,[22] is that a country relying heavily on income taxes and not using a value-added tax, such as the United States, is placed at a relative disadvantage competing in world markets with countries using the value-added tax, and thus such a country can increase its exports and improve its balance-of-payments position by shifting from a corporate income tax. Therefore, U.S. producers are at a disadvantage in competing with firms in countries using the value-added tax, it is argued.

This argument has been subjected to a number of criticisms.[23] In the first place, it has validity, at least in the short run, only if the corporate income tax is reflected in higher prices (or if the value-added tax is not fully shifted); as discussed in Chapter 13, the extent of shifting of the corporate tax is unknown. Even if it is reflected in higher domestic prices, it is not necessarily reflected in higher export prices, where world competition is significant. If the corporate tax is not shifted and the value-added tax is, replacement of the former by the latter would not aid exports, despite the refund of value added tax on exports.

The greatest weakness in the argument, however, lies in the implicit assumption that the countries introducing the tax have reduced or eliminated corporate income taxes as a result of its use and have corporate income taxes lower than our own. The levies have been introduced to replace other forms of sales tax, not income taxes, and the corporate income levies of other industrial countries are, in fact, comparable to or, in some cases, higher than ours. Exact comparison is

---

[21] D. T. Smith, *Excise Tax Compendium*, Committee on Ways and Means, U.S. House of Representatives, 1964, pp. 89–98.

[22] Richard Lindholm, "National Tax System and International Balance of Payments," *National Tax Journal*, vol. 19 (June 1966), pp. 163–72.

[23] A detailed analysis is presented in the paper by R. A. Musgrave and Peggy Richman, "Allocation Aspects, Domestic and International," *The Role of Direct and Indirect Taxes in the Federal Revenue System* (Princeton: Princeton University Press, 1964), pp. 81–140.

difficult because of differences in definition of taxable income, but the levy of Germany—a chief competitor in world markets—is on the whole higher than ours. Thus, even if our corporate income tax is reflected in higher prices, we are not at a competitive disadvantage in world markets so long as corporate taxes of other countries are also reflected in higher prices. Given the greater degree of cooperation permitted competing companies in most countries, shifting is even more likely than in the United States. If we were to replace our corporate tax by a value-added tax, this would inevitably be regarded as an effort to create an unfair artificial advantage for our producers in world markets and would lead to retaliation.

Thirdly, the value-added taxes—like all sales taxes—are more likely to generate wage increases by increasing the cost of living. To the extent this occurs—given the exchange rates—the export position of the country will be weakened.

A final consideration relates to exchange rates. The tax structures of the various countries, to the extent that they affect export and import prices, influence the levels of exchange rates if the rates are flexible. Thus a country relying heavily on income taxes that are not refundable at export but are reflected in higher prices will over time have a lower foreign-exchange value for its money relative to countries with other tax structures. A change in the tax structure not accompanied by changes in exchange rates will of course alter the international-payments situation. And in practice, exchange rates have not been allowed to move freely. But any continuing foreign-exchange deficit experienced by the United States or any other country can be attributed to failure to devalue as appropriately as to the nature of the tax structure. Thus, in a sense, shift from a corporate income tax to a value-added tax may be regarded as identical with devaluation (or with a deliberate export subsidy).[24] A strong argument can be made for the position that balance-of-payments problems should be solved by foreign-exchange measures rather than by altering the tax structure.

Economic Efficiency

A second line of reasoning defends the value-added proposals on the grounds of greater economic efficiency. There are several aspects. The first, as stressed by Arnold Harberger, is that the corporate income tax produces numerous distortions in the economy—against the corporate sector, in favor of housing, and in favor of petroleum and other industries receiving special tax treatment.[25] These, presumably,

---

[24] C. E. McLure, Jr., "Taxes and the Balance of Payments: Another Alternative Analysis," *National Tax Journal*, vol. 21 (March 1968), pp. 57–69.

[25] Arnold Harberger, "Let's Try a Value Added Tax," *Challenge*, vol. 15 (November–December 1966), pp. 16–23.

would all be eliminated by a value-added tax, which would apply to corporate and noncorporate sectors and uniformly to all industries. Hopefully, of course, these inefficiencies could be eliminated by changes in the income tax structure, but this appears unlikely.

A second aspect of efficiency relates to the possible effect of the income tax in lessening pressures to efficiency, since the government shares about half of any losses. The significance of this argument is of course open to question. A related argument is that the income tax holds an umbrella over the inefficient firm, allowing it to continue because it pays no tax and penalizing the efficient profitable firms. Shift to the value-added tax will force the inefficient firm to improve its methods or go out of business. Transfer of resources from the less efficient to the more efficient will be speeded up. This analysis, of course, is based upon the dubious assumption that differences in profitability primarily reflect differences in efficiency rather than monopoly power, unanticipated changes in environment, and the age of the business. The value-added tax would—if not shifted—bear particularly hard on the new, growing, still unprofitable firm and the one struggling to maintain itself. If the tax is universally shifted, it will have no effect on the marginal firms.

The greatest weakness in the efficiency argument is that replacement of all or part of the corporate tax by a value-added tax would create serious distortion and inequity unless undistributed corporate profits were brought within the scope of the personal income tax; otherwise, such profits would escape income taxation completely. The difficulties of doing this were outlined in Chapter 13. If this were not done, tremendous incentive would be provided to shift to the corporate form of organization; strong incentive would be given to retain additional earnings in the business; and a large portion of income would escape income taxation on a current basis.

Other Arguments

Investment and Economic Growth. The third line of reasoning is the traditional one for consumption-related taxes—the lesser adverse effect on work and investment incentives and the higher savings-income ratio. These arguments need not be repeated.

Fiscal Policy Instrument. Arnold Harberger and others have argued for the tax as an additional weapon of fiscal policy—as an additional weapon to use to fight inflation and to finance sharp increases in spending; but the levy offers no great advantage over the income tax on this score and the danger of anticipatory effects of rate changes is more serious.

Objections to the Proposals

The objections to use of a federal value-added tax to replace the corporate income tax are primarily the objections to increased reliance on consumption-related taxation of any form: the less acceptable pattern of distributional effects, particularly the burden on the poor; the probable adverse effect upon maintaining full employment; and interference with the major source of state and local taxation. The tax, while basically anti-inflationary in terms of its effects on demand, would tend to push money wages up and aggravate inflation from the cost push side. These objections are particularly relevant when the federal income tax has just been significantly reduced.

The other major type of objection to a value-added tax is that if the federal government is to rely more heavily on indirect taxation, the value-added tax offers no significant advantages over the retail sales tax and has major disadvantages. As noted earlier in the chapter, the spreading out of the impact of the value-added tax throughout the production and distribution channels, highly important in many countries, offers no advantage in the United States. Introduction of the tax would result in substantial work for business firms, in handling a new tax different in many respects from present levies, whereas they are familiar with retail sales taxes and could handle a federal retail tax in the same fashion as they now handle the state levies. The retail sales tax is a very familiar form of levy; the value-added tax is not. While retailers would have less tax obligation directly to the government, more of their working capital would be tied up in tax on their purchases.

Forty-five of the states, with over 98 percent of the population of the country, employ sales taxes, with local supplements or separately collected local sales taxes in a number of them (including several of the largest—New York, California, Texas, Illinois). If a federal sales tax were imposed on the retail level, substantial coordination of operation of the two taxes would be possible. Records required would be the same for the two taxes and tax return forms would be similar. In fact, both taxes could be collected on the basis of a single tax return (as is, common now with the state-local levies), and joint auditing, or at least reliance by one level of government on the audits of the other (as with the corporate income tax), would be possible. The value-added tax would require two separate sets of sales tax records and two types of tax returns (although theoretically they could still be included on the same form), and auditing would be different. A federal retail sales tax would encourage greater uniformity among the state sales taxes, while a value-added tax would have no such effect. The opposite argument sometimes made, that the use of the retail tax by the states makes it necessary for the federal government to use a different form of sales tax, has no merit; the value-added tax in the end is carried forward into retail prices and from the standpoint of the consumers (and taxpayers) is no different from a retail sales tax.

Other difficulties of the value-added tax were noted earlier in the chapter: The greater complexity in handling exemptions and the complications created if the tax is not applied to certain sectors, such as agriculture. The tax works best if applied uniformly to all types of economic activity at a uniform rate, but to do so would create serious nuisance problems with farmers and place a much heavier burden on the consumption of certain services, particularly professional ones, local transportation, and so on, than is usually regarded as desirable.

REFERENCES

Due, J. F.   *State and Local Sales Taxation.* Chicago: Public Administration Service, 1971.

McLure, C. E., and Ture, N.   *Value Added Tax: Two Views.* Washington: American Enterprise Institute, 1972.

Musgrave, R. A., ed.   *Broad Based Taxes.* Baltimore: Johns Hopkins University Press, for Committee for Economic Development, 1973, pp. 133–227.

Schiff, E.   *Value Added Taxation in Europe.* Washington: American Enterprise Institute, 1973.

Tait, A. A.   *Value Added Tax.* London: McGraw-Hill U.K. Ltd., 1972.

A Value Added Tax, Symposium volume, Tax Institute. Princeton: Tax Institute, 1972.

The Value Added Tax and Alternative Sources of Federal Revenue. Washington: Advisory Commission on Intergovernmental Relations, 1973. The ACIR report on a federal value-added tax.

16

The Taxation of Wealth; The Property Tax

The prize for the most unpopular levy in the United States today goes to the property tax. It is condemned from all sides as inequitable and regressive, as an obstacle to economic development and elimination of slum housing; it is labeled with virtually every condemnatory adjective conceivable. Several state supreme courts, commencing with that of California in the case of *Serrano* v. *Priest*, held that the tax is unconstitutional as a basis for financing of education because it favors wealthy areas over poor ones.[1] Yet the tax continues as a major source of revenue. This chapter explores the question of the property tax: how it operates, how objectionable it actually is, what can be done to improve it.

The property tax is one principal form of a broader category of wealth taxes—taxes related to the wealth persons have at any particular time, rather than the income they receive over a period of time, the amount they spend on consumption, or other measures. The property tax as it operates in the United States and Canada is essentially an *in rem* (on objects rather than people) levy, imposed upon property per se, on gross value without regard to claims outstanding against it or the personal circumstances of the owners.

The alternative form of wealth-related taxation is the net-wealth tax, imposed upon individuals on the basis of their net wealth. This form of tax, while not used in the United States, will be considered first to serve as a basis for evaluation of the property tax.

---

[1] 487 P. 2d 1241, 96 Cal. Rptr. 601(1971).

NET-WEALTH TAXES[2]

A net-wealth tax is a levy imposed upon individuals, not corporations, on the basis of their net wealth, that is, the total value of all assets they own, including cash and bank deposits, securities, and real property, less debts or other claims outstanding against them. Corporate property is reached via the securities outstanding in the hands of the owners and creditors. Certain items could, of course, be exempted or, as is more consistent with the philosophy of the taxes, a minimum exemption could be provided, comparable to that of the personal exemptions under the income tax. This figure can be adjusted for the number of dependents. The rate can be proportional or progressive as desired.

Use

Net-wealth taxes are used in at least 14 countries of the world: the Scandinavian countries, Germany, Luxembourg, Switzerland, the Netherlands, Japan, India, Ceylon and Pakistan, Uruguay and Colombia.[3] Other Latin American countries and Japan have used it, at least for limited periods. Several major characteristics of the taxes can be noted briefly:

1.   The family is typically the unit for the tax, the holdings of the wife and minor children being combined with those of the husband. Four countries do apply the tax to corporations, thus deviating from the basic principle of a net-wealth tax.

2.   Normally all assets are included, with minor exceptions, such as personal effects.

3.   Exemptions are provided for small amounts of property in all countries. In most countries, the figures are relatively low—from two to four times the per capita income of the country, but in India and Pakistan, where the taxes were aimed at large concentrations of wealth, the figures range from 500 to 1,000 times the per capita income.

4.   The rates are proportional in several, progressive in others, particularly in those where the levies are aimed mainly at the very wealthy. The proportional rates have in recent years been either 0.5 percent or 1 percent, the progressive rates ranging from 0.5 or 1 percent to 2 or 3 percent, and thus sufficiently low that the tax can usually be paid from annual income.

5.   The taxes are, for the most part, administered nationally and in

---

[2] A strong plea for net-wealth taxation is presented by L. C. Thurow in his book *The Impact of Taxes on the American Economy* (New York: Praeger, 1971).

[3] N. Tanabe, "The Taxation of Net Wealth," *I.M.F. Staff Papers*, vol. 14 (March 1967), pp. 124–67.

conjunction with income tax administration; often the same return forms are used. Local net-wealth taxes, are, however, used in Switzerland, Norway, and Denmark.

6. In no instance are the net-wealth taxes major revenue sources, the figures typically being from 1 to 2 percent of total tax revenues. Of all the users, Colombia has been the most successful, the yield reaching 5 percent of total revenue.

Economic Effects

Given the limited experience with net-wealth taxes and the relatively low rates, little or no empirical evidence of economic effects is available. But some observations can be offered on the basis of economic analysis.

Effects on Savings and Investment. A net-wealth tax differs from an income tax in two basic ways. First, the tax applies to the entire stock of wealth a person has rather than the amount acquired during the year. Since the total base is much larger, the rate is lower for a given revenue. Secondly, as with a consumption tax, there is no direct connection between the earning of the income and the liability for tax; only if the person adds the sum to wealth is tax liability created, and then only in subsequent periods, not directly in full during the period.

In brief summary, there are several possible consequences arising out of these differences.

1. Since savings, regardless of the form in which it is kept, will create additional tax liability, a wealth tax is almost certain to reduce savings to a greater extent than a consumption-related tax, the exact extent depending upon the response of the volume of savings to changes in the net return from savings. As compared to an income tax, however, the net difference is not obvious. Savings does give rise directly to additional wealth tax liability, whereas savings increases income tax liability only if the savings is placed in income-yielding assets. On the other hand, the wealth tax rate is very much lower than the income tax for a given sum of revenue.

2. The wealth tax will have less deterring effect on investment decisions than an income tax per dollar of revenue and thus facilitates attainment of full employment. The wealth tax applies to personal assets whether they are income-yielding or not; the income tax applies only to the income earned from additional assets acquired. The wealth tax will therefore not only have less deterring effect on investment decisions generally, but it will discourage persons from holding cash, vacant land for speculative purposes, and low-yield investments, and encourage them to purchase assets that involve or lead to real investment activity. Some persons would be forced to turn to higher-yield equity investments in order to be able to pay the tax without disposal

of assets. The net effect is to increase the willingness to take risk. The income tax reaches only the cash earnings from financial investments and not the liquidity and security advantages; the wealth tax avoids this penalty on high-yield investments. Essentially, the wealth tax encourages holders of assets to seek to increase the earnings of their assets since increasing the monetary yield does not in itself increase tax liability. The net result is to facilitate attainment of full employment.

Labor Supply. Like any tax, the wealth tax has an income effect, encouraging persons to work more to offset the decline in after-tax income. But unlike the income tax there is no offsetting substitution effect since tax liability is not affected by the income earned, except to the extent that a portion may be saved.

On the whole, therefore, wealth taxes are likely to produce somewhat less factor excess burden than income taxes, but the difference cannot be calculated.

Distortion of Production Methods and Consumption Patterns. As noted, the net-wealth tax is likely to have less unfavorable effects on investment than an income tax, in part because it should make persons more willing to supply money capital on an equity basis. But at the same time, the more capital intensive the production methods, the greater the tax liability; the net effect might be to encourage the use of somewhat more labor intensive methods by noncorporate forms of business. Given the usual rates of a net-worth tax, the possibility is slight, but with heavier burdens the effect might be significant.

Taxes on net wealth may likewise distort consumption patterns away from durable consumer goods that give rise to wealth tax liability in favor of nondurable goods. The magnitude of such change is unknown; at net-wealth tax rates actually used, one would not expect to see significant changes.

Distributional Effects. The net-wealth tax is a personal levy directly related to the person's net wealth. If factor supplies are not affected at all and all markets are perfectly competitive, the burden will rest upon the persons upon whom it is imposed. Therefore, the tax will reduce the return to capital, including the implicit return on owner-occupied homes. This is the most likely consequence in a short-run period, with a relatively fixed supply of capital. If, however, the supply of savings is reduced relative to that with other forms of tax, as suggested in the preceding section, then the rate of return on capital will rise and a portion of the tax will be shared with labor. In addition, if the tax affects the relative attractiveness of various forms of investment, including that in various types of consumer durables, there will be some readjustment of burden away from the initial pattern.

To the extent that the burden is distributed in the pattern of the initial impact, persons with large incomes relative to their net wealth will pay relatively less with the net-wealth tax than with the income tax, while the reverse is true with those with disproportionate amounts of net wealth. Thus in higher income levels the progressivity will be greater with a wealth tax than an income tax with given rate patterns since wealth is much more unequally distributed than income at the higher levels. The lowest income groups have higher ratios of wealth to income than those in middle-income groups, however, as shown in Table 16–1, with some consequent regressivity at low-income levels. There is not a high correlation of income and wealth among families in particular income levels, and thus there is extensive dispersion of wealth tax relative to income.

TABLE 16–1
Ratios of Wealth to Income by Income Groups

Income Bracket	Average Family Wealth	Ratio of Wealth to Income
$0 –2,999	$ 7,609	5.1
3,000 –4,999	10,025	2.5
5,000 –7,499	13,207	2.1
7,500 –9,999	19,131	2.2
10,000–14,999	28,021	2.2
15,000–24,999	62,996	3.1
25,000–49,999	291,317	7.8
50,000–99,999	653,223	8.7
100,000 and over	1,698,021	–

Source: U.S. Department of Commerce, Bureau of the Census, *Statistical Abstract of the United States, 1968*, p. 333.

Equity

The strongest case for a net wealth tax is on equity grounds. While income is generally accepted to be the most satisfactory single measure of tax capacity, it is not, used alone, an entirely satisfactory measure, because tax capacity obviously depends upon the amount a person has already accumulated—net wealth—as well as current income. If two persons each have $10,000 income a year, but one has accumulated $30,000 and the other nothing, clearly the first person has more tax capacity. The first person has a reserve for emergency and old age and therefore has less obligation to save and feels able to maintain a higher order of consumption with the given income. The possession of wealth is in itself a source of satisfaction and prestige. Consumption-related taxes compensate to some degree for this inadequacy of the income tax but not fully so. Many expenditures cannot easily be reached by the consumption tax, and this type of levy cannot possibly reach the miser—the person with large accumulated wealth who has little current income and spends relatively little—sitting on the bare floor of a delapidated house counting his gold.[4]

Second, the use of a net wealth tax has the effect of placing a higher tax burden on property income than on wage and salary income. This is commonly defended on equity grounds, on the argument that property income is more permanent than labor income and does not require direct human effort to acquire.

Third, the net-wealth tax compensates for the discrimination of the income tax against the returns from more risky types of assets. The liquidity and security returns from cash and low-yield assets are not reached by the income tax, which favors persons who prefer this type of investment. The net-wealth tax reaches all wealth equally regardless of the yield on it.

Finally, and closely related, the net-wealth tax with progressive rates can more effectively break up large concentrations of wealth, if this is regarded as equitable. As noted, wealth is distributed much more unevenly than income. This argument is particularly pertinent in some developing economies in South America and Southeast Asia characterized by extreme inequality of wealth.

This equity argument, however, should not be exaggerated. Of the two measures, income is the most satisfactory, since income is the primary determinant of family living levels and the primary source from which tax is paid. To rely heavily on net-wealth taxes as compared to income taxes would place severe burden on some groups of persons—ones with large investments in assets not currently yielding money income and persons owning their homes but having relatively little current income—the elderly, particularly. The primary argument is that a combination of the income and net-wealth bases, with dominant reliance on the former but partial use of the latter, can produce an overall pattern of distributional effects more closely conforming with usual standards of equity than either tax used alone.

Administrative Considerations

On the positive side, it is often argued that a net-wealth tax would facilitate administration of the income tax, since the two taxes would reinforce each other from an operational standpoint. Since persons would be required to list all assets for the net-wealth tax, it would be more difficult for them to escape tax on capital gains or from property earnings; the reported dividends, interest, and other items of property income would facilitate enforcement of the net-wealth tax.

This argument undoubtedly has some validity. But, nevertheless, the net-wealth tax in itself is a much more difficult tax to operate than

---

[4] If transfer at death were defined as consumption, the consumption tax would be more effective in reaching wealth, but not on a current basis.

the income tax, even if the two are used in conjunction with each other. Income and consumption taxes are levies upon flows—upon transactions during a period of time. The values are therefore the values of the transactions—with some modifications, primarily arising out of depreciation of capital. But a net-wealth tax is a levy upon an accumulated stock, not on a transaction, and constructive valuation is necessary. The values of many properties, particularly common stock, fluctuate frequently and widely.

Discovery. A primary problem is to ascertain the existence of property for which there is no registered title or other external indication of its existence. Cash is the extreme example, but jewelry, non-registered bonds, and even stock of small closely held businesses create problems, although the stock can be tracked down if sufficient effort is made. The others are extremely hard to find.

The cross-check with the income tax is probably less advantageous than it might appear to be. The obvious items can be checked—but with much property, a cross-check, even with modern computers, would be a difficult, time-consuming, and costly process.

Valuation. The most fundamental problems center around valuation. Many types of property do have current ascertainable values—cash, bonds, stock of widely held corporations, and even real property of a type of which some parcels are frequently being sold. But other forms of real estate and holdings in closely held businesses have no current ascertainable value; all that can be done is to construct a figure—and this is extremely difficult to do in any accurate fashion. The inevitable consequence will be substantial inequality in assessment among various persons, the same problems now encountered with the property tax. This is the fundamental difficulty with the net-wealth tax, as has been demonstrated by experience in Japan and elsewhere. It is not a conclusive argument against the use of the tax, but it constitutes a major weakness and one that inevitably limits the revenue potentiality of the tax. A related problem centers around the need for selecting a particular date for the year; any one selected may not be representative of the value over the year and use of an average greatly adds to complications.

In conclusion: A net-wealth tax, if effectively operated, could make a significant contribution to the overall effectiveness of a tax system, supplementing the income tax. Of necessity, it would have to be a national tax; it would be impossible for local or even state governments to operate a net-wealth tax effectively. And even at the national level there are serious doubts about the potential effectiveness of operation. Much of the potential equity would be lost if all property were not discovered and valued with equal effectiveness. Because of these problems, the tax at present is not a serious contender as a major revenue source. It is a form of levy that improved administration in the future may make possible. Meanwhile it serves as a standard with which the property tax may be compared.

THE PROPERTY TAX

While net-wealth taxes have not been used in the United States or Canada another form of wealth taxation, the property tax, is a major source of revenue. In 1975 in the United States the yield of the property tax was $51 billion, providing 82 percent of local government tax revenue, and 12 percent of total federal, state, and local tax revenues. The Canadian percentages are 87 percent and 8 percent respectively. Somewhat similar levies, called rates, are major sources of local government revenue in Great Britain and the Commonwealth countries of East and Central Africa, as well as Australia and New Zealand. We will be primarily concerned with the tax in the United States, with some reference to that elsewhere.

Development of the U.S. Property Tax

In Colonial days, taxes were imposed upon particular types of property—land, houses, carriages—often at specific rates. These were carried over into the new states. During the early part of the 18th century, partly to gain additional revenue, partly to accord with the philosophy that all property should be treated alike, the taxes became general ad valorem levies on all forms of property; real (land and improvements permanently affixed to land), tangible personal (movable property having intrinsic value, such as furniture), and intangible personal (property not desired for its intrinsic value but as a claim against, title to, evidence of ownership in, or means of acquiring other property).[5] For many decades, the tax was a major source of state revenue and the primary source of local revenue. As subsequently explained, in the United States the states came to rely less and less heavily on the tax until today many do not use it at all; the local governments have continued to rely primarily upon it, although supplementing it by other levies. Thus the relative role of the tax has declined somewhat, but it is still the fourth most important tax in the country as a whole.

Steps in the Operation of the Tax

Since the property tax functions in a substantially different fashion from other levies, a brief summary is desirable. In part the differences

---

[5] In Canada, similar levies have been confined, with a few exceptions, to real property only; personal property was never brought within the scope of the tax.

arise from the importance of valuation, in part from the fact that the tax serves as the residual revenue source for local governments, the rate being adjusted each year to provide the desired revenue.

Assessment. The first step is assessment of property, that is, of the placing of a value for tax purposes upon all property in the taxing jurisdiction. This task is performed by a local tax assessor, frequently chosen by election.[6] The initiative in the assessment of the real property rests with the assessor, who places a value upon all such property, using the title records of the property as guide to the ownership.[7] Assessment is performed as of a certain date, usually early in the spring. Annual assessment is often required by law but rarely occurs in practice, the figure of the preceding year being carried on to the next. As noted below, assessment is often very carelessly done.

Review or Appeal. The taxpayer has the right to appeal any assessment to a board of review, usually the county commissioners or a similar body sitting ex officio for this purpose for a few days during the year.[8]

Determination of the Tax Rate. Once assessment is complete, the individual assessments are summed to determine the total assessed valuation of all property in each taxation jurisdiction—county, township, city, town, or village, school district, special district. Each of these jurisdictions then determines its own property tax rate by dividing the figure of the total assessed valuation in the area into the sum to be collected from the property tax. The rate, which is a percentage, is usually expressed as mills of tax per dollar of assessed value or dollars per $100. The property tax is essentially the residual levy, being adjusted to obtain the money needed to meet expenditures that is not provided by other revenue sources.

The figure set must not exceed the maximum rate allowed by state constitution or law or city charter. Furthermore, in determining expenditures, the local legislative body will be influenced by political repercussions that may arise from any change in tax rate that will be required. Thus the process of determining the rate is not in fact merely

---

[6] The assessor is typically a county official in the West and South and a township official in the East. In some areas, cities assess property for city taxes separately from the county or township assessment.

[7] In most states, the initiative in the assessment of personal property rests upon the taxpayer, who must file a statement of such property owned and place a value (subject to change by the assessor) upon it.

[8] Following this appeal, the taxpayer may contest the assessment in court, but rarely is this action successful unless the procedure of assessment has been faulty or the property is clearly assessed in excess of its sale value. The courts typically, but not universally, take the position that the property owner is not entitled to legal redress of assessment so long as his or her assessment does not exceed the percentage of value specified by law, even though the assessment may be relatively much higher than that of other property in the taxing jurisdiction. In recent years, however, in several states courts have ordered overall reassessment because of individual inequities.

a process of arithmetic, as might at first appear. If the planned expenditures require a tax rate that exceeds the legal or politically feasible limit, either the expenditures must be reduced or other sources of revenue must be found.

Calculation of Each Tax Bill. In most states, each of the local units in the area reports its rate to a county official, who then figures the total tax bill on each piece of property by summing the various rates (school district, city, county, etc.) to which the property is subject and applying this figure to the assessed value.

Treatment of Delinquency. If the tax is not paid by the due date, the tax becomes a lien against the property, which is ultimately sold at public auction. [9]

State Assessment

At a relatively early date, it became apparent that local assessors could not adequately determine the value of segments of railroad lines and, later, public utility facilities within their jurisdictions. A five-mile stretch of railway line crossing a county has no value distinct from its role as a segment in the entire system. As a consequence, toward the end of the last century, most states assumed the task of assessing railways and, in many states, all public utility property. State assessment, often called central assessment, permitted the task to be performed by experts in the field and use of the unit rule, that is, assessment of the entire railroad or utility as a unit. Following assessment, the property is allocated back to the local units, largely on a mileage basis, for taxation along with other property. [10] In Hawaii the state assesses all property. The province of Ontario has also taken over all assessment work.

Economic Effects

The tax will have economic effects somewhat similar to those of a net-wealth tax, as contrasted to an income tax, but there are significant differences.

---

[9] The buyer usually receives only a temporary deed for a period of years, during which time the original owner has a chance to redeem the property by paying the taxes due and penalties. Eventually, in most states the buyer obtains a clear title if no redemption occurs.

[10] State assessment gave rise to numerous debates over the question of the appropriate method of valuing the property of the enterprises involved. The aim is to obtain a figure for which the property would be sold in an open market sale, but since such property rarely sells, the task of ascertaining a suitable figure is a troublesome one. The states stress the capitalization of earnings basis, largely on the premise that the selling price of a property basically depends upon the amount the property can earn. In order to ensure some tax revenue from enterprises yielding no profit, an arbitrary minimum figure, per mile in the case of railways, is frequently employed for such companies. In 1966, the states assessed $42 billion of the total assessment of $484 billion.

Factor Supplies. 1. Investment: As with the net-wealth tax, earning of additional income per se does not give rise to additional tax liability. Furthermore, with the property tax, savings do not give rise to tax liability unless they are placed in assets actually subject to tax. Accordingly, the tax would appear to have less substitution effect on savings-consumption decisions than an income tax or a net-wealth tax.

Unlike the net-wealth tax, however, the property tax does not divert holders of wealth away from cash and other liquid low-yield assets toward equity investments and thus has less effect in encouraging risk-taking and the making of funds available for real investments. It does divert investors from speculative holding of land, which is encouraged by the capital gains features of income taxes.

2. Labor supply: The property tax, like the net-wealth tax, should have less potential effects upon labor supply than the income tax. While, as with all taxes, there is an income effect leading persons to work more, there is little or no substitution effect, since earning additional labor income does not give rise to tax liability unless the funds are invested in assets subject to tax.

3. Land: A substantial portion of the tax rests upon land. By definition, the supply of land available to society is fixed, but the tax can affect the intensity with which land is utilized. The tax increases the cost of holding land idle for speculative purposes relative to the effect of an income tax. Since the amount of tax on the land is independent of the actual earnings of the land, the tax encourages the owner to seek to make more efficient use of it. Like a lump-sum tax, the tax on land, unlike the tax on capital goods, has only an income effect; it has no substitution effect since the earning of additional income does not raise the tax liability.

Allocative and Efficiency Effects. The property tax as it operates inevitably shifts investment away from real property, upon which it bears with particular severity. Much of the burden rests on owner-occupied homes; this portion cannot be shifted, and thus persons are discouraged from making this form of investment (although the effect is offset in part or entirely in the upper income levels by the favorable treatment given owner-occupied homes under the federal income tax). Another major portion rests on rental housing; given potential rents, there may be difficulty in shifting the tax, and thus the total volume of investment in rental housing is undoubtedly reduced below what it would be with a net-wealth or income tax used in lieu of the property tax.[11] The same may be true to some extent of other forms of investment in real property construction—store and office buildings, fac-

---

[11] Orr concludes, on the basis of rental data in the Boston area, that differentially higher rates on rental housing are not shifted. L. L. Orr, "The Incidence of Differential Property Taxes on Urban Housing," *National Tax Journal,* vol. 21 (September 1968), pp. 253–62.

tories, and so on—although in some of these instances the potentiality of shifting appears to be greater. In general, the tax encourages relatively greater use of labor intensive methods of production.

The tax also distorts relative investment and output among various industries. Unlike the income tax, the property tax, imposed on the value of business property as well as personal property, is heavier relative to sales of the firms in the capital-intensive industries than in the labor-intensive industries. It is particularly high per dollar of receipts on public utilities, railroads, timber owners, and similar establishments and low on many service industries, for example. The inevitable effect is to raise the prices of products of the capital-intensive industries and reduce their relative outputs compared to other industries.

Netzer and others have concluded that the adverse effects are most serious on the railroads, because of their heavy investment in real property and the competition to which they are subject from motor transport, which pays relatively little property tax. The burden on the railroads is reduced somewhat by the tendency in most states to assess them primarily on the basis of capitalization of earnings, a method not used for other types of business. But even so, there is bound to be some artificial reallocation of resources away from the railroad industry because of the property tax.

Because the levy is a local tax, rates (and assessment standards) differ among various local jurisdictions. As a consequence, location decisions, particularly of fabricating and warehousing activity, may be affected. Various studies of location decisions generally suggest that taxes are not a major factor. But within a metropolitan area, the effects may be significant. Particularly attractive are "industrial enclaves," industrial suburbs with few functions to perform but substantial industrial property. Experience suggests that the tax on business inventory has greater significance in location decisions than that on real property.

The tax produces distortions in particular industries based on the character of the industry. For example, a tax tends to encourage premature cutting of timber if it is assessed on the usual basis against standing timber; the lumber companies are given an incentive to cut the trees quickly and abandon the land instead of logging indefinitely on a selective basis. Most timber states have adjusted the tax to eliminate this effect by relating the tax to output rather than the value of the standing timber. Somewhat similar effects may arise with mines; the companies are given incentive to get the high-grade ore out as quickly as possible and abandon the low-grade ore, instead of taking low-grade ore out with high-grade ore.

The use of one particular date during the year likewise has peculiar distorting effects. The one-day inventory rule in California results in the jamming of railway freight yards in Nevada shortly before April 1 as shippers have the cars held back from entering California until after April 1.

Finally, the tax is often charged with deterring improvements to homes and other real property. Property owners may defer painting their buildings and making other repairs in fear that doing so will lead to higher property assessments.

Distributional Impact—The Traditional View

The issue of the incidence and thus distributional impact of the property tax has become a highly controversial one in recent years.

The issue is complicated by the fact that the tax is made up essentially of several elements, the distributional impact of the various elements being different.

Owner-Occupied Housing.   Because the payment of property tax is not related to the earning of a person's income, this portion cannot be shifted forward to anyone else and reduces incomes in relation to actual amounts paid.

Land.   By definition, the supply of land is fixed; it has no cost of production, and prices are determined in somewhat imperfect but nevertheless relatively purely competitive markets. As a consequence, since supply is not reduced, the tax cannot be shifted forward

Figure 16–1
Response of Rental Charges to Property Taxation

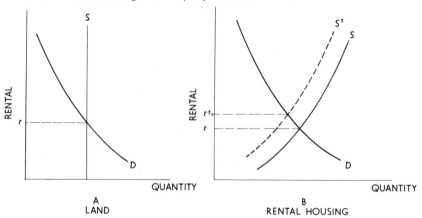

A
LAND

B
RENTAL HOUSING

(Figure 16–1A). Instead, the tax capitalizes: It reduces the selling price of the land by the capitalized sum of the tax. Selling prices of land are determined by the capitalization of expected returns; with a 5 percent interest rate, a parcel of land yielding, net, $500 a year to infinity will sell for $10,000 (subject to variations depending upon the diversity of expectations about future returns). A tax of $100 a year is imposed; the sale price will fall to $8,000, or by the capitalized sum of the $100. The market does not function this perfectly, but certainly such a tendency is to be expected. If the tax were universal and actually reduced the overall net rate of return, the selling price might not fall, but this is unlikely. A study of property values in San Francisco when property taxes on homes were increased sharply supports the capitalization hypothesis; property values did fall below the otherwise prevailing figures when tax was increased.[12] Even more complete capitalization was found in a study by A. M. Church of single-family residences in Martinez, California; a study of farmland values by E. C. Pasour concluded that property taxes are largely capitalized into farm property values.[13] But a study by T. J. Wales and E. G. Wiens, which seeks to eliminate various biases, concluded that there is no evidence of capitalization, in a municipality in the Vancouver, British Columbia, area, and a study by A. T. King found only limited evidence of capitalization in New Haven.[14]

Rental Housing. Another major segment of the tax rests upon rental housing. Given the expected rate of return, the property tax on rental housing will lead to a reduction in supply of such housing, which in turn will lead to higher rents and a forward shifting of part of the tax to the tenants (Figure 18–1B). A portion of the tax is likely to shift backwards to the landowner because the demand for land falls. The forward-shifting process may take considerable time, however; if there is a temporary surplus of such housing, landlords will not be able to raise rents in the usual housing market. Not only will they bear the current tax but the selling prices of their buildings will fall. Landlords may find it impossible to shift differentially higher taxes when taxes vary in metropolitan areas; this is borne out by work of Larry Orr for the Boston area.[15]

---

[12] R. S. Smith, "Property Tax Capitalization in San Francisco," *National Tax Journal*, vol. 23 (June 1970), pp. 177–93. Smith also summarizes other empirical studies of capitalization. The primary difficulty in the studies has been that of excluding the effects on land values of the increased government expenditures financed by the higher property taxes. The San Francisco experience was particularly significant because the tax changed very sharply with no significant changes in government services. Capitalization is also demonstrated in the work of W. F. Oates, "The Effect of Property Taxes and Local Public Spending on Property Values," *Journal of Political Economy*, vol. 77 (November–December 1969), pp. 957–71.

[13] "Capitalization of the Effective Property Tax Rate on Single Family Dwellings," *National Tax Journal*, vol. 27 (March 1974), pp. 113–22; "The Capitalization of Real Property Taxes Levied on Farm Real Estate," *American Journal of Agricultural Economics*, vol. 57 (November 1975), pp. 539–48.

[14] T. J. Wales and E. G. Wiens, "Capitalization of Residential Property Taxes: An Empirical Study," *Review of Economics and Statistics*, vol. 56 (August 1974), pp. 329–33; A. T. King, *Property Taxes, Amenities and Residential Land Values.* Cambridge, Mass.: Ballinger, 1973.

[15] Orr, "Incidence of Differential Property Taxes."

Other Business Property. A large portion of the tax rests initially on business property of all types. Here a less clear-cut answer is possible. The tax becomes a business expense and can be expected, at least over time, to be reflected in higher prices to the consumers of the products. But the ratio of tax to sales will not be uniform among or within industries. Capital intensity varies, as well as property tax assessments and tax rates. Firms subject to high taxes relative to sales will find great difficulty in shifting the differential. The small, uneven annual increments likewise make the uniformity of action that is common under sales and excise taxes difficult if not impossible. Thus much less precise and uniform shifting will occur; portions will rest for a time on monopoly profits and on other returns to the owners.

One other element in the picture may be important for both commercial property as well as urban housing, particularly in urban areas; the reduced demand for sites for construction will tend to reduce the rents earned by the landowners, so that a portion of the tax applied to buildings will end up on the landowners, with consequent capitalization.[16]

Empirical Studies of Distributional Effects by Income Level

A number of studies have been made of the distributional effects of the property tax, under the traditional assumptions about incidence. Two of these are illustrated on Figs. 16–2 and 16–3, and the results of several are shown in Table 16–2, reproduced from a Brookings study.

The principal conclusions reached are as follows:

1. The burden of the tax on residential property is distributed in a highly regressive fashion at the lower income levels, more or less proportional in the middle income levels, and, in most studies, somewhat regressive at high income levels.

2. The portion of the tax on tenants appears to be highly regressive.

3. The pattern of the tax as a whole, under the incidence assumptions employed, appears to be regressive, but less sharply so at the lower income levels than the tax on residential property.

The basic reason for regressivity, so far as housing is concerned, is that family expenditures on housing as a percentage of current income fall as family incomes rise. This is true of both owner-occupied and rental housing, and is explainable in part by the fact that housing decisions are often made for long periods and not reconsidered as income changes. Older families often have housing outlays all out of proportion to their current incomes as they have not adjusted housing downward after they have retired. Regressivity, so far as tenants are concerned, is increased by the fact that the ratio of rent to income falls

---

[16] R. L. Richmond, in "The Incidence of Urban Real Estate Taxes," *Land Economics*, vol. 63 (May 1967), pp. 172–80, argues that virtually all the tax on improvements will fall on the owners of the land.

FIGURE 16–2

Total Property Taxes as Percentage of Family Income, Massachusetts 1967

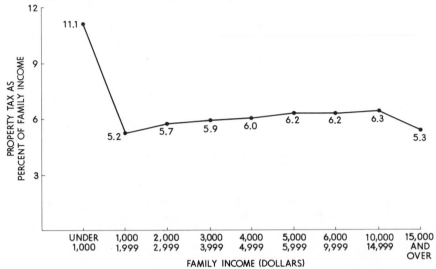

Source: S. H. Beer and R. E. Barringer, eds. *The State and the Poor* (Cambridge, Mass. Winthrop, 1970), p. 289.

FIGURE 16–3

Property Tax Payments as Percent of Income by Income Bracket, 1968

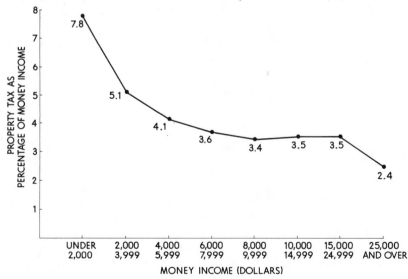

Source: A.C.I.R., unpublished material, 1972.

TABLE 16-2

Estimates of the Property Tax as a Percentage of Income under the Traditional View, by Income Class, Various Years, 1957–1970 (classes income in thousands of dollars; other figures in percent)

	Netzer—1957			Musgrave—1968		Pechman-Okner—1966		ACIR—1970	
Money Income Class	Nonresidential Property	Residential Property	Total Property	Income Class	Total Property	Family Income Class	Total Property	Family Income Class	Residential Property
Less than 2	4.0	3.3	7.3	Less than 4	6.7	Less than 3	6.5	Less than 2	16.6
2–3	3.4	1.6	5.0	4.0–5.7	5.7	3–5	4.8	2–3	9.7
3–4	3.2	1.4	4.6	5.7–7.9	4.7	5–10	3.6	3–4	7.7
4–5	3.4	1.4	4.8	7.9–10.4	4.3	10–15	3.2	4–5	6.4
5–7	2.2	1.7	3.9	10.4–12.5	4.0	15–20	3.2	5–6	5.5
7–10	1.6	2.0	3.6	12.5–17.5	3.7	20–25	3.1	6–7	4.7
10–15	1.3	2.7	4.0	17.5–22.6	3.3	25–30	3.1	7–10	4.2
15 and over	1.7	1.6	3.3	22.6–35.5	3.0	30–50	3.0	10–15	3.7
				35.5–92.0	2.9	50–100	2.8	15–25	3.3
				92.0 and over	3.3	100–500	2.4	25 and over	2.9
						500–1,000	1.7		
						1,000 and over	0.8		
Average, all classes	—	—	4.6	Average, all classes	3.9	Average, all classes	3.4	Average, all classes	4.9

Source: H. J. Aaron, *Who Pays the Property Tax?* Washington, D.C.: The Brookings Institution, 1975, p. 26. Aaron himself, of course, does not accept the traditional view.

significantly as incomes rise—although this effect is offset in part by the fact that the ratio of value to rent of rental buildings rises as income rises. Cheaper rental accommodations tend to be in deteriorating areas in which property values are low relative to the rents that can be obtained.[17] There is some evidence, however, that assessors determine sale value of deteriorated housing by applying a multiplier to gross rents; if they do, these properties will be overassessed relative to sale value, thus weakening or eliminating this force tending to lessen regressivity.

The same question is raised with the property tax as with the sales tax about the significance of the permanent component doctrine involving consideration of lifetime incomes rather than incomes in particular years. Decisions about purchases of consumer durables, including houses, appear to be governed more by expected lifetime incomes—"permanent" or "normal" incomes—than by incomes of particular years. Lifetime incomes show less variation among families than incomes in a particular year. The work of Margaret Reid suggests an income elasticity of 2 for housing expenditures when related to permanent component income.[18] Further evidence is provided by study of the relationship between the value of owner occupied housing and the incomes of the owners, averaged over a five-year period; the distribution was somewhat progressive.[19]

Accordingly, it may be argued, the tax is less regressive than it might appear to be. Apart from questions that may be raised about the permanent income hypothesis itself, there are two replies that may be made to the argument that regressivity is less in view of the hypothesis. First, there is now substantial evidence to indicate that a large portion of the poor is permanently poor; it is the ghetto resident who is primarily burdened by the property tax. Second, taxes must be paid on a current-year basis, and current income is the item of direct concern to the taxpayer. Many of the permanently poor are the elderly—for whom the property tax burden is a very severe one relative to incomes—yet they are most reluctant to sell their homes and move into rental housing.

Distributional Impact—Application of the Harberger Model

As stressed in recent years by Peter Mieszkowski[20] and Henry Aaron,[21] application of the Harberger model results in a substantially

---

[17] H. J. Aaron, *Who Pays the Property Tax?* (Washington, D.C.: The Brookings Institution, 1975), pp. 37–38.

[18] M. G. Reid, *Housing and Income* (Chicago: University of Chicago Press, 1962).

[19] Aaron, *Property Tax*, p. 37.

[20] "The Property Tax: An Excise Tax or a Property Tax," *Journal of Public Economics*, vol. 1 (April 1972), pp. 73–96.

[21] Aaron, *Property Tax.*

different distributional pattern and in overall progressivity. Under the assumptions of perfect factor mobility, perfectly inelastic factor supply, perfect competition in all markets, and the income-maximization goal, a geographically uniform property tax will be borne by all capital owners in the form of reduced return, and thus in a progressive fashion. Capital will flow from the taxed forms of real investment, including that in owner-occupied housing, to the untaxed forms, reducing the overall rate of return on all capital by a uniform amount. The consequence is that the tax distribution is progressive, as shown in Table 16–3. There will be an "excise tax" effect; the consumers of products of capital intensive high-property-tax industries will experience a relative reduction in real income, but this will be offset, in total magnitude, by a reduced burden on other consumers. Under the Harberger model, consumers, per se, do not bear tax burden.

Even under this approach, however, it is recognized that when the property tax is not geographically uniform, as it is not, any differentials will rest on the owners of the higher-taxed property, as capital flows out of the area into a lower-taxed one; this in turn will cause land values to fall, and capitalization of tax will occur.

To some, including Henry Aaron, the Harberger-model findings are of sufficient relevance to lead to the conclusion that the property tax is basically a progressive levy. But some serious questions can be raised about the relevance of the assumptions upon which the analysis is based:

1. *Factor mobility.* Question can be raised about the mobility of capital between owner occupied housing and other investments. The purchase of a house involves both consumption and investment decision-making; the ownership of a home and a home of a given type is so important to many persons from a strictly consumption standpoint as to restrict the flow of capital away from owner-occupied housing as a consequence of the tax, and thus the return on all capital will not equalize.

2. *Nonperfectly competitive markets.* The Harberger model assumes perfectly competitive markets. But many markets are not of the character. This is true of parts, at least, of the rental housing market and of many product markets. As a consequence, firms may simply be able to raise rentals and prices of their products. This is particularly likely to happen in two situations: where a firm has a dominant position in a local area without effective competition, or when it completely dominates a national market. If the firm has maximized monopoly profits prior to the tax, of course, complete shifting would not be possible, but it is likely that this is often not the case.

In conclusion: The property tax is probably not as regressive as is often argued, given the possibility of some shifting to capital owners generally. But there remains of the traditional analysis several threads of validity:

1. A large portion of the tax, under any theory of shifting, rests on property owners–whether in their capacity as capital owners, as such, or as homeowners as such. It is this absolute burden that is of concern. Older persons frequently have homes of values disproportionate to their current incomes, and as a matter of social policy it is difficult to argue that they should be forced to dispose of them and move into smaller quarters. At any rate, such action is politically intolerable.

2. Differential elements of tax are substantial, given the variations in tax rates–and, by any theory of incidence, these differentially higher elements burden persons in the high-tax areas relative to incomes.

The difference in distributional patterns between the traditional and Harberger-Aaron theories of incidence is illustrated in Table 16–3.

TABLE 16–3
Effective General Property Tax Rates under Alternative Incidence Assumptions, by Income Classes, 1972
(income classes in thousands of dollars; other numbers in percent)

| | *Effective Property Tax Rate Assuming that the Tax on Improvements Is Borne by* | |
Income Class	*Capital*	*Renters and Consumers*
0–3	7.2	13.0
3–5	5.4	8.0
5–10	3.6	5.9
10–15	2.6	4.9
15–20	2.9	4.7
20–25	3.7	4.4
25–50	5.7	4.4
50–100	14.1	3.7
100–500	22.4	3.5
500–1,000	24.5	3.0
1,000 and over	18.2	2.1
All classes	5.0	5.0

Source: C. L. Schultze et al., *Setting National Priorities: the 1973 Budget* (Washington, D.C.: The Brookings Institution, 1972), p. 445.

Evaluation: Economic Effects

Of all taxes, the property tax has been subjected to the most violent criticism. Yet the tax continues to be a major revenue source. This dilemma requires consideration. A substantial part of the criticism of the tax has centered around economic effects.

Perpetuation of Deteriorated Areas in Central Cities. One of the major socioeconomic problems of the day is the urban ghetto with its deteriorated buildings, poor housing, run-down commercial properties—many standing empty in a state of dilapidation. One major aspect is the cutting up of old houses and apartments into numerous small apartments. Frequently, if the owner were to remodel these buildings or replace them by new ones, the tax would rise to a much greater extent than the potential return. The result is direct discouragement of reconstruction. Aggravating the effects is the influence, noted below, of the higher tax levels in the central cities compared to those in the surrounding suburbs, which make investment in housing, commercial, or industrial property more attractive in the suburbs than in the central city. The significance of the property tax in encouraging and perpetuating central city blight is impossible to calculate, but many students of the blight problem are convinced that it is a major contributing factor.

Reduction in Total Housing. A second and major objectionable effect of the tax is that of reducing total consumer outlay on housing. The result is inevitably some reduction in total housing available to society. When a person is considering the purchase of a home, for example, the key element is the monthly payments, which typically include the property tax. The higher the tax, the less expensive the house that the person can afford to buy. There is objection to any form of distortion of consumption patterns without specific justification, and under the value judgments of many people, reduction in housing facilities is particularly undesirable. At the higher and middle income levels, the advantageous treatment given housing under the income tax compensates for the property tax—but for the lower income groups and for tenants generally there is no income tax offset. The overall result of the two taxes, therefore, is to reduce the amount of housing available for the lower income groups both in absolute terms and relative to that of the higher income levels—a consequence completely contrary to usual standards.

This influence is, of course, offset in part at least by federal programs that encourage housing construction, particularly the FHA program. The net effect is difficult to determine.[22]

Locational Effects Generally. Since the property tax is a local levy, the rates (and frequently the assessment levels) vary among jurisdictions. In general, in a metropolitan area, they are lowest in industrial suburbs having large amounts of business property; they are highest in the central city and in low-income suburbs. While there have been few definitive empirical studies of the question, inevitably within a metropolitan area, location decisions for real-property-intensive types of enterprises will be affected by relative tax levels. The process of course is reinforcing; as more industries locate in one area, the tax rate

---

[22] H. J. Aaron, *Shelter and Subsidies* (Washington, D.C.: The Brookings Institution, 1972).

may go down still further while the problems of the low-income residential suburbs are aggravated.

This reasoning is not valid, of course, to the extent that the property tax is a payment for inputs into the production process—for services provided by the community to the business firm. If property taxes are higher in one suburb than in another because the town provides better police and fire protection and other services to business firms, the higher tax will have no deterring effect. But this is not typically the source of the difference, which is attributable primarily to variation in tax base relative to functions and particularly to the number of children in school.

Tax rates may also affect residential location, particularly within a metropolitan area. Persons may build outside city boundaries in order to obtain lower tax rates and then resist annexation to the city. There are, however, other considerations as well that influence decisions. The Tiebout effect, as explained in Chapter 19, suggests that persons who prefer high levels of government activities and thus are willing to pay higher taxes will tend to congregate in those suburbs that follow such policies. A study by Wallace Oates, based on New Jersey experience, shows that high levels of expenditures on education offset, or more than offset, the effects of the higher tax rates necessary to finance them so far as property values are concerned.[23] Other studies likewise have shown that high-quality municipal services constitute an important element in decisions about residential location.

Other Distortions.   As noted earlier in the chapter, the tax causes a number of distortions which are likely to reduce efficiency in the use of resources. Output of property-intensive industries is reduced relative to others and efficiency in transportation is reduced by the excessive relative burden on the railroads. Various wasteful practices, such as premature cutting of timber and cyclical depletion of inventories, are encouraged.

Evaluation: Equity

Much of the most severe criticism of the property tax is based upon equity considerations. There are several aspects.

Regressivity.   Whether or not the tax is regressive in overall distribution depends upon the particular theory of shifting that is accepted. Even with the Aaron "reduced return on capital" conclusion, there is some regressivity at the lowest levels. But in any event, regardless of the theory accepted, the absolute burden on persons in the lowest income groups is substantial; it is of little solace to a low-income family trying to meet its property tax bills that the wealthy, under one

---

[23] Oates, "The Effect of Property Taxes."

theory of incidence, may be paying a higher percentage of their income in taxes. For example, an elderly couple owns a home that would sell for $16,000—certainly very modest with present-day values. With a 50 percent assessment ratio, the home will be assessed at $8,000; with a $5 (5 percent) tax rate, the annual tax will the $400. If the couple has, say, $5,000 a year retirement income, federal income tax will be perhaps $300, sales tax perhaps (assuming a 5 percent rate) $150. The property tax is the largest tax the couple must pay, one very substantial in relation to the income, already squeezed in real terms by inflation in the last decade.

The tax likewise becomes a severe burden when income falls sharply; the tax liability continues unchanged, unlike the income and sales taxes.

Some regressivity is introduced within metropolitan areas by the concentration of low-income persons in jurisdictions with relatively high tax rates—rates that are high because the amount of property is low compared to the expenditure needs.

Geographical Nonuniformity. As noted, the tax rates vary widely among taxing jurisdictions, even within a given metropolitan area. In part, of course, these reflect varying preferences for public services; wealthy suburbs often have relatively high property tax rates because they wish to have high-quality schools and other services. But in large part the differentials arise out of varying tax capacity—total property—relative to standard levels of functions. Thus either the rates must be higher in the poor areas than in the wealthier suburbs or the services of poorer quality. This issue is reviewed in Chapter 19.

Quite apart from individual homeowners, the property tax rests in an inequitable fashion on various persons. Some business firms will be able to shift the tax in the short run; others will not, and the incomes of the owners will be reduced. Ultimately a large portion of the tax on business property is likely to be shifted forward to the consumers; thus this portion of the tax has the undesirable characteristics of a sales tax and, since industries vary in property-intensiveness (the ratio of real property to sales volume), the burden will not be uniform on various consumption expenditures—thus producing the discrimination of excise tax systems.

Inequity from Nonuniform Assessment. There is widespread belief, borne out by numerous empirical studies, that the ratio of assessed value to sale value varies widely. As a consequence, serious inequity arises. If two persons own homes of equal value but one home is assessed at 60 percent of its sale value and the other at 30 percent, the first person will pay twice as much tax as the second, even though the actual wealth involved is the same. Most of the studies show not only a very wide range of assessments but a substantial scattering; the situation is not one of merely a few properties being incorrectly assessed but of numerous deviations. The measure usually employed is the coefficient of dispersion, the average deviation of assessments from sale value from the median ratio divided by the median. A 20 percent coefficient, for example, sometimes regarded as a minimum acceptable figure, indicates that the taxpayer knows that the bill he or she receives is, if typical, 20 percent smaller or larger than it should be. ACIR studies show that standards improved up to 1968 but not since. For 1971, the range by county for the country as a whole is from 1.1 (Warren, Kentucky) to 85.2 for Washington, Pennsylvania. These figures are not entirely accurate, since the actual sales figures used for comparison are not always open-market sales figures and the samples are sometimes small. But they give some indication of the degree of dispersion.

Some studies have shown a tendency to value less-expensive homes closer to the sale value than more-expensive homes, probably because the assessor is more familiar with such homes, but other studies show the opposite; there is no conclusive evidence. The most significant evidence, that provided in the 1967 Census of Governments, does not show any general tendency toward regressive assessment.

There are also wide variations in assessment by type of property. Some of this is deliberate though illegal; assessors simply decide to assess business property, for example, closer to the sales value than residential property. There has been a tendency for the courts to overthrow this differentiation in recent years, but a substantial amount remains. One basic objection is that the assessors have taken over legislative powers unto themselves, quite contrary to constitutional requirements. Beyond this, the tendency to assess business property more heavily not only results in a larger portion of the levy taking on the characteristics of an unequal sales tax but also aggravates the effects of the tax on location decisions.[24]

Sources of Poor Quality Assessment. There are several explanations of the poor quality of assessment:

1. *The inherent task.* A constructive value must be derived, in contrast to other taxes. With types of property where similar parcels sell frequently, there is little difficulty; with more complex properties that do not sell, the task is an extremely difficult one at best. In a sense the assessor has to do the impossible—find out what the property would sell for if it sold, when neither it nor any similar property actually sells. This is especially true of much business property. If several expert appraisals of such property are made for any purpose, a wide range of figures usually results.

---

[24] Evidence is presented in Aaron, *Property Tax*, p. 60. In the 25 largest cities, single-family homes were assessed at lower figures (relative to sale value) than commercial-industrial property in all except eight. In New York and Boston, the differential was over 2 to 1.

2. *The limited qualifications of assessors.* Frequently assessors, who are often elected, have few qualifications for the task. Salaries are often inadequate to lure competent persons, many of whom will not run for an elected office anyway. With few qualifications, the assessors have little idea about appraisal techniques and do not particularly care about learning. This is not universally true, but it is only too frequently true. The situation is usually the worst in smaller jurisdictions, in which assessors are part time and poorly paid.

3. *Political considerations.* While outright political interference and bribery are probably less common than they were a century ago, they are not unknown.

Underassessment. Not only are assessments uneven, but there is general underassessment. Many states require by law assessment at full commercial value. But rarely do assessors follow this rule. In 1966 the overall ratio of assessed value to sale value for properties as a whole in the United States was 33.[25] The range by state extended from 84 in Kentucky, a state well known for high standards of tax administration, to 5 percent in South Carolina. Chronic underassessment is a product of several factors. When there is a state property tax, any jurisdiction that underassesses more than the average reduces the state tax burden on its property owners. More frequently today, when state grants for schools vary inversely with the amount of assessed valuation per student in the school district, strong incentive is provided to underassess. Assessors tend to let assessments lag behind increases in property values, partly from inertia, partly because they believe the increases to be only temporary. Underassessment is often politically attractive; each person thinks he or she is getting a break, although for purely local taxes, lower levels of assessment simply mean higher tax rates with no net gain or loss. The main objection to underassessment, apart from state taxes or school grants, is that underassessment is likely to encourage uneven assessment. Persons with relatively high assessments are denied relief in the courts because their assessments are still less than sale value as required by law. It is widely believed that if assessors would aim for exact full value instead of some rule-of-thumb figure below it, the results would be more uniform.

Some states have tried to meet the problem by lowering the legal figure to coincide with practice. But this only results in a further drop in the actual figure, although a few states have moved law and practice closer together by this means.[26] Other states have given the state revenue agency the power to raise the level of assessment in each county to 100 percent by applying a multiplier based on test checks, as discussed below.

[25] Advisory Commission on Intergovernmental Relations, *State–Local Finances,* 1972 ed. (Washington, D.C.: 1972), p. 244.

[26] California, Colorado, Georgia, Iowa, Nebraska.

Tangible personal property is also difficult to assess. Household furniture, for example, has no ready sale figure. Motor vehicles pose fewer difficulties because of the used car dealer "blue book" compilation.

Inequity from Escape of Property.   Real property can escape the tax rolls completely only if there are defects in property rolls or the assessors are grossly inefficient. But many types of personal property easily escape, particularly valuable items such as jewelry, as well as cash and intangible property if these are subject to tax. If the taxpayer does not voluntarily report them it is almost impossible for the assessor to discover them.

Evaluation: Other Criticisms

Two other criticisms are often advanced.

Lump-Sum Nature.   The property tax usually must be paid in one, two, or in a few states four installments. Given the present magnitude of the tax—several hundred dollars at the least, frequently up to a thousand dollars on a modest home—the task of accumulating funds is a serious one for many families. FHA-type mortgages, in which the property tax is paid in monthly installments along with mortgage payments, lessen the scope of the problem but do not eliminate it.

Revenue Elasticity.   The yield of the property tax does not automatically rise with increased incomes or inflation; the assessments must be altered or the rates raised, and the latter are subject to state imposed limits. The actual picture is not as bad as claimed, however. Most estimates of the figure range from 0.8 to 1.3, and thus not substantially lower than the sales tax. This measure is somewhat different for the property tax than for other levies, since it reflects changes in both base and rate. Part of the elasticity—given the lag in assessments—results from the ability to adjust the rate each year by small increments up to the maximum figures set by the state without the usual legislative fight over changes in rates.

PROPERTY TAX REFORM

Given the endless complaints about the property tax, it is not surprising that numerous proposals for reform have been advanced, ranging all the way from minor structural and administrative changes to complete elimination of the tax.

Classification of Property

The property tax has functioned more satisfactorily with some types of property than others and taxation of some appears to give rise to more inequity than taxation of others. The result has been some tendency to classify property, exempting some classes or taxing them at different rates than others.

Personal Property. As the property taxes developed in the last century, they applied to intangible and tangible personal property as well as to real property, and, to some extent, they still do. The two types of personal property created different problems. Intangible property was difficult if not impossible for the local assessors to locate, and persons soon learned that if they did not report it no one would discover it. While theoretically deposits in local banks could be ascertained, at least with some changes in legislation, this would lead persons to move their accounts to other localities. Since much intangible property could not be found, assessors—quite reasonably—ceased looking for it at all. When it was found, by accident or otherwise, undervaluation was difficult and the result was, given undervaluation of other property, gross discrimination. But it also came to be recognized that taxation of most intangible property would result in a form of double taxation; the real property of a corporation would be taxed as well as the stock that represented ownership of it, while noncorporate property would be taxed only once. To tax both a house and a mortgage on it at gross value was obviously discriminatory against mortgaged property.

The combination of theoretical objections on the basis of double taxation and the practical difficulties of finding the property resulted in almost complete disappearance of intangibles from the tax rolls and eventual exemption of such property in most states. Thirty-four states make no effort to tax intangibles and most of the others make little serious effort.

Some states, particularly Ohio, have had considerable success with use of a low rate on intangibles; with low rates, many persons will report their securities and bank deposits. But once the pattern of not reporting intangibles is widespread in a state, an attempt to lure them back on to the tax rolls by low rates is not likely to be successful. Taxation of the income from them is a preferable alternative.

Tangible personal property, which currently constitutes about 14 percent of all assessed values, presents a somewhat different picture. This property consists of several distinct types:

1. Business personal property: inventories of merchants, manufacturers, and other business firms, and farm livestock.

2. Household furniture and effects.

3. Motor vehicles, taxed at regular property tax rates in 21 states, by some form of special levy in most of the others.

The trend has been away from taxation of such property. It is difficult for the assessor to discover many household and personal effects, even more difficult to value them. How, for example, is household furniture to be valued? This problem has led to popular support for exemption; about half the states exempt all such property and many others exempt it in part. Pressure to exempt commerical and industrial property, a trend that has been slower because it has less political appeal, has arisen primarily from recognition of the adverse effects of taxation of inventory on location within the jurisdiction and some recognition that inventory is a poor measure of tax capacity of business firms.

The question of the desirability of inclusion of tangible personal property within the base of the tax—given the property tax in its present form—is not easily resolved; a few general conclusions are offered.

1.   Exclusion of household furniture and personal effects and consequent use of somewhat higher real property taxes simplifies the operation of the tax and likely has little impact on distributional patterns. The taxation of these items involves considerable nuisance and inequity.

2.   Exclusion of motor vehicles[27] can be seriously questioned. Complete enforcement is possible if the payment of the tax is made in conjunction with or as a prerequisite for licensing. A number of families have considerable wealth in automobiles but not real property and disproportionately low rental expenditures. There is little justification for freeing them from payment of property tax on their cars, thus loading more burden on real property.

3.   Tax treatment of business and farm inventory and livestock is debatable. As an element in business expense, much of this tax is likely to shift forward—but not all of it, particularly as some states exempt it. As noted, inventory is a very poor measure of wealth of the owners or of benefits received from government, and there is evidence to suggest that taxation does have substantial influence on location decisions and produces other distortions. Tax on inventory is often substantial in many lines of business—half or more of the amount paid on real property. Exemption of this property and raising the same sum from additional levies on real property are, of course, subject to the objections against high taxes on real property, and part of the burden will be shifted onto householders. The preferable alternative is exemption and replacement of the revenue by other types of taxes, such as income taxes.

General Classification.   A few states have gone far beyond classification of intangibles to set up by law different rates or bases of assessment for different forms of real property. In Arizona, for example, there are four classes. Residential, farm, and vacant land and livestock are assessed at 18 percent of the sale value; commercial and industrial real property and equipment at 25 percent; public utilities at 40 percent; and railroads, mines, and standing timber at 60 percent. The Arizona

---

[27] Also private planes, power boats, and other registered property.

pattern involves gross discrimination, reflecting little more than the old attempt to push more burden onto business and free the homeowner-voter, a policy that is politically attractive but is self-defeating. High rates on utility companies, for example, merely result in higher rates to the consumers—the poor as well as the wealthy—and higher rates on business generally may retard economic development.

The inherent difficulty with real property classification is that there is no logical basis for any distinctions; the consequence is that the rates depend upon relative lobbying strength of various groups, with disregard of equity and potential economic effects. The argument often advanced that income-yielding property should pay more tax than nonincome property makes no sense in a system characterized by substantial income taxes (it would make some sense otherwise); one of the prime objectives of taxing wealth is to reach tax capacity that is reflected by wealth yielding little or no current income.

Administrative Improvements

While change in administration is difficult to measure, on the whole gradual improvement has occurred. Detailed examination of the changes is beyond the scope of this book but major ones can be noted. Local governments—especially urban—have moved slowly to greater use of trained personnel, with civil service or merit systems, more adequate salaries, and tenure. With more competent personnel, improved appraisal techniques have been introduced. The consequence without question has been greater uniformity, although this is difficult to measure precisely. Between 1956 and 1966, for the country as a whole, the coefficient of dispersion in assessment fell from 29.9 to 19.2—but since 1966 there has been no further improvement.[28]

At the same time, the states have increased their role in property tax assessment, a role many of them relinquished when they abandoned state property taxes several decades earlier. State aid has involved preparation of manuals and operation of training schools for assessors, provision in some states of aid for reassessment of all property, and development of the multiplier system in others, such as Illinois. With this system, the state each year determines the typical level of assessment by sales-ratio studies for property that has sold and applies a multiplier to all assessments in the county to bring the level to a uniform figure. If the general level in a state is presumed to be 50 percent, a county in which the actual level was 25 percent would get a multiplier of 2, and the assessment of each parcel of property would be doubled. This does not in itself eliminate individual inequities but it tends to make them more obvious by raising the overassessed property figures over 100 percent. It also serves to equalize between locally

---

[28] Aaron, *Property Tax*, p. 16.

assessed and state assessed property (e.g., railroads) and to eliminate underassessing to obtain greater school grants.

There are inherent problems in improving administration, however, apart from political obstacles and the basic difficulty of constructive valuation. One is the size of the assessing unit. Many local jurisdictions are too small for effective assessment at reasonable cost. The only solution is transfer of assessment to large units—at least the counties, when the township is the present unit—or to the state. Political obstacles to such a transfer are often strong.

Drastic revision in relative tax burdens also will cause capital gains for some and losses for others. These persons affected are not the ones that initially were discriminated against or favored if the property has changed hands, since the original differentials were reflected in the purchase prices.

Exemptions and Circuit Breakers

Complaints about regressivity, burden on the poor, and the particular problems of the elderly have led all states to make some concessions for the elderly, and in some for all low-income persons.[29]

Homestead Exemptions. Several states, of which Florida is by far the most important in terms of revenue involved, exempt so-called homesteads, that is, owner-occupied homes of less than a certain value. While this exemption lessens the burden on the poor homeowner, it does nothing for the tenant who presumably bears at least some of the tax imposed upon the landlord. The system is also the source of serious financial difficulties for communities losing most of their tax base because of the dominance of low-value owner-occupied homes.

Circuit Breakers.[30]   In the last decade the so-called circuit breaker approach has spread rapidly and is now used by most states. Under this system, a credit is given to the low-income taxpayer, usually in the form of a deduction from income tax, with cash refund for those owing less income tax than the amount of the credit; a few provide cash refunds to all beneficiaries and some provide a direct reduction in the property tax bill. The plans differ so much that generalizations are difficult. There are two basic approaches:

---

[29] U.S. Department of Housing and Urban Development, *Property Tax Relief Programs for the Elderly*, 3 vol. (Washington, D.C.: 1976.)

[30] A detailed description and analysis of circuit breakers is to be found in the ACIR publication, *Property Tax Circuit Breakers: Current Status and Policy Issues* (Washington, D.C.: 1975). Opposition to the principle is to be found in Aaron, *Property Tax*, chap. 5. Note also M. Bendick, "Designing Circuit Breaker Property Tax Relief," *National Tax Journal*, vol. 27 (March 1974), p. 19–29; B. D. Cook and K. E. Quindry, "Humanization of Property Tax for Low Income Households," *National Tax Journal*, vol. 22 (September 1969), pp. 367–67.

1. *The threshold approach.* If the property tax exceeds a specified percentage of the taxpayer's income, the taxpayer receives a credit for all or part of the excess.

2. *The sliding scale approach.* All taxpayers in a given income class receive a percentage reduction in property tax liability, the percentage being lower for successively higher income classes.

In five states, benefits are available regardless of age; in the remainder they are available only for the elderly.

Several states allow credits for tenants as well as homeowners, with the assumption that a specified percentage—typically around 20—of rent payments reflects the landlord's property tax.

This general approach is obviously far more satisfactory than homestead exemptions. Credit can be given to the tenant as well as the homeowner; benefits are adjusted on the basis of the family income rather than the value of the property alone; they are typically financed by the state, and thus do not create serious financial problems for communities with many low-value homes. The programs are successful in removing the property tax burden from the groups covered. It can be argued that they should not be confined to the elderly, as in a number of states, but broadening the coverage, of course, materially increases the cost of the program.

The system, however, has been subject to some criticism. Under the more recent theories of distribution of property tax burden, the tax is not regressive because it rests on the owners of capital, and therefore there is no need for circuit breakers. But this regressivity argument is actually not the relevant issue at all, as the circuit breakers are primarily designed to alleviate the absolute burden on the lower income groups rather than regressivity. It is true that as many of the systems operate they do provide more relief, at a given income level, to owners of more expensive homes or tenants in more expensive quarters than those spending less on housing—and this feature could be eliminated. But it is included primarily because of the objective that the elderly not be forced to sell their homes because of the inability to pay property tax. The suggestion of Aaron and others that the property tax on the elderly be deferred until death rather than being canceled is so completely contrary to increasingly accepted principles that children should not have to bear the property tax of their parents that it does not receive serious attention.

The Single Tax: Site Value Taxation

For nearly a century, one group of critics of the property tax has been arguing for a fundamental reform: the replacement of the present tax, which applies equally to land and improvements, to one on land value only. This is often called site value taxation, or more popularly, the single tax—as the first proponent, San Francisco newspaperman Henry George, advocated it as the sole tax to be used. The proposal has attracted a strong band of zealots, some of whom lose professional rationality in their vehement support of the levy.

The proponents advance four principal arguments:

Cheaper Land.   Because of the capitalization effect, land values would fall if the tax were shifted entirely onto land. As a consequence, land for economic development—for expansion of industry, for stores, for homes—would be cheaper and less money capital would be required to acquire land.

Greater Holding Costs.   While land would become cheaper, the costs of holding it would sharply increase because of the higher taxes. Speculation in land around the outskirts of cities would become prohibitively expensive; such speculation—holding large blocks of land idle in the hope of increases in value—is regarded as one of the principal obstacles in the way of optimal economic development of communities. Idle blocks of land force development to leapfrog, increasing dispersion and therefore adding to costs of various facilities— water, sewers, transportation, and the like. Failure to utilize land for purposes optimal from a development standpoint would become prohibitive because of the high annual tax; owners would be compelled by economic forces to make the most effective use of it. This is equally true of farmland and urban property.

The Tax Costs of Making Improvements Would Be Eliminated. Persons would pay the same tax whether they held the land idle, used it as a parking lot, retained an old ramshackle building on it or put up a 50-story apartment. Under the property tax, the tax would rise sharply with the improvements. Thus a major obstacle to rebuilding of deteriorated area would be eliminated. At the same time, the urban sprawl would be lessened.

Equity.   The equity argument for site value taxation is based upon the thesis that increases in land values are "unearned increments"; they are not attributable to the efforts of the landowner, but to the general growth of the community. Thus, they constitute a form of parasitic income, which represents particular taxpaying capacity. This is a position completely contrary to the usual thesis that in the interests of equity all income should be treated uniformly regardless of source. No equity argument can be refuted, but it can be pointed out that many other incomes in society are in a sense unearned—monopoly profit, for example—and that present-day landowners are not necessarily the ones who gained from the growth in land values; they may have worked hard all their lives to be able to buy the land at already inflated prices.

Available data do not provide accurate figures of total assessments of land and improvements. The California figures show a total of $25 billion of land, $35 billion of improvements, $10 billion of personal property, but the division made by the assessors between the two items is not always careful.[31] Improvements exceed land values in urban areas, but the difference is not great, while land values dominate in rich agricultural counties with little industry. If these data are representative, the rates on land values would roughly double if improvements were freed of tax.

Site value taxation has received only limited use in the United States, in the cities of Pittsburgh and Scranton, which for many years have taxed land values at twice the rate as that on improvements (for city taxes only, not school taxes). The four western provinces of Canada tax land more heavily than improvements. Hawaii has introduced a system for increase in the relative levy on land. Site value taxation in its purest form is found in Australia, New Zealand, and the cities of east, central and southern Africa.[32] Experience in all of these jurisdictions shows that the system will function and may have played some role in rapid expansion of the cities since buildings are free of tax, but there is no conclusive evidence of substantial influence on developent.

Several objections are raised against site value taxation. Almost inevitably a greater burden would be shifted to farmers; present owners of farmlands would suffer a disproportionate reduction in real income. The same argument can, of course, be raised with regard to all existing landowners; they are not necessarily the ones who experienced the gain in values but may have purchased the land at high prices. The present owners in a sense bear the full burden and subsequent owners are able to buy the land more cheaply.

From the standpoint of economic effects, critics of the proposal maintain that the change would have little actual impact on development. This argument cannot be scientifically refuted, but inevitably some change in the desired direction would occur. The critics also charge that the change would increase the intensity of building in urban areas and force the elimination of open spaces. This could well happen, but only because the present property tax favors the holding of property in less-intensive uses. Direct governmental action to acquire land for parks and other open areas is probably a more effective way of preserving open spaces.

A further argument relates to costs of services provided. Many local government services are directly related to improvements, not to vacant land: fire, police, street lighting, sewerage, and so forth. With the present property tax, as additional buildings are erected, property tax

---

[31] California State Board of Equalization, *Annual Report*, 1972–73. A study by Allan Manvel shows that land accounts for 40 percent of all assessments; see "Trends in the Value of Real Estate and Land," 1956–66, in National Committee on Urban Problems, *Three Land Research Studies* (Washington, D.C.: Government Printing Office, 1968).

[32] A. M. Woodruff and L. L. Ecker-Racz, "Property Taxes and Land Use Patterns in Australia and New Zealand," *Tax Executive*, vol. 28 (October 1965), pp. 16–63.

revenue rises accordingly; with the site value tax it does not. The tax on land values can, of course, be pushed up—but the direct correlation between revenues and benefits is lost.

Without question site value taxation offers some advantages over the property tax as it now stands. But despite the recent partial adoption of the system in Hawaii, where the land area is very limited and most of it is owned by a very few holders,[33] the site value approach has little political support in the United States—partly because of the fanatical claims of many of its supporters.

Conversion to a Net Wealth Tax

All of the reforms thus far discussed and those implemented, except for the exemptions provided persons with low incomes, are based on the impersonal concept of the property tax. The other basic avenue of reform would be to convert the tax into a true tax on net wealth, as a personal levy complementary to the income tax. Some of the problems, particularly those related to assessment, would remain and might even become worse; but the overall equity would be tremendously increased since net wealth is a much better measure of tax capacity than property, and the economic effects would likely be less severe. Disincentives to the making of improvements in low-income areas, for example, would be eliminated.

The main obstacle to the change is the fact that the property tax is mainly a local tax; local assessors cannot hope to ascertain persons' net wealth. Furthermore, the change would drastically alter the geographical distribution of the tax revenue. More of the revenue would go to the wealthy suburbs where the owners live and less to the jurisdictions of location of the business activity. Only if the tax were converted to a national levy would effective administration and acceptable jurisdictional allocation of revenue be possible. But this change would not only require a constitutional amendment but is completely contrary to the philosophy of local financial autonomy, to which so many persons adhere. The change would also appear to shift burdens off corporations per se, a shift that has no political appeal despite the logic of the change.

Economic Policy Concessions

Exemption from property tax has long been provided governmental units, and religious, charitable, and comparable institutions, for the same reasons that contributions are deductible for income tax purposes. But in recent decades other concessions have been

---

[33] Twelve owners hold 52 percent of the entire land area of Hawaii; 60 own 80 percent of the land. See J. Hulten, "Hawaii's Modified Property Tax Base Law," *Proceeding of the National Tax Association for 1969*, pp. 52–65.

provided as well. Tax "holidays" or tax reduction has been provided in some areas to new industry in an effort to aid economic development—a policy that can easily become self-defeating if followed by a number of areas. Some cities have made concessions for slum-clearance projects.

More than half the states now provide special treatment of farm land close to urban areas, requiring that the land be assessed on the basis of its value for farming use, not the higher market-value figure representing potential use for subdivisions. The measures are designed to protect farmers against tax bills they could not meet without selling the property, and to aid in keeping land surrounding urban areas in agricultural use, preventing premature development.

CONCLUSION

The property tax is clearly an unpopular levy in the United States. There are serious complaints against the tax on both equity and economic-efficiency grounds. Most of the complaints center around regressivity—yet the tax is, on the whole, probably not significantly regressive. But in traditional form it does place substantial absolute burden on the lowest income groups, particularly the elderly. The introduction of "circuit breakers" in a number of states has greatly reduced the burden on the poor and complaints of this type, even though the systems used are by no means ideal. Continued reliance on the tax is essential if the local governments are to enjoy substantial fiscal autonomy. The alternatives—local sales or income taxes—are likely to have more adverse effects than the property tax. There is great need for further improvements in administration and perfection of the circuit-breaker systems. Change to a net-wealth tax would be desirable, but is clearly not feasible. The site value approach offers merits in theory, but sudden change to it would have drastic effects on relative property values.

REFERENCES

Aaron, H. J. *Who Pays the Property Tax?* Washington, D.C.: The Brookings Institution, 1975. A strong argument that the burden of the tax rests on capital owners.

Financing Schools and Property Tax Relief. Washington, D.C.: Advisory Commission on Intergovernmental Relations, 1973. A review of the property tax and its use for the financing of schools.

Ladd, Helen F. "The Role of the Property Tax: A Reassessment," in *Broad Based Taxes*, ed. R. A. Musgrave, Baltimore: John Hopkins Press, 1973. A review of the property tax question.

Peterson, G. E., ed. *Property Tax Reform.* Washington, D.C.: Urban Institute, 1973. A collection of papers on various aspects of reform of the tax.

Netzer, D. "The Incidence of the Property Tax Revisited," *National Tax Journal,* vol. 26 (December 1973), pp. 515–35. A review of the incidence issue.

Netzer, D. *Economics of the Property Tax.* Washington, D.C.: The Brookings Institution, 1966. Now out of date, but the best overall summary of the tax.

Data on assessments and rates are to be found in the 1967 Census of Governments volume, *Taxable Property Values;* Advisory Commission on Intergovernmental Relations, *State–Local Finances,* 1973–74 ed. (Washington: Advisory Commission on Intergovernmental Relations, 1974), *The Property Tax in a Changing Environment,* 1974; and U.S. Bureau of the Census, *Property Values Subject to Local General Property Taxation in the United States: 1975.* (Washington: 1976.)

The TRED Series

A series of volumes consisting of papers presented at annual conferences on various aspects of property taxation, published by the University of Wisconsin Press, Madison. The volumes (though not all of the papers in them) have a single tax orientation.

Becker, A. P. (ed.) *Land and Building Taxes.* 1969.

Holland, D. M. (ed.) *The Assessment of Land Value.* 1970.

Lindholm, R. W. (ed.) *Property Taxation U.S.A.* 1967.

Lynn, A. D. *Property Taxation, Land Use and Public Policy.* 1976.

Lynn, A. D., Jr. (ed.) *The Property Tax and Its Administration.* 1965.

17

Taxes upon the Transfer of Wealth

Receipt of bequests or gifts constitutes income under the broad Simons definition noted in Chapter 10. But in the United States, as in almost all countries, bequests and gifts are specifically excluded by law from taxable income and subjected instead to special levies, which in the United States preceded, historically, the income taxes. There are several primary forms:

1. Estate taxes, imposed, technically, upon the entire estate in excess of a specified exemption without regard to the number of bequests or the relationship of the recipients to the deceased.

2. Inheritance taxes, imposed separately upon the individual bequests, the rates progressive according to the size of the bequest without regard to the size of the total estate, the rates and exemptions varying with the relationship of the heir to the decedent.

3. Succession taxes, common in Canada, hybrids between estate and inheritance taxes, rates varying with the size of the estate, the size of the individual bequests, and the family relationship.

The gift taxes are supplementary but often separate levies, imposed upon gifts between living persons. The U.S. federal gift tax was merged with the estate tax in 1976.

Gift taxes are imposed upon the donor; estate taxes, technically, are imposed upon the estate per se, inheritance taxes on the bequests. The death taxes must be paid before the heirs can obtain their bequests.

The Levies in the United States

The Federal Estate and Gift Tax. After decades of inaction on the issue, Congress, in the Tax Reform Act of 1976, drastically altered the federal estate and gift tax structure. The tax is now imposed upon the cumulated figure of gifts and bequests. A person is liable for gift tax each year on the lifetime cumulated sum of gifts; at death, the amount of the estate is added to the cumulated sum of gifts and the tax rate applied to the sum. In each year and at death, the tax actually due is the sum determined by applying the tax rate to the cumulated sum and then subtracting the cumulated sum of gift taxes paid to date. There are several features that require explanation:

1.   Only gifts in excess of $3,000 per year per recipient ($6,000 for a married couple) are taxable.

2.   Gifts made prior to 1977 (in excess of the $3,000 or $6,000 figure) are included in the cumulated total, and credit given for tax that would have been paid if the present system had been in effect prior to 1977, in determining liability for tax on gifts. This rule does not apply at death; the tax applies only to the cumulated sum of gifts from 1977 on plus the estate.

3.   In addition to the $3,000 (or $6,000) exemption on gifts, a single unified credit-against-tax is provided, on the following schedule:

1977	$30,000
1978	34,000
1979	38,000
1980	42,000
1981 and thereafter	47,000

These figures, which are credits against tax, are higher than those of the pre-1977 law. A person has only one of these for his lifetime.

4.   Tax applies when the funds in trusts are transferred to the heirs; a defect in the old law was the ability to eliminate one application of tax by leaving property in trust for a son, the property to pass to a grandson upon the son's death.

5.   Subject to certain restrictions, farms will be valued on the basis for farm use rather than other possible higher-value uses (e.g. real estate development).

6.   Any gift given within three years of death is held to be a gift in contemplation of death and treated as a part of the estate.

7.   A marital deduction is provided; property can be given to the surviving spouse up to $100,000 tax free; the second $100,000 is fully taxable; beyond this, one half of the amount can be given or bequeathed tax free.

8.   In specified cases where hardship from forced sale would result, tax payment can be deferred for up to 10 years and in some instances 15 years.

The rates, now the same on gifts as estates, commence at 18 percent on the first $10,000 of taxable gifts or estate, and progress steadily, to, for example, a rate of 30 percent at $100,000, 37 percent at $500,000, 49 percent at $2 million, and a high of 70 percent for the excess over

$5 million. Only typical figures are given; the brackets are relatively narrow.

The change effective in 1977 was primarily designed to close major loopholes in the old structure; since there was no integration of gift tax and estate tax, there was strong incentive to give property away prior to death, and to use generation-skipping trusts. There is now only limited gain from making gifts prior to death.

The taxable estate includes the entire legal estate (including municipal bonds) plus the proceeds of life insurance policies and any death-bed gifts—ones held to be in contemplation of death. Bequests to charitable and related organizations are excluded as well as legal costs for transference of the estate.

State death taxes constitute a credit against federal tax, the percentage credit rising with the size of the estate up to 16 percent of the federal tax due. This feature, introduced in the 1920s, was designed to eliminate interstate competition in the field. Several states— particularly Florida—were seeking to lure old, wealthy persons to the state by not using the tax. The credit feature ensures that, so long as the state rates do not exceed the amount of the federal credit, the total tax will be the same whether a person lives in a state with the tax or not. Smaller estates subject to state but not federal rates of course will escape tax if the state does not levy one, but these are not the persons the states are anxious to lure.

The State Levies. The state levies take two forms. The estate tax is used in 14 states, in five of which the tax liability is the precise magnitude of the federal credit. In six others the rates differ but there is a supplemental "pickup tax" designed to collect any difference between the estate tax and the federal credit.

The inheritance tax is used in 36 states, in two of these in conjunction with an estate tax. All but a few of these states also use pickup taxes, the liability for which is the difference between the sum of the inheritance taxes on the individual shares and the amount of the federal credit.

As noted, with the inheritance tax the exemptions and rates vary with the relationship of the heir to the decedent. For example, in California, the exemptions and rates[1] are as follows:

Relationship	Exemption	Rates, Percent
Widow	$ 5,000	3–14
Minor child	$12,000	3–14
Adult child	$ 5,000	3–14
Brother, sister	$ 2,000	6–20
Other or unrelated	$ 300	10–24

---

[1] The rates increase as the size of the taxable bequest increases. The figure for the widow is low because only half the property passes to a widow from her spouse.

While the patterns are comparable in various states, the figures differ widely; the exemption for a widow ranges from $150 in Maryland to $75,000 in Kansas; for unrelated persons, from none in a number of states to $1,000 in several. The highest rate in any state is 40 percent, in Wisconsin on bequests to unrelated persons in excess of $500,000.

The state levies reach many smaller estates not subject to the federal tax, particularly for persons other than direct heirs, but the tax is small over a substantial range. The liability is much less than the federal tax at the higher brackets.

Only 14 states tax gifts. The goal of these levies is primarily to discourage deliberate giving away of property to escape estate tax and the states believe the federal tax to be adequate for this purpose.

Total collections from state death and gift taxes in 1975 were $1.4 billion, or 2 percent of total state tax collections.

Economic Effects

So far as labor and risk-taking are concerned, it would appear that death duties would have less effect than income taxes yielding equivalent revenue. The fact that a death tax will be collected on a person's estate in some distant future is presumably less likely to enter into decisions to work and to undertake the risks of investment than a tax that affects the current income earned. There could conceivably be an income-type effect if persons seek to pass to their heirs a given-after-tax sum—but the possibility of significant influence appears to be rather remote.

Death taxes, however, do increase demand for liquidity and shift investment in more conservative, less risky directions. First, the need for money to meet death tax obligations undoubtedly causes many wealthy persons to shift portfolios into more liquid forms.[2] Tax considerations are considerably more significant in encouraging the transfer of property to children; both of these changes result in more conservative types of investments (at least where minor children are concerned).[3] Management of the estate becomes particularly conservative during the period of settling the estate, which may run several years.

While the tax may have less effect on incentives than an income tax, it may, per dollar of revenue, have more impact on the savings/income ratio and therefore the potential rate of capital formation. It would

---

[2] Some—but limited—evidence was found in the Barlow study of tax influences on behavior of the wealthy. See R. Barlow, H. E. Brazer, and J. N. Morgan, *Economic Behavior of the Affluent* (Washington, D.C.: The Brookings Institution, 1966), pp. 109–11.

[3] Ibid. The estate tax gains from use of trusts have been reduced by the 1976 legislation.

appear that of all taxes, the death duty, a one-time levy on a capital sum transferred, is most likely to be paid out of the sum itself, with little reduction in consumption on the part of the recipients. If the income tax, or even more so, a consumption tax, were used, some persons would of necessity curtail consumption and others would do so to maintain given savings rates. But even a death tax may result in persons consuming less than they would have had they received the bequest tax free; consumption is a function of wealth as well as of income. The issue is basically one of relative response of savings and consumption to a reduction in disposable "normal" income and reduction in "transitory" income, that is, irregular, unanticipated elements in income. By the Friedman hypothesis, all transitory income will be saved. This is not necessarily valid, but there is good reason to argue that the *MPS* of transitory income is greater than that of normal income, and so death taxes will directly reduce savings to a greater degree than other levies.

Death duties may also affect the savings patterns of persons during their lifetimes, but there are conflicting considerations depending upon the savings motives. On the one hand, if persons wish to leave a given sum to their heirs, they will save more rather than less because they know that a death tax must be paid. On the other, knowledge that taxes will take a good portion of an estate may cause the person to decide that accumulation of an estate is not worthwhile. The overall effect cannot be predicted.

Little is known about the distributional pattern of death duties. But given the much greater inequality of wealth than income, the concentration of large bequests in the higher income levels, the high exemptions, and the progressive rates, the distribution is likely to be progressive but haphazard among higher income persons, partly because some persons take greater advantage of loopholes than others.

Justification

A tax on the transfer of property at death or by gift has strong justification under usual standards of taxation. The receipt of property by bequest obviously represents taxpaying capacity—at least under most circumstances. An adult who inherits $50,000 from a father or an uncle is obviously better off economically than if he or she had not done so. Many bequests are windfall gains—basically even more suitable measures of tax capacity than ordinary income and less likely to produce excess burdens. The tax, with usual exemptions, rests primarily on the higher income groups, and it can be an effective instrument for breaking up large fortunes, in a fashion other taxes do not do. As explained in Chapter 6, wealth is more unequally distributed than income, and death taxes therefore are potentially more effective than income taxes in reducing inequality of wealth and of income gained from wealth. The tax therefore increases equality of opportunity. It is in part a substitute for an effective net-wealth tax and for failure to tax accrued capital gains.

From the standpoint of economic effects, it can be presumed, as noted above, that the tax will have less adverse effects on incentives than most other forms of tax. While it may reduce savings to a greater extent, this is a desirable result under circumstances in which the maintenance of full employment is difficult. All in all, while no substitute for the income tax, the death tax is a useful supplement.

An Optimal Death Tax Structure—A Separate Levy

Definition of an optimal death tax structure requires establishment of criteria for this purpose, derived from the usually accepted standards of taxation.

Let us assume initially, in conformity with typical approaches thus far used, that the tax will be regarded as a separate levy, the burden unrelated to the income or the wealth of the recipients. Four goals are commonly accepted.

1. The taxes should be progressive relative to the size of the gift, estate, or inheritance by usual standards of society. This objective is based in part on the argument that tax capacity rises more rapidly than the sum of the bequest or gift, in part on the deliberate desire to break up large fortunes.

2. The taxes should be adjusted on the basis of the relationship of the heir to the decedent. Receipt of a bequest by a widow or minor children from the deceased spouse or parent represents less tax capacity than the receipt of a similar amount from a distant relative or unrelated person or receipt by an adult child. The widow's or child's economic well-being is not increased by the bequest while that of other persons is.

3. The amount of tax should be the same, taking interest into consideration, regardless of time of giving or the form in which the property is given (for example, gift or bequest; trust versus direct gift). Otherwise the tax will affect the choice of methods of giving property.

4. The tax structure should minimize adverse economic effects, such as forced liquidation of closely held businesses.

To some extent, the present taxes do attain these objectives. The tax rates are progressive and the levies are borne primarily by persons in the higher income groups. To some extent, they do restrain the growth of large fortunes. With the inheritance taxes, the levy is adjusted according to the relationship of the heir to the decedent and the federal tax adjusts for the surviving spouse, while the high exemptions make other relationship adjustments unnecessary. The taxes would appear, at present rates, to have few adverse effects on economic behavior; to the extent that they reduce the savings/income ratio, they may aid in lessening unemployment.

Some of the worst defects of the old law were eliminated in the Tax Reform Act of 1976. By combining the gift and estate taxes and making the tax liability depend upon the cumulated sum of gifts and estates, the overall tax burden was made much more equitable, and there is now much less incentive to give property away prior to death. Only the additional $3,000 per year per recipient exemption offers any advantage, while the use of the funds is lost. The incentive to use generation skipping trusts was largely eliminated.

However, certain defects remain.

1. Incentive is provided to skip generations; one imposition of the tax will be avoided by giving property to grandchildren rather than children.

2. While the tax is progressive, the progression relates to the amounts given by a person, not the amounts received by particular persons. Two persons inherit $500,000, one in a lump sum from one person, the other in ten $50,000 bequests from different persons. With the inheritance levies, the tax will be much less on the latter than on the former. With the estate tax the total tax will be much less on the latter unless the ten bequests are parts of estates averaging $500,000 or more. As noted below, liability is not affected by the wealth or income of the recipient.

3. While the present taxes appear to have relatively little adverse economic effect, they do encourage owners of closely held businesses to sell prior to death to avoid danger of forced liquidation or overvaluation of property for death tax purposes, therefore increasing mergers and concentration of economic power. Criticism has been mounting about the adverse effects of the tax on the preservation of the family farm, and changes made in 1976 were designed to lessen this problem.

Solutions. To eliminate the generation skipping incentive, William Vickery developed the bequeathing power approach, which would adjust the tax rate according to the excess of the age of the decedent over that of the heir; accordingly, the burden would be the same regardless of the path the bequest followed, that is, whether it went initially to the child or directly to the grandchild.[4] The plan has merit within the framework of separate taxation of gifts and bequests, but its complications have precluded serious consideration.

Another alternative approach, which would make the operation of

---

[4] W. Vickrey, *Agenda for Progressive Taxation* (New York: Ronald Press Co., 1947), chap. 8.

progression more effective, is the accessions tax.[5] The tax would be placed upon the recipient, on a cumulative basis, on all gifts and bequests received over his or her lifetime from all donors, with a lifetime exemption plus a small exemption on each individual gift and bequest. The tax would therefore be related to the sum of a person's gratuitous receipts, and the taxation of gifts and bequests would be integrated. Enforcement would be somewhat more complex than that of the estate tax. The most serious problem relates to certain forms of discretionary trust, the taxation of which might be postponed more or less indefinitely.

Taxation of Gifts and Bequests as Income

No matter how well gift and death taxes are designed within the present framework, certain objectionable features would persist as a result of the divorce of the taxation of gifts and bequests from the taxation of income. One consequence of the separate tax treatment is the problem of delineation between income and gratuitous transfers. An example is the distinction between graduate fellowships and assistantships, with the absurd consequence that the recipients must pay tax only if they work for the income. Similar problems arise in distinguishing awards and prizes from payments for services and with the tax status of business gifts to customers and employees.

Second, tax liability is related only to the size of the gift, estate, or inheritance, and in some instances to the relationship of the heir to the decedent, with no recognition of the wealth or income of the recipient. Thus a penniless person pays more tax on an inheritance from a distant relative than a millionaire does on the receipt of the same sum from a brother. Tax capacity reflected in an inheritance cannot appropriately be considered in a vacuum without regard to the economic position of the recipients.

Taxation as income of all gifts and bequests received would avoid the problem of delineation and make the tax treatment accord much more fully with usually accepted standards of equity. Some adjustments would be necessary, however, for equity and administrative reasons. A separate form, such as that used for capital gains, would be required of taxpayers receiving gifts and bequests, the taxable amount being transferred to the basic return. Spreading of the gift or bequest over a period of several years would be essential to avoid severe tax penalty, unless a general system of averaging of income were employed. Small gifts would be exempted to avoid taxing persons on Christmas and birthday presents and similar items. Finally, either all gifts within the family unit would be exempt (husband to wife, or

---

[5] See H. J. Rudick, "What Alternative to Estate and Gift Taxes?," *California Law Review*, vol. 36 (March 1950), pp. 150–82.

parent to minor child), as proposed by the Canadian Royal Commission, which endorsed this approach,[6] or granted partial exemption because of the lack of a clear distinction between gift and support.

This system, while avoiding some of the problems and inequities of the present policy, would not be entirely free of problems:

1. The worst difficulty would center around precise delineation between gifts and partial support of persons outside the family unit: the aged parents; the young married couple in college partially supported by their parents. Taxation of these support payments would violate usual standards of equity, but delineation of them from pure gifts would be troublesome. If the family unit rule were employed, great incentive would be provided to make gifts before the child left the unit.

2. Gifts in kind. Noncash gifts of considerable value (for example, old paintings) could create serious difficulties to the recipients and require embarrassing refusals of the gifts. The more basic problem for the economy is the receipt by bequest of a large interest in a closely held business—a problem that arises now with the estate tax and could be more serious with income tax treatment. Special provisions to allow deferment of payment would be required in income tax legislation to avoid forced liquidation.

3. Enforcement. While bequests are easy to detect because of the necessity for court approval of the transfer, gifts are not, even larger ones. Some evasion would be inevitable.

4. Choice in timing. Typical gifts differ from regular income in one major respect: They are optional on the part of the donor (and the donee) and they can be timed to suit the convenience of all concerned and minimize tax. Thus persons systematically giving away property to their heirs would concentrate gifts in the years in which the recipients' incomes were low. This is not too serious a problem and can scarcely be avoided.

Of these problems, without question the first is the most serious. It is largely avoided under present death taxes by the high exemptions, relatively low rates compared to those of income taxes on moderate amounts, and adjustment of the exemption and rate to the relationship of the heir to the decedent. The problem is not insuperable, but meeting it would without question give rise to a number of complications in the treatment.

---

[6] *Report of the Royal Commission on Taxation* (Ottawa: Queen's Printer, 1966), vol. 3, chap. 17. The proposal was not followed; instead, the federal estate and gift taxes were repealed.

Prior to 1972, Ontario, Quebec, and British Columbia levied their own succession taxes, the tax rate depending upon the relationship of the beneficiary to the decedent, the aggregate value of the estate, and the size of each bequest. The other provinces shared in the proceeds of the federal estate tax. When the latter was repealed as of the end of 1971, the provinces followed different policies.

The Disintegration of Death Taxes in Canada[7]

Following the report of the Royal Commission, the Canadian government, in 1969 and 1970, completely redesigned its estate tax to eliminate tax on transfers between spouses and to integrate the estate and gift taxes, producing a greatly improved structure. Then, suddenly in 1971, the government reversed its position completely and repealed all death duties at the same time that capital gains realized at death were made taxable under the income tax. As one consequence of this policy, four provinces proceeded to repeal their death duties (and Alberta had never used one). Thus, as of 1975, only half the provinces use the levy at all. Ontario and Quebec use so-called successions taxes, imposed on the transmission of property, the rate varying with the aggregate value of the estate, the relationship of the heir to the decendent, and the amount received by each beneficiary—thus combining features of the estate and inheritance taxes. The British Columbia tax is similar. Manitoba and Saskatchewan, on the other hand, use the accessions tax approach. All levies are now provincially collected.

REFERENCES

Jantscher, G. R. *Trusts and Estate Taxation.* Washington, D.C.: The Brookings Institution, 1967.

Shoup, Carl S. *Federal Estate and Gift Taxes.* Washington, D.C.: The Brookings Institution, 1966.

Tait, A. A. *The Taxation of Personal Wealth.* Urbana: University of Illinois Press, 1967.

---

[7] J. Bossons, "The Effect of Income Tax Reform on Estate Taxes in Canada," *Proceedings of the National Tax Association for 1973,* pp. 148–59; Canadian Tax Foundation, *Provincial and Municipal Finances,* 1975 (Toronto: Canadian Tax Foundation, 1975), pp. 86–93.

PART III

Fiscal Federalism

18

Fiscal Federalism

Few questions of public finance have received more attention in Congress, at the state level, and in popular discussions in this decade than revenue sharing and other questions relating to the fiscal relationships of various levels of government. Much of the concern has arisen out of the serious problems facing city governments—particularly the large metropolitan-area cities—and their financial inability to cope with them. The lag of state and local activities behind the preferences for them, while the federal government clearly had potential for more than ample funds, played a major role as well. The interest culminated in enactment of revenue sharing in 1972, and revived in 1975–76 with consideration of renewal of sharing. Renewal legislation was enacted in 1976.

ALLOCATION OF FUNCTIONS

Complete Centralization

These problems would not arise if all governmental activities were concentrated in the hands of a single national government, as occurs in a very few small countries.[1] The central government would make all decisions about governmental activities and revenues on the basis of the preferences of the persons of the country as a whole. The revenue structure would be uniform throughout the country, and the effects of unequal taxing resources of various regions and tax competition among taxing jurisdictions arising out of mobility of labor and capital

---

[1] This was essentially true in Newfoundland prior to its absorption by Canada.

would be avoided. Full economies of scale in the production of all governmental activities would be attained.

Clearly some functions of government must be performed at the national level. First, stabilization policy must be conducted on a nationwide basis. If local units attempted to lessen unemployment by fiscal policy, much of the gain would be lost to other areas. Local units cannot employ monetary policy nor obtain funds by money creation and they can run at deficits only by borrowing, largely from the outside, creating burdens for future periods.

Second, effective income redistribution is possible only at the national level. If a local unit seeks to lessen inequality by providing large benefits for the poor and placing high taxes on the rich, it will drive wealthy persons out of the jurisdiction and lure the poor in from other areas, thus sabotaging the attainment of the objectives. As indicated by Oates, income will be equalized—the jurisdiction will now contain only the poor.[2] But this was not the intent.

Third, the national government must provide those public goods of such nature that the benefits accrue to the people of the country as a whole. Foreign affairs and national defense are the classic cases; national unity is possible only if these functions are in the hands of the national government.[3]

Merits of Decentralization

The areas of benefits of many activities are much smaller than the entire country. Many public goods directly affect only the persons in local or regional areas. There are important advantages to the conduct of such activities by subordinate units of government.

First, to the extent that preferences for public goods vary among persons, the decentralization of government permits closer adaptation of the levels of governmental activities to the preferences of society. This adaptation lessens the adverse feature of all governmental activity, that the amounts of each activity cannot be adjusted separately for each person on the basis of that person's preference schedule. Each local unit can adjust the level of its activity to meet the preferences of its residents. The gains from decentralization therefore are greater, the greater the diversity in preference levels among persons in various areas. Furthermore, persons may tend to congregate in those local units that provide the mixture of activities and taxes they prefer—the

---

[2] W. E. Oates, *Fiscal Federalism* (New York: Harcourt Brace Jovanovich, 1972), p. 7.

[3] The earlier experience of the Swiss confederation demonstrated this most clearly; in the Napoleonic wars, various cantons became allied with opposite sides. As a consequence, Bern fell to the enemy for the first time in 800 years and the ceremonial bears of Bern were paraded through the streets of Paris. With the end of the war, the confederation was given powers over foreign affairs and national defense.

Tiebout effect, named for the economist who first popularized it.[4] This phenomenon increases still further the adaptation of the levels of governmental activity to the varying preferences of subsets of the population.

Second, decentralization allows more effective collective decision-making. The numbers of persons involved are smaller; knowledge of costs and benefits may be greater; there is a more direct tie between the benefits to be received and the real resource costs of providing the services. Greater popular control can be exercised over the precise manner in which the services are provided.

Third, experimentation and innovation are facilitated; various units will try different approaches to problems, and the successful techniques will be adopted by other units. There will be pressures on the various local units to match the efficiency of comparable units. The dangers of diseconomies of scale are avoided.

The Optimal Structure of Allocation of Functions

The theoretically optimal structure would assign to the federal government the stabilization and redistributional activities and those allocational activities whose benefits are nationwide in scope. Other activities would be allocated to governmental units coinciding in size with the group that directly benefits from the service involved.[5] Thus, for example, fire protection would be provided by cities, urban-area rapid transit by metropolitan transit districts.

This rule, however, must be modified in light of several constraints:

1. *Economies of scale in production.* While many services, such as police and fire protection and education, can be provided with full attainment of the economies of scale at the local government level, others may require larger units than those optimal on the basis of homogeneity of preferences. In such instances, compromise is necessary among the conflicting considerations. Scale economies are not believed to be significant for most government activities above a relatively low threshold, however.[6]

2. *Costs of decision-making.* An excessively large number of units, each coinciding with the group benefiting from the particular activity,

---

[4] Charles M. Tiebout, "A Pure Theory of Public Expenditures," *Journal of Political Economy*, vol. 64 (October 1956), pp. 416–24. Some confirmation of the Tiebout hypothesis is found by J. R. Aronson and E. Schwartz, "Financing Public Goods and the Distribution of Population in a System of Local Governments," *National Tax Journal*, vol. 26 (June 1973), pp. 137–60.

[5] Oates, *Fiscal Federalism*, chap. 2.

[6] D. Netzer, "State-Local Finance and Intergovernmental Fiscal Relations," in *The Economics of Public Finance*, A. S. Blinder *et al.* (Washington, D.C.: The Brookings Institution, 1975) pp. 381–84.

would be intolerable from the standpoints of administration and time taken for voting for members of governing bodies.

3. *Interjurisdictional externalities or geographic spill-overs.* The groups of persons benefiting from particular activities cannot be clearly delineated into mutually exclusive groups. As explained below, benefits of many governmental activities accrue primarily to one group but also spill over into other groups. Therefore, the various local units cannot be completely autonomous in their expenditure and revenue decisions. This question is discussed in greater detail below.

4. *Geographic mobility.* As noted, the tendency of persons and capital to move from one subordinate governmental unit to another facilitates the overall adjustment of governmental activities on the basis of preferences. But it may also result in excessive numbers of persons moving into certain areas, thus creating congestion costs relating to crime, fire, transport, and the like, and it seriously interferes with the establishment of acceptable tax structures. Ideally, in terms of economic efficiency, each local unit should finance its activities by benefit-related taxes. But such levies are often unworkable and unacceptable on equity grounds; and the taxes actually selected have some effect in encouraging persons and capital to move out of the area. The overall fiscal framework must take this tendency into consideration.

These constraints suggest that there is no system for division of governmental activities among several levels of government that does not interfere with the attainment of optimal overall government expenditure and revenue programs. These difficulties in turn have led to a variety of solutions, some of which have produced new problems.

EXTERNAL BENEFITS AND COSTS

As noted, many governmental services that can be performed most efficiently at lower levels of government and primarily benefit persons in the particular jurisdictions nevertheless produce *spill-overs*— geographically external benefits—to persons in other areas. Education is the classic example. Higher levels of education promote more stable and effective political processes and effective functioning of democracy; they bring more rapid technological change and economic growth and higher levels of per capita real income. These benefits extend to the country as a whole, not merely to the particular school district or area. Second, persons are highly mobile, especially in countries such as the United States. Persons educated in one area migrate to other areas, which benefit from the education. This effect is illustrated by the migration of large numbers of poorly educated persons from southern states to northern cities in recent years, bringing to the cities many problems that would have been avoided if the migrants had been better educated. There are numerous other examples; visitors to a city or state benefit from roads and police protection; treatment of sewerage by one city avoids pollution of the water supply of another; preservation of forests in one state lessens floods in its neighbors; urban slums increase crime problems in neighboring states.

When some benefits are external, the level of activity is likely to be too small relative to the interests of the country as a whole if the activity is financed locally and decisions about quantity to produce are left in local hands. In making decisions about the activity, persons will stress those benefits they themselves receive and ignore or at least give little attention to those spilling over into other communities.[7]

There is an exception to the rule that activities with spill-over will be underproduced. If a community has very strong preference for a particular level of a certain activity and some of the benefits are lost to other areas, the community will spend more, rather than less, than it would if there were no spill-overs, in order to attain the desired levels.[8] This reaction is comparable to the income-effect reaction of an individual to a change in a factor price.

Equivalent *spill-ins* from governmental activities of other jurisdictions will not bring adjustment of expenditures to the optimum, unless the spill-ins are induced by the spill-outs. Otherwise, persons will enjoy benefits of the spill-ins without considering the spill-outs in determining expenditure levels; in fact, awareness of spill-ins may reduce still more the amount of the activity provided by the unit. Why produce as much as otherwise if the area benefits from services produced by other areas? Likewise, ability to shift cost of governmental activities to outsiders will not necessarily be regarded as an offset against external benefits, but rather as a means of attaining a net increase in benefits for the community. In fact, if substantial revenue can be obtained from outsiders,[9] the overall level of activity may become excessive relative to the optimum but without increase in activities that yield external benefits. Examples of tax exporting include taxation of tourist expenditures and taxation of an industry concentrated in the state and selling outside the state.[10]

---

[7] Several empirical studies provide evidence. See, for example, the article by R. F. Adams, "On the Variation in the Consumption of Public Services," *Review of Economics and Statistics*, vol. 47 (November 1965), pp. 400–405; and B. A. Weisbrod, *External Benefits of Public Education* (Princeton, N.J.: Princeton University, 1964), pp. 107–15. These studies show significant inverse correlation between expenditure levels and the extent of subdivision of local governments into small units.

[8] Alan Williams in "The Optimal Provision of Public Goods in a System of Local Government," *Journal of Political Economy*, vol. 74 (February 1966), pp. 18–33, demonstrates this possibility.

[9] Examples include localities with extensive outside-owned industrial property and few residents; the residents can easily increase the services that benefit themselves at the expense of the outsiders. Or, if a local government operates a commercial facility, such as a toll bridge used largely by outsiders, expenditures may be increased beyond the optimal level.

[10] Note the work of Charles McLure, "The Interstate Exporting of State and Local Taxes," *National Tax Journal*, vol. 20 (March 1967), pp. 49–77.

Functional Grants as a Solution[11]

If the residents of each jurisdiction were to base expenditure decisions upon benefits to the entire country rather than those to their own areas alone, the problem would be avoided. This is not a realistic assumption. The only feasible solution, short of transferring the activity to higher levels of government, is the *conditional* or, more appropriately, *functional* grant. The higher level of government grants funds to the subordinate unit for a particular function to induce it to raise the level of the service.

If the objective is to be attained, obviously the grant must lead to net increase in spending on the activity. But any grant from one level of government to another may have both an income effect and a substitution effect. The income effect—the provision of more revenue to the recipient government—inevitably operates in the direction of leading the recipient government to reduce its own tax revenues. This is obviously contrary to the objective. But a grant may also have a substitution effect: It may lead the recipient government to increase spending from its own sources rather than reduce them. The net effect, in the absence of provisions noted below designed to ensure that spending increases, depends on the elasticity of the demand for the service as seen by the recipient government. If it appears to be high, total spending will rise; if it is low, spending with fall. The grantor government can ensure that spending will rise only if the terms of the grant are designed to ensure this effect. This result is generally accomplished by providing incentives through matching or other provisions to induce the recipient to spend more, rather than by imposing penalties to prevent them from spending less.

The principal technique to accomplish the goal is the matching rule; the recipient must match on an established formula the granted funds or it loses the grant.[12] The percentage of matching support is adjusted on the basis of the relative external and internal benefits. The open-end type of grant, whereby the expenditures of the recipient unit will be matched without limit as to amount, is desirable since the external benefits may be expected to continue to rise in total as the expenditures and the internal benefits rise. A fixed-sum grant presumes that externalities cease beyond a certain level. But grantor governments are often reluctant to provide an open-end blank check because of their own budget constraints.

Several empirical studies have been made of the actual effects of

---

[11] See George F. Break, *Intergovernmental Fiscal Relations in the United States* (Washington, D.C.: The Brookings Institution, 1967).

[12] The effectiveness of matching in increasing expenditures by the recipient government is demonstrated by John H. Bowman, "Tax Exportability, Intergovernmental Aid and School Finance Reform," *National Tax Journal*, vol. 26 (June 1974), pp. 163–74.

federal grants on state spending. One of the most thorough studies concludes that the grants programs have led to increased state expenditures in the fields covered by grants and state expenditures in total but have reduced expenditures on other state functions.[13]

With the functional grants inevitably go some measure of control of use of the funds, to make certain that the recipient unit employs them effectively. Extensive debate has occurred over the extent to which controls interfere with the autonomy of the recipient unit. The rule that controls should go no farther than is essential for accomplishment of the purposes is not easy to interpret, and reasonableness of the controls in the grants program in the United States has been debated extensively.

The related complaint, that grant programs distort state/local expenditure patterns from the optimum, is not valid if the grants are properly designed; on the contrary by financing the costs of the external benefits, they enable the recipient units to approach the optimum more precisely. Improperly designed grants may well lead states and local governments to spend more than the preferred optimum simply to obtain the grant money and to spend less than optimal amounts on other activities.

Over the years the United States federal government has developed an extensive grant program (summarized in Appendix I). Many questions have been raised about the programs. Some questions reflect lack of understanding of the basic role of the grants, such as the charge that nothing is gained and much is lost by having funds channeled from local areas to Washington and back again. Other more legitimate complaints have centered around the questions of whether grants are limited to situations of significant external benefits, whether magnitudes are properly adjusted in terms of the external benefits, and whether the nature and extent of controls are acceptable. The large number of separate programs has been criticized. Consolidation of grants, which would simplify operation, would be warranted for activities with similar ratios of internal and external benefits, and was again proposed in the 1977 budget.

Minimum Standards

Even when externalities are absent, the social welfare function of the society as a whole may require certain minimum levels of activities throughout the country. Thus, even if there were no geographical spill-overs from education, the majority of persons in the

---

[13] Thomas O'Brien, "Grants in Aid: Some Further Answers," *National Tax Journal*, vol. 24 (March 1971), pp. 65–78. Note also the article by E. M. Gramlich, "Alternative Federal Policies for Stimulating State and Local Expenditures," *National Tax Journal*, vol. 21 (June 1968), pp. 119–29.

country as a whole may feel that every child is entitled to a certain minimum quality of education, even though the majority in a particular locality might feel that universal education is not desirable. If the functions are such that society as a whole wishes them performed at the local level, it can ensure minimum provision most easily by lump-sum conditional grants.

FRAGMENTATION OF TAXATION, UNEQUAL FISCAL CAPACITY, AND BLOCK GRANTS

Division of governmental activities among several levels of government requires fragmentation of the overall tax structure in the sense that portions of the overall structure are levied and administered by several units of government. Fragmentation is necessary if each level is to have autonomous financial resources rather than merely serving as an agency to spend money collected by the national government. Division of taxation between the central government and the subordinate units results in collection at both levels (vertical fragmentation) and by a number of separate subordinate units (horizontal fragmentation). In addition to allowing fiscal autonomy, tax fragmentation does offer certain advantages. The tax structures can be adapted to voter preferences. Experimentation is facilitated, as illustrated in the United States by the pioneering work of such states as Michigan, Illinois, and Florida in the use of EDP equipment. Some taxes may be administered more effectively by a small unit than by a larger one, and possible diseconomies of scale are avoided. These diseconomies are apparently less serious than those of expenditure activities.

Consequences of Fragmentation

Fragmentation, however, does give rise to a number of major difficulties.

Attainment of Optimal Tax Structures. When tax policy is determined independently by various levels of government, attainment of an optimal *overall* structure is obviously complex. The optimal tax structure for each unit depends upon the policies of the others, and a simultaneous adjustment is required. In practice, this is virtually impossible to attain. Some units must act first; others consider this action in making their decision, and then the first may readjust, requiring further adjustments in the others. The largest jurisdictions may preempt certain fields, making use of these taxes by other units politically difficult and economically dangerous. Yet these forms may be well suited to the subordinate units, whereas other types are not. The subordinate units will be forced to use unsatisfactory taxes, or the combined burden on some levies may be so great as to produce adverse consequences and, at the minimum, duplication of collection facilities. At state or local levels, the failure of some units to use a particular tax may make it difficult for others to do so and agreement on uniform action may be impossible.

Reduction in Tax Capacity. Fragmentation of the tax structure reduces the total tax capacity of the subordinate units compared to the ability of a unified government to finance the same level of activity. This reduction is a reflection of the basic rule that the larger the taxing jurisdiction relative to the country as a whole, the more effectively it can operate a tax, for both administrative and economic reasons. First, some types of taxes cannot be administered by relatively small jurisdictions because these governments do not have access to the information necessary to assess the taxpayer or the ability to reach the taxpayer by legal means to enforce payment. A local government cannot discover property owned by residents but located in other areas and cannot require a vendor located outside of the unit and having no property or activity in the unit to collect and remit sales tax on a sale to a resident of the area. While payment could legally be enforced against the purchaser, this procedure is usually too costly to be worthwhile.

Second, various subordinate units are fearful of tax competition of other areas because of the mobility of capital and labor. Given the levels of taxation of other states, a particular state will be reluctant to raise its taxes above these levels for fear of loss of business and population. There is some real danger, and legislatures are inclined to exaggerate it. State legislatures are more fearful of locational effects of income taxes than of sales, excise, and other taxes. The most serious effects are likely to be found among local units in a metropolitan area, where choice of place of residence and location of manufacturing, distribution, and retailing activity may be substantially influenced by tax differences. Or a state may deliberately hold tax levels below those of other states to attract industry to the state or may seek to do so by special tax concessions, such as exemption of new firms from property tax for a period of years. These policies aggravate the problems of the other states.

This reduction in fiscal capacity has several consequences. The most serious is the restriction in the level of services of the states and local governments below desired levels. Another is the disproportionate reliance placed upon forms of taxes least affected by interstate competition. Many states undoubtedly rely more heavily on sales taxes and less heavily on income taxes than otherwise for fear that income taxes will impair economic development of the state.

Unequal Fiscal Capacity. Given the division of functions among various levels of government, the fragmentation of the tax structure results in varying tax capacity of local units relative to their expenditure needs. Potential tax base and expenditure needs are unevenly distributed by local unit. One local unit may contain only low-income families, with large numbers of children and heavy demands for funds for welfare, education, and housing, but very little tax capacity. A neighboring community may contain only wealthy persons with high incomes and little need for welfare services, while another may have very few inhabitants but extensive business property and thus substantial per capita wealth. Even among the states, the per capita income of the highest income state (Connecticut) is nearly twice that of the lowest (Mississippi). Within states the difference in per capita income, sales, or property among local units is very much greater. In Michigan, the wealthiest school district has 24 times the assessed value per pupil as the poorest district;[14] in California, the range is from $103 to $952,156, or 1 to 10,000.[15] In New Jersey, the average assessed valuation per pupil in school for the state as a whole is $41,026; the figure ranges from $432,084 in Mantoloking and $145,312 in Englewood Cliffs to $19,815 in Newark and $10,709 in Lakehurst.[16] In Maryland, per capita property values range from $57 in Baltimore City to $194 in Worcester country, sales tax per capita from $35 in Somerset to $177 in Worcester.

This difference in tax capacity has several consequences. The overall pattern of adjustments of activities will be very different from that arising if the central government conducted all activities and raised all revenue. Activities will be carried farther in wealthy areas than in poor. Taxes must be higher in poor areas even to maintain levels of activity that are far lower than those in the wealthy areas. Not only may these differences be regarded as inequitable but by retarding development in the poor areas they perpetuate and aggravate the differences.

Administrative and Compliance Problems.   Fragmentation of the tax structure between higher and subordinate units of government results in duplicating tax administration and compliance activities. Two sets of administrative staffs are required and two sets of returns must be filed by taxpayers. Overall costs of administration and compliance are increased. The tasks of taxpayers are aggravated if the bases of the two taxes are not identical.

Operational problems arising at subordinate levels from the interjurisdictional nature of economic activity will be discussed in a subsequent section, since the solutions are different from those for vertical fragmentation.

---

[14] Harvey Brazer, "Federal, State and Local Responsibility for Financing Education," in *Economic Factors Affecting the Financing of Education* eds. R. L. Johns *et al.* (Gainesville, Fla.: National Education Finance Project, 1970), p. 255.

[15] *Tax Administrators News*, vol. 35 (September 1971), p. 97.

[16] *Business Week* (Feb. 12, 1972), p. 53.

Unconditional or Block Grants

The reduction in overall fiscal capacity and the unequal fiscal capacity of various subordinate units are so closely related that solutions must be considered in terms of both problems. Functional grants determined solely on the basis of external benefits make only limited contribution to the solution of these problems, which are related to the financing of the services that benefit the residents of each local area. Functional grants could be extended to meet the problem by increasing the payments beyond the amounts related to external benefits. To lessen inequality of fiscal capacity the functional grant programs would require equalizing features; the amount of the grant would be adjusted on the basis of a measure of the local unit's capacity to finance the activity itself, relative to need. For example, state grants to school districts are often adjusted according to the figure of assessed value of property per child in school in each district. Use of functional grants to meet the tax capacity problem is open to the basic criticism against any functional grant program not directly related to external benefits. The grants are accompanied by controls that are unjustifiable in terms of relative responsibilities of the donor and recipient governments and they distort expenditure patterns of the recipients away from those regarded as optimal in the local area.

The logical solution of the fiscal-capacity problem is the unconditional or block grants, adjusted in terms of fiscal capacity and provided without specifications as to use or control. The allocation formula can be based upon population weighted by the reciprocal of per capita income and perhaps also by an index of the tax effort of the recipient unit to lessen the danger that the recipients simply reduce their own tax levies and to give a bonus to units that prefer a higher level of activity. Tax effort can be ascertain by a comparison between actual tax collection and the potential yield of a "standard" tax program in the area.[17]

While all units would receive some money, the payments to the poorer units would be relatively greater. Accordingly, not only would the overall fiscal capacity of the subordinate units be increased, but the inequality in fiscal capacity would be lessened or eliminated. The absence of specification of use and of controls would protect the financial autonomy of the recipient governments and avoid distorting their budget patterns. Substantial use of the unconditional grant system has been made for many years in Canada, at both dominion and provincial levels.

---

[17] See Advisory Commission of Intergovernmental Relations, *Measures of State and Local Fiscal Capacity and Tax Effort* (Washington, D.C.: 1962), and *Measuring the Fiscal Capacity and Effort of State and Local Areas* (Washington, D.C.: 1971).

One objection raised against unconditional grants, which also applies to a lesser extent to functional grants, is the danger that governments are less careful to attain efficiency in the spending of money given to them than they are in spending their own money, especially if they are not subject to supervision. This argument is difficult to evaluate but is probably of limited merit. Waste in the use of granted funds means higher taxes if given functions are to be performed, since taxes imposed by the jurisdiction must provide the marginal revenue. Standards of efficiency developed for use of the government's own funds are likely to be applied to granted funds as well. Furthermore, provision of granted funds may make effective planning feasible since without them the government may be forced into a hand-to-mouth existence that produces inefficiency and use of inexpensive, incompetent personnel.

Another question relates to the general utilization of the funds; will they be allocated to attain overall optimization of use of governmental resources? If subordinate governments are to continue to play a role in the overall structure, they must be allowed some freedom in the choices of expenditures, except for those supported by functional grants because of external benefits. If the states are not to be allowed discretion, the federal structure might as well be eliminated.

The final question is the danger that unconditional grants (as well as functional grants) will perpetuate poor areas that have lost their economic base, such as mining or timber resources. The best use of national resources may require that people move out of these areas, whereas grants may enable them to stay, supported by the government. Minimum welfare grants may produce this result. But grants for such purposes as education will facilitate movement out of the area since educated persons are much more mobile than the uneducated. Furthermore, elimination of poverty areas does not necessarily require outward movement of population because of inadequate resources. Some need additional skilled workers to bring about development of resources that are available, and the grants may facilitate inflow of such persons. Poverty tends to be self-perpetuating and some stimulus to better utilization of resources, rather than out-migration, may be the best answer.

FEDERAL REVENUE SHARING—A PARTIAL SHIFT FROM CONDITIONAL GRANTS TO BLOCK GRANTS

Increasing concern in the United States with conditional grants, coupled with reluctance to go all the way to block grants, led to the introduction, in 1972, of a system called revenue sharing—actually a modified system of block grants with some control exercised by the federal government over the use of the funds. The original proposals were called revenue sharing because they did provide for the sharing of a portion of the federal income tax with the states and local governments. The initial proposal was the Heller-Pechman plan, named for the two proponents, Joseph Pechman of Brookings Institution in Washington, and Walter W. Heller, former chairman of the Council of Economic Advisers and Professor of Economics in the University of Minnesota. A number of variants were developed, the idea was endorsed in principle by the Nixon administration, and finally, enacted by Congress, in modified form, in 1972 for an initial five-year period, and extended, in 1976, with some modifications, for 3¾ years.

The primary features of the system are as follows:

1. Congress provided initially for a five-year program of grants, with a trust fund, thus ensuring that for this period the states and local governments would be able to plan on the assurance of receiving the funds without the need for annual federal appropriations—a sharp break with precedent. The amounts have ranged between approximately $5–$7 billion a year, a minor item in the federal budget. In 1976, the trust fund was eliminated but the funds guaranteed, $6.65 billion per year, through 1980.

2. Distribution among the states is made on the basis of two formulas, each state getting the amount resulting from the formula most favorable to it:

a. The Senate formula: population, tax effort, and relative per capita income (inversely).

b. The House formula, which added to the Senate formula the percentage of urbanized population and state income tax collections, designed to increase the relative share going to the states with large urban populations and to encourage state use of income taxes.

3. One third of the funds remain with the states; two thirds is passed through to the local governments, all general (as distinguished from special district) local units participating.

Allocation to the local units is based essentially on the Senate formula noted above (population, per capita income, net nonschool taxes for general purposes, and aggregate personal income). After the amounts are allocated to the counties on this basis, part remains with the county government, part goes to the municipalities, part to the townships, the amount going to each depending on the nonschool taxes collected by each. The sum is then allocated among the various units on the Senate formula.

There are, however, several major constraints; for example, no unit can receive more than 145 percent of the state per capita average, and no unit can receive less than 20 percent (except counties).

States are free to spend the money as they wish, but local governments were restricted for current expenditure to certain basic activities: safety, environment, transport, health, recreation, libraries, social services, financial administration, but not education. Restriction to these categories was eliminated in 1976. Any capital outlays are eligible.

There are several other restrictions:

1. A separate fund must be used, with standard accounting and audit procedures.

2. The activities must be nondiscriminatory.

3. The funds could not be used for matching purposes for federal conditional grants; this rule was dropped in 1976.

4. Wage payments are subject to certain rules.

Thus the system is broadly one of block grants, but differs primarily in the restrictions on use so far as the local governments are concerned, and the other restrictions noted. But there is a wide area of freedom, particularly as compared to the traditional conditional grant.

The Accomplishments. There is general agreement that the program has in considerable measure attained the desired objective: [18]

1. Recipient governments find, with exceptions, that they do have substantial freedom in the use of the funds—partly because the restrictions on use are difficult to implement. Use of revenue sharing funds for one activity frees local funds for ineligible functions.

2. There is a substantial degree of equalization of fiscal capacity among rich and poor states. The rich states get much less—about half as much, per capita—as the poor states, because of the significance of per capita income in the allocation formula.

3. The major central cities benefit more, per capita, than the wealthier suburbs—four to seven times as much.

4. The development of the system has had some dampening effect on the further expansion of conditional-grant programs.

The Limitations and Criticisms. The program has not been without its criticisms, and various defects have become apparent in the structure of the system:

1. The restrictions have been criticized by those who are strongly committed to a true block-grant system. The restrictions particularly affect use of funds by those local governments whose spheres of activity are narrowly limited by state law. Restrictions, in turn, may lead to changes in policies of local governments that are not intended.

2. The formulas may affect financing; one of the most serious effects is to discourage the use of charges, which do not enter into the tax-effort formula, in favor of taxes—a result that may have undesirable

---

[18] Note particularly Advisory Commission on Intergovernmental Relations (ACIR), *General Revenue Sharing* (Washington, D.C.: 1974); R. P. Strauss, "General Revenue Sharing: How Well Is It Working?" *Proceedings of the National Tax Association for 1974*, pp. 172–208.

consequences. The program, however, has not induced greater use of state income taxes, as sought.

3. While the central cities receive relatively greater amounts per capita, the 145 percent rule drastically constrains the amounts that they get. The system has done little to solve the desperate financial situation of New York City and some other large cities.

4. There is substantial complaint that the federal government has cut back certain conditional programs, particularly those aiding the poor and the central cities, so that the problems of the central cities have been aggravated rather than being lessened, and there has been little improvement in the position of the lowest income groups.

5. Obsolete governmental units, primarily townships in the Midwest and counties in New England, have been propped up by the system. They often receive funds for which there is little apparent need. One consequence is to preserve governmental units that by any standards no longer are justified, and to pull funds away from units that urgently require additional money.

6. A substantial amount of the funds—about 45 percent—has been used to reduce or avoid increases in state-local taxes. Whether this effect is desirable or undesirable depends upon one's philosophy about the appropriate level of governmental activity.

7. Some disappointment is expressed over the failure of the program to accomplish more in the way of lessening discrimination and increasing popular participation in decision-making (though the law does not requires this), though there has been some gain.

8. Per capita income is not an ideal measure of tax capacity; there has been argument for a more complex formula that considers other elements, such as property values, affecting the capacity.

The basic argument for continuing revenue sharing is that for block grants generally. The states, and to a much greater degree the local governments, have inadequate revenues to meet demands for services, whereas the federal government has much greater potential. The result of the inadequacies has been constant fiscal crises, such as that in New York City in 1975–76. Mayors and governors, legislatures and city councils are caught between rising expenditure demands on the one side and the blame that falls upon them for raising tax rates on the other. The inherent disadvantages of the property tax limit its use, and the interstate competition fears restrict income tax increases and even sales tax increases to some extent. At the same time, the fiscal resources of local governments and of the states are very unequal; poorer jurisdictions must either use higher tax rates or provide poorer-quality services, thus making economic growth and improvement in the fiscal position of the areas more difficult. Poverty tends to be self-perpetuating for governmental units just as it is for families.

Given the pressures for additional services and the resistance to tax increases at the state-local level, the inevitable tendency has been for the federal government to provide more and more conditional grants and assume direct responsibility for more and more functions. Both of these trends reduce the financial autonomy of the states and local governments; more and more the federal government is taking over decision making that is regarded as appropriately belonging to lower levels. At the same time, the continuous increase in conditional grants has also produced an increasingly complex network of grants—now in the hundreds. The result is a great drain of money and manpower simply in keeping up with the availability of grants and conformity with the rules established.

Shared revenues are therefore seen as a means of checking the trend toward excessive centralization in decision-making, preserving the autonomy of the states and localities and thus the basic federal structure of the country, and allowing the meeting of pressing expenditure demands without excessive centralization or continued expanding of second-best taxes.

The basic criticisms come from those who favor much more aggressive federal action, especially in the poverty field, on the one hand, and those that object to further expansion of all governmental activity and believe that states and local governments will waste funds given to them, on the other. Others point to the federal deficit as evidence of the lack of fiscal capacity of the federal government—an argument that has no merit, given the great tax capacity at the federal level.

MINOR SOLUTIONS

Objections to grants and shared revenues have led to search for alternative solutions to the problems that would provide greater financial resources for the subordinate governments and reduce duplication of administration yet preserve financial autonomy. Some use is made of these alternatives, in part because of the unwillingness to date to make adequate unconditional grants.

Tax Sharing on Origin Basis

The higher unit of government may share a portion of a tax that it imposes and administers on the basis of the geographic origin of revenue. This procedure increases the fiscal capacity of the subordinate units by giving them access to revenue from taxes barred from their direct use at equivalent rates by competitive and administrative considerations and avoids the distorting effects on location that might arise from differential use of the levies. But the technique does not meet the problems of unequal fiscal capacity and varying preferences among communities for use of the particular revenue source. Nor does it meet the argument that governments are less careful about the use of taxes they do not themselves impose. While this technique lessens duplication of tax administration and compliance, taxpayers must still segregate tax liability by local units, with inevitable allocation problems. The origin basis of allocation, while satisfactory for the personal income tax once relative claims of the jurisdiction of residence and source of income are established, is unworkable with some forms of tax. For example, a motor fuel tax may be collected from refineries located in one county, whereas the motor fuel is used over a wide area.

Tax Supplements

To meet the problem of variation in need for revenue and the objection that governments are less careful in the use of revenue from taxes that they do not impose, a tax supplement system may be used in lieu of tax sharing. The larger unit collects, along with its own levy, a supplement imposed by the local unit. A number of states employ this technique with sales taxes. Tax supplements allow for diversity in rates among local units and, like tax sharing on an origin basis, avoid duplication of administration and compliance activities and ensure uniformity of base of the tax. But the supplement system does not avoid the tax competition problem since some local units may be unwilling to impose the tax for fear of loss of economic activity to other jurisdictions. The system works best when rates of the supplement are so low that there is little fear of this result or when use of the tax is universal. [19] Except where there is variation in need, the preference for the supplement system over origin-shared revenue rests entirely on the rather questionable argument that units must impose the taxes that provide them revenue if the funds are to be used most efficiently. Tax supplements, of course, do nothing to meet the problem of unequal fiscal resources.

Tax Credit

Full credit of tax paid to the subordinate unit against tax due to the larger unit eliminates tax competition problems and thus increases tax capacity of the subordinate units, but does not, per se, eliminate duplication of administration. [20] This system has been used for many years for state inheritance and estate taxes in the United States (with a

---

[19] In California, local sales tax supplements to the state sales tax are universal, and in Illinois most local units employ the supplement. Once a levy of this type becomes universal, the uniformity advantage of the shared revenue approach is attained.

[20] The Canadian federal government has used this system for a number of years for income taxation; see *The Financing of Canadian Federation* (Toronto: Canadian Tax Foundation, 1966). The provinces are given the option of federal collection.

maximum deductible figure established in terms of a percentage of federal tax due) and has been employed in Canada for both personal and corporate income taxes, with a maximum set in terms of percentage points of the federal rate. The fear of the smaller units to impose the tax because of loss of economic activity is eliminated; if a particular unit does not impose the tax, its residents will pay no less tax, but the central government will receive all the revenue. Introduction of the system without an increase in the central government tax rates increases the tax capacity of the subordinate units relative to that of the central government.

With credit of only a portion of the tax instead of the full amount, the tax competition influence is only partially removed. If the tax is merely deductible from income instead of from tax, for example, the larger unit government bears only a portion of the cost of subordinate unit tax increases.

Other Measures [21]

Some of the compliance and administrative inefficiencies arising out of overlapping of taxes can be lessened by rather simple devices that do not reduce the fiscal autonomy of the smaller units. For example, a state may adjust the base of its income tax to correspond with that of the federal tax or, as a few states have done, define the liability for state income tax as a percentage of federal tax. Joint operation of portions of tax administration and exchange of audit information lessen administrative duplication. The larger unit of government can also avoid using taxes that are suitable for the subordinate units yet unnecessary for its own use and avoid unnecessary departure from separation of tax sources and duplication of administrative effort. This consideration is a major argument against the use of a federal sales tax in the United States.

On the other hand, a proposal for complete separation of all revenue sources, whereby no tax would be used by more than one level of government, is unrealistic unless supplemented by extensive grant programs since there are not enough "acceptable" taxes available for the subordinate units. The result of attempted separation would be use by the subordinate units of less-satisfactory levies.

INTERJURISDICTIONAL PROBLEMS FROM HORIZONTAL FRAGMENTATION

Horizontal fragmentation of the tax structure creates major jurisdictional questions for the subordinate units, because much economic activity extends beyond the boundaries of a particular taxing jurisdic-

[21] See Break, *Intergovernmental Fiscal Relations*, chap. 2.

tion. When the base of the tax is in any way interjurisdictional in nature, not only do questions of principle arise about the allocation of the base among the various units but the task of compliance and enforcement may be more difficult and costly. Some retail sales are interstate in nature, made by a vendor in one state to a purchaser in another. Decision must be reached about the claim to the tax: Does the state of the vendor or the state of the purchaser have jurisdiction? In terms of the principle of the tax as a levy on consumption the state of the purchaser is entitled to the tax, but effective enforcement by this state is possible only if the vendors can be made to collect and remit tax. Even when states have legal power to force payment by vendors, they find collection difficult from out-of-state vendors who make only a few sales in the state, and the firms selling into a number of states experience substantial cost in collecting and remitting tax. In practice the states are limited in their power to firms doing business in the state or selling through agents in the state.[22] Even when they have legal power, they usually do not enforce this power effectively, so that revenue is lost, inequity created, and interstate selling encouraged. Some double taxation arises when an article is purchased in one state subject to tax and then taxed again when transferred to another state. Most states now provide credit for sales tax paid another state.

With state personal and corporate income taxes, allocation and enforcement problems arise when a person lives in one state and earns income from work or investment in another and when business firms operate in more than one state. With individuals, most states tax on the basis of both residence and source of income, and double taxation would be widespread were it not for reciprocal provisions whereby credit is allowed for tax paid to another state. With corporations, there are two major questions of principle: determination of the nature of activity in a state necessary to give it jurisdiction over the corporation, and the allocation of the income among the various states. Most states use a three-element formula (property owned, payrolls, sales), but some do not, and the definition of sales varies; accordingly some companies may pay tax on more than their entire income and others on less. Enforcement is a less-serious problem than it is with sales taxation; the main source of additional cost is that of compliance with a number of state laws.

With estate and inheritance taxes, problems similar to those with personal income taxes are encountered, although the rule is usually

---

[22] Attempts of the states to require collection by firms selling only through mail-order catalogs and other advertising sent into the state were blocked by the U.S. Supreme Court action in 1967 in the National Bellas Hess case (*National Bellas Hess, Inc.* v. *Dept. of Revenue of the State of Illinois*, 386 US 753, 18th ed. 2d 505). The large mail-order houses collect tax because they also have places of business in the state. Previous court decisions barred the states from requiring firms merely delivering in the state to collect tax.

accepted that the state of residence of the decedent, not that of the heir, has jurisdiction. On corporate securities, however, the state of incorporation has been held to have claim as well, although frequently this right is not exercised.

The consequences of these interstate collection problems include higher cost of tax administration and higher compliance costs for business firms, especially those operating in a number of states with diverse laws and subject to both income and sales tax requirements, and for individuals complying with the tax laws of several states. At the same time, effectiveness of collection is reduced and evasion is increased. Compliance problems may affect business decisions; a firm may decide not to place an office or distribution warehouse in a particular state because to do so would make the firm liable to collection of sales tax on sales made into the state. On the other hand, the inability of the states to enforce payment on certain types of interstate sales, such as those by mail-order catalog, encourages this form of business activity.

Excessive fragmentation reduces efficiency in tax operation by placing administration in the hands of governmental units too small to attain economies of scale. The most extreme example is assessment of property by jurisdictions too small to hire full-time trained personnel.

Reduction of Administrative and Compliance Problems

Some of the major difficulties encountered by both taxpayers and state and local governments can be lessened by cooperation of the units or by action of the higher level of government.

First, use of standard rules of allocation of tax lessens multiple taxation and escape from tax. Second, cooperative administrative action can benefit all concerned except the tax evaders. Sales taxation offers many possibilities for joint effort; states may agree on cooperative audit, whereby each state, in its own audit work, ensures that tax due another state has been paid. Or agreements can be devised whereby one state collects and remits to other states the sales tax due them by vendors located in the state.

Fear of adverse federal legislation plus concern about interstate complications led the states to develop the Multistate Tax Compact in 1967. The primary purpose of the compact is to bring about greater cooperation among the states to meet the complaints of business firms, facilitate tax administration, and deter federal legislation by meeting the problems through cooperative effort. The compact itself provides for certain rules relating to sales and income taxes designed to promote uniformity and lessen the danger of multiple taxation. The Multistate Tax Commission, established by the compact, seeks to devise techniques to simplify the tasks of business firms on the one hand and to improve the effectiveness of the administration on the other. Without congressional sanction, the compact has no power to enforce any actions, but it has brought improvements in interstate cooperation. Unfortunately many of the larger states have not joined the compact.

The Special Case of Education

The unequal fiscal capacity of various school districts and the geographical externalities of education long ago led to state grants to the school districts to ensure minimum levels and somewhat equalize the educational opportunities in various areas. But despite these state grants, school districts have varied widely in their ability to finance the portion of school costs for which they have been responsible. Examples were given above of the widely varying ratios among school districts of assessed value of property per pupil in attendance. The result has been that the poor districts must impose a much higher tax rate to raise a given sum per pupil than the wealthy districts, and frequently, they were unable to raise sums equivalent to those collected in the wealthy areas. As a consequence, persons in the poor districts were burdened more heavily yet their children received poorer-quality education. Innumerable examples could be given; one will illustrate the point. In New Jersey, for example, Audubon Park imposes a rate of $5.59 but raises only $771 per pupil, while nearby Haddenfield raises $1,065 per pupil from a rate of $2.33.

Complaints had long been made about this situation but early lawsuits had proved unsuccessful. Finally, however, in 1971 a suit in California carried to the state supreme court proved successful.[23] The suit was brought on the basis that the higher tax rates and lower expenditures in the poor districts (Baldwin Park, in the case) discriminated against the children of these districts compared to those in wealthy districts. The state supreme court accepted this argument, holding that school financing based on the local property tax was unconstitutional because it resulted in discrimination against children in the poorer districts; the expenditures for education cannot be dependent upon the wealth per pupil in the district. Federal courts in Minnesota and Texas rendered similar decisions, as did the state superior court in New Jersey. But the U.S. Supreme Court overruled the state courts so far as the federal constitution is concerned.[24] But in some states, readjustments are still required on the basis of the state constitution.

One alternative is simply to replace local school property taxes by a state property tax, thus providing a uniform rate throughout the state

---

[23] *Serrano* v. *Priest*, 487 P. 2d 1241 96 Cal. Rptr. 601 (1971).

[24] *San Antonio Independent School District* v. *Rodriguez*, 93 S.Ct. 1278 (1973).

and allocating the money to the school districts on a per pupil or similar basis. Such a step would have the incidental advantage of leading to better property assessment, whether it is taken over by the state or state supervised. Alternatively, the states may replace the local property tax by increases in state sales or income taxes, but the magnitudes of the increase in these levies would be so great that few legislatures are likely to follow this path.

METROPOLITAN AREAS[25]

Several of the basic problems arising out of fragmentation of governmental activities and taxation are most apparent in metropolitan areas, which typically include large numbers of local governments, often spreading across state lines. These areas witness the most spectacular failure of governments to solve the problems of the contemporary world; slums with substandard housing and juvenile delinquency and crime; severe and self-perpetuating poverty; poor quality of education in the core cities; traffic congestion and air pollution, largely a product of the motor vehicle; urban sprawl with its unsightliness and poor land utilization.

The Problems

More specifically, the metropolitan area problem has several major aspects:

Expenditure Needs Per Capita. The central city faces to an increasing extent much greater expenditure needs per capita than do the suburbs as a whole. First, the central city typically has a much higher percentage of very low-income groups. This is not a new phenomenon, but the importance has increased relatively. The evidence is provided very clearly by the much higher welfare load relative to population in the central city. Baltimore, for example, has 27 percent of the population of Maryland but 71 percent of the welfare load; Boston has 14 percent of the population of Massachusetts but 28 percent of the welfare load.[26]

The concentration of poverty in the central cities plus the much higher degree of concentration of persons and buildings result in higher per capita police and fire protection costs and sanitation costs

[25] Advisory Commission on Intergovernmental Relations, *Fiscal Balance in the American Federal System* (Washington, D.C.: 1967); *American Federal System* (Washington, D.C.: 1967); *Metropolitan Disparities* (1970); *Improving Urban America* (Washington, D.C.: 1976); S. M. Miller and W. K. Tabb, "A New Look at a Pure Theory of Local Expenditures," *National Tax Journal*, vol. 26 (June 1973); pp. 161–76; *Urban Fiscal Problems* NTA-TIA Symposium, *National Tax Journal*, vol. 29 (September 1976) pp. 233–367.

[26] Advisory Commission on Intergovernmental Relations, *Fiscal Balance*, vol. 2, p. 5.

and as yet unsolved crime problems. The inflow of commuters to be served likewise increases expenditure needs per capita.[27] Education requirements are likewise in a sense greater because of the higher costs of providing quality education in the low-income areas and the lesser tendency to send children to private schools. In the last five years powerful and aggressive labor unions have pushed up municipal wage levels sharply in central cities.

Tax Base. At the same time that expenditure needs have been growing relative to those in the suburbs, the tax base has tended to diminish relative to that of the outlying areas. Higher-income population has been fleeing to the suburbs for a variety of reasons; retailing has been shifting to suburban shopping centers; and manufacturing has been moving out into outlying areas from the congested downtown areas. A number of factors have been responsible: overall higher income levels; greater ease in buying homes; and the development of motor vehicles, which makes suburban living simpler and increases the traffic-congestion problems of the downtown areas and lessens dependence of light industry upon rail facilities.

As a consequence, the tax base of the central cities has fallen relative to the expenditure needs, as compared to the suburban areas. On the one hand, this means poorer services; school expenditures are less per capita in the central cities than in the outlying areas whereas needs are actually greater. On the other hand, tax rates are typically higher. For the central cities as a whole, state and local taxes constitute 7.6 percent of personal incomes; for the outlying areas, 5.6 percent.[28] At the same time many urban requirements are neglected and many large cities face recurrent financial crises—aggravated in some instances by financial mismanagement and policies that merely postponed solution.

The New York City situation—the city simply reached the point in 1975 at which it could no longer meet its obligations and drastic state action was required—has been the most severe.[29] The city continued to operate at a deficit for 15 years, borrowing for current expenditures and building up increasing debt obligations. Underlying the situation was a somewhat higher per capita expenditure level than is typical, and very much greater outlays on activities that are not significant for most cities, particularly welfare, transit-system deficits, pensions, and hospitals. Basically the city tried for a decade to live beyond its means,

---

[27] W. B. Neenan concluded that six Detroit suburbs in effect "exploit" Detroit in terms of use by their residents of Detroit services. See his "Suburban Central City Exploitation Thesis," *National Tax Journal*, vol. 23 (June 1970), pp. 117–39.

[28] Advisory Commission on Intergovernmental Relations, *Urban America and the Federal System* (Washington, 1969), p. 10.

[29] E. Gramlich, "Ripple or Tidal Wave?", *Proceedings of the American Economic Association for 1975* (May 1976), pp. 415–29.

and tried to carry on more redistributive activity than is feasible at the local level. While other cities have major problems, none have as yet gotten themselves into as deep a morass as New York.

The net effect is not only inequity but aggravation of the problem: The higher tax rates and the poorer services drive more residents and industry and retailing out of the central cities, thus leading to further deterioration.

Disparities among the Suburbs. The previous discussion related to the central cities versus the suburbs. But there are great disparities among the suburbs. There are high-income, high-wealth suburbs, often with a low population density per square mile. There are low-income, low-property suburbs with little business property. There are industrial suburbs, with large amounts of business property and few services to perform. In the Chicago metropolitan areas, for example, assessed value per capita ranges from $7,122 in Winnetka to $1,205 in Robbins. In Los Angeles county, the range is from $7 in Artesia to $20,430 in Vernon. Retail sales vary much more drastically—in the Chicago area from $1.35 per capita in Flossmoor (which fortunately has high wealth and income) to $166 in Oakbrook; in Los Angeles country, from $1 in Hidden Hills to $29,279 in Vernon. The sales differences are largely a product of location of shopping centers. In the Boston metropolitan area, the median family income ranges from $13,000 in Weston to $5,298 in Chelsea.[30]

The net result is the same as between the central city and the suburbs; the poor areas become poorer, the rich richer. Children growing up in the poorer areas receive much less in the way of education than those in the rich areas; the poorer are squeezed to maintain even a minimum level of services. Any tendency that might occur toward equalization is in part blocked by various restrictions. The rich high-income suburbs block the flow of population by various zoning restrictions that keep lot sizes large, and they resist any effort toward equalization.

Land Use. One final aspect of metropolitan area development is the "scatterization" and "leapfrogging" of real estate developments, spreading the subdivisions over excessive land areas, jumping over large blocks of land to get into further outlying areas where land is cheap. The net result is to increase the cost of provision of utilities, to destroy the chances for retention of open spaces, and to increase reliance on the automobile by making effective rapid transit uneconomic.

---

[30] Advisory Commission on Intergovernmental Relations, *Urban America and the Federal System* (Washington, 1969), p. 10. These figures are taken from A.C.I.R. *Fiscal Balance*, and R. D. Reischauer, "In Defense of the Property Tax," *Proceedings of the National Tax Association for 1974*, pp. 288–306.

Thus more and more metropolitan areas have become "balkanized," divided into separate governmental units with widely differing racial and economic composition. The advantaged localities are determined to protect their advantages, the poor ones are helpless to improve their situation. So the rich areas become richer and the poor become poorer.

The Organizational Structure

Inability to solve metropolitan-area problems is basically a product of faulty governmental organization—the large number of autonomous local governments—in a metropolitan area. There are, for example, over 1000 local governments in the Chicago metropolitan area. Many of the functions are areawide in nature. Some cannot be undertaken at all by small units, others only very inefficiently, without adequate regard to the interests of the area as a whole. Spill-over benefits are widespread within a metropolitan area, yet no one local unit can take them into consideration in its own decision-making. There is no means of balancing the overall governmental needs of the area. The tax base is unevenly divided, industrial and high-income residential suburbs having high tax capacity relative to those of low-income residential character. Because of the limited size of the taxing jurisdictions and the relative equality of other forces affecting location within metropolitan areas, tax competition may have severe effects upon the tax capacity of each unit. The governmental structures are carry-overs from earlier years when they were more suitably adapted to the circumstances. Change is often difficult because of sheer inertia, vested interests of existing local units, and domination of state legislatures by suburban and rural representatives.

Several general solutions to the problem are available; all have been utilized in limited degree, with slow but definite trend in the direction of positive action.

Consolidation

An obvious solution is the merger of the various small units into a single metropolitan government. Consolidation, however, is difficult politically and sacrifices the advantages of smaller units: greater popular participation in government and adjustment of activities to the wishes of the people of the areas. Some of the political objection to consolidation centers around the fear of domination by the central city political machine. More significantly, however, the suburbs—high income or low—seek to preserve neighborhood schools and the high-income ones seek to avoid flow of lower-income families into the jurisdiction.[31] As with any merger of governmental units, residents and officials of each city inevitably resist loss of their political identities, and merchants fear the loss of business. Despite these obstacles, some movement toward merger of contiguous small units could help to lessen the problems of metropolitan areas, increasing efficiency and the ability to meet some of the major problems.[32]

The Metropolitan Federation

A compromise, which retains the smaller units for purely local activity but establishes a metropolitan government, such as that of Toronto, to undertake functions requiring conduct and financing on an areawide basis, has more political appeal and offers some advantages of each system. The metropolitan government can undertake activities requiring areawide operation for efficiency and those with significant spill-over benefits. The metropolitan government can also levy its own uniform tax throughout the area, lessening tax competition and providing more adequate support for schools. The local units retain the purely local activities, with continued popular participation and the important political advantage of retention of identity. Even if exact optimal allocation of functions cannot be attained, the system is an improvement over the present disorganization. The main difficulty is the political objection to transference of functions. There is also danger that the metropolitan government will be merely a confederation, with paralyzing veto powers retained by the various local units. When the metropolitan area covers more than one state, political obstacles to the formation of an overall metropolitan government are serious.

When one county covers all or a large portion of a metropolitan area (as for example Los Angeles), the county may serve as the metropolitan government, with perhaps less political difficulty.

More common in practice than metropolitan governments or federations are metropolitan councils, representing the various local jurisdictions, seeking better coordination of policy. These organizations accomplish little because of lack of power.

Metropolitan Area Sharing of Revenues

The state of Minnesota, by provisions of 1971 legislation, established a system whereby 40 percent of all new commercial and indus-

---

[31] Consolidation in rural areas would often increase governmental efficiency. Townships are too small for efficient operation, and in many states even counties are excessively small. Alpine, in California, has a population of 430; King, Texas 460; Esmeralda, Nevada 600. The same identity and prestige concepts impede merger; lobbies of township officials are often very influential in state legislatures.

[32] One of the few examples of this type of merger was the formation of the city of Fremont, California, bringing together a number of towns and unincorporated urban areas.

trial property in the seven-county St. Paul-Minneapolis area will be redistributed for property tax purposes to the local governments in the area on an equalizing basis. This system shares the increase in the base, lessens the competition of various jurisdictions for new industry, and lessens fiscal inequalities in the area. It does not meet the problem of areawide provision of the governmental services.

Special-Purpose Districts [33]

An alternative approach is the formation of special-purpose districts. Historically these first developed in the field of education, often contiguous with the basic local governmental unit, established to free education from the control of local political machines. Other districts have frequently been formed to escape bond and tax-rate limitations or restrictions on existing local governments and have contributed little except additional fragmentation, interfering with coordination of policies and optimal adjustment of activities.

Special districts covering an entire metropolitan area, however, can make significant contributions to the improvement of the conduct of governmental functions and financing and aid in attainment of the objective that the size of a governmental unit should coincide with the group benefiting from the activity of the unit. Such units can undertake areawide functions and provide a uniform basis of financing. They may even include parts of more than one state, as does the New York Port Authority. The districts are usually relatively easy to form, especially if no major functions are transferred away from existing governmental units. As a practical matter, they constitute an effective device for improving governmental organization, but they are not without defects. Their formation to meet the most pressing problems may retard more basic reforms. Special districts interfere with evaluation of the benefits and costs of overall governmental activities. The officials of an aggressive special district, armed with substantial taxing powers, may push their activity far beyond the level reflecting comparative consideration of benefits from other activities as well. Other districts may lie moribund, accomplishing nothing. Voters may take little interest. An infinite number of elections for officials of special districts (on different days) is sufficient to discourage the most responsible citizen from voting. On the whole, special-purpose districts represent a feasible, simple method of accomplishing in part what broader approaches could do much better; they may gradually become metropolitan gov-

---

[33] Other techniques are used on a limited scale. One government may contract to supply certain functions for another government, as various communities of the Los Angeles area have done for one another (the so-called Lakewood plan). Several counties may set up joint multicounty health units or other joint projects. These arrangements allow greater efficiency in specific instances by allowing small units access to the economies of scale, but do little to meet the overall problems.

ernments if diverse functions are given to them or, in time, they may be replaced by broader units.

Stabilization and Intergovernmental Relations

A final problem arising out of the division of functions and revenue sources is the potentially perverse stabilization behavior of state and local finance. To prevent this reaction from offsetting federal fiscal policy, adjustments are required in federal grant programs.

Unconditional grants or increased revenue sharing to support basic state-local expenditures in depression would avoid cutbacks in these functions, even though in full-employment periods there was no justification for federal aid for these activities. Second, grants for public works expenditures, as a partial substitute for direct conduct of the public works by the federal government, would facilitate better project selection since many state-local functions offer good opportunities for capital investment.

Such an approach could be systematized by a formal program whereby the federal government would grant to the states and localities the difference between predepression revenues and expenditures, similar to the Canadian stabilization grants, provided that the recipients did not raise taxes or cut expenditures. If the states would liberalize their debt limits, they could themselves lessen their fiscally perverse behavior.

Restriction of increases in state-local expenditures in inflationary periods is more difficult. Monetary policy has some restrictive effect by increasing the total cost of state-local borrowing. Reduction in grants can also curtail spending, but must be employed in such a way as to avoid curtailing basic activity.

CONCLUSION

There are several philosophical issues in the sphere of intergovernmental fiscal relations that can be decided only on the basis of value judgments. One is the resolution of conflict between local and national preference functions. The national function may, for example, desire a certain minimum level of educational opportunities available to all. But the preferences in a particular community may be for a much lower level—because the residents regard education as offering little benefit, because other activities are given greater priority, or because of limited financial resources. This divergence takes its starkest form on school-integration questions: A large majority of voters in a school district may strongly prefer nonintegrated schools, but a strong national majority may prefer that schools throughout the country be integrated. The question is: Which majority shall rule, that of the local area or that of the state or nation as a whole? Where there are externalities the answer is relatively clear: The local preferences must give way to the national one to the extent of the externalities— although the larger unit of government is obligated to provide a portion of the finance. Beyond externalities the answer is less obvious. The general statement is widely accepted that local preferences should dominate except when there is strong national consensus that a certain level of activity is essential on grounds of equity; then the national will must take precedence. But this is a difficult rule to interpret, and implementation must rest primarily on social philosophy.

A second question is that of the relative effectiveness with which state and local governments will ascertain and respond to preference patterns and the relative efficiency with which they will administer their programs compared to the federal government. Here views differ widely, as they have since the founding of the country. To many, the local governments and the states are not in fact highly responsive to voter preferences despite the theoretical advantages of smaller size and closer contact with the public. These governments, it is argued, are dominated by various interest groups concerned only about their own welfare; the quality of personnel is low; and programs are badly executed. By contrast the federal government is more conscious of national goals, attracts much higher-caliber personnel, and operates with a higher degree of efficiency. To the opponents, this is little short of nonsense; the states and localities are much more responsive to the voters and conscious of popular preferences; the federal government suffers from the twin evils of vast bureaucracy and remoteness from the public—a remoteness that furthers the Santa Claus attitude that services provided by the federal government are costless to the taxpayer. These issues cannot now, if ever, be solved on a scientific basis.

APPENDIX I—GRANT PROGRAMS IN THE UNITED STATES

Federal Grant Programs

The United States federal government until late 1972 used only the functional (conditional) grant system, the grants primarily designed to stimulate state activity in fields in which externalities are important; since then revenue sharing has been introduced. The programs have expanded over the year, the payments constituting in 1976 about 14 percent of total federal spending. Most of the programs are matching, but the traditional 50 percent is giving way to a greater variety of figures. All programs are accompanied by some control and supervision of the use of the funds.

TABLE 18A–1

Federal Grant-In-Aid and Revenue Sharing Outlays by Function (in millions of dollars)

Function	1975 actual	1976 estimate	1977 estimate
National defense	74	76	67
Natural resources, environment, and energy	2,479	3,088	4,505
Agriculture	404	499	556
Commerce and transportation	5,872	8,227	8,990
Community and regional development	3,335	4,008	3,917
Education, training, employment, and social services	11,638	14,422	12,497
Health	8,810	10,032	10,188
Income security	9,279	11,212	11,434
Veterans benefits and services	32	73	80
Law enforcement and justice	725	838	805
General government	102	145	135
Revenue sharing and general purpose fiscal assistance	6,971	7,166	7,349
Total outlays	49,723	59,787	60,523

As shown in Table 18A–1 most of the money is granted for a relatively few programs, particularly public assistance, health, housing, highways, and, to a growing extent, education. Some of the welfare grants have equalizing features, the amounts given being determined in part by the tax capacity of the recipient states. Table 18A–2 shows the relative share of each function, and Table 18A–3 relative importance of grants in the overall spending program.

TABLE 18A–2

Percentage Function Distribution of Federal Grants-In-Aid

	Actual						Estimates	
	1952	1957	1962	1967	1972	1975	1976	1977
Natural resources, environment and energy	1	1	2	2	2	5	5	7
Agriculture	4	9	6	3	1	1	1	1
Commerce and transportation	18	24	36	27	15	12	14	15
Community and regional development	1	1	3	6	9	7	7	6
Education, training, employment and social services	9	8	8	25	26	23	24	21
Health	8	4	5	10	17	18	17	17
Income security	57	49	38	25	26	19	19	19
Revenue sharing and general purpose fiscal assistance	2	3	2	2	1	14	12	12
Other	—	1	—	—	1	2	2	2
Total	100	100	100	100	100	100	100	100

Source: *Budget of the United States Government*, 1977.

TABLE 18A–3
Impact of Federal Grant Outlays (dollar amounts in millions)

		Federal grants as a percent of		
		Federal outlays		State and local expenditures[2]
	Grants	Total	Domestic[1]	
1950	$ 2,253	5.3	8.8	10.4
1955	3,207	4.7	12.1	10.1
1960	7,020	7.6	15.9	14.7
1965	10,904	9.2	16.6	15.3
1969	20,255	11.0	20.1	18.0
1970	24,018	12.2	21.1	19.4
1971	28,109	13.3	21.4	19.9
1972	34,372	14.8	22.8	22.0
1973	41,832	17.0	24.8	24.3
1974	43,308	16.1	23.3	22.7
1975	49,723	15.3	21.3	23.4
1976 estimate	59,787	16.0	21.7	25.2
1977 estimate	60,523	15.4	21.1	23.0

[1] Defined for this purpose as excluding national defense and international programs.
[2] As defined in the National Income Accounts.
Source: *Budget of the United States Government, 1977.*

State Grant Programs

Three functions account for most of the state grants to the local governments: education, roads, and welfare; the first comprises two thirds of the total. Grants to the school districts for education were established primarily because of their limited tax resources, the wide variation in tax capacity among districts, and the desire to stimulate them to provide better-quality education. In many states, part of the grant is on a uniform ADA (average daily attendance) basis, part on an equalizing basis. The districts with low figures of total assessed valuation of property per child in school receive larger sums, in order to obtain better equalization of fiscal capacity of the various districts.

Total state grants to local governments in 1974 totaled $45.9 billion,

TABLE 18A–4
State Grants to Local Governments, by Function, 1975 (in billions of dollars)

Function	Amount
Education	31.1
Highways	3.2
Welfare and health	8.1
General	5.1
Other	2.3
Total	51.0

Source: U.S. Bureau of the Census, *State Government Finances in 1975.*

or 35 percent of total state spending. Grants by function are shown in Table 18A–4. Some states share revenues from particular taxes with the local governments, thus providing a payment very similar to an unconditional grant.

APPENDIX II—CANADIAN EXPERIENCE

Federal Conditional Grants

Canada was much slower to develop conditional grant programs than the United States, primarily because of greater fear of the effects of such grants on provincial autonomy. Quebec, until 1960, flatly refused to accept the grants for this reason. There is as yet, for example, no general highway grant program, and the number of grant systems is much smaller than in the United States. The total provided in 1975 was $3.4 billion. The major grants are those for hospital insurance, medicare, and welfare.

Federal Unconditional Grants

The story of the Canadian block grants and other intergovernmental techniques is an extremely complicated one and can only be summarized here. There are several distinct elements.

1. *The statutory or constitutional subsidies.* When the Dominion was formed in 1867, the powers of the provinces to levy indirect taxes were taken from them. Since they had relied heavily on these taxes, the Dominion gave them annual subsidies to replace the lost revenue. The amounts were intended to remain fixed, but were increased somewhat and have continued down to the present time. The total in 1975 was only $34 million.

2. Equalization grants designed to equalize the relative fiscal position of the various provinces. The provinces receive equalization grants if the per capita revenues they can derive from standard tax rates for some 23 taxes are less than the national average. The total in 1975 was $1.9 billion (including stabilization grants). Ontario, Alberta, and British Columbia typically received little or nothing.

3. Stabilization grants are made when necessary to bring the current year's revenue at previous-year tax rates up to the previous year's revenues.

Federal Tax Collection and Tax Credits

In addition, the federal government collects personal and corporate income taxes for all provinces that wish it to do so (all except Quebec, and, for Ontario, except corporate income tax). An abatement or tax credit of 24 percent is allowed for provincial income taxes against federal tax liability.

Provincial Grants to Municipalities [34]

Conditional grants to municipal governments totaled $4.9 billion in 1974, of which $3.6 billion was given for education. Unconditional grants totaled $606 million. The total figure was one third of total provincial expenditures.

APPENDIX III—INTERNATIONAL TAX RELATIONSHIPS

The fragmentation of tax structures within a country is paralleled, in a sense, by the use of separate tax structures by various countries, but the consequences are less serious. Economic activity of an international character is much less significant, relative to total economic activity, than that of an interstate or interlocal nature. While some persons gain incomes from outside the country, the percentage of total income so derived is less than the percentage gained outside state or local units. Furthermore, because of control over the borders of the country, the operation of fiscal frontiers, and the unrestricted taxing power of a country over its nationals and over all activity within or crossing its borders, the enforcement of tax on international activity is much easier than enforcement against interstate or interlocal activity. Nevertheless, several problems arise.

Income Tax Complications

Income earned in one country by residents of another is difficult for the country of residence to discover, although it has legitimate claim to tax the earnings. Frequently the country of origin will subject the income to at least partial tax, so the person will not escape completely. The opposite result is also possible: The person may be fully taxed by both countries. This result is usually avoided by tax treaties, under the terms of which each country frees from tax the income earned in the country by residents of the other. The United States allows a credit for tax paid other countries even without a tax treaty, but many countries are not so liberal. Corporate taxes give rise to less difficulty, since usually a separate subsidiary corporation must be formed for operation in each country, subject to the tax laws of that country. Questions do arise about such items as payments by the subsidiary to the parent company in excess of the commercial value of the service rendered.

Commodity Taxes

International transactions have for centuries been the object of discriminatory commodity taxation in the form of customs duties, partly

---

[34] Canadian Tax Foundation, *Provincial and Municipal Finances, 1975* (Toronto: 1975).

because customs are relatively easy to enforce so long as smuggling can be prevented, partly because of protective aspects. National sales taxes can be applied to imported goods without great difficulty, either in conjunction with customs or at a later transaction, with problems less serious than those posed by interstate sales.

Countries usually free exports from sales or excise taxes in order to protect the international competitive position of their producers. On the other hand, developing countries frequently levy special export taxes on basic primary products designed to tax the income of the producers of the products rather than to hamper the exports of the country.

Tax Harmonization[35]

Since 1960, increased efforts have been made to develop common market areas in Europe, in Latin America, and the Caribbean. With this development has arisen concern about harmonization of tax relationships among countries forming the common market, that is, adjustments in the tax structures of the countries to ensure that taxes do not interfere with attainment of the objectives of the common market. A common market requires, by its nature, the removal of internal tariffs among the countries so that trade can move freely and industry can develop on the basis of comparative advantage, as it does within a country. But removal of tariffs alone may not be adequate. Internal tax structures, particularly commodity taxes, can interfere with the free functioning of the common market and prevent full attainment of its advantages. Differences in rates of manufacturers sales taxes or value-added taxes will affect location decisions. Turnover taxes are virtually impossible to make uniform in practice, because of differences in structures of industry and distribution. If a country seeks to eliminate turnover tax on sales into the other common market countries, it finds the cumulative amount of tax affecting export prices hard to determine. Inadequate refund of tax on exports will harm production in the country, while refunds in excess of the actual tax on export sales will give artificial advantage and invite retaliation. While these differences can be offset by tariffs in the absence of a common market, they cannot be within such a market.

Accordingly, some uniformity of policy is imperative for sales taxes. The European Common Market countries agreed upon the use of the value-added form, which allows equal treatment of imported and domestic goods and full refund on exports. It will also allocate revenue among the countries automatically in terms of the value added

---

[35]This question is discussed at length in C. S. Shoup, ed. *Fiscal Harmonization in Common Markets*, 2 vols. (New York: Columbia University Press, 1967).

within the country when the origin basis, noted below, is ultimately used. Since a value-added tax must be more or less uniform in all of the countries to avoid affecting location, the countries may use supplementary retail sales taxes to adjust for differences in revenue needs. Variations in retail taxes do not cause serious distortions. Retail activity is market-oriented and cannot shift to any extent to escape taxes. The Central American common market countries have introduced retail sales taxes in preference to the other forms for the same reason.

With both the value-added tax and the retail tax, decision must be made about the jurisdiction for taxation on intercountry sales; should the tax of the originating country or the destination country apply? The latter rule, as used within the United States, is most logical since the tax is intended to be a levy on consumption spending. But this rule requires the maintenance of fiscal frontiers, that is, control over goods coming into the country from other common market countries, or some alternative technique. The origin rule is much simpler to operate and with equivalent tax rates and comparable flows of goods in both directions will produce much the same overall distribution of revenues, even if the "wrong" country gets the tax on particular transactions. If the tax rates are not uniform, the tax revenue distribution will be different and producers in high-tax countries are placed at a competitive disadvantage. The European Common Market countries plan ultimate use of the origin base for the value-added tax but do not expect to attain it until the rates are more nearly uniform.

REFERENCES

Advisory Commission on Intergovernmental Relations Publications (Washington):
Fiscal Balance in the American Federal System. 2 vols., 1967.
Urban America and the Federal System. 1969.
Measuring the Fiscal Capacity and Effort of State and Local Areas. 1971.
In Search of Balance: Canada's Intergovernmental Experience. 1971.
General Revenue Sharing. 1974.
American Federalism: Toward a More Effective Partnership. 1975.
Federal State Local Finances, 1974–75. 1976.
Significant Features of Federalism, 1976.
Improving Urban America: A Challenge to Federalism, 1976.
Break, George F. Intergovernmental Fiscal Relations in the United States. Washington, D.C.: The Brookings Institution, 1967.
Carter, G. E. Canadian Conditional Grants Since World War II. Toronto: Canadian Tax Foundation, 1971.
Dommel, P. R. The Politics of Revenue Sharing. Bloomington, Ind.: Indiana University Press, 1975.
Inman, R. P., et al. Financing the New Federation. Washington, D.C.: Resources for the Future, 1975.

Nathan, R. P., Manvel, A. D., and Calkins, S. E.   *Monitoring Revenue Sharing*. Washington, D.C.: The Brookings Institution, 1975.

Netzer, D.   *State-Local Finance and Intergovernmental Fiscal Relations*, in *The Economics of Public Finance*. A. S. Blinder et al. (Washington, D.C.: The Brookings Institution, 1974), pp. 316–422.

Oates, Wallace.   *Fiscal Federalism*. New York: Harcourt Brace Jovanovich, 1972.

Urban Fiscal Problems, NTA-TIA Symposium, National Tax Journal, vol. 29 (September 1976), entire.

PART IV

The Overall Impact of the Fiscal Structure on the Economy

19

The Theory of Income Determination

The previous chapters of this book have primarily concerned themselves with problems of microeconomics: how the government affects decisions regarding how goods are produced, what goods are produced, and for whom they should be produced to achieve both an efficient and equitable allocation of resources in the economy. We have assumed, either implicitly or explicitly, that society maintains full employment, price stability, and the desired rate of growth through appropriate government activity and that the problem facing government is to achieve what society considers to be an equitable and efficient allocation of resources. But just as the free market will generally fail to permit society to achieve an equitable or efficient allocation of resources without government intervention, it will also generally fail to ensure full employment, price stability, or the desired rate of growth without government intervention. It is with these latter macroeconomic problems that this section is concerned.

This chapter discusses questions of income determination in a world without government and shows why the market mechanism may not in itself ensure the full employment of resources. Chapter 20 analyzes ways in which government fiscal policy can help stabilize the economy and discusses some of the problems facing government in this respect. Chapter 21 then considers governmental efforts to stabilize the United States economy during the postwar period. Finally, Chapter 22 considers problems of economic growth, how government can in principle affect the rate of growth through fiscal and monetary policy, and discusses the experience of the United States in the postwar period in this respect.

Before we can understand the way in which government affects any of these problems, however, we must understand the basic mechanics of income determination: what comprises the components of aggregate demand and how they are determined. Only then can we understand how government can influence the behavior of the components of aggregate demand or national income through its fiscal and monetary policies.

By fiscal policy, we refer to the governmental determination of the level and structure of taxes and expenditures and the manner of financing a budgetary surplus or deficit to achieve the various macroeconomic goals of full employment, price stability, growth, a balance-of-payments equilibrium, and so forth. By monetary policy, we refer to the regulation of the money supply and interest rates by the Federal Reserve Board. Since this is a book about fiscal economics, its discussion concentrates on fiscal policy. But fiscal policy cannot be neatly separated from monetary policy. The components of aggregate demand are usually affected by interest rates; and interest rates are not only affected by changes in the money supply that are regulated by the Federal Reserve Board, but also by changes in taxes or expenditures and the way in which a budgetary surplus or deficit is financed. Therefore the roles of fiscal and monetary policy are intertwined.[1] Although we do not investigate how the government can affect interest rates in great detail, we analyze the interrelationships among the money supply, taxes, expenditures, and the level of aggregate demand.

The Analysis of Income Determination

Until the 1930s and the so-called Keynesian revolution, it was generally accepted that if the economy suffered an exogenous shock, such as an unforeseen downward shift in investment demand, the economy would return by itself to a full-employment equilibrium. This notion was perhaps best expressed by the so-called Say's Law, which claimed that "supply creates its own demand." This presumes that if there were a fall in aggregate demand for any reason, prices, wages, and interest rates would also adjust so as to leave each market in equilibrium. Since there would never be an excess supply of goods and services and particularly of labor at the existing prices or wages, full employment would necessarily prevail. While the real wage might fall as a result of a change in demand, unemployed resources would never

---

[1] In this connection, it is useful to recognize that the government effectively operates under a budget constraint in which changes in expenditures cannot be made without concomitant changes in taxes, the money supply, or the amount of debt. Therefore changes in government expenditures that are not financed by changes in taxes must necessarily be financed by changes in the money supply or by changes in government debt that will generally affect the interest rate structure. The following chapter will discuss these interrelationships in greater detail.

exist; machines and men would never be idle. By hypothesis, there would always be some level of prices, wages, and interest rates at which all resources would be fully employed. Equally important, it was assumed that there were no institutional constraints to prevent these variables from reaching their equilibrium levels. This theory of income determination is generally attributed to the so-called "classical economists."

This is not to say that the classical economists ignored the possibility or fact of business cycles. But they generally felt that the economic system had self-stabilizing mechanisms that would prevent periods of long depression and unemployment. According to them, government was not needed to stabilize the economy, although it might mitigate the excesses of the business cycle. Nevertheless, as long as wages, prices, and interest rates were fully flexible, the system was capable of maintaining a full employment equilibrium in the absence of governmental intervention.

The Great Depression of the 1930s brought these beliefs sharply into question. Not only did the economies of the United States and other industrialized countries throughout the world fail to recover from their high levels of unemployment, but the depressed conditions seemed to get worse and worse. Prices, wages, and interest rates fell, but no general movement toward recovery ensued. It was at this time that Keynes published his *General Theory*,[2] which analyzed why economies need not have the self-regulating mechanisms believed to exist by the classical economists. According to Keynes, even with flexible wages and prices, it was possible for the relationships in the economy to be such that government intervention was needed to restore the economy to full employment through fiscal policy measures, such as increased expenditures or reduced taxes. Not only was government intervention needed, but monetary policy alone would not necessarily be sufficient. This was the essence of the Keynesian revolution, which legitimized and eventually institutionalized the role of fiscal policy in achieving and maintaining full employment. Just as laissez-faire had been shown to fail in allocating goods efficiently or equitably, laissez-faire had been shown to fail in maintaining full employment. When President Nixon announced in 1971 that he had become a "Keynesian," the Keynesian revolution became in effect complete.

The Keynesian model contains many subtleties, only some of which we discuss here. We start with the basic model of income determination and then discuss the integration of the monetary and the real sectors to show how income is determined and equilibrium achieved in the various markets.

---

[2] J. M. Keynes, *The General Theory of Employment, Interest and Money* (New York: Harcourt, Brace and World, 1935).

The Simple Analytics of Income Determination

The essence of the Keynesian revolution was that the economic system need not contain self-equilibrating mechanisms to ensure that planned savings equal planned investment at full employment. Moreover, since the savings-investment decision determines the level of income in the Keynesian world, it is possible to maintain an unemployment equilibrium indefinitely. We show how this is possible in a simplified world of extreme assumptions about the nature of investment, savings, and consumption. Even if these assumptions are modified, however, it is still possible for the basic conclusions to remain: Under certain plausible conditions the economic system will not contain self-equilibrating mechanisms to ensure that full employment is always reached.

The Consumption Function.   A cornerstone of the Keynesian analysis is the consumption function. This states that, in the aggregate, consumption will remain a stable function of income. We assume for the time being that consumption is a function of income alone, although later in this chapter we modify this assumption somewhat.[3] Specifically, let us assume that the consumption function takes the form specified in Figure 19-1, given by the line *CC*. This implies that consumption is a linear function of income. At low levels of income,

FIGURE 19-1
Consumption Function

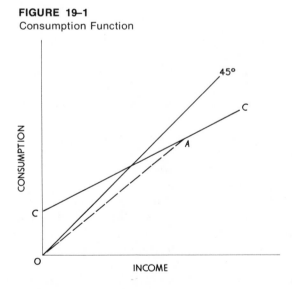

---

[3] The specific form and nature of the consumption function have been the subject of considerable theoretical and empirical work, which we shall not attempt to summarize here. For a good summary of the literature, see G. Ackley, *Macroeconomic Theory*, (New York: Macmillan Company, 1961), chaps. 10, 11, 12.

consumption will be greater than income as people dissave to maintain their consumption standards. This dissaving is shown by the algebraic difference between the consumption function CC and the 45° line. At high levels of income, consumption will be less than income as people satisfy their consumption demands and then accumulate saving. Algebraically this relationship can be expressed by the simple expression

$$C = a + bY. \tag{19-1}$$

It is important to distinguish between the average propensity to consume (*apc*) and the marginal propensity to consume (*mpc*). The average propensity to consume is given by the ratio of consumption to income at any given level of consumption and income and is shown graphically by the slope of the line emanating from the origin, for example, the slope of the line OA in Figure 19–1. Algebraically, the *apc* can be found by dividing both sides of the consumption function by income, which yields the relationship $C/Y = a/Y + b$. This is the proportion of total income that is consumed. The marginal propensity to consume is given graphically by the slope of the consumption function CC in Figure 19–1 and is given algebraically by the expression $\Delta C/\Delta Y = b$, where the "Δ" sign reflects change. Thus the expression $\Delta C/\Delta Y$ gives the change in consumption divided by the change in income. As long as the consumption function has a positive intercept, dissaving takes place at low levels of income. This can take place through borrowing, spending accumulated wealth, and so forth. As long as the consumption function is linear and dissaving can occur, the marginal propensity to consume will always be less than the average propensity to consume.

Savings. Since total income equals consumption plus savings, savings are given by the expression $Y - C$:

$$\begin{aligned} S &= Y - C \\ &= Y - (a + bY) \\ &= -a + (1 - b)Y \end{aligned} \tag{19-2}$$

Graphically, this can be shown in Figure 19–2. The savings function SS indicates that savings will be negative at low levels of income.[4] The marginal propensity to save (*mps*) is given by $(1 - mpc)$ while the average propensity to save is given by $(1 - apc)$.

Investment. For the time being let us assume that investment is autonomously determined. This means that investment is given by factors outside of the scope of this simplified economic model and is independent of variations in the level of income, interest rates, and so forth. Although we modify this assumption shortly, it is useful to illus-

---

[4] Although Figure 19–2 assumes that savings are independent of the rate of interest, this assumption is not necessary. Thus, we could draw a family of curves relating savings to income at different rates of interest.

FIGURE 19–2
Savings Function

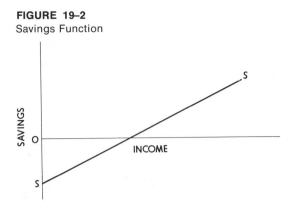

trate the essence of the Keynesian system and the possibility of an unemployment equilibrium. Let us assume that investment is given as $\bar{I}$ and is a constant for any level of income.

The Mechanics of Income Determination. We now have sufficient information to determine the equilibrium level of income in this very simple model of the economy. We can do this by either considering the determinants of the income expenditure equilibrium: aggregate demand, or consumption plus investment; or by considering the equilibrium condition that savings equal investment. Because of the relationship between saving and consumption, the two are equivalent.

1. *The income-expenditure approach.* Let us consider first the determination of income by the income-expenditure relationship $Y = C + I$. This is shown in Figure 19–3. The consumption function is plotted as CC corresponding to Figure 19–1. Investment is assumed to be given by a constant OI. As the schedule II makes clear, investment is assumed to be independent of income. Total aggregate demand is given by the vertical sum of the consumption and investment schedules, shown by the line $C + I$. In equilibrium, aggregate demand must equal total income. This is given by the intersection of the line $C + I$ with the 45° line emanating from the origin. Total income is given by OY on the horizontal axis. There is nothing in the system as we have outlined it, however, that indicates that when aggregate demand equals income, the two must also equal aggregate or potential supply. Consequently, the income actually produced may not equal the income that society is capable of producing at full employment.

When aggregate demand is less than aggregate supply or potential output, we say that a deflationary gap exists. Similarly, when aggregate demand is greater than aggregate supply or potential output, we say that an inflationary gap exists. In either case, we define the deflationary or inflationary gap as the difference between actual autonomous expenditures (investment plus government spending) and the level of autonomous expenditures needed to ensure equilibrium between

FIGURE 19-3
Income Equilibrium, Expenditure Approach

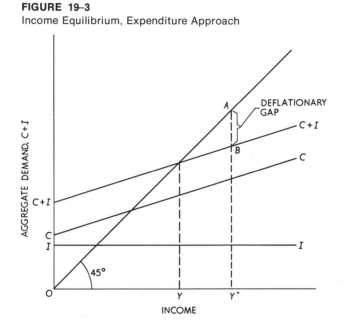

aggregate demand and potential output. In Figure 19–3, for example, a deflationary gap equal to AB exists; autonomous spending must be increased by AB to ensure full employment.

2. *The savings-investment approach.* The equilibrium level of income can also be determined by the requirement that planned savings equal planned investment. This is shown in Figure 19–4, where equilibrium income is determined by the intersection of the savings line SS and the investment line II. Note that if investment is greater than

FIGURE 19-4
Income Equilibrium, Savings-Investment Approach

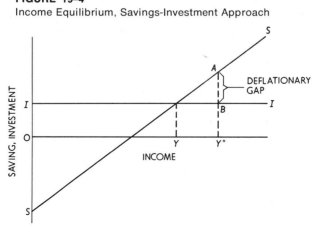

savings, income will rise, while if it is less than savings, income will fall. This can be seen in Figure 19–4. At the assumed full-employment level of income OY^*, savings are greater than investment. Hence this does not represent an equilibrium level of income. Only if savings equal investment will an equilibrium level of output occur. As drawn, this takes place at OY, which is less than potential income OY^*. Again, additional autonomous expenditures equal to AB are needed to ensure that full employment is achieved.

3. *Algebraic analysis.* That the two approaches yield identical levels of equilibrium income can easily be shown by considering the algebra of the situation. Consider first, income determination through the income-expenditure approach.

$$Y = C + I \qquad\qquad (19\text{–}3)$$
$$C = a + bY \qquad\qquad (19\text{–}4)$$

Therefore,

$$Y = \frac{a + I}{1 - b} \qquad\qquad (19\text{–}5)$$

Alternatively, consider income determination through the savings-investment equilibrium.

$$I = S \qquad\qquad (19\text{–}6)$$
$$S = -a + (1 - b)Y \qquad\qquad (19\text{–}7)$$

Therefore,

$$Y = \frac{a + I}{1 - b} \qquad\qquad (19\text{–}8)$$

Equilibrium income is identical under either approach. The equivalence arises because savings equal income minus consumption $(S = Y - C)$. By subtracting C from both sides of Equation 19–3 it is easy to see that the condition $Y = C + I$ is identical to the condition $S = I$. Therefore, in terms of income determination in this simple model, it does not matter whether we look at the problem in terms of the savings-investment equilibrium or in terms of the income expenditure equilibrium $Y = C + I$.

The Monetary Sector

While the previous section outlined a model that contained nothing inherent to ensure that the equilibrium level of income would be a full-employment level of income, the model included some extreme simplifying assumptions: namely, that savings and consumption are completely independent of the interest rate and that investment is autonomously given and is, in particular, independent of the interest rate or the level of income. The Keynesian conclusion that full-employment equilibrium need not occur, however, does not depend on these assumptions. In fact, we can assume that investment is a function of the interest rate, and that savings are a function of income and the interest rate, and still have a system that does not necessarily produce a full-employment equilibrium. In this alternative model, however, the nature of the monetary sector becomes of crucial importance. In fact, probably the most important innovation of the Keynesian model lies in linking the real and the monetary sectors in such a way that it is possible that there is no interest rate that can simultaneously equilibrate the supply and demand for investable funds and the supply and demand for money to produce a full-employment equilibrium. This possibility arises from the assumption about the nature of the demand for money, which we now consider.

The Transactions Demand. People need money in the form of cash or demand deposits to meet their ordinary expense of living. Thus there is a transactions demand for money, which reflects the role of money as a medium of exchange. This is postulated to be proportional to the value of money income. Algebraically, this can be stated as:

$$M_t = PY/V \qquad (19\text{--}9)$$

where M_t = the transactions demand for money, P = the absolute price level, Y = the level of real income, and V = the velocity of money. Thus the transactions demand represents the money needed to enable people to purchase final goods and services. The velocity of money V is taken as an institutional constant that roughly corresponds to the reciprocal of the average cash balances held in the economy. If the average cash balances were one fourth of the value of final transactions in the economy, the velocity of money would be 4. The value of final transactions in the economy or the level of money income is given by the product of the average price level P, and the level of real income Y and is thus given by PY, which can also be expressed as Y_m. The transactions demand for money M is proportional to the value of final transactions, with the factor or proportionality being the average cash balance or the reciprocal of velocity.

The Asset Demand. In addition to the transactions demand for money, there is an asset demand for money. The rationale behind this is fairly easy to see. As interest rates rise money held in idle balances undergoes increasing opportunity costs, since it could be earning income if transferred to income-producing assets. At some point, in fact, the interest rate will become sufficiently high that no money is held for asset purposes;[5] the only money demanded is for transactions pur-

---

[5] Strictly speaking, as the interest rate rises, there may still be some minimum amount of money held for asset purposes. It simplifies the graphical analysis, however, to assume that this minimum amount is zero.

poses, and the total demand for money becomes interest inelastic. As interest rates fall the opportunity cost of holding money as an asset falls, and people become increasingly willing to hold money as an asset. At some low interest rate, people believe that interest rates will not fall any more and, in effect, the opportunity cost of holding money as an asset is zero. The asset demand for money becomes infinitely elastic at this point.

Figure 19–5 illustrates the asset demand for money. At a high inter-

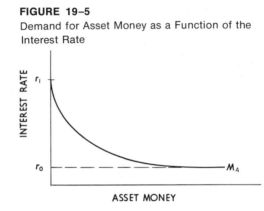

FIGURE 19–5

Demand for Asset Money as a Function of the Interest Rate

ASSET MONEY

est rate, say r_1, people are unwilling to hold any money for asset purposes; the only demand for money is the transactions demand. Similarly, at some low interest rate, say r_0, the demand for asset money becomes infinitely elastic since people do not believe that any reduction in the interest rate below r_0 is possible. Alternatively stated, since the price of an income-producing asset is inversely related to its yield or rate of interest, when interest rates reach r_0, people feel that assets have reached their maximum price possible. They are, therefore, unwilling to purchase any more assets at a higher price or a lower interest rate since they are certain that asset prices will fall and interest rates will rise. The demand for assets becomes totally inelastic at this point while the demand for money as an asset becomes infinitely elastic. Since people do not feel that interest rates can fall below r_0, when interest rates reach this point, people hold all of their assets in money in expectation of a rise in interest rates.

The Total Demand for Money. The total demand for money (M) is given by the sum of the transactions demand (M_t) and the asset demand (M_a). Thus,

$$M = M_a + M_t \qquad (19\text{--}10)$$

Since the transactions demand is constant for any given level of real income, prices, and velocity, it is possible to draw a family of total-

FIGURE 19-6

Total Money Demand as a Function of the Interest Rate

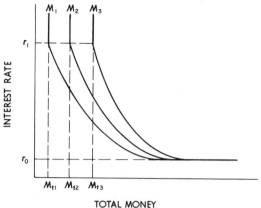

TOTAL MONEY

money demand curves as a function of the rate of interest and the level of real income. There are shown in Figure 19-6, for a given price level (P) and income velocity (V). As the real level of income shifts out from Y_1 to Y_2 to Y_3, the total demand for money shifts out from M_1 to M_2 to M_3. Each curve reflects a parallel shift of the asset curve drawn in Figure 19-5. The point where each total-money demand curve becomes totally inelastic marks the point where money is only held for transactions purposes. Thus, the transactions demand for money is given by M_{t1} for income level Y_1, M_{t2} for income level Y_2, M_{t3} for income level Y_3, and so on.

From the relationship between the total demand for money and its components, it is also possible to express the money level of income in terms of the asset demand for money and the total supply of money. In equilibrium $M_D = M_S$, i.e., the total money demanded must equal the total money supplied. For a fixed supply of money, as the asset demand for money increases, there must necessarily be less money available for transactions purposes. The transactions demand for money is positively related to prices and income and inversely related to the velocity of money. For a given level of real income and a given velocity of money, as the amount of money available for transactions purposes falls, the price level must also fall. Consequently, the level of money income must fall. Therefore, the level of money income must be positively related to the total money supply and negatively related to the asset demand for money. This can be shown by the following relationship:

$$Y_m = V(M_S - M_a) \qquad (19\text{–}11)$$

where Y_m = money income or PY, V = the velocity of money, M_S = the

FIGURE 19-7
Relationship between Asset Money and the Level
of Money Income

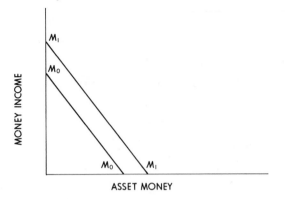

total money supply, and M_a = the asset demand for money.[6] Given the total supply of money, there is a unique linear relationship between the asset demand for money and the money level of income.

This relationship is shown in Figure 19-7. The line M_0M_0 reflects a money supply equal to M_0, while the line M_1M_1 reflects a greater money supply equal to M_1. For a given interest rate, as the money supply increases, the transactions demand for money must increase, causing a parallel shift in the line relating the asset demand for money to the level of money income. Note that if we assume that prices are given, this also reflects a unique relationship between the asset demand for money and real income.

The Determination of Income

Given these relationships, we can now illustrate how income is determined in this Keynesian system.[7] This is given in Figure 19-8.

Attaining Equilibrium Income. Consider first graph *(a)*. As is true of the classical system, investment is assumed to be a function of the interest rate. But unlike the classical system, at low levels of the interest rate, the elasticity of investment to the interest rate is assumed to be quite low. Thus, over a fairly broad range of relatively low interest rates, the investment-demand schedule is assumed to be quite interest inelastic. Let us assume that the interest rate is given by r_0. Then investment is equal to I_0.

---

[6] This can be derived as follows: $M_S = M_D$ and $M_D = M_t + M_a$. Moreover $M_t = (1/V)PY = (1/V)Y_m$. Thus, $M_S = M_a + (1/V)Y_m$ and $Y_m = V(M_S - M_a)$.

[7] The full Keynesian system contains a labor sector, specifying the relationships between employment, output, and wages.

FIGURE 19–8

Determination of Income in the Keynesian System

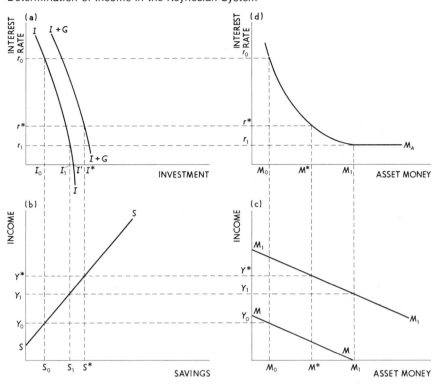

The savings function *(SS)* is drawn in graph *(b)*. This is analogous to the savings function drawn in Figure 19–4, but the axes are reversed. Thus income is drawn on the vertical axis and savings are drawn on the horizontal axis. Unlike the classical system, savings are assumed to be a function of income alone and are therefore assumed to be independent of the interest rate. Since savings must equal investment in equilibrium, if investment equals I_0, savings must equal S_0. This implies that income must equal Y_0.

We can then move to graph *(c)* of Figure 19–8 to determine the asset demand for money. Let us assume that the initial money supply is such that the relationship between real income and asset money is given by the line *MM*. If this relationship holds, an income level Y_0 is consistent with an amount of asset money equal to M_0. Finally, we can move to graph *(d)* and find what interest rate is consistent with this amount of asset money from the demand curve for asset money M_A. This is given by r_0. Moving back to graph *(a)* we see that this is consistent with the arbitrarily chosen interest rate r_0. Thus the system is in equilibrium. The supply of and demand for investable funds and the supply of and demand for asset money is such that the investable funds market and the money market are in simultaneous equilibrium with an interest rate equal to r_0 and an income level equal to Y_0.

Attaining Full Employment.   Suppose, however, that Y_0 is not a full-employment level of income, which is given by Y^*. How can we reach this full-employment equilibrium? Because of the nature of the asset demand for money, the minimum attainable interest rate is given by r_1. Suppose that the monetary authorities increase the money supply sufficiently that this interest-rate floor is reached. This is shown in Figure 19–8 by the shifted line $M_1 M_1$ portraying the relationship between real income and asset money in graph *(c)*. In this case, the following relationships hold. Investment is given by I_1, savings are given by S_1, and income is given by Y_1. The amount of asset money demanded is given by M_1, and the interest rate is given by r_1. Again an equilibrium holds since the investment-savings market and the money market are in a unique equilibrium at a given interest rate (r_1) and income level (Y_1).

But Y_1 is still below the full-employment level of income Y^*. Since interest rates have reached their floor, increases in the money supply will only serve to increase the amount of asset money held. Because interest rates cannot fall, however, no more investment will be forthcoming. Unless some means can be found to shift the savings or investment curves, income will have to remain at Y_1, the maximum income attainable through monetary policy alone. This is precisely where fiscal policy must come into play.[8] Suppose the government increases expenditures, thereby moving the effective investment curve out to $I + G$.[9] It can be seen then that a new equilibrium interest rate will be given by r^*, which is above the interest-rate floor. At this interest rate, sufficient investment plus government spending will be forthcoming to enable income to reach its equilibrium level Y^*. At this income level and the new money curve $M_1 M_1$, the amount of asset money held will equal M^*. This is consistent with an interest rate r^*. Thus for a given investment and savings curve, only through fiscal policy (in this case increased government expenditures) can income reach its full-employment equilibrium.

Summary.   What, then, are the lessons of this analysis? First, be-

---

[8] If consumption is positively related to wealth so that savings are negatively related to wealth, reductions in price and interest rates will cause the value of assets to increase, thus reducing the amount of savings forthcoming at any level of income. Therefore, it is theoretically possible to restore equilibrium through monetary policy alone if the wealth effect on savings is sufficiently strong. As a practical matter, however, this effect does not appear to be very strong, thus making fiscal policy necessary to ensure a full-employment equilibrium.

[9] The precise way in which government spending or tax policy can take place to shift the effective investment curve or saving curve will be discussed in the following chapter.

cause people not only hold money for transactions purposes, but also for speculative or asset purposes, the real and the monetary sectors are linked through the interest rate. The equilibrium in the investable funds market (savings and investment) is no longer independent of the equilibrium in the money market (the demand for and supply of money). Because there is a floor to the interest rates at which people are willing to hold nonmonetary assets, however, there is a limit to which interest rates can fall. If the amount of investment forthcoming at this interest rate is insufficient to generate full employment, increases in the money supply will have no effect on income levels but only serve to increase the amount of money held for asset purposes. In this case full employment can only be reached by fiscal policies that must either shift the saving function by changes in the tax structure or shift the effective investment function through increases in government expenditures or perhaps through tax changes. Fiscal policy is only mandatory, however, when the interest floor is reached. Until that point, monetary policy can be used to reduce interest rates and, therefore, increase investment and real income. There is, however, one exception. If the investment demand schedule is so shaped that it intersects the horizontal axis at a point where the savings-investment equilibrium yields less than full employment, monetary policy could not enable society to reach full employment even in the absence of an interest-rate floor. The reader should verify this by assuming that (on Figure 19–8) the curve *II* intersects the horizontal axis at point *I'* in graph *(a)* and assuming that there is no interest-rate floor in graph *(d)*.

A GENERAL EQUILIBRIUM ANALYSIS

The Keynesian system analyzed above can be summarized by graphs of the so-called *IS-LM* curves. The *IS* curve plots the interest rates and income levels that equilibrate the savings-investment market, while the *LM* curve plots the interest rates and income levels that equilibrate the money market. Since general or full equilibrium requires that the investable funds and money markets be in equilibrium, a general equilibrium is reached where both curves intersect.[10] The *IS-LM* curve analysis consequently provides a shortcut analysis for determining the equilibrium level of interest and the equilibrium level of income. Moreover, if this equilibrium is not at full employment, it can be shown that the curves can be shifted by appropriate monetary or fiscal policies or a combination of the two to achieve a full-employment equilibrium.

Because the derivation of each curve is based on the partial equilib-

---

[10] It should be pointed out that this ignores the labor makret and, hence, is not a full general-equilibrium solution.

rium in the specific investable funds or money market, an understanding of their derivation and the way in which each curve responds to changes in fiscal or monetary policy is necessary for an understanding of macroeconomic policy.

The *IS* Curve

The *IS* curve shows the levels of interest rate and income that equilibrate the investable-funds market for a fixed supply of money. Let us assume that investment is a function of the interest rate and that savings are a function of the level of income. The derivation of the *IS* curve is shown in Figure 19–9. The curve *II* in quadrant *(d)* portrays the familiar investment schedule, which is postulated to be a function of the interest rate. Note that as the interest rate falls, the investment demand becomes increasingly inelastic, that is, a given decline in the interest rate will bring forth proportionately less investment. The line *SS* in quadrant *(b)* shows the savings function, which is assumed to be a function of income alone. Since dissaving is assumed to occur at low

FIGURE 19–9
Derivation of *IS* Curve

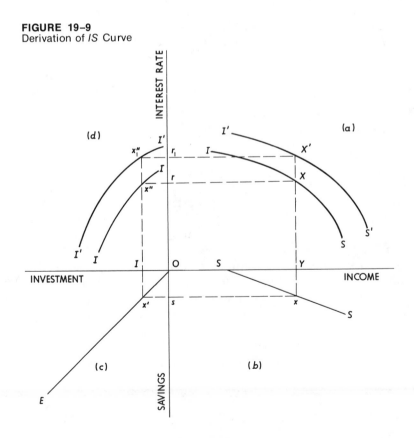

levels of income, savings only become positive at point S on the horizontal axis. The slope of the savings curve represents the marginal propensity to save. Since savings must equal investment in equilibrium, the line OE in quadrant (c) has a slope of 45°, indicating that a given level of savings must be associated with an equal amount of investment. Finally, the line IS in quadrant (a) shows the levels of interest rate and income that equilibrate savings and investment.

A given point on the IS curve, say X, can be derived as follows. Consider point x on the savings schedule in quadrant (b), where income is equal to OY and savings are equal to Os. If savings equal Os, line OE in quadrant (c) indicates that investment must equal OI. The investment schedule II in quadrant (d) shows that an amount of investment equal to OI is associated with an interest rate equal to Or. Thus, an interest rate equal to Or and an income level equal to OY are consistent with savings equal to Os and investment equal to OI. This defines a point X on the IS curve. By choosing points along the savings curve and moving around Figure 19–9 in a counterclockwise direction, it is possible to trace out the locus of points on the IS curve.

If the investment curve shifts out to I'I', it is easy to show that the IS curve must shift out to I'S'. To see this, let us consider point x on the savings schedule again. At point x, income equals OY, savings equals Os, and investment equals OI. The investment schedule I'I' indicates that investment equal to OI is associated with an interest rate Or_1, which is higher than the interest rate Or associated with the investment curve II. Thus, with the new investment curve I'I', any given level of income must be associated with a higher interest rate. Consequently, an outward shift in the investment curve will lead to an outward shift in the IS curve to I'S'.

The *LM* Curve

The LM curve plots the levels of the interest rate and income that produce equilibrium in the money market. Its derivation is shown in Figure 19–10. In quadrant (d) the asset demand for money is shown by the line M_A. At some high interest rate the asset demand becomes zero as all available money is used for transactions purposes, while at some low interest rate, the asset demand for money becomes infinitely elastic, indicating that individuals believe that interest rates will fall any more and the opportunity cost of holding money is zero. The transactions demand for money is plotted as the line OT in quadrant (b). Since the transactions demand for money is proportional to income, the line OT is a straight line, whose slope represents the proportion of income that people wish to hold for transactions purposes.[11] In equilibrium,

---

[11] Since $M_t = (P/V)Y$, the factor of proportionality is given by the price level, divided by the velocity of money. As the price level rises, the line OT gets steeper.

FIGURE 19–10
Derivation of *LM* Curve

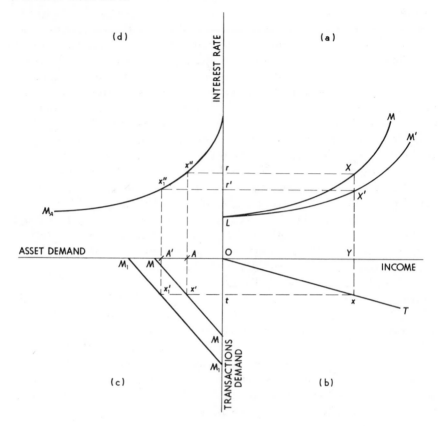

the supply of money must equal the demand for money. Since the total amount of money must be used for either transactions or asset purposes, the line *MM* in quadrant *(c)*, relating the total supply of money to the asset and transctions demand for money, must have a slope of minus one. As the money supply shifts out, this line shifts out; e.g., the line M_1M_1 represents a larger supply of money than the line *MM*.

To see how a point on the *LM* curve is determined let us start with the point *x* on the line *OT* in quadrant *(b)*. At this point income is *OY* and *Ot* of transactions money is demanded. The line *MM* indicates that if *Ot* of money is demanded for transactions purposes, *OA* is available for asset purposes. The line M_A in quadrant *(d)* indicates that an asset demand of *OA* is consistent with an interest rate *Or*. Thus an interest rate equal to *Or* and an income equal to *OY* are consistent with equilibrium in the money market; the point *X* on the *LM* curve is therefore defined. By choosing any point on the line *OT* and moving in a counterclockwise direction, it is possible to generate the locus of points on the *LM* curve.

If the authorities increase the money supply, the money line in quadrant *(c)* will shift to M_1M_1. In this case, the point x in quadrant *(b)* that is associated with income *OY* and a transactions demand *Ot*, will be consistent with an asset demand *OA'*, an interest rate *Or'*, and a point on the *LM* curve *X'*. Thus an increase in the money supply will cause the *LM* curve to shift out to *LM'*; any given level of income will be associated with a lower interest rate.

Equilibrium of the *IS* and *LM* Curves

We now have sufficient information to determine the equilibrium values of income and interest rates. This can be seen by considering Figure 19–11 where the curves *IS* and *LM* are assumed to hold initially. Equilibrium is given by their intersection where income is Y_0 and the interest rate is r_0. Suppose, however, that full employment income is given by Y^*. Although increasing the money supply can shift the *LM* curve to any desired point to the right of *LM*, the maximum income attainable is reached when the *IS* curve intersects the elastic portion of the *LM* curve. This is given by an *LM* curve equal to *LM'*. In this case, the equilibrium is given by Y_1 and r_1, which is still less than the full-employment level of income.

Thus, as long as the interest rate floor is fixed, full employment can only be reached by shifting the *IS* curve. But just as there is a limit to the extent that increasing the money supply to shift the *LM* curve can increase income for a given *IS* curve, there are limits to the amount that increasing government expenditures to shift the *IS* curve can increase income along a given *LM* curve. This can be seen in Figure 19–11, where the initial *LM* curve is assumed to hold. This reaches its inelastic range at an interest rate r_m; any increases in the *IS* curve beyond that shown by *I'S'* will only increase interest rates without increasing income since all of the available money is being used for transactions purposes at this point. In this case, the maximum income is given by Y_1', which is also less than full employment.

As shown in Figure 19–11, if full employment is to be reached, a combination of monetary policy to shift the *LM* curve to *LM'* and fiscal policy to shift the *IS* curve to *I'S'* must be used.[12] In this case, full

---

[12] Again, it should be pointed out that if there is a strong wealth effect, the savings curve may shift in as interest rates fall, causing the *IS* curve to shift out. Similarly, reductions in prices will cause the *LM* curve to shift out. Consequently, it is theoretically possible for interest rate and price changes to ensure a full-employment equilibrium. Nevertheless, Keynes felt that price reductions were not a viable adjustment mechanism since they might also adversely affect expectations, profits, and investment. Similarly, the empirical impact of the wealth effect seems to be relatively small. Thus, these qualifications do not substantively alter the conclusion that monetary and fiscal policy are needed to ensure a full-employment equilibrium.

FIGURE 19–11

Equilibria between *IS* and *LM* Curves

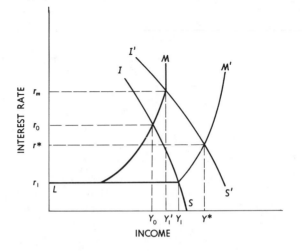

employment at Y^* can be reached with an equilibrium level of interest at r^*. This implies that although monetary or fiscal policy alone may be inadequate to enable society to reach full employment, together they can always ensure full employment. Moreover, together they can ensure that society can always achieve full employment and any desired rate of interest and level of capital formation in this simplified model.

CONCLUSION

This chapter has attempted to summarize the theory of income determination. If wages are rigid downward or if savings and investment are insensitive to the interest rate, full-employment equilibrium need not occur. But, even if wages are flexible and savings and investment are interest elastic, if the speculative or asset demand for money becomes infinitely elastic at some point, full-employment equilibrium also need not occur. This assumption about the demand for money is crucial to the Keynesian system for it not only serves to tie the real and the monetary sectors together, but also is the basic cause why full-employment equilibrium may not necessarily occur. In this case, however, there is only so much that monetary policy or changes in the money supply can do to increase income. Fiscal policy to increase the effective level of investment demand and/or to shift the savings schedule is necessary to enable society to reach full employment.

Thus the Keynesian revolution not only made fiscal policy respectable but showed it to be essential for the maintenance of full employment. It demonstrated that deficits may be required at certain times and that surpluses may be required at others. It showed that tax policy to shift the slope of the saving or consumption function may be used in conjunction with expenditures to achieve full employment. Just how this can be done will be the subject of the next chapter.

REFERENCES

Ackley, G.   *Macroeconomic Theory.* New York: Macmillan Company, 1961.

Keynes, J. M.   *The General Theory of Employment Interest and Money.* New York: Harcourt Brace and World, 1936.

Patinkin, Don.   *Money, Interest, and Prices.* 2d ed. New York: Harper and Row, 1965.

20

The Theory of Economic Stabilization

The previous chapter discussed why the market mechanism may fail to provide a full-employment equilibrium and why governmental action may be necessary to ensure that resources are fully employed. This chapter explores how government can stabilize the economy by changing the level of taxes or expenditures. The analysis throughout this chapter is static in the sense that it assumes that the economy adjusts instantaneously to changes in government expenditures or taxes. In the following chapter, when we discuss economic policy in the postwar period, we will discuss how governmental lags of recognition and of action can affect the stability of the economy.

This chapter takes the following form: The first part analyzes the impact of changing government expenditures or taxes in an economy in which the monetary authorities are assumed to adjust the money supply to keep interest rates constant and derives what we call the pure fiscal multipliers resulting from tax or expenditure changes. Because, however, the way in which changes in expenditures are financed can affect interest rates and the money supply, the actual multiplier effect of changing taxes or expenditures will usually be different from those implied by the pure fiscal multipliers. The second part considers this question explicitly and analyzes the way in which changes in taxes or expenditures affect the equilibrium level of income. Finally, it is important to realize that income or GNP is only one of a number of variables with which the government is concerned. Thus, the final section of this chapter considers how the government should set policy to satisfy a range of policy goals.

THE SIMPLE THEORY OF INCOME STABILIZATION

In the previous chapter, we discussed the theory of income determination in the Keynesian model to show why government activity is needed to ensure the maintenance of full employment. This section expands the simplified analysis presented there and analyzes how government can influence the level of national income through expenditures, tax policy, or a combination of the two, while maintaining a balanced budget.

In terms of the *IS-LM* diagrams discussed in the previous chapter, it is important to remember that changes in expenditures or taxes affect the *IS* schedule, while changes in the money supply affect the *LM* schedule. Throughout this section we assume that monetary policy alters the supply of money in response to changes in taxes or expenditures in such a way that interest rates are left unchanged.[1] This is shown in Figure 20–1 where the *IS* and *LM* curves initially are as-

FIGURE 20–1
Change in Income with Accommodating Monetary Policy

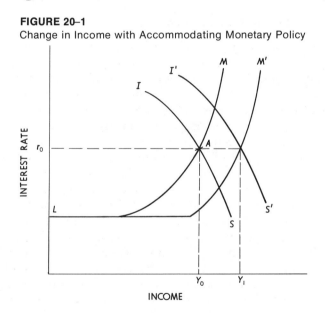

sumed to intersect at point *A* where the equilibrium level of income is given by Y_0 and the equilibrium interest rate is given by r_0. Let us assume that government expenditures increase, shifting the *IS* curve out to *I'S'*, and that monetary policy reacts in such a way that the *LM* curve shifts to *LM'*. The new equilibrium income level is given by Y_1, while the equilibrium interest rate remains at r_0. Because the interest

---

[1] We could alternatively assume that the interest rate was at its floor and, hence, that the intersection of the *IS* and *LM* curves always took place along the horizontal portion of the *LM* curve.

rate is assumed to remain constant, any changes in income arise from tax- or expenditure-induced changes in the *IS* curve alone. Thus, the multipliers derived in this section can be referred to as pure fiscal multipliers.

Because we assume in this section that monetary policy is accommodating and that the interest rate remains constant, we can ignore the interrelationships between the investable-funds market and the money market that the *IS-LM* diagrams highlight. Instead, we can illustrate the expansionary or contractionary impact of changing expenditures or taxes by using the income-expenditure approach outlined in the discussion of the Keynesian system in Chapter 19. In the next section when we relax the assumption of a constant interest rate, we utilize the *IS-LM* diagrams to analyze the impact of changing expenditures or taxes upon the equilibrium level of income in the economy.

The Impact of Government Expenditures

The expansionary impact of government expenditures arises from their so-called "multiplier effect," which means that each dollar of government expenditures will give rise to more than a dollar of income. The factor by which total income is increased over the initial government expenditures is called the multiplier. The multiplier effect arises because the marginal propensity to consume *(mpc)* lies between zero and one. Suppose that, for example, people on the average consume $0.75 out of every additional dollar of income. If government increases its expenditures by $1 billion, this money enters the income stream immediately as wage and salary payments, payments for materials, and so on. If the *mpc* is 0.75, then $750 million of this money is respent, while $250 million is withdrawn from the income stream and placed in savings. As long as the *mpc* is 0.75, three quarters of the $750 million will be respent, while one quarter will leave the income stream in savings. This multiplier process will continue until eventually the $1 billion of increased government expenditures will give rise to $4 billion of additional income.[2] Thus the multiplier is given by the following expression:

$$\text{Expenditure multiplier} = \frac{1}{1 - mpc}$$

This phenomenon can be shown graphically in Figure 20–2, which is similar to the simple graphs of income determination outlined in the

---

[2] The *mpc* represents the marginal propensity to consume. Then each additional dollar of government expenditures gives rise to the following expansion: $1 + mpc + (mpc)^2 + (mpc)^3 + \ldots$. By the rules for developing a sum of a geometric series, it is straightforward to show that this is equal to $1/(1 - mpc)$.

FIGURE 20–2

Change in Income Resulting from Increase in Governmental Expenditures

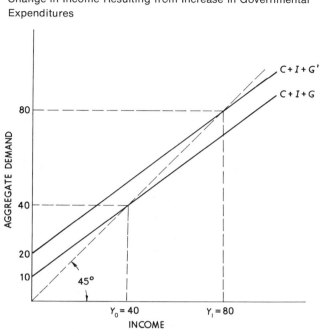

previous chapter. The vertical axis shows aggregate demand: the sum of consumption expenditures (C), investment (I) and government expenditures (G). Consumption is assumed to be an increasing linear function of income while investment and government expenditures are assumed to be independent of the level of income. Investment is assumed to be a function of the interest rate. Since, however, the interest rate is assumed to remain constant, investment can be taken as a constant for the purpose of the present analysis. While constraining, this assumption highlights the pure impact of fiscal policy upon the economy. In the following section, we relax this assumption and see how the multiplier analysis of this section must be altered when interactions between the investable funds market and the money market are taken into account.

The horizontal axis shows the level of income. In equilibrium, aggregate demand must equal income, so the intersection of the aggregate demand line $C + I + G$ with the 45° line gives the equilibrium level of income. This is shown as Y_0. The graph is drawn so that the mpc is 0.75. Thus, a \$10 billion increase in government expenditures, raising the aggregate demand line to $C + I + G'$, will increase income by \$40 billion.

These relationships can also be shown algebraically and are given as follows:

$$Y = C + I + G \tag{20-1}$$

$$C = a + bY \tag{20-2}$$

$$I = \bar{I} \tag{20-3}$$

$$G = \bar{G} \tag{20-4}$$

Equation (20–1) states the usual national income equilibrium condition that income equals the sum of consumption (C), investment (I), and government expenditures (G). Equation (20–2) states a behavioral relationship between consumption and income, while Equations (20–4) and (20–5) state that investment and government expenditures are some predetermined constants and are independent of the level of income. Substituting Equations (20–2), (20–3), and (20–4) into Equation (20–1) and solving for income (Y) yields the following expression:

$$Y = \frac{a + \bar{I} + \bar{G}}{1 - b} \tag{20-5}$$

In Figure 20–2 we assumed that $b = 0.75$, while the sum of $a + \bar{I} + \bar{G} = \$10$ billion. Hence $Y = \$40$ billion. If government expenditures rises by another \$10 billion, income will reach a level of \$80 billion, or Y_1 in Figure 20–2. The multiplier equals 4.

Algebraically this can be shown by the equation:

$$\Delta Y = \frac{\Delta G}{1 - b} \tag{20-6}$$

Therefore,

$$\frac{\Delta Y}{\Delta G} = \frac{1}{1 - b} \tag{20-6a}$$

or

$$\frac{dY}{dG} = \frac{1}{1 - b} \tag{20-6b}$$

Equations (20–6), (20–6a), and (20–6b) are equivalent and show the change in income that would result from a change in government expenditures, with all other things being held constant. This is the familiar multiplier. Since the parameter "b" equals the marginal propensity to consume, this says that the multiplier is equal to $1/(1 - mpc)$.

Of course, this expression for the multiplier is an oversimplification based on our simple model of the economy. Typically, income will rise by more than government expenditures, but by less than that indicated by the simple multiplier given above. This is true for several reasons.

First, the mpc may not be constant but may fall as income rises. Hence, the multiplier will depend upon the distribution of government expenditures among different income groups Second, personal savings are not the only "leakage" out of income. Different kinds of taxes, corporate saving, and imports all cause the net amount actually consumed out of an additional dollar of GNP to be less than that indicated by the additional amount consumed out of personal disposable income. In the simplified economy that we have been considering, GNP and personal disposable income are equivalent. But in the real world, the marginal propensity to consume out of personal disposable income is considerably greater than that consumed out of GNP; and in terms of estimating the multiplier effect of a change in government expenditures, it is the latter that is important rather than the former. Third, changes in government expenditures or taxes typically will lead to changes in interest rates, causing investment levels to change, affecting the equilibrium level of income. And fourth, investment may be a function of the level of income (or consumption) or of change in the level of income (or consumption), which will also affect the ultimate equilibrium level of income.

The Impact of Tax Changes

Again we assume that monetary policy accommodates to maintain a constant interest rate and that investment is independent of the level of income. Hence investment can be taken as autonomously given. The impact of changes in personal taxes is somewhat different from that of government expenditures because all of the changes in government expenditures enter the income stream directly, while some of the changes in tax revenues are saved. Compare, for example, the impact of an increase in government expenditures of $1 billion with that of a personal tax cut of $1 billion, with an assumed mpc of 0.75. With government expenditures, $1 billion enters the income stream directly. This then generates $750 million of additional consumption expenditures. In the case of tax reductions, however, $1 billion in tax savings reach the consumers, but only $750 million enter the income stream directly; $250 million of the tax saving enters the saving stream. Thus the multiplier effect of tax changes has an opposite sign and a smaller magnitude than that of government expenditures. In the example given here, the multiplier effect of the $1 billion revenue loss is 3. In general, it is given by the expression

$$\text{Tax multiplier} = -\frac{mpc}{1 - mpc}.$$

The difference between the tax multiplier and the expenditure multiplier can be seen the most clearly in its algebraic formulation. Consider first, a lump sum tax. Thus the following relationships hold:

$$Y = C + I + G \tag{20-7}$$

$$C = a + b\,Y_D \tag{20-8}$$

$$Y_D = Y - T \tag{20-9}$$

$$I = \bar{I} \tag{20-10}$$

$$G = \bar{G} \tag{20-11}$$

$$T = \bar{T} \tag{20-12}$$

This model differs from that given in the previous section in that consumption is now postulated to be a function of disposable income (Y_D), which equals total income or GNP less taxes. Substituting Equation (20-9) into Equation (20-8) and then Equations (20-8), (20-10), and (20-11) into Equation (20-7) and solving for income (Y) yields the following expression:
2700

$$Y = \frac{a + \bar{I} + \bar{G} - b\bar{T}}{1 - b}. \tag{20-13}$$

Thus, a change in taxes with everything else held constant will yield the following change in income:

$$\Delta Y = - \frac{b}{1 - b} \Delta T; \tag{20-14}$$

or

$$\frac{\Delta Y}{\Delta T} = - \frac{b}{1 - b}; \tag{20-14a}$$

or

$$\frac{dY}{dT} = - \frac{b}{1 - b}. \tag{20-14b}$$

This is the multiplier resulting from a change in taxes and is equal to $-mpc/(1 - mpc)$. In this simplified model of the economy, the multiplier resulting from a change in taxes will always be less in absolute value than that resulting from a change in government expenditures because all of the government expenditures enter the income stream directly, while only the portion of the tax change that actually affects consumption enters the income stream directly.

Graphically, the introduction of a lump-sum tax has the effect of shifting the intercept of the consumption function while leaving the *mpc* unchanged. This is formally equivalent to a change in government expenditures. But, while the intercept is shifted by the full amount of the expenditure change, it is only shifted by the negative of the tax change multiplied by the *mpc*. Since the *mpc* is less than one, the shift in the intercept is less than the revenue loss. This can be seen in Figure 20–3, where the initial intercept is assumed to equal $10 billion, and the *mpc* is assumed to be 0.75. Thus the initial level of

FIGURE 20–3
Impact of Change of Taxes on Equilibrium Income

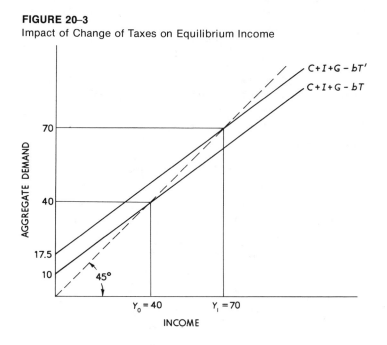

income is given by $40 billion, corresponding to the initial situation depicted in Figure 20–2.

Suppose that taxes are reduced by $10 billion. Instead of increasing the new intercept by $10 billion, the tax change only leads to a net increase in the intercept of $7.5 billion. The new level of income is given by $70 billion instead of $80 billion attained with a $10 billion increase in government expenditures. In terms of this simple model, government expenditures will always have more impact than tax changes per dollar of increase in the government deficit or reduction in its surplus. Of course, these expenditures must be direct payments for goods and services. If they are transfer payments, such as social security benefits or unemployment compensation which are given directly to consumers, they will have the same effect as tax changes, although of opposite sign.

It is unrealistic, however, to assume that the government can adjust taxes in a lump-sum manner. Tax revenues must be related to some base: income, corporate profits, retail sales, and others. For simplicity, let us assume that the only tax in the economy is a flat-rate tax on income. Instead of being predetermined, the tax function takes the following form:

$$T = tY. \tag{20-15}$$

Consumption is still assumed to be a function of disposable income $(Y_D = Y - T)$. Substituting the tax formula into the consumption function yields the following expression:

$$C = a + b(1 - t)Y \tag{20-16}$$

The effective *mpc* out of GNP has been reduced by the factor $(1 - t)$. The parameter "b" remains the *mpc* out of disposable income, while the expression $(1 - t)b$ equals the *mpc* out of GNP. Substituting Equations (20-15) and (20-16) for Equations (20-8) and (20-12) and solving for income yields the following expression:

$$Y = \frac{1}{1 - b(1 - t)}(a + \bar{I} + \bar{G}) \tag{20-17}$$

The change in income resulting from a change in government expenditures is now given by

$$\Delta Y = \frac{1}{1 - b(1 - t)} \cdot \Delta G \tag{20-18}$$

or

$$\frac{\Delta Y}{\Delta G} = \frac{1}{1 - b(1 - t)} \tag{20-18}$$

or

$$\frac{dY}{dG} = \frac{1}{1 - b(1 - t)} \tag{20-18b}$$

The effective expenditures multiplier has been reduced from that in the world in which there were only lump-sum taxes. The existence of taxes makes the *mpc* out of disposable income, which is equal to b, differ from the *mpc* out of GNP, which is equal to $b(1 - t)$. Thus the *mpc* out of GNP is lower than the *mpc* out of disposable income. This, of course, leads to a reduction in the multiplier effect of government expenditures. This implies, however, that personal taxes create a stabilizing effect upon the economy; for any change in government expenditures or investment, the resulting change in equilibrium income will be smaller in an economy with personal taxes than in one without. This can be seen by comparing the multipliers of Equations (20-6b) and (20-18b). The implications of the existence of personal taxes and other taxes that increase the built-in stability of the economy will be discussed in Chapter 21.

These relationships can be seen graphically in Figure 20-4. The

FIGURE 20-4

Impact of Personal Taxes on Equilibrium Income

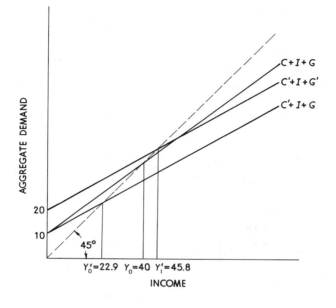

line $C + I + G$ represents the relationship between aggregate demand and income in a world without personal taxes and corresponds to similar lines in Figures 20–2 and 20–3. If we assume an initial intercept of $10 billion and an initial mpc of 0.75, income is given by $40 billion. The introduction of taxes reduces the effective mpc by a factor of $(1 - t)$. If $t = 0.25$, so that taxes comprise 25 percent of income, the effective mpc becomes 0.5625 and the aggregate demand curve is given by the line $C' + I + G$. The multiplier becomes 2.29. Instead of an initial equilibrium level of income equal to $40 billion, the initial equilibrium level of income is $22.9 billion. The existence of personal taxes reduces the multiplier effect of a change in government expenditures. This can be seen from the line $C' + I + G'$, which postulates an increase in government expenditure of $10 billion, leading to a net increment of income of $22.9 billion, or a new equilibrium income level of $45.8 billion.

The impact of a change in taxes can no longer be directly compared to the impact of a change in government expenditures because the tax changes now represent rates instead of dollar amounts. It is possible to make the two comparable, however, by asking what change in rates (Δt) is required to make the same change in income as that resulting from a change in revenue (ΔT).[3]

---

[3] The answer to this question can be derived algebraically as detailed in Additional Note 1 at the end of the chapter.

Figure 20–5
Impact on Equilibrium Level of Income by Changes in
Personal Taxes

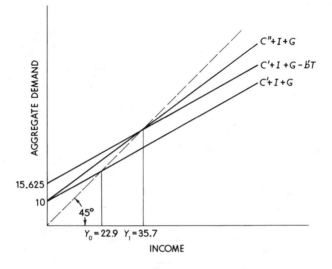

This can be seen in Figure 20–5. The line $C' + I + G$ is drawn on the assumption that the *mpc* out of disposable income (the parameter "*b*") is 0.75 and that the initial tax schedule (t_0) is 0.25. Thus the effective *mpc* out of GNP is 0.5625 and the initial level of income (Y_0) is given by \$22.9 billion. The impact of a \$10 billion cut in taxes is shown by the line $C' + I + G' - b'T$, which reflects a parallel shift in the line $C' + I + G'$ equal to the change in taxes multiplied by a factor of $(1 - t_0)b$, which is equal to 0.5625. The new level of income is given by \$35.7 billion.

This same income level could be attained by reducing the tax rate to increase the effect *mpc* out of GNP to that indicated by the line $C' + I + G$, which intersects the line $C' + I + G - b'T$ at the same level of income. The reader should verify that such a shift in the *mpc* out of GNP would require a new tax rate of 4.0 percent. Since government can only reduce taxes by reducing rates, in terms of policy it is the line $C' + I + G$ that is relevant, for this shows how the *mpc* out of GNP would have to change through the reduction of tax rates to be equivalent in impact to a tax reduction of \$10 billion. A comparison of Figures 20–5 and 20–4 will indicate that a tax reduction of \$10 billion generates less additional income than an increase in expenditures of \$10 billion. This arises, of course, since part of the tax reduction fails to enter the income stream directly because of savings.

Balanced-Budget Changes

If the government seeks to increase government expenditures and taxes simultaneously to maintain a balanced budget, this action will have a net expansionary effect. Again, we assume that the interest rate is constant and that investment is independent of the level of income, as are government expenditures. Hence investment and government expenditures can be assumed to be exogenously given outside of the system. Under these assumptions, the multiplier resulting from a balanced budget change in revenues and expenditures is exactly equal to one. This can be seen intuitively by considering that the entire amount of government expenditures enters the income stream directly, while only revenues multiplied by the *mpc* leave the income stream because some of the increased revenues would have been saved. Thus there is a net increment of $(1 - b)B$, where B equals the balanced-budget change in revenue and expenditures. In the example we have used, b is taken to be 0.75, and the expenditure multiplier is 4. If the government makes a balanced budget change of $10 billion, the net increment to the income stream is $2.5 billion, which will lead to an increase in total income of $10 billion. Thus the balanced-budget multiplier is one.

This can be seen in the case of lump-sum taxes by combining the expenditure multiplier, Equation (20–5), with that of the tax multiplier, Equation (20–14), to yield

$$\Delta Y = \frac{1}{1 - b}[\Delta G - b\,\Delta T] \qquad (20\text{–}19)$$

If $\Delta G = \Delta T = \Delta B$, the multiplier must be equal to one, i.e.,

$$\Delta Y = \frac{1 - b}{1 - b}\,\Delta B \qquad (20\text{–}19a)$$

and

$$\frac{\Delta Y}{\Delta B} = 1 \qquad (20\text{–}19b)$$

Figure 20–6 shows the derivation of the balanced-budget multiplier with a lump-sum tax. The initial equilibrium is given by the intersection of the 45° line with line $C + I + G$ at income $Y_0 = \$40$ billion. Suppose that tax revenues and government expenditures are simultaneously raised by $10 billion. The increase in tax revenues shifts the aggregate demand line down to $C + I + G - bT$, while the increase in government expenditures raises it to the line $C + I + G' - bT$. Because more income directly enters the income stream via expenditures than is taken out in taxes, the net first-round increase in the level of

FIGURE 20–6

Impact of Balanced-Budget Change on Equilibrium Level of Income

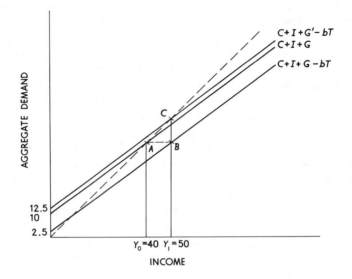

aggregate demand is $2.5 billion. With the assumed *mpc* of 0.75, the total increment in income is $10 billion; the new equilibrium level of income is at $50 billion. That the balanced-budget multiplier is one can be seen from the figure. The vertical distance CB shows the balanced budget change, while the horizontal distance AB shows the increase in income. Since $CB = AB$, the balanced-budget multiplier is one.

Figure 20–7 shows the balanced-budget impact with tax rates rather than with lump-sum tax changes. The line $C' + I + G$ is drawn on the assumption that the *mpc* out of disposable income is equal to 0.75 while the tax rate $t = 0.25$. The initial income equilibrium is given by $22.9 billion. An income tax that would yield revenues equal to $10 billion is imposed, shifting the aggregate demand function to $C'' + I + G$, while government expenditures are increased by $10 billion, further shifting the aggregate demand schedule to $C'' + I + G'$. This intersects the 45° line at an income level equal to $32.9 billion. Thus the increase in income (AB) is exactly equal to the balanced-budget change (CB). Again, the balanced-budget multiplier equals one. The demonstration that the balanced-budget multiplier is equal to one in this simplified model of the economy is often referred to as the balanced-budget theorem.

The balanced-budget theorem indicates that a balanced-budget increase in the government sector will be expansionary, while a balanced-budget reduction in the government sector will be restric-

FIGURE 20–7
Impact of Balanced-Budget Change with Personal Taxes on
Equilibrium Income

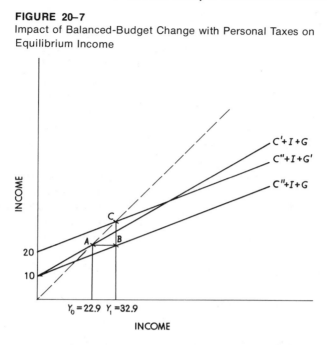

tive; and the net impact of the balanced-budget change upon the
economy will be precisely equal to that change. This conclusion, however, rests on several simplifying assumptions, the most important of
which are the following. First, the marginal propensities to consume
are identical for all people. If the recipients of the expenditures have
different $mpcs$ from the payers of the taxes, the two effects would fail to
cancel out. For example, if the government expenditures go to individuals with high $mpcs$ while the taxes are paid by people with low
$mpcs$ the net expansionary impact will be greater than one, since the
proportion of the expenditures that enters the income stream directly
is greater than the proportion of the funds removed from the income
stream by those paying the taxes. Second, prices are assumed to be
constant. Thus, there is no difference between changes in real and
money income. Third, investment is constant, or at least independent
of income, consumption, government expenditures, and the tax functions. Changes in income, consumption, or the government sector do
not affect investment, leading to secondary changes in income. Fourth,
the analysis ignores any growth considerations but is static in the sense
that it is solely concerned with comparing two levels of income under
two different assumptions about the behavior of government. Finally,
the analysis assumes that compensatory monetary policy takes place to
ensure that the interest rate remains constant.

Clearly, the entire analysis in this section has been highly simplified. It does suggest the following, however: First, a change in government expenditures will change the level of income by some multiplier. Second, a change in tax revenue will change income in an opposite direction, by some multiplier that is less than the expenditure multiplier. Third, changes in expenditures and taxes of equal magnitudes but opposite directions may have an impact on income equal to the balanced budget change. The precise magnitude of the multipliers involved depends upon the marginal propensity to consume out of GNP, which in turn depends upon the *mpc* out of disposable income, the nature of the tax function, the relationship between GNP, personal income, disposable income, and so on. Thus the model used here, which assumes away the importance of the corporate sector and corporate taxation and assumes that investment is independent of the level of income, is a gross simplification of reality. Nevertheless, it does illustrate the pertinent points about the expansionary or restrictive effects of changes in expenditures or taxes. From these, more realistic models of the economy can be constructed. We make a modest step in this direction in the next section by relaxing the assumption that interest rates remain constant.

A GENERAL ANALYSIS OF INCOME STABILIZATION

In general, the impact of fiscal policy upon income depends upon the way in which a change in the government surplus or deficit is financed. This is made clear by realizing that the government must operate under an effective budget constraint which states [4]

$$\Delta G = \Delta T + \Delta D + \Delta H \qquad (20\text{--}20)$$

where ΔG represents the change in government expenditures; ΔT represents the change in tax revenues; ΔD represents the change in the government's debt; and ΔH represents the change in the monetary base, which is also referred to as high-powered money.[5] Thus, any change in government expenditures must be financed by a change in tax revenues, government debt, or the monetary base. In general, the impact that the change in government expenditures will have upon the equilibrium level of income depends upon the way in which it is financed. Money creation is the most expansionary, while tax finance is the least expansionary. To understand the relationships between changes in

---

[4] For a full discussion of the implications of this point see Carl F. Christ, "A Simple Macroeconomic Model with a Government Budget Constraint," *Journal of Political Economy*, vol. 76 (February 1968), pp. 53–67; Frank G. Stendl, "Comment," *Journal of Political Economy*, vol. 79 (May 1971), pp. 675–79.

[5] Only in an economy in which the banking system must hold all of its deposits in reserves will the change in the monetary base equal the change in the money supply. As long as banks must keep only some fraction of their deposits in reserves, a change in the monetary base will generate change in the money supply.

government expenditures and the way in which they are financed, we will analyze the problem of financing a deficit. The impact of a tax increase or expenditure reductions to create a surplus can be analyzed in a similar fashion. This analysis will be left to the reader, however.

The model used in the previous section assumed that the monetary authorities keep the interest rate constant by adjusting the money supply. Since investment was assumed to be a function of the interest rate alone, a constant interest rate implied a constant level of investment. Once this assumption is relaxed, the interactions between the investable funds market and the money supply must be considered. Although a given increase in government expenditures will shift the IS curve out by the full multiplier analyzed in the previous section, the equilibrium level of income will be determined by the relative shifts in the IS and the LM curves. As long as interest rates are not at their floor, if the LM curve shifts less than the IS curve, the change in the equilibrium level of income will be less than that implied by the pure fiscal multiplier; if the LM curve shifts more than the IS curve, the change in the equilibrium level of income will be greater than that implied by the pure fiscal multiplier; finally, if the IS and LM curves shift out by an equal amount, the interest rate will remain constant and the change in the equilibrium level of income will be that implied by the pure fiscal multiplier. This section analyzes how the IS and the LM curves could be expected to shift under different methods of financing an increase in expenditures.

Money Creation

If increased government expenditures are financed by money creation, the government must increase the monetary base by the amount of the increased government expenditures. It can do this by putting new money into circulation or by drawing down its accounts held at the Federal Reserve banks. In either case, the change in government expenditures will affect the IS curve, while the change in the monetary base will affect the LM curve. The ultimate impact of the increased expenditures upon the equilibrium level of income will depend upon the relative magnitudes of the shifts in the two curves, assuming, of course, that the interest rate is not at its floor.

Changes in the IS Curve. The IS curve traces out the levels of income and interest rate that equalize planned savings and planned investment. The way in which the IS curve can be expected to move with a change in government expenditure can be seen by considering the following relationships:

$$I = I(r) \tag{20-21}$$

$$S = -a + s(Y - T) \tag{20-22}$$

$$I + G = S + T \qquad (20\text{–}23)$$

$$G = \bar{G} \qquad (20\text{–}24)$$

$$T = \bar{T} \qquad (20\text{–}25)$$

Equation (20–21) states that investment is a function of the rate of interest, while Equation (20–22) states that savings are a linear function of disposable income. The coefficient s represents the marginal propensity to save. Equation (20–23) states that in equilibrium the planned saving plus taxes in the economy must equal the sum of planned investment and government expentitures,[6] while Equations (20–24) and (20–25) state that the levels of government expenditures and of taxes are given outside of the system. Of course, if the government's budget is balanced so that $\bar{T} = \bar{G}$, this equilibrium condition reduces to the familiar one that planned savings must equal planned investment. Substituting the revelant equations into (20–23) and solving for equilibrium income yields the familiar expression for the level of income

$$Y = \frac{a + I(r) + \bar{G} - (1 - s)\bar{T}}{s}. \qquad (20\text{–}26)$$

Since investment is a function of the interest rate, each interest rate determines a particular level of investment. Equation (20–26) associates each level of the interest rate and its corresponding level of investment with a given level of income. Letting the interest rate vary over its feasible range of values makes it possible to trace out the associated levels of equilibrium income. The pairs of the interest rate and the level of income that equilibrate planned savings and planned investment are plotted by the curve IS in Figure 20–8. This curve is such that at high interest rates, planned investment would be relatively low and equilibrium income would be relatively low. As the interest rate falls, planned investment and therefore equilibrium income rise. But this rise in equilibrium income occurs at a diminishing rate because investment is assumed to be relatively interest inelastic at low interest rates.

By assuming that interest rates remain constant, Equation (20–26) indicates at what rate equilibrium income changes with given changes in government expenditures, taxes, or both. These are given by the familiar fiscal multipliers we analyzed in the previous section, where $(1 - mpc)$ has been replaced by $s = mps$, or $s = 1 - b$.

---

[6] This can easily be derived from the equilibrium condition that $Y = C + I + G$. Consumption plus saving equals disposable income (Y_D); and disposable income plus taxes equals national income. Thus $Y_D = C + S$ and $Y = Y_D + T$. Therefore $C = Y - S - T$. Substituting this into the equilibrium condition that $Y = C + I + G$ yields the equivalent equilibrium condition that $I + G = S + T$.

FIGURE 20–8

Shift in *IS* Curve Due to Change in Government
Expenditures

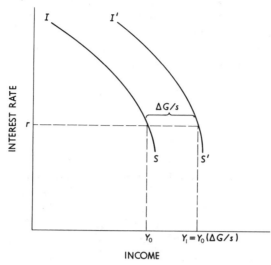

$$\Delta Y = \frac{\Delta G}{s} \tag{20-27a}$$

$$\Delta Y = \frac{1-s}{s} \Delta T \tag{20-27b}$$

$$\Delta Y = \Delta B \tag{20-27c}$$

Equation (20–27a) states that if interest rates and taxes remain constant, the equilibrium level of income will change by $(1/s)$ times the change in government expenditures (ΔG). Equation (20–27b) states that if interest rates and government expenditures remain constant, the equilibrium level of income will change by the fraction $(1-s)/s$ times the change in taxes (ΔT). Equation (20–27c) states that if interest rates remain constant, the equilibrium level of income will change by the amount of the balanced budget change (ΔB).

Because interest rates are assumed constant, each of these expressions can be interpreted as a horizontal *shift* in the *IS* curve caused by the policy change. Thus Equation (20–27a) indicates that a given increase in government expenditures will shift the *IS* curve at each interest rate to the right by $(1/s)$ $\Delta G/s$. This is shown in Figure 20–8 where an increase in government expenditures has shifted *IS* to *I'S'*. At a given interest rate (r), income was initially Y_0. After the increase in government expenditures, income is now given by $Y_0(\Delta G/s)$.

The shifts with tax or balanced budget changes are qualitatively the same, although the shifts in the *IS* curve will be smaller in magnitude than those under an expenditure change. The horizontal amount of these shifts is specifically given by Equations (20–27b) and (20–27c).

Shifts in the LM Curve. Because the equilibrium level of income is determined by the intersection of the *IS* and *LM* curves, it is necessary to analyze how a change in the money supply will affect the *LM* curve. The demand for money is given by the following relationships, which were developed in Chapter 19.

$$M_D = M_t + M_a \qquad\qquad (20\text{--}28)$$

$$M_t = (1/V)PY \qquad\qquad (20\text{--}29)$$

$$M_a = M(r) \qquad\qquad (20\text{--}30)$$

Equation (20–28) states that the total demand for money (M_D) is the sum of the transactions demand (M_t) and the asset demand (M_a). In Equation (20–29) the transactions demand is assumed to be proportional to the level of money income, with the factor of proportionality given by the reciprocal of the income velocity of money $(1/V)$. This can also be thought of as the average cash balances held in the economy over time or over the accounting period. The asset demand for money, shown in Equation (20–30), is assumed to be a function of the interest rate.

The money supply is related to the monetary base by the average reserve requirements in the banking system and can be expressed by

$$M_s = H/k \qquad\qquad (20\text{--}31)$$

where H represents the monetary base and k represents the average reserve requirements. Since only a fraction of an increase in the monetary base need be held as reserves, the rest can be loaned to the public. These funds in turn will be deposited, but again, only a fraction need be held in reserves. Thus just as an increase in government expenditure has a multiplier effect on income, an increase in the monetary base has a multiplier effect upon the money supply. Suppose, for example, that the average reserve requirements are 20 percent. If the government increases the monetary base by $1 billion, $200 million must be held in reserve, while the remaining $800 million can be loaned to the public. If this money is then deposited, $160 million must be held in reserve and $640 million can be loaned to the public. As long as banks hold no excess reserves or borrow so as to incur negative free reserves, the final increase in the money supply will be $5 billion. Thus as long as banks maintain their legal reserve requirements, an increase in the monetary base will increase the money supply by the reciprocal of the average reserve requirements.[7]

---

[7] The actual relationship between the monetary base and the money supply is somewhat more complicated than this because different banks have different reserve requirements. Thus, the potential increase in the money supply depends upon the distribution of funds between the different banks. Moreover, banks may choose to hold re-

In equilibrium, the money supply (M_S) must equal the demand for money (M_D). Hence

$$M_S = M_D \qquad (20\text{--}32)$$

Substituting Equations (20–28), (20–29), (20–30), and (20–31) into Equation (20–32) and solving for income yields the relationship

$$Y = \left[\frac{H}{k} - M(r) \right] \frac{V}{P} \qquad (20\text{--}33)$$

This states that the level of real income is positively related to the monetary base and negatively related to the asset demand for money. This is similar to the relationship between the level of money income and the money supply and the asset demand for money developed in Chapter 19. Each interest rate implies a unique asset demand for money. Since the price level is assumed to be constant, it can be set equal to one without any loss of generality. Thus for a given interest rate, the change in income generated by change in the money supply is given by

$$\Delta Y = V \, \Delta H / k \qquad (20\text{--}34)$$

The change in income is equal to the change in the monetary base multiplied by the ratio of the income velocity of money and the average reserve ratio.

Figure 20–9 shows the initial LM curve that relates the interest rate and the level of income that equilibrate the supply of and demand for money. With a fixed interest rate, an increase in the monetary base will shift the LM curve out to LM' by an amount $V \, \Delta H / k$. Thus at an interest rate r, the intial equilibrium level of income is given by Y_0. With an increase in the monetary base equal to ΔH, the new income level is given by $Y_0 V \, \Delta H / k$.

The Determination of the Equilibrium. If the government expenditures are financed by money creation, the monetary base must increase by the amount of the government expenditures. The IS curve will shift to the right by an amount equal to $\Delta G / s$, while the LM curve will shift by an amount equal to $V \, \Delta H / k$. By assumption, the change in expenditures equals the change in the monetary base, i.e., $\Delta H = \Delta G$. Since savings must equal investment, the savings ratio s must equal the proportion of total income that is invested. Over the postwar period in the United States this has been approximately 15 percent. V represents the income velocity of money and can be calculated by the ratio

serves in excess of those required by law, in which case the actual monetary expansion will be less than the potential expansion. Alternatively, they may choose to borrow from the Federal Reserve banks in which case they can actually loan out more funds than those resulting from the increase in the monetary base. In this case, the actual increase in the money supply will be greater than the estimated potential expansion.

FIGURE 20–9

Shifts in *LM* Curve Due to Increase in Monetary Base

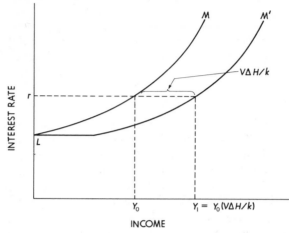

of GNP to the money supply, defined as currency plus demand deposits. For the United States, this is approximately 3. Reserve requirements are approximately 20 percent. Therefore, the shift in the *IS*
curve will be approximately 6.67 ΔG while the shift in the *LM* curve
will be approximately 15ΔH or 15 ΔG. Therefore, if interest rates are
not at their floor, increases in government expenditures financed by
money creation will lead to a greater increase in the equilibrium level
of income than that implied by the pure fiscal multiplier.

This is shown in Figure 20–10 where the *IS* and *LM* curves are
assumed to be in initial equilibrium at Y_0 and r_0. Since the *LM* curve
shifts to the right by more than the *IS* curve, the interest rate must fall,
stimulating investment. Therefore, the increase in income is greater
than it would be if interest rates had remained constant. In the new
equilibrium the interest rate is given by r_1 while income is given by
Y_1. It should be pointed out that if interest rates were initially at their
floor, the greater shift in the *LM* curve relative to the *IS* curve would
not have affected interest rates. In this case income have increased by
the amount implied by the pure fiscal multiplier since there would not
have been any interest rate effects.[8]

---

[8] If the velocity of money is an increasing function of the interest rate, the situation is
somewhat different. In this case, an increase in the money supply will cause a nonparal-
lel shift in the *LM* curve, with the curve shifting out more at higher interest rates. At low
interest rates, it is possible that 1/s > V/h and that the *IS* curve would shift not more than
the *LM* curve. With money creation, the usual situation, however, is one where 1/s < V/h
and the *IS* curve shifts less than the *LM* curve. At high interest rates, an equal increase
in government expenditures and the money supply will probably lead to an increase in
income greater than that predicted by the simple multiplier alone, while at low levels of
interest rates, an equal increase in government expenditures and the money supply may
lead to an increase in income less than that predicted by the simple multiplier alone.

FIGURE 20–10

Change in Income Resulting from Increased Government
Expenditures Financed by Money Creation

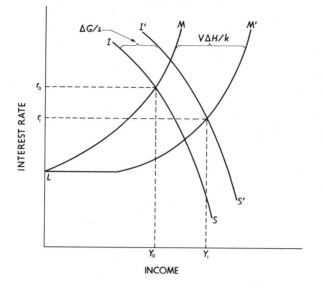

INCOME

Debt Finance

If the government sells bonds to finance the deficit, the result will generally be less expansionary than if it had printed new money. By increasing its purchase of goods and services by ΔG, the government puts additional funds into the income stream by the same amount, which ultimately causes the change in the money supply to be greater than the increase in expenditures. By selling bonds to finance this increase in expenditures, it then takes an equal amount of funds out of the income stream. If the funds are borrowed simultaneously with the expenditures, the monetary base and therefore the money supply and the LM curve remain constant.

As previously discussed, the IS curve shifts by an amount equal to $(1/s)(\Delta G)$. Thus the impact of a change in government expenditures, financed by issuing new debt by the same amount, upon the equilibrium level of income depends upon the IS curve shifting along a fixed LM curve. The resulting equilibrium is shown in Figure 20–11. Let us assume that the initial equilibrium is given by the intersection of the initial IS curve, given by the curve IS, and the LM curve, at point A. If government expenditures increase by ΔG, the IS curve is shifted out to the right to $I'S'$ by an amount equal to $\Delta G/s$. Since, however, the LM curve remains stationary, the resulting equilibrium will be at an interest rate r_1, which is higher than the initial rate r_0, and an income level Y_1, which is less than that implied by the shift in the IS

curve. In the limiting case when the *LM* curve is totally inelastic, no increase in income occurs and the interest rate and investment bear the full burden of the adjustment. In this case, all asset money that can be freed has been shifted to transactions demand. The money supply is fully used to support transactions. Since investment is inversely related to the interest rate, the interest rate will rise sufficiently to cause investment to fall by the full increase in government expenditures. Consequently, income will remain unchanged.

If interest rates are very low, the *LM* curve will be elastic and the increase in equilibrium income may be as great as that implied by the pure fiscal multipliers. Let us assume, for example, that the initial equilibrium occurred at point *B* in Figure 20–11 where the *IS* curve marked *is* intersects the *LM* curve. The initial level of income is given by y_0 and the interest ratio is given by r_0'. An increase in government expenditure of ΔG shifts the curve marked *is* to the right by an amount $\Delta G/s$, to the curve marked $i's'$. The interest rate remains constant and income rises to y_1; the increase in income is given by the full shift in the curve *is* and is equal to $\Delta G/s$, which is also equal to the pure expenditure multiplier derived earlier in this chapter.

Thus, when fiscal changes are financed by debt, the multiplier effect of these changes depends upon where the initial equilibrium occurs. If it occurs on the elastic portion of the *LM* curve, the impact of

FIGURE 20–11

Change in Income Resulting from Increase in Government Expenditures Financed by Debt

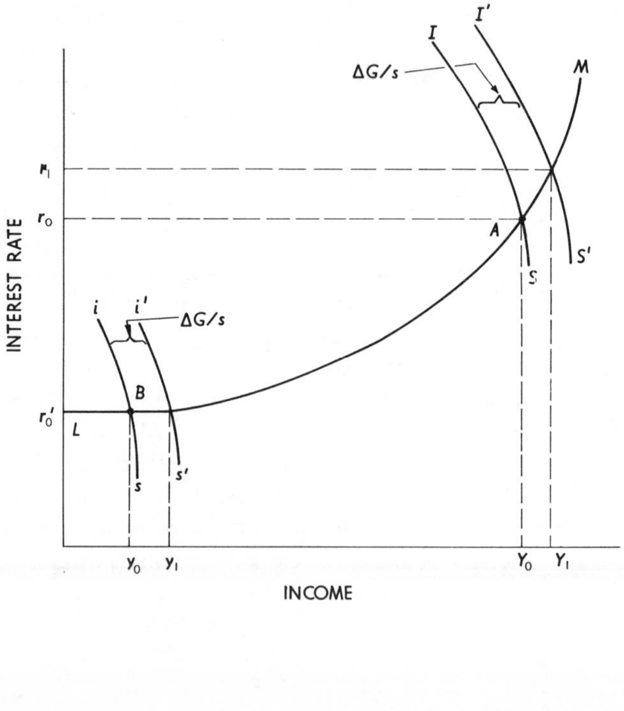

INCOME

fiscal change may be as great as those implied by the pure fiscal multiplipliers. If it occurs on the inelastic portion of the *LM* curve, the impact of fiscal changes will be less than those implied by pure fiscal multipliers. In either case, however, the impact of fiscal changes financed by debt creation will generally be less than those financed by money creation.

Balanced-Budget Changes

Just as the expenditure multiplier under debt finance will generally be less than $1/(1 - mpc)$, the balanced-budget multiplier will generally be less than 1. With debt finance the money supply remains constant because the government removes the same amount of funds in debt that it puts into the income stream as expenditures. With tax finance, the money supply remains constant because the government removes the same amount of funds in taxes that it puts into the income stream as expenditures. Since the money supply remains constant in both cases, the *LM* curve does not change.

Under a balanced-budget change, the nature of the new equilibrium is similar to that described in the case of debt creation. The balanced-budget change shifts the *IS* curve by the increase in the government sector ΔG. Since the *IS* curve shifts by ΔG instead of by $\Delta G/s$, the increase in equilibrium income will be less if the expenditures are financed by taxes than if they had been financed by debt. Moreover, unless the economy is in an initial equilibrium at the interest floor, the balanced-budget multiplier will be less than one. The analysis is formally identical to that of debt creation and need not be repeated. In general the balanced-budget change in income will be less than that given by the pure balanced-budget multiplier, since interest rate increases will curtail investment.

The Need for Coordination

This section has stressed the importance of the interrelationships between fiscal policy and monetary policy and the need for policy coordination. If increased expenditures are financed by money creation, the money supply will rise by more than government expenditures and the *LM* curve will shift by more than the *IS* curve. Hence interest rates will fall, stimulating new investment, and the new equilibrium level of income will be greater than that implied by the pure fiscal multipliers. Of course, if interest rates are initially at their floor, shifts in the *IS* or *LM* curves will not alter interest rates and income will change by the amount implied by the pure fiscal multipliers. If, however, government expenditures are financed by debt or taxes, the money supply and the *LM* curve do not change. As long as interest rates are not at their floor, the interactions of the investable funds market and the money market will generate an increase in interest rates, which will reduce investment, counteracting the impact of the fiscal policy change. Thus in the absence of accommodating changes in monetary policy, changes in government expenditures will lead to smaller changes in the equilibrium level of income than that implied by the pure fiscal multipliers alone.

The magnitude of these offsetting impacts in large part depends upon the level of interest rates and the elasticities of investment and the asset demand for money with respect to the interest rate. As we discussed in Chapter 19, at high interest rates, the elasticity of investment is fairly high while the elasticity of the asset demand for money is fairly low; at low interest rates, the opposite is true. Consequently, at low levels of interest rates, these offsetting considerations should lead to relatively small reductions in investment demand and hence in the equilibrium level of income. At high interest rates, however, these offsetting considerations could curtail investment and the equilibrium level of income considerably.

If the government wants to obtain a maximum impact from a given change in expenditures or taxes, it is important that the monetary authorities let the money supply change in a direction consistent with the expenditure or tax change. In general, fiscal policy moves the *IS* curve while monetary policy moves the *LM* curve. Thus, if the government wants to maximize the change in income resulting from a given change in taxes or expenditures, it should make sure that the monetary authorities adjust the money supply in a way consistent with this change.

THE THEORY OF ECONOMIC STABILIZATION

The previous section assumed that the government was solely interested in maintaining income at its potential level. Typically, however, the government has several macroeconomic goals. Of these, the most important appear to be the maintenance of full employment, that is, of income at its potential level; price stability; the desired rate of growth; and the proper external balance. Unfortunately these goals may not be entirely consistent. For example, as the economy approaches full employment, pressures are put on prices, causing them to rise. Similarly, the maintenance of a positive balance of payments may conflict with the goal of a high rate of growth if high interest rates are needed to keep capital from leaving the country. Thus the policy-maker's problem is considerably more complicated than that of using combinations of tax or expenditure changes to ensure that actual income equals potential income to maintain full employment. Instead the policy-maker is generally faced with a wide range of not necessarily consistent goals and a limited number of policy instruments. Thus this section outlines the nature of the problem by discussing a simple model that outlines the nature of the possible trade-off between price stability and full employment and analyzes under what conditions these targets can be achieved.

The Nature of the Trade-Off

To understand the nature of the problem, let us consider a simple example in which the policy-maker is assumed to be concerned about the degree of price stability and the degree of unemployment that exist in the economy. We furthermore assume that the following relationships describe the rate of price change and the unemployment rate that exist in the economy at any given time.[9]

$$E = \epsilon Y \tag{20–34}$$

$$U = N - E \tag{20–35}$$

$$u = U/N = 1 - E/N \tag{20–36}$$

$$p = \Delta p/p = \beta \left(\frac{Y - Y^*}{Y} \right) \tag{20–37}$$

$$Y = C + I + G \tag{20–38}$$

$$C = cY \tag{20–39}$$

$$N = \bar{N} \tag{20–40}$$

$$I = \bar{I} \tag{20–41}$$

$$G = \bar{G} \tag{20–42}$$

$$Y^* = \bar{Y}^* \tag{20–43}$$

Equation (20–34) states that employment (E) is directly related to income (Y) by some constant (ϵ) which can be taken to represent some aggregate labor/output ratio. Equation (20–35) states the identity that unemployment (U) equals the labor force (N) less total employment (E), while Equation (20–36) states that the unemployment rate (u) equals the percentage of the work force that is unemployed. Equation (20–37) gives the relationship between the rate of changes of prices $(\dot{p})$ and the gap between actual and potential income $(Y - Y^*)$ and indicates that the rate of change in prices is porportional to the percentage gap between actual and desired income. Equation (20–38) gives the

---

[9] In Chapter 21, we explore the nature of the trade-off in more detail. This simplified example is primarily given to pose the problem facing the policy-maker rather than to describe the reasons why certain unemployment rates and rates of change of prices may be inconsistent.

familiar income-equilibrium condition, which states that total income (Y) is equal to the sum of expenditures on consumption (C), investment (I), and government (G). Equation (20–39) states that consumption is assumed to be proportional to income. Finally, Equations (20–40)–(2–43) state that the labor force (N), investment (I), government expenditures (G), and potential income (Y^*) are given exogenously outside of the system.

If the values of all of the exogenous or predetermined variables are known, the values of all of the endogenous variables can be determined as long as the system has a unique solution. When all of the endogenous variables are expressed solely in terms of the exogenous or predetermined variables, the system is said to be in its reduced form. Although this terminology may seem tedious in this simplified example, a familiarity with it will be useful when we consider more complex models of the U.S. economy.

The policy-maker is not generally concerned with the entire spectrum of the endogenous variables, but only with a few. Suppose in this case that he is only concerned with the rate of unemployment (u) and the rate of change of prices $(\dot{p})$. Using Equations (20–38), (20–39), (20–41), and (20–42), it is possible to solve for income and then to derive the other relationships by substitution. Thus, the reduced-form equations of the unemployment rate and the rate of change of prices are given by:

$$u = \frac{(1 - c)\bar{N} - \epsilon(\bar{I} + \bar{G})}{(1 - c)N} \tag{20–44}$$

$$\dot{p} = \beta \left[\frac{\bar{I} + \bar{G} - (1 - c)\bar{Y}^*}{\bar{I} + \bar{G}} \right] \tag{20–45}$$

Since these structural equations are not generally known with certainty,[10] the reduced forms of these equations are not generally known with certainty. It is acceptable, however, to replace the structural parameters (ϵ, β, C) with their estimated values and the exogenous variables (I, G, N, Y^*) with their expected values and proceed as if we knew these relationships with certainty[11] (note that we drop the bars in recognition that the values of these variables are not constants, but were in fact exogenously determined variables). Thus, Equations (20–44) and (20–45) state that if the values of the labor force (N), potential income (Y^*), investment (I), and government expenditures (G) are

---

[10] The structural equations are usually estimated with an error term. Hence the parameters in the structural equations are not known with certainty, but subject to some probability distirbution. Moreover, for forecasting purposes the exogenous variables are not known with certainty.

[11] For a good discussion of this point see H. Theil, "Linear Decision Rules for Macrodynamic Policy Problems," in *Quantitative Planning of Economic Policy*, ed. Bert G. Hickman (Washington, D.C.: The Brookings Institution, 1965), pp. 18–42.

known, and if the values of the structural parameters (ϵ, β, C) are known, the values of the unemployment rate (u) and the rate of change of prices $(\dot{p})$ can be uniquely determined.

Suppose, however, that the policy-maker has a desired value for each of the two target variables: the unemployment rate (u) and the rate of changes of prices $(\dot{p})$. Given these desired values which we can denote by u^* and p^*, we can then determine what value of government expenditures (G) is needed to achieve either of these goals by using Equations (20–44) and (20–45) to solve for G. This is given in Equations (20–46) and (20–47), which show the level of government expenditures needed to achieve the desired value of the unemployment rate (u^*) or the desired value of the rate of change of prices $(\dot{p}^*)$, given the expected values of the other predetermined variable and the structural parameters.

$$G = -I + \frac{N(1-c)(1-u^*)}{\epsilon} \qquad (20\text{–}46)$$

$$G = -I - \frac{\beta Y^*(1-c)}{(\dot{p}^* - \beta)} \qquad (20\text{–}47)$$

Clearly, however, Equations (20–46) and (20–47) are not independent since the level of government expenditures that applies to one must also apply to the other. Consequently, it is possible to link the two equations and express the rate of change of prices as a function of the unemployment rate. This is given in Equation (20–48):

$$\dot{p} = \beta - \frac{\epsilon \beta Y^*}{N(1-u)} \qquad (20\text{–}48)$$

This states that the rate of change of prices is a nonlinear function of the unemployment rate. The general shape of the relationship is given by the line PP in Figure 20–12. When the rate of change of prices is zero, unemployment will be positive. As unemployment drops, the rate of change of prices increases sharply. Similarly, large increases in the unemployment rate are needed to get further price reductions. This relationship is generally called the Phillips curve after the man who first discovered this relationship empirically. [12] While the specific shape of this curve will be discussed in the following chapter, the ensuing discussion will be simplified if we refer to it as the Phillips curve.

In this simplified world, the Phillips curve describes the possible combinations of the rate of change of prices and the unemployment rate that can be attained by society. If, for example, the policy-

---

[12] A. W. Phillips, "The Relation between Unemployment and the Rate of Change of Money Wage Rates in the United Kingdom, 1861–1957," *Economica*, vol. 25 (November 1958), pp. 283–99.

FIGURE 20-12
Welfare Maximization Subject to the Phillips Curve

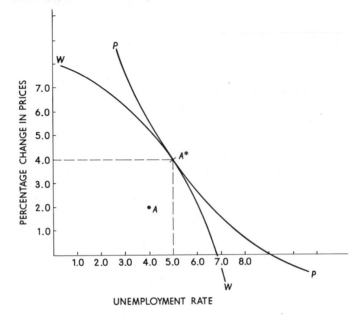

maker wanted society to achieve a 4 percent rate of unemployment and a 2 percent rate of change of prices, this would not be possible. This is shown by the point *A* which is off the Phillips curve, If a 2 percent rate of price increase is to be achieved, the policy-maker must settle at best for a 6.5 percent rate of unemployment; if a 4 percent rate of unemployment is to be achieved, the policy-maker must settle for at least a 5.5 percent rate of price increase. Thus, the goals of a 4 percent rate of unemployment and a 2 percent rate of price increase are consistent.

Given that the policy-maker is constrained to stay on the Phillips curve *PP*, what is the preferred point? This can be determined by an analysis similar to that used in consumer theory, where the consumer maximizes welfare subject to budget constraint. Here the policy-maker is assumed to maximize his or her welfare subject to the target possibility constraint, which in this case is given by the Phillips curve *PP*.

Since price increases and increases in the rate of unemployment are both "bads" instead of "goods," the policy-maker's indifference curves take the general form shown by the curve *WW* in Figure 20–12. This is the opposite in curvature of those given by most indifference curves and shows that the policy-maker is only willing to accept higher price rises if unemployment is reduced or higher unemployment rates if price increases are reduced. The curvature of the slope indicates a diminishing rate of substitution; as prices rise, the policy-maker requires increasingly large reductions in the unemployment rate; as the unemployment rate rises, the policy-maker requires increasingly large reductions in the rate of increases in prices. Given the shape of the indifference curve WW and the target possibility curve or the Phillips curve *PP*, society's welfare is maximized at point *A**, where the unemployment rate is 5 percent and the rate of price increase is 4 percent. If these values are inserted into Equations (20–46) or (20–47), a unique level of government expenditures is determined that gives the constrained target levels of unemployment and rate of increase of prices that can be achieved simultaneously.

The Relationship between the Targets and the Instruments

The constraints imposed upon the economy as expressed through the Phillips curve arise from the underlying structural relationships and the way in which they are affected by the policy instruments. It is often claimed, for example, that if the number of policy instruments equals the number of target variables, it is possible to satisfy the desired values of the target variables simultaneously.[13] The rationale behind this thinking is intuitively obvious. If there are more targets than instruments, some compromise must be reached between the desired targets since the number of policy instruments is insufficient to permit the simultaneous realization of the desired values of all of the target variables. If, however, the number of policy instruments is equal to or greater than the number of target variables and if the equations relating the targets to the policy instruments are linearly independent and consistent, the policy-maker should have sufficient degrees of freedom to permit the simultaneous determinations of the desired values of the target variables.[14] In particular, if the number of policy instruments equals the number of target variables, there should be a unique set of instruments that will enable the simultaneous determination of any set of desired values of the target variables; if the number of policy instruments exceeds the number of target variables, there should be a multitude of values that the policy instruments can take on to achieve the desired set of target variables.

A little reflection should indicate, however, that the equality of the number of target variables with the policy instruments is a necessary but not a sufficient condition for the simultaneous satisfaction of any set of desired values of the target instruments. In addition, the reduced-form equations that link the target variables to the policy

---

[13] For a full discussion of this problem, see L. Johansen, *Public Economics* (Chicago: Rand-McNally & Co., 1965), chap. 2.

[14] This is detailed in Additional Note 1 at the end of this chapter.

instruments should be linear and independent.[15] Thus, the various policy instruments should work upon different variables.

This can be seen in the context of our simplified economy. Suppose, for example, that the government has at its disposal a lump sum income tax as well as government expenditures. Consumption becomes a function of disposable income, and the consumption function is altered to read

$$C = c(Y - T) \qquad (20\text{--}49)$$

Given a desired value of the unemployment rate and a desired value of the rate of change of prices, what values of government expenditures (G) and of taxes (T) can we use to achieve these targets? Instead of expressing each policy instrument as a function of the desired target variables, we can express both policy instruments as a function of the desired values of the target variables. Thus

$$-\epsilon G + \epsilon cT = (1 - c)(1 - u^*)N - \epsilon I \qquad (20\text{--}50)$$

$$G(\dot{p}^* - \beta) - (\dot{p}^* - \beta)cT = I(\beta - \dot{p}^*) - \beta(1 - c)Y^* \qquad (20\text{--}51)$$

An inspection of Equations (20–50) and (20–51) should indicate that they are not independent, since by multiplying Equation (20–50) by $-(\dot{p}^* - \beta)$ and by multiplying Equation (20–51) by ϵ, the coefficients on the two unknown variables $(G$ and $T)$ become identical. Thus, the relationship between the unemployment rate and the rate of change of prices remains unchanged and is given by Equation (20–48), i.e., $\dot{p} = \beta - \epsilon\beta Y^*/N(1 - u)$. Since taxes operate upon income in an identical fashion as government expenditures, the introduction of taxes does not increase the degrees of freedom available to the policy-maker. Moreover, the basic constraints between the attainable unemployment rate and the attainable rate of change of prices are unaltered. The optimal solution for the economy remains at the point of tangency between the social welfare function and the target-possibility curve. Although the policy-maker can now achieve the desired value of the attainable targets by a combination of taxes and expenditures, he or she can only achieve values of the targets delineated by the Phillips curve. Even though there are two targets and two instruments, the underlying structure of the economy is such that he or she cannot attain a 4 percent unemployment rate and a 2 percent price rise.

The inability of the policy-maker to achieve any desired value of the targets simultaneously, even when there are as many policy instruments as target variables, arises because the equations that relate the targets to the policy instruments are not linearly independent. If they are to be made independent, the policy instruments must act

---

[15] In terms of econometric model building, this requirement is equivalent to the one that the model be linear and identified.

independently upon the relevant variable and not in the same way, as they did with government expenditures and lump-sum, personal taxes. Suppose, for example, that the capacity level of income (Y^*) could be altered by the appropriate tax structure. Let us assume that instead of being exogenous or predetermined, potential income is given by the relationship $Y^* = Y^*(T)$. In this case the policy-maker has two independent policy instruments, government expenditures (G) and the tax structure (T). Then the relationship between the desired values of the target variables and the policy instruments can be given by

$$\epsilon G = N(1 - c)(1 - u^*) - \epsilon I \qquad (20\text{--}52)$$

$$\beta(1 - c)Y^*(T) + (\dot{p}^* - \beta)G = -I(\dot{p}^* - \beta). \qquad (20\text{--}53)$$

These two equations are independent. Given any value of the desired unemployment rate (u^*) and the desired rate of change of prices $(\dot{p}^*)$, there is a unique level of government expenditures (G) and a unique tax structure $Y^*(T)$ that will enable these values of the target variables to be simultaneously determined.

Consequently, the requirement that the number of policy instruments be greater than or equal to the number of target variables is a necessary and sufficient condition to ensure that the desired values of the target variables can be achieved if the equations that determine the underlying structure of the economy are independent, linear, and consistent. This can be stated alternatively that the policy instruments must act upon different target variables so that they are in some sense independent. Mere equality of the number of policy instruments with the number of target variables will not generally be sufficient to ensure that any values of the target variables can be attained.

Constraints upon the Policy Instruments

The previous analysis has indicated that if the equations that relate the policy instruments to the target variables are linear and independent and if the number of policy instruments is greater than or equal to the number of target variables, there are values of the policy instruments that will permit the simultaneous attainment of any desired values of the target variables. Since, however, there are often constraints upon the policy instruments themselves, it may be impossible to attain the desired values of the targets, regardless of the relationship between the policy instruments and the target variables. For example, the political considerations in the mid-1960s were such that tax increases in the face of rising excess demand were politically unacceptable. Moreover, because of the rising expenditures on the Vietnam War, it was politically impossible to reduce expenditures sufficiently to counteract the rising excess demand. Therefore, even though the policy tools were in principle available, in fact, they were not; and the bulk of stabilization policy fell on monetary policy, which proved inadequate to the task.

Although the Vietnam War placed a unique set of constraints upon the policy-maker in the mid-1960s, the general observation that the policy instruments are not independent of constraints is valid. Congress is often unwilling to change tax structures; the government is often unwilling or unable to change the level of expenditures substantially; political considerations impose constraints upon the level or structure of interest rates; and so forth.

Thus, the policy-makers must not only maximize their preference function subject to the relationships of the economy but also subject to political and administrative constraints placed upon attainable values of their policy instruments. While they can generally find a set of policy instruments that will permit them to maximize their social welfare function subject to these constraints, it will not generally be possible to achieve the desired values of all of the target variables, regardless of the relationship between the number of policy instruments and target variables. Some compromise among the conflicting goals must be determined.

CONCLUSION

Just as the analyis of the economy becomes increasingly complicated as simplifying assumtions are dropped, so does the analysis of stabilization policy. The simplest framework used to evaluate fiscal policy assumes that investment is independent of the interest rate and of income (or alternatively that the monetary authorities maintain a constant interest rate). Since income is only affected by changes in fiscal variables, the multipliers derived from this analysis can be called pure fiscal multipliers. The expenditure multiplier equals $1/(1 - mpc)$; the tax multiplier equals $-mpc/(1 - mpc)$; and the balanced-budget multiplier equals 1.

Once the assumption is dropped that investment is independent of the interest rate (or that the monetary authorities adjust the money supply to maintain a constant interest rate), the impact of fiscal changes upon income is less predictable. If the government finances increases in expenditure by increasing the monetary base through the creation of money, the ultimate increase in the money supply will generally be greater than the increase in expenditures. This will cause the interest rate to fall, which will stimulate investment and cause the ultimate increase in income to be greater than that implied by the pure expenditure multiplier alone. If the government finances increases in expenditures by selling debt, however, the money supply remains constant and interest rates rise. Thus investment will be curtailed, and the ultimate increase in income will be less than that implied by the pure expenditure multiplier. Finally, if no accommodating changes are made in the money supply, interest rates will rise under a balanced-budget increase in government expenditures, and the balanced-budget multiplier will be less than one. Similar conclusions hold in the case of reductions in government expenditures.

Thus it is important to coordinate monetary and fiscal policy in trying to affect the level of income. If the policy-maker concentrates on fiscal impacts alone, he or she neglects the linkage between the real and the monetary sector through the interest rate. Depending upon the way in which the fiscal change is financed, its ultimate impact upon the economy may be greater or less than that predicted by the pure fiscal multipliers alone.

It is important to remember that the government typically has a number of macroeconomic goals, of which income is only one. Full employment, price stability, growth, and the external balance are also important macroeconomic goals. Unfortunately, the structure of the economy and the available policy instruments may be such that the desired values of these target variables may not be simultaneously achievable. Therefore the role of the policy-maker must be to determine how the government can best achieve its alternative goals, subject to the constraints of the structure of the economy and the available policy tools. Since it is generally impossible to achieve simultaneously the desired values of all of the policy goals, the policy-maker must coordinate the available policy instruments to achieve the best mix of goals under the circumstances.

ADDITIONAL NOTES

1. By the standard rules of calculus, it is straightforward to show that a change in income resulting from a change in the tax rate is given by

$$\Delta Y = \frac{-bY_0}{1 - b(1 - t)} \Delta t \text{ or} \tag{a}$$

$$\frac{dY}{dt} = \frac{-b}{1 - b(1 - t)} \cdot Y_0, \tag{a'}$$

where Y_0 represents the initial equilibrium level of income. The multiplier resulting from a change in the tax rate equals the expenditure multiplier, multiplied by the factor $-bY_0$.

We now want to determine the change in tax rates that will yield the same change in income as that resulting from the change in revenues. Equation (20–14) related income to revenues and stated that

$$\Delta Y = -\frac{b}{1 - b} \Delta T \tag{20–14}$$

Since the change in income resulting from a revenue change must be the same as the change in income resulting from a rate change, we can set Equation (a) equal to Equation (20–14) and derive the relationship between revenue changes and rate changes. Thus

$$- \frac{b}{1-b}\Delta T = - \frac{bY_0}{1-b(1-t)}\Delta t \tag{b}$$

and

$$\Delta t = \frac{1-b(1-t)}{(1-b)Y_0}\Delta T \tag{b'}$$

The change in income (ΔY) resulting from a change in total tax revenue (ΔT) can be given by the following expression

$$\frac{\Delta Y}{\Delta T} = \frac{\Delta Y}{\Delta t}\ \frac{\Delta t}{\Delta T} \tag{c}$$

where $\dfrac{\Delta Y}{\Delta t}$ represents the change in income resulting from a change in tax rates and $\dfrac{\Delta t}{\Delta T}$ represents the change in rates that would be required to generate a change in total revenues.

Therefore substituting (a) and (b) into (c) yields

$$\frac{\Delta Y}{\Delta T} = \frac{-b}{1-b} \tag{d}$$

This, of course, is precisely the expression given by Equation (20–14). Thus it is possible to transform the impact of rate changes into the impact of revenue changes and vice versa, given the relationship between rates and revenues.

2. Formally, assume there are K target variables whose desired values are given by $X_1^*, \ldots , X_K^*$. In addition, assume that there are a total of I unknown or endogenous variables. Finally, assume that the government has at its disposal J policy instruments, $t_1 \ldots , t_J$. Thus, the economic system can be described by the following system of equations.

$$f_1(X_1^*, \ldots , X_K^*; X_{K+1}, \ldots , X_I; t_1, \ldots , t_J) = 0$$
$$\vdots$$
$$f_I(X_1^*, \ldots , X_K^*; X_{K+1}, \ldots , X_I; t_1, \ldots , t_J) = 0$$

The variables $X_1^*, \ldots X_K^*$ can be taken as given, while the policy instruments $t_1, \ldots t_J$ can be taken as unknowns whose values must be determined to permit the solution of the system. There are $I - K + J$ unknowns: $X_{K+1}, \ldots, X_I; t_1, \ldots t_J$; and there are I equations. If we assume that the equations are independent and not contradictory, then the following possibilities exist: *(a)* $I - K + J > I$ so that $J > K$; *(b)* $I - K + J = I$ so that $J = K$; *(c)* $I - K + J > I$ so that $J < K$. In case *(a)* there are more unknowns than equations and the system has many ranges of solutions. In case *(b)* the number of equations equals the number of unknowns and there is a unique solution to the system. In case *(c)* the number of equations is greater than the number of unknowns and the system does not have any solution unless the target variables are related by something akin to the Phillips curve. Since the relationship between the number of equations and the number of unknowns is given by the relationship between the number of target variables *(K)* and the number of policy instruments *(J)*, the relationship between the targets and the instruments determines whether the system has a unique solution. If the number of targets just equals the number of instruments there is a unique way in which all of the targets can be simultaneously achieved. If the number of targets is less than the number of instruments, there are a multitude of ways in which the targets can be achieved. If the number of targets is greater than the number of instruments, the targets can only simultaneously be achieved if they lie on the target possibility constraint. For a full analysis of these points, see Johansen, *Public Economics*, pp. 9ff.

REFERENCES

Branson, Willian H. *Macroeconomic Theory and Policy*. New York: Harper and Row, 1972.

Dernberg, Thomas F. and McDougall, Duncan M. *Macroeconomics*. New York: McGraw-Hill, 1976.

Johansen, L. *Public Economics*. rev. ed: Chicago: Rand McNally & Co., 1976.

Keiser, Norman F. *Macroeconomics*. New York: Random House, 1971.

Phillips, A. W. "The Relation between Unemployment and the Rate of Change of Money Wage Rates in the United Kingdom, 1861–1957," *Economica*, vol. 25 (November 1958), pp. 283–99.

Shapiro, Edward. *Macroeconomic Analysis*. 3d ed. New York: Harcourt Brace Jovanovich, 1974.

Theil, Henri. "Linear Decision Rules for Macrodynamic Policy Problems," in *Quantitative Planning of Economic Policy*, ed. Bert G. Hickman, Washington, D.C.: The Brookings Institution, 1965, pp. 18–42.

21

Economic Stabilization in the Postwar Period

Having discussed the theory of economic stabilization in the previous chapter, we now consider governmental attempts to stabilize the United States economy during the postwar period. The first part gives a brief description of the behavior of key macroeconomic variables during this period: income, employment, and prices. The second part then considers the record of the government with regard to stabilizing income and discusses the behavior of built-in stabilizers and the government's countercyclical discretionary behavior. The final section analyzes the specific problems of achieving price stability and full employment.

THE BEHAVIOR OF INCOME, EMPLOYMENT, AND PRICES

The Employment Act of 1946 made official a government policy of promoting "maximum employment, production, and purchasing power." This has generally been interpreted as the maintenance of full employment, price stability, and a desirable rate of economic growth. Since the United States controlled the bulk of the world's monetary reserves at that time, no mention was made of balance-of-payments considerations, which became increasingly important after the late 1950s. Moreover, the Employment Act was solely concerned with macroeconomic goals and hence ignored such things as the allocation of resources or the distribution of income. The extent to which the government has succeeded in achieving these macroeconomic goals will be the subject of the remainder of this chapter and the following one. In this chapter, we discuss the extent to which the government has enabled actual income to move along its potential growth path through both its fiscal structure and its discretionary policy, and we consider problems of achieving full employment and price stability simultaneously. Chapter 22 is concerned with problems of growth, or the way in which the government can influence the growth path of potential and actual output.

Some Definitional Problems

Before discussing the behavior of income, employment, and prices during the postwar period, it is useful to consider some problems associated with defining full employment, potential income, and price stability.

Measuring Unemployment. The notion of full employment is not as simple as it may sound. Ideally, it means that every person who is looking for a job is able to find it in a reasonably short time. This does not imply, however, that everyone is fully employed at any given time. Typically, a certain amount of frictional unemployment exists. This refers to the temporary unemployment of people who have either quit their jobs or have been laid off and are looking for work but have expectations of finding new work reasonably quickly. Thus at any given time, a certain percentage of the work force will be unemployed and between jobs. The amount of unemployment that can be attributed to frictional causes can range anywhere from 2 to 4 percent of the labor force and depends upon the mobility of the work force and the tightness of the labor market. The more geographically mobile the labor force and the tighter the labor market, the smaller should be the amount of frictional unemployment. In assessing the degree of unemployment, frictional unemployment should probably be discounted. Although the frictionally unemployed represent unemployed resources, they do not represent a cost to society in the same way that the hard-core unemployed do because their unemployment is relatively short-lived.

At the other extreme are the hard-core unemployed who can only find work in an extremely tight job market. This group consists of people who have relatively low skills, who generally belong to minority groups, who generally are not members of a union. They are typically the last to be hired and the first to be laid off. Members of this group may have been out of work for six months or more and have exhausted their unemployment benefits—if any were initially available to them. While these people form a relatively small percentage of the work force, they create a disproportionate share of the costs of unemployment. In human terms, these people pose a pressing social problem.

In between these two extremes lies the remainder of the unemployed: people who have been laid off or who have quit their jobs and are actively seeking work but have no expectations of finding immediate employment. Finally, there are people who have been unemployed so long that they have dropped out of the labor force, and there are people who have not entered the labor force because they despair of finding work. While these people do not show up on the unemployment rolls, they are, in some sense, as unemployed as the hard-core unemployed. Were the job situation to improve, they would probably enter the labor market in the hopes of finding work. Indicative of this is the observed phenomenon that as the labor market tightens, the labor force participation rate rises. This implies, however, that the actual unemployment figures probably underestimate the true unemployment figures since they do not take into account those who would enter the labor force if the prospects for finding a job were brighter.

Table 21–1 gives the unemployment rates for different groups for two years: the recession year of 1975 and the recent peak-employment year of 1969. As expected, the figures indicate that unemployment rises sharply in recession. But the unemployment rates of the disadvantaged groups (teen-agers, nonwhites, women) tend to rise relatively more than those at the top of the labor pool (white adult males, experienced workers, and the like). It is interesting to note, moreover, that, even during the marked expansion the economy experienced between 1965 and 1969, the unemployment rate failed to fall below 3.5 percent. This figure can probably be taken to represent the residual amount of frictional unemployment that will exist regardless of the conditions in the labor market.

What then can be taken as a measure of full employment? Clearly a zero unemployment rate will never be achieved, since some people will always be between jobs. It is important to make sure, however, that those people who have difficulty finding jobs are considered to be unemployed in terms of the "full-employment level" of the unemployment rate. As an operational concept, full employment has generally been taken to be that level of unemployment that is consistent

TABLE 21–1
Selected Unemployment Rates, 1969 and 1975.

	1969	1975
All workers	3.5	8.5
Both sexes, 16–19 years	12.2	19.9
Men, 20 years and over	2.1	6.7
Women, 20 years and over	3.7	8.0
White	3.1	7.8
Nonwhite	6.4	13.8
Experienced wage and salary workers	3.3	8.2
Blue-collar workers	3.9	11.7

Source: *Economic Report of the President*, 1976, Table B–24, p. 199.

with a tolerable increase in prices. During the postwar period in the United States, this has been thought of as a 4 percent rate of unemployment. In recent years, however, as the United States economy has been plagued by high levels of unemployment and a rapid increase in prices, the definition of full employment as a 4 percent unemployment rate has come under increasing question. If a general concensus develops that a 4 percent unemployment rate is incompatible with acceptable price increases, it is quite conceivable that the "full-employment" unemployment rate could be in excess of 4 percent. Thus, in periods of inflation with high unemployment rates, the definition of full employment becomes quite ambiguous.

Potential Output. Just as full employment is a relative concept that depends upon the rate of unemployment consistent with price stability, so is potential output, which is usually defined as that level of output that the economy can produce under conditions of noninflationary full employment. Although the economy would probably be the most productive in a situation of inflationary pressures where excess demand existed in many sectors, the goal of maximum output is constrained by society's desire for price stability. As such, it is a supply concept and serves as a standard by which actual income can be measured. When actual income lies below potential income, resources are not fully employed and a deflationary gap exists. When actual income lies above potential income, the unemployment rate must be below the "full-employment" unemployment rate. This implies that when actual output exceeds potential output, resources are used sufficiently intensively to create bottlenecks and scarcities that cause prices to rise. Consequently, actual output in excess of potential output will generally be accompanied by rising prices and inflationary pressures. [1]

Price Stability. Just as the notion of full employment and potential output are somewhat ambiguous, so is the notion of price stability. This arises from three sources: first, there are a number of different price indices that have different rates of change; second, a certain amount of price increase may be acceptable to society; and third, price changes may incorporate quality changes, making evaluation of real price changes difficult.

There are three main price indices that economists study: the wholesale price index (WPI), the consumer price index (CPI), and the implicit GNP deflator (GPI). The WPI measures changes in the price of goods and raw materials in wholesale transactions. The CPI measures changes in the price of a representative "market" of retail goods and services that are purchased by representative consumers. And the

---

[1] For a good discussion of the way in which potential income is measured, see A. M. Okun, "Potential GNP: Its Measurement and Significance," in *Readings in Money, National Income, and Stabilization Policy*, eds. W. L. Smith and R. L. Teigen, rev. ed. (Homewood, Ill.: Richard D. Irwin, 1970), pp. 313–23.

GPI measures a weighted average of the price change of the components of aggregate demand: consumption, investment, government expenditures, and exports less imports.

Since each of these covers a wide spectrum of goods and services, it is not clear which is the relevant price index. The WPI generally acts as a bellwether for other price changes, since the commodities and raw materials that enter the WPI enter into the CPI and the GPI at a later date. In terms of consumer welfare, the CPI is probably the most relevant, since it measures changes in the prices of the bundle of goods and services purchased by a "typical" consumer. The GPI has the widest coverage since it includes all components of aggregate demand. Thus, in terms of measuring the extent of overall price changes, it is probably the most relevant. For that reason, economists tend to concentrate upon the GPI. But it should be clear that the relevant price index to consider primarily depends upon what the economist is trying to measure.

Because price indices only take product changes into account with a considerable lag, if at all, there tends to be an upward bias to price indices. For example, when a new car is introduced, it typically incorporates new design, engineering, and safety devices; and it is more expensive. Since there is no real way to adjust the price rise for the automobile's new features, the price analyst simply records that the cost of the car has risen by so much percent. While some of the price increase is due to cost changes, some of it is also due to product changes.[2] What is needed is a measure of what last year's car would have cost this year if it had continued to be produced. Unfortunately, however, this figure is rarely available. While this difficulty is not as severe for machinery as for consumer goods, some increase in measured prices should be expected due to product changes.

Just as full employment is a relative term, price stability is a relative term and measures the rate of change in prices that is considered to be socially acceptable. Besides incorporating price increases due to product change, it also incorporates the position of the United States relative to its major trading partners. If their prices are increasing at a rate of 5 to 6 percent a year, a 2 to 3 percent rate of price increase in the United States is more acceptable than if their prices were constant. In fact, a rate of price increase of 2 to 3 percent per year is generally considered acceptable, given the recent rate of product improvement and the rate of inflation in other countries. While clearly not reflecting

---

[2] Many would argue that not all of these product changes are desirable. In the case of automobiles, for example, style changes or increases in horsepower may add to the vehicle's cost without increasing the efficiency or safety of automotive transport. For this point of view, see E. J. Mishan, *The Costs of Economic Growth* (London: Staples Press, 1967), and J. K. Galbraith, *The Affluent Society*, 2d ed. (Boston: Houghton Mifflin, 1969).

absolutely stable prices, this increase reflects a range of price increases that society appears to be willing to live with.

Income, Employment, and Prices in the Postwar Period

The postwar period has not been marked by periods of steady growth, but rather by periods of expansion or contraction in which the economy failed to reach or exceeded the level of potential output. The unemployment rate has generally moved with the size of the inflationary or deflationary gap that existed in the economy or the difference between potential and actual GNP. As the gap between potential and actual income widened, the rate of unemployment rose, while as the gap between potential and actual income narrowed, the rate of unemployment fell. The behavior of prices during the postwar period has been less predictable. Although prices generally rose as the gap between actual and potential output narrowed, they also rose at times as the gap between potential and actual output widened. Thus in the postwar period, output, employment, and prices have not moved in a steady or necessarily predictable fashion.

Figure 21–1 indicates that although the trend in income has been upward during the past twenty years, income has rarely moved along at its potential level. Instead, income has moved in a cyclical pattern. Recessions occurred in 1957–58, 1960–61, 1970–71, and 1974–75, where the level of actual income was substantially below that of potential income. Moreover, between 1956 and 1965, a substantial gap existed between actual and potential output. Periods of excessive expansion, where actual output has exceeded noninflationary full-employment output, have occurred in 1955–56, 1965–70, and 1972–1973. It is significant that the longest of these periods occurred during the Vietnam War. Thus in the past twenty years, periods of peacetime expansion have been relatively short-lived.[3]

Figure 21–2 shows the behavior of prices and Figure 21–3 shows the behavior of the unemployment rate during the post-World War II period. The unemployment rate has generally moved with contraction and expansion. During the recessions of 1948–49, 1953–54, 1955–58, 1960–61, 1970–71, and 1973–74, the unemployment rate rose, while during periods of expansion it fell. Thus during the recession years when the gap between actual and potential income was quite large, the unemployment rate usually exceeded 6 percent and reached 8.5

---

[3] For a good discussion of governmental policy in the postwar period, see G. L. Bach, *Making Monetary and Fiscal Policy* (Washington, D.C.: The Brookings Institution, 1971); Wilfred Lewis, *Federal Fiscal Policy in Postwar Recessions* (Washington, D.C.: The Brookings Institution, 1962); A. E. Holmans, *United States Fiscal Policy, 1945–1959* (London: Oxford University Press, 1961); G. R. Canterbury, *Economics on the New Frontier* (Belmont, Calif.: Wadsworth Publishing Company, 1968); A. M. Okun, *The Political Economy of Prosperity* (Washington, D.C.: The Brookings Institution, 1969).

FIGURE 21–1

The Trend of Output—Quarterly Totals at Annual Rates[1]
Seasonally Adjusted

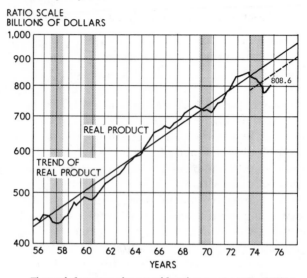

RATIO SCALE
BILLIONS OF DOLLARS

The trend of output was determined from the regression in Q = 5.7292 + .0092t, which was estimated from quarterly data for the 1/1947–11/1971 period. The coefficient (.0092) is the estimate of the trend rate of increase of output for the period. The line has been extrapolated beyond 11/1971.
[2] Gross National Product of 1953 prices.
[3] Dashed line is an estimate of the trend of real growth after the supply constraints. The new trend rate of growth of capacity is tentative at this time.
The shaded area in 1973–75 represents the recent economic contraction. The first section (1973–74) represents the period of constraints on aggregate supply, while the portion since late 1974 was induced by restriction of aggregate demand. The remaining shaded areas represent periods of business recessions as defined by the National Bureau of Economic Research.
Latest data plotted: third quarter.
Source: Bowsher, Norman L., "1975—Year of Economic Turnaround," Federal Reserve Bank of St. Louis, *Review*, vol. 58, no. 1 (January 1976), p. 3.

percent during the recession of 1974–75. Moreover, the unemployment rate is generally strongly correlated with the gap between actual and potential output. Thus, during the period between 1957 and 1964, when income fell far below its potential, the unemployment rate remained well above 5 percent. In contrast, during the boom years of 1953, 1956, and the period 1966–68 when actual income exceeded estimated potential income, the unemployment rate fell below 4 percent, reaching a recent minimum of 3.5 percent in 1969.

The behavior of prices during the postwar period has not been as cyclical as that of income or employment.[4] Figure 21–2 shows that, except for the recession years of 1948–49, prices have risen throughout the postwar period. Moreover, prices have also risen substantially

---

[4] In this discussion, we refer to the GNP deflator as representing price changes.

FIGURE 21–2

Change in Prices, 1948–1975

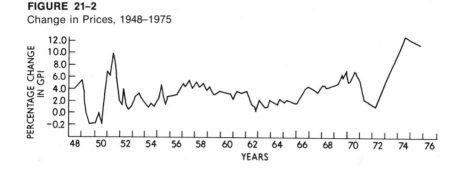

during the recession years of 1957–58, 1970–71, and 1974–75. While the reasons for this rise in prices in the face of slack demand will be discussed later in this chapter, Figure 21–3 clearly indicates that price stability has not occurred in the postwar period. If price stability is considered to be anything less than a 2 percent increase in prices, only the period between 1958 and 1965 experienced price stability.

Although the government has not been successful in achieving full stability of income, employment, or prices during the postwar period, its actions have for the most part been stabilizing. Its efforts to achieve stability and some of the reasons why it has not been more successful will be the subject of the remainder of this chapter.

Stabilizing Income in the Postwar Period

When the economy experiences an excessive contraction or expansion, there are certain factors that offset part of the change in income. These are called automatic stabilizers, indicating that they are an inherent part of the tax or expenditure structure. Since, however, automatic stabilizers cannot offset the entire change in economic activity, certain discretionary actions may be needed to maintain noninflationary full employment. This section first considers the efficiency of

FIGURE 21–3

Unemployment Rate, 1948–1971

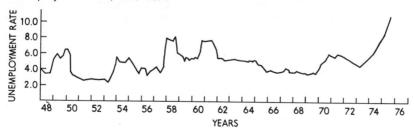

built-in stabilizers in mitigating the impact of an exogenous shock upon income and then considers the behavior of the policy-maker with respect to discretionary action. Finally, it discusses the merits of rules versus discretionary action.

Built-In Flexibility

The discussion on the impact of taxes upon income in the context of the simple models considered in the previous chapter indicated that income changes would be greater in the absence of taxes than they actually are in a world with taxes. Given a shock to the system, such as an unexplained reduction in investment, income will fall by less in a world with taxes than in a world without them. By reducing the effective *mpc* out of GNP, personal or corporate taxes increase the built-in stability of the economy.

A simple measure of built-in flexibility provided by the fiscal structure can be given by the following expression:

$$F = 1 - \frac{\Delta Y_a}{\Delta Y} \tag{21-1}$$

where ΔY_a = the actual change in income resulting from a change in government expenditures or investment and ΔY = the change in income that would have resulted from a change in government expenditures or investment in a world without taxes.

Of course, the change in income depends crucially upon the model used to depict the economy. In the real world there are many different kinds of taxes (personal, corporate, excise, among others) whose revenues react differently to changes in income levels. Moreover, there is a wide range of government transfer payments, such as social security benefits, unemployment insurance, and the like, that also react to changes in the level of income. In measuring the built-in flexibility of the United States economy, all of these taxes and transfer payments should be taken into account.

Built-In Flexibility in a Simplified World. The nature of the problem and the kind of measurements involved can be seen in the following simplified model. Let the no-tax world be given by

$$Y = C + I + G \tag{21-2}$$

$$C = cY \tag{21-3}$$

$$I = \bar{I} \tag{21-4}$$

$$G = \bar{G} \tag{21-5}$$

thus

$$Y = \frac{1}{1 - c} (\bar{I} + \bar{G}) \tag{21-6}$$

and

$$\Delta Y = \frac{1}{1 - c} \Delta A \tag{21-7}$$

where ΔA represents the change in autonomous expenditures, investment (I) or government (G).

Let us assume that the government imposes personal taxes and that consumption is a function of disposable income. Thus

$$Y_a = C + I + G \tag{21-8}$$

$$C = cY_D \tag{21-9}$$

$$Y_D = Y - T \tag{21-10}$$

$$T = tY \tag{21-11}$$

$$I = \bar{I} \tag{21-12}$$

$$G = \bar{G} \tag{21-13}$$

Actual income Y_a can be given by

$$Y_a = \frac{1}{1 - c(1 - t)} (\bar{I} + \bar{G}) \tag{21-14}$$

and

$$\Delta Y_a = \frac{1}{1 - c(1 - t)} \Delta A \tag{21-15}$$

The measure of built-in flexibility is given by the proportion by which income changes are damped as a result of the tax structure, i.e.,

$$F = 1 - \frac{\Delta Y_a}{\Delta Y}.$$

Making the appropriate substitutions yields

$$F = \frac{ct}{1 - c(1 - t)}. \tag{21-16}$$

Suppose that the *mpc* out of disposable income equals 0.75 and that the ratio of taxes to income (t) is 0.25. Then $F = 0.43$. In this simplified world, over 40 percent of potential changes in income are dampened by the tax structure.[5]

---

[5] For a somewhat more elaborate measure of built-in flexibility, see R. A. Musgrave, *The Theory of Public Finance* (New York: McGraw-Hill, 1959), pp. 508–10.

Measures of Built-In Flexibility in the United States. As we indicated earlier, the actual fiscal structure of the United States is considerably more complicated than that indicated in this simplified model of the economy. The government incorporates a wide range of taxes and expenditures that serve to offset potential changes in income. The most significant of these are the personal income tax, social security contributions, and corporate tax payments. Most empirical studies of the effectiveness of built-in stabilizers estimate that approximately 50 percent of a downswing and approximately 35 percent of an upswing can be offset by the existing tax and expenditure structure.[6] Thus, the figure of 40 percent derived by the simple model given above does not appear to be a bad approximation of reality.

Nevertheless, if cycles are to be offset completely, so that income will move along its growth path, discretionary action is needed. The past record with regard to discretionary action is somewhat contradictory, however. In some instances, governmental action was too little or too late and actually proved destabilizing, while in others, it was stabilizing more by accident than design.

Discretionary Action

In assessing the impact of the government on economic stability, it is useful to consider two types of budgetary changes: first, those changes in taxes or expenditures that were instituted in direct response to changing economic considerations; and, second, the totality of nonautomatic tax or expenditure changes. The two are rarely equivalent since expenditure and tax schedules not only change in response to economic considerations, but also in response to political or defense considerations. While discretionary action of the former type indicates how the government reacts to purely economic forces, discretionary action of the latter type indicates the total impact of governmental activity upon the economy; and for the overall evaluation of economic policy this measure is probably the more relevant.

The Overall Impact of Discretionary Action. The surplus or deficit of the so-called full-employment budget is a useful device to measure the overall impact of the fiscal structure on economic activity. This is the surplus or deficit that would be generated by the fiscal structure if the economy were operating at its potential or full-employment level of income. This concept is illustrated in Figure 21–4 which shows the relationship between two budgets and the level of economic activity. Since Budget *A* achieves a higher level of surplus for any given level

---

[6] See, for example, W. Lewis, *Federal Fiscal Policy in Postwar Recessions*, (Washington, D.C.: The Brookings Institution, 1962), chap. 3; and Peter Eilbott, "The Effectiveness of Automatic Stabilizers," *American Economic Review*, vol. 56 (June 1966) pp. 450–65.

FIGURE 21–4
Relationship between Budgets and Level of Economic Activity

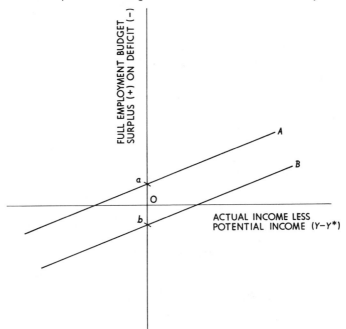

of actual income relative to potential income (i.e., $Y - Y^*$), it is more restrictive than Budget *B*. When actual income equals potential income, Budget *A* is in surplus while Budget *B* is in deficit. Thus Budget *B* is basically expansionary, while Budget *A* is basically restrictive.

Changes in the full-employment budget indicate basic changes in overall fiscal policy. For a given tax structure and level of expenditures, the surplus or deficit of the full-employment budget should remain constant (e.g., at points *a* and *b* in Figure 21–4). Changes in the surplus or deficit of the full-employment budget occur when the government changes its overall budgetary policy and moves, for example, from a restrictive budget indicated by a full-employment budget surplus of *Oa* to an expansionary budget, indicated by a full-employment budget deficit of *Ob*.

Thus over the business cycle, the behavior of the surplus or deficit of the full-employment budget gives some indication of the responsiveness of the federal government to changing economic conditions. During periods of high employment when actual GNP is close to potential GNP, the full-employment budget should probably be in surplus, while during periods of contraction or slack when actual GNP is below potential GNP, the full-employment budget should probably be in

FIGURE 21–5
Surplus or Deficit of Full-Employment Budget, 1948–1971

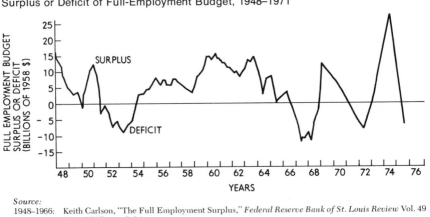

Source:
1948–1966:   Keith Carlson, "The Full Employment Surplus," *Federal Reserve Bank of St. Louis Review* Vol. 49
             (June 1967), pp. 6–14.
1967–1968:   A. Okun and N. Teeters, "The Full Employment Surplus Revisited," *Brookings Papers* (1970–71),
             pp. 104–5.
1970–1971:   *Economic Report of The President, 1971*, p. 24.
1969–1975:   *Economic Report of the President, 1976*, Table 8, p. 55.

deficit. In any event, the behavior of the surplus or deficit of the full-employment budget should probably move with the business cycle, with its surplus falling as employment or income falls and rising as employment or income rises. Figure 21–5 shows that during the postwar recessions, the surplus or deficit of the full-employment budget generally followed this behavior.

In the recession of 1948–49, the surplus or deficit of the full-employment budget followed the business cycle fairly closely. Throughout this period, however, it was generally restrictive, with its surplus ranging from values of $5 to $15 billion. Therefore, even though the full-employment surplus fell throughout the recession, the overall impact of the budget was quite deflationary. Governmental action cannot be said to have contributed substantially to the recovery that took place.

In contrast, the behavior of the full-employment budget indicates that governmental action was stabilizing during the 1953–1954 recession. During the period when the economy was contracting, the full-employment budget was in deficit, while as the economy began to expand, the full-employment budget was in surplus. Thus it appears that the government did respond to changing economic conditions in such a way as to help stabilize the economy, although it appeared to do so more by accident than by design, as we will discuss below.

During the recessions of 1957–58 and 1960–61, the full-employment budget was always in surplus, although the surplus did fall during the recessions and thus moved in a countercyclical way. Nevertheless, the fiscal structure imposed a net drag while the economy was experiencing slack and recovery.

During the recent recessions of 1970–71 and 1974–75, the behavior of the full-employment surplus has been somewhat perverse. Thus, even though income began to rise in 1971, the full-employment surplus fell, reaching a deficit of $8.5 billion in 1972. At that time, fiscal policy became very restrictive, and the full-employment budget reached a surplus of $7.5 billion and $25.4 billion in 1973 and 1974. Since 1974 marked the postwar period's most severe recession, it seems clear that such restrictive policy was highly destabilizing. It is interesting to note that fiscal policy then became quite expansive in 1975, and the full-employment budget fell to a deficit of $7.5 billion. Thus during the 1970s, the behavior of the full-employment surplus indicates that discretionary fiscal policy has tended to follow the level of economic activity and thus be destabilizing rather than stabilizing.

More generally, although the behavior of the full-employment budget indicates that the government usually reacts to changing economic conditions, the timing of the changes in the full-employment budget have tended to be destabilizing rather than stabilizing. Of course, the full-employment budget cannot separate the impact of expenditure and tax changes induced by purely economic considerations, such as changing income or employment levels, and the impact of tax or expenditure changes induced by other factors, such as increased defense pressures from abroad. It is, nevertheless, useful in assessing the overall impact of budgetary policy upon the economy; and the evidence indicates that the government's actions have often been perverse with respect to the economic stability of the economy.

Countercyclical Discretionary Action. To assess the behavior of the government's response to changing economic conditions alone, it is necessary to consider the purely discretionary changes in taxes or expenditures that were made in response to those conditions. It is important to realize, however, that purely discretionary action of this nature is hampered by lags of recognition, action, and implementation. Forecasts of economic activity are typically sufficiently inaccurate that policy-makers are unwilling to make budgetary changes on the basis of prediction alone. But, if they wait until changing economic conditions have become established, several months or quarters have typically elapsed since the change in economic activity took place. At least one and possibly two quarters must elapse after a downturn has occurred before economists can determine that it has in fact taken place. Similar problems present themselves with an economic expansion. Thus the lags of recognition are such that at least one and possibly two or three quarters have elapsed after a turning point in the economy before policy-makers can agree that it has occurred. Only then can they recommend that the government take action.

The lags of action, however, are generally as long as the lags of recognition. Some expenditures or tax changes can be made by administrative fiat: Expenditures can be speeded up, corporate tax payment periods can be changed, depreciation guidelines can be altered, mortgage rates on federally backed loans can be changed, and so on. But the scope for purely administrative action is limited. Most discretionary action, whether increases in expenditures via public works or transfer payments, such as social security or unemployment compensation, or changes in personal or corporate tax rates must be approved by Congress. Thus the lags of action usually extend for one or two quarters. They can often take considerably longer as was the case of the tax cut of 1964 or the income tax surcharge of 1968. Moreover, once a countercyclical program has been passed, some time must usually elapse before it affects the income stream. These lags of implementation are usually a quarter at the minimum.

The lags of recognition, action, and implementation are such that usually at least a year must elapse between the turning point in the economy and the time when discretionary governmental action affects the economy. Only in the recession of 1960–61 did some discretionary action take place before income had actually started to rise. Even in this case, however, the bulk of the countercyclical action took place when income was actually rising. Thus with respect to timing, antirecession discretionary action has tended to be procyclical rather than countercyclical.[7]

The timing of these antirecession actions has not been terribly important, however, because the magnitude of these actions has been quite limited. Antirecession discretionary actions have been confined to the following: During the 1953–54 recession, defense expenditures and public works projects; during the 1957–58 recession, highway expenditures, public works speedups; during the 1960–61 recession, unemployment compensation, veterans' dividends, speedup of defense procurements and other construction, and increased farm price supports. The overall magnitude of these actions has generally been less than $2 billion on an annual basis. Thus the behavior of discretionary actions during the postwar recessions has been limited and somewhat perverse.

Rules versus Discretion

In view of the rather spotty record of discretionary fiscal policy and the inability of econometric models to forecast the behavior of economic activity accurately, it seems reasonable to ask whether discre-

---

[7] For a good formal presentation of the importance of timing fiscal changes, see W. J. Baumol, *Economic Dynamics*, 3d ed. (New York: Macmillan Company, 1970), pp. 437 ff.

tionary action is desirable at all.[8] Should the fiscal system be structured in such a way that discretionary action is not used at all, but instead that stabilization measures are built into the system? This could take several forms: automatic stabilizers or rules or guidelines that the fiscal authorities should follow.

While automatic stabilizers can help to offset swings in income, they are inadequate to offset all income changes. Moreover, they work in both directions; the more effective automatic stabilizers are in offsetting unwanted rises and declines in income, the more effective they are in offsetting desired upward and downward movements. Thus totally effective automatic stabilizers would cause income to remain at a stable, stagnant equilibrium.

This raises the question of the desirability of introducing certain fiscal rules or guidelines for the government to follow. Over the years, several possibilities have been suggested.

The Annually Balanced Budget. This is the policy prescription of fiscal conservatives who regard deficits per se as the sign of irresponsible fiscal management. But we have seen in this and the previous chapters that economic forces make an annually balanced budget incompatible with the maintenance of full employment. If aggregate demand is insufficient to maintain full employment without deficit spending, the responsible action of government is to increase expenditures relative to taxes and to make its budgetary changes in deficit. Although the balanced-budget theorem discussed in Chapter 20 indicates that the government could in principle achieve any desired increase in aggregate demand while maintaining a balanced budget, often the size of the deflationary gap is such that the government sector would have to expand considerably to achieve full employment. Since expenditures and tax changes of this magnitude would create expenditure levels that are probably not politically tenable, the need for unbalanced budgets must be recognized. While the fiscal conservatives dislike deficits, it is likely that they dislike an increase in the size of government expenditures even more.

The Cyclically Balanced Budget. One rule that has received considerable attention over the years is the notion that, while the budget need not be balanced for any one year, the budget should be balanced over the business cycle. Presumably the budget would be in deficit during periods of recession and in surplus during period of expansion. In the downswing the government would stimulate the economy while during the upswing the government would act as a brake. In

---

[8] For a strong argument in favor of this view, see M. Friedman, *A Program for Monetary Stability* (New York: Fordham University Press, 1959); and M. Friedman, "The Supply of Money and Changes in Prices and Output," in *The Relationship of Prices to Economic Stability and Growth*, Joint Economic Committee (Washington, D.C., 1958), pp. 241–56.

principle this sounds reasonable, but its implementation poses certain problems. Basically there is no reason why the magnitude of the deficits should be offset by that of the surpluses. If the economic contraction were particularly severe, substantial deficits would probably be needed to ensure the recovery. Unless the ensuing recovery were particularly strong, however, governmental efforts to restore the cyclical budget balance by running substantial surpluses could well kill off the recovery and be self-defeating. Whether the budget should be balanced in any one year depends upon the economic conditions existing in that year and cannot be determined by arbitrary budgetary rules.

A Full-Employment Budget Surplus of Zero. Under this rule the government would attempt to have an annually balanced full-employment budget or a full-employment surplus of zero. This implies that if the economy were operating at its potential, the net impact of the government would be neutral, neither expansionary nor restrictive. While this approach appears attractive, it too has certain rigidities. The composition of private aggregate demand may be such that the level of potential GNP can only be maintained if the full-employment budget is either in surplus or deficit. In the first case, aggregate private demand would be chronically high, and restrictive governmental action would be needed to ensure that inflationary pressures are avoided. In the second case, aggregate private demand would be chronically low, and expansionary government action would be needed to ensure that a chronic slack does not develop in the economy. Again, it is important that governmental policy be sufficiently flexible to meet the demands of the changing economic situation.

Need for Flexible Discretionary Action. The economy is never in a stationary equilibrium, but is constantly being subjected to various shocks, whether arising from changing consumer tastes, changing investment demand, changing foreign demand, or changing government expenditures. Appropriate fiscal action requires a constant assessment of the state of the economy and changing action to meet the existing situation. This is not to say, however, that the economy should be subjected to constant "fine tuning" or changes in taxes and expenditures to meet small changes in projected aggregate demand. As we discussed previously, the policy-maker cannot predict the behavior of economic variables with sufficient accuracy to permit such fine tuning. It is important, nevertheless, to maintain as many policy options as possible; and rules must necessarily eliminate a degree of freedom from the policy-maker. What is needed are changes to expand his or her freedom of action rather than restrict it. The answer to the problems of uncertainty facing the policy-maker is not to adopt inflexible rules, but to adopt stabilization policies on the basis of the available evidence. Policies based on an understanding of the economic system should prove to be more effective in stabilizing the economy than those based on rules of questionable empirical validity.

In this connection, it has often been suggested that the president be granted discretionary action to increase or decrease personal income tax rates subject to a congressional veto.[9] This change would be highly desirable. The lags of recognition and action are currently sufficiently long that tax changes are effectively prohibited as countercyclical measures. This change would reduce the lags to those of recognition. Thus as soon as the president was aware of a substantive change in economic conditions, he could order a tax change. Because of the withholding system, changes in tax rates could be felt almost immediately and affect spending patterns accordingly. This would be a highly desirable change in the fiscal structure and increase its flexibility considerably.

PRICE STABILITY AND FULL EMPLOYMENT

While the government typically has many macro policy goals that it attempts to achieve, it appears to give the most weight to the maintenance of full employment and of price stability. The maintenance of full employment is important because it is a prerequisite for the efficient utilization of resources. If resources are unemployed—whether they be men or machines—society cannot achieve its potential output and will produce inside of the production possibility frontier. With appropriate governmental policies, more of some commodities could be produced without reducing the output of others. Moreover, the output lost through unemployment is lost forever. While society can achieve full employment at some later date, it can never replace the output that could have been produced during the period of slack. Thus unemployment imposes a deadweight loss upon society in terms of output and income that the society could have had if resources had been fully utilized.

The maintenance of price stability is also thought to be important. First, inflation of any significant magnitude is considered to be undesirable per se. Although a moderate amount of inflation is generally acceptable, price increases in excess of 2 to 3 percent per year arouse specters of runaway inflation. Visions of the Weimar Republic in Germany are conjured up where people literally had to take bushels of money to market with them. A hyperinflation of that order of magnitude clearly threatens the basic stability of the economy and the

---

[9] See, for example, Commission on Money and Credit, *Money and Credit: Their Influence on Jobs, Prices and Growth* (Englewood Cliffs, N.J.: Prentice-Hall, 1961); G. L. Bach, *Making Monetary and Fiscal Policy* (Washington, D.C.: The Brookings Institution, 1971).

structure of society. It is perhaps the fear that a little inflation will lead to a hyperinflation that gives inflation its special role as a target variable. Second, even a moderate amount of inflation can impose considerable costs on people with fixed incomes as their real income falls. Since these people are typically the elderly or the nonworking poor, they are generally the least able to cope with a reduced standard of living. Just as unemployment tends to impose the most hardship on the poor and the unskilled, so does inflation. Third, inflation tends to increase labor strife as workers try to maintain their absolute and relative levels of income. The losses in output and income caused by strikes impose just as much of a dead weight loss upon society as those created by unemployment. Fourth, there is some evidence that during inflationary periods, investment is channeled into speculative real estate or financial ventures of dubious real value at the expense of productive investments in men and machines. Finally, price stability has come to receiver high priority as a goal during the last 10 or 15 years with the development of the chronic balance-of-payments problem facing the United States. If U.S. prices rise relative to those in other countries. U.S. goods will become more expensive and their competitive position will deteriorate. Thus, price stability is important for the maintenance of a favorable balance-of-payments position of the U.S. economy at given exchange rates. Whether the fear of hyperinflation, the allocational and human costs of inflation, or the balance of payments position of the U.S. economy is more important in determining the desirability of maintaining price stability is difficult to say. Their combined effect, however, makes the maintenance of price stability a high-priority governmental goal.

The Causes of Inflation

The causes of unemployment are usually straightforward: a lack of aggregate demand which makes the value of goods and services purchased less than the value that the economy is capable of producing. While some structural unemployment probably exists in the sense that some industries or skills are the victims of changes in tastes or techniques that make them obsolete, the bulk of unemployment can be cured by increasing aggregate demand. Thus the cure of unemployment is usually quite straightforward: undertake government policies to increase aggregate demand.[10]

Unfortunately, the causes and cures of inflation are much less straightforward. This arises because there are several sources and kinds of inflation that tend to interact once an inflation has begun.

---

[10] For a good discussion of whether unemployment is caused by structural factors or a lack of aggregate demand, see R. Solow, *The Nature and Sources of Unemployment in the United States* (Stockholm: Almquist and Wicksell, 1964).

Demand Pull. Perhaps the most familiar and easiest form of inflation to understand is the so-called demand pull inflation. This arises from an inflationary gap, as previously explained, where aggregate demand is greater than the available goods and services in the economy at full employment. As such, it is analogous to a disequilibrium condition in a given market where an excess demand occurs. Suppose. for example, that a given market were in equilibrium at a given price. If the demand curve shifts out, an excess demand for the product will exist at the old price. Prices must rise for equilibrium to be restored, unless supply is perfectly elastic.

When aggregate demand exceeds aggregate supply, the same phenomenon that occurs in a single market is repeated throughout the economy. The purchasing power in the hands of business firms making investments, consumers buying goods and services, and the government is greater than the value of goods and services capable of being produced at existing prices. Aggregate demand exceeds potential output. Since excess demand would develop in the various markets at existing price levels, prices must rise to restore equilibrium.

When society is faced with a general demand pull inflation, the government attempts to restore the equilibrium between aggregate demand and aggregate supply. Insofar as productive capacity cannot meet total aggregate demand, one cure for the inflation is to increase capacity so that aggregate supply rises to meet aggregate demand. But increasing investment is hardly a short-term cure for inflation, since it contributes to aggregate demand until the new capacity becomes operational. Thus in the short run, equilibrium can best be restored by fiscal and monetary policies that curb aggregate demand: consumption, investment, or government expenditures.

Reducing consumption by temporary increases in personal taxes has proven to be somewhat difficult. Because consumers appear to adjust their expenditures in terms of what they consider to be their permanent or lifetime incomes, they may not react to temporary tax increases. Thus, they may continue their expenditures in the face of tax increases, vitiating the effectiveness of these increases as anti-inflation devices. This apparently occurred in response to the anti-inflationary tax surcharge of 1968.

Just as the impact of a dollar of increased personal tax revenues may have a limited impact in curtailing inflation, the impact of a dollar of increased corporate tax revenues may be limited. First, insofar as the corporate tax is shifted, increases in taxes will not have a substantive impact on profits and cash flow and, therefore, will not lead to a reduction in investment. Moreover, the price rises caused by the shifting of the profits tax will contribute to inflationary pressures. While consumers might curtail consumption of commodities produced in the corporate sector in favor of those produced in the noncorporate sector, it is unlikely that there will be much net reduction in consumption as a result of the shifting of the profits tax.

There is some evidence that aggressive use of monetary policy can curtail investment. The impact of monetary policy is very selective, however, and primarily falls upon residential construction. Since the housing stock is generally thought to be inadequate, one can certainly question the desirability of using monetary policy to curtail investment. More generally, insofar as productive capacity cannot meet total aggregate demand, curtailing investment and the growth of capacity may be self-defeating in terms of establishing a long-run equilibrium.

Since efforts to curtail consumption by tax increases may not be successful and since curtailing investment may be counterproductive, the most effective means of reducing aggregate demand probably lies in reducing government expenditures.

But reducing inflation is rarely the only goal facing the policy-maker. Distributional and allocational considerations are usually intertwined with those of reducing inflation. Consequently, large-scale reductions in government expenditures may be neither politically nor socially desirable. In the mid-1960s anti-inflationary reductions in government expenditures were concentrated on the War on Poverty. In view of the extent of poverty that still exists in the United States, one can certainly question if this reflected the proper priorities. But given the structure of government programs there is usually little leeway for cuts except in relatively new or controversial programs.

Obviously there is no clear-cut answer as to which component of aggregate demand should be reduced in response to a demand pull inflation. The policies adopted usually reflect a combination of what is politically, socially, and economically feasible and desirable. In some instances investment may be curtailed; in others, consumption or government expenditure may be curtailed. The proper policy thus in large part reflects society's view toward the continuing inflation and its view toward the policies adopted to curtail it.

Sectoral Inflation. When excess aggregate demand exists throughout the economy, the traditional fiscal and monetary measures used for fighting inflation are useful. But inflation is often caused by a sectoral disequilibrium rather than by a general excess demand. For example, the demand for services usually rises more rapidly than income, while the change in productivity in the service industries is generally quite low compared to that in manufacturing. Consequently, the demand for services tends to rise relative to its supply and prices will tend to rise in the service sector. Similarly, bad crops in certain key agricultural commodities, like wheat or corn, can cause prices for a whole host of agricultural commodities to rise. Thus, price indices can rise because large parts of their components rise, rather than because of a general situation where aggregate demand exceeds aggregate supply.

In this situation efforts to counter inflationary pressure by traditional measures can cause problems. The proper cure is to increase supply or to curtail demand in those sectors where demand exceeds supply rather than to curtail demand throughout the economy. But policy tools are usually not sufficiently selective to permit either the expansion of supply or the reduction in demand in the affected sectors. Thus the government is faced with the unpleasant task of having to curtail aggregate demand to restore balance in certain key sectors.

Unfortunately, when the government curtails aggregate demand, expenditures for all consumption goods and services are cut back rather than those in the affected industries alone. If, for example, excess demand exists in the service industries, a general tax increase will reduce the demand for automobiles as well as for services. Consequently, to restore an equilibrium in one market, the government may be forced to create excess supply and unemployment in another.

The overall unemployment rate will, therefore, rise even while prices may still be rising. If labor were perfectly mobile between industries and between sectors, the sectoral disequilibrium would probably only be temporary. Labor laid off in the automobile industry would move into one of the service industries, and the supply in the former industry would contract while that in the latter would expand. But the skills and wage structure that are appropriate to an industry like automobile manufacturing may not be compatible with the service industries. If labor is not readily transferable between industries it is entirely possible to have prices rising in one sector and severe unemployment in another. While this kind of sectoral inflation can eventually be cured if aggregate demand is sufficiently curtailed, it may do so at the cost of generating considerable unemployment in the noninflationary sectors of the economy.

Cost Push and Incomes Inflation. After an economy has experienced a period of demand pull inflation and pressures from excess demand have abated, it may find that it still experiences inflation caused by pressures on costs. These can arise from firms' and workers' efforts to restore their absolute or relative income shares. Inflation arising from efforts to restore absolute income levels can be referred to as cost push inflation; inflation arising from efforts to restore relative income levels can be referred to as incomes inflation.

In both instances, inflationary pressures primarily arise from imperfections in the labor and product markets. As prices rise, firms may find that the prices of their materials rise faster than the prices of their output. Consequently, to maintain their profit levels, firms may introduce further price increases, even in the face of falling demand for their products. Similarly, as workers find their real incomes falling as prices increase faster than wages, they may demand large wage increases to restore their real income levels. Even after the initial excess in aggregate demand has abated, prices can continue to rise as firms attempt to restore their profit margins and workers attempt to restore their real income levels. This inflation can only exist in imperfectly competitive product and labor markets. If firms were perfectly competitive, they would not be able to raise prices in the face of falling demand; similarly if labor unions had no monopoly power, they would not be able to increase wages in the face of rising unemployment. But to the extent that many firms and labor unions have some monopoly power, they can increase their prices and wages even if the demand for their goods and services is falling.

A related source of inflation also arises from noncompetitive market structures and is due to the desires of firms and labor unions to restore their relative income shares. During periods of demand pull inflation, profits generally rise faster than wages. Even if real wages do not fall, they may fall relative to profits. In this situation, labor unions may attempt to restore the relative share of labor income through wage increases. But firms may attempt to maintain their new relative profit share and raise prices to offset the reduction in profits arising from the wage increases. An interaction between firms and unions may be created in which each attempts to raise its income share relative to the other. As long as this process continues, wages and prices will tend to rise, even if aggregate demand is falling and unemployment is rising. Thus, long after the pressures that created demand pull inflation have abated, prices can continue to rise through the efforts of unions and firms to maintain what they consider to be their proper income share.

The problem may become exacerbated by a "demonstration effect" with regard to unions. Suppose, for example, industry A makes a large wage settlement that is consistent with productivity gains and is, therefore, not inflationary. The union in industry B may then demand similar wage increases even though productivity gains in industry B may be substantially less than those in industry A. The result will be pressure on wages, profits, and prices in industry B that might not have existed if unions had not been sensitive to the magnitude of their settlements relative to those of other unions.

It should be stressed that cost push or incomes inflation can only exist in a situation of administered prices in the product and labor markets. If all markets were perfectly competitive, price would equal marginal cost for all products and wages would be determined by labor's marginal product. Prices and wages would be determined by forces outside of the control of a given firm or a given union. But this situation does not correspond to a large part of American industry. A union with considerable monopoly power and a firm with considerable monopoly power essentially form a bilateral monopoly that can set wages and prices in such a way as to maximize their joint welfare. In this way, prices can continue to rise in the face of considerable excess capacity and unemployment throughout the economy.

When cost push or incomes inflation has become established, the traditional cure of inflation by reducing aggregate demand may be ineffective; alternatively stated, the degree of unemployment and excess capacity that is required to restore price equilibrium in the product and labor markets may be politically or socially unacceptable. In this case, other alternatives are needed. From 1962 to 1964, the government introduced guidelines or "jawboning" techniques to maintain prices in the noncompetitive industries. These guidelines stated that wages should not rise by more than demonstrable productivity gains. If the profit share remained constant, this would be adequate to ensure that prices remained stable. Just how effective the guidelines were in controlling inflation is a debatable point; but a large number of economists feel that the rate of price increase was less than it would have been in the absence of the guidelines.

The government undertook a program of wage-price controls in the early 1970s, when the economy was confronted by rising unemployment rates and high rates of inflation. In the summer of 1971, the government imposed a brief wage-price freeze, followed by fairly rigid guidelines concerning wage and price increases. When the rate of change of prices began to decline in late 1972 however, the controls were relaxed, and the economy then experienced its most severe period of price inflation in the postwar period. Unfortunately, however, there remains considerable controversy over the impact of the wage-price controls upon inflation during this period. It is likely that the general decline in aggregate demand in 1971 contributed to a reduction in inflationary expectations and thus caused the rate of price level increase to decline in 1972. Similarly, it is likely that the Arab oil embargo and the worldwide grain shortage had a major impact upon prices in late 1973 and 1974, when the rate of inflation began to accelerate. Thus, whether the wage-price controls of 1971–72 had a major impact upon the behavior of prices is an unresolved issue. Some economists feel that if the wage-price controls had continued in existence during 1973–75, the economy would have experienced a somewhat lower rate of price inflation. Other economists feel, however, that the distortions caused by controls would have exacerbated the existing inflationary pressures.

The Phillips Curve

In the previous chapter, we described a simplified model of the economy that postulated the existence of a trade-off between the rate of change of prices and the unemployment rate. In this section, we have discussed why sectoral inflation, cost push, or income inflation could lead to rising prices with high unemployment rates. Moreover, the recent experience of the United States economy gives ample proof that such trade-offs do exist in the United States. The policy options facing the government in the face of the unemployment-inflation trade-off are the subject of the remainder of this chapter.

The Shape and Behavior of the Phillips Curve.   As previously noted, the curve depicting the relationship between wage changes, price changes, and the unemployment rate is called the Phillips curve, which takes the general shape shown in Figure 21–6. The percentage

FIGURE 21–6
Phillips Curve for the United States

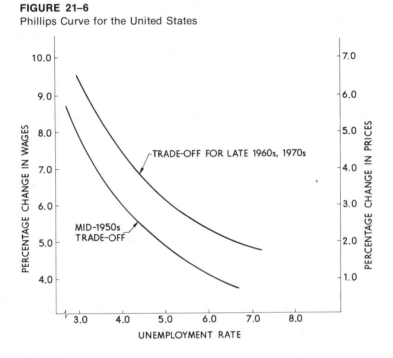

change in wages is measured on the left-hand vertical axis, and the percentage change in prices is shown on the right-hand vertical axis. The unemployment rate is plotted on the horizontal axis. If the profit share is constant, any increase in wages in excess of productivity changes, which are assumed to be 3 percent in the figure, must be translated into price increases.

The previous chapter described a simple macroeconomic model of the economy that was consistent with the observed shape of the Phillips curve. Price changes were related to the gap between actual and potential income as a percentage of actual income and government expenditures were the only policy tool available to the government. In the context of this simple model, the Phillips curve was derived as a result of the structure of the economy and the limited policy tools.

While enlightening, this analysis did not shed any real insight into the underlying behavioral relationships that would relate price changes and unemployment rates in such a way that would explain the observed behavior of the Phillips curve. While there is no entirely satisfactory theory to explain why price changes are related to the level of unemployment, several hypotheses are possible.

One explanation arises from the sectoral theory of inflation. If some industries have more excess demand than others and if an anti-inflation policy affects all sectors more or less equally, efforts to control inflation must lead to unemployment. Another explanation arises from the existence of noncompetitive pricing elements in the economy. If firms and unions attempt to maintain their absolute or relative levels of profits and incomes, they will tend to interact to cause price increases greater than those caused by excess demand alone. As prices begin to rise above some acceptable level, labor and firms in noncompetitive industries will tend to interact to create an accelerating rate of inflation. In this situation, unemployment may have to reach very high levels to enable price stability to be maintained. Both of these explanations are sufficient to explain the nonlinearities observed in the Phillip's curve. As unemployment falls, prices will rise at increasing rates; to achieve price stability, unemployment must rise more than proportionately.

The Phillips Curve and Economic Policy. The economic policy of the 1960s and 1970s has been marked by efforts to alter the behavior of the economy with respect to the Phillips curve. During the early 1960s when unemployment was excessive, the government attempted to reduce the unemployment rate without raising prices. During the latter part of the 1960s and 1970s when price increases were excessive, the government attempted to reduce the rate of price increase without reducing unemployment. Unfortunately, these efforts were only partially successful.

The economy of the early 1960s was characterized by a chronic gap between actual and potential output, an unemployment rate in excess of 5 percent, essentially stable prices, and a substantial surplus in the full employment budget. In view of the existing excess capacity and stable prices, the government felt that expansionary policies would be noninflationary. Consequently, the government instituted two programs to counteract the fiscal drag imposed by the tax structure and to stimulate income and employment.

First was the investment tax credit of 1962, whose impact will be discussed in Chapter 22. The goal of this was twofold: in the short run, to increase investment and, therefore, to stimulate income and employment; in the longer run, to increase the rate of growth of the economy. While the evidence is somewhat contradictory, on balance, it appears that the tax credit had a more than marginal impact upon investment and income. More important, however, was the Revenue

Act of 1964, which reduced tax liabilities by some $14 billion. Within a year after the passage of this act, the full-employment budget surplus had dropped from $15 billion to almost zero, indicating that the impact of the fiscal structure upon the economy had switched from being highly restrictive to being essentially neutral. The tax cut of 1964 probably marks the full acceptance of discretionary fiscal policy on the part of government to help stimulate a lagging economy.

Because 1965 also marked the beginning of the buildup of the Vietnam War, it is somewhat difficult to disentangle the effects of the tax cut from those of increased defense outlays. What is clear, however, is that by the end of 1965 the full-employment budget was in deficit, where it was to remain until 1969. During this time, actual GNP reached the level of potential GNP for the first time in a decade and, in fact, surpassed its estimated potential until it began to fall shortly prior to the recession of 1970–71. During 1965, however, prices began to creep upward and rose at an increasing rate thereafter.

By 1966, unemployment had fallen to its target level of 4 percent; prices were beginning to rise substantially; and actual GNP had surpassed the estimated value of potential GNP. All the evidence suggested that, instead of being faced with the deflationary gap that had existed for the past decade, the government was faced with a rising inflationary gap. Between 1966 and 1968, the unemployment rate fell to below 4 percent while the rate of change in prices rose from 3.5 percent to 5.1 percent.

Given the behavior of prices, employment, and income during this period, the standard fiscal procedure would have been to raise taxes to reduce the inflationary pressures emanating from the massive increase in defense spending. The government was unwilling to do this, however, because of its basic unwillingness or inability to state what the costs of financing the war were. Since fiscal policy was not being used to restrain inflationary pressures, the bulk of the efforts to stabilize the economy fell to monetary policy. The result was a credit crunch, unprecedentedly high interest rates, and a concomitant recession in home building and other sectors of the economy that were sensitive to interest rates. Although the government did impose a 14 percent tax surcharge in 1968, it was by then a question of too little, too late, since the surcharge had virtually no impact in reducing consumer demand. This can probably be attributed to its temporary nature. Because it was only initially enacted for a year, consumers reduced their savings instead of their consumption. [11]

---

[11] For a good discussion of the failure of the surcharge, see R. A. Eisner, "What Went Wrong?" *Journal of Political Economy*, vol. 79 (May 1971), pp. 629–41. Also see A. Blinder and R. M. Solow, "Analytical Foundations of Fiscal Policy," in *The Economics of Public Finance*, eds. Blinder et al. (Washington, D.C.: The Brookings Institution, 1974), pp. 3–118.

The Nixon administration was faced with a legacy of considerable inflation. During 1969, the unemployment rate averaged 3.5 percent, while the rate of price increase averaged 6.7 percent. Realizing that restrictive fiscal policy was needed, the administration attempted to cut expenditures and extend the surcharge. In the first six months of the Nixon administration, the full-employment budget swung from a deficit of $7.6 billion to a surplus of $12.1 billion—a net change toward contraction of almost $20 billion. The result of this dramatic change in budgetary policy was a decline in the rate of growth of income, increasing unemployment, which reached 6 percent by 1971, but unfortunately no significant decline in the rate of change in prices.

Part of the inability of the Nixon administration to reduce the rate of price increase by increasing unemployment can be attributed to the apparent shift in the Phillips curve in recent years, which means that any given level of unemployment will be associated with a higher rate of price increase than in previous years.

There are several hypotheses to explain this shift. One is based on expectations. As the inflation has continued, households and businesses expect it to continue. Thus, any level of unemployment must be associated with higher rates of inflation. Another hypothesis explains the shift in the Phillips curve by the changing composition of the labor force. As the proportion of unskilled workers in the labor force rises, relatively larger increases in unemployment are needed to create a given amount of excess capacity and, hence, downward pressure on wages and prices. During the past few years, the proportion of teen-agers and women in the labor force has risen. Since these groups tend to be less skilled and have a lower productivity than their adult male counterparts, a given unemployment rate will be associated with less excess capacity now than it has been in the past. This could cause the Phillips curve to shift to the right. A third hypothesis is based on the nature of the recession of 1970–71, which was largely concentrated in the defense and aerospace industries. Thus, a large amount of unemployment was generated in a few industries without having much negative impact on aggregate demand. Consequently, prices kept rising at a substantial rate in the face of considerable unemployment. Finally, a fourth hypothesis stresses the increased mobility of capital relative to that of labor. In particular, the rise in conglomerate mergers has made it much easier to transfer capital both between regions and industries. Since labor remains much less mobile, this should generate a secular rise in the unemployment rate; any given rate of price increase should be associated with a higher unemployment rate.

The observed shift in the Phillips curve poses a dilemma for society if there is no combination of price increase and unemployment that it deems fully acceptable. For example, current evidence indicates that a rate of inflation of at least 5 to 6 percent per year will accompany a rate of unemployment of 5 percent. While the rate of inflation could probably be reduced by creating higher unemployment rates, this is politically and socially unacceptable. Similarly, while unemployment could be reduced to 4 percent, this would probably be accompanied by price increases of 6 percent or more.

Whatever the reasons for the observed shift in the Phillips curve, none of them appears to be self-correcting. Thus faced with an unacceptable trade-off between unemployment and price rises, the Nixon administration instituted the so-called New Economic Policy in August 1971. Briefly, this involved a wage-price freeze for 90 days, followed by limited price and wage controls, proposed reductions in taxes and expenditures by equal amounts, a devaluation of the dollar, and the institution of a 10 percent surcharge on imports.

The goal of the New Economic Policy was to reduce unemployment without increasing prices. As explained above, this appeared to be moderately successful as the unemployment rate fell to 5.6 percent in 1972 and the rate of growth in the CPI fell to 3.3 percent. When the wage-price controls were removed in 1973, the government undertook an extremely restrictive fiscal policy, causing the full-employment surplus to grow from $7.5 billion to $25.4 billion. This had relatively little immediate impact upon price or unemployment, however, since, in 1973, the unemployment rate fell to 4.9 percent and the CPI increased by 6.2 percent.

Nevertheless, it is generally agreed that the sharply restrictive fiscal policy had a major impact in triggering the extremely severe recession of 1974–75. Unemployment began to rise rapidly in mid-1974 and hit a peak in excess of 9 percent in early 1975. Unfortunately, however, this rising unemployment rate was also accompanied by accelerating inflation in 1974. Thus, by the end of 1974, it appeared that the Phillips curve had shifted out even further.

While the behavior of prices and unemployment in 1974–75 was extremely disquieting, it now appears that a number of unique occurrences caused the rapid increase in inflation that took place at that time. The Arab oil embargo and subsequent rise in oil prices that occurred in late 1973 and early 1974 essentially represented a one-shot impact of higher energy costs upon prices. Similarly, the worldwide grain shortage that took place in 1973 caused the United States grain reserves to be largely depleted and hence made the United States more vulnerable to shifts in the world grain market than it had previously been. Finally, the increase in prices caused by the oil embargo and grain shortage led to an increase in inflationary expectations, which, in turn, tended to generate more inflation.

Thus, we can argue that the unpleasant combination of high unemployment rates and high inflation rates that the economy experienced during 1973–75 was more a result of bad luck than either bad management or a fundamental shift in the Phillips curve. Indeed, the experience of early 1976 suggests that the economy may be returning to more traditional behavior. During the first half of 1976, the unemployment rate fell steadily to 7.5 percent, and the rate of price inflation fell to 6 percent.

Nevertheless, it is clear that once inflationary pressures have become established, they are extremely hard to eliminate. Thus, although there is some evidence that the Phillips curve may be returning to its general shape of the late 1960s, there is little evidence that it is returning to its shape of the early 1960s. Therefore, it may be impossible to achieve simultaneously a rate of unemployment of 4 percent and a 3 percent rate of inflation in the near future. While the unemployment-inflation trade-off appears to have shifted inward somewhat by mid-1976, it is impossible to tell at this time whether this trend will continue or not.

CONCLUSION

This chapter has indicated that the government has not been generally successful in maintaining a stable growth of income, full employment, or price stability. With respect to income, automatic stabilizers that are built into the tax and expenditure structure can be expected to offset between 30 and 50 percent of the changes in GNP in either an upswing or a downswing. Further countercyclical action must take place through discretionary policies aimed at offsetting specific expansions or contractions. The record of discretionary fiscal policy is not particularly bright. Lags of recognition and of action have often been sufficiently long that countercyclical actions have had procyclical rather than countercyclical impacts. Moreover, budgetary changes that are not specifically connected to the change in the economy have generally had a greater impact upon income than specific countercyclical actions.

Nevertheless, discretionary fiscal policy is probably preferable to the adoption of specific budgetary rules aimed at stabilizing the economy. Rules by their very nature are confining and limit the policymaker's degrees of freedom. As forecasting techniques improve, so should the application of discretionary fiscal policy.

The record with respect to price stability and full employment has not been particularly encouraging during the postwar period. Inflations that have started from pressures of excess demand have tended to become subject to pressures from the cost side, which have been difficult to mitigate. Stated alternatively, demand pull inflations, initially cost push inflations that have proved difficult to counteract. Thus, the past decade has seen an actual shift in the Phillips curve, indicating an increasingly high trade-off between unemployment and price stability.

REFERENCES

Bach, G. L. *Making Monetary and Fiscal Policy.* Washington, D.C.: The Brookings Institution, 1971.

Blinder, A. S., and Solow, R. M. "Analytical Foundations of Fiscal Policy," in *The Economics of Public Finance,* eds. Blinder et al. Washington, D.C., The Brookings Institution, 1974.

Eilbott, Peter. "The Effectiveness of Automatic Stabilizers," *American Economic Review,* vol. 61 (June 1966).

Friedman, Milton. *A Program for Monetary Stability.* New York: Fordham University Press, 1969.

Lewis, Wilfred. *Federal Fiscal Policy in Postwar Recessions.* Washington, D.C.: The Brookings Institution, 1962.

22

Growth and Fiscal Policy

This book has largely ignored the problem of growth until this chapter. We have generally assumed that the government determines the appropriate rate of growth through the expression of collective desires via the social welfare function and adjusts monetary and fiscal policy to ensure that this growth rate is achieved. The maintenance of a given growth path, however, is not always a straightforward matter. This chapter explores the determinants of the rate of growth and analyzes how the government can help society maintain an equilibrium growth path. It should be pointed out that this chapter considers the problem of maintaining the desirable growth path in the context of a developed economy. The problems posed by the LDCs are somewhat different and will be considered in Chapter 23.

Just as the models of income determination that we have studied in the previous chapters are simplified abstractions of reality, so are growth models. While the income determination models attempt to isolate the essential determinants of the equilibrium level of income, the growth models attempt to isolate the essential determinants of the equilibrium rate of change of income. In particular, growth theory investigates four questions. First, what determines the rate of growth of productive capacity? Second, what determines the rate of growth of demand? Third, what conditions are needed to ensure that capacity, demand, and the labor force all grow in equilibrium? Fourth, how can governmental action help to ensure the maintenance of equilibrium? The answers to these questions can be developed in the context of either of two basic models: the so-called Harrod-Domar model and the so-called neoclassical model.

The opening section analyzes these questions in the context of the Harrod-Domar model, which assumes that capital bears a fixed relation to output and that investment is totally interest inelastic. These questions are then considered in the context of the so-called neoclassical model, which assumes that investment is interest elastic and that the capital output ratio can change. Finally, these models are related to the experience of the United States in the postwar period, evaluating governmental policy with respect to its stated growth objectives.

THE HARROD-DOMAR MODEL [1]

In the Harrod-Domar model three growth paths must be considered: the rate of growth of capacity, the rate of growth of demand, and the rate of growth of the labor force. We proceed by considering the determinants of each of these rates of growth and then analyze their interaction to see under what conditions the economy can sustain an equilibrium growth path.

The Warranted Rate of Growth

The rate of growth of capacity, or what is called the "warranted rate of growth" in the Harrod-Domar model, is determined by the answer to the following question. Given society's desired saving ratio and the relationship between output and the capital stock, how much investment is required to ensure that investment will equal planned saving? The warranted rate of growth is that rate of growth of income that ensures over time a succession of levels of investment that just equal desired savings.

Suppose, for example, that society's saving rate is 12 percent and that there is a constant capital-output ratio of 3. Thus $12 is saved out of every $100, and every $100 of output requires a capital stock of $300 to produce it. Given these relationships, what rate of growth of income is needed to ensure that savings and investment remain in equilibrium? To be concrete, let us assume an initial level of income of $100. Thus $12 of saving will be forthcoming. For the economy to be in equilibrium, $12 of investment is required to absorb this saving. The equilibrium growth rate is found by asking what increase in income would require $12 of additional investment. In this example, equilibrium could only occur if income grew by $4 or if the rate of increase in income were 4 percent. If the rate of growth of income were 3 percent, investment would equal $9; if it were 5 percent, investment would equal $15. In the first case, planned saving would be greater than

[1] The so-called Harrod-Domar model was developed and independently by Sir Roy F. Harrod and Evsey D. Domar. See R. F. Harrod, *Toward a Dynamic Economics* (London: Macmillan Company, 1948); E. D. Domar, "Expansion and Employment," *American Economic Review*, vol. 37 (March 1947), pp. 34–55, reprinted in *Essays in the Theory of Economic Growth* (Oxford: Oxford University Press, 1957), pp. 83–108.

investment; in the second case, planned saving would be less than investment. Given this example, only if the rate of growth of income equals 4 percent would investment equal planned saving and the economy be in equilibrium.

The relationships expressed in this example can be generalized by considering the algebra of the situation. In equilibrium, planned savings must equal planned investment,

$$S = I \tag{22-1}$$

Total savings are assumed to be proportional to income

$$S = sY \tag{22-2}$$

Investment is derived by the relationship between capital and output. Specifically, it is assumed that the capital-output ratio is a constant,

$$K/Y = v \tag{22-3}$$

If the capital-output ratio is constant, the average capital-output ratio must also equal the marginal capital-output ratio, i.e.,

$$\Delta K/\Delta Y = v \tag{22-3a}$$

Since investment equals the change in capacity or ΔK, equation (22-3a) implies that

$$I = v \, \Delta Y \tag{22-4}$$

This states that investment is proportional to the change in income. Consequently, this investment function embodies the familiar accelerator principle that relates planned investment to change in income.

By substituting Equations (22-4) and (22-2) into Equation (22-1) and solving for the percentage change in income, we can derive the warranted rate of growth (g_w):

$$g_w = \frac{\Delta Y}{Y} = \frac{s}{v} \tag{22-5}$$

Thus the warranted rate of growth is equal to the savings ratio divided by the capital-output ratio.[2]

The Actual Rate of Growth

The warranted rate of growth is defined as the rate of growth of output that would require an amount of investment just equal to the forthcoming level of savings. If investment were determined by an

---

[2] The warranted rate of growth can be determined somewhat more rigorously in terms of time periods as shown in Additional Note 1 at the end of the chapter.

accelerator principle and if income grew at the warranted rate of growth, planned saving would just equal planned investment, and income could maintain that growth path indefinitely. As such, it gives an equilibrium rate of growth of capacity. But businessmen do not necessarily plan their investment according to the accelerator principle. Expectations, profits, income or sales levels, etc. can all affect investment demand. Hence, the determinants of aggregate demand may be such that desired aggregate demand as expressed by desired consumption and desired investment based on profits, expectations, and the like may differ from aggregate supply or the income level that is determined by the rate of growth of capacity. In this case, planned saving could differ from planned investment, and the economy would deviate from its equilibrium growth path.

Specifically, let us assume that the following expenditure relationships hold in the economy:

$$Y_t = C_t + I_t \qquad (22\text{–}6)$$
$$C_t = (1 - s)Y_t \qquad (22\text{–}7)$$
$$I_t = \bar{I}_t \qquad (22\text{–}8)$$

Equation (22–6) states the familiar income-equilibrium relationship that in equilibrium (Y_t) must equal the sum of consumption (C_t) and investment (I_t). Equation (22–7) states that consumption is proportional to income. Because it is definitionally true in this simplified economy that savings plus consumption equals income (i.e., $Y_t = C_t + S_t$) this factor of proportionality must equal one minus the savings ratio (i.e., $c = 1 - s$).[3] Equation (22–8) states that investment is arbitrarily given as equal to $\bar{I}_t$ for the time being. Substituting Equations (22–7) and (22–8) into Equation (22–6) yields the condition that

$$sY_t = \bar{I}_t \qquad (22\text{–}9)$$

Since, however, $sY_t = S_t$, this states the familiar equilibrium condition that planned savings must equal planned investment.

If investment demand were given by the accelerator principle, investment could be expressed according to Equation (22–4); the equilibrium condition (22–9) would yield the warranted rate of growth. But if investment demand is not given by the accelerator principle given in Equation (22–4), the rate of growth of demand or the actual rate of growth will generally differ from the warranted rate of growth. This can be seen by considering an alternative investment demand function. Specifically, let us assume that investment in any time period is equal to some proportion (α) of last period's income plus an adjustment

---

[3] By assumption, $C_t = cY_t$ and $S_t = sY_t$. By definition, $Y_t = C_t + S_t$. Therefore, substituting C_t and S_t into the definitional relationship yields $Y_t = Y_t(c + s)$ or $1 = c + s$.

factor (β) that attempts to close the gap between the desired and actual capital stock in the previous period. This can be expressed symbolically as

$$I_t = \alpha Y_{t-1} + \beta(K_{t-1}^d - K_{t-1}^a) \qquad (22\text{--}10)$$

where K_{t-1}^d represents the desired capital stock in the previous period and K_{t-1}^a represents the actual capital stock in the previous period. The desired capital stock in period t is equal to the capital stock required to produce the actual level in period t and is derived by the capital-output ratio. The actual capital stock in period t is given by the previous period's capital stock plus the investment that took place in period t.[4]

Substituting Equation (22–10) in Equation (22–9) and solving for the current level of income yields

$$Y_t = \frac{\alpha}{s} Y_{t-1} = \frac{\beta}{s}(K_{t-1}^d - K_{t-1}^a) \qquad (22\text{--}11)$$

From this expression, it is straightforward to derive the actual rate of growth of income or the rate of growth of demand which we denote by g_a[5]

$$g_a = \frac{Y_t - Y_{t-1}}{Y_{t-1}} = \left(\frac{\alpha}{s} - 1\right) + \frac{\beta}{s}(v_{t-1}^d - v_{t-1}^a) \qquad (22\text{--}12)$$

where v_{t-1}^d represents the desired capital-output in period $t - 1$ and v_{t-1}^a represents the actual capital-output ratio in period $t - 1$. This states that the actual rate of growth of income is given by two elements: The first is the ratio of the propensity to invest out of last period's income and the savings rate minus one; the second is given by the ratio of the adjustment factor (β) and the savings rate, multiplied by the difference between the desired or optimal capital-output ratio (v^d), which is determined by the production relationships in the economy, and the actual capital-output ratio (v^a), which may be greater or less than the optimal capital-output ratio if income is below or above its equilibrium level. In equilibrium, the actual capital output ratio (v^a) must equal the desired capital output ratio (v^d), and the actual rate of growth is given by

$$g_a = \frac{\alpha}{s} - 1 \qquad (22\text{--}12a)$$

---

[4] Formally, these relationships can be expressed as follows:

$$K_t^d = vY_t$$
$$K_t^a = K_{t-1}^a + I_t$$

[5] Subtract Y_{t-1} from both sides of the equation and divide by Y_{t-1}.

The Relationship between the Warranted Rate of Growth and the Actual Rate of Growth

As long as income grows in equilibrium so that the actual rate of growth equals the warranted rate of growth, there will be no divergence between the income demanded and the capacity income supplied. The optimal capital stock will equal the actual capital stock and the actual capital-output ratio will equal the desired capital-output ratio. The economy will maintain a stable, equilibrium growth path.

Because of the inflexibility of the desired capital-output ratio, however, this economy is characterized by potential instability. If the actual and warranted rates of growth diverge for even one period, the economy will go into an extended expansion or contraction. If, for example, the actual rate of growth fails to equal the warranted rate of growth in one period, desired investment will fall below planned savings available in that period. Since planned savings exceeds planned investment, businessmen's sales expectations will not be realized. Hence, they find that they accumulate undesired inventories and that the actual investment, which must equal planned savings, exceeds desired investment. Consequently, the actual capital stock will rise above the capital stock needed to produce the actual level of output. In the next period, businessmen will try to adjust the actual capital stock to the desired capital stock and reduce investment accordingly. In this period, even though planned savings equals planned investment, the actual capital stock still exceeds the desired capital stock. Hence investment and savings will be reduced still further in the following period. The result of one period's disequilibrium where planned saving exceeded planned investment is a perpetual fall in income that can presumably only be stopped when investment becomes negative and capital is actually used up in the production process.

The story is similar if desired investment exceeds planned savings in a given period. In this case, firms will find that actual investment falls short of desired investment as inventories are depleted. In subsequent periods the desired capital stock will exceed the actual capital stock, which will cause desired investment to increase. The increasing gap between the desired and the actual capital stock will cause investment, savings, and income to rise at an ever-increasing rate, and the economy will experience an ever-increasing expansion.

Thus, the Harrod-Domar model portrays an economy of dynamic instability. As long as the growth rates in demand and capacity happen to coincide, balanced growth is possible. But if they once diverge, there is no self-equilibrating mechanism to return them to the equilibrium growth path. Income will either exceed or fall short of its equilibrium level by ever-increasing amounts.

The Natural Rate of Growth

There is still another rate of growth to consider: the rate of growth of the labor force adjusted for technical change. This is called the natural rate of growth because it measures the rate of growth over which the government has little, if any, control.[6] It is desirable to express this rate of growth in efficiency units rather than in physical units. By physical units we mean the actual number of workers, while by efficiency units we mean the number of workers adjusted by their productivity. Hence, the efficiency labor force represents the actual labor force multiplied by some productivity factor. This concept can easily be translated into growth terms. For example, if the actual labor force grows by 1 percent per year and labor productivity increases by 3 percent per year, the natural rate of growth would be 4 percent per year. This would reflect the rate of growth of the labor force in efficiency units rather than in physical units. Thus the natural rate of growth should be thought of as the rate of growth of the labor force plus the rate of growth of technological change, rather than the rate of growth of the labor force alone.

This rate of growth sets the ultimate limit to the equilibrium rate of growth of income. In the Harrod-Domar model, production requires fixed units of labor per unit of output and fixed units of capital per unit of output. Consequently, the capital-labor ratio is also fixed. This implies that the maximum possible increase in output is given by the increase in the labor force since this is determined exogenously outside of the system.[7] For a full equilibrium, the rate of growth of capital must be such that the rate of growth of capacity, the rate of growth of demand, and the rate of growth of labor force are all equal. Alternatively stated, the warranted rate of growth and the actual rate of growth and the natural rate of growth must all be equal.

Since we have already analyzed what happens when the warranted and the actual rates of growth diverge, we need only relate them to the natural rate of growth. Specifically, let us assume that the natural rate of growth is greater than the warranted rate of growth. This means that the rate of growth of the efficiency labor force is greater than the rate of growth of capacity. Since the increase in the efficiency labor force should be reflected in higher income and higher aggregate demand, the excess of the natural rate of growth over the warranted rate of growth should lead to an excess of the actual rate of growth over the

---

[6] Of course, the government can apply family-planning measures to affect the birth rate or introduce measures to affect technical change. Nevertheless, these measures are likely to have only a marginal impact upon the natural demographic and technological factors that determine the natural rate of growth.

[7] Strictly speaking, the assumption of fixed production coefficients is not necessary for this conclusion. When the capital-labor ratio is variable, the maximum rate of growth will still be given by the rate of growth of the labor force. This will be discussed in the following section.

warranted rate of growth. As we have seen, this should lead to an ever-increasing expansion in which income, savings, investment, and the capital stock rise at an ever-increasing rate.

Alternatively, let us assume that the natural rate of growth falls short of the warranted rate of growth. In this case, the economy is constrained by a ceiling on the expansion of the efficiency labor force. Hence the rate of growth of demand or the actual rate of growth is limited by the natural rate of growth. In this case, a deflationary spiral will develop since the warranted rate of growth exceeds the actual rate of growth. Income, investment, savings, and the capital stock will fall at an ever-increasing rate.

The Role of Government

The Harrod-Domar model is a model of a highly unstable economy that is capable of sustained growth if the rates of growth of capacity, demand, and the labor force are equal. But, if one of these growth rates once diverges from the others, the economy will enter a deflationary or an inflationary spiral.

The source of the instability of the Harrod-Domar model lies in the rigid capital-output ratio. Because the desired capital-output ratio is assumed fixed, there is no mechanism such as the interest rate to bring desired savings and investment or the desired and actual capital stock into equality. Consequently, there is no self-equilibrating mechanism to ensure that capacity, demand, and the labor force will grow together. This rigidity can be seen by considering the following equilibrium condition:

$$s/v = (\alpha/s - 1) = n \qquad (22-13)$$

The expression s/v represents the warranted rate of growth; the expression $(\alpha/s - 1)$ represents the actual rate of growth;[8] and n represents the rate of growth of the labor force, measured in efficiency units. Since all of these parameters are behavioral or technical constants, these equalities will hold only by chance.

The natural rate of growth can be assumed to be exogenously given and cannot be influenced by government tax or expenditure policy. Thus the role of government is to assure that the warranted rate of growth equals the actual rate of growth and that these both equal the natural rate of growth.

The warranted rate of growth is given by s/v and is equal to the

---

[8] The actual rate of growth is actually given by $[\alpha/s - 1 + \beta/s(v_{t-1}^d - v_{t-1}^a)]$ where v^d represents the desired capital-output ratio and v^a represents the actual capital-output ratio. In equilibrium, however, the actual capital-output ratio must equal the desired or optimal capital-output ratio so that the second term of the actual rate of growth equals zero.

savings ratio divided by the desired capital-output ratio. By assumption the desired capital-output ratio is fixed and cannot be influenced by governmental policy. As we saw in previous chapters, however, the savings ratio can be influenced by personal taxes and government expenditures. Thus in principle, the savings ratio s can take on any values through appropriate tax and expenditure policy. Consequently, the warranted ratio of growth is not immutable, but can be expressed as

$$g_w' = \frac{\sigma}{v} \tag{22-14}$$

where the σ denotes the savings ratio that is dependent upon government tax and expenditure policy.[9]

When the government does not utilize tax or expenditure policy we have seen that the actual rate of growth in equilibrium is given by $\alpha/s - 1$, where α represents the marginal propensity to invest out of last period's income and s represents society's savings ratio. We have just discussed how the government can alter society's savings ratio through its tax and expenditure policy. But if investment is related to profits and if the government can utilize a profits tax, it can also affect the propensity to invest by changing the profits tax. If investment is related to profits and profits are related to income, changing the profits tax can change profits and hence the amount of desired investment in the economy. Then we can rewrite the actual rate of growth in equilibrium as

$$g_a' = \frac{a}{\sigma} - 1 \tag{22-14a}$$

where a represents the effective marginal propensity to invest out of last period's income that is dependent upon the profits tax; and σ represents the effective savings ratio that depends upon the tax and expenditure parameters.[10]

In equilibrium, the warranted rate of growth (g_w'), the actual rate of growth (g_a'), and the natural rate of growth

$$\frac{\sigma}{v} = \left(\frac{a}{\sigma} - 1 \right) = n \tag{22-15}$$

$(g_n = n)$ must all be equal. Moreover, in equilibrium, the actual capital-

---

[9] The model described in Additional Note 2 at the end of the chapter, derives these relationships rigorously and is based on the article by Warren L. Smith, "Monetary-Fiscal Policy and Economic Growth," *Quarterly Journal of Economics*, vol. 71 (February 1957), pp. 36–55.

[10] These relationships can be formally derived as shown in Additional Note 3.

output ratio must always equal the desired capital-output ratio. Thus, the following condition is required for balanced growth:

$$\frac{\Delta K}{K} = \frac{\Delta L}{L} \qquad (22\text{--}17)$$

Since the savings rate (σ) and the propensity to invest out of last period's income (a) depend upon fiscal parameters, we can set the warranted rate of growth and the actual rate of growth both equal to the natural rate of growth and solve for the values of the policy parameters that will enable equilibrium to be achieved.[11]

Thus the introduction of government into the Harrod-Domar model can enable the economy to maintain a given rate of growth of income by altering the effective savings rate and the propensity to invest out of last period's income. Therefore, the dramatic instability that previously characterized the Harrod-Domar economy no longer exists. By choosing the appropriate fiscal parameters the government can always ensure that the warranted rate of growth, the actual rate of growth, and the natural rate of growth are equal. Through proper governmental actions, any equilibrium growth path can be maintained.

Of course, the Harrod-Domar model is a highly unrealistic view of the economy, since investment and the capital stock are assumed to be totally unresponsive to equilibrating factors, such as the interest rate. When the equilibrium capital-output ratio is allowed to vary in response to the interest rate, the instability that characterized the Harrod-Domar model vanishes. Nevertheless, even though the economy does contain self-equilibrating mechanism in this case, there is still a role for government.

GROWTH UNDER NEOCLASSICAL ASSUMPTIONS

As we have indicated, the Harrod-Domar model contains no self-equilibrating mechanism to ensure that the economy moves along its equilibrium growth path. Although savings and investment can maintain an indefinite equilibrium if the warranted rate of growth happens to equal the actual rate of growth, once planned savings and desired investment diverge for only one period, the economy will enter a sustained upward or downward spiral without government intervention. This conclusion follows primarily from the inability of the capital stock and actual investment to adjust to changing economic conditions. Because the desired capital stock is assumed to bear a fixed relationship to income (and labor), when the actual capital-output ratio diverges from its equilibrium level for any reason, there are no forces inherent

---

[11] This is detailed in Additional Note 4.

in the system to restore it to its equilibrium level. In fact, efforts to restore the equilibrium capital-output ratio are self-defeating and lead to sustained expansion or sustained contraction of income and a widening gap between the desired and actual capital-output ratios. In the absence of governmental intervention, the Harrod-Domar economy tends to lapse into periods of prolonged contraction or prolonged expansion.

Obviously, the Harrod-Domar assumptions overstate the rigidities under which the real world economies operate. Although the United States economy has never maintained a balanced growth path, neither has it experienced sustained inflationary or deflationary spirals. While part of the observed relative stability of the growth of the United States economy may have arisen from the application of appropriate monetary and fiscal policy, a greater part probably also arose from the ability of the capital stock to adjust toward its desired level in response to changes in the level of income and to changes in interest rates. Since the assumed rigidity of the capital-output ratio is the primary source of instability in the Harrod-Domar model, let us consider how adjustments in the desired capital stock and the desired capital-output ratio can ensure the attainment of a stable growth path. Again, we first discuss the rate of growth of capacity and the rate of growth of demand in an economy without government and analyze the nature of the equilibrium. We then introduce government to determine how its fiscal activities affect the nature of the equilibrium.

The Rate of Growth of Capacity [12]

As in all macroeconomic models, equilibrium requires equality of planned savings and planned investment. But since equilibrium with respect to capacity may not represent equilibrium with respect to demand, it is important to distinguish between capacity investment and desired investment. Capacity investment is the level of investment that determines the rate of growth of capacity and thus is a supply concept. Desired investment is the investment that determines the rate of growth of demand and thus is a demand concept. Full equilibrium requires that the two levels of investment be equal. It was the inability of the economy to bring these two levels of investment into equality that created the instability of the Harrod-Domar model. In the neoclassical model such an equilibrating mechanism exists, so that the economy should always grow along its balanced growth path.

In the neoclassical model, output is assumed to be related to inputs

---

[12] This analysis follows that of Solow. See R. M. Solow, "A Contribution to the Theory of Economic Growth," *Quarterly Journal of Economics*, vol. 70 (February 1956), pp. 65–94. For a good summary, see W. J. Baumol, *Economic Dynamics*, 3d ed. (New York: Macmillan Co., 1970), pp. 381–93.

of capital and labor.[13] Since the rate of growth of the labor force is given outside of the system, the capital stock must adjust to the rate of growth of the labor force to maintain an equilibrium in the factor or input markets. Equilibrium in the factor or input markets implies that factor returns are constant. This will occur if labor and capital grow at the same rate. Capacity investment is rigorously defined as the level of investment that enables equilibrium to be maintained in the factor markets and occurs when the capital stock and the labor force grow at the same rate. Equilibrium in the factor market requires that

$$\frac{\Delta K}{K} = \frac{\Delta L}{L} \qquad (22\text{--}17)$$

But investment is precisely the change in the capital stock, and the rate of growth in the labor force can be denoted by n. Thus $\Delta K = I$ and $\Delta L/L = n$. Therefore, equilibrium in the factor market implies that

$$I = nK \qquad (22\text{--}18)$$

Since investment equals the change in the capital stock, Equation (22–18) is merely a restatement that equilibrium with respect to capacity requires that the rate of growth of the labor force and the rate of growth of capacity are equal. Moreover, if labor and capital growth at the same rate, the capital-labor ratio must remain constant. Therefore, capacity investment can also be defined as the amount of new capital required to maintain a constant capital-labor ratio.

For a full equilibrium, however, capacity investment consistent with the rate of growth of the labor force must also be consistent with planned saving. Thus we must utilize the familiar equilibrium condition used in income-expenditure analysis that planned savings equal capacity investment. Savings are assumed to be a fixed proportion of income and are written as

$$S = sY \qquad (22\text{--}19)$$

Since equilibrium requires that savings equal investment, setting Equation (22–19) equal to Equation (22–18) yields the condition needed for a full equilibrium

$$sY = nK \qquad (22\text{--}20)$$

---

[13] In this discussion, we abstract from technical change. Technical change could be introduced quite easily, however, in which case the labor force would be expressed in efficiency units. The rate of growth of the efficiency labor force would equal the rate of growth of the work force plus the rate of growth of technical change. In a model that incorporates technical change, in equilibrium the capital-labor ratio and the wage rate would remain constant for labor in efficiency units, but would rise for labor expressed in physical units. For these results to be shown rigorously, it is necessary to assume that the economy is subject to labor augmenting technical change, which increases the productivity of labor relative to that of capital.

This equilibrium condition should look quite familiar. We can rearrange terms and state the equilibrium in the familiar Harrod-Domar terms:

$$\frac{sY}{K} = n \qquad (22\text{--}20a)$$

or

$$\frac{s}{v} = n \qquad (22\text{--}20b)$$

where $v = K/Y$, the capital-output ratio. The left side of this equation is precisely the Harrod-Domar warranted rate of growth, while the right side is the rate of growth of the labor force. Equation (22–20b) states that in equilibrium the rate of growth of capacity must equal the rate of growth of the labor force. But in the neoclassical economy, the capital-output ratio (v) is variable. Therefore, if for some reason, the warranted rate of growth or the rate of growth of capacity were to diverge from the rate of growth of the labor force, the system would return to its equilibrium growth path, which is given by the exogenously determined rate of growth of the labor force.

The Role of Demand

The model that we have described is primarily concerned with supply or the equilibrium rate of growth of capacity. The rate of growth of the labor force, which is given outside of the system, determines the maximum rate of growth attainable by society. The equilibrium conditions, $sY = nK$, requires both that the level of savings and investment be equal and that the level of investment be sufficient to enable capital and labor to grow in tandem and thus to maintain a constant capital-labor ratio. If investment equals nK, the rate of growth of capital will equal the rate of growth of the labor force and balanced growth can be maintained. But the factors that determine desired investment may differ from those that determine capacity investment. Nevertheless, in the neoclassical model the interest rate acts as an equilibrating mechanism to ensure that capacity investment equals desired investment. [14] Therefore, the neoclassical model describes an inherently stable economy, while the Harrod-Domar model does not.

At any given time, it is possible to define a desired capital stock that enables a representative firm to maximize its profits for any given level of output. This desired capital stock is equal to be capital stock that

---

[14] This discussion is based on the paper by R. R. Nelson, "Full Employment Policy and Economic Growth," *American Economic Review*, vol. 56 (December 1966), pp. 1178–92.

equates the marginal revenue product of an additional unit of capital with the interest rate, which reflect the cost of capital to the firm. If output is a function of capital and labor, this desired capital stock is related to the interest rate and the labor employed by the firm. By aggregating over all firms, we can extend the argument and postulate that the desired capital for the economy is related to the interest rate and the labor force.[15]

Since capital cannot adjust instantaneously to changes in demand at any given time, it is unlikely that the economy's desired capital stock equals the economy's actual capital stock. Thus investment takes place to restore the actual capital stock to its desired level. Therefore, investment can be postulated to be related to the gap between the desired capital stock and the actual capital stock. Since the desired capital stock is a function of the labor force and the interest rate, investment must be a function of the existing capital stock, the interest rate, and the labor force.

In equilibrium, the rate of growth of investment must equal the rate of growth of savings. But since the savings ratio is assumed to be constant, the rate of growth of investment must also equal the rate of growth of income.[16] Moreover, in equilibrium, the rate of interest must be constant since the investment demand and the supply of funds available for investment from savings must be growing at the same rate. But if the rate of interest is constant, there is no pressure for the capital-labor ratio or the capital-output ratio to change. Consequently, the rate of growth of income, the rate of growth of capital, and the rate of growth of the labor force must be equal. Therefore, if the rate of interest is constant, the following equilibrium conditions will hold:

$$\frac{\Delta K}{K} = \frac{\Delta Y}{Y} = \frac{\Delta L}{L} \qquad (22\text{--}21)$$

The rate of growth of the labor force ($\Delta L/L$) is given by n, while $\Delta K = I$. In equilibrium $I = sY$. Thus, the relationship in Equation (22–21) also states that in equilibrium $\Delta Y/Y = n = s/v$; the rate of growth of income will equal the rate of growth of the labor force and the warranted rate of growth.

It is important to realize, however, that this condition is derived by considering investment demand rather than by determining the amount of investment needed to maintain a constant capital-labor or capital-output ratio. In particular, investment is specified to be a gen-

---

[15] This is stated formally in Additional Note 5.

[16] This can be derived more formally as detailed in Additional Note 6 at the end of the chapters.

eral function of labor, capital, and the interest rate, and the rate of growth of investment is set equal to the rate of growth of savings or income. Under the neoclassical assumptions, the interest rate works as an equilibrating mechanism that ensures that investment demand equals the capacity investment required to utilize the labor force as efficiently as possible. If, for example, capacity investment exceeds desired investment at the existing interest rate, planned savings will exceed desired investment. Since there is an excess supply of funds for investment at the existing interest rate, the interest rate will fall, causing an increase in investment demand. Thus under the neoclassical assumptions, there will always be an interest rate that will ensure that the rate of growth of demand, the rate of growth of capacity, and the rate of growth of the labor force will all be equal. [17]

The Role of Government

If the neoclassical conditions are satisfied, there is no need for government to enable the economy to maintain an equilibrium growth path. As long as investment is sensitive to the interest rate, there will always be some interest rate at which the rate of growth of demand will equal the rate of growth of capacity and at which the rate of growth of output, capital, and labor will be equal. Since the interest rate bears the burden of adjustment in this model, any rigidities in the interest rate or any insensitivity of investment to the interest rate can affect the ability of the economy to maintain an equilibrium growth path. Suppose, for example, that instead of being fully flexible, the interest rate is subject to some Keynesian, liquidity-trap floor or that investment becomes interest inelastic at some level of the interest rate. In either case, the interest rate no longer serves to equilibrate investment demand with planned savings or capacity investment. Nevertheless, governmental fiscal policies can be introduced to alter society's effective savings rate and ensure that the economy maintains its equilibrium growth path. Moreover, even if the interest rate is fully flexible and investment is fully sensitive to the interest rate so that equilibrium can be maintained without governmental intervention, the government may still want to alter the savings ratio to affect the consumption-investment ratio. [18] If we call σ society's effective savings

---

[17] This is shown in Additional Note 7.

[18] In particular, it can be shown that there is one savings ratio and an associated growth path that will enable society to maximize its discounted consumption stream. Since this golden age savings ratio will only equal the actual savings ratio by chance, the government may want to alter the actual savings ratio to conform to the golden age savings ratio by appropriate tax and expenditure policies. For a full discussion of this point see Baumol, *Economic Dynamics*, pp. 393–400.

rate that take government spending and taxes into account, the equilibrium rate of growth of output occurs when $\sigma Y = nK$.[19]

Since government can alter society's effective savings rate and thus ensure that $\sigma Y = nK$, the government can ensure that society stays on its balanced growth path, even if there are rigidities in the interest rate to prevent it from achieving its equilibrium level or if investment is insensitive to the interest rate. Moreover, even if society is capable of maintaining a balanced growth rate without governmental intervention, society may still want to act collectively through government and utilize fiscal policy to alter its effective savings rate and hence its mix of consumption and investment. Thus even in a neoclassical world, there is some scope for governmental fiscal action.

It should be clear, however, that whether we are thinking of a neoclassical or a Harrod-Domar model, the primary scope of government fiscal activity is to ensure that society moves along an equilibrium growth path rather than to alter the nature of that growth path. The natural rate of growth or the rate of growth of the labor force and technological change determines the maximum rate at which the economy can grow in a sustained fashion. While the government can adopt policies to influence the rate of growth of the labor force or the rate of growth of technology, the impact of these policies will be relatively marginal upon these growth rates. Since the rates of growth of the labor force and technical change are largely determined outside of the system, the function of government with respect to growth is to ensure that the rate of growth of capacity and the rate of growth of demand equal the rate of growth of the labor force and technical change. In a world in which investment is not responsive to the interest rate, this becomes a crucial role since there is no equilibrating mechanism to equalize the various growth rates. In a neoclassical world, however, the interest rate would serve to maintain an equilibrium between the various growth rates. Nevertheless, if the interest rate is rigid, governmental action may be required to enable society to maintain a balanced growth path. Moreover, government may still be needed to adjust the savings ratio and, hence, the mix of consumption and investment in the economy.

RECENT GROWTH IN THE UNITED STATES

Having analyzed the determinants of growth in the abstract Harrod-Domar and neoclassical models, we now discuss the behavior of the determinants of growth in the United States. We first consider what factors have contributed to the rate of growth in the United States

---

[19] The role of government can be developed more rigorously by considering the model shown in Additional Note 8.

and then assess the behavior of government in achieving its stated growth objectives.

The Determinants of Growth in the United States

Since the United States economy has rarely experienced a period of a balanced equilibrium in which the labor force, capacity, and demand all grow proportionately, the actual rate of growth observed over time reflects pressures from both capacity and demand. When aggregate demand is generally sluggish, as it was during the period from 1955 to 1964, the observed rate of growth will be rather low; when aggregate demand is buoyant, as it was from 1964 to 1969, the rate of growth will be high. During the former period, for example, the growth of real income averaged 2.8 percent per year, while during the latter period it averaged 3.5 percent per year, a 25 percent increase in the rate of growth of the economy. Of course, if excess capacity prevails as it did in the beginning of 1964, the economy can maintain a much higher rate of growth than if the capacity is fully employed. When full capacity is reached, the growth rate must slow down since it will be constrained by the amount of net capital formation and the growth in the labor force.

At full employment, the rate of growth of income is influenced by three factors: the rate of growth of capital, the rate of growth of labor, and the rate of growth of technological change. If income can be expressed as a function of labor, capital, and technical change at any given moment of time, the rate of growth of income can be given by the following expression:[20]

$$\frac{\Delta Y}{Y} = F_k \frac{\Delta K}{K} + F_L \frac{\Delta L}{L} + T.C. \tag{22-22}$$

where F_k represents the share of capital out of total income; F_L represents the share of labor out of total income; $T.C.$ represents technical change; and Y, L, and K represent income, labor, and capital respectively. Suppose, for example, that labor receives 75 percent of national income and that capital receives 25 percent. Suppose, moreover, that the rate of growth of labor is 2 percent, the rate of growth of capital is 4 percent, and the rate of technical change is 2 percent. Then total output will increase at a rate of 4.5 percent per year [(¾)(2%) + (¼)(4%) + 2.0% = 4.5%].

---

[20] This expression is derived by assuming that income can be expressed by a production function that takes the form $Y = F(K, L, A)$, where A represents a technical change factor. Technical change is assumed to be neutral in the sense that it does not affect the relative marginal productivities of labor and capital. For a full discussion of the derivation of Equation (22-22) from the production function, see R. M. Solow, "Technical Change and the Aggregate Production Function," *Review of Economics and Statistics*, vol. 39 (August 1957), pp. 312–20.

Alternatively, we can analyze per capita growth. This enables us to abstract from the impact that the rate of growth of the labor force has upon the rate of growth of income and concentrate, instead, on the impact that capital deepening, that is the impact that changing the capital-labor ratio has upon growth. When we express the rate of growth in per capita terms, the following expression holds:[21]

$$\% \text{ change in } Y/L = F_K(\% \text{ change in } K/L) + t.c. \qquad (22\text{–}23)$$

where F_k represents the share of capital and *t.c.* represents per capita technical change. This states that the rate of growth of per capita income is given by the percentage change in the capital-labor ratio multiplied by the capital share, plus the increase per capita technical change. This relationship indicates the capital deepening or increasing the capital stock relative to the supply of labor will not lead to a proportionate increase in output. For example, if capital's share is 25 percent of income, the increase in per capita income will only be one fourth as great as the increase in the capital-labor ratio. This arises from the diminishing returns that result when one factor is increased relative to the other.

In pioneering work, Robert Solow estimated a relationship similar to that given in Equation (22–22) for the United States for the period between 1929 and 1955 and concluded that more than half of the increased output over the past few decades is due to technical change or increased productivity due to technological advances.[22] Capital deepening per se accounted for only one eighth to one tenth of the observed growth, while the growth of the labor force accounted for the rest.

Following Solow's lead, Edward Denison analyzed the source of growth in the United States between 1929 and 1969 in more detail.[23] His conclusions are interesting, and are summarized in Table 22–1. Between 1929 and 1969, the rate of growth of potential output of the United States economy averaged 3.41 percent per year. Of this, approximately 53 percent was accounted for by increases in the quantity and quality of capital and labor, while 47 percent was accounted for by technical change or productivity increases. Increases in the quality

---

[21] This expression can be derived by altering society's production function to read $y = f(k, a)$ where $y = Y/L$; $k = K/L$, and $a = A/L$. Because we assume that the production function is subject to constant returns to scale, this expression for the production function is equivalent to the more familiar one $Y = F(K, L, A)$. By differentiating $y = f(k, a)$ with respect to time and making the appropriate transformations to determine growth rates, we can derive Equation (22–23).

[22] Solow, "Technical Change."

[23] Edward F. Denison, *Accounting for United States Economic Growth, 1929–1969* (Washington, D.C.: The Brookings Institution, 1974).

TABLE 22-1

Sources of Growth of Potential National Income in the United States, 1929–1969

	Percentage Points in Growth Rate	Percent of Growth Rate
National income	3.41	100.0
Total factor input	1.82	53.4
Labor	1.32	38.7
Employment	1.09	32.0
Hours	−0.22	−6.5
Age-sex composition	−0.05	−1.5
Education	0.41	12.0
Unallocated	0.09	2.6
Capital	0.50	14.7
Inventories	0.09	2.6
Nonresidential structures and equipment	0.20	5.9
Dwellings	0.19	5.9
International assets	0.02	0.6
Land	0.06	0.0
Productivity change	1.59	46.6
(Output per unit of input)		
Advances in knowledge	0.92	27.0
Improved resource allocation	0.30	8.8
Economies of scale	0.36	10.6
Dwellings occupation ratio	0.01	0.3

Source: E. F. Denison, *Accounting for United States Economic Growth, 1929–1969* (Washington, D.C.: The Brookings Institution, 1974) pp. 127–28.

and quantity of the work force were responsible for 39 percent of the increase in income. Of this, changes in employment and working hours accounted for 25 percent of the total growth, while improvements in the quality of labor—primarily through rising educational standards—accounted for 12 percent of the total growth that took place. Increases in the total amount of capital only contributed to 15 percent of the economy's total growth. The bulk of technical change, which accounted for 47 percent of total growth, came from the general advance of knowledge that permitted more to be produced with a given fixed input. This contributed to 27 percent of the total growth. Finally, economies of scale, which permitted more efficient production as the size of the market grew, accounted for 11 percent of total growth.

The main determinants of past growth appear to be the following: improvements in the quantity and quality of the labor force (39 percent); technical change that permits more output for a given unit of input (27 percent); and increases in the physical capital stock (15 percent). Thus the evidence indicates that increase in the capital stock will have relatively little impact upon the long-run rate of growth of output.

The Role of Government

The theoretical discussion of the previous sections and the empirical research of Solow, Denison, and others indicate relatively little scope for governmental activity to stimulate the rate of growth in a period of full employment. If the government wants to raise the equilibrium growth rate, the empirical evidence suggests that the most effective way of doing this is by increasing the productivity of labor by improving the quality of the labor force. This primarily means improving the degree of education or human capital available in the economy. The available evidence indicates that a large proportion of the economy's past growth has been due to improved educational levels. While diminishing returns may set in with respect to further improvements in education, it is likely that improved education will continue to exert a positive force in growth. Efforts on the part of the government to improve the educational standards in the country are important not only in terms of raising the income of the poor, but in terms of increasing the growth of income and thereby the standard of living to all members of society.

In a period of full employment, Denison's research indicates that the efficacy of other governmental policies aimed at raising the equilibrium growth rate is limited. The impact of R and D expenditures appears to be relatively limited, while efforts to increase the aggregate savings ratio and hence the level of investment and the rate of capital formation should have relatively little effectiveness. Of course, if the economy were in a situation of secular stagnation with a large gap between actual and potential output, the traditional governmental policies to stimulate income could obviously cause the growth rate to rise substantially. As we saw in the previous chapter, the economy has operated below its potential during much of the postwar period. Consequently, it is not surprising that the bulk of explicit governmental effort aimed at increasing the rate of growth of income has been aimed at increasing the amount of investment. These efforts have included the following: accelerated depreciation, investment tax credits, and reductions in the corporate income tax. [24]

The Impact upon Investment in Theory. The general impact of these policies can be seen in Figure 22–1 which portrays a supply and a demand curve for investable funds by a representative firm. The demand curve is the marginal efficiency of investment curve, which expresses the demand for investable funds at different interest rates. This curve reflects decreasing returns as the amount of capital increases. In this formulation, investment demand is assumed to be a function of the interest rate alone. The supply curve has a horizontal

---

[24] See Chapter 13 for a formal analysis of the impact of these policies upon the investment decision.

FIGURE 22–1

Demand for and Supply of Capital to a Representative Firm

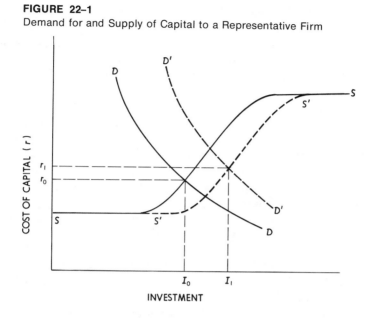

portion reflecting the firm's internal supply of funds consisting of retained earnings, depreciation, and what the firm considers to be its
safe debt limit. As it accumulates more debt, however, its cost of
borrowing increases. At some point, the cost of issuing equity should
be less than that of accumulating debt, and the firm will choose to
issue equity. At this point, the firm's supply curve may level off or
become more elastic since the cost of raising equity capital rises only
slightly over a wide range.

The effect of accelerated depreciation, investment credits, or corporate tax reductions will be to raise the investment demand or *mei*
curve proportionately by reducing the effective tax burden imposed on
the firm. Thus the investment demand curve should shift to $D'D'$
These policies will shift the supply curve to the right by increasing the
amount of depreciation reserves and/or retained earnings, causing the
investment supply schedule to shift to $S'S'$. Since both the demand
and the supply curves have shifted to the right, more investment
should be forthcoming. Specifically, in Figure 22–1 the equilibrium
amount of investment has risen from I_0 to I_1. If the economy is not at
full employment, this increase in investment should lead to increases
in income and hence facilitate the attainment of the equilibrium
growth path. Of course, if the economy is already at full employment,
the increase in investment demand will generate inflationary pressures
and no increase in either income or the equilibrium growth rate.

The Impact upon Investment in Practice. Having outlined how changes in profits taxes, accelerated depreciation, or investment credits can in principle affect investment, let us briefly survey the major changes made to stimulate investment during the postwar period and review the evidence concerning their efficacy. The major changes that took place are given as follows.

1. *Accelerated depreciation.* Prior to 1954, virtually the only method of depreciation permitted was straight line. Under this formula, a firm deducts a constant proportion of any investment during its taxable lifetime. In 1954, the government permitted firms to utilize accelerated depreciation methods, enabling them to increase the amount of depreciation claimed in the early years of the investment.[25] Since the depreciation allowance is greater in the early years under accelerated depreciation than under straight-line depreciation, the present value of the tax savings on depreciation is greater under accelerated depreciation than under straight-line depreciation. Moreover, insofar as a firm's investments keep growing, the size of the discounted tax savings keeps growing. Thus, under accelerated depreciation, the government in effect gives growing firms an increasing tax-free loan.

2. *Depreciation life guidelines.* In 1962, the Treasury permitted firms to adopt shorter lifetime of equipment. By shortening the taxable lifetime of investments, the government increased the present value of the reduction in the tax liability arising from depreciation allowances. This should increase the profitability of any given investment.[26]

3. *Investment tax credit.* In 1962, the government also adopted a tax credit equal to 7 percent of the cost of investments in equipment with useful lives of eight years or more. Reduced credits were given for investments with useful lives of four to eight years, while no credit was given for investments with useful lives of less than four years. Utilities only received tax credits of 3 percent. Moreover, credits amounting to more than $25,000 were limited to a maximum reduction of total tax liability by 50 percent; amounts in excess of this limitation could be carried forward for five years to reduce tax liabilities in the future. As the tax credit was initially enacted, the tax credit had to be deducted from the depreciable value of the asset. For example, if the investment cost $1,000, the firm would receive a credit equal to $70. But the depreciable cost of the asset would be $930 instead of $1,000. This provision, which is known as the Long Amendment, was repealed in 1964. Obviously the value of the tax credit is greater if it does not have to be deducted from the depreciable cost of the investment. In October 1966, the tax credit was suspended until December 1967 to counteract inflationary pressures; but this suspension was repealed

---

[25] See Chapter 13 for a discussion of the specific form of accelerated depreciation allowed.

[26] In 1972, the Canadian government shortened the depreciation lifetime for manufacturing equipment to two years, in a drastic effort to increase investment.

after only five months when the pace of economic activity appeared to slacken. Finally, as inflationary pressures continued, the tax credit was repealed in April 1969. As part of the New Economic Policy, Congress reinstated the investment credit effective in 1972. The rate was ultimately raised to 10 percent and the credit extended to 1981. Canada introduced a 5 percent investment credit in 1976.

4. *Tax reductions.* In 1964, the government reduced the marginal tax rate on corporate profits from 52 percent to 48 percent.[27] This was part of a general tax reduction that also reduced personal income taxes substantially. Unlike accelerated depreciation, the change in the depreciation guidelines and the investment credit, the tax reduction was part of a package aimed at stimulating economic activity in general rather than investment per se. Nevertheless, by reducing corporate tax liabilities the reduction in the corporate income tax should have increased the present value of investments and thus increased investment expenditures.

A number of recent studies have attempted to quantify the impact of these various incentives upon investment expenditures.[28] While the specific methodologies and assumptions in each of these studies differ, they all indicate that tax incentives had a fairly sizable effect upon investment demand. Between 1954 and 1966, it is estimated that the shift in the investment demand curve amounted to between 47 percent and 27 percent of total investment. Even if we take the lower figure as representative, this indicates a substantial shift in the investment demand schedule.[29]

In terms of specific incentive effects, it appears that accelerated depreciation and the tax credit gave the greatest boost to investment. Shortening the taxable life of investments or reducing corporate profit taxes had relatively little impact on investment. Per dollar of revenue loss, policies to accelerate allowable depreciation or to permit tax credits for investments appear to have had the greatest impact upon the investment demand schedule.

In assessing the impact of these policies to stimulate investment

---

[27] In May 1972, the Canadian government reduced its tax rates on corporations in the manufacturing sector from 46.5 percent to 40 percent in an effort to stimulate investment.

[28] R. E. Hall and Dale W. Jorgenson, "Application of the Theory of Optimum Capital Accumulative"; C. W. Bischoff, "The Effect of Alternative Long Distributions"; R. M. Coen, "The Effect of Cash Flow on Speed of Adjustment," in *Tax Incentives and Capital Spending*, ed. Gary Fromm (Washington D.C.: The Brookings Institution, 1971); R. M. Coen, "Investment Behavior, The Measurement of Depreciation, and Tax Policy," *American Economic Review* vol. 65 (March, 1975), pp. 59–74.

[29] It should be pointed out that these studies estimated the shift on the investment demand function resulting from the tax incentives, rather than the net change in investment. This latter figure depends upon the interaction of the supply of investable funds as well as the investment demand function and will only equal the shift in the investment demand schedule if the supply schedule is infinitely elastic.

upon the rate of growth of the economy, it is important to distinguish between their impact upon the actual growth rate and the equilibrium growth rate. Most of these investment stimuli took place between 1954 and 1965. During most of this period, the economy was suffering from a substantial gap between actual and potential GNP. While their specific numerical estimates differ, the authors of all of these studies conclude that the various policies aimed at stimulating investment did in fact have a substantial impact upon investment. Because of problems associated with the specific lag relationships, it is difficult to estimate by how much investment in any one year would have been less if these investment stimuli had not been in effect. The evidence suggests, however, that for the entire period, 1954 to 1966, the total level of investment was raised by at least 25 percent. During the period 1954 through 1966, investment averaged $80 billion a year, while GNP averaged approximately $500 billion a year. If 25 percent less investment had taken place, the average level of income would have fallen by $50 billion on the assumption that the multiplier for the economy is 2.5. Thus, on the average, without the investment stimuli, GNP would have been 10 percent less and the average rate of growth of income would have been 10 percent less. This implies that on the average 10 percent of the rate of growth of the economy that took place during this period was due to accelerated depreciation, the investment credit, and the tax cut.

This estimate reflects the impact of the investment stimuli upon the actual rate of growth. If we attempt to estimate the impact of the investment stimuli upon the equilibrium rate of growth, we reach some different conclusions. For example, following Denison, let us assume that total investment accounted for 15 percent of the economy's growth during the period 1954–66 and that the policies to stimulate investment accounted for 25 percent of all investment during this time period. This implies that the investment generated by accelerated depreciation, the investment credit, and the tax cut accounted for slightly less than 4 percent of the total growth that took place between 1954 and 1966.

The difference between these two estimates can be interpreted as differences between the actual and the equilibrium growth rates. In the short run, when actual income lies below potential income, the economy is capable of growing at a faster rate than when actual income equals potential income. During most of the period between 1954 and 1966, the economy was at less than full employment and actual income fell short of potential income. Thus efforts to increase investment raised aggregate demand and led to sizable increases in real income.

Although the economy rarely moves along a balanced growth path where actual income equals potential income, the analyses of Solow and Denison are based on the implicit assumption that the observed average growth rate reflects a balanced growth rate. Thus their re-search is primarily concerned with the sources of growth from the supply side, since demand is implicitly assumed to adjust to supply. Alternatively stated, their estimates of the source of growth are not based on a short-run Keynesian demand model, but on a long-run equilibrium growth model that receives primary impetus from the supply side instead of the demand side.

Since the period between 1954 and 1966 was largely marked by excess capacity, the impact of the investment stimuli upon demand was probably greater than its impact upon capacity. Consequently, the estimate that the investment stimuli contributed 10 percent to the overall rate of growth is probably more accurate than the estimate that they contributed 4 percent to the overall growth rate. If, however, this period had been marked by full employment, the analysis based on the equilibrium growth path would have been more appropriate and the estimate of 4 percent would have been more accurate.

CONCLUSION

This chapter has considered the problem of enabling an economy to maintain a stable growth path of income. In an economy where in-vestment is not responsive to the interest rate, the rate of growth of capacity is apt to equal the rate of growth of demand only by chance, since the economy contains no self-equilibrating mechanism to bring these two together. If investment is responsive to the interest rate, however, an interest rate will always exist that could equilibrate the growth of capacity and the rate of growth of demand, enabling the economy to maintain a stable growth path. If, however, society is sub-ject to an interest rate floor or if investment is interest inelastic, this self-equilibrating mechanism will fail and the growth of capacity will not necessarily equal the growth of demand. In this case, govern-mental action is needed to alter the savings ratio and society's invest-ment propensities to bring the growth of capacity and of demand to-gether. Moreover, even if investment is interest elastic, governmental action may still be desirable to alter the savings ratio to change the savings-consumption mix.

It should be stressed that whether investment is interest elastic or not, the ultimate determinant of the rate of growth of capacity is the rate of growth of the labor force and technical change. Thus unless government can act to increase productivity in society, it cannot alter the basic long-run equilibrium growth path. It can, however, adopt policies to enable the rate of growth of capacity, demand, and the labor force to grow in tandem.

An analysis of the sources of growth in the United States indicates that investment and savings play a relatively minor role in contributing to the equilibrium growth path. During the period between 1929 and 1957, capital formation accounted for approximately 15 percent of the growth of the economy. Thus the efforts on the part of the government to increase the savings ratio and to stimulate investment by tax credits, accelerated depreciation, or reductions in the corporate profits rate should have relatively little impact upon the long-run equilibrium growth path. Nevertheless, in periods of excess capacity and slack aggregate demand, efforts to stimulate investment can have a substantial impact upon aggregate demand and upon the actual rate of growth. In this connection, investment stimuli act much like any other expansionary fiscal policy.

Thus, in analyzing the impact of government upon the rate of growth of the economy, it is important to distinguish between the equilibrium or potential growth rate and the actual growth rate. While there is little the government can do to alter the natural rate of growth or the equilibrium rate of growth, it can bring its full arsenal of fiscal and monetary policies to bear to ensure that the actual rate of growth coincides with the long-run equilibrium growth rate. Thus its main role should be seen as ensuring that the equilibrium growth rate is attained rather than attempting to alter it.

ADDITIONAL NOTES

1. The warranted rate of growth in terms of time periods is determined as follows:

In equilibrium, at any time period, savings must equal investment, i.e.,

$$S_t = I_t \tag{a}$$

Savings in any period is a constant proportion of income. Thus

$$S_t = sY_t \tag{b}$$

There is a fixed relationship between capital (K) and income (Y) such that

$$K_t/Y_t = v \tag{c}$$

Since this relationship holds for all time periods, Equation (c) implies

$$K_t = vY_t \text{ and} \tag{c.1}$$
$$K_{t+1} = vY_{t+1} \tag{c.2}$$

Subtracting (c.1) from (c.2) yields

$$K_{t+1} - K_t = v(Y_{t+1} - Y_t) \tag{d}$$

But the difference between the capital stock in period $t + 1$ and period

t represents investment in period t, that is

$$I_t = K_{t+1} - K_t \qquad (e)$$

Substituting (d) into (e) yields

$$I_t = v(Y_{t+1} - Y_t) \qquad (f)$$

Therefore, substituting (f) and (b) into (a) and solving for income yields

$$Y_t = \frac{v}{s}(Y_{t+1} - Y_t) \qquad (g)$$

Therefore, the rate of growth of income is given by

$$g_w \equiv \frac{Y_{t+1} - Y_t}{Y_t} = \frac{Y_t - Y_{t-1}}{Y_{t-1}} = \frac{s}{v} \qquad (h)$$

2. Let us assume that the government has three policy tools: expenditures, a personal income tax, and a tax on profits. The relationships between the fiscal variables and the other variables in the economy are given as follows:

$$
\begin{aligned}
Y_t &= C_t + I_t + G_t & (a) \\
C_t &= (1 - s)(Y_t - T_t) & (b) \\
T_t &= T_t^y + T_t^p & (c) \\
T_t^y &= tY_t & (d) \\
T_t^p &= \rho P_t & (e) \\
P_t &= pY_t & (f) \\
G_t &= gY_t & (g) \\
I_t &= \bar{I}_t & (h)
\end{aligned}
$$

Equation (a) states the familiar equilibrium condition that income must equal the sum of aggregate demand: consumption, investment, and government expenditures. Equation (b) indicates that consumption is proportional to income net of taxes, with the factor of proportionality being the marginal propensity to consume or one minus the savings ratio. Note that $Y_t - T_t$ does not equal disposable personal income because the existence of profits (P_t) drives a wedge between national income and personal income. Equation (c) defines total tax revenue as the sum of personal taxes (T_t^y) and profits taxes (T_t^p). According to Equation (d), personal tax revenues are a constant proportion of income, while according to Equation (e) profits tax revenues are a constant proportion of profits (P_t). Equations (f) and (g) indicate that profits and government expenditures are respectively constant proportions of income. Finally, Equation (h) states that investment is as yet an undetermined constant. As was true in the model of the no-government economy, the nature of the investment function determines the nature of the equilibrium rate of growth.

By making the necessary substitutions into Equation (a) and solving for income, it is straightforward, if somewhat tedious, to show that in equilibrium

$$\sigma Y_t = I_t$$

where

$$\sigma = s(1 - \tau) + (\tau - g) \tag{i}$$

and

$$\tau = (t + \rho p)$$

The parameter σ should be interpreted as the total proportion of income that is saved by society: individuals plus the government. Thus Equation (i) states the familiar condition that in equilibrium, total savings (σY_t) must equal investment. (The parameter τ represents the ratio of total tax revenue to GNP. Thus the first term of σ represents the propensity to save out of GNP while the second term represents the net impact of government upon society's saving ratio. If the government's budget is balanced, expenditures equal revenue and $\tau = g$; the government is neutral with respect to the aggregate savings ratio. If expenditures exceed revenues, g is greater than τ and the government reduces the aggregate savings ratio. Similarly, if revenues exceed expenditures, τ is greater than g and the government adds to the savings ratio.)

The nature of the equilibrium growth path can be determined by the nature of the investment function. If we assume that investment is determined by the accelerator principle, we can derive the rate of growth of capacity or the warranted rate of growth. Specifically, let us assume that investment takes the form previously discussed in connection with the warranted rate of growth.

$$I_t = v(Y_{t+1} - Y_t)$$

Substituting this expression into the equilibrium condition (i) and solving for the equilibrium rate of growth yields

$$g_w' \equiv \frac{Y_t - Y_{t-1}}{Y_{t-1}} = \frac{\sigma}{v} \tag{k}$$

This states the familiar relationship that the warranted rate of growth is equal to the savings ratio divided by the capital-output ratio. But, unlike the warranted rate of growth in the no-government economy, the warranted rate of growth in this economy (g_w') is flexible since it can be altered by changing the fiscal parameters in the economy, g and t, and ρ.

3.   Let us assume that investment demand is a constant proportion

of the net profits in the previous period, plus an adjustment factor that attempts to close any gap between the desired and the actual capital stock that existed in the previous period:

$$I_t = b(P_{t-1} - T_{t-1}{}^p) + B(K_{t-1}{}^d - K_{t-1}{}^a) \qquad \text{(a)}$$

By substituting Equations (e) and (f) from Additional Note 2 into Equation (a) of this Note we can derive a simplified expression for investment demand:

$$I_t = aY_{t-1} + \beta(K_{t-1}{}^d - K_{t-1}{}^a) \qquad \text{(a.1)}$$

where $a = bp(1 - \rho)$. The parameter "a" can be interpreted as the propensity to invest out of last period's income. Thus this investment function is analogous to the investment demand function specified in the no-government economy [see Equation (22–10)]. But in this investment function, the propensity to invest depends upon the profits tax rate ρ and hence can be manipulated by the government.

By substituting Equation (a.1) into the equilibrium condition $S = I$ [Equation (i) in Additional Note 2] and solving for the rate of growth, we can derive the actual rate of growth in this economy:

$$g_a' \equiv \frac{Y_t - Y_{t-1}}{Y_{t-1}} = \frac{a}{\sigma} - 1 + \frac{\beta}{\sigma}(v_{t-1}{}^d - v_{t-1}{}^a) \qquad \text{(b)}$$

This states that the actual rate of growth must equal the sum of two terms: the first represents the propensity to invest out of last period's income divided by the savings rate minus one, while the second term represents an adjustment factor for divergences between the desired capital-output ratio (v^d) and the actual capital-output ratio (v^a). This is entirely analogous to the actual rate of growth derived in the no-government economy given by Equation (22–12). The only difference is that the propensity to invest out of last period's income (a) and society's saving ration (σ) not only depend upon behavioral constants, but also depend upon fiscal variables that can be changed by the government.

4.   The ability of the government to achieve any growth path can be seen rigorously by setting the warranted rate of growth (g_w') and the actual rate of growth (g_a') equal to the natural rate of growth (g_n) and solving for the fiscal parameters. This yields the following set of equations:

$$(n + 1)(1 - s)t - (n + 1)g + [(n + 1)(1 - s) + b]p\,\rho = bp - (n + 1)s \qquad \text{(a)}$$

$$(1 - s)t - g + (1 - s)p\,\rho = vn - s \qquad \text{(b)}$$

The following parameters are behavioral constant and presumably are known by the policy-maker: the natural rate of growth (n); the capital-output ratio (v); the private-savings rate (s); the profits share (p); and the propensity to invest out of after-tax profits (b). Given these, we can solve for the value of the share of government expenditures (g); the income tax rate (t); and the profits tax rate (ρ) that will enable equilibrium to be maintained.

Note that there are only two equations but three unknown policy variables. Inspection of Equation (a) should indicate, however, that only two of the policy tools are independent. For example, if we take the profits tax rate (ρ) as given, there will be no solution to the equations since the Equations (a) and (b) will no longer be independent. (Formally, when $\rho = \bar{\rho}$ and is given, the determinant of the left-hand side of the equation will equal zero.) This happens because income taxes and government expenditures influence the equilibrium level of income in the same way. The government should fix its rate of expenditures or its rate of income taxes and then solve for the rate of profit taxes and income taxes or expenditures that will enable equilibrium to occur.

5. The desired capital stock can be derived from the condition $\partial Y/\partial K = r$, where we assume that the price index is standardized to equal one. For example, if output can be expresed by a Cobb-Douglas production function, $Y = K^a L^{1-a}$, then $\partial Y/\partial K = \alpha K^{a-1} L^{1-a}$. The desired capital stock is given by $K^* = [(r/\alpha(L^{\alpha-1})]^{1/(\alpha-1)}$.

6. In equilibrium

$$\frac{dT/dt}{I} = \frac{dS/dt}{S}.$$

But

$$S = sY.$$

Therefore $dS/dt = (dS/dY)(dY/dt)$. Substituting the expression for dS/dt into the above equilibrium condition yields

$$\frac{dT/dt}{I} = \frac{dS/dt}{S} = \frac{s\,dY/dt}{sY} = \frac{d\,Y/dt}{Y}$$

7. Under fairly general assumptions, it can be shown that this rate of interest is given by

$$r = \frac{\alpha}{s}n$$

where α represents the share of profits in the economy or the ratio of profits to income. If, by chance, the profit share also equals the savings ratio, the equilibrium rate of interest will equal the rate of growth of the labor force. In this case the economy will be in a long-run equilibrium that maximizes consumption. But, regardless of the relationship between saving and profits, the above interest-rate equation indicates that there should always be an interest rate that equates the rate of growth of capacity with the rate of growth of demand. For a good summary of this and other "golden age" results, see Baumol, *Economic Dynamics*, pp. 393–400.

8.   The role of government can be developed by using the following model:

$$Y = C + I + G \tag{a}$$
$$C = (1 - s)(Y - T) \tag{b}$$
$$T = tY \tag{c}$$
$$G = gY \tag{d}$$
$$I = \bar{I} \tag{e}$$

Equation (a) states the familiar equilibrium condition that income must equal the sum of aggregate demand: consumption, investment, and government. Equation (b) state that consumption is proportional to income net of taxes, while Equations (c) and (d) state that tax revenue (T) and expenditures (G) are proportional to income. Finally, Equation (e) indicates that investment is an unspecified constant.

By substituting Equations (b)–(e) into Equation (a) we derive the equilibrium condition that planned savings equals investment.

$$\sigma Y = \bar{I} \tag{f}$$

where $\sigma = s(1 - t) + t - g$. Thus σ reflects society's effective savings rate.

Again, let us consider the equilibrium rate of growth given by capacity investment and that given by desired investment. Capacity investment is defined to be that investment that enables society to maintain a constant capital-labor ratio. As we showed previously, this requirement is met when $I = nK$. Thus the equilibrium rate of growth of capacity takes place when

$$\sigma Y = nK \tag{g}$$

But since σ represents society's effective savings rate, this condition is precisely equivalent to the equilibrium condition $sY = nK$ given in Equation (22–20).

The equilibrium investment demand can also be determined in a similar fashion. If desired investment equals planned savings, the interest rate will be constant. This implies that the capital-labor ratio and the capital-output ratio are constant. But this in turn implies that the rate of growth of capital, the rate of growth of labor, and the rate of growth of output are all equal (i.e., $\Delta K/K = \Delta L/L = \Delta Y/Y$). But since the change in the capital stock equals investment ($\Delta K = I$), and the rate of growth of the labor force equals $n (\Delta L/L = n)$, this implies that $I = nK$. For equilibrium, savings must equal investment or $\sigma Y = nK$. This, again, is the equilibrium condition required for balanced growth.

REFERENCES

Denison, Edward F. *Accounting for United States Economic Growth, 1929–1969.* Washington, D.C.: The Brookings Institution, 1974.

Domar, Evsey D. "Expansion and Employment," in *Essays in the Theory of Economic Growth.* Oxford: Oxford University Press, 1957, pp. 83–108.

Fromm, Gary, ed. *Tax Incentives and Capital Spending.* Washington, D.C.: The Brookings Institution, 1971.

Harrod, Sir Roy F. *Toward a Dynamic Economics.* London: Macmillan Company, 1948.

Nelson, R. R. "Full Employment Policy and Economic Growth," *American Economic Review,* vol. 56 (December 1966), pp. 1178–92.

Smith, Warren L. "Monetary—Fiscal Policy and Economic Growth," *Quarterly Journal of Economics,* vol. 71 (February 1957), pp. 36–55.

Solow, R. M. "A Contribution to the Theory of Economic Growth," *Quarterly Journal of Economics* vol. 70 (February 1956), pp. 65–94.

Solow, R. M. "Technical Change and the Aggregate Production Function," *Review of Economics and Statistics,* vol. 39 (August 1957), pp. 312–20.

PART V

Development

23

Public Finance in the Developing Economies

As explained in the previous chapter, the potential or equilibrium growth path is dependent upon the rate of capital formation, the capital-output ratio, the rate of technological change, and the growth of the labor force (in numbers and skill). In highly industrialized countries, governments can do little to influence the potential rate of growth, as explained; the government's primary task is to seek to ensure that the actual growth coincides with the potential growth path—that full employment is attained. While such a government can to a limited extent affect the potential rate of capital formation, changes in this rate have little impact upon growth; the capital-output ratio is largely beyond the government's control; and small changes in the ratio are not likely to influence growth to any great extent. Technological change is little affected by government policy and the rate of growth of the labor force is even less affected, except through governmental programs of education.

THE DEVELOPING ECONOMIES

In the developing countries—the LDCs, as they are commonly known today—there is much greater opportunity for altering the equilibrium rate of growth and much more pressure to do so. There is also more need to alter the capital-labor ratio, largely self-adjusting in the more developing economies. On the other hand, while lag of the actual growth rate behind the potential rate, with consequent "Keynesian" unemployment—unemployment arising from inadequate aggregate demand—does occur, it is thought to be much less of a problem. Unemployment and underemployment in the LDCs primarily result from inadequate capital goods, not inadequate aggragate demand.

The Characteristics of the LDCs

While there are wide differences among the LDCs, as a group they display major characteristics:

Low Per Capita Real Incomes.   While there are serious difficulties in comparing incomes among countries with different cultures, by any standards the per capita GNPs of the LDCs are very low—some under $100 a year, many under $200. Such a figure means that most families are living at bare subsistence of a most meager sort. By contrast, the income figures of the developed economies run well over $4,000 a year; the 1975 GNP figure for the United States is $7,034.

Limited Stock of Capital Goods.   A second major characteristic is the relatively small quantity of capital goods compared to labor. Crude hand methods are dominant in agriculture and other fields of endeavor. As a consequent, physical output per person is much less than in developed countries. In large measure, the shortage of capital is a result of a very low savings-income *(S/Y)* ratio; persons have such limited incomes that margin for savings is almost nil.

Dominance of Subsistence Agriculture in the Least-Developed Countries.   A high percentage of the population is dependent upon their own agricultural produce for their livelihood, while the commercial and industrial sectors of the economy are small in scope compared to that of agriculture. Except for those LDCs fortunate enough to have oil or mineral resources, exports consist primarily of unprocessed agricultural products.

Relatively Low Levels of Education and Health.   Formal education is limited, with widespread illiteracy and lack of other skills important for modern economic development. Public health standards are frequently low, with limited numbers of doctors and widespread endemic diseases, which reduce output of the labor force.

The Primary Determinants of Economic Growth

Precise analysis of the role of governmental expenditures and revenues on economic growth requires use of a model of economic growth applicable to the LDCs. The simplified models of Chapter 22 are of little use and refinement of them is not fruitful for this purpose, given the complete absence of knowledge of the functional relationships involved in the equations in the LDCs. Therefore, there is little merit in attempting to go farther than merely identifying some of the major determinants that appear to influence economic growth in the LDCs.

As a consequence, no quantitative estimates of the effects of various alternatives are possible.

The primary determinants of the rate of economic growth in LDCs appear to be as follows:

The Rate of Capital Formation. The potential or capacity level depends upon the ratio of savings to income at full employment *(S/Y)*. The actual level, or desired investment, which cannot exceed the potential level, is a function of present and expected rates of return from additional investment; attitudes toward the security of the investment; availability of entrepreneurship and the willingness to undertake risk; and availability of money capital to those who wish to undertake investment. Capital formation is a much more significant determinant of growth in an LDC than in a developed economy because the availability of underutilized labor minimizes the importance of the labor supply constraint.

The Incremental Capital Output Ratio. The greater the additional output available from additional investment, the lower is the incremental capital-output ratio and the higher is the rate of increase in output from a given volume of investment. This question, normally ignored in a highly developed economy, is of utmost importance in an LDC in which too often scarce capital will be used, unless prevented by the government, for investments that contribute little to economic growth.

Ability to Import. A major constraint on the ability to increase the rate of capital formation and utilize the optimal forms of capital goods is the amount of foreign exchange available to pay for imported capital goods. Most LDCs cannot produce more complex forms of capital equipment. Unfortunately they have only limited exports and foreign loan or aid potential and they suffer from a high propensity to import consumption goods as incomes rise.

Technological Change. As in developed countries, the rate of technological change is an element in determining increases in per capita output. Technology can, of course, be imported from the outside, but often technology originating in the highly developed labor-scarce economies is not well suited to the LDCs.

Growth of the Labor Force. Increases in total output also depend on increases in labor supply, involving a larger number of available workers and increased skills. The former, of course, increases the number of persons over whom the greater output must be divided, while the latter results in a clear gain. Of particular importance in a developing economy is improved managerial skills—ones that are particularly scarce because the subsistence economy provides no experience of this type.

Environment. In the least-developed economies, attitudes toward change from old traditions, family relationships, legal framework, tribal hostilities, and so on may be of great importance.

The overall ingredient necessary for attainment of the goals of development is the appropriate balance among the various elements. An increase in the rate of capital formation without skilled workers to use the equipment will result in a high capital-output ratio. But even worse is an increase in numbers of educated persons beyond the capacity of the economy to absorb them. The result is frustration and political instability.

Goals of the Developing Economies

In the period since World War II, the LDCs have become increasingly concerned about their plight; independence, increased knowledge of the outside world on the part of at least a portion of the population, and increased competence on the part of the policy-makers have led virtually all LDCs to seek to improve their economic positions. Specifically, the LDCs have sought to speed the rate of growth and to increase per capita income closer to the levels of the developed countries.

Second, LDCs seek to ensure that development accompanies growth—that the benefits of growth spread beyond a small group. Closely related, they seek to retain or attain a pattern of distribution of income regarded as acceptable and particularly to avoid or eliminate the high degree of inequality that has occurred in many countries in the past as output rose rapidly. Attitudes vary; countries such as Tanzania and Zambia place great stress on maintaining a high degree of equality of income, while others, particularly in Latin America and southeast Asia, have been less concerned.

Third, given the scarcity of resources, the LDCs are more concerned about the utilization of resources in a manner that will contribute most to the satisfaction of the wants of the community. Waste of capital or foreign exchange, for example, is of much greater concern than in a highly developed economy. Finally, but to a lesser degree, LDCs are concerned about the maintenance of reasonable price stability.

With the strong stress on development and the realization that private enterprise has lagged in providing development, the LDCs stress the role of government in the economy much more than do most of the Western developed countries.

GOVERNMENTAL ACTIVITY AND ECONOMIC DEVELOPMENT

In a number of ways, governments of LDCs may be able to speed the rate of economic development.

Rate of Capital Formation

As noted previously, the potential rate of capital formation is controlled by the S/Y ratio—the percentage of income saved. Governments may increase this ratio in several ways.

Governmental Savings. The government may collect more in taxes than its spends for current operations (consumption expenditures of government), providing the remainder for private investment on a loan basis or for direct governmental investment.

Alternatively, this goal may be accomplished by financing of government investment (or of loans to private firms) by money creation, with consequent inflation; those persons whose incomes lag behind the price level increase are thus compelled to save to finance the government's real investment. Most LDCs, however, regard the avoidance of inflation as a significant, if secondary, goal.

Measures to Increase Private Saving. The government may encourage private savings by providing more suitable outlets for holding savings (e.g., mobile banks that visit villages weekly) and by taxes that provide incentive to save. Thus the case for consumption-related taxes is much stronger than it is in countries that do not seek to increase the S/Y ratio. Similarly, the case against highly progressive income taxes is stronger if the higher-income groups are, in fact, saving substantial portions of their incomes.

Finally, governments may be able to increase savings by providing greater assurance of the security of holding of savings, by promoting political and economic stability.

Measures to Increase Investment

While capital formation is restricted severely in an LDC by the low level of savings, it may also be restricted by inadequate willingness to undertake real investment, so that the actual or desired rate of capital formation lags behind the potential rate. LDCs frequently suffer from lack of adequate entrepreneurship, from inadequate mobilization of such money capital as is available, and from lack of security for future earnings from investments.

There are several steps governments can take. One is to provide entrepreneurship through government—perhaps initially with the aid of foreign management and technical experts—by undertaking investment directly in industry, in hotels, in other essentially commercial facilities. Second, governments may facilitate private investment by providing infrastructure: roads, electric power, communications, and the like, without which industrial development cannot succeed but which cannot be provided profitably by private enterprise, at least in the earlier years of development. Externalities and natural monopoly characteristics justify governmental action. Third, by developing banking systems, governments may aid in mobilizing money capital for those who are willing to undertake private investment.

Finally, governments may encourage private investment through tax concessions of various kinds, including those noted in the previous chapter, plus "tax holidays"—complete exemption from taxes for new enterprises for a period of years.

Type of Investment

As noted, in LDCs the type of investment undertaken has significant influence for the capital-output ratio. Private enterprise, left to its own devices, tends to concentrate in investment in facilities yielding high short-term returns (partly because of fears of security over a longer period) and in prestige-type investments, such as office buildings, many of which have a high capital-output ratio.

If governments undertake investment themselves, they may direct the investment along the lines maximizing contribution to economic growth. As subsequently noted, they may not in fact do so; governments make mistakes and they too are influenced by prestige considerations and invest in uneconomic jet planes and steel mills.

Governments may also influence the type of private investment via tax adjustment much more effectively, in fact, than they can influence the overall level of private investment by this means. Provision of accelerated depreciation or tax credits for investments in desired lines and limitation or even complete denial of depreciation deductions for unwanted types of investment can significantly alter investment patterns. Excise taxes on the sale of goods not considered important for development can reduce the sales of these products and thus investment in facilities to produce them.

Finally, governments can facilitate investment requiring imported capital equipment by restricting imports of less essential goods via tariffs or direct control through licensing of imports.

Technological Change

Directly, LDCs can do little to alter technological change, except by sponsoring research for methods more suited to the circumstances of the country. In agriculture, governments may be able to develop new varieties of crops and livestock through experimentation under the conditions of the country. The so-called Green Revolution is an example of what can be done. They may also be able to encourage introduction of new methods in agriculture through farm extension and demonstration work.

Labor

As in the developed economies, governments may be able to make their greatest contributions to growth by increasing the quality of the labor force. Partly this can be attained by public health measures, which reduce the impact of endemic diseases that so curtail output in many tropical countries. Partly it can be attained by providing additional education, not only of the more scholastic type, but also of the trade-school and commercial-college variety. Few skills are as scarce in many LDCs as those of carpenters, machinists, secretaries, and book-keepers. Management skills are of prime importance as well but have received somewhat less attention. In early years of development, governments find it necessary to contract management and high-level technical skills from abroad pending the training of indigenous personnel. Finally, provision of passenger transport—improved roads and cheap public transportation—may prove highly important in increasing the availability of workers. At least in the past, poll taxes and similar levies that must be paid in money have the desirable effect of forcing persons out of purely subsistence agriculture, making their labor services available and increasing labor supply.

Use of Natural Resources

While, by definition, governments cannot increase the supply of natural resources, they may be able to influence the extent to which the owners use the resources or make them available to others. Land is subject to varying degrees of exploitation; owners may allow land to lie idle or they may use it with a low degree of intensity—for range fattening of cattle, for example—while the country imports food products. A relatively heavy tax based on the value of land rather than on the income from it or on the improvements on it will force the owners to use it more intensively and thus contribute to economic development.

Distributional Goals

The LDCs, to varying degrees, seek to restrict the development of income inequality and to improve the economic position of the poor. Thus they seek to improve housing, education, and health for the poor and to establish relatively progressive tax structures. Some of these policies, as for example, improved education, are consistent with the objective of economic growth. But others may not be. Resources used for housing, for example, however meritorious this use may appear to be from an equity standpoint, may be diverted from investment in industry with a much greater payoff. And, as noted, highly progressive income tax systems designed to check the growth of large incomes may seriously reduce the ratio of savings to income and the incentive to undertake investment. This is not necessarily an objection; the government may decide to undertake most investment and to ensure savings from tax collections. But it may be a serious objection if the government relies heavily on private investment. Where conflicts of these types arise, the decision must be made on the basis of weighing of relative objectives.

INSTITUTIONAL CONSTRAINTS

Despite possible conflict among objectives, at least theoretically, the government of an LDC through expenditure and tax policy should be able to facilitate economic growth. But there are serious obstacles in the way of implementing such a program.

First, on the expenditure side, the determination of benefits and costs from various government activities and investments is subject to all the difficulties encountered in a developed economy plus the lack of trained personnel. Theoretically government can direct investment toward the channels that will provide the greatest payoff, avoiding investments that contribute little to development such as office buildings and concentrating on those that do. But, in practice, it may be difficult to select the projects that will actually make the greatest contribution; in fact it is not impossible that the governmental choices may be worse than those of an unregulated private sector. Hopefully the government can do better, but attainment of an optimal program is obviously impossible. With governmental investment there is the additional danger of loss of efficiency arising out of the absence of the profit motive and the high proclivity in some, but by no means all, LDCs toward corruption on the part of government officials.

On the taxation side, attainment of the objective requires a rather complex system of taxes providing, for example, investment incentives for industrial expansion yet incentives to use manpower in preference to capital equipment. An effective system of consumption-related taxation encounters the difficulty that many vendors, even at the manufacturing level, are relatively small, are often illiterate, and keep few records. As noted, the retail sales tax is the preferred form of sales tax, but it cannot possibly be administered in a country in which retailing is carried on by thousands of small illiterate peddlers and market and sidewalk sellers. Similarly, an effective income tax is difficult to operate in a society characterized by illiteracy, absence of records, and a tradition of tax evasion. The governments of LDCs are likewise very short of trained audit and inspection personnel and, in some countries, bribery is difficult to prevent. Thus drastic simplification of tax structures is necessary if they are to function with any degree of effectiveness, yet doing so causes loss of attainment of other objectives.

Quite apart from these difficulties are those common to all countries: the lack of knowledge of the income and price elasticities of demand for various commodities; of the response of labor to reductions in real wages; of the effectiveness of investment credits and other devices for increasing investment.

Finally, and in a sense most significantly, the potential tax capacity of a developing economy relative to total GNP is much less than that of a highly developed one. When most families are at a bare subsistence level, there is little margin that can be paid in taxes. A large portion of total income in the least-developed countries is derived from subsistence agriculture and provides no basis for taxation. The problems noted above, of limited education and record-keeping and lack of trained administrative and audit personnel, further restrict the ability to collect revenues. But the basic problem is the very limited margin over bare subsistence.

THE EXPENDITURE SYSTEMS OF THE LDCs

The actual expenditures systems of the LDCs reflect the objectives and the constraints.

Level of Expenditures

Despite the urgent demands for governmental activities to speed the process of development, the constraints upon the ability to expand the government sector are such that tax revenues in LDCs as a percentage of GNP are relatively low compared to those in highly developed economies. The picture is illustrated in Table 23–1. Whereas the typical figures of the highly industralized countries range from 20 to 35 percent (exclusive of social security), and average 25 percent; the LDC typical figure is from 10 to 20 percent, with an average of 15 percent. The figures cannot be regarded as precisely accurate, in part because the figures of GNP are not known with any high degree of precision. There is little correlation between the actual level of GNP and the tax-GNP ratio, except when comparison is made between the LDCs as a whole and the highly developed countries. Differences among the LDCs are attributable, on the basis of statistical analysis, primarily to three considerations: the degree of openness, that is, the relative importance of foreign trade; the extent of mining and petroleum production; and, inversely, the share of agriculture in GNP. Foreign trade provides a convenient basis for taxation, on imports or exports. Mining is concentrated in a few large firms, and substantial revenues can be collected without affecting the living standards of the

TABLE 23–1
Tax Revenue as Percentage of GNP

Country	Taxes as Percentage of GNP	
	Excluding Social Security	*Including Social Security*
Typical industrial countries (1973)		
Denmark	41.8	44.1
Sweden	34.8	43.5
Norway	32.4	45.9
Finland	31.6	36.9
Canada......................................	31.0	33.9
New Zealand	29.9	29.9
Netherlands	27.8	43.8
Ireland......................................	27.3	32.8
United Kingdom	27.3	32.8
Belgium......................................	25.6	36.6
Germany	24.4	37.3
United States	21.9	28.0
France	21.8	36.9
Switzerland	19.2	26.4
Japan	18.5	22.6
Italy	17.2	29.2
Average 21 OECD countries	25.4	
Typical LDCs (1969–71)		
Brazil	22.9	
Iran...	21.6	
Jamaica	19.4	
Egypt..	19.2	
Sudan..	18.2	
Ghana	15.8	
Kenya	14.4	
Tanzania	13.9	
India..	13.4	
Mali	13.2	
Colombia	10.6	
Honduras	11.3	
Paraguay	10.9	
Indonesia	10.0	
Philippine...................................	9.1	
Ethiopia	8.6	
Guatemala	7.9	
Mexico......................................	7.1	
Nepal	4.4	
Average, 47 LDCs	15.1	

Source: *Canadian Tax Journal*, vol. 24 (March–April 1976), p. 154; R. J. Chelliah, H. J. Baas, and M. R. Kelly, "Tax Ratios and Tax Effort in Developing Countries, 1969–71," *IMF Staff Papers*, vol. 22 (March 1975), pp. 192–93.

typical persons in the country. The agricultural sector is difficult to tax.[1]

Expenditure Patterns

It is impossible to provide meaningful statistics on expenditures by function for LDCs as a group. But examination of the budgets of various LDCs suggests the importance of the following functions.

Education. Particularly in Africa, education is a major expenditure item, frequently accounting for one fourth or more of the budget. Many of the African countries have accomplished excellent results in providing elementary education for a high percentage of children of school age—up to 90 percent in some countries. The great bottleneck has been at the secondary level, where lack of trained teachers has seriously restricted the number of openings and caused a major "school-leaver" problem. Children who have had some education are reluctant to return to the family subsistence farm but lack sufficient education for the jobs that are available. Yet to restrict elementary education would contribute little toward increasing the ability to expand secondary education and politically is extremely unpopular.

Transport and Other Forms of Infrastructure. Many developing countries, particularly in Africa but in Latin America and elsewhere as well, suffer seriously from lack of transport facilities necessary for moving products to market, integrating the economy as a whole, and facilitating exports. Thus road construction has received very high priority, plus extension of railroad lines where traffic volume is heavy.

Public Health. While accounting for relatively less in money terms than some of the other functions, high priority is being given to eliminate endemic diseases and to lessen infant mortality. The rapid spread of improved medical facilities has sharply reduced the death rate but with the unfortunate side effect of stepping up the rate of population growth, a major obstacle in many countries to increased per capita GNP. In many LDCs, increased governmental attention is being given to dissemination of birth-control information.

Agriculture. The outlays on agriculture are substantial in many LDCs, partly for extension work to spread information on improved methods, partly for research, partly to improve farm organization and output by developing state or cooperative farms. Where land has been held in large blocks, acquiring the land and dividing it up into small landholder parcels has been a major activity. This has occurred, for example, in Kenya and Chile, among others. In most of

---

[1] R. J. Chelliah, "Trends in Taxation in Developing Countries," *I.M.F. Staff Papers*, vol. 18 (July 1971), pp. 254–331; R. J. Chelliah, H. J. Baas, and M. S. Kelly, "Tax Ratios and Tax Effort in Developing Countries, 1969–71," *I.M.F. Staff Papers*, vol. 22 (March 1975), pp. 187–205.

Africa, land is not privately owned and is farmed on a small-scale basis, in contrast to the large estates characteristic of much of Latin America. Some countries suffer from excessively small holdings, and concentration or cooperation rather than breaking up of large estates is required for greater efficiency.

Industry.   Some LDCs have left industrial development largely in private hands. Others, however, have taken an active role directly through government corporations or, more commonly, through joint government and foreign private ventures. Automobile assembly plants in LDCs are often developed on this basis, for example.

THE TAX STRUCTURES IN LDCs

The objectives and the constraints in LDCs have several implications for the overall tax structures of the LDCs and the evolution of the structures as development continues.

Dominance of Consumption Taxation

Table 23–2 below shows the relative importance of consumption-related (indirect) taxes (import duties, sales and excise taxes primarily) in LDCs and developed economies. The consumption-related taxes constitute roughly two thirds of the revenue of the countries with incomes estimated to be under $500 a year, half for the countries between $500 and $850, and one third for the highly developed countries. A study by R. J. Chelliah and others shows that, for a sample of 43 LDCs, income taxes yield 27 percent of tax revenue; import, excise, and sales taxes, 56 percent; export taxes, 8 percent; property taxes, 5 percent; others 4 percent.[2] This heavy reliance on consumption taxes is

TABLE 23–2
Relative Revenues from Consumption and Other Taxes, 1968–1970

Estimated Per Capita GNP, (U.S. dollars)	Number of Countries Included	Percentage of Tax Revenue From	
		Consumption-Related Taxes[1]	Other Taxes[2]
Under $101	20	68	32
$101–200	11	64	36
$201–500	19	64	36
$501–850	9	50	50
Over $850	15	32	68

[1] Customs duties, sales taxes, excise taxes, miscellaneous indirect taxes.
[2] All other taxes, including export duties.
Source: J. F. Due, *Indirect Taxation in Developing Economies* (Baltimore: Johns Hopkins Press, 1970), p. 178. Reproduced by permission of Johns Hopkins Press.

[2] Chelliah, et al. "Tax Ratios," p. 197.

a product primarily of two forces—administrative and economic. In an LDC, use of income taxation is severely restricted by the lack of education and record-keeping on the part of the individual household and small shopkeeper and the lack of trained administrative personnal. The indirect taxes, collected at importation or from a small number of manufacturers or large vendors, are much easier to enforce.

Second, from the standpoint of economic policy, consumption-related taxes offer the great advantage of placing a tax penalty on luxury consumption, thus discouraging purchases of luxuries, most of which are imported. The net effect is to encourage savings, of vital importance for economic development, and to avert foreign exchange crises, and free foreign exchange for the purchase of needed capital goods. Since the lowest income groups purchase little or nothing subject to tax and purchases of taxed goods appear to rise more than proportionately with income, such a system, if properly devised, accords reasonably well with standards of equity under the circumstances—better, perhaps than a poorly enforced income tax.[3] At the same time, emphasis on consumption taxes lessens the danger that high income taxes might adversely affect savings and investment incentives.

Optimal consumption-related taxation in LDCs is obviously different in structure from that regarded as optimal in highly developed countries. First, substantially higher rates are necessary on goods consumed primarily in the higher income groups than on items of general consumption, in order to restrain luxury consumption and to provide progression, which is provided by income taxes in developed countries. Secondly, relatively broad-based taxes on all consumption except the most essential necessities, such as basic unprocessed food, are required if substantial amounts of revenue are to be obtained and a damper placed on consumption generally.

At the same time, even greater simplicity is required in the taxes than in developed countries because of compliance and administrative constraints, and avoidance of distortion in production and distribution is more important, given the strong desire to raise per capita real income.

Forms of Consumption-Related Taxation—Customs Duties. In the earliest years of development, customs duties are the only feasible significant consumption levy and one that accords reasonably well with the objectives. So long as a country can prevent smuggling, customs can be enforced more effectively than domestic taxes on transactions, since goods can be forced to pass through the bottlenecks of custom houses and are not admitted into the country until duties are paid. Fewer trained administrative personnel are required for given

---

[3] A recent study of the tax system in Tanzania shows it to be progressive, for example, despite the high reliance on indirect taxes. Y. Huang, "Distribution of the Tax Burden in Tanzania," *Economic Journal*, vol. 86 (March 1976), pp. 73–86.

TABLE 23-3
Relative Importance of Various Types of Consumption-Related Levies 1968–1970

Estimated Per Capita GNP (U.S. dollars)	No. Countries Included	Number of Countries Using Sales Tax	Percent Total Tax Revenue from:					Percent Total Indirect Taxes from:			
			All Indirect Taxes[2]	Customs Duties	Excise Taxes	Sales Taxes		Customs Duties	Excises	Excises Plus Miscellaneous Indirect Taxes	Sales Taxes
						All	Users				
Under $101	20	13	68	35	15	14	21	52	24	28	20
$101–200	11	8	64	32	17	11	15	50	29	33	17
$201–500	19	9	64	33	20	8	16	51	29	36	13
$501–850	9	4	50	18	15	9	19	38	36	42	16
Over $850	15	14	32	4	15	13	14	12	47	[1]	41

[1] Miscellaneous included in other categories.
[2] Including miscellaneous excise taxes.
Source: J. F. Due, *Indirect Taxation in Developing Economies* (Baltimore: Johns Hopkins Press, 1970), p. 178. Reproduced by permission of Johns Hopkins Press.

revenue. Furthermore, customs duties applying to imported goods are particularly effective means of restricting importation of luxury goods, which drains foreign exchange away from imports more essential for economic growth. Importation of capital goods that contribute to economic development can be freed of duty. Since virtually all goods that may be regarded as nonnecessities are imported, the duties likewise effectively reduce luxury consumption and provide incentive for increased savings. For the same reason, they accord reasonably well with accepted standards of equity, since few imported goods are used by the lower income groups. To the extent that duties do provide incentive for domestic production, development is aided, so long as the domestic production that results is in accord with development objectives.

As development continues, however, customs duties deteriorate as a source of revenue.[4] As industrial production develops within the country, the ratio of imports of finished products to GNP falls and thus the tax potential is reduced. The increased use of duties for deliberate protective purposes likewise lessens the revenue potential. Increased domestic production of certain types of luxury goods reduces the equity of customs as a means of reaching the higher income groups. Furthermore, high duties for revenue purposes will produce some unwanted import substitution; domestic production expands along lines contrary to development objectives. But once these industries develop, politically it is very difficult to kill them off by eliminating protection.

As shown in Table 23–3, customs revenues constitute about half of total indirect tax revenues and one third of total tax revenues up to the $500 per capita GNP level; beyond this they fall rapidly, to reach the low of 4 percent of total tax revenues for the highly developed countries.

Excises.[5] The decline in the revenue potential of customs duties as a revenue source is accompanied by rising capacity to levy taxes on domestic production and sales. Typically domestic indirect taxation first takes the form of excise taxes on the production of commodities that are widely consumed yet are regarded as nonessentials—ones that were major producers of customs revenue. Cigarettes, beer, liquor, and motor fuel (partly justified on the benefit basis to finance roads) are the principal excises in the LDCs, just as they are in the more developed countries. There is also a tendency to extend excise taxation beyond these categories to more and more manufactured goods and

---

[4] Marion A. O'Connor, "The Growth of Direct Taxes in Developing Countries 1958–68." Discussion paper, Research Program in Economic Development, Princeton University, 1972.

[5] S. Cnossen, "Revenue Aspects of Excise Systems," and "Sales and Excise Systems of the World," *IMF Departmental Memos, 1974.*

some services (e.g., hotels) as domestic production increases, essentially compensating for the loss in customs revenue. Rates are usually specific and thus problems of valuation are avoided. So long as the number of excises is not too great, administration is feasible because the number of manufacturers is relatively small.

As industrial production continues to expand, however, excises become progressively less satisfactory. As more and more are introduced, the number of separate taxes complicates administration and specific rates are not feasible in many fields (e.g., hardware) with numerous different items. Likewise, excises inevitably discriminate against consumers of taxed goods compared to those of untaxed ones. Revenue potentials are restricted because many items will slip through the net; as new products are developed, they are not taxed until the law is changed.

Sales Taxes.   The need for supplementing customs revenue and the inadequacies of excise taxation as development continues have led a number of LDCs to introduce sales taxes. Of the larger Latin American countries, for example, only Venezuela does not use a sales tax. Most of the countries of southeast Asia use the tax. India makes extensive use at the state level and virtually all ex-French and several British Commonwealth countries of Africa have introduced sales taxes.

The optimal form and structure of a sales tax are obviously different in an LDC than in highly developed countries. In the lowest per capita GNP countries, use of the retail tax, the basically optimal form, is impossible because of the large number of very small, uneducated, often itinerant shopkeepers. Only countries with relatively high levels of development and substantial retailing can use the retail tax,[6] and these countries frequently exclude small retailers, applying tax to sales to these firms rather than to sales by them. The manufacturers sales tax of the Canadian type is the form preferred in a number of LDCs;[7] the number of manufacturers is relatively small, most are of substantial size, and control is easier. Much of the tax is collected at the point of importation, since the tax applies to both imported and domestic goods, but the evils of customs duties—provision of incentive toward unwanted import substitution and progressive loss of revenue on domestic products—are avoided.

As noted in Chapter 15, there are several inherent difficulties with the manufacturers tax, particularly the discrimination against certain forms of distribution channels and the attainment of equality of treatment of domestic and imported goods. Furthermore, the elimination of distribution margins from the tax greatly reduces the revenue potential at a given rate. But in the earliest years of development these are

---

[6] Barbados is one of the few LDCs to use retail tax.

[7] For example, Ghana, Uganda, Tanzania, Kenya, Pakistan, Phillippines, Zambia.

not regarded as significant relative to the important merit of ease of collection.

Another group of LDCs, some of the ex-French countries of Africa, several states in India, and Mexico, use the multi-stage or turnover tax, under the belief that the easiest way to collect substantial revenue is to apply a relatively low rate to all transactions at all stages of production and distribution. In fact, some sales are usually excluded, particularly those by farmers. This approach results in an unnecessarily large number of taxpaying firms and soon gives rise to strong complaints of discrimination against nonintegrated firms. The tax causes serious economic distortion by encouraging vertical integration in manufacturing and distribution. It produces unjustifiable variation in ratio of tax to final consumer expenditures and implementation of the desired distributional pattern is difficult. One of the greatest weaknesses of the tax in LDCs is the impossibility of providing equal treatment of domestic and imported goods (the latter typically pass through fewer domestic sales than the former) and in completely excluding the tax from export prices. As a consequence, several LDCs that used this tax have shifted to some form of nonmultiple tax.

In order to avoid the evils of the turnover tax yet not concentrate the impact of the tax on one level of production and distribution, several more-developed LDCs have turned to the value-added tax and others are considering it. Present LDC users include the Argentine, Chile, Malagasy, Ecuador, and Brazil.[8] The primary objection to the levy, certainly in the least-developed countries, is the greater complication and the larger numbers of vendors. Much of the advantage is lost if retailers are excluded, yet including them adds materially to administrative costs. The usual rule is to exclude at least the smallest ones. In Malagasy, the urban retailers are included, the rural ones excluded. While the tax may be regarded as acceptable in the most advanced of the LDCs, such as Chile and Mexico, which require large amounts of money from the tax and have relatively highly developed commercial sectors, the complexities suggest that the least-developed countries avoid it.

In summary: While the use of sales taxation has strong justification in LDCs except in the very early years of development, no one form is necessarily optimal. The manufacturers tax is perhaps the most suitable when an LDC first moves into the sales tax field, but the levy may well evolve into a retail tax with small retailers excluded or into a value-added tax as development continues. The turnover tax should be avoided at all costs, since once it is introduced it is difficult politically to abandon it because of the relatively low rate needed for given

---

[8] A number of ex-French African countries use taxes called value-added taxes, but they are essentially manufacturers sales taxes.

revenue, but it grows progressively more unsatisfactory as development continues.

Income Taxation

While consumption-related taxes offer substantial advantages in LDCs, virtually all LDCs use income taxation as well, and there are strong justifications for doing so. The income tax provides greater revenue potential from the higher income groups and is the only effective means of obtaining payments from these persons consistent with standards of equity accepted in many LDCs. Substantial use of income taxation is particularly important in countries with a high degree of inequality, much of the wealth and income concentrated in a few wealthy families (e.g., Peru)—but unfortunately in some of these countries the rich are so powerful politically as to block effective income taxation. In any country, highly developed or less developed, the income tax offers other important advantages as well. As the economy expands the coverage of the tax continues to increase automatically. More and more families come within the scope of the tax and more and more incomes are subjected to the higher rates. Just as development tends to destroy customs duties as a revenue source, it increases the effectiveness of income taxation.[9] The tax can be used to influence use of income if desired, concessions being offered if the income is reinvested in business expansion, for example.

Administrative problems plus incentive considerations, however, restrict the revenue potentiality of the tax in earlier years of development. The tax can be applied successfully to wage and salary receivers and stockholders in larger businesses, recipients of interest, and owners of large businesses. Clearly the small semisubsistence farmer, illiterate and without records, cannot be reached by the tax, and traders, even larger ones, are a source of considerable evasion. Yet some payments can be obtained from these groups, and continued administrative effort can bring ultimate success.

These considerations suggest the need for excluding the lowest income groups and limiting the marginal rates to reasonable figures. Incentive considerations also require reasonable rates; high marginal rates are likely to produce little revenue but give rise to adverse incentive effects. But egalitarian goals are so stressed in some countries that marginal rates up to 90 percent or more are employed.

Simplicity in the structure of the tax is of greater importance than in economies with higher levels of education; many developing economies have unfortunately copied the complex income taxes of mature economies, making compliance and enforcement much more difficult. On the other hand, withholding has proven to be feasible.

---

[9] O'Connor, "Growth of Direct Taxes," provides empirical evidence.

The Personal Tax

Since income taxation in its usual form cannot be applied to the majority of the population in a developing economy, some other form of direct tax is desirable to gain revenue and to acquaint all families with the need for making direct tax payments to the government and paving the way for their eventual entry into the income tax structure. Several African countries have developed graduated personal taxes for these purposes. These are outgrowths of the old head taxes, the sums paid adjusted very roughly according to actual or presumed income. These taxes have several characteristics: coverage of all families (rather than individuals as such) except those exempted by local officials as completely destitute; application to all income (net, in the case of businesses) without deductions, exemptions, or allowances; assessment, at least in part, on presumptive income as determined, for example, by the number of livestock or cocoa trees; simple graduation in rate by blocks of taxpayers (a flat money rate within each block) up to the level at which the income tax becomes effective; and administration primarily local. Local committees familiar with the circumstances of each family do the assessing. Typically most taxpayers are subject to the basic rate (which may be the equivalent of $2 or $3 per family).

Such a tax brings almost all families within the scope of direct taxation and facilitates their integration into the income tax system as their incomes rise. Yield is greater than from any alternative levy reaching most of the population, with greater equity. If honesty can be maintained, local administration increases the possibility of obtaining equitable assessment and facilitates local fiscal responsibility and financial autonomy.

The graduated personal tax is less likely to have adverse incentive effects than typical income taxes, since the rates are relatively low. When the taxes are levied upon presumptive rather than actual income they encourage additional economic activity. They provide incentive to subsistence farmers to move into the commercial sector to earn money income.

The most significant weakness of the taxes is the danger of inadequate administration. In urban areas particularly, it is difficult to ensure that all persons pay, and in both rural and urban areas assessment may not be equitable.[10]

Taxation of Corporate Income

Corporate income taxation is essential to reach income earned in the corporate form of business on a current basis when it is not paid out as

---

[10] K. Davey, *Taxing a Peasant Society* (London: Knight, 1974).

dividends or is paid to foreign stockholders. This case for such taxation is particularly strong when the corporations are foreign-owned and operate in enclaves, contributing little to the development of the country. Corporate taxation is relatively easy to administer compared to personal taxation and in many developing economies can make an important contribution to government revenue. Politically, such taxation has great appeal (too much in some instances) and is without doubt an ingredient necessary to obtain general acceptance of the tax structure. Given the tax laws of the home countries, the overall tax burden on the firms may not be increased, the developing economy enjoying some of the revenue otherwise going to the country of the owners. Finally, company taxation offers possibilities for directing investment along lines regarded as most important for economic development.

On the other hand, a country can easily overdo corporate taxation if private investment is desired. If company taxation is not held to moderate levels, investment from both domestic and foreign sources will be discouraged and funds will merely be diverted from private investment to government. Absorption of funds that would be used for domestic investment may hamper development; absorption of funds that otherwise would be paid to foreign investors and not reinvested in the country or used for investments that do not aid growth encourages development.

The exact structure of the company taxation may have a marked influence upon its developmental effects. Adjustments in the tax that lessen risk encourage additional investment activity. One of the incisive tax policies with this effect is the allowance of full loss carry forward, so that losses incurred in early years of operation can be deducted for tax purposes from profits earned in later years. Similarly, provisions allowing rapid depreciation of equipment purchases lessen the risk that full deduction for tax purposes will never be attained, but encourage excessive use of capital equipment relative to manpower.

Tax Incentives. [11] Special tax concessions, such as investment credit and tax holiday provisions, may aid development. The tax holidays exempt from taxes for a period of years new firms found by the government to contribute to economic development. These policies have two major functions: (1) They lessen the impact of the corporate taxes upon funds and incentives for investment by reducing tax burden, and (2) they provide a means to channel investment into preferred outlets. The credits or the holidays are granted only for industries where investment is desired.

Such programs are not without difficulties. The investment credit approach, made applicable automatically to all firms in the industries

---

[11] G. E. Lent, "Tax Incentives for the Promotion of Industrial Employment in Developing Countries," *IMF Staff Papers*, July 1971, pp. 400–419.

covered, is simpler to operate than the usual tax holiday approach but favors the capital-intensive type of investment, a policy that may be questioned in a labor-surplus economy. But the tax holiday approach may bog down in administrative difficulties, with long delays in granting the concession. The effectiveness of the overall program depends upon the ability of the government to select the most advantageous types of investment. The government always runs the risk of choking off some kinds of investment without stimulating others; investments in breweries may be preferred to no investment at all. Tax revenue is sacrificed, much of it on gains from investment that would have been undertaken anyway. There is always the danger that adjacent countries will escalate concessions in competition with one another for industry, all in the end losing revenue and gaining nothing.

Little attention has been given in most countries to the adjustment of company tax liability according to the use made of the earnings. Tax concessions could be made on earnings reinvested within the country (not necessarily in the same industry), with substantially heavier burden on earnings transferred outside the country. Such a policy is not difficult to administer, at least for the larger companies, those that typically earn most of the total profits in a developing economy. The significance for development may be as great as governmental absorption of the funds, while the overall adverse incentive effects will be very much less.

Export Duties [12]

Taxes on the exportation of particular products may serve as a partial substitute for income taxes in a developing economy and as a means of capturing windfall gains due to sharp increases in world prices. The taxes are presumably borne by the producers of the taxed products when prices are determined in world markets. As a substitute for income taxes on farmers, as for example in Ghana, the tax offers the advantage of administrative simplicity. When goods are exported through marketing boards or a few large dealers, collection of tax is easier than taxing income from numerous small farmers. But used in this fashion, the tax is not only inequitable, since other incomes will not be taxed to the same extent, but it may also have serious adverse incentive effects, shifting farmers to domestic products or to export products not subject to tax, with consequent overall loss of efficiency and foreign exchange. As a means of obtaining additional revenue from large foreign-owned producers, income taxation is likely to be more effective and less likely to discourage marginal production.

As a means of taxing windfall gains from sharp increases in world

---

[12] R. Goode, G. E. Lent, and P. D. Ojha, "Role of Export Taxes in Developing Economies," *I. M. F. Staff Papers*, vol. 13 (November 1966), pp. 453–503.

market prices for the country's exports, export duties have greater merit. They can absorb a substantial portion of the increase in domestic incomes without adverse incentive effects. At the same time they can check domestic inflation, which will otherwise arise because the increase in incomes will not be accompanied by comparable increases in domestic production (and should not, in the interests of economic development, be accompanied by an equivalent increase in consumer goods imports). For this purpose, the export duties must have rates that are nominal so long as world prices are more or less normal but that climb steeply with an increase in prices. There is still some danger that marginal operations, particularly in mining, will be discouraged when cost of production is not taken into consideration in determining liability. Since the revenues will fluctuate widely, these levies must be regarded as supplementary sources of funds available in certain periods for development purposes rather than as normal regular sources governmental revenue.

Taxation of Wealth

Taxation of wealth in developing countries is typically taxation of real property, primarily land, in view of the difficulties in operating a tax on net wealth, however advantageous the latter might be in minimizing incentive effects and checking the growth of large fortunes. Taxation of land offers several advantages. The danger of adverse incentive effects is slight, if the taxes are designed and operated properly, since a tax on land value encourages more, not less, intensive use of the land. The tax recovers for society a portion of the increase in land values arising from economic growth and thus conforms with usual equity standards.

The issues are somewhat different with urban and rural property. In urban areas, increases in land values are often very rapid and a major source of large fortunes. Heavy taxes will not retard development but may facilitate it by preventing the holding idle of land for speculative purposes. There are problems in some areas arising from lack of land titles, and valuation may be difficult if trained personnel are not available. The issue of whether the tax should apply only to land values or to land and improvements must be resolved. Taxing land values only is particularly advantageous in encouraging more effective use of the land and discouraging the holding idle of land. On the other hand, there is a close correlation between building construction and the demand for governmental services, and some tax on improvements may be justified to finance these additional services.[13]

---

[13] G. E. Lent, "The Taxation of Land Value," *I.M.F. Staff Papers*, vol. 14 (March 1967), pp. 89–123.

The taxation of agricultural land is a much more complex one.[14] Generalization are difficult, in part because of great differences in land tenure systems, from the communal ownership typical of much of tropical Africa, where individuals do not own land, to vast plantation holdings characteristic of portions of Latin America. With private ownership of land, particularly in large estates, taxation of land values may be highly effective in bringing about more effective use of the land and greatly improve the equity of the overall tax system, since it is difficult to reach the higher income farmers effectively by income taxation, and the income tax may discourage additional output. But experience has shown that in fact very few developing countries tax agricultural land effectively; the only ones that do succeed in placing much tax on farmers are those using heavy export duties, and as noted these duties probably have serious undesirable effects. Failure to tax land effectively is due in part to administrative problems of valuation, particularly to keep assessed values up-to-date, in part to political influence of large landowners, and in part to sheer inertia. In some countries the attempt to make the taxes more "personal" and to couple them with land reform and other objectives has resulted in such great complexities that they have accomplished nothing.

The argument, widely found in literature on economic development, that heavy land taxes are essential to drive resources from agriculture to industry is now seriously questioned. It has become evident that economic development requires increased emphasis on agriculture; that agriculture requires more capital and labor, not less; and that any attempt to force resources away from it will hamper growth. Thus the inadequacy in taxing agricultural land has been perhaps preferable to excessive taxation of it—but clearly in most countries there is substantial potential that is not being exploited, and great need to move from export taxes on farm products to taxation of the land values. But effective land taxation can come only slowly, in simple form, adapted to the circumstances of the country, and separated from other measures such as land-tenure reform.

Overall Revenue Elasticity and Distributional Effects

Given the urgency of additional tax revenues and the inevitable political tensions created by continuing tax rate increases, a high degree of revenue elasticity relative to economic growth is obviously highly desirable. Some studies suggest that the typical LDC tax structures do have substantial income elasticity, with an overall figure for a

---

[14] A recent thorough study of the question is that by Richard Bird, *Taxing Agricultural Land in Developing Countries* (Cambridge: Harvard University Press, 1974).

selected group of countries of 1.4 percent.[15] The highest elasticity, 2.4 percent, is shown by sales and excise taxes, essentially because of rapid increases in industrial production relative to imports and to GNP—a trend not found, of course, in highly developed economies. Income taxes, the most elastic in developed countries, show a lower figure, 1.4 percent, partly because of poor enforcement. Over time, as development continues, this figure rises relative to the figure for taxes on domestic production and sales.

An increasing number of studies have been made of the distributional impact of taxes in developing countries.[16] Contrary to what is commonly believed, there is substantial evidence of progressivity in the tax structure in the majority of LDCs, although this often does not extend to the highest income levels, and does not always occur at the lowest levels. In another group of countries, the system appears to be more or less proportional; in only two of the studies were the results regressive (Greece and the Philippines). Given the high reliance on indirect taxes, this suggests that the indirect systems are not as regressive as they appear to be in many developed countries. There are several reasons: the importance of untaxed subsistence production; the fact that the lowest income groups purchase very few goods subject to tax; and the use of higher rates of tax on goods consumed primarily in the upper income groups.

REFERENCES

Bird, R. M.   *Taxing Agricultural Land in Developing Countries.* Cambridge: Harvard University Press, 1974.

Bird, Richard, and Oldman, Oliver eds.   *Readings on Taxation in Developing Countries*, 3d ed. Baltimore: Johns Hopkins Press, 1975.

Due, J. F.   *Indirect Taxation in Developing Economies.* Baltimore: Johns Hopkins Press, 1970.

Heller, P. S.   "A Model of Public Fiscal Behavior in Developing Countries", *American Economic Review*, vol. 65 (June 1975), pp. 429–45.

Hinrichs, H. H.   *A General Theory of Tax Structure Change During Economic Development.* Cambridge, Mass.: Harvard Law School, 1966.

Musgrave, R. A.   *Fiscal Systems.* New Haven, Conn.: Yale University Press, 1969.

---

[15] Chelliah, "Trends in Taxation," p. 263.

[16] R. M. Bird and L. H. DeWulf, "Taxation and Income Distribution in Latin America: A Critical Review of Empirical Studies," and L. H. DeWulf, "Fiscal Incidence Studies in Developing Countries; Survey and Critique," both in *IMF Staff Papers*, vol. 21 (November 1972), pp. 639–82 and vol. 22 (March 1975), pp. 61–131

Musgrave, R. A., and Gillis, S. M. *Fiscal Reform for Colombia.* Cambridge, Mass.: Harvard Law School, 1971.

Prest, A. R. *Public Finance in Underdeveloped Countries.* New York: Halsted Press, 1972.

Wang, N. T. *Taxation and Development.* New York: Praeger, for United Nations, 1976.

INDEX

Index

*This book has been set in 10 and 9 point
Caledonia, leaded 2 points. Part numbers and
titles are 16 point Helvetica italic. Chapter
numbers are 30 point Helvetica and chapter
titles are 16 point Helvetica. The size of the
type page is 27 by 46½ picas.*